Lecture Notes in Computer Scien

T0238112

Commenced Publication in 1973
Founding and Former Series Editors:
Gerhard Goos, Juris Hartmanis, and Jan van Leeuwen

Tarmo Uustalu (Ed.)

Mathematics of Program Construction

8th International Conference, MPC 2006
Kuressaare, Estonia, July 3-5, 2006
Proceedings

 Springer

Volume Editor

Tarmo Uustalu
Institute of Cybernetics
Akadeemia tee 21, 12618 Tallinn, Estonia
E-mail: tarmo@cs.ioc.ee

Library of Congress Control Number: 2006927705

CR Subject Classification (1998): F.3, F.4, D.2, F.1, D.3

LNCS Sublibrary: SL 1 – Theoretical Computer Science and General Issues

ISSN   0302-9743
ISBN-10   3-540-35631-2 Springer Berlin Heidelberg New York
ISBN-13   978-3-540-35631-8 Springer Berlin Heidelberg New York

Springer is a part of Springer Science+Business Media

springer.com

© Springer-Verlag Berlin Heidelberg 2006
Printed in Germany

Typesetting: Camera-ready by author, data conversion by Scientific Publishing Services, Chennai, India
Printed on acid-free paper   SPIN: 11783596   06/3142   5 4 3 2 1 0

Preface

This volume contains the proceedings of the 8th International Conference on Mathematics of Program Construction, MPC 2006, held at Kuressaare, Estonia, July 3–5, 2006, colocated with the 11th International Conference on Algebraic Methodology and Software Technology, AMAST 2006, July 5–8, 2006.

The MPC conferences aim to promote the development of mathematical principles and techniques that are demonstrably useful and usable in the process of constructing computer programs. Topics of interest range from algorithmics to support for program construction in programming languages and systems.

The previous MPCs were held at Twente, The Netherlands (1989, LNCS 375), Oxford, UK (1992, LNCS 669), Kloster Irsee, Germany (1995, LNCS 947), Marstrand, Sweden (1998, LNCS 1422), Ponte de Lima, Portugal (2000, LNCS 1837), Dagstuhl, Germany (2002, LNCS 2386) and Stirling, UK (2004, LNCS 3125, colocated with AMAST 2004).

MPC 2006 received 45 submissions. Each submission was reviewed by four Programme Committee members or additional referees. The committee decided to accept 22 papers. In addition, the programme included three invited talks by Robin Cockett (University of Calgary, Canada), Olivier Danvy (Aarhus Universitet, Denmark) and Oege de Moor (University of Oxford, UK).

The review process and compilation of the proceedings were greatly helped by Andrei Voronkov's EasyChair system that I can only recommend to every programme chair.

MPC 2006 had one satellite workshop, the Workshop on Mathematically Structured Functional Programming, MSFP 2006, organized as a "small" workshop of the FP6 IST coordination action TYPES. This took place July 2, 2006.

Tallinn, April 2006   Tarmo Uustalu

Conference Organization

Programme Chair

Tarmo Uustalu (Institute of Cybernetics, Estonia)

Programme Committee

Roland Backhouse (University of Nottingham, UK)
Eerke Boiten (University of Kent, UK)
Venanzio Capretta (University of Ottawa, Canada)
Sharon Curtis (Oxford Brookes University, UK)
Jules Desharnais (Université de Laval, Canada)
Jeremy Gibbons (University of Oxford, UK)
Lindsay Groves (Victoria University of Wellington, New Zealand)
William Harrison (University of Missouri, USA)
Ian J. Hayes (University of Queensland, Australia)
Johan Jeuring (Universiteit Utrecht, The Netherlands)
Dexter Kozen (Cornell University, USA)
Christian Lengauer (Universität Passau, Germany)
Lambert Meertens (Kestrel Institute, USA)
Shin-Cheng Mu (Academia Sinica, Taiwan)
Bernhard Möller (Universität Augsburg, Germany)
José Nuno Oliveira (Universidade do Minho, Portugal)
Alberto Pardo (Universidad de la República, Uruguay)
Ross Paterson (City University London, UK)
Ingrid Rewitzky (University of Stellenbosch, South Africa)
Varmo Vene (University of Tartu, Estonia)

Additional Referees

José Bacelar Almeida	Tyng-Ruey Chuang	Colin Fidge
Ian Bayley	Michael Claßen	Sergei Gorlatch
Yves Bertot	Robert Colvin	Jonathan Grattage
Marc Bezem	Phil Cook	Dan Grundy
Ana Bove	Silvia Crafa	E. C. R. Hehner
Carlos Camarão	Alcino Cunha	John Hughes
David Carrington	Ellie D'Hondt	Peter Höfner
Manuel Chakravarty	Andreas Dolzmann	Benjamin Kelly

Shriram Krishnamurthi
Peeter Laud
Carlos Luna
Ralf Lämmel
Clare Martin
Larissa Meinicke
Diethard Michaelis
Till Mossakowski
Härmel Nestra

Milad Niqui
John O'Donnell
Bruno C. d. S. Oliveira
Jorge Sousa Pinto
Fermin Reig
Gunter Ritter
Eike Ritter
Ando Saabas
Lutz Schröder

Olha Shkaravska
Graeme Smith
Kim Solin
Barney Stratford
Georg Struth
Femke van Raamsdonk
Joost Visser
Da-Wei Wang
Meng Wang

Organizing Committee

Juhan Ernits, Monika Perkmann, Ando Saabas, Olha Shkaravska, Kristi Uustalu, Tarmo Uustalu (Institute of Cybernetics, Estonia).

Host Institution

Institute of Cybernetics at Tallinn University of Technology, Estonia.

Sponsors

National Centers of Excellence Programme of the Estonian Ministry of Education and Research.

Table of Contents

Invited Talks

Contributed Papers

What Is a Good Process Semantics?
(Extended Abstract)

Robin Cockett

Dept. of Computer Science, University of Calgary,
2500 University Drive NW, Calgary, Alb. T2N 1N4, Canada
robin@cpsc.ucalgary.ca

Abstract. Current mathematical tools for understanding processes predominantly support process modeling. In particular, they faithfully represent all the things that can go wrong (deadlock, livelock, etc.). However, for the development of good programming abstractions in concurrent (and other) setting it is important to focus on formal systems in which things do not go wrong. So what are the formal models of processes where nothing goes wrong?

For those involved in trying to understand the mathematics of program construction the new challenge is to understand the mathematics of concurrent programs. The era of simple input/output computation has been completely superseded by an expectation of connectivity from which there is no return.

After some four decades of intense effort to provide a good calculus of processes, Robin Milner's π-calculus [5, 6] and its variants have emerged as a core paradigm. The π-calculus evolved directly from CCS and may be regarded as a response to the desire to pass information between processes beyond the mere fact of communication. To achieve this it was necessary to introduce the notion of a channel along which information could be passed and this involved solving the syntactic scope and substitution issues inherent in interaction along such channels.

A considerable portion of the theoretical effort which went into these ideas was inspired by operational considerations. In particular, the underlying paradigm for equality hinged on behavioural equivalence and the notion of bisimulation. The preoccupation with how the solution of these local technical issues lead to a coherent global notion of equality based on bisimulation seemed to an observer, such as myself, to be in tension with the desire to understand the structure of processes.

Of course, equality given through operational considerations as embodied in notions of bisimulation is a crucial sanity check: without it the production of an operational system is impossible. However, these operational considerations do not of themselves lead to a well-clothed mathematical understanding of processes. In particular, they do not directly inform us of what the manipulations of processes should be or how these manipulations should be organized. To make progress on this front it is necessary to turn to algebraic rather than operational sources for guidance.

T. Uustalu (Ed.): MPC 2006, LNCS 4014, pp. 1–3, 2006.

The λ-calculus [1] is a basis for simple input/output computations and the model of reduction in this calculus undoubtedly provided inspiration for reduction of the π-calculus. However, the λ-calculus transcended being a mere mechanism to model computation and became intimately connected into mathematics when the Curry-Howard-Lambek isomorphism was established. Terms of the typed λ-calculus correspond precisely to proofs of propositions which, in turn, form a cartesian closed category.

Lambek's contribution to this was the categorical end, but it was also really much broader: for it was categorical proof theory itself [4]. He understood that the cut-elimination process is the operational semantics of composition. Furthermore he realized that there is a correspondence between proof theories and categorical doctrines. While one of Lambek's motivation was to use the reduction processes from proof theory to throw light on categorical coherence issues, his observation opened up a connection through which ideas could flow in both directions. Examples of categorical doctrines occur throughout mathematics and they can (and have) been used as a rich source from which to develop a deeper understanding of the corresponding proof theories.

So what is the categorical proof theory of processes? I will argue that it is, in fact, an old and thorny friend: multiplicative additive linear logic. This is a thorn friend as the coherence issues of this logic are still the subject of active research [7]. Indeed, at this time, it is not clear that the definitive view of even these most basic issue has yet emerged. Equality of proofs, however, is known to be decidable [3]and one way to show this is to use a term logic reminiscent of the π-calculus. These ideas go right back to Bellin and Scott's early work [2].

Recalled the proof theoretic systems for typed λ-calculi are powerful enough to secure good termination properties. However, these formal properties are bought at a cost to expressiveness and consequently programmability. It is still open, for example, whether the loss of expressiveness due to the imposed type discipline can be successfully arranged in a manner to satisfy a significant programming community.

To make the proof theory for concurrent processes usable as a language in which reasonable concurrent problems can be programmed it is necessary to add datatypes and value passing. Datatypes, in the process world, correspond to protocols. The resulting type systems for the proof theory of linear logic do actually secure all the good properties one wants: progressiveness, deadlock freedom, and livelock freedom.

Unfortunately I do not claim to know (yet) how to turn this into something which approaches a practical programming language! This is still seems a distant goal. However, the motivation for formally based languages to support concurrent computation, when compared to that for simple input/output computations, is much greater. This simply because so much more can go wrong. Furthermore, the paradigms for expressing concurrent computation are still relatively crude and this means there is much to be gained, even for todays programs, from studying the mathematical structure of these formal systems.

References

1. Barendregt, H. P.: The Lambda Calculus: Its Syntax and Semantics. Revised edn. Vol. 103 of Studies in Logic and the Foundations of Mathematics. North-Holland (1984)
2. Bellin, G., Scott, P. J.: On the pi-calculus and linear logic. Theor. Comput. Sci. **135**(1) (1994) 11–65
3. Cockett, J. R. B., Pastro, C.: A language for multiplicative-additive linear logic. In Proc. of 10th Conf. on Category Theory and Computer Science, CTCS 2004. Vol. 122 of Electron. Notes in Theor. Comput. Sci. Elsevier (2005) 23–65.
4. Lambek, J.: Deductive systems and categories II. Proc. of Conf. on Category Theory, Homology Theory and Their Applications, Vol. 1. Vol. 87 of Lect. Notes in Math. Springer-Verlag (1969) 76–122
5. Milner, R., Parrow, J., Walker, D.: A calculus of mobile processes I. Inform. and Comput. **100**(1) (1992) 1–40
6. Milner, R., Parrow, J., Walker, D.: A calculus of mobile processes II. Inform. and Comput. **100**(1) (1992) 41–77
7. van Glabbeek, R. J., Hughes, D. J. D.: Proof nets for unit-free multiplicative-additive linear logic. ACM Trans. on Comput. Logic **6**(4) (2005) 784–842

Refunctionalization at Work

Olivier Danvy

BRICS,
Department of Computer Science, University of Aarhus,
IT-parken, Aabogade 34, DK-8200 Aarhus N, Denmark
danvy@brics.dk

Abstract. First-order programs are desired in a variety of settings and for a variety of reasons. Their coming into existence in first-order form may be unplanned or it could be the deliberate result of a form of "firstification" such as closure conversion, (super)combinator conversion, or defunctionalization. In the latter case, they are higher-order programs in disguise, just as iterative programs with accumulators are often recursive programs in disguise.

This talk is about Reynolds's defunctionalization [1, 2]. Over the last few years, we have observed that a number of existing first-order programs turn out to be in the range of defunctionalization, and therefore they directly correspond to higher-order programs, even though they were designed independently of any higher-order representation. Not all first-order programs, however, are in defunctionalized form.

The goal of this talk is to refine our earlier characterization of what it means to be in defunctionalized form [3], and to investigate how one can tease a first-order program into defunctionalized form. On the way, we present a variety of independently known programs that are in (or can be teased into) defunctionalized form, and we exhibit their functional counterpart—a process we refer to as 'refunctionalization' since it is a left inverse of defunctionalization.

References

1. Reynolds, J. C.: Definitional interpreters for higher-order programming languages. In: Proc. of 25th ACM Nat. Conf. ACM Press (1972) 717–740 // Reprinted in Higher-Order and Symb. Comput. **11**(4) (1998) 363–397
2. Reynolds, J. C.: Definitional interpreters revisited. Higher-Order and Symb. Comput. **11**(4) (1998) 355–361
3. Danvy, O., Nielsen, L. R.: Defunctionalization at work. In Proc. of 3rd Int. ACM SIGPLAN Conf. on Principles and Practice of Declarative Programming PPDP'01. ACM Press (2001) 162–174

T. Uustalu (Ed.): MPC 2006, LNCS 4014, p. 4, 2006.

Aspects and Data Refinement

(Extended Abstract)

Pavel Avgustinov[1], Eric Bodden[2], Elnar Hajiyev[1], Oege de Moor[1], Neil Ongkingco[1], Damien Sereni[1], Ganesh Sittampalam[1], and Julian Tibble[1]

[1] Oxford University Computing Laboratory,
Wolfson Building, Parks Road, Oxford OX1 3QD, United Kingdom
[2] School of Computer Science, McGill University,
Montréal, Québec H3A 2A7, Canada

Abstract. We give an introduction to aspect-oriented programming from the viewpoint of data refinement. Some data refinements are conveniently expressed via aspects. Unlike traditional programming language features for data refinement, aspects conceptually transform run-time events, not compile-time programs.

1 Introduction

Data refinement is a powerful tool in program construction: we start with an existing module, adding some new variables related to the existing ones via a *coupling invariant*, and possibly adding new operations as well. Next we refine each of the existing operations so that the coupling invariant is maintained. Finally, if any existing variables have become redundant, they are removed [1].

The idea is pervasive, and it is no surprise, therefore, that numerous researchers have attempted to capture it in a set of programming language features. An early example of this trend can be found in the work of Bob Paige, who advocated the use of a program transformation system to achieve the desired effect [2]. The idea was again raised by David Gries and Dennis Volpano in their design of the *transform* in the Polya programming language [3]. Very recently, Annie Liu and her coworkers [4] breathed new life into this line of work by updating it to the context of object-oriented programming.

All these systems are very powerful, and they are complete in that all data refinements can be expressed, at least in principle. In another community, a set of programming language features has been proposed that is less powerful, but still suitable for direct expression of simple data refinements. These features are collectively known under the name of 'aspects' [5].

In this talk, we shall examine some examples of data refinement expressed as aspects. Conceptually aspects transform run-time computations, unlike the above systems, which are all based on the idea of compile-time transformation. For efficiency, aspect compilers do as much transformation as possible at compile-time [6], but that is an implementation technique, not the semantics. We argue that to write reusable data refinements, which are independent of the syntactic details of the program being refined, the run-time view offered by aspects is preferable.

T. Uustalu (Ed.): MPC 2006, LNCS 4014, pp. 5–9, 2006.

2   Data Refinement

Consider an interface in Java for bags (multisets) of integers; an example of such an interface is shown in Figure 1. It includes an operation that returns an iterator over the elements of a bag; the order of such an iteration is not further specified.

```
interface Bag {
    void add(int i);
    void remove(int i);
    java.util.Iterator  iterator ();
}
```

Fig. 1. *Bag* interface in *Java*

Now suppose we wish to augment this interface, and all classes that implement it, with an operation that returns the average of the bag of integers. A naive implementation would be to re-calculate the average each time, but that requires time proportional to the size of the bag.

To achieve a contant-time implementation of *average*, we introduce two new variables via data refinement, namely *sum* and *size*. The coupling invariant is that *sum* holds the sum of the abstract bag, and *size* the number of elements.

```
1   public aspect Average {
2       private int Bag.sum;
3       private int Bag.size;
4       public float Bag.average() {
5           return (size == 0 ? ((float)sum) / ((float)size)  :  0);
6       }
7       after(Bag b,int i) returning() :
8           execution(void Bag.add(int)) &&
9           this(b) &&
10          args(i)
11      {
12          b.sum += i;
13          b. size  += 1;
14      }
15      after(Bag b,int i) returning() :
16          execution(void Bag.remove(int)) &&
17          this(b) &&
18          args(i)
19      {
20          b.sum −= i;
21          b. size  −= 1;
22      }
23  }
```

Fig. 2. Aspect for data refinement

Once we have these two variables, it is easy to define an efficient implementation of the *average* function, as it just returns their quotient (provided the bag is not empty). Of course *sum* and *size* have to be kept up-to-date when *add* and *remove* are called: these operations must be data-refined accordingly.

Figure 2 shows how to code this data refinement in AspectJ, an aspect-oriented extension of the Java programming language [7]. First note how it introduces the two new variables into all implementations of the *Bag* interface, on Lines 2 and 3. Next we define the new *average* operation, on Lines 4 to 6. The remainder of the aspect is devoted to refining the *add* operation (Lines 7–14) and the *remove* operation (Lines 15–22). Let us examine the refinement of *add* in a little bit more detail. It says that whenever we have completed executing the body of *add*, on a bag *b*, with argument *i*, the sum should be increased by *i* and the size should be increased by 1.

Note that the aspect is generic, in that it applies the data refinement to any implementation of the *Bag* interface. Obviously this is a desirable property, as we can now reuse the same piece of code without having to replay the same data refinement each time a new implementation of bags is introduced.

3   Compile-Time Transformations

An obvious way to view aspects is as program transformations, which insert extra code into an existing program. Indeed, that has been the prevailing view in all previous works that sought to provide language support for data refinement.

The disadvantage of such a wholly syntactic approach is that it is very hard to write reusable data refinements, that are independent of the implementation details of the program being refined. To illustrate, consider changing the original *Bag* interface by adding a method *addAll*(*Bag c*); this new method adds all elements of another bag *c* to the given *Bag*. Formally, the call *b.addAll*(*c*) implements the assignment (writing + for bag union)

$$b := b + c$$

Now consider how the aspect should be modified, if at all, to take account of *addAll*. First observe that if we know that *addAll* is always implemented by iterating over *c*, calling the *b.add* method, no changes to our aspect are necessary. It is conceivable, however, that a more efficient implementation is used. For instance, when both the collection and the bag happen to be stored as sorted lists, a simple list merge would be cheaper than repeated element insertions.

It follows that for the aspect to remain reusable across all implementations of the *Bag* interface, we need to implement the data refinement of the new *addAll* method separately:

```
after(Bag b, Bag c) returning() :
  execution(void addAll(Bag)) &&
  this(b) &&
  args(c)
```

```
{
    b.sum += c.sum;
    b.size += c.size;
}
```

It is not enough to add this piece of code to our aspect, however. If *addAll* is implemented via repeated calls to *add*, we would now add the sum of *c* twice to that of *b*. The data refinement of *add* itself therefore needs to be amended. Intuitively it is clear what amendment is required: when *add* is executed at the top-level, we use the refined code described earlier, and when part of other routines in *Bag* (such as *addAll*), the unrefined version of *add* is used. But this is a run-time distinction and not a compile-time one.

4   Run-Time Transformations

Motivated by this type of example, the designers of AspectJ advocate that aspects are viewed as run-time observers, which intercept events based on their run-time characteristics. In our running example, we only want to transform top-level method executions: in particular, the data refinement should apply to *add* when called on its own, but not when it is called from within another method of *Bag* like *addAll*. To achieve that objective in AspectJ, we can add the conjunct

!**cflowbelow**(**execution**(∗ Bag.∗(..)))

to the pattern of Lines 8–10 in Figure 2. In words, it says the currently executing method invocation is not properly nested inside another method of *Bag*. Specifying the same behaviour as a compile-time transformation could be exceedingly painful. The *cflowbelow* primitive requires, in general, run-time observation of the state of the program, in particular the control stack. However, in practice this can often be statically determined by control-flow analysis [8] for efficiency.

The view of a data refinement in this setting is that an aspect checks the coupling invariant, and when the invariant may be violated, the aspect runs some extra code to restore the invariant. Much remains to be done to arrive at this point, however, and the challenges include:

Completeness. What class of data refinements can be expressed via aspects? The example in this abstract only illustrates adding code before or after an operation on an abstract data type, and on its own it is clearly not enough to express all data refinements. What is a minimal set of aspect-oriented features needed to achieve completeness?

Diminution. We have ignored the process of *diminution*, where auxiliary variables are removed from a data-refined program. While it is tempting to just rely on mechanical dead-code elimination in a compiler, it is unlikely that will always succeed. Aspects do offer a feature (so-called *around advice*) where operations can be replaced by others, in particular by *skip*.

Semantic patterns. The patterns of interception should be less syntactic in nature, instead expressing properties like: 'the state of this object may have changed'. Again this is important for aspects to be reusable.

We are investigating these and other challenges related to the design and implementation of aspect-oriented programming languages in the *abc* project [9]. We hope others will join us in exploring this new area, and in developing a rigorous basis for the use of aspects in program construction.

Acknowledgements. Richard Bird, Carroll Morgan, Jeff Sanders and Bernard Sufrin provided helpful feedback on a draft of this abstract.

This work was supported, in part, by IBM, and by EPSRC in the United Kingdom, and NSERC in Canada.

References

1. Morgan, C.: Programming from Specifications. International Series in Computer Science. 2nd edn. Prentice Hall (1994) `http://users.comlab.ox.ac.uk/carroll.morgan/PfS/`.
2. Paige, R.: Programming with invariants. IEEE Software **3**(1) (1986) 56–69
3. Gries, D., Volpano, D. M.: The transform—a new language construct. Structured Programming **11**(1) (1990) 1–10
4. Liu, Y. A., Stoller, S. D., Gorbovitski, M., Rothamel, T., Liu, Y. E.: Incremental-ization across object abstraction. In Proc. of 20th Ann. ACM SIGPLAN Int. Conf. on Object-Oriented Programming, Systems, Languages and Applications, OOPSLA 2005. ACM Press (2005) 473–486
5. Kiczales, G., Lamping, J., Menhdekar, A., Maeda, C., Lopes, C., Loingtier, J. M., Irwin, J.: Aspect-oriented programming. In Aksit, M., Matsuoka, S., eds.: Proc. of 11th European Conf. on Object-Oriented Programming, ECOOP '97. Vol. 1241 of Lect. Notes in Comput. Science. Springer-Verlag (1997) 220–242
6. Masuhara, H., Kiczales, G., Dutchyn, C.: A compilation and optimization model for aspect-oriented programs. In Hedin, G, ed.: Proc. of 12th Int. Conf. on Compiler Construction, CC 2003. Vol. 2622 of Lect. Notes in Comput. Sci. Springer-Verlag (2003) 46–60
7. Kiczales, G., Hilsdale, E., Hugunin, J., Kersten, M., Palm, J., Griswold, W.G.: An overview of AspectJ. In Knudsen, J. L., ed.: Proc. of 15th European Conf. on Object-Oriented Programming, ECOOP 2001. Vol. 2072 of Lect. Notes in Comput. Sci. Springer-Verlag (2001) 327–353
8. Avgustinov, P., Christensen, A.S., Hendren, L., Kuzins, S., Lhoták, J., Lhoták, O., de Moor, O., Sereni, D., Sittampalam, G., Tibble, J.: Optimising AspectJ. In Proc. of ACM SIGPLAN 2005 Conf. on Programming Language Design and Implementation, PLDI 2005. ACM Press (2005) 117–128
9. abc: The AspectBench Compiler. Home page with downloads, FAQ, documentation, support mailing lists, and bug database. `http://aspectbench.org/`.

Towards Generic Programming with Sized Types

Andreas Abel[*]

Institut für Informatik, Ludwigs-Maximilians-Universität München
Oettingenstr. 67, D-80538 München, Germany
abel@informatik.uni-muenchen.de

Abstract. Instances of a polytypic or generic program for a concrete recursive type often exhibit a recursion scheme that is derived from the recursion scheme of the instantiation type. In practice, the programs obtained from a generic program are usually terminating, but the proof of termination cannot be carried out with traditional methods as term orderings alone, since termination often crucially relies on the program type. This problem is tackled by an adaption of type-based termination to generic programming, and a framework for sized polytypic programming is described.

1 Introduction

In the last decade, *polytypic* or *generic* programming has been explored for functional programming languages [34, 7, 25, 28, 29, 30]. With polytypic programming, many repetitive tasks, like writing a `size`-function for data structures of type A, can be mechanized by writing a generic `size`-function which then can be instantiated to all sorts of types A. Over the years, many useful examples of generic programs have been put forth, like parsing and unparsing, map and zip functions, and even finite maps for key type A. When generic programs are defined by recursion on type A, then the resulting programs have often a recursion structure that corresponds to the recursion structure of type A; and it is the rule that they terminate, if applied to finite input. However, because of the high degree of abstraction that generic programs usually involve, termination cannot be proven with conventional methods like term orderings or initial algebras alone. It is the purpose of this article to outline a systematic solution to the termination problem of many generic programs.

As an example, we take Hinze's [24] generic definition of finite maps. If instantiated to key type *list of A*, in Haskell syntax `[a]`, we get the following definition of a finite map:

```
data MapList f v = Leaf
                 | Node (Maybe v) (f (MapList f v))
```

[*] Research supported by the coordination action *TYPES* (510996) and thematic network *Applied Semantics II* (IST-2001-38957) of the European Union and the project *Cover* of the Swedish Foundation of Strategic Research (SSF).

T. Uustalu (Ed.): MPC 2006, LNCS 4014, pp. 10–28, 2006.

Herein, v is the range of the finite map, and f w represents the finite maps from a to w. Instantiating a with Char and f w with Char→w, we would get finite maps over strings. Such a finite map is either totally undefined (Leaf) or a pair of maybe a piece of data associated with the current key (Maybe v) plus a finite map for each extension of the current key by one character (f (MapList f v)).

Merging finite maps is a completely generic operation. Again for the key type of lists, we get the following instance. Let

```
comb :: (v -> v -> v) -> Maybe v -> Maybe v -> Maybe v
```

be a conflict resolution function for up to two candidate values of a finite map at a certain key. Then the following Haskell program merges two finite maps over lists:

```
mergeList ::
  (forall w. (w -> w -> w) -> f w -> f w -> f w) ->
  (v -> v -> v) ->
  MapList f v -> MapList f v -> MapList f v
mergeList mergeF c Leaf t = t
mergeList mergeF c t Leaf = t
mergeList mergeF c (Node m1 t1) (Node m2 t2) =
  Node (comb c m1 m2) (mergeF (mergeList mergeF c) t1 t2)
```

This function has an extraordinary recursion behavior: As a recursive "call", the whole function mergeList mergeF c is passed to one of its arguments, mergeF. It is not immediately obvious that mergeList is a total function. Indeed, if we disregard its type, we can create a non-terminating execution: Define

```
mf m t1 t2 = m (Node Nothing t1) (Node Nothing t2)
```

and run mergeList mf fst (Node Nothing t1) (Node Nothing t2)! However, mf does not have the right type, and the polymorphic nature of the argument mergeF is a critical ingredient for termination.

This example demonstrates that term-based termination arguments do not suffice for generic programs. We need a method for establishing termination which takes the *type* of a program into account. Such a method is *type-based termination*, which has been developed by Hughes, Pareto, and Sabry [31], and independently by Giménez [20] who advanced the pioneering work of Mendler [37]. Since then, type-based termination has been considered by several authors [1, 2, 8, 9, 14, 15, 18].

In this work, we show that type-based termination can be successfully applied to generic programs. To this end, we have extended the approach to higher-order data types, arriving at System $F_{\hat{\omega}}$, which is the object of the author's thesis [3]. We will briefly introduce the necessary concepts to the reader in Section 2 and then outline a framework for total generic programming in Sect. 3. More related work and directions for future research are discussed in Sect. 4.

1.1 Preliminaries

We assume that the reader is firm in the higher-order polymorphic lambda-calculus, System F^ω (see Pierce's text book [46]). Additionally, some familiarity with generic programming would be helpful [29].

Generic programming takes a minimalistic view on data types: Each ground type can be constructed using the unit type 1, disjoint sum type $A + B$, product type $A \times B$ and recursion. The following terms manipulate these types:

$$
\begin{aligned}
&() \quad : 1 \\
&\mathsf{pair} : \forall A \forall B.\ A \to B \to A \times B \\
&\mathsf{fst} \quad : \forall A \forall B.\ A \times B \to A \\
&\mathsf{snd} \ : \forall A \forall B.\ A \times B \to B \\
&\mathsf{inl} \quad : \forall A \forall B.\ A \to A + B \\
&\mathsf{inr} \quad : \forall A \forall B.\ B \to A + B \\
&\mathsf{case} : \forall A \forall B \forall C.\ A + B \to (A \to C) \to (B \to C) \to C
\end{aligned}
$$

Pairs $\mathsf{pair}\, r\, s$ are written (r, s). We assume the usual reduction rules, for instance, $\mathsf{fst}\,(r, s) \longrightarrow r$. Sometimes it is convenient to introduce abbreviations for derived data constructors. For instance:

$$
\begin{aligned}
\mathsf{Nat} &= 1 + \mathsf{Nat} \\
\mathsf{zero} &= \mathsf{inl}\,() \\
\mathsf{succ} &= \lambda n.\,\mathsf{inr}\, n
\end{aligned}
$$

To improve readability, we will freely make use of the pattern matching notation

$$
\mathsf{match}\ r\ \mathsf{with}\ p_1 \mapsto t_1 \mid \cdots \mid p_n \mapsto t_n
$$

for patterns p_i generated from both elementary and derived data constructors. Similarly, we use a non-recursive $\mathsf{let}\ p = r\ \mathsf{in}\ t$.

2 Sized Types in a Nutshell

We use sized types for type-based termination checking, as described by Hughes, Pareto, and Sabry [31, 44] and Barthe, Frade, Giménez, Pinto, and Uustalu [8]. In comparison with the cited works, our system, $F_{\widehat{\omega}}$, also features higher-order polymorphism and heterogeneous (nested) and higher-order data types. In this section, we quickly introduce the most important features of $F_{\widehat{\omega}}$ [3].

Inductive types are recursively defined types which can only be unfolded finitely many times. The classical example are lists which are given as the least fixed-point of the type constructor $\lambda X.\, 1 + A \times X$, where A is the type of list elements. If the type constructor underlying an inductive type is not covariant (monotone), non-terminating programs can be constructed without explicit recursion [37]. Therefore we restrict inductive types to fixed-points of covariant constructors. We write

$$* \xrightarrow{+} * \quad \text{or} \quad +* \to * \quad \text{for the kind of covariant,}$$
$$* \xrightarrow{-} * \quad \text{or} \quad -* \to * \quad \text{for the kind of contravariant, and}$$
$$* \xrightarrow{\circ} * \quad \text{or} \quad \circ* \to * \quad \text{for the kind of mixed-variant}$$

type constructors, the last meaning constructors which are neither co- nor contravariant, or the absence of variance information. For example, $\lambda X.\, X \to 1$ is contravariant, and $\lambda X.\, X \to X$ is mixed-variant. The notion of variance is extended to arbitrary kinds and p-variant function kinds are written as $p\kappa \to \kappa'$ or

$$\kappa \xrightarrow{p} \kappa'.$$

For instance, we have the following kindings for disjoint sum, product, function, and polymorphic type constructor:

$$+ \;\; : \;\; * \xrightarrow{+} * \xrightarrow{+} * \qquad \text{disjoint sum}$$
$$\times \;\; : \;\; * \xrightarrow{+} * \xrightarrow{+} * \qquad \text{cartesian product}$$
$$\to \;\; : \;\; * \xrightarrow{-} * \xrightarrow{+} * \qquad \text{function space}$$
$$\forall_\kappa \;\; : \;\; (\kappa \xrightarrow{\circ} *) \xrightarrow{+} * \qquad \text{quantification}$$

We assume a *signature* Σ that contains the above type constructor constants together with their kinding, plus some base types 1, Char, Int ... The signature Σ is viewed as a function, so $\Sigma(C)$ returns the kind of the constructor constant C. A bit sloppily, we write $C \in \Sigma$ if C is in the domain of this function, $C \in \text{dom}(\Sigma)$. Also, we usually write $\forall X : \kappa.A$ for $\forall_\kappa \lambda X.A$, or $\forall X A$, if the kind κ is inferable.

Sized Inductive Types. We write inductive types as $\mu^a F$, where F is a covariant constructor and a a constructor of special kind ord. This kind models the stage expressions of Barthe et. al. [8], which are interpreted as ordinals, and has the following constructors:

$$\text{s} \;\; : \;\; \text{ord} \xrightarrow{+} \text{ord} \qquad \text{successor of ordinal}$$
$$\infty \;\; : \;\; \text{ord} \qquad \text{infinity ordinal}$$

The *infinity ordinal* is the closure ordinal of all inductive types considered, i.e., an ordinal big enough such that the equation

$$F\,(\mu^\infty F) = \mu^\infty F$$

holds for all type constructors which are allowed as basis for an inductive type. If F is first-order, i.e., does not mention function space, then the smallest infinite ordinal ω is sufficient. However, if we allow higher-order datatypes like the infinitely-branching $\mu^\infty \lambda X.1 + (\text{Nat} \to X)$, higher ordinals are required.[1]

In the following, we will only make use of ordinal constructors that are either ∞ or $\imath + n$, where $\imath$ is a constructor variable of kind ord and n a natural number

---

[1] More details can be found in the forthcoming thesis of the author [3, Sect. 3.3.3].

and $a + n$ is a shorthand for prepending the constructor a with n successor constructors s.

Sized inductive types are explained by the equation $\mu^{a+1} F = F (\mu^a F)$. Viewing inductive types as trees and F as the type of the node constructor, it becomes clear that the size index a is an upper bound on the height of trees in $\mu^a F$. Hence, inductive types are covariant in the size index, and their instances stand in the subtyping relation

$$\mu^a F \leq \mu^{a+1} F \leq \mu^{a+2} F \leq \cdots \leq \mu^\infty F.$$

Some examples for sized inductive types are:

$$\text{Nat} : \quad \text{ord} \xrightarrow{+} *$$
$$\text{Nat} := \lambda \imath.\ \mu^\imath \lambda X.\ 1 + X$$

$$\text{List} : \quad \text{ord} \xrightarrow{+} * \xrightarrow{+} *$$
$$\text{List} := \lambda \imath \lambda A.\ \mu^\imath \lambda X.\ 1 + A \times X$$

$$\text{Tree} : \quad \text{ord} \xrightarrow{+} * \xrightarrow{-} * \xrightarrow{+} *$$
$$\text{Tree} := \lambda \imath \lambda B \lambda A.\ \mu^\imath \lambda X.\ 1 + A \times (B \to X)$$

Nat^a denotes the type of natural numbers $< a$, $\text{List}^a A$ the type of lists of length $< a$, and $\text{Tree}^a B A$ the type of B-branching A-labeled trees of height $< a$. For lists, we define the usual constructors:

$$\text{nil} \quad := \text{inl}\,() \qquad\qquad : \forall \imath \forall A.\ \text{List}^{\imath+1} A$$
$$\text{cons} := \lambda a \lambda as.\ \text{inr}\,(a, as) : \forall \imath \forall A.\ A \to \text{List}^\imath A \to \text{List}^{\imath+1} A.$$

Heterogeneous Data Types. Nothing prevents us from considering inductive types of higher kind, i.e., such $\mu^a F$ where F is not of kind $* \xrightarrow{+} *$, but, for instance, of kind $(* \xrightarrow{+} *) \xrightarrow{+} (* \xrightarrow{+} *)$. For such an F we get an inductive *constructor*, or a heterogeneous data type [6], in the literature often called nested type [4, 11, 12, 13, 36, 22, 24, 26, 41, 42, 43]. In general, the least-fixed point constructor μ_κ can be used on any $F : \kappa \xrightarrow{+} \kappa$ where κ must be a pure kind, i.e., must not mention special kind ord. Examples for heterogeneous types are:

$$\text{PList} : \quad \text{ord} \xrightarrow{+} * \xrightarrow{+} *$$
$$\text{PList} := \lambda \imath.\ \mu^\imath_{+*\to*} \lambda X \lambda A.\ A + X\,(A \times A)$$

$$\text{Bush} : \quad \text{ord} \xrightarrow{+} * \xrightarrow{+} *$$
$$\text{Bush} := \lambda \imath.\ \mu^\imath_{+*\to*} \lambda X \lambda A.\ 1 + A \times X\,(X\,A)$$

The type $\text{PList}^a A$ implements lists with exactly 2^n elements of type A for some $n < a$. The second type, *bushy* lists, is an example of a *truly nested* type. It is well-defined since we can infer covariance of $X\,(X\,A)$ in X from the assumption that X is covariant itself.[2]

---

[2] The constructor underlying Bush fails a purely syntactical covariance test, like the test for *strict positivity* in Coq [32].

Example 1 (A powerlist). Let $a_0, a_1, a_2, a_3 : A$ and $\imath$: ord. We can construct the powerlist $\mathsf{PList}^{\imath+3} A$ containing these four elements as follows:

$((a_0, a_1), (a_2, a_3))$	:	$((A \times A) \times (A \times A)) =: A^4$
$\mathsf{inl}\,((a_0, a_1), (a_2, a_3))$	:	$A^4 + \mathsf{PList}^{\imath}\,(A^4 \times A^4)$
$\mathsf{inl}\,((a_0, a_1), (a_2, a_3))$	:	$\mathsf{PList}^{\imath+1}\,A^4$
$\mathsf{inr}\,(\mathsf{inl}\,((a_0, a_1), (a_2, a_3)))$	:	$A \times A + \mathsf{PList}^{\imath+1}\,A^4$
$\mathsf{inr}\,(\mathsf{inl}\,((a_0, a_1), (a_2, a_3)))$	:	$\mathsf{PList}^{\imath+2}\,(A \times A)$
$\mathsf{inr}\,(\mathsf{inr}\,(\mathsf{inl}\,((a_0, a_1), (a_2, a_3))))$	:	$A + \mathsf{PList}^{\imath+2}\,(A \times A)$
$\mathsf{inr}\,(\mathsf{inr}\,(\mathsf{inl}\,((a_0, a_1), (a_2, a_3))))$	:	$\mathsf{PList}^{\imath+3}\,A$

Structural Recursion. Since we are considering a terminating programming language, recursion cannot be available without restriction. In the following we give a typing rule for structurally recursive functions. Herein, we interpret *structurally recursive* in the context of sized types: A function is structurally recursive if the recursive instance is of smaller size than the calling instance. As typing rule, this definition reads:

$$\frac{\imath : \mathsf{ord}, \; f : A\,\imath \vdash t : A\,(\imath + 1)}{\mathsf{fix}\,(\lambda f.t) : \forall \imath. \, A\,\imath}$$

Of course, the type $A\,\imath$ must mention the size variable $\imath$ in a sensible way; with the constant type $A\,\imath = \mathsf{Nat}^\infty \to \mathsf{Nat}^\infty$ one immediately allows non-terminating functions. Barthe et. al. [8, 9] suggest types of the shape $A\,\imath = \mu^\imath F \to C$ where $\imath$ does not occur in F and only positively in C. In this article, we want to consider recursive functions that simultaneously descent on serveral arguments, and also polymorphic recursion. Hence, we consider types of the shape

$$\forall X_1 \ldots \forall X_k. \; \mu^\imath F \to B_1 \to \cdots \to B_m \to C,$$

where $\imath$ does not occur in F, index $\imath$ occurs only positively in C, and each of the B_i is either $\imath$-free or of the shape $\mu^\imath F_i$ with F_i $\imath$-free. More valid shapes for the type $A\,\imath$ are described by Hughes, Pareto, and Sabry [31], in Pareto's thesis [44], my thesis [3] and previous work of mine [1].

To obtain a strongly normalizing system, unrolling of fixed-point has to be restricted to the case

$$\mathsf{fix}^\mu s\,v \longrightarrow s\,(\mathsf{fix}^\mu s)\,v,$$

where v is a value (an injection, a pair, a λ-abstraction, an under-applied function symbol). For convenience, we define the fixed-point combinator fix^μ_n that takes n non-recursive arguments before the first recursive argument:

$$\begin{aligned}
\mathsf{back}_n &:= \lambda g \lambda t_1 \ldots \lambda t_n \lambda r. \; g\,r\,t_1 \ldots t_n \\
\mathsf{front}_n &:= \lambda g \lambda r \lambda t_1 \ldots \lambda t_n. \; g\,t_1 \ldots t_n\,r \\
\mathsf{fix}^\mu_n &:= \lambda s. \; \mathsf{back}_n\,(\mathsf{fix}^\mu\,(\lambda f. \, \mathsf{front}_n\,(s\,(\mathsf{back}_n\,f))))).
\end{aligned}$$

Example 2 (Merge sort). Assume a type A with a comparison function $\leq: A \to A \to \mathsf{Bool}$, a function $\mathsf{merge} : \mathsf{List}^\infty A \to \mathsf{List}^\infty A \to \mathsf{List}^\infty A$ which merges two ordered lists into an ordered output list and a function $\mathsf{split} : \forall \imath. \, \mathsf{List}^\imath A \to \mathsf{List}^\imath A \times$

$\text{List}^i A$ which splits a list into two parts of roughly the same size. The type of split expresses that none of the output lists is bigger than the input. We can encode merge sort $\text{msort}\, a\, as$ for non-empty lists $\text{cons}\, a\, as$ in $\mathsf{F}_{\widehat{\omega}}$ as follows:

$$
\begin{aligned}
\text{msort} &: \quad \forall i.\, A \to \text{List}^i A \to \text{List}^\infty A \\
\text{msort} &:= \text{fix}_1^\mu\, \lambda msort \lambda a \lambda xs.\ \text{match } xs \text{ with} \\
&\qquad\qquad \text{nil} \qquad \mapsto \text{cons}\, a\ \text{nil} \\
&\qquad\qquad \text{cons}\, b\, l \mapsto \text{let } (as, bs) = \text{split}\, l \\
&\qquad\qquad\qquad\qquad\qquad \text{in } \text{merge}\, (msort\, a\, as)\, (msort\, b\, bs)
\end{aligned}
$$

The recursive calls to $msort$ are legal because of the typing of split. Indeed, we can assign the following types:

$$
\begin{aligned}
msort &: A \to \text{List}^i A \to \text{List}^\infty A \\
a, b &: A \\
xs &: \text{List}^{i+1} A \\
l &: \text{List}^i A \\
as, bs &: \text{List}^i A
\end{aligned}
$$

The termination of msort depends on the fact that split is non size-increasing. This information could have been established by other means than typing, e. g., by a term ordering as usual for termination of term rewriting systems. However, for the generic programs we consider in the next section, the typing will be essential for termination checking.

3   A Framework for Generic Programming with Sized Types

Hinze [25] describes a framework for generic programming which is later extended by Hinze, Jeuring, and Löh [30] and implemented in *Generic Haskell* [29]. In this framework, both types and values can be constructed by recursion on some index type. The behavior is only specified for the type and constructor constants like Int, 1, + and ×, and this uniquely defines the constructed type or value. In the following we propose an extension by sized types, *sized polytypic programming*, and demonstrate its strength by giving termination guarantees for Hinze's generalized tries [24].

Observe the following typographic conventions:

Capital	$\text{Type}\langle A\rangle$	a type Type indexed by type A
UPPERCASE	$\text{TYPE}\langle\kappa\rangle$	the kind TYPE of type Type indexed by kind κ of type A
lowercase	$\text{poly}\langle A\rangle$	a polytypic program poly instantiated at type A
Capital	$\text{Poly}\langle\kappa\rangle$	the polykinded type Poly of program poly instantiated at kind κ of type A

3.1 Type-Indexed Types

In generic programming as proposed by Hinze, Jeuring, and Löh [30], one can define a family $\mathsf{Type}\langle A\rangle$ indexed by another type A. For instance, one can define the type $\mathsf{Map}\langle A\rangle V$ of finite maps from A to V generically for all index types A, by analyzing the structure of A. To this end, one specifies what $\mathsf{Map}\langle A\rangle$ should be for base types A_0 and for the standard type constructors, e. g., $+$ and $\times$. Then, $\mathsf{Map}\langle A\rangle$ is computed for a specific instance of A, where recursion is interpreted as the infinite unfolding. We differ from this setting in that we deal with inductive types instead of recursive types, thus, in our case, $\mathsf{Map}\langle A\rangle$ for an inductive type A will be itself an inductive type. In general, a type-indexed type $\mathsf{Type}\langle A\rangle$ will obey the following laws:

$$
\begin{aligned}
\mathsf{Type}\langle C\rangle &= \textit{user-defined} &&\text{for } C \in \{1, +, \times, \mathsf{Int}, \mathsf{Char}, \dots\} \\
\mathsf{Type}\langle X\rangle &= X \\
\mathsf{Type}\langle \lambda X F\rangle &= \lambda X.\, \mathsf{Type}\langle F\rangle \\
\mathsf{Type}\langle F\, G\rangle &= \mathsf{Type}\langle F\rangle\ \mathsf{Type}\langle G\rangle \\
\mathsf{Type}\langle \mu_\kappa\rangle &= \mu_?
\end{aligned}
$$

What should the kind index to μ be in the last equation? We can answer this question if we look at the kind $\mathsf{TYPE}\langle \kappa\rangle$ of a type-indexed type $\mathsf{Type}\langle F\rangle$. (Actually, the term *constructor-indexed constructor* would be more appropriate, but we stick to the existing terminology.) The kind $\mathsf{TYPE}\langle \kappa\rangle$ depends on the kind κ of constructor F. The given equations for abstraction and application dictate the following laws for function kinds.

$$
\mathsf{TYPE}\langle \kappa_1 \xrightarrow{p} \kappa_2\rangle = \mathsf{TYPE}\langle \kappa_1\rangle \xrightarrow{p} \mathsf{TYPE}\langle \kappa_2\rangle
$$

The kind $\mathsf{TYPE}\langle *\rangle$ has to be chosen such that $\mathsf{Type}\langle C\rangle : \mathsf{TYPE}\langle \Sigma(C)\rangle$ for all basic type constructors $C \in \Sigma$. (Of course, $\mathsf{Type}\langle C\rangle$ can be undefined for some C, typically for $C = \rightarrow$ and $C = \forall_\kappa$.) For instance, the kind $\mathsf{MAP}\langle \kappa\rangle$ for the type of finite maps $\mathsf{Map}\langle F : \kappa\rangle$ is defined by $\mathsf{MAP}\langle *\rangle = * \xrightarrow{+} *$. We can now complete the construction law for types indexed by inductive types.

$$
\mathsf{Type}\langle \mu_\kappa\rangle = \mu_{\mathsf{TYPE}\langle \kappa\rangle}
$$

Remark 1. Note that the presence of polarities restricts the choices for $\mathsf{Type}\langle C\rangle$. However, if index types are constructed in a signature without polymorphism and function space, as it is usual in the generic programming community, all function kinds are covariant and we do not have to worry about polarities.

We extend the framework to sized types by giving homomorphic construction rules for everything that concerns sizes:

$$
\mathsf{TYPE}\langle \mathsf{ord}\rangle = \mathsf{ord}
$$

$$
\begin{aligned}
\mathsf{Type}\langle s\rangle &= s \\
\mathsf{Type}\langle \infty\rangle &= \infty
\end{aligned}
$$

Theorem 1 (Well-kindedness of type-indexed types). *Let Σ be a signature of constructor constants. If* $\mathsf{Type}\langle C \rangle : \mathsf{TYPE}\langle \kappa \rangle$ *for all* $(C : \kappa) \in \Sigma$, *and* $X_1 : p_1 \kappa_1, \dots, X_n : p_n \kappa_n \vdash F : \kappa$, *then* $X_1 : p_1 \mathsf{TYPE}\langle \kappa_1 \rangle, \dots, X_n : p_n \mathsf{TYPE}\langle \kappa_n \rangle \vdash \mathsf{Type}\langle F \rangle : \mathsf{TYPE}\langle \kappa \rangle$.

Proof. By induction on the kinding derivation.

Example Finite Maps Via Generalized Tries. Hinze [24] defines generalized tries $\mathsf{Map}\langle F \rangle$ by recursion on F. In particular, $\mathsf{Map}\langle K : * \rangle V$ is the type of finite maps from domain K to codomain V. The following representation using type-level λ can be found in his article on type-indexed data types [30, page 139].

$$\mathsf{MAP}\langle * \rangle \quad := * \xrightarrow{+} *$$

$$\mathsf{Map}\langle \mathsf{Int} \rangle := \lambda V.\ \textit{efficient implementation of } \mathsf{Int} \to_{\mathsf{fin}} V$$
$$\mathsf{Map}\langle \mathsf{Char} \rangle := \lambda V.\ \textit{efficient implementation of } \mathsf{Char} \to_{\mathsf{fin}} V$$
$$\mathsf{Map}\langle 1 \rangle \quad := \lambda V.\ 1 + V$$
$$\mathsf{Map}\langle + \rangle \quad := \lambda F \lambda G \lambda V.\ 1 + F V \times G V$$
$$\mathsf{Map}\langle \times \rangle \quad := \lambda F \lambda G \lambda V.\ F (G V)$$

Well-kindedness of these definitions is immediate, except maybe for $\mathsf{Map}\langle \times \rangle$ which must be of kind $(* \xrightarrow{+} *) \xrightarrow{+} (* \xrightarrow{+} *) \xrightarrow{+} (* \xrightarrow{+} *)$. For $\mathsf{Map}\langle + \rangle$ we have used the variant of *spotted products* (or lifted products) which Hinze mentions in section 4.1 of his article [24]. This way we avoid that certain empty tries have an infinite normal form (see [24, page 341]) which requires lazy evaluation. The constructor for finite maps over strings can now be computed as follows:

$$\mathsf{Map}\langle \lambda \imath.\ \mathsf{List}^\imath \mathsf{Char} \rangle$$
$$= \mathsf{Map}\langle \lambda \imath.\ \mu^\imath_* \lambda X.\ 1 + \mathsf{Char} \times X \rangle$$
$$= \lambda \imath.\ \mu^\imath_{* \xrightarrow{+} *} \lambda X.\ \mathsf{Map}\langle + \rangle\ \mathsf{Map}\langle 1 \rangle\ (\mathsf{Map}\langle \times \rangle\ \mathsf{Map}\langle \mathsf{Char} \rangle\ X)$$
$$= \lambda \imath.\ \mu^\imath_{* \xrightarrow{+} *} \lambda X \lambda V.\ 1 + (1 + V) \times \mathsf{Map}\langle \mathsf{Char} \rangle\ (X V)$$

The matching kind is

$$\mathsf{MAP}\langle \mathsf{ord} \xrightarrow{+} * \rangle = \mathsf{ord} \xrightarrow{+} * \xrightarrow{+} *.$$

Note that the type $\mathsf{Map}\langle \lambda \imath.\ \mathsf{List}^\imath \mathsf{Char} \rangle$ of sized, string-indexed tries involves a higher-kinded inductive type $\mu_{* \xrightarrow{+} *}$. However, it is not heterogeneous, but homogeneous, meaning that X is always applied to the variable V. Thus, we have the option to simplify it using λ-*dropping* and obtain an ordinary inductive type:

$$\mathsf{Map}\langle \lambda \imath.\ \mathsf{List}^\imath \mathsf{Char} \rangle = \lambda \imath \lambda V.\ \mu^\imath_* \lambda Y.\ 1 + (1 + V) \times \mathsf{Map}\langle \mathsf{Char} \rangle\ Y)$$

It is easy to interpret this type as a trie for strings with prefix p: The trie is either "()" (first 1), meaning that strings with this prefix are undefined in the finite map, or it is a pair of maybe a value v (the value mapped to p) and of one trie for strings with prefix $p \cdot c$ for each $c \in \mathsf{Char}$. A trie for strings with empty prefix is then a finite map over all strings.

3.2   Type-Indexed Values

The key ingredient to generic programming are type-indexed values, meaning, programs $\mathsf{poly}\langle F \rangle$ which work for different type constructors F but are uniformly (generically) constructed by recursion on F. Again, the user supplies the desired behavior $\mathsf{poly}\langle C \rangle$ on base types and type constructors C, and the polytypic program $\mathsf{poly}\langle F \rangle$ is then constructed by the following laws:

$$
\begin{aligned}
\mathsf{poly}\langle C \rangle & = \textit{user-defined} \\
\mathsf{poly}\langle X \rangle & = x \\
\mathsf{poly}\langle \lambda X F : \kappa_1 \to \kappa_2 \rangle & = \lambda x.\,\mathsf{poly}\langle F \rangle \\
\mathsf{poly}\langle F\, G \rangle & = \mathsf{poly}\langle F \rangle\, \mathsf{poly}\langle G \rangle \\
\mathsf{poly}\langle \mu_\kappa \rangle & = \mathsf{fix}
\end{aligned}
$$

(This definition is sensible if we consider all bound variables in F distinct and require $\mathsf{poly}\langle C \rangle$ to be a closed expression.)

Hinze [27] has observed that type-indexed values $\mathsf{poly}\langle F : \kappa \rangle$ have kind-indexed types $\mathsf{Poly}\langle F, \dots, F : \kappa \rangle : *$ with possibly several copies of F, obeying the following laws:

$$
\begin{aligned}
\mathsf{Poly}\langle A_1, \dots, A_n : * \rangle & = \textit{user-defined} \\
\mathsf{Poly}\langle F_1, \dots, F_n : \kappa \xrightarrow{p} \kappa' \rangle & = \forall G_1 : \kappa \dots \forall G_n : \kappa. \\
& \quad \mathsf{Poly}\langle G_1, \dots, G_n : \kappa \rangle \to \mathsf{Poly}\langle F_1\, G_1, \dots, F_n\, G_n : \kappa' \rangle
\end{aligned}
$$

For example, three copies of F are required for a generic definition of zipping functions [27, Sect. 7.2].

Hinze works in a framework where only covariant type constructors serve as indices, i.e., $p = +$ in the above equation. However, with polarity information at hand, it is sometimes useful to depart from Hinze's scheme. One example is a generic map function (monotonicity witness, functoriality witness, resp.):

$$
\begin{aligned}
\mathsf{GMap}\langle A, B : * \rangle & := A \to B \\
\mathsf{GMap}\langle F, G : \kappa \xrightarrow{-} \kappa' \rangle & := \forall X \forall Y.\ \mathsf{GMap}\langle Y, X : \kappa \rangle \to \mathsf{GMap}\langle F\, X,\ G\, Y : \kappa' \rangle \\
\mathsf{GMap}\langle F, G : \kappa \xrightarrow{p} \kappa' \rangle & := \forall X \forall Y.\ \mathsf{GMap}\langle X, Y : \kappa \rangle \to \mathsf{GMap}\langle F\, X,\ G\, Y : \kappa' \rangle \\
& \qquad \text{for } p \in \{+, \circ\}
\end{aligned}
$$

With this refined definition of kind-indexed type, a generic map function is definable which also works for data types with embedded function spaces, e.g., Tree.

$$
\begin{aligned}
\mathsf{gmap}\langle 1 : * \rangle & := \lambda u.\, u \\
\mathsf{gmap}\langle + : * \xrightarrow{+} * \xrightarrow{+} * \rangle & := \lambda f \lambda g \lambda s.\ \mathsf{case}\ s\ (\lambda x.\,\mathsf{inl}\,(f\,x))\ (\lambda y.\,\mathsf{inr}\,(g\,y)) \\
\mathsf{gmap}\langle \times : * \xrightarrow{+} * \xrightarrow{+} * \rangle & := \lambda f \lambda g \lambda p.\ (f\,(\mathsf{fst}\,p),\ g\,(\mathsf{snd}\,p)) \\
\mathsf{gmap}\langle \to : * \xrightarrow{-} * \xrightarrow{+} * \rangle & := \lambda f \lambda g \lambda h \lambda x.\ g\,(h\,(f\,x))
\end{aligned}
$$

For the main example we want to consider, generic operations for tries, types $\mathsf{Poly}\langle F : \kappa \rangle$ indexed by a single constructor F are sufficient, hence, we will restrict the following development to this case.

In $F_\omega^\wedge$, there is a second base kind, ord. Since ordinals are only used to increase the static information about programs, not to carry out computations, the occurrence of kind ord in a kind which indexes a type should not alter this type. Thus, the following laws are sensible:

$$\mathsf{Poly}\langle A:* \rangle \qquad\qquad = user\text{-}defined$$
$$\mathsf{Poly}\langle F:\mathsf{ord} \xrightarrow{p} \kappa\rangle = \forall\imath:\mathsf{ord}.\, \mathsf{Poly}\langle F\,\imath:\kappa\rangle$$
$$\mathsf{Poly}\langle F:\kappa_1 \xrightarrow{p} \kappa_2\rangle = \forall G:\kappa_1.\, \mathsf{Poly}\langle G:\kappa_1\rangle \to \mathsf{Poly}\langle F\,G:\kappa_2\rangle$$

Kinds suitable as indexes must fit into the grammar: $\kappa ::= * \mid \mathsf{ord} \xrightarrow{p} \kappa \mid \kappa_1 \xrightarrow{p} \kappa_2$. Size expressions appearing in the type A of a generic program $\mathsf{poly}\langle A\rangle$ should not influence the program. We only consider types A which are normalized and contain size expressions only as index to an inductive type. Then we can refine the generation laws for type-indexed programs as follows:

$$\mathsf{poly}\langle C\rangle \qquad\qquad = user\text{-}defined$$
$$\mathsf{poly}\langle X\rangle \qquad\qquad = x$$
$$\mathsf{poly}\langle \lambda\imath F : \mathsf{ord} \to \kappa\rangle = \mathsf{poly}\langle F\rangle$$
$$\mathsf{poly}\langle \lambda X F : \kappa_1 \to \kappa_2\rangle = \lambda x.\, \mathsf{poly}\langle F\rangle \qquad \text{where } \kappa_1 \neq \mathsf{ord}$$
$$\mathsf{poly}\langle F\,G\rangle \qquad\qquad = \mathsf{poly}\langle F\rangle\,\mathsf{poly}\langle G\rangle$$
$$\mathsf{poly}\langle \mu_\kappa^a\rangle \qquad\qquad = \mathsf{fix}_n^\mu \qquad\qquad \text{for some } n$$

In the last equation, n has to be chosen such that the nth argument to the resulting recursive function is of an inductive type whose size is associated to a. The choice of n depends on the definition of the type $\mathsf{Poly}\langle A:*\rangle$ of the type-indexed program given by the user. For the example of map lookup functions (see below), the polytypic program is of type

$$\mathsf{Lookup}\langle K:*\rangle := \forall V.\ K \to \mathsf{Map}\langle K\rangle\,V \to 1 + V.$$

Hence, we set $n = 0$, because the recursive argument of the function that is generated in case $K = \mu^a F$ is the first one, of type K. In the example of finite map merging to follow, we will have the type

$$\mathsf{Merge}\langle K:*\rangle := \forall V.\ \mathsf{Bin}\,V \to \mathsf{Bin}\,(\mathsf{Map}\langle K\rangle\,V)$$

with $\mathsf{Bin}\,V = V \to V \to V$. Since $\mathsf{Map}\langle K\rangle$ is an inductive type for inductive K, the second argument is the recursive one and we have $n = 1$.

Example Finite Map Lookup. In the following, we implement Hinze's generic lookup function in our framework. The definitions on the program level are unchanged, only the types are now sized, and we give termination guarantees. We use the bind operation $\gg=$ for the *Maybe* monad $\lambda V.\,1 + V$. It obeys the laws $(\mathsf{inl}() \gg= f) \longrightarrow \mathsf{inl}()$ and $(\mathsf{inr}\,v \gg= f) \longrightarrow f\,v$.

$\mathsf{Lookup}\langle K : * \rangle := \forall V.\ K \to \mathsf{Map}\langle K \rangle\, V \to 1 + V$

$\mathsf{lookup}\langle 1 \rangle \quad : \quad \forall V.\ 1 \to 1 + V \to 1 + V$

$\mathsf{lookup}\langle 1 \rangle \quad := \lambda k \lambda m.\, m$

$\mathsf{lookup}\langle + \rangle \quad : \quad \forall A : *.\ \mathsf{Lookup}\langle A \rangle \to \forall B : *.\ \mathsf{Lookup}\langle B \rangle \to$
$\qquad\qquad\qquad \forall V.\ A + B \to 1 + (\mathsf{Map}\langle A \rangle\, V) \times (\mathsf{Map}\langle B \rangle\, V) \to 1 + V$

$\mathsf{lookup}\langle + \rangle \quad := \lambda la \lambda lb \lambda ab \lambda tab.\ tab \gg= \lambda(ta, tb).$
$\qquad\qquad\qquad$ match ab with
$\qquad\qquad\qquad\qquad$ inl $a \mapsto la\ a\ ta$
$\qquad\qquad\qquad\qquad$ inr $b \mapsto lb\ b\ tb$

$\mathsf{lookup}\langle \times \rangle \quad : \quad \forall A : *.\ \mathsf{Lookup}\langle A \rangle \to \forall B : *.\ \mathsf{Lookup}\langle B \rangle \to$
$\qquad\qquad\qquad \forall V.\ A \times B \to \mathsf{Map}\langle A \rangle\, (\mathsf{Map}\langle B \rangle\, V) \to 1 + V$

$\mathsf{lookup}\langle \times \rangle \quad := \lambda la \lambda lb \lambda(a, b) \lambda tab.\ la\ a\ tab \gg= \lambda tb.\ lb\ b\ tb$

All these definitions are well-typed, which is easy to check since there are no references to sizes.

Example Lookup For List-Shaped Keys. The previous definitions determine the instance of the generic lookup function for the type constructor of lists.

$\mathsf{lookup}\langle \mathsf{List} \rangle$
$:\ \mathsf{Lookup}\langle \mathsf{List} \rangle$
$:\ \forall \imath \forall K : *.\ \mathsf{Lookup}\langle K \rangle \to \mathsf{Lookup}\langle \mathsf{List}^\imath\, K \rangle$
$:\ \forall \imath \forall K : *.\ \mathsf{Lookup}\langle K \rangle \to \forall V.\ \mathsf{List}^\imath K \to \mathsf{Map}\langle \mathsf{List}^\imath K \rangle \to 1 + V$
$:\ \forall \imath \forall K : *.\ \mathsf{Lookup}\langle K \rangle \to \forall V.\ \mathsf{List}^\imath K \to (\mu^\imath \lambda Y.\ 1 + (1 + V) \times Y) \to 1 + V$

$\mathsf{lookup}\langle \mathsf{List} \rangle$
$= \mathsf{lookup}\langle \lambda \imath \lambda K.\ \mu^\imath \lambda X.\ 1 + K \times X \rangle$
$= \lambda lookup_K.\ \mathsf{fix}_0^\mu\, \lambda lookup.\ \mathsf{lookup}\langle + \rangle\, \mathsf{lookup}\langle 1 \rangle\, (\mathsf{lookup}\langle \times \rangle\, lookup_K\, lookup)$
$= \lambda lookup_K.\ \mathsf{fix}_0^\mu\, \lambda lookup \lambda l \lambda m.\ m \gg= \lambda(n, c).$
$\qquad$ match l with
$\qquad\qquad$ nil $\qquad \mapsto n$
$\qquad\qquad$ cons $k\, l' \mapsto lookup_K\, k\, c \gg= \lambda m'.\ lookup\, l'\, m'$

Note that the type of $\mathsf{lookup}\langle \mathsf{List} \rangle$ mentions the size variable $\imath$ twice, as index to both inductive arguments. This makes sense, since the length of the search keys determines the depth of the trie. Welltypedness can be ensured on an abstract level:

$$\begin{array}{ll} lookup_K & : \mathsf{Lookup}\langle K \rangle \\ lookup & : \mathsf{Lookup}\langle \mathsf{List}^\imath K \rangle \\ \mathsf{lookup}\langle \times \rangle\, lookup_K\, lookup =: r & : \mathsf{Lookup}\langle K \times \mathsf{List}^\imath K \rangle \\ \mathsf{lookup}\langle + \rangle\, \mathsf{lookup}\langle 1 \rangle\, r \quad =: s & : \mathsf{Lookup}\langle 1 + K \times \mathsf{List}^\imath K \rangle \\ & : \mathsf{Lookup}\langle \mathsf{List}^{\imath+1} K \rangle \\ \mathsf{fix}_0^\mu\, \lambda lookup.\, s & : \mathsf{Lookup}\langle \mathsf{List}^\imath K \rangle \end{array}$$

Finally, the type $\mathsf{Lookup}\langle \mathsf{List}^\imath K \rangle$ is valid for recursion with fix_0^μ, according to criterion given in Sect. 2.

Trie Merging. Hinze [24] presents three elementary operations to construct finite tries: empty, single, and merge. In the following we replay the construction of merge in our framework, since it exhibits a very interesting recursion scheme.

First we define the type Bin V for binary operations on V and a function comb which lifts a merging function for V to a merging function for $1 + V$.

$$\text{Bin} \quad : \quad * \xrightarrow{\circ} *$$
$$\text{Bin} \quad := \lambda V.\, V \to V \to V$$

$$\text{comb} : \quad \forall V.\, (V \to V \to V) \to (1 + V \to 1 + V \to 1 + V)$$
$$\text{comb} := \lambda c \lambda m_1 \lambda m_2.\ \text{match } (m_1, m_2) \text{ with}$$
$$\begin{array}{ll}
(\text{inl}(), \_) & \mapsto m_2 \\
(\_, \text{inl}()) & \mapsto m_1 \\
(\text{inr}\, v_1, \text{inr}\, v_2) & \mapsto \text{inr}\, (c\, v_1\, v_2)
\end{array}$$

The following definitions determine a generic merging function.

$$\text{Merge}\langle K:*\rangle := \forall V.\, \text{Bin}\, V \to \text{Bin}\, (\text{Map}\langle K\rangle\, V)$$

$$\begin{array}{ll}
\text{merge}\langle 1\rangle & : \quad \text{Merge}\langle 1\rangle \\
\text{merge}\langle 1\rangle & := \text{comb}
\end{array}$$

$$\begin{array}{ll}
\text{merge}\langle +\rangle & : \quad \forall A.\, \text{Merge}\langle A\rangle \to \forall B.\, \text{Merge}\langle B\rangle \to \forall V.\, \text{Bin}\, V \to \\
& \qquad \text{Bin}\, (1 + \text{Map}\langle A\rangle\, V \times \text{Map}\langle B\rangle\, V)
\end{array}$$

$$\begin{array}{ll}
\text{merge}\langle +\rangle & := \lambda ma \lambda mb \lambda c.\ \text{comb} \\
& \qquad \lambda(ta_1, tb_1)\lambda(ta_2, tb_2).\ (ma\, c\, ta_1\, ta_2,\ mb\, c\, tb_1\, tb_2)
\end{array}$$

$$\begin{array}{ll}
\text{merge}\langle \times\rangle & : \quad \forall A.\, \text{Merge}\langle A\rangle \to \forall B.\, \text{Merge}\langle B\rangle \to \forall V.\, \text{Bin}\, V \to \\
& \qquad \text{Bin}\, (\text{Map}\langle A\rangle\, (\text{Map}\langle B\rangle\, V))
\end{array}$$

$$\begin{array}{ll}
\text{merge}\langle \times\rangle & := \lambda ma \lambda mb \lambda c.\ ma\, (mb\, c)
\end{array}$$

The instance for list tries can be computed as follows:

$$\begin{array}{l}
\text{merge}\langle \text{List}\rangle \\
\quad : \text{Merge}\langle \text{List}\rangle \\
\quad : \forall \imath \forall K.\, \text{Merge}\langle K\rangle \to \text{Merge}\langle \text{List}^\imath K\rangle \\
\quad : \forall \imath \forall K.\, (\forall V.\, \text{Bin}\, V \to \text{Bin}\, (\text{Map}\langle K\rangle\, V)) \to \\
\qquad \quad \forall W.\, \text{Bin}\, W \to \text{Bin}\, (\text{Map}\langle \text{List}^\imath K\rangle\, W)
\end{array}$$

$$\begin{array}{l}
\text{merge}\langle \text{List}\rangle \\
\quad = \text{merge}\langle \lambda \imath \lambda K.\, \mu^\imath \lambda X.\, 1 + K \times X\rangle \\
\quad = \lambda merge_K.\ \text{fix}_1^\mu\, \lambda merge.\ \text{merge}\langle +\rangle\, \text{merge}\langle 1\rangle\, (\text{merge}\langle \times\rangle\, merge_K\, merge) \\
\quad = \lambda merge_K.\ \text{fix}_1^\mu\, \lambda merge \lambda c.\ \text{comb} \\
\qquad \lambda(mv_1, t_1)\lambda(mv_2, t_2).\ (\text{comb}\, c\, mv_1\, mv_2,\ merge_K\, (merge\, c)\, t_1 t_2) \\
\quad [= \lambda merge_K \lambda c.\ \text{fix}_0^\mu\, \lambda merge.\ \text{comb} \\
\qquad \lambda(mv_1, t_1)\lambda(mv_2, t_2).\ (\text{comb}\, c\, mv_1\, mv_2,\ merge_K\, merge\, t_1 t_2)]
\end{array}$$

In the last step, we have decreased the rank of recursion by λ-dropping. Surprisingly, recursion happens not by invoking *merge* on structurally smaller arguments, but by *passing the function itself* to a parameter, $merge_K$. Here, type-based termination reveals its strength; it is not possible to show termination of merge⟨List⟩ disregarding its type. With sized types, however, the termination proof is again just a typing derivation, as easy as for lookup⟨List⟩. We reason again on the abstract level:

$$
\begin{array}{lll}
merge_K & & : \mathsf{Merge}\langle K\rangle \\
merge & & : \mathsf{Merge}\langle \mathsf{List}^\imath K\rangle \\
\mathsf{merge}\langle\times\rangle\, merge_K\, merge =: r & : \mathsf{Merge}\langle K \times \mathsf{List}^\imath K\rangle \\
\mathsf{merge}\langle+\rangle\, \mathsf{merge}\langle 1\rangle\, r \quad =: s & : \mathsf{Merge}\langle 1 + K \times \mathsf{List}^\imath K\rangle \\
& & : \mathsf{Merge}\langle \mathsf{List}^{\imath+1} K\rangle \\
\mathsf{fix}_1^\mu\, \lambda merge.\, s & & : \mathsf{Merge}\langle \mathsf{List}^\imath K\rangle
\end{array}
$$

The type $\mathsf{Merge}\langle\mathsf{List}^\imath K\rangle$ is admissible for recursion on the second argument (the first argument is of type $\mathsf{Bin}\,V$): The whole type is of shape $\forall V.\,\mathsf{Bin}\,V \to \mu^\imath F \to \mu^\imath F \to \mu^\imath F$ for some F which does not depend on the size variable $\imath$. Hence, the type has the required shape.

Merging Bushy Tries. An even more dazzling recursion pattern is exhibited by the merge function for "bushy" tries, i.e., finite maps over bushy lists.

$$
\begin{array}{ll}
\mathsf{Bush} & : \quad \mathsf{ord} \xrightarrow{+} * \xrightarrow{+} * \\
\mathsf{Bush} & := \lambda\imath.\, \mu^\imath_{*\xrightarrow{+}*}\, \lambda X \lambda K.\, 1 + K \times X\,(X\,K)
\end{array}
$$

$$
\begin{array}{ll}
\mathsf{Map}\langle\mathsf{Bush}\rangle : & \mathsf{ord} \xrightarrow{+} (* \xrightarrow{+} *) \xrightarrow{+} (* \xrightarrow{+} *) \\
\mathsf{Map}\langle\mathsf{Bush}\rangle = & \lambda\imath.\, \mu^\imath_{(*\xrightarrow{+}*)\xrightarrow{+}(*\xrightarrow{+}*)}\, \lambda X \lambda F \lambda V.\, 1 + (1 + V) \times F\,(X\,(X\,F)\,V)
\end{array}
$$

The merge function for bush-indexed tries can be derived routinely:

$$
\begin{aligned}
\mathsf{merge}&\langle\mathsf{Bush}\rangle \\
&= \mathsf{merge}\langle\lambda\imath.\, \mu^\imath\, \lambda X \lambda K.\, 1 + K \times X\,(X\,K)\rangle \\
&= \mathsf{fix}_2^\mu\, \lambda merge \lambda merge_K. \\
&\qquad \mathsf{merge}\langle+\rangle\, \mathsf{merge}\langle 1\rangle\, (\mathsf{merge}\langle\times\rangle\, merge_K\, (merge\,(merge\, merge_K))) \\
&= \mathsf{fix}_2^\mu\, \lambda merge \lambda merge_K \\
&\qquad \lambda c.\, \mathsf{comb}\, \lambda(mv_1, t_1)\lambda(mv_2, t_2). \\
&\qquad\quad (\mathsf{comb}\, c\, mv_1\, mv_2,\; merge_K\,(merge\,(merge\, merge_K)\, c)\, t_1\, t_2)
\end{aligned}
$$

The recursion pattern of merge⟨Bush⟩ is adventurous. Not only is the recursive instance *merge* passed to an argument to the function $merge_K$, but also this function is modified during recursion: it is replaced by $(merge\, merge_K)$, which involves the recursive instance again! All these complications are coolly handled by type-based termination!

4   Conclusions and Related Work

We have seen a polymorphic λ-calculus with sized higher-order data types, $\mathsf{F}_{\widehat{\omega}}$, in which all programs are terminating. This calculus is strong enough to certify termination of arbitrary instances of generic programs, provided the generic programs themselves do not use unrestricted recursion. A systematic method to certify termination using the framework of sized polytypic programming has been sketched. The approach of type-based termination we have seen can handle convoluted recursion patterns that go far beyond schemes of iteration and primitive recursion stemming from the initial algebra semantics of data types. The recursion patterns of many examples for generic programming [28, 29] can be treated in $F_\omega^{\widehat{}}$, and I am still looking for sensible examples that exceed the capabilities of $F_\omega^{\widehat{}}$. It seems promising to pursue this approach further.

In this article, we have not addressed the problem of type-checking sized types. However, some solutions exist in the literature: Pareto [44], Barthe, Gregorie, and Pastawski [9], and Blanqui [15] have given constraint-based inference algorithms for sized types.

System $F_\omega^{\widehat{}}$ is strongly normalizing [3], as is its non-polymorphic predecessor $\lambda^{\widehat{}}$ [8]. More suitable for functional programming seems an interpretation of types as sets of closed values or finite observations—this, however, is future work. Hughes, Pareto, and Sabry [31] have presented a similar calculus, with ML-polymorphism, and given it a domain-theoretic semantics. In my view, this semantics has the flaw that it introduces undefinedness ($\bot$), only to show later that no well-typed program is undefined. I would like to find a tailored semantics that can handle infinite objects (coinductive types) but speaks of neither strong normalization nor undefinedness.

Related Work on Termination. The research on *size-change termination* (SCT), which is lead by Neil Jones, has received much attention. Recently, Sereni and Jones have extended this method to higher-order functions [48]. Is SCT able to check termination of the generic programs presented in this work? No, because SCT analyses only the *untyped* program, and without typing information termination of, e. g., `mergeList` cannot be established, as explained in the introduction (`mergeList` diverges on ill-typed arguments). Neither can the methods developed for higher-order term rewriting systems, as for instance bundled in the tool AProve [19], be applied to the generic program, since they disregard typing. (According experiments were carried out by the author in Fall 2005.)

Related Work on Generic Programming. We have considered generic programming in the style of *Generic Haskell* which has been formulated by Hinze, Jeuring, and Löh [23, 25, 27, 28, 29, 30]. Another philosophy of generic programming is rooted in in the initial algebra semantics for data types (see the introductory text by Backhouse, Jansson, Jeuring, and Meertens [7]). Jansson and Jeuring [33, 34, 35] present *PolyP*, a polytypic extension for Haskell which gives more control in defining polytypic functions, for instance, "recursion" is a type constructor one can treat in a clause of the polytypic program, whereas in *Generic Haskell* and our extension to sized types, recursion on types is always mapped to a recursive program.

Pfeifer and Rueß [45] study polytypic definitions in dependent type theory where all expressions are required to terminate. Termination is achieved by limiting recursion to the elimination combinators for inductive types, which correspond to the scheme of primitive recursion or *paramorphism*. This excludes many interesting generic programs we can treat, like merging of tries, that do not fit into this scheme. Benke, Dybjer, and Jansson [10] extend the approach of Pfeifer and Rueß to generic definition over inductive families. They also restrict recursion to iteration and primitive recursion. Altenkirch and McBride [5] pursue a similar direction; they show that generic programming is dependently type programming with tailored type universes. They construct a generic fold for members of the universe of Haskell types, which allows to define generic *iterative* functions (catamorphisms).

Norell and Jansson [39] exploit the type class mechanism to enable polytypic programming in Haskell without language extensions. They also present an approach to generic programming using template Haskell [40]. Finally, Norell [38] describes an encoding of generic programs in dependent type theory. None of these works considers the problem of termination of the generated programs.

Generic programming within an intermediated language of a typed compiler has been studied under the names *intensional polymorphism* and *intensional type analysis* by Harper and Morrisett [21] and Crary, Weirich, and Morrisett [17]. The gist of this approach is to have a *type case* construct on the level of programs, in later developments even also on the level of types. This way, certain compiler optimizations such as untagging and unboxing can be performed in a type-safe way. Crary and Weirich [16] even enrich the kind language by inductive kinds and the constructor language by primitive recursion. Saha, Trifonov, and Shao [47] consider intensional analysis of polymorphism. To this end, they introduce polymorphic kinds. For our purposes, this would be contraproductive since a language with two impredicative universes on top of each other is non-normalizing (Girard's paradox).

Acknowledgments. The idea to apply type-based termination to generic programming was born in discussions with Ralph Matthes. Thanks to the anonymous referees for helpful comments which helped to improve the presentation.

References

1. Abel, A.: Termination and guardedness checking with continuous types. In Hofmann, M., ed.: Proc. of 6th Int. Conf. on Typed Lambda Calculi and Applications, TLCA 2003. Vol. 2701 of Lect. Notes in Comput. Sci. Springer-Verlag (2003) 1–15
2. Abel, A.: Termination checking with types. Theor. Inform. and Appl. **38** (2004) 277–319.
3. Abel, A.: A Polymorphic Lambda-Calculus with Sized Higher-Order Types. PhD thesis, Ludwig-Maximilians-Universität München (2006)
   Draft available at http://www.tcs.ifi.lmu.de/~abel/diss.pdf
4. Abel, A., Matthes, R., Uustalu, T.: Iteration schemes for higher-order and nested datatypes. Theor. Comput. Sci. **333** (2005) 3–66
5. Altenkirch, T., McBride, C.: Generic programming within dependently typed programming. In Gibbons, J., Jeuring, J., eds.: Proc. of IFIP TC2/WG2.1 Working Conf. on Generic Programming, WCGP '02. Vol. 243 of IFIP Conf. Proceedings. Kluwer (2003) 1–20

6. Altenkirch, T., Reus, B.: Monadic presentations of lambda terms using generalized inductive types. In Flum, J., Rodríguez-Artalejo, M., eds.: Proc. of 13th Int. Wksh. on Computer Science Logic, CSL '99. Vol. 1683 of Lect. Notes in Comput. Sci. Springer-Verlag (1999) 453–468

7. Backhouse, R., Jansson, P., Jeuring, J., Meertens, L.: Generic programming — an introduction. In Swierstra, S.D., Henriques, P.R., Oliveira, J.N.: Revised Lectures from 3rd Int. School on Advanced Functional Programming, AFP '98. Vol. 1608 of Lect. Notes in Comput. Sci. Springer-Verlag (1999) 28–115

8. Barthe, G., Frade, M. J., Giménez, E., Pinto, L., Uustalu, T.: Type-based termination of recursive definitions. Math. Struct. in Comput. Sci. **14** (2004) 1–45

9. Barthe, G., Grégoire, B., Pastawski, F.: Practical inference for type-based termination in a polymorphic setting. In Urzyczyn, P., ed.: Proc. of 7th Int. Conf. on Typed Lambda Calculi and Applications, TLCA 2005. Vol. 3461 of Lect. Notes in Comput. Sci. Springer-Verlag (2005) 71–85

10. Benke, M., Dybjer, P., Jansson, P.: Universes for generic programs and proofs in dependent type theory. Nord. J. of Comput. **10** (2003) 265–289

11. Bird, R., Meertens, L.: Nested datatypes. In: Jeuring, J., ed., Proc. of 4th Int. Conf. on Mathematics of Program Construction, MPC '98. Vol. 1422 of Lect. Notes in Comput. Sci. Springer-Verlag (1998) 52–67

12. Bird, R., Paterson, R.: Generalised folds for nested datatypes. Formal Asp. Comput. **11** (1999) 200–222

13. Bird, R. S., Paterson, R.: De Bruijn notation as a nested datatype. J. Funct. Program. **9** (1999) 77–91

14. Blanqui, F.: A type-based termination criterion for dependently-typed higher-order rewrite systems. In van Oostrom, V., ed.: Rewriting Techniques and Applications, RTA 2004. Vol. 3091 of Lect. Notes in Comput. Sci. Springer-Verlag (2004) 24–39

15. Blanqui, F.: Decidability of type-checking in the Calculus of Algebraic Constructions with size annotations. In Ong, C.-H. L., ed.: Proc. of 19th Int. Wksh. on Computer Science Logic, CSL 2005. Vol. 3634 of Lect. Notes in Comput. Sci. Springer-Verlag (2005) 135–150

16. Crary, K., Weirich, S.: Flexible type analysis. In Proc. of 4th ACM SIGPLAN Int. Conf. on Functional Programming, ICFP'99. ACM Press (1999) 233–248

17. Crary, K., Weirich, S., Morrisett, J. G.: Intensional polymorphism in type-erasure semantics. In Proc. of 3rd ACM SIGPLAN Int. Conf. on Functional Programming, ICFP '98. ACM Press (1998) 301–312

18. Frade, M. J.: Type-Based Termination of Recursive Definitions and Constructor Subtyping in Typed Lambda Calculi. PhD thesis, Dep. de Informática, Universidade do Minho (2003)

19. Giesl, J., Thiemann, R., Schneider-Kamp, P., Falke, S.: Automated termination proofs with AProVE. In van Oostrom, V., ed.: Proc. of 15th Int. Conf. on Rewriting Techniques and Applications, RTA 2004. Vol. 3091 of Lect. Notes in Comput. Sci. Springer-Verlag (2004) 210–220

20. Giménez, E.: Structural recursive definitions in type theory. In Larsen, K.G., Skyum, S., Winskel, G., eds.: Proc. of 25th Int. Coll. on Automata, Languages and Programming, ICALP '98. Vol. 1443 of Lect. Notes in Comput. Sci. Springer-Verlag (1998) 397–408

21. Harper, R., Morrisett, J. G.: Compiling polymorphism using intensional type analysis. In Conf. Record of 22nd ACM SIGPLAN-SIGACT Symp. on Principles of Programming Languages, POPL'95. ACM Press (1995) 130–141

22. Hinze, R.: Numerical representations as higher-order nested datatypes. Technical Report IAI-TR-98-12, Institut für Informatik III, Universität Bonn (1998)

23. Hinze, R.: Polytypic programming with ease (extended abstract). In: Middeldorp, A., Sato, T., eds.: Proc. of 4th Fuji Int. Symp. on Functional and Logic Programming, FLOPS '99. Vol. 1722 of Lect. Notes in Comput. Sci. Springer-Verlag (1999) 21–36

24. Hinze, R.: Generalizing generalized tries. J. of Funct. Program. **10** (2000) 327–351

25. Hinze, R.: A new approach to generic functional programming. In Proc. of 27th ACM SIGPLAN-SIGACT Symp. on Principles of Programming Languages, POPL 2000. ACM Press (2000) 119–132

26. Hinze, R.: Manufacturing datatypes. J. of Funct. Program. **11** (2001) 493–524

27. Hinze, R.: Polytypic values possess polykinded types. Sci. of Comput. Program. **43** (2002) 129–159

28. Hinze, R., Jeuring, J.: Generic Haskell: Applications. In Backhouse, R. C., Gibbons, J., eds.: Generic Programming - Advanced Lectures. Vol. 2793 of Lect. Notes in Comput. Sci. Springer-Verlag (2003) 57–96

29. Hinze, R., Jeuring, J.: Generic Haskell: Practice and Theory. In Backhouse, R. C., Gibbons, J., eds.: Generic Programming - Advanced Lectures. Vol. 2793 of Lect. Notes in Comput. Sci. Springer-Verlag (2003) 1–56

30. Hinze, R., Jeuring, J., Löh, A.: Type-indexed data types. Sci. of Comput. Program. **51** (2004) 117–151

31. Hughes, J., Pareto, L., Sabry, A.: Proving the correctness of reactive systems using sized types. In Conf. Record of 23rd ACM SIGPLAN-SIGACT Symp. on Principles of Programming Languages, POPL '96. ACM Press (1996) 410–423

32. INRIA: The Coq Proof Assistant Reference Manual, version 8.0 edition (2004) http://coq.inria.fr/doc/main.html

33. Jansson, P.: Functional Polytypic Programming. PhD thesis, Dept. of Computing Science, Chalmers University of Technology (2000)

34. Jansson, P., Jeuring, J.: PolyP—a polytypic programming extension. In Conf. Record of 24th ACM SIGPLAN-SIGACT Symp. on Principles of Programming Languages, POPL '97. ACM Press (1997) 470–482

35. Jansson, P., Jeuring, J.: Polytypic data conversion programs. Sci. of Comput. Program. **43** (2002) 35–75

36. Martin, C., Gibbons, J., Bayley, I.: Disciplined, efficient, generalised folds for nested datatypes. Formal Asp. of Comput. **16** (2004) 19–35

37. Mendler, N. P.: Recursive types and type constraints in second-order lambda calculus. In Proc. of 2nd Ann IEEE Symp. on Logic in Computer Science, LICS '87. IEEE Computer Soc. Press (1987) 30–36

38. Norell, U.: Functional Generic Programming and Type Theory. Master's thesis, Computing Science, Chalmers University of Technology (2002). Available from http://www.cs.chalmers.se/~ulfn

39. Norell, U., Jansson, P.: Polytypic programming in Haskell. In Trinder, P.W., Michaelson, G., Pena, R., eds.: Revised Papers from 15th Int. Wksh. on Implementation of Functional Languages, IFL 2003. Lect. Notes in Comput. Sci. Springer-Verlag (2004) 168–184

40. Norell, U., Jansson, P.: Prototyping generic programming in Template Haskell. In: Kozen, D., Shankland, C., ed., Proc. of 7th Int. Conf. on Mathematics of Program Construction, MPC '04. Vol. 3125 of Lect. Notes in Comput. Sci. Springer-Verlag (2004) 314–333

41. Okasaki, C.: Purely Functional Data Structures. Ph.D. thesis, Carnegie Mellon University (1996)

42. Okasaki, C.: From fast exponentiation to square matrices: An adventure in types. In Proc. of 4th ACM SIGPLAN Int. Conf. on Functional Programming, ICFP '99. ACM Press (1999) 28–35

43. Okasaki, C.: Red-black trees in a functional setting. J. of Funct. Program. **9** (1999) 471–477

44. Pareto, L.: Types for Crash Prevention. PhD thesis, Dept. of Computing Science, Chalmers University of Technology (2000)

45. Pfeifer, H., Rueß, H.: Polytypic proof construction. In: Bertot, Y., Dowek, G., Hirschowitz, A., Paulin, C., Théry, L., eds., Theorem Proving in Higher Order Logics, TPHOLs '99. Vol. 1690 of Lect. Notes in Comput. Sci. Springer-Verlag (1999) 55–72

46. Pierce, B. C.: Types and Programming Languages. MIT Press (2002)

47. Saha, B., Trifonov, V., Shao, Z.: Intensional analysis of quantified types. ACM Trans. on Program. Lang. and Syst. **25** (2003) 159–209

48. Sereni, D., Jones, N. D.: Termination analysis of higher-order functional programs. In Yi, K., ed.: Proc. of 3rd Asian Symp. on Programming Languages and Systems, APLAS 2005. Vol. 3780 of Lect. Notes in Comput. Sci. Springer-Verlag (2005) 281–297

Relational Semantics for Higher-Order Programs

Kamal Aboul-Hosn and Dexter Kozen

Department of Computer Science, Cornell University,
Ithaca, NY 14853-7501, USA
kamal@cs.cornell.edu, kozen@cs.cornell.edu

Abstract. Most previous work on the semantics of higher-order programs with local state involves complex storage modeling with pointers and memory cells, complicated categorical constructions, or reasoning in the presence of context. In this paper we show how a relatively simple relational semantics can be used to avoid these complications. We provide a natural relational semantics for a programming language with higher-order functions. The semantics is purely compositional, with all contextual considerations completely encapsulated in the state. We show several equivalence proofs using this semantics based on examples of Meyer and Sieber (1988).

1 Introduction

Reasoning about higher-order programs with local state is an important and difficult problem that has garnered much attention over the years. Most previous work involves complex storage modeling with pointers and memory cells or complicated categorical constructions to capture the intricacies of programming with state. Reasoning about the equality of such programs typically involves the notion of *contextual* or *observable equivalence*, where two programs are considered equivalent if either can be put in the context of a larger program and yield the same value. Pitts [1] explains that these notions are difficult to define formally, because there is no clear agreement on the meaning of *program context* and *observable behavior*. A common goal is to design a semantics that is *fully abstract*, where observable equivalence implies semantic equivalence, although this notion makes the most sense in a purely functional context (see for example [2, 3]).

Work in modeling local state dates back over thirty years. Early seminal work by Meyer and Sieber [12] used the store model of Halpern-Meyer-Trakhtenbrot to prove equivalence of ALGOL procedures with no parameters. Their goal was to formalize informal arguments about the contextual equivalence of programs with block structure. One of the most important contributions of their work was the introduction of seven examples that exemplify the subtleties in reasoning about programs with local state. These classical examples have become the preferred standard against which to evaluate models that address the problem.

Much early attention focused on the use of denotational semantics to model a set of storage locations [4, 5, 6, 7]. The inability to prove some simple program equivalences using traditional denotational techniques led several researchers to

T. Uustalu (Ed.): MPC 2006, LNCS 4014, pp. 29–48, 2006.

take a categorical approach [8, 9, 10]. See [11] for more information regarding the history of these approaches.

More recently, several researchers have investigated the use of operational semantics to reason about ML programs with references. While operational semantics can be easier to understand, their use makes reasoning about programs more complex. Mason and Talcott [13, 14, 15] considered a λ-calculus extended with state operations. By defining axioms in the form of contextual assertions, Mason and Talcott were able to prove the equivalence of several examples of Meyer and Sieber. Pitts and Stark [1, 16, 17, 18] also use operational semantics.

Others have used game semantics to reason about programs with local state [19, 20, 21, 22]. Several full abstraction results have come from using game semantics to represent languages with state and higher-order constructs.

In this paper, we wish to explore the extent to which *relational semantics* can be used to avoid intricate memory modeling, category theory, and the explicit use of context in program equivalence proofs. Relational semantics combine the expressiveness of denotational semantics with the more intuitive understanding of operational semantics. Our objective is to define a notion of local variable scoping, along with a purely compositional semantics based on binary relations, such that all contextual considerations are completely encapsulated in the semantics.

We provide a natural relational semantics for a programming language with higher-order functions in Section 3. This treatment contrasts sharply with other contemporary functional or denotational approaches (see for example [23, 24, 25]). One distinguishing aspect of our approach is that functions and data are not conflated; we distinguish between expressions that can denote values and those that can denote programs. This allows us to give a development that aligns more closely with the procedural view of computation (computation as state manipulation) without abandoning the functional view (computation as evaluation). This is useful even for languages such as ML that are nominally functional. Our semantics allows destructive updates, but no aliasing.

Fully compositional relational semantics have been quite popular for first-order imperative programs (see for example [26] and references therein), but to our knowledge this is the first attempt to provide semantics in this style to higher-order programs.

We are ultimately interested in moving toward a more axiomatic treatment of program equivalence and partial correctness for higher-order programs in the style of Hoare logic or Kleene algebra with tests [27]. Our compositional program operators are based on the Kleene algebra operators (see [27, 26]), which have well-understood relational models and are simpler and more amenable to axiomatic treatment than conventional programming constructs. We take some initial steps in this direction in Section 4, in which we prove six of Meyer and Sieber's seven examples using relational semantics. The only example we cannot handle is the one involving aliasing, since our semantics does not treat aliasing at present.

2 Syntax

2.1 Types

A *type* is either a *base type* denoting an individual element of the domain of computation or a *functional type* of the form s → t, where s and t are types or void. The notation void is to accommodate methods with no arguments and/or no return value, but it is not itself a type. We assume the existence of infinitely many variables of each type.

Expressions are either *value expressions* or *program expressions*. These two sets of expressions are disjoint and are defined by mutual induction.

2.2 Value Expressions

Value expressions must be well-typed. Let Σ be a first-order signature consisting of a collection of function, relation, and constant symbols. A *value expression* is either

(i) a variable,
(ii) a symbol of the signature Σ,
(iii) a λ-term of the form $\lambda x.p$, $\lambda x.p; e$, $\lambda().p$, or $\lambda().p; e$, where x is a variable, p is a program expression, and e is a value expression,
(iv) an application $P(d)$, where P is a value expression of functional type with non-void return type and d is a value expression of the appropriate input type for P,
(v) an application $P()$, where P is a value expression of functional type with non-void return type and void input.

Evaluation of an expression of the form (i)–(iii) is immediate and without side effects. In (iii), the forms $\lambda x.p$ and $\lambda().p$ are for methods with no return value (or return value void) and the forms $\lambda x.p; e$ and $\lambda().p; e$ are for methods with return value e. The forms $\lambda().p$ and $\lambda().p; e$ are parameterless methods. In general, the process of evaluating a value expression (iv) or (v) can have side effects, which manifest themselves as a change of state.

2.3 Program Expressions

Program expressions differ from value expressions in that they do not yield a value. However, their execution generally results in a change of state.

Syntactically, a *program expression* is either

(i) an assignment $x := d$, where x is variable and d is a value expression of the same type,
(ii) a test $R(d)$, where R is a relation symbol of the signature Σ and d is a value expression of the appropriate input type for R,
(iii) a nondeterministic choice $p + q$, where p and q are program expressions,
(iv) a sequential composition $p \, ; \, q$, where p and q are program expressions,
(v) an iteration p^*, where p is a program expression,

(vi) an application $P(d)$, where P is a functional expression with void return type and d is a value expression of the appropriate input type for P,

(vii) an application $P()$, where P is a functional expression with void input and return type.

As mentioned, $\lambda x.p$, $\lambda x.p; e$, $\lambda().p$, and $\lambda().p; e$ are only value expressions, not program expressions. The application $(\lambda x.p)(d)$ is a program expression, but the application $(\lambda x.p; e)(d)$ is a value expression.

In the presence of higher-order functions, we can encode let expressions by a standard encoding:

$$\text{let } x = d \text{ in } p \text{ end} = (\lambda x.p)(d)$$
$$\text{let } x = d \text{ in } p; e \text{ end} = (\lambda x.p; e)(d).$$

3   Relational Semantics

The *domain of computation* is a first-order structure $\mathfrak{A}$ of signature Σ. Each symbol of Σ is interpreted as a function, relation, or constant of $\mathfrak{A}$ of the appropriate type.

3.1   Closure Structures

Before we can give the semantics, we must define what we mean by a state of execution. Informally, a state is a structure that contains all the variable/value bindings that have been created up to that point, along with specific rules for lookup, new binding creation, and destructive update. We will call these *closure structures*. Programs will be interpreted as relations on closure structures. The definition is directly motivated by the operational semantics of ML, Scheme, and other languages with static binding, in which the environment of a method declaration is saved with the compiled method for the purpose of evaluating free variables when the method is called; see for example [28, Ch. 10].

Formally, a *closure structure* is a triple $\sigma = (T, \alpha, s)$, where T is a tree, α is a reference to a node in T, and s is a stack of references to nodes in T.

Each node of T (except the root) is an object containing

– a binding of the form $x = c$, where x is a variable and c is a value of the same type, and
– a reference to its parent in T.

Distinct nodes are different objects, but may represent the same binding and may have the same parent. We use $\alpha, \beta, \ldots$ to refer to nodes of T and $\sigma, \tau, \ldots$ to refer to closure structures.

Every node α of T uniquely determines an *environment*, which is the list consisting of α and all its ancestors back to the root of T. We denote this environment also by α. This slight abuse of notation should cause no confusion, since there is a one-to-one correspondence between nodes in T and the environments they determine.

It is important to note that we have not defined an environment as a list of bindings. As distinct nodes can represent the same binding, so can distinct environments represent the same list of bindings.

The root of T, denoted ε, represents the empty environment with no bindings. It is the terminal node of all environments in T.

The empty closure structure is $(\varepsilon, \varepsilon, [\,])$, where ε is the root and $[\,]$ is the empty stack.

The environment α in a closure structure $\sigma = (T, \alpha, s)$ is called the *active environment* of σ and is denoted $\mathsf{actv}(\sigma)$. In Section 3.4 below, we will describe the operations of lookup and rebinding on closure structures. These operations are always performed in the active environment.

The set of closure structures is denoted CS.

3.2 Values

The values c occurring in bindings are either

(i) elements and functions of the domain of computation $\mathfrak{A}$, or
(ii) pairs (t, β), where t is a λ-expression of the form $\lambda x.p$, $\lambda x.p; e$, $\lambda().p$, or $\lambda().p; e$ and β is a reference to a node in T.

Values of class (i) are called *intrinsic values*, and those of class (ii) are called *closures*.

A closure (t, β) is created when the expression t is evaluated. The reference β is included in order to recall the environment that was active at the time of the evaluation. That environment will be used in future calls to interpret the free variables of t. Although the bindings in this environment may change over the lifetime of the object due to variable assignments, the reference β does not.

Symbols $f, g, \ldots$ range over intrinsic functions. Since we have postulated Σ as a first-order signature, closures, which are of functional type, cannot be arguments of intrinsic functions. All higher-order functions must be constructed using λ-expressions.

The set of values is denoted Val.

3.3 Accessibility

A node of a closure structure is *accessible* if it is reachable starting from the active environment or from a reference on the stack and following parent references or references β in closures (t, β). Note that any descendant of an inaccessible node is inaccessible. Two closure structures are considered equivalent if their accessible substructures are isomorphic; that is, if there is a one-to-one correspondence between accessible nodes of their trees and between their stack entries and active environments that preserves stack order and all reference relationships and binding values (environment references in closures are mapped appropriately under the isomorphism). Equivalence modulo accessibility can be viewed as a kind of mathematical garbage collection, although we do not postulate any explicit mechanism for garbage collection.

The purpose of the stack is to ensure the persistence of nodes across computations in which those nodes might otherwise become inaccessible. We will give a more precise explanation when we give the relational semantics below.

3.4 Operations on Closure Structures

Our relational semantics is defined in terms of the following low-level operations on closure structures.

If x is variable, c is a value, and α is an environment in σ, then $x = c : \alpha$ denotes the environment obtained by creating a new node with binding $x = c$ and prepending it to α. Whenever this occurs, a reference to α is available on top of the stack of σ, along with a reference to γ in the case c is a closure (t, γ). These references are popped (or just the reference to α, if c is an intrinsic value) and a reference to the newly created node is pushed onto the stack.

If σ is a closure structure and β is an environment in σ, then $\beta + \sigma$ denotes the result of popping β off the stack (it will always be there when this operation is applied), pushing the current active environment on the stack, and making β the new active environment. Thus we can think of this operation simply as switching the active environment with the environment on top of the stack.

These two operations are most commonly used in tandem to create a new binding. In this case, $(x = c : \alpha) + \sigma$ denotes the closure structure obtained from σ by creating a new node with binding $x = c$, prepending this node to α, then making this the new active environment. Before this operation, references to α and γ if c is a closure (t, γ) are available on top of the stack. In the special case in which $\alpha = \mathsf{actv}(\sigma)$, we abbreviate this by $(x = c) + \sigma$. The cumulative effect on the stack is to pop one or two elements, depending on whether c was an intrinsic value or a closure, respectively, and pushing the old active environment.

All evaluation of and assignment to variables is done in $\mathsf{actv}(\sigma)$, the active environment of σ. When evaluating a variable x, the value is the one bound to the first (most recently bound) occurrence of x in $\mathsf{actv}(\sigma)$. This value is denoted $\sigma(x)$. If x is not bound in $\mathsf{actv}(\sigma)$, then $\sigma(x)$ is undefined. When assigning to a variable x, we destructively rebind the first occurrence of x in $\mathsf{actv}(\sigma)$ to its new value. It is important to note that this is done destructively, not functionally: the list of nodes in $\mathsf{actv}(\sigma)$ is not changed, but only the value in the binding of one of the nodes. We denote the result of rebinding x to the new value a in closure structure σ by $\sigma[x/a]$. In addition, if a is a closure (t, β), then the stack is popped; in this case the top element will always be β. If x is not bound in $\mathsf{actv}(\sigma)$, the rebinding operator $[x/a]$ has no effect.

In real life, any attempt to evaluate or assign to an undefined variable (one that is not in the domain of the active environment) would result in a runtime error. The relational semantics to be given below will ensure that there will be no tuple in the relation corresponding to the program with that input state.

The value of a term t in the language of $\mathfrak{A}$ in a closure structure σ is denoted $\sigma(t)$ and is defined by structural induction on t in the usual way. Note that $\sigma(t)$ is defined iff x is bound in $\mathsf{actv}(\sigma)$ for all variables x occurring in t.

The operation $\mathsf{rest}(\sigma)$ just restores an earlier active environment by popping the stack and setting the active environment to that value. The current active environment is discarded. Curiously, $\mathsf{rest}(\beta + \sigma)$ is not necessarily equivalent to σ, since β may no longer be accessible.

We give a skeleton implementation in the appendix for illustrative purposes. Equivalence of closure structures modulo accessibility could be implemented by a deep equality test, although care must be taken due to circularities that can be introduced by destructive updates.

3.5   Semantics

Let CS denote the set of closure structures and Val the set of values. Each value expression e denotes a binary relation

$$[e] \subseteq \mathsf{CS} \times (\mathsf{CS} \times \mathsf{Val}) \tag{1}$$

relating input states with (output state, value) pairs. We write $(\sigma, (\tau, c))$ simply as (σ, τ, c). Each program expression p denotes a binary relation

$$[\![p]\!] \subseteq \mathsf{CS} \times \mathsf{CS} \tag{2}$$

relating input states with output states. The definitions are mutually inductive. Value expressions e also denote binary relations of the form (2), but these are derived immediately from (1) by projecting out the value:

$$[\![e]\!] = \{(\sigma, \tau') \mid (\sigma, \tau, c) \in [e]\},$$

where $\tau' = \tau$ if c is an intrinsic value, and is τ with the stack popped if c is a closure (t, β). In the latter case, the value that is popped will always be β.

3.6   Value Expressions

(i) If x is a variable, $[x] = \{(\sigma, \sigma', \sigma(x)) \mid \sigma \in \mathsf{CS}, \ \sigma(x) \text{ is defined}\}$, where $\sigma' = \sigma$ if $\sigma(x)$ is an intrinsic value, or σ with β pushed on the stack if $\sigma(x)$ is a closure (t, β).

(ii) If f is a symbol of the signature of $\mathfrak{A}$, $[f] = \{(\sigma, \sigma, f^{\mathfrak{A}}) \mid \sigma \in \mathsf{CS}\}$.

(iii) If t is a λ-expression of the form $\lambda x.p$, $\lambda x.p; e$, $\lambda().p$, or $\lambda().p; e$, then

$$[t] = \{(\sigma, \sigma', (t, \mathsf{actv}(\sigma))) \mid \sigma \in \mathsf{CS}\},$$

where σ' is σ with $\mathsf{actv}(\sigma)$ pushed onto the stack.

(iv) If P is a functional expression with non-void return type and d is a value expression of the appropriate input type for P, then

$$
\begin{aligned}
[P(d)] = \{(\sigma, \mathsf{rest}(\tau), b) \mid & \ \exists \rho \ \exists v \ \exists c \ \exists (\lambda x.p; e, \beta) \\
& (\sigma, \rho, (\lambda x.p; e, \beta)) \in [P], \ (\rho, v, c) \in [d], \\
& ((x = c : \beta) + v, \tau, b) \in [\![p]\!] \circ [e]\} \\
\cup \ \{(\sigma, \tau, f(c)) \mid & \ \exists \rho \ (\sigma, \rho, f) \in [P], \ (\rho, \tau, c) \in [d]\}.
\end{aligned}
$$

(v) If P is a functional expression with non-void return type and no parameter, then

$$[P()] = \{(\sigma, \mathsf{rest}(\tau), b) \mid \exists \rho \; \exists(\lambda().p; e, \beta)$$
$$(\sigma, \rho, (\lambda().p; e, \beta)) \in [P], \; (\beta + \rho, \tau, b) \in [\![p]\!] \circ [e]\}$$
$$\cup \; \{(\sigma, \tau, f()) \mid (\sigma, \tau, f) \in [P]\}.$$

In (iv) and (v), the composition operator in the expression $[\![p]\!] \circ [e]$ is ordinary binary relation composition; recall that $[e]$ is officially a binary relation. Thus

$$[\![p]\!] \circ [e] = \{(\sigma, \tau, c) \mid \exists \rho \; (\sigma, \rho) \in [\![p]\!], \; (\rho, \tau, c) \in [e]\}.$$

The definition of $[P(d)]$ in (iv) captures the following operational intuition. Given an initial execution state described by a closure structure σ, the halting states and output values are all those obtained as follows. First, we evaluate P in the state σ to obtain a value, say $(\lambda x.p; e, \beta)$, consisting of a value expression $\lambda x.p; e$ and a reference β to the active environment at the time the value $(\lambda x.p; e, \beta)$ was created. For instance, if P is a variable, we might previously have executed an assignment $P := \lambda x.p; e$, where β was the active environment at the time of the assignment. We also obtain a new state ρ. In general the new state may be different, since the evaluation of P might have had side effects. There may be several possible values and states obtained in this way due to nondeterminism in the evaluation of P, but the set of all such values and states we might obtain are given by all elements of $[P]$ with first component σ.

Then we evaluate the argument expression d in the resulting state ρ to obtain a value c and an output state v. The stack is used to preserve β across this computation. We then create a new node with binding $x = c$, where x is the formal parameter and c is the argument value just computed, and prepend this binding to the environment β to obtain the environment $x = c : \beta$. This becomes the new active environment, and the state is now $(x = c : \beta) + v$. We run $p; e$ starting in this state until it halts, yielding an output state τ and value b. The stack is then popped to restore the previous active environment, giving $\mathsf{rest}(\tau)$, and this is the final output state.

3.7   Program Expressions

(i) $[\![x := d]\!] = \{(\sigma, \tau[x/a]) \mid (\sigma, \tau, a) \in [d], \; \sigma(x) \text{ is defined}\}$. Recall that if a is a closure, then the stack of τ is popped in the formation of $\tau[x/a]$.

(ii) $[\![R(d)]\!] = \{(\sigma, \tau) \mid (\sigma, \tau, a) \in [d], \; R^{\mathfrak{A}}(a)\}$.

(iii) $[\![p + q]\!] = [\![p]\!] \cup [\![q]\!]$.

(iv) $[\![p \, ; \, q]\!] = [\![p]\!] \circ [\![q]\!]$.

(v) $[\![p^*]\!] = \bigcup_{n \geq 0} [\![p]\!]^n = $ the reflexive transitive closure of $[\![p]\!]$.

(vi) If P is a functional expression with void return type and d is a value expression of the appropriate input type for P, then

$$[\![P(d)]\!] = \{(\sigma, \mathsf{rest}(\tau)) \mid \exists \rho \; \exists v \; \exists c \; \exists(\lambda x.p, \beta)$$
$$(\sigma, \rho, (\lambda x.p, \beta)) \in [P], \; (\rho, v, c) \in [d],$$
$$((x = c : \beta) + v, \tau) \in [\![p]\!]\}$$
$$\cup \; \{(\sigma, \tau) \mid \exists \rho \; \exists f \; (\sigma, \rho, f) \in [P], \; (\rho, \tau) \in [\![d]\!]\}.$$

(vii) If P is a functional expression with void return type and no parameter, then

$$\llbracket P() \rrbracket = \{(\sigma, \mathsf{rest}(\tau)) \mid \exists \rho \; \exists(\lambda().p, \beta)$$
$$(\sigma, \rho, (\lambda().p, \beta)) \in [P], \; (\beta + \rho, \tau) \in \llbracket p \rrbracket\}$$
$$\cup \; \{(\sigma, \tau) \mid \exists f \; (\sigma, \tau, f) \in [P]\}.$$

The Kleene algebra operators $+, ; , ^*$ have been used here for mathematical simplicity. It is well known how to define more conventional programming constructs such as conditional branches and while loops from them; see for example [27, 26].

3.8   Discussion

The shape of the tree can change during a computation, as new nodes can be added or previously accessible nodes can become inaccessible. This is the reason we must consider equivalence modulo accessibility. However, there are strong invariants on the active environment and the stack:

- For $\llbracket p \rrbracket$, both the active environment and the stack are preserved from input to output.
- For $[p]$, the active environment is preserved from input to output. The stack is also preserved if the output value is intrinsic. Otherwise, if the output value is a closure (t, β), then the output stack consists of the input stack with a reference to β pushed on top.

These can be verified by induction on the structure of p.

The stack is needed to preserve active environments across function calls. It is also needed to preserve β across the evaluation of the argument d in 3.6(iv) and 3.7(vi) when the function to be applied is a closure (t, β).

One might well ask: In the preservation of β across calls, why is it not necessary to preserve t as well? This is certainly a legitimate question. The answer is that it *would* be necessary in any real implementation. However, here we are only trying to define a binary input/output relation, and the mathematical definitions 3.6(iv) and 3.7(vi) do this adequately without any explicit mechanism in closure structures for remembering t.

So why then does the same argument not apply to β? In an earlier version of this work, we thought that it did. However, there is a subtlety related to our assumption regarding equivalence modulo accessibility. We must ensure that in any triple $(\sigma, \rho, (t, \beta)) \in [P]$, the node β is accessible in ρ and remains accessible throughout the calculation $(\rho, v, c) \in [d]$. Otherwise, the subsequent operation $(x = c : \beta) + v$ would not make sense, since the formalism does not keep track of the correspondence between nodes of ρ and those of v. The value expression let $x = 0$ in $\lambda().x$ end provides an example of a P for which this is an issue. The corresponding closure contains a reference to the binding $x = 0$, but this node would be inaccessible after the evaluation of the expression if not for the stack.

3.9   Eliminating Context

The relational semantics presented in Sections 3.6 and 3.7 captures all contextual information in the state, allowing us to reason about programs with local state in a purely compositional way without considering their context. Formally, a *context* $C[\text{-}]$ is just a program or value expression with a distinguished free program variable. It is easy to see that for any program expressions p and q, $[\![C[p]]\!] = [\![C[q]]\!]$ for all contexts $C[\text{-}]$ iff $[\![p]\!] = [\![q]\!]$. For the direction ($\Rightarrow$), take $C[\text{-}]$ to be the trivial context consisting of a single program variable. The converse follows from an inductive argument, observing that the semantics is fully compositional, the semantics of a compound expression being completely determined by the semantics of its subexpressions.

3.10   An Example

Consider the program

$$\begin{aligned} \text{let} \quad & y = 4 \\ & f = \lambda z.(y := y + z \,;\, x := y) \\ \text{in} \quad & f(1)\,;\, x \\ \text{end} \end{aligned} \tag{3}$$

where x, y, z, and f are all distinct variables. Translating this program into a λ-expression, we obtain

$$\lambda y.(\lambda f.(f(1)\,;\, x) \ \ \lambda z.(y := y + z \,;\, x := y)) \tag{4}$$

First we give an operational account of the computation. Suppose the input state is σ with active environment α. The expression is an application of a function of type int $\rightarrow$ int, thus 3.6(iv) applies. We first evaluate the outermost λ-expression t, which according to 3.6(iii) yields the value (t, α). Then the argument 4 is evaluated, giving value 4. The formal parameter y is bound to the argument 4 and prepended to the environment α in the closure, giving a new active environment $y = 4 : \alpha$, which we call β. The old active environment α is saved on the stack.

Next, we look at the body of the λ-expression t, namely

$$\lambda f.(f(1)\,;\, x) \ \ \lambda z.(y := y + z \,;\, x := y).$$

This is another application, but in this case, the argument is itself a function. We prepend the binding $f = (\lambda z.(y := y + z \,;\, x := y), \ \beta)$ to the active environment β to get a new active environment γ.

The semantics of the body of the function we are applying is the composition $[\![f(1)]\!] \circ [\![x]\!]$. For $f(1)$, we look up f in the active environment γ, retrieve its value $(\lambda z.(y := y + z \,;\, x := y), \ \beta)$, prepend the binding $z = 1$ to β to get the environment δ, then evaluate the body in the environment δ. Note that y and z are bound in δ but not f (unless f was bound in the original active environment of σ). Now $[\![y := y + z \,;\, x := y]\!]$ will rebind x and y in δ to the value 5, provided x was bound in the original active environment of σ. If not, then there is no output state corresponding to σ. Let τ be the resulting state. The active environment of τ is δ, so $\tau(x) = \tau(y) = 5$.

Now x has value semantics $[x] = \{(\sigma, \sigma, \sigma(x)) \mid \sigma \in \mathsf{CS}\}$. One of these tuples is $(\tau, \tau, 5)$. Composing with $[\![f(1)]\!]$, we get an output state τ and corresponding value $\tau(x) = 5$. The stack is popped twice, yielding $\mathsf{rest}(\mathsf{rest}(\tau)) = \sigma[x/5]$ after garbage-collecting the inaccessible bindings of f and y. The value semantics of the entire program contains the tuple $(\sigma, \sigma[x/5], 5)$.

Now we do the same thing calculationally, using the algebraic properties of relations and properties of closure structures. Substituting

$$\lambda y.(\lambda f.(f(1)\,;\,x)\ \lambda z.(y := y + z\,;\,x := y))$$

for P and 4 for d in 3.6(iv) and simplifying, we obtain

$$
\begin{aligned}
&[\lambda y.(\lambda f.(f(1)\,;\,x)\ \lambda z.(y := y + z\,;\,x := y))\ (4)] \\
&= \{(\sigma, \mathsf{rest}(\tau), b) \mid ((y = 4) + \sigma, \tau, b) \in \\
&\qquad\qquad [\lambda f.(f(1)\,;\,x)\ \lambda z.(y := y + z\,;\,x := y)]\}.
\end{aligned}
\tag{5}
$$

Using the same rule with $\lambda f.(f(1)\,;\,x)$ for P and $\lambda z.(y := y + z\,;\,x := y)$ for d, we obtain

$$
\begin{aligned}
&[\lambda f.(f(1)\,;\,x)\ \lambda z.(y := y + z\,;\,x := y)] \\
&= \{(\theta, \mathsf{rest}(\eta), b) \mid (f = (\lambda z.(y := y + z\,;\,x := y), \mathsf{actv}(\theta))) + \theta, \eta, b) \\
&\qquad\qquad \in [\![f(1)]\!] \circ [x]\}.
\end{aligned}
\tag{6}
$$

Now by 3.7(vi) and 3.6(i), we have

$$
\begin{aligned}
[\![f(1)]\!] &= \{(\sigma, \mathsf{rest}(\tau)) \mid \exists(\lambda x.p, \beta) \\
&\qquad\qquad \sigma(f) = (\lambda x.p, \beta),\ ((x = 1 : \beta) + \sigma, \tau) \in [\![p]\!]\} \\
&\quad \cup\ \{(\sigma, \sigma) \mid \sigma(f) \text{ exists and is intrinsic}\} \\
[x] &= \{(\sigma, \sigma, \sigma(x)) \mid \sigma(x) \text{ exists}\}.
\end{aligned}
$$

Composing these two relations and using the distributivity of composition over union, we have

$$
\begin{aligned}
[\![f(1)]\!] \circ [x] &= \{(\sigma, \mathsf{rest}(\tau), \mathsf{rest}(\tau)(x)) \mid \exists(\lambda x.p, \beta)\ \sigma(f) = (\lambda x.p, \beta), \\
&\qquad\qquad ((x = 1 : \beta) + \sigma, \tau) \in [\![p]\!], \\
&\qquad\qquad \mathsf{rest}(\tau)(x) \text{ exists}\} \\
&\quad \cup\ \{(\sigma, \sigma, \sigma(x)) \mid \sigma(f) \text{ exists and is intrinsic, } \sigma(x) \text{ exists}\}.
\end{aligned}
$$

Combining this with (6) and simplifying yields

$$
\begin{aligned}
&[\lambda f.(f(1)\,;\,x)\ \lambda z.(y := y + z\,;\,x := y)] \\
&= \{(\theta, \mathsf{rest}(\eta), b) \mid \exists\rho\ \exists\tau\ \eta = \mathsf{rest}(\tau),\ b = \mathsf{rest}(\tau)(x), \\
&\qquad\qquad \rho = (f = (\lambda z.(y := y + z\,;\,x := y), \mathsf{actv}(\theta))) + \theta, \\
&\qquad\qquad ((z = 1 : \mathsf{actv}(\theta)) + \rho, \tau) \in [\![y := y + z\,;\,x := y]\!]\}.
\end{aligned}
\tag{7}
$$

Using 3.7(i) and (iv),

$$[\![y := y + z]\!] = \{(\sigma, \sigma[y/\sigma(y) + \sigma(z)]) \mid \sigma(y), \sigma(z) \text{ exist}\}$$
$$[\![x := y]\!] = \{(\sigma, \sigma[x/\sigma(y)]) \mid \sigma(x), \sigma(y) \text{ exist}\}$$
$$[\![y := y + z \,;\, x := y]\!] = [\![y := y + z]\!] \circ [\![x := y]\!]$$
$$= \{(\sigma, \sigma[y/\sigma(y) + \sigma(z)][x/\sigma(y) + \sigma(z)]) \mid \sigma(x), \sigma(y),$$
$$\sigma(z) \text{ exist}\}.$$

Using this, the last condition of (7) simplifies to

$$((z = 1 : \mathsf{actv}(\theta)) + \sigma, \tau) \in [\![y := y + z \,;\, x := y]\!]$$
$$\Leftrightarrow \tau = ((z = 1 : \mathsf{actv}(\theta)) + \sigma)[y/\theta(y) + 1][x/\theta(y) + 1]), \quad \theta(x), \theta(y) \text{ exist.}$$

Plugging this into (7) and simplifying further, we obtain

$$[\lambda f.(f(1) \,;\, x) \ \lambda z.(y := y + z \,;\, x := y)]$$
$$= \{(\theta, \theta[y/\theta(y) + 1][x/\theta(y) + 1], \theta(y) + 1) \mid \theta(x), \theta(y) \text{ exist}\}.$$

This allows us to simplify the last condition of (5):

$$((y = 4) + \sigma, \tau, b) \in [\lambda f.(f(1) \,;\, x) \ \lambda z.(y := y + z \,;\, x := y)]$$
$$\Leftrightarrow \tau = (y = 5) : (\sigma[x/5]), \ b = 5, \ \sigma(x) \text{ exists.}$$

Finally, plugging this back into (5) and simplifying, we obtain the desired result:

$$[\lambda y.(\lambda f.(f(1) \,;\, x) \ \lambda z.(y := y + z \,;\, x := y)) \ (4)]$$
$$= \{(\sigma, \sigma[x/5], 5) \mid \sigma(x) \text{ exists}\}.$$

Although this calculation is much abbreviated, we have used nothing beyond elementary logic, set theory, and relational algebra, along with a few self-evident properties of closure structures.

4   Relational Semantics in Program Equivalence Proofs

In this section we prove six of the seven equivalences of Meyer and Sieber [12].

We begin with a general bisimulation result. Let $\sigma, \hat{\sigma}$ be closure structures. Let $f : \sigma \to \hat{\sigma}$ be a function mapping nodes in σ to nodes in $\hat{\sigma}$ and stack entries in σ to stack entries in $\hat{\sigma}$. We say that f *embeds* σ *in* $\hat{\sigma}$ if

- f is one-to-one on both nodes and stack entries,
- $f(\mathsf{actv}(\sigma)) = \mathsf{actv}(\hat{\sigma})$,
- f preserves stack order,
- f preserves all reference relationships and node labels in the following sense:
  - $f(\mathsf{parent}(\alpha)) = \mathsf{parent}(f(\alpha))$,
  - $f(\mathsf{root}(\sigma)) = \mathsf{root}(\hat{\sigma})$,
  - if i is a stack entry of σ containing a reference to α, then $f(i)$ contains a reference to $f(\alpha)$,

- if the node α contains the binding $x = c$ and c is an intrinsic value, then $f(\alpha)$ contains $x = c$,
- if the node α contains a binding to a closure $x = (t, \beta)$, then $f(\alpha)$ contains $x = (t, f(\beta))$.

Thus $\widehat{\sigma}$ contains an isomorphic copy of σ, possibly with some extra stack entries and accessible nodes. However, the subtree of σ consisting of nodes accessible from the active environment is isomorphic to that of $\widehat{\sigma}$, and this determines all computational behavior from those input states. This intuition is captured in the following bisimulation property.

Lemma 1. *Suppose f embeds σ in $\widehat{\sigma}$. Let p be a program expression.*

(i) *If $(\sigma, \tau) \in [\![p]\!]$, then there exist $\widehat{\tau}$ and f' such that $(\widehat{\sigma}, \widehat{\tau}) \in [\![p]\!]$ and f' embeds τ in $\widehat{\tau}$.*

(ii) *If $(\widehat{\sigma}, \widehat{\tau}) \in [\![p]\!]$, then there exist τ and f' such that $(\sigma, \tau) \in [\![p]\!]$ and f' embeds τ in $\widehat{\tau}$.*

Moreover, in both cases f and f' agree on the stack (recall from Section 3.8 that the stacks of σ and τ are the same, as are the stacks of $\widehat{\sigma}$ and $\widehat{\tau}$).

Proof. The proof is by induction on p, with the induction hypothesis suitably strengthened to include $[\![e]\!]$ for value expressions. We argue (i) for cases 3.7(i) and (vii) explicitly.

For 3.7(i), suppose $(\sigma, \tau) \in [\![x := a]\!]$. Then there exist ρ and c such that $(\sigma, \rho, c) \in [\![a]\!]$, $\sigma(x)$ exists, and $\tau = \rho[x/c]$. Then $\widehat{\sigma}(x)$ exists, since σ and $\widehat{\sigma}$ have isomorphic active environments. By the induction hypothesis on a, there exist $\widehat{\rho}$ and an embedding $f' : \rho \to \widehat{\rho}$ such that $(\widehat{\sigma}, \widehat{\rho}, \widehat{c}) \in [\![a]\!]$, where $\widehat{c} = c$ if c is an intrinsic value, and if c is a closure (t, β), then $\widehat{c} = (t, f'(\beta))$. Letting $\widehat{\tau} = \widehat{\rho}[x/\widehat{c}]$, we have that f' embeds τ in $\widehat{\tau}$ and $(\widehat{\sigma}, \widehat{\tau}) \in [\![x := a]\!]$.

For 3.7(vii), suppose $(\sigma, \tau) \in [\![P()]\!]$. Then there exist ρ and υ such that $(\sigma, \rho, (\lambda().p, \beta)) \in [\![P]\!]$ (say), $(\beta + \rho, \upsilon) \in [\![p]\!]$, and $\tau = \text{rest}(\upsilon)$. By the induction hypothesis on P, there exist $\widehat{\rho}$ and embedding $f' : \rho \to \widehat{\rho}$ such that $(\widehat{\sigma}, \widehat{\rho}, (\lambda().p, f'(\beta))) \in [\![P]\!]$. Form the new closure structure $f'(\beta) + \widehat{\rho}$ and extend f' to an embedding $\beta + \rho \to f'(\beta) + \widehat{\rho}$ (the extension is uniquely determined), which we still denote it by f'. By the induction hypothesis on p, there exist $\widehat{\upsilon}$ and embedding $f'' : \upsilon \to \widehat{\upsilon}$ such that $(f'(\beta) + \widehat{\rho}, \widehat{\upsilon}) \in [\![p]\!]$. Defining $\widehat{\tau} = \text{rest}(\widehat{\upsilon})$, we have $(\widehat{\sigma}, \widehat{\tau}) \in [\![P()]\!]$ and f'' an embedding of τ in $\widehat{\tau}$. □

The first two examples of Meyer and Sieber examine the inability of procedures to access variables not in scope at the time of their declaration.

Example 1. For a procedure identifier P of type void $\to$ void, x distinct from P, and c a constant, the following two programs are equivalent.

$$\text{let } x = c \text{ in } P() \text{ end} \qquad P().$$

Proof. From 3.6(iii) and (iv), after simplification we have

$$[\![\text{let } x = c \text{ in } P() \text{ end}]\!] = [\![\lambda x.P() \ c]\!]$$
$$= \{(\sigma, \text{rest}(\tau)) \mid ((x = c) + \sigma, \tau) \in [\![P()]\!]\}. \qquad (8)$$

Similarly, from 3.7(vii) and 3.6(i), we have

$$[\![P()]\!] = \{(\sigma, \mathsf{rest}(\tau)) \mid \sigma(P) = (\lambda().p, \beta), \ (\beta + \sigma, \tau) \in [\![p]\!]\} \qquad (9)$$
$$\cup \ \{(\sigma, \sigma) \mid \sigma(P) \text{ exists and is an intrinsic value}\}.$$

Substituting (9) in (8) and simplifying, we obtain

$$[\![\mathsf{let}\ x = c\ \mathsf{in}\ P()\ \mathsf{end}]\!]$$
$$= \{(\sigma, \mathsf{rest}(\mathsf{rest}(\eta))) \mid \sigma(P) = (\lambda().p, \beta), \ (\beta + (x = c) + \sigma, \eta) \in [\![p]\!]\} \qquad (10)$$
$$\cup \ \{(\sigma, \sigma) \mid \sigma(P) \text{ exists and is an intrinsic value}\}.$$

To show (9) and (10) are equal, it suffices to show that for all ρ, the following two statements are equivalent:

$$\exists \eta\ \rho = \mathsf{rest}(\mathsf{rest}(\eta)), \ (\beta + (x = c) + \sigma, \eta) \in [\![p]\!],$$
$$\exists \tau\ \rho = \mathsf{rest}(\tau), \ (\beta + \sigma, \tau) \in [\![p]\!].$$

This follows directly from Lemma 1 once we have constructing an embedding $\beta + \sigma \to \beta + (x = c) + \sigma$. The embedding is the identity on the tree of σ and maps the stack elements of $\beta + \sigma$ to the stack elements of $\beta + (x = c) + \sigma$ in order, but skipping the top element, which is $\mathsf{actv}((x = c) + \sigma)$. $\qquad \square$

Example 2. For a procedure identifier P of type $\mathsf{void} \to \mathsf{void}$, x distinct from P, and c a constant, the following two programs are equivalent.

```
let  x = c        let  x = c
in   P() ; u      in   P() ; (x = c) ; u
end               end
```

Proof. The equation asserts that the test $x = c$ is redundant after the evaluation of $P()$. The proof is similar to that of Example 1. After expanding the definitions and simplifying, it comes down to showing that if $\sigma(P) = (\lambda().p, \beta)$, and if $(\beta + (x = c) + \sigma, \rho) \in [\![p]\!]$, then $\rho(x) = c$. This follows from Lemma 1 by constructing an embedding of $\beta + \sigma$ in $\beta + (x = c) + \sigma$, giving a bisimilar computation that cannot change the value of x. $\qquad \square$

The next example demonstrates that the effect of a function does not depend on the names of the arguments. This is a feature of the call-by-value parameter passing mechanism.

Example 3. Let x, y, and Q be distinct variables and b, c constants. The following two programs are equivalent:

```
let  x = b, y = c       let  x = c, y = b
in   Q(x)(y)            in   Q(y)(x)
end                     end
```

Proof. It suffices to show that both programs are equivalent to $Q(b)(c)$; that is, this is an instance of when call-by-value and call-by-name (β-reduction) give the same result. We can do this in stages: to show the first program is equivalent to $Q(b)(c)$, it suffices to show that

$$\text{let } y = c \text{ in } Q(x)(y) \text{ end} = Q(x)(c)$$
$$\text{let } x = b \text{ in } Q(x)(c) \text{ end} = Q(b)(c).$$

Let us argue the former.

Suppose both Q and x are defined in σ, say $\sigma(Q) = (\lambda z.q; e, \beta)$ and $\sigma(x) = b$. To calculate $[\![\text{let } y = c \text{ in } Q(x)(y) \text{ end}]\!]$, we expand the definition and simplify. Prepending the binding $y = c$ to $\mathsf{actv}(\sigma)$ and evaluating $Q(x)$ in that environment, we would get (say)

$$((z = b : \beta) + (y = c) + \sigma, \rho, (\lambda w.p, \gamma)) \in [\![q; e]\!], \tag{11}$$

and we wish to apply $(\lambda w.p, \gamma)$ to y in the active environment of $\mathsf{rest}(\rho)$.

The corresponding calculation for $[\![Q(x)(c)]\!]$ starts in state $(z = b : \beta) + \sigma$. But there is an embedding of this state in $(z = b : \beta) + (y = c) + \sigma$ that omits the top stack element containing the binding $y = c$. By Lemma 1, we have

$$((z = b : \beta) + \sigma, \upsilon, (\lambda w.p, \gamma)) \in [\![q; e]\!] \tag{12}$$

with an embedding $f : \upsilon \to \rho$, and we wish to apply $(\lambda w.p, \gamma)$ to c in the active environment of $\mathsf{rest}(\upsilon)$. Now f restricted to $\mathsf{rest}(\upsilon)$ is not an embedding in $\mathsf{rest}(\rho)$, since the active environment is not mapped correctly; but it is an embedding in $\mathsf{rest}(\mathsf{rest}(\rho))$. Moreover, the stack sizes of $\mathsf{rest}(\upsilon)$ and $\mathsf{rest}(\mathsf{rest}(\rho))$ are the same, so the embedding is an isomorphism. This says that $\mathsf{rest}(\mathsf{rest}(\rho)) = \mathsf{rest}(\upsilon)$. Furthermore, the value of y was not changed in (11), since there is a bisimilar computation (12) in which it was not changed. This says that

$$\mathsf{rest}(\rho) = (y = c) + \mathsf{rest}(\upsilon).$$

It remains to argue that the final application of $(\lambda w.p, \gamma)$ yields the same result in both cases. Again we have an embedding and can apply Lemma 1. The two expressions are

$$((w = c : \gamma) + (y = c) + \mathsf{rest}(\upsilon), \theta) \in [\![p]\!]$$
$$((w = c : \gamma) + \mathsf{rest}(\upsilon), \eta) \in [\![p]\!]$$

with an embedding $f : \eta \to \theta$. The final output states are $\mathsf{rest}(\mathsf{rest}(\theta))$ and $\mathsf{rest}(\eta)$, which are isomorphic because f embeds $\mathsf{rest}(\eta)$ in $\mathsf{rest}(\mathsf{rest}(\theta))$ and the stack sizes are the same. □

The remaining examples look at the higher-order case in the presence of local variables. The goal of these examples is to prove that procedures that have as arguments procedures with private data cannot access that private data.

In this example, we look at a procedure with two local variables that only alters one of them.

Example 4. For distinct variables x, y, Q, and T, the following two programs are equivalent:

let $x = 0,\ y = 1,\ T = \lambda().y := 2y$ let $x = 0,\ y = 1,\ T = \lambda().y := 2y$
in $Q(T)\,;\ (x = 0)\,;\ u$ in $Q(T)\,;\ u$
end   end

Proof. Let

$$\rho = (y = 1) + (x = 0) + \sigma,$$
$$\gamma = \mathsf{actv}(\rho),$$
$$\xi = (T = (\lambda().y := 2y, \gamma) + (y = 1) + (x = 0) + \sigma.$$

Starting in state σ, ξ is the state after binding x, y, and T in the let expression. Suppose $\sigma(Q) = (\lambda R.p, \beta)$. This is also $\xi(Q)$. After substituting the definitions and simplifying, the proof comes down to showing that if

$$((R = (\lambda().y := 2y, \gamma) : \beta) + \xi, \eta) \in [\![p]\!],$$

then $\eta(x) = 0$. By Lemma 1, removing all stack elements, there is a bisimilar computation

$$((R = (\lambda().y := 2y, \gamma) : \beta) + \varepsilon, \theta) \in [\![p]\!],$$

where ε is an abbreviation for the empty closure structure. As β is a node of σ, the only reference to the binding $x = 0$ in this closure structure is via the closure $(\lambda().y := 2y, \gamma)$. All that can be done with this object is to apply it or assign it to a variable, and neither operation changes the value of x or changes the fact that the only reference to $x = 0$ is via γ in the closure. This is clear for assignments. An application $R()$ in a state τ in which R is bound to $(\lambda().y := 2y, \gamma)$ yields output state $\mathsf{rest}(v)$, where $(\gamma + \tau, v) \in [\![y := 2y]\!]$. The value of x is unchanged due to the form of the assignment, and the reference to γ on the stack during this calculation is transitory. $\square$

In the next example, we want to know that if an invariant on a local variable is maintained by a function, then that invariant is maintained for the entire program if the variable is only accessed through that function.

Example 5. For distinct variables x, Q, and A_2, the following two programs are equivalent:

let $x = 0,\ A_2 = \lambda().x := x + 2$ let $x = 0,\ A_2 = \lambda().x := x + 2$
in $Q(A_2)\,;\ (x \bmod 2 = 0)\,;\ u$ in $Q(A_2)\,;\ u$
end   end

Proof. This example is very similar to the previous. In this case, we note that if $\sigma(x) \bmod 2 = 0$ and $(\sigma, \tau) \in [\![A_2]\!]$, then $\tau(x) \bmod 2 = 0$. $\square$

The final example demonstrates that the behavior of a procedure is not affected by the values of another procedure's local variables.

Example 6. Let x, Q, A_1, and A_2 be distinct variables. The following two programs are equivalent:

let $x = 0, A_1 = \lambda().x := x + 1$	let $x = 0, A_2 = \lambda().x := x + 2$
in $Q(A_1)$	in $Q(A_2)$
end	end

Proof. In this example, it is important to note that A_1 and A_2 have void return type. The argument is very similar to the argument in Example 5. We use Lemma 1 to obtain bisimilar computations in which x is not accessible except via the closures bound to A_1 and A_2, therefore can only be altered by calls to A_1 and A_2. The execution of Q is always in a preexisting environment with no other access to x. Finally, the bindings of x, A_1 and A_2 are discarded at the end, leaving equivalent output states. □

The one example from Meyer and Sieber that our system cannot currently handle deals with the inability of local variables to be aliased by variables declared elsewhere. We currently have neither the means to alias a location nor to test for aliasing.

5 Conclusion and Future Work

We have presented a compositional relational semantics that captures all contextual information in the state, allowing us to reason about programs with local state in an equational way without consideration of context. We have shown how to reason in this framework by proving several benchmark examples of Meyer and Sieber [12].

While we do not deal with the more intricate issue of aliasing, there is no reason to believe our approach could not be extended to do so. We are currently attempting to expand the definition of closure structure to allow explicit references as values.

Using relational semantics for higher-order programs does not solve problems that many other methods cannot, it simply allows one to reason in a natural equational style that is mathematically based, yet true to the underlying operational intuition.

Acknowledgments. We are grateful to Jules Desharnais, Matthew Fluet, Riccardo Pucella, and three anonymous reviewers for their valuable input.

References

1. Pitts, A. M.: Operational semantics and program equivalence. In Barthe, G. et al, eds.: Advanced Lectures from Int. Summer School on Applied Semantics, APPSEM 2000. Vol. 2395 of Lect. Notes in Comput. Sci. Springer-Verlag (2002) 378–412
2. Plotkin, G.: Full abstraction, totality and PCF (1997)

3. Cartwright, R., Felleisen, M.: Observable sequentiality and full abstraction. In Conf. Record of 19th Ann. ACM SIGPLAN-SIGACT Symp. on Principles of Programming Languages, POPL '92. ACM Press (1992) 328–342
4. Milne, R., Strachey, C.: A Theory of Programming Language Semantics. Halsted Press, New York (1977)
5. Scott, D.: Mathematical concepts in programmng language semantics. In: Proc. of 1972 Spring Joint Computer Conferences. AFIPS Press (1972) 225–34
6. Stoy, J.E.: Denotational Semantics: The Scott-Strachey Approach to Programming Language Theory. MIT Press (1981)
7. Halpern, J.Y., Meyer, A.R., Trakhtenbrot, B.A.: The semantics of local storage, or what makes the free-list free? (preliminary report). In Conf. Record of 11th Ann. ACM Symp. on Principles of Programming Languages, POPL '84. ACM Press (1984) 245–257
8. Stark, I.: Categorical models for local names. LISP and Symb. Comput. 9(1) (1996) 77–107
9. Reyonlds, J.: The essence of ALGOL. In de Bakker, J., van Vliet, J.C., eds.: Algorithmic Languages. North Holland (1981) 345–372
10. Oles, F.J.: A category-theoretic approach to the semantics of programming languages. PhD thesis. Syracuse University (1982)
11. O'Hearn, P.W., Tennent, R.D.: Semantics of local variables. In Fourman, M.P., Johnstone, P.T., Pitts, A.M., eds.: Applications of Categories in Computer Science. Vol. 177 of London Math. Soc. Lect. Note Series. Cambridge Univ. Press (1992) 217–238
12. Meyer, A.R., Sieber, K.: Towards fully abstract semantics for local variables. In Conf. Record of 15th ACM Symp. on Principles of Programming Languages, POPL '88. ACM Press (1988) 191–203
13. Mason, I.A., Talcott, C.L.: Axiomatizing operational equivalence in the presence of effects. In Proc. of 4th Ann. IEEE Symp. Logic in Computer Science, LICS '89. IEEE Comput. Soc. Press (1989) 284–293
14. Mason, I.A., Talcott, C.L.: Equivalence in functional languages with effects. J. of Funct. Program. 1 (1991) 287–327
15. Mason, I.A., Talcott, C.L.: References, local variables and operational reasoning. In Proc. of 7th Ann. IEEE Symp. on Logic in Computer Science, LICS '92. IEEE Comput. Soc. Press (1992) 186–197
16. Pitts, A.M., Stark, I.D.B.: Observable properties of higher order functions that dynamically create local names, or what's new? In Borzyszkowski, A.M., Sokolowski, S., eds.: Proc. of 18th Int. Symp. on Mathematical Foundations of Computer Science, MFCS 93. Vol. 711 of Lect. Notes in Comput. Sci. Springer-Verlag (1993) 122–141
17. Pitts, A.M.: Operationally-based theories of program equivalence. In Dybjer, P., Pitts, A.M., eds.: Semantics and Logics of Computation. Publications of the Newton Institute. Cambridge Univ. Press (1997) 241–298
18. Pitts, A.M., Stark, I.D.B.: Operational reasoning in functions with local state. In Gordon, A.D., Pitts, A.M., eds.: Higher Order Operational Techniques in Semantics. Cambridge Univ. Press (1998) 227–273
19. Abramsky, S., Honda, K., McCusker, G.: A fully abstract game semantics for general references. In Proc. 13th Ann. IEEE Symp. on Logic in Computer Science, LICS '98. IEEE Comput. Soc. Press (1998) 334–344
20. Laird, J.: A game semantics of local names and good variables. In Walukiewicz, I., ed.: Proc. of 7th Int. Conf. on Foundations of Software Science and Computation Structures, FoSSaCS 2004. Vol. 2987 of Lect. Notes in Comput. Sci. Springer-Verlag (2004) 289–303

21. Abramsky, S., McCusker, G.: Linearity, sharing and state: a fully abstract game semantics for idealized ALGOL with active expressions. Proc. of Linear Logic 1996 Tokyo Meeting. Vol. 3 of Electron. Notes on Theor. Comput. Sci. Elsevier (1996) 2–14

22. Abramsky, S., McCusker, G.: Call-by-value games. In Nielsen, M., Thomas, W., eds.: Proc. of 11th Int. Wksh. on Computer Science Logic, CSL '97. Vol. 1414 of Lect. Notes in Comput. Sci. Springer-Verlag (1997) 1–17

23. Riecke, J.G., Sandholm, A.: A relational account of call-by-value sequentiality. In Proc. of 12th Ann. IEEE Symp. on Logic in Computer Science, LICS '97. IEEE Comp. Soc. Press (1997) 258–267

24. Riecke, J.G., Viswanathan, R.: Isolating side effects in sequential languages. In Conf. Record of 22th ACM SIGPLAN-SIGACT Symp. on Principles of Programming Languages, POPL '95. ACM Press (1995) 1–12

25. Fiore, M.P., Plotkin, G., Turi, D.: Abstract syntax and variable binding. In Proc. of 14th Ann. IEEE Symp. on Logic in Computer Science, LICS '99. (1999) IEEE Comp. Soc. Press 193–202

26. Harel, D., Kozen, D., Tiuryn, J.: Dynamic Logic. MIT Press (2000)

27. Kozen, D.: Kleene algebra with tests. ACM Trans. on Program. Lang. and Syst. **19**(3) (1997) 427–443

28. Abadi, M., Cardelli, L.: A Theory of Objects. Springer-Verlag (1996)

Appendix Skeleton Implementation of Closure Structures

For illustrative purposes, we provide here a skeleton of a simple untyped implementation of closure structures in ML that is faithful to the description in Section 3. The type `cs` represents the active environment and stack of a closure structure; the tree is implicit. The second component of a `binding` is declared as a reference to allow destructive updates.

```
type var = string
type lambdaExpr = string

datatype value = Int of int | Closure of lambdaExpr * environment
withtype binding = var * value ref
and environment = binding list

type cs = environment * environment list

fun newCS () : cs = ([],[])

fun lookup (v:var) ((act,s):cs) : value option =
  let fun lookup' (v:var) (env:environment) : value option =
    case env of [] => NONE
        | (u,c)::t => if u=v then SOME (!c) else lookup' v t
  in lookup' v act
  end
```

```
fun update (v:var) (d:value) ((act,s):cs) : unit =
  let fun update' (v:var) (d:value) (env:environment) : unit =
    case env of [] => ()
         | (u,c)::t => if u=v then c := d else update' v d t
  in update' v d act
  end

fun createBinding (v:var) (c:value) ((act,s):cs) : cs =
  let val b = (v,ref c) : binding
      val env = b::(hd s) : environment
  in (env, act::(tl s))
  end
```

Proofs of Randomized Algorithms in Coq

Philippe Audebaud[1] and Christine Paulin-Mohring[2]

[1] ENS Lyon and INRIA Sophia-Antipolis,
2004 route des lucioles - BP 93, F-06902 Sophia Antipolis, France
philippe.audebaud@sophia.inria.fr
[2] LRI, Université Paris Sud and INRIA Futurs,[*]
Bât. 490, Université Paris Sud, F-91405 Orsay Cedex, France
christine.paulin@lri.fr

Abstract. Randomized algorithms are widely used either for finding efficiently approximated solutions to complex problems, for instance primality testing, or for obtaining good average behavior, for instance in distributed computing. Proving properties of such algorithms requires subtle reasoning both on algorithmic and probabilistic aspects of the programs. Providing tools for the mechanization of reasoning is consequently an important issue. Our paper presents a new method for proving properties of randomized algorithms in a proof assistant based on higher-order logic. It is based on the monadic interpretation of randomized programs as probabilistic distribution [1]. It does not require the definition of an operational semantics for the language nor the development of a complex formalization of measure theory, but only use functionals and algebraic properties of the unit interval. Using this model, we show the validity of general rules for estimating the probability for a randomized algorithm to satisfy certain properties, in particular in the case of general recursive functions.

We apply this theory for formally proving a program implementing a Bernoulli distribution from a coin flip and the termination of a random walk. All the theories and results presented in this paper have been fully formalized and proved in the Coq proof assistant [2].

1 Introduction

Randomized algorithms are widely used either for finding efficiently approximated solutions to complex problems such as the primality test, or in order to obtain good average behavior, for instance in distributed computing. Proving properties of such algorithms requires subtle reasoning both on algorithmic and probabilistic aspects of the programs. Providing tools for the mechanization of reasoning is consequently an important issue.

Models. The first problem is to find an appropriate mathematical representation of a randomized algorithm. Methods for modeling randomized programs

---

[*] ProVal Project (http://proval.lri.fr/), Pôle Commun de Recherche en Informatique du plateau de Saclay CNRS, École Polytechnique, INRIA, Université Paris-Sud.

T. Uustalu (Ed.): MPC 2006, LNCS 4014, pp. 49–68, 2006.

go back to the early work of D. Kozen [3, 4] which proposes to interpret randomized imperative programs as measure transformers. This approach has been studied further by A. McIver and C. Morgan [5] which extend the interpretation to non-deterministic as well as probabilistic choices and define a refinement relation. Using an extension of weakest-precondition computation to randomized programs, they propose a method to analyze the probability for the result of the program to satisfy a given property by simple rules on the structure of the program and algebraic properties.

Studying the semantic foundations of probabilistic languages has been the concern of many works. There are at least two different approaches.

The first one is an operational view using access to an arbitrary number of independent random variables following a given distribution (which can be a coin flip or a uniform distribution as in [6]). This interpretation is a monadic transformation. If Ω denotes the type of infinite sequences of independent random values, then a computation of type A will be interpreted as a function of type $\Omega \rightarrow A \times \Omega$: it computes a value of type A and modifies the global state of type Ω after consuming a finite prefix of the sequence of random values. Reasoning on randomized programs using this approach requires to model the base probability distribution on Ω.

The second approach is to use directly the monadic structure of probability distributions in order to interpret directly a randomized program of type A as a distribution over the set of possible values in A. This is also a monadic interpretation but with a different space: a probability distribution can essentially be seen as a function from a set of subsets of A into the interval $[0, 1]$, an alternative [1] is to use the monad corresponding to expectations which is a functional which maps functions of type $A \rightarrow \mathbb{R}$ to $\mathbb{R}$.

Proofs. The second problem is to reason about probabilistic programs. There are few works on actually mechanizing the proofs in this area.

J. Hurd, A. McIver and C. Morgan designed a mechanization of the quantitative logic for probabilistic guarded commands using the proof assistant HOL [7].

In the domain of distributed protocols, the group of M. Kwiatkowska in Birmingham has designed a probabilistic model-checker PRISM [8], which uses Markov's chains as the underlying model and a probabilistic temporal logic for queries. Reasoning in this framework requires complex computations.

In the domain of algorithms, J. Hurd [9, 10] showed how to model and prove properties of randomized programs in the HOL proof assistant using a monadic transformation of programs, where he assumes access to an infinite sequence of independent coin flips.

Our work has the same goals as J. Hurd's development, to provide tools for interactive reasoning on probabilistic programs. We choose a different monadic transformation of probabilistic programs, interpreting directly programs as measures. One good thing about this method is that it does not require a complicated development within probability theory: the measure can be treated abstractly as a function with algebraic properties. Also the framework does not rely on a particular choice of a primitive randomized function, both discrete and uniform distributions can be manipulated. We propose an axiomatic semantics in the spirit of the work of C. Morgan et al. [5] and prove the validity of rules with respect to our semantics.

Outline. The paper is organized as follows. In section 2, we introduce the input language and its semantics: an interpretation of programs as measures using a monadic transformation. We analyze our monadic interpretation from the functional point of view. In section 3 we introduce the basic CoQ theories for representing measures. In section 4, we show the derived rules for estimating the probability for a randomized program to satisfy a given property. In section 5, we apply our method to proofs of simple probabilistic properties of programs.

Remark. The possible interpretation of random functional programs as probabilistic distributions using a monadic interpretation is not new, it appears in many theoretical works on semantics, or more concretely for representing random programs in Haskell in [1]. To our knowledge, however, the approach of mechanizing reasoning on random functional expressions is new. In [1], the interpretation does not cover general recursive programs and its inefficiency is criticized, the authors propose instead an alternative method which only cover discrete distributions. The possibility to cover recursion was however studied in [11] and we shall take the same approach in this paper. That the interpretation can lead to inefficient or even unfeasible computations in practice will be illustrated in section 2.6. Our work advocates that operational behavior is not relevant, as our model allows anyway for abstract reasoning on programs, using the general rules presented in section 4 and illustrated on examples in section 5. This is to be related to Hoare rules for axiomatic semantics, which do not rely on computations per se, but to denotational semantics. From this point of view, we compare with Kozen's second semantics in [3].

2   Monadic Interpretation of Randomized Algorithms

2.1   Randomized Programs as Measure Transformers

In works by D. Kozen [3, 4], G. Plotkin & C. Jones [12, 11], C. Morgan & A. McIver [13] and others, the basic idea is to interpret randomized programs as measure transformers instead of the usual interpretation of programs as state transformers.

The intuitive idea is that a randomized algorithm introduces a form of non-determinism in the sense that, for a given input state, it may produce different output states. One is interested in the distribution of these output states. If this distribution is known, given a property P on the state, we can compute the probability for the result of the program to satisfy P. A randomized program uses basic randomized primitives such as a `random` function which, given a natural number n, produces a number between 0 and n with uniform probability $\frac{1}{n+1}$, or a more basic `flip` function which produces `true` (resp. `false`) with probability $\frac{1}{2}$. Another classical operator is probabilistic choice P $_p$+ Q which behaves like the program P with probability p and as Q with probability $1 - p$.

The implicit assumption is that any access to a random operator in the program is independent of the others.

In this work, we start from a functional language. We do not have to consider a global state: programs are functions which are computing values, and we want to estimate the distribution of these values.

2.2   Representation of Distributions

In this section, we explain our choice for a mathematical representation of probability distributions. We introduce the notation $[0, 1]$ for the set of real numbers between 0 and 1.

The probability point of view. From the mathematical point of view, a probability distribution on a set A is defined by a set of *events* $\mathcal{E}$ which is a set of subsets of A with good closure properties, and a function Pr from $\mathcal{E}$ to $[0, 1]$ such that the following properties hold:

$$\mathsf{Pr}(A) \quad = 1$$
$$\mathsf{Pr}(\textstyle\bigcup_i E_i) = \Sigma_i \mathsf{Pr}(E_i) \text{ when } (E_i)_i \text{ is a denumerable set of disjoint sets}$$

The measure point of view. A (positive) measure on a set A, is a linear functional μ which given a (measurable) function f from A to $\mathbb{R}^+$, computes a non-negative real number, its integral $\int f d\mu$. In the following, we shall use the notation $\mu(f)$ instead of $\int f d\mu$.

Characteristic functions. If X is a subset of A, $\mathbb{I}_X \in A \to [0, 1]$ will denote the characteristic function of X such that $\forall x \in A, \mathbb{I}_X(x) = 0 \Leftrightarrow x \notin X \wedge \mathbb{I}_X(x) = 1 \Leftrightarrow x \in X$. We write simply $\mathbb{I}$ for the function which is 1 everywhere. If $P(x)$ is a formula with a free variable x, we write $\mathbb{I}_{P(.)}$ for the characteristic function of the set X such that $x \in X \Leftrightarrow P(x)$. For instance, $\mathbb{I}_{.=k}$ is the characteristic function of the singleton $\{k\}$.

Measure and probability. There is a well-known correspondence between measures and probability.

Given a probability Pr on a set A, the functional which, given a function $f : A \to \mathbb{R}^+$, computes its expectation defines a measure.

For instance, if A is a finite set, the set of events can be generated by the singletons $\{x\}$ for $x \in A$. The expectation of a function f is defined by:

$$\mu(f) \;=\; \Sigma_{x \in A} f(x) \times \mathsf{Pr}(\{x\})$$

In the other direction, given a measure μ on a set A such that $\mu(\mathbb{I}) = 1$, one can define an associated probability Pr. The events are subsets X of A, such that $\mathbb{I}_X$ is measurable and $\mathsf{Pr}(X) = \mu(\mathbb{I}_X)$.

Our abstract notion of measure. In this development, probability distributions are represented as positive bounded measures.

In order to define a probability distribution, it is sufficient to be able to measure functions which take values in the unit interval $[0, 1]$. We can remark that if $\forall x.f(x) \in [0, 1]$ then $\mu(f) \in [0, 1]$ because a probability distribution is bounded by one. Hence, a measure μ can be interpreted as a function of type $(X \rightarrow [0, 1]) \rightarrow [0, 1]$ satisfying some extra algebraic properties, to be precised in section 3.2.

2.3   Basic Language for Randomized Programs

In the following, we shall be interested in a simple functional language with the following constructions:

- Primitive constants and functions: c
- Conditional: **if** b **then** e_1 **else** e_2
- Local binding: **let** $x = e_1$ **in** e_2
- Abstraction: **fun** $(x : \tau) \Rightarrow e$
- Application: $(e_1 \; e_2)$

The term τ in the abstraction denotes a type. We assume given a simple (non-polymorphic) type system on this language, containing (at least) the base types **bool** for boolean values and **int** for integer as well as function types $\tau_1 \rightarrow \tau_2$.

A fixpoint construction will be introduced later in our language.

In order to deal with probabilistic programs, we add primitive functions to this language, such as the **random** function which given a positive integer n, computes with uniform distribution an integer k such that $0 \leq k \leq n$ and the **flip** function which computes a boolean which is **true** with probability $\frac{1}{2}$.

In the following, we use the same language for expressions representing randomized computations and terms representing their functional interpretation instead to introduce a monadic meta-language as in [14] or [15]. There will be in general no possible confusion.

For the sake of simplification, this paper assumes that abstraction and application in programs are only done on objects in base (non-functional) types; in a local binding as well, the introduced variable has a base type. In the meta-theory and in the interpretation, however, we shall use the same notations for higher-order functions, in particular when writing fixpoints.

2.4   Interpretation of Random Expressions

A (random) expression e in a base type τ actually represents a set of values of type τ, as different evaluations of the expression will lead to different values in general.

As pointed out above, for analyzing the distribution of these values, we interpret $e : \tau$ as a measure on τ, i.e. a function of type $(\tau \rightarrow [0, 1]) \rightarrow [0, 1]$.

We write $[e]$ to represent the measure associated to the expression e. If we know $[e]$, given a property Q on τ, it is possible to compute the probability for the evaluation of e to satisfy Q, it is just $[e](\mathbb{I}_Q)$, namely the application of the measure associated to the expression e to the characteristic function of the predicate Q, interpreted as a subset of τ.

2.5 Monadic Transformation

The computation of the measure $[e]$ is defined by case analysis on the structure of the expression e, following a monadic transformation.

We extend the interpretation to expressions denoting functions and not just expressions in base types. Each random expression representing a computation of type τ is interpreted as a purely functional expression of type $[\tau]$.

For a base type τ, $[\tau]$ is defined as $(\tau \to [0, 1]) \to [0, 1]$ the type of measures on τ. For a functional type $\tau = \tau_1 \to \tau_2$, we define $[\tau] = \tau_1 \to [\tau_2]$, as our study is restricted to the first-order case where τ_1 is a base type.

In the monadic approach, it is sufficient to define two operators

$$\mathsf{unit} : \tau \to [\tau] \quad \mathsf{bind} : [\tau] \to (\tau \to [\sigma]) \to [\sigma],$$

and for each non-functional construction of type τ (for instance **random**), its functional interpretation of type $[\tau]$.

Then the interpretation of expressions follows naturally:

Computation $p : \tau$	Functional value $[p] : [\tau]$
let $x = a$ **in** b	(bind $[a]$ **fun** $(x : \sigma) \Rightarrow [b]$)
fun $(x : \sigma) \Rightarrow t$	**fun** $(x : \sigma) \Rightarrow [t]$
$(t\ u)$	(bind $[u]\ [t]$)
if b **then** e_1 **else** e_2	(bind $[b]$ **fun** $(x : \mathtt{bool}) \Rightarrow$ **if** x **then** $[e_1]$ **else** $[e_2]$)

Definition of unit and bind. Given an expression e of base type τ, we want $[e]$ to be a measure, that is a functional object of type $(\tau \to [0, 1]) \to [0, 1]$. The transformation $[e]$ is analogous to the monadic interpretation of continuations. Assume τ and σ are base types, one defines:

$$
\begin{aligned}
\mathsf{unit}_\tau\ :\ & \tau \to [\tau] \\
= & \mathbf{fun}\ (x : \tau) \Rightarrow \mathbf{fun}\ (f : \tau \to [0, 1]) \Rightarrow (f\ x) \\
\mathsf{bind}_\sigma\ :\ & [\tau] \to (\tau \to [\sigma]) \to [\sigma] \\
= & \mathbf{fun}\ (\mu : [\tau]) \Rightarrow \mathbf{fun}\ (M : \tau \to [\sigma]) \Rightarrow \\
& \mathbf{fun}\ (f : \sigma \to [0, 1]) \Rightarrow (\mu\ \mathbf{fun}\ (x : \tau) \Rightarrow (M\ x\ f))
\end{aligned}
$$

This definition obviously satisfies the expected monadic properties, for instance (bind (unit$_\tau$ x) M) = (M x) and (bind (bind μ M_1) M_2) = (bind μ (**fun** $x \Rightarrow$ (bind $(M_1 x)$ M_2)). It is actually possible to extend these operators to functional types:

$$
\begin{aligned}
\mathsf{unit}_{\tau_1 \to \tau_2}\ :\ & (\tau_1 \to \tau_2) \to [\tau_1 \to \tau_2] \\
= & \mathbf{fun}\ (f : \tau_1 \to \tau_2) \Rightarrow \mathbf{fun}\ (x : \tau_1) \Rightarrow \mathsf{unit}_{\tau_2}(f\ x) \\
\mathsf{bind}_{\sigma_1 \to \sigma_2}\ :\ & [\tau] \to (\tau \to [\sigma_1 \to \sigma_2]) \to [\sigma_1 \to \sigma_2] \\
= & \mathbf{fun}\ (\mu : [\tau]) \Rightarrow \mathbf{fun}\ (M : \tau \to [\sigma_1 \to \sigma_2]) \Rightarrow \\
& \mathbf{fun}\ (y : \sigma_1) \Rightarrow \mathsf{bind}_{\sigma_2}\ \mu\ (\mathbf{fun}\ (x : \tau) \Rightarrow (M\ x\ y))
\end{aligned}
$$

Notice that, since we are only manipulating first-order programs in this paper, these generalized operators will not be needed in the examples. Following the translation scheme, if f has type $\tau_1 \to \tau_2 \to \sigma$, the binary application $((f\ a)\ b)$ should be translated into $\mathrm{bind}_\sigma\ [b]\ (\mathrm{bind}_{\tau_2 \to \sigma}\ [a]\ [f])$ but it is always possible, and probably more readable, to use the equivalent expanded form: $\mathrm{bind}_\sigma\ [b]$ (**fun** $(y : \tau_2) \Rightarrow \mathrm{bind}_\sigma\ [a]\ \mathbf{fun}(x : \tau_1) \Rightarrow ([f]\ x\ y))$.

Interpretation. From the measure point of view, $(\mathrm{unit}_\tau\ x)$ is the Dirac measure at point x. If x is an expression of type τ with no randomized construction then it evaluates deterministically to a value v and the probability of the result to satisfy P is one when $P(v)$ is true and zero otherwise.

In the definition of bind_σ, μ is a measure on τ, and M is a family of measures on σ parameterized with $x \in \tau$. Given a function f on σ, bind $\mu\ M$ measures with μ the function which associates with x the measure of f given by $(M\ x)$. For example, assume a is a randomized expression of type τ and e is a function which associates with $x : \tau$ a randomized expression of type σ. Given a property P on σ, we want to evaluate the probability for $(e\ a)$ to satisfy P. Interpreting e as a parameterized measure M we can compute, for a given value x, the probability for $(e\ x)$ to satisfy P. Then if we integrate this function with respect to x, using the measure associated with the expression a, we end up with the probability for $(e\ a)$ to satisfy P. That is exactly what bind is doing. This definition of bind captures the independence of random choices done in f and a.

Interpretation of randomized constructions. For the additional primitives, we get

$$\begin{aligned}
\mathrm{random}(n) : [\mathrm{int}] &= \mathbf{fun}\ (f : \mathrm{int} \to [0,1]) \Rightarrow \Sigma_{i=0}^{n} \tfrac{1}{n+1}(f\ i) \\
\mathrm{flip}() \quad : [\mathrm{bool}] &= \mathbf{fun}\ (f : \mathrm{bool} \to [0,1]) \Rightarrow \tfrac{1}{2}(f\ \mathrm{true}) + \tfrac{1}{2}(f\ \mathrm{false}) \\
e_1\ {}_p{+}\ e_2 \quad : [\tau] &= \mathbf{fun}\ (f : \tau \to [0,1]) \Rightarrow p \times ([e_1]\ f) + (1-p) \times ([e_2]\ f)
\end{aligned}$$

2.6   Functional Interpretation: An Example

Now that the monadic translation is defined, we can transform an expression e which computes a value randomly into an expression $[e]$ which does a deterministic computation of the measure associated with the expression e. Before looking at this interpretation for proofs, we can use it simply for computation, in a functional language like Caml.

In this part, we introduce a fixpoint construction in our language (written **let rec f = e**) with the idea that the interpretation $[f]$ of f will be a functional (still named f) defined by **let rec f = $[e]$**. We shall come back on this interpretation of fixpoints in section 3.3.

A basic example of a randomized algorithm is the primality test. The principle of this algorithm is the following. We want to check whether a number p is prime. There is a deterministic test (**test**) which applies to $1 \le k < p$ and p such that:

- If p is prime then (**test** $k\ p$) evaluates to **true** for all k
- If p is not prime then (**test** $k\ p$) evaluates to **true** for a limited number of k, say N less than $\frac{p-1}{2}$.

We choose k randomly and run the test: if the answer is false, then p is not prime; if the answer is true then p is not prime with a probability $\frac{N}{p-1}$ which is less than $\frac{1}{2}$. Iterating the test improves the level of confidence, provided the random choices of k are independent.

In our language, the function which iterates n times the primality test for p can be written: [1]

```
let rec prime_test p n =
    if n = 0 then true
    else if test (random' (p-1)) p then prime_test p (n-1)
    else false
```

Using the monadic transformation, and monadic simplification laws, we get the functional computation of the associated measure:

```
let rec prime_test_fun p n =
    if n = 0 then (unit true)
    else bind (random' (p-1))
             fun a ⇒ if (test p a) then (prime_test_fun p (n-1))
                     else (unit false)
```

Now if we want to evaluate the probability for our program to give a correct answer, we define the characteristic function of the correctness predicate, which says that the result is true exactly when p is prime, and which is encoded as:

```
let prime_correct p b = if b = exact_prime p then 1. else 0.
```

One can now explicitly compute the probability that our program gives a correct answer after n iterations:

```
let evaluate p n = prime_test_fun p n (prime_correct p)
```

The function can be run in Caml and gives the following results.

```
# evaluate 23 1;;
- : float = 1
# [evaluate 9 0;evaluate 9 1;evaluate 9 2;evaluate 9 3];;
- : float list = [0.;0.75;0.9375;0.984375]
```

If the number is prime (example $p = 23$), then the result will be correct with probability one. On the other hand, if p is not prime (example $p = 9$) then the probability that the program gives a correct answer after 0 iteration is 0, after 1 iteration, we get the good answer 3 times out of 4 and it goes to more than 98% of good answers after 4 iterations.

One nice point is that we have been able to compute these probabilities with a simple ML program without any specific knowledge on probability theory nor number theory. On the other hand, if we analyze the program, we remark that it is very inefficient:

---

[1] We use a function **random'** defined as **random'** n = **random** $(n-1) + 1$ in order to get a number between 1 and n.

- in order to build the characteristic function to be tested we need to know (or to test) exactly if p is prime or not;
- because of the interpretation of `random`, the program is executed for all the values of k between 1 and $p - 1$ before computing the average number of good answers.

Furthermore, this computational approach does not work in all cases. Our previous program uses a structural recursion which always terminates. Many interesting probabilistic programs only terminate with probability one, which is a weaker requirement. For instance the following function flips a coin and returns how many flips it took to get `false`, this is a typical example of a random walk:

let rec walk x = **if** flip () **then** walk (x+1) **else** x

If we test this function in Caml several times, we get small number answers such as $1, 2, 3$. We may apply our translation scheme:

let rec walk_fun x =
    bind flip (**fun** (b:bool) $\Rightarrow$ **if** b **then** walk_fun (x+1)
                                  else (unit x))

and measure the function which is 1 everywhere:

```
# walk_fun 1 (fun n -> 1.);;
Stack overflow during evaluation (looping recursion?).
```

it loops because our interpretation tests all the cases, in particular the one where the result of `flip` is always true. . .

    This example shows that, when general fixpoints are involved, we cannot anymore use computation of the monadic interpretation for analyzing the probability of events. We shall need to reason about these programs instead. For that, we first define a CoQ theory for representing distributions, then we prove several theorem for analyzing programs.

3   Coq Representation of Randomized Programs

We present now our model of randomized programs in the proof assistant CoQ. We follow the ideas presented in the previous section in order to associate with each program a measure and to reason directly on these measures.

3.1   The Set [0, 1]

Our model is based on measures seen as functionals of type $(A \rightarrow [0,1]) \rightarrow [0,1]$. For constructing this model in CoQ, we have chosen to axiomatize a type U which corresponds to the interval $[0,1]$.

Definitions. Let two special constants 0 and 1 in U. The basic operations are multiplication, addition and a special inversion function. The addition is bounded: it gives the minimum of addition on reals and 1. The inversion function associates $1 - x$ with x. We have also two predicates on U, $x \leq y$ and $x = y$, with the standard meaning.

For each natural number n, we introduce a special element $\frac{1}{n+1}$ in U.

To deal with unbounded computations, we also need the least-upper bound (*lub*) of any denumerable set of elements of U, represented as a function from `nat` to U: we consequently adjoin a parameter `lub` with type $(\texttt{nat} \rightarrow U) \rightarrow U$. If f is an expression with a free variable n, we write $\texttt{lub}(f)_n$ instead of $\texttt{lub}\,(\textbf{fun } n \Rightarrow f)$.

Axioms. We have axioms which say that $\forall x : U, 0 \leq x \leq 1$ and that $0 \neq 1$.

As expected, the previous operators come with the usual axioms stating that addition and multiplication are symmetric and associative, with 0 and 1 as their respective neutral elements, and so on.

Our inversion function enjoys good properties such as $1 - (1 - x) = x$. Some properties of addition are only valid when there is no overflow during addition. The non-overflow condition is expressed in our formalism as $x \leq 1 - y$. For instance, assuming $x \leq 1 - y$, we have:

$$(1 - (x + y)) + x = 1 - y \qquad (x + y) \times z = x \times z + y \times z \qquad x + y \leq x + z \Rightarrow y \leq z$$

The axioms for least upper bounds include the two basic properties of *lubs* and the fact that *lubs* are compatible with addition and multiplication

$$\texttt{lub}\,((f\ n) + k)_n = \texttt{lub}\ f + k \qquad \texttt{lub}\,((f\ n) \times k)_n = \texttt{lub}\ f \times k$$

We also need two extra properties: $\neg\neg(x \leq y) \rightarrow x \leq y \qquad x \leq y \vee y \leq x$.

The first property is required because CoQ implements an intuitionistic logic in which $\neg\neg A \Rightarrow A$ is not satisfied for all propositions. The second property states that the order is total.

The operation $\frac{1}{n+1}$ satisfies the axiom $\frac{1}{n+1} = 1 - n \times \frac{1}{n+1}$ where $n \times \frac{1}{n+1}$ is a generalized sum defined by induction on n.

Finally the fact that U is archimedian is axiomatized by the property

$$\forall x, x \neq 0 \Rightarrow \exists n, \frac{1}{n+1} \leq x$$

Remarks. Our modeling of randomized programs does not depend on our particular axiomatization of $[0, 1]$. Our choices are somehow arbitrary, we tried to find an axiomatization with a few number of operations and axioms such that the theory could be easily instantiated by different representations of real numbers. We are interested in particular by constructive reals, and we are currently investigating a possible encoding using the reals defined in [16] or the axioms proposed for interval objects as described in [17]. We use the functor mechanism of CoQ in order to keep the axiomatization of $[0, 1]$ as a parameter of the theory.

Derived operators. The usual minus operation $x - y$ (which is zero when $x \leq y$) can be defined using our special inverse by: $x - y = 1 - ((1 - x) + y)$ The operator `max` can be defined as $(x - y) + y$. It is also easy to define $n \times x$ and x^n for an integer n by induction on n. In [5], C. Morgan and A. McIver use an operator $x \& y$ defined on non-negative real numbers as the maximum of 0 and $x + y - 1$. The same operator can be defined in our theory using the inverse operator and addition by $x \& y \equiv 1 - ((1 - x) + (1 - y))$. It is the dual operation of addition because we have $(1 - (x \& y)) = (1 - x) + (1 - y)$ and $(1 - (x + y)) = (1 - x) \& (1 - y)$. This operator captures intersection of properties because $\mathbb{I}_{P \cap Q} = \mathbb{I}_P \& \mathbb{I}_Q$.

3.2   Definition of a Distribution

In the following, we extend in a standard way the operations and relations on U, to operations and relations on functions of type $A \to U$ using the same notations: $f \leq g$ will stand for $\forall x, f\, x \leq g\, x$ and $f + g$ is the function **fun** $x \Rightarrow f\, x + g\, x$.

Given a type A, we define a distribution on A to be a measure μ of type $(A \to U) \to U$ which furthermore satisfies stability properties, namely:

- monotonicity : $\forall f\ g : A \to U, f \leq g \Rightarrow \mu(f) \leq \mu(g)$
- compatibility with addition :
  $\forall f\ g : A \to U, f \leq 1 - g \Rightarrow \mu(f + g) = \mu(f) + \mu(g)$
- compatibility with inverse : $\forall f : A \to U, \mu(1 - f) \leq 1 - \mu(f)$
- compatibility with multiplication : $\forall (k : U)(f : A \to U), \mu(k \times f) = k \times \mu(f)$

In CoQ, we use a dependent record type in order to introduce a type (`distr A`) which contains the measure μ plus the proofs of compatibility properties for μ.

Remarks. Because the addition is bounded, the compatibility with respect to addition is only assumed when there is no overflow in the addition of f and g. We also need the extra condition of compatibility with respect to inversion which is usually derived from linearity.

We allow a distribution to be a sub-probability with possibly $\mu(1 - f) < 1 - \mu(f)$ (i.e. $\mu(\mathbb{I}) < 1$). This is useful for interpreting non terminating programs.

Monotonicity could be replaced by compatibility with respect to equality $\forall f\ g : A \to U, (f = g) \Rightarrow \mu(f) = \mu(g)$. Assuming this property, monotonicity comes from the fact that $g = (g - f) + f$ and stability with respect to addition.

Derived properties. From this definition, we can deduce further properties, such as $\mu(\textbf{fun}\ x \Rightarrow 0) = 0$, or $\mu(1 - f) = \mu(\mathbb{I}) - \mu(f)$. The inequality $\mu(f + g) \leq \mu(f) + \mu(g)$ is valid without extra non-overflow condition and, in a dual manner, we have $\mu(f) \& \mu(g) \leq \mu(f \& g)$.

Monadic operators. We define the monadic operators on distributions: `Munit` of type $\forall A, A \to \text{distr } A$ and `Mlet` of type $\forall A\ B, \text{distr } A \to (A \to \text{distr } B) \to \text{distr } B$. These operations are based on the transformations unit and bind for measures, while including extra proofs stating that these operations are stable with respect to the expected properties of distributions.

Properties. We can define an order and an equality on the type (distr A) by a simple extensions of the relations on U. This leads to proofs of monadic equalities, as well as monotonicity of the bind operation. In particular we prove [18]:

- $\forall(\mu : \text{distr } A), \text{Mlet } \mu \ (\textbf{fun } (x : A) \Rightarrow \text{Munit } x) = \mu$
- $\forall(\mu : \text{distr } A) \ (M : A \rightarrow \text{distr } B) \ (N : B \rightarrow \text{distr } C),$
  $\text{Mlet } (\text{Mlet } \mu \ M) \ N = \text{Mlet } \mu \ (\textbf{fun } (x : A) \Rightarrow \text{Mlet } (M \ x) \ N)$
- $\forall(\mu_1 \ \mu_2 : \text{distr } A) \ (M_1 \ M_2 : A \rightarrow \text{distr } B),$
  $\mu_1 \leq \mu_2 \Rightarrow (\forall x, (M_1 \ x) \leq (M_2 \ x)) \Rightarrow \text{Mlet } \mu_1 \ M_1 \leq \text{Mlet } \mu_2 \ M_2$

Random distributions. Following the interpretation of random primitives we gave in section 2.5, we can define in CoQ the corresponding distributions, we have to formally prove the stability properties.

The primitive flip has type (distr bool), random has type int $\rightarrow$ (distr int) and the choice operator has type $U \rightarrow$ (distr A) $\rightarrow$ (distr A) $\rightarrow$ (distr A).

The framework is not limited to discrete distributions. While defining completely a measure on U could require the development of a non-trivial part of analysis, it is already possible, for example as found in [6], to introduce as a parameter a new distribution uniform of type (distr U) with the extra assumption that for all $a, b \in U$, the measure of the interval $[a, b]$ is equal to $b - a$, i.e. $(\text{uniform } \mathbb{I}_{a \leq . \leq b}) = b - a$.

Interpretation of simple programs. The constructors Mlet, Munit, flip, random are sufficient for interpreting simple random programs. Following our general monadic translation scheme, one can also define a conditional operation Mif of type (distr bool) $\rightarrow$ (distr A) $\rightarrow$ (distr A) $\rightarrow$ (distr A) by

$$\text{Mif } \mu_b \ \mu_1 \ \mu_2 \equiv \text{Mlet } \mu_b \ (\textbf{fun } b \Rightarrow \textbf{if } b \textbf{ then } \mu_1 \textbf{ else } \mu_2).$$

We use this operator for interpreting conditional programs:

$[\textbf{if } b \textbf{ then } e_1 \textbf{ else } e_2] \equiv \text{Mif } [b] \ [e_1] \ [e_2]$

3.3   Interpretation of Fixpoints

As expected, the difficult part is the interpretation of general fixpoints. This is achieved through the following steps.

Limit of distributions. In order to interpret recursive functions, we need to take limits of sequences of distributions.

We assume given a denumerable family of distributions $(\mu_n)_{n \in \mathbb{N}}$ of type distr A, such that $\forall n \ m, n \leq m \Rightarrow \mu_n \leq \mu_m$. Then we can define a new distribution as the least upper bound of $(\mu_n)_n$. The associated measure, $\mu_{\text{lub}}(\mu_n)_n$, is defined by $\mu_{\text{lub}}(\mu_n)_n \ (f) \equiv \text{lub } (\mu_n \ (f))_n$.

Fixpoints. Let us consider we want to define a function which satisfies the equation

let rec f x = F f x

where f is assumed to take an argument in type A, and returns a random value of type B, so that it is interpreted as a function of type $A \rightarrow \mathtt{distr}\ B$. Thus, F will have type $(A \rightarrow \mathtt{distr}\ B) \rightarrow A \rightarrow \mathtt{distr}\ B$, and we assume this functional to be monotonic: $f \leq g \Rightarrow F\ f \leq F\ g$.

Let us define the sequence M_n of functions of type $A \rightarrow \mathtt{distr}\ B$, by repeated iterations of F from the null distribution:

$$M_0\ x = \mathbf{fun}\ f \Rightarrow 0 \quad M_{n+1}\ x = F\ M_n\ x$$

The limit distribution $\mathtt{Mfix}$ is defined, for each given x, as the least upper bound of the sequence which associates with n the distribution $(M_n\ x)$:

$$\mathtt{Mfix}\ F\ x \equiv \mu_{\mathtt{lub}}(M_n\ x)_n$$

We can derive the inequalities

$$\mathtt{Mfix}\ F\ x \leq F\ (\mathtt{Mfix}\ F)\ x \quad \text{and} \quad F\ (\mathtt{Mfix}\ F)\ x \leq \mathtt{Mfix}\ F\ x$$

The second inequality requires an extra hypothesis of continuity namely that for all monotonic sequences $(g_n)_{n \in \mathbb{N}}$ of type $A \rightarrow \mathtt{distr}\ B$,

$$F\ (\mathbf{fun}\ y \Rightarrow \mu_{\mathtt{lub}}(g_n\ y)_n)\ x \leq \mu_{\mathtt{lub}}(F\ g_n\ x)_n$$

However, as we will see in section 4.2, estimating programs built with fixpoints can be done without using this rule.

4 Derived Rules for Reasoning on Programs

For reasoning about programs, it is convenient to use an axiomatic semantics that provides rules by induction on the structure of the program, stating as usual, how some post-condition is satisfied after execution, provided some precondition holds. In fact, in the context of probabilistic programs, we are interested (see also [4]) in deriving that the probability for a certain property to hold is greater than a certain value.

Thus we look forward deriving judgements of the form $k \leq [e](f)$ where $k \in [0, 1]$, e is an expression of type A and f is a function of type $A \rightarrow [0, 1]$.

The meaning of this judgement is that the measure associated with the program e computed on the function f is no less than k. Usually f will be the characteristic function $\mathbb{I}_P$ of some predicate P of type $A \rightarrow \mathtt{bool}$. The judgement $k \leq [e](\mathbb{I}_P)$ therefore means that the probability for the result of e to satisfy P is at least k.

4.1 Basic Rules

We can prove the following rule for application:

$$\frac{k \leq [a](f) \quad \forall x, f\ x \leq [e\ x](g)}{k \leq [e\ a](g)}$$

For the case of conditional, we can prove the rule:

$$\frac{k_1 \leq [e_1](f) \quad k_2 \leq [e_2](f)}{k_1 \times [b](\mathbb{I}_{.=\mathtt{true}}) + k_2 \times [b](\mathbb{I}_{.=\mathtt{false}}) \leq [\mathbf{if}\ b\ \mathbf{then}\ e_1\ \mathbf{else}\ e_2](f)}$$

4.2   Rule for Fixpoints

We now justify the rule for estimating fixpoints which follows the ideas presented in [11]. We assume F has type $(A \rightarrow \mathtt{distr}\ B) \rightarrow A \rightarrow \mathtt{distr}\ B$ and is monotonic. We take a monotonic sequence $(p_i)_i$ of functions of type $A \rightarrow U$ such that $\forall x, p_0\ x = 0$. The following rule is valid:

$$\frac{\forall f : A \rightarrow \mathtt{distr}\ B, (\forall x, p_n\ x \leq [f\ x](q)) \Rightarrow (\forall x, p_{n+1}\ x \leq [F\ f\ x](q))}{\forall x, \mathtt{lub}\ (p_n\ x)_n \leq [\mathbf{fix}\ F\ x](q)}$$

No continuity condition on F is required to validate this rule. The sequence $(p_n)_n$ can be seen as a generalized invariant for randomized programs: assuming that the recursive goal establishes a post-condition Q with probability at least p_n, we prove that one further iteration establishes Q with probability at least p_{n+1}, and we finally get that the recursive program establishes Q with a probability which is at least the $\mathtt{lub}$ of $(p_n)_n$.

4.3   Other Rules

We can derive in our formalism useful schemes which generalize reasoning on deterministic programs. For instance, if we have established that an expression a satisfies a predicate P with probability 1, then it is possible to reason subsequently exactly as if P was true for the result of the computation of a.

This is stated in the following derivable rule:

$$\frac{1 \leq [a](\mathbb{I}_P) \qquad \forall x, (P\ x) \Rightarrow k \leq [b](f)}{k \leq [\mathbf{let}\ x = a\ \mathbf{in}\ b](f)}$$

5   Applications

We apply our approach for proving properties of simple randomized programs.

5.1   Probabilistic Termination

We return to our example of section 2.6, a random walk which illustrates probabilistic termination.

```
let rec walk x = if flip() then walk (x+1) else x
```

We show that this program terminates with probability one. For that it is enough to prove that:

$$\forall x, 1 \leq [\mathtt{walk}\ x](\mathbb{I}).$$

We shall apply the fixpoint rule with a functional F defined by

$$F\ f\ x \equiv \mathtt{Mif}\ \mu_{\mathtt{flip}}\ (f(x+1))\ (\mathtt{Munit}\ x)$$

We introduce a sequence p_i defined by $p_0 = 0$ and $p_{i+1} = \frac{1}{2}p_i + \frac{1}{2}$. It is easy to show that $p_n = 1 - \frac{1}{2^n}$ and that the least upper bound of the sequence $(p_i)_i$ is 1. In order to prove $1 \leq [\texttt{Mfix } F \ x](\mathbb{I})$, we use the fixpoint rule and show:

$$\forall f, (\forall x, p_i \leq [f \ x](\mathbb{I})) \Rightarrow \forall x, p_{i+1} \leq [F \ f \ x](\mathbb{I})$$

We assume $\forall x, p_i \leq [f \ x](\mathbb{I})$ and we simplify as follows

$$p_{i+1} \leq [F \ f \ x](\mathbb{I}) \Leftrightarrow \tfrac{1}{2}p_i + \tfrac{1}{2} \leq [\texttt{Mif } \mu_{\texttt{flip}} \ (f(x+1)) \ (\texttt{Munit } x)](\mathbb{I})$$
$$\Leftrightarrow \tfrac{1}{2}p_i + \tfrac{1}{2} \leq \tfrac{1}{2}f(x+1)(\mathbb{I}) + \tfrac{1}{2}\mathbb{I}(x)$$

This is trivially true because $p_i \leq f(x+1)(\mathbb{I})$ by hypothesis and $\mathbb{I}(x) = 1$.

5.2 The Bernoulli Distribution

We now apply our technique to the proof of an algorithm to simulate a Boolean function following Bernoulli's distribution (which is **true** with some probability p and false with probability $1 - p$) using only a coin flip. The algorithm which is also taken as an example in [19] uses a simple idea : write p in binary form $\Sigma_{i=1}^{\infty} p_i \frac{1}{2^i}$, if we flip a coin and get a sequence $(q_i)_{i \geq 1}$ then the first time we get $q_i \neq p_i$, we answer true when $q_i < p_i$ and false otherwise. Now this function can be expressed recursively. If $p < \frac{1}{2}$ then $p_1 = 0$ and the remainder of the sequence corresponds to $2 \times p = p + p$. If $\frac{1}{2} \leq p$ then $p_1 = 1$ and the remainder of the sequence corresponds to $2 \times p - 1 = p\&p$ (using the special operation $x\&y$ we introduced in section 3.1). Our Bernoulli program can be written as

```
let rec bernoulli p =
    if flip() then if p < ½ then false else bernoulli (p & p)
             else if p < ½ then bernoulli (p + p) else true
```

We directly translate this definition into a distribution, as was done in the case of the random walk. In order to analyze this program, we use the fixpoint rule and prove that

$$\forall p, \mathbf{lub}_n \ (p - \frac{1}{2^n}) \leq [\texttt{bernoulli } p](\mathbb{I}_{.=\texttt{true}}).$$

Assuming $\forall p, (p - \frac{1}{2^n}) \leq [\texttt{bernoulli } p](\mathbb{I}_{.=\texttt{true}})$, we just simplify the expression corresponding to the body of **bernoulli**. In case $p < \frac{1}{2}$, we have to show that

$$p - \frac{1}{2^{n+1}} \leq \frac{1}{2}\texttt{bernoulli}(p + p)$$

and in case $\frac{1}{2} \leq p$, we have to show that

$$p - \frac{1}{2^{i+1}} \leq \frac{1}{2}\texttt{bernoulli}(p\&p) + \frac{1}{2} \times 1$$

this follows easily using the fixpoint rule hypothesis and algebraic properties. The same reasoning allows to prove:

$$\forall p, \mathbf{lub}_n \ ((1 - p) - \frac{1}{2^n}) \leq [\texttt{bernoulli } p](\mathbb{I}_{.=\texttt{false}}).$$

Using the fact that $\mathbb{I}_{.=\mathtt{false}} = 1 - \mathbb{I}_{.=\mathtt{true}}$ and the property of measures of inverse functions, we conclude that $[(\mathtt{bernoulli}\ p)]\mathbb{I}_{.=\mathtt{true}} = p$.

Using $\mathbb{I}_{.=\mathtt{true}} + \mathbb{I}_{.=\mathtt{false}} = \mathbb{I}$, we also have $[(\mathtt{bernoulli}\ p)]\mathbb{I} = 1$ which shows that the process terminates with probability one.

5.3 Improving Precision

Another example is an abstract version of a program scheme where a randomized program is executed twice in order to improve the probability of getting a correct result. The implicit assumption is that given two runs on the program we can choose the better of the two answers. In case of primality for instance, if one of the test answers that p is not prime, we are sure that p is not prime; only when the two programs assert that p is prime, we can still pretend (but with higher confidence) that p is prime.

We want to compute a value in a type A which satisfies a property Q with a certain probability. The hypotheses are that we have two programs p_1 and p_2 of type A, thus interpreted as objects of type distr A. We want to combine p_1 and p_2 in order to get a better program i.e. we want to improve the probability that the result is correct.

We assume we have a function choice of type $A \to A \to A$ such that $(Q\ x) \Rightarrow Q\ (\mathtt{choice}\ x\ y)$ and $(Q\ y) \Rightarrow Q\ (\mathtt{choice}\ x\ y)$ are provable.

In case of a Boolean test for primality of p, we have $(Q\ b)$ defined as $(b = \mathtt{true} \Leftrightarrow p\ \mathtt{is\ prime})$ and $(\mathtt{choice}\ b_1\ b_2)$ defined as $(b_1\ \mathtt{and}\ b_2)$.

Now we build a new program p:

let x = p_1 **in let** y = p_2 **in** choice x y

We want to show that $k_1 \le [p_1](\mathbb{I}_Q)$ and $k_2 \le [p_2](\mathbb{I}_Q)$ implies $k_1(1 - k_2) + k_2 \le [p](\mathbb{I}_Q)$. The new estimation $k_1(1 - k_2) + k_2$ (also equal to $k_2(1 - k_1) + k_1$) is greater than both k_1 and k_2.

Actually we established a more general result, using an arbitrary function q of type $A \to U$ instead of the characteristic function $\mathbb{I}_Q$ of a predicate Q. We assume that $\forall x\ y, (q\ x) + (q\ y) \le q\ (\mathtt{choice}\ x\ y)$ (with bounded addition). It is easy to see that when q is the characteristic function $\mathbb{I}_Q$, then the assumptions $(Q\ x) \Rightarrow Q\ (\mathtt{choice}\ x\ y)$ and $(Q\ y) \Rightarrow Q\ (\mathtt{choice}\ x\ y)$ are equivalent to $(\mathbb{I}_Q\ x) + (\mathbb{I}_Q\ y) \le \mathbb{I}_Q\ (\mathtt{choice}\ x\ y)$. We also need the fact that both programs p_1 and p_2 terminate with probability one, otherwise our choice function could give a result which is not as good as p_1 and p_2. Now, the property to be shown amounts to

$$k_1(1 - k_2) + k_2 \le [p_1](\mathbf{fun}\ x \Rightarrow [p_2](\mathbf{fun}\ y \Rightarrow (q\ (\mathtt{choice}\ x\ y))))$$

Using the fact that

$$(q\ x) \times (1 - (q\ y)) + (q\ y) \le (q\ x) + (q\ y) \le (q\ (\mathtt{choice}\ x\ y))$$

the proof reduces to

$$k_1(1 - k_2) + k_2 \le [p_1](\mathbf{fun}\ x \Rightarrow [p_2](\mathbf{fun}\ y \Rightarrow (q\ x) \times (1 - (q\ y)) + (q\ y)))$$

Algebraic properties of measures lead to simplification of the right-hand side:

$$[p_1](q) \times [p_2](1 - q) + [p_2](q)$$

Because p_2 terminates, we have $[p_2](1 - q) = 1 - [p_2](q)$ (only the inequality is true in general) so we have to show:

$$k_1(1 - k_2) + k_2 \leq [p_1](q)(1 - [p_2](q)) + [p_2](q)$$

which is true because $k_1(1 - k_2) + k_2 = k_2(1 - k_1) + k_1$ is monotonic with respect to both k_1 and k_2.

This example illustrates the possibility to do abstract modular reasoning in our framework.

6 Related Work

In [6], Park and al. propose a functional language, named $\lambda_\bigcirc$ which extends the ML functional kernel on the basis of the monadic metalanguage developed by Pfenning and Davies [15]. It is a reformulation of Moggi's monadic metalanguage (the **let...in...** construction) which augments the λ-calculus, consisting of terms, with a separate syntactic category, consisting of expressions which denote probabilistic computations. A term can be cast to a (random) expression. From any expression E, the operator **prob** E builds the image measure. In our work, both terms and (random) expressions are not distinguished, unit providing the corresponding operator from terms to random expression. Besides, the current bind operation is represented by **sample** x **from** M **in** E in $\lambda_\bigcirc$. The language introduces a new constant S which denotes an expression, i.e. a random variable which follows the uniform law on the real interval $[0, 1]$. The system is simply typed, where types are limited to arrows and pairs, enriched with the monadic construction $\bigcirc A$ for each type A.

We do not have these two syntactic levels in our system where we chose to represent in CoQ only the level of terms. The $\bigcirc A$ type play the role of (distr A) in our formalism and the value **prob**(E) corresponds to our definition of $[E]$. Their formalism allows to build distributions on arbitrary types (possibly functional), an extension we did not investigate yet.

$\lambda_\bigcirc$ is mainly designed toward expressiveness as a programming language, for which the paper provides a small steps operational semantics. This corresponds to Kozen's first semantics in [3], where any computation involved in a reasoning step about a program requires the user to refer to the measurable space of random streams over $[0, 1]$. As far as reasoning on programs is concerned, this is not of great help, since axiomatic semantics relies on denotational semantics. Therefore, examples developed with $\lambda_\bigcirc$ are better analysed through simulation techniques. Both approaches are complementary: we are not able to simulate the programs as sampling functions but we can directly and easily reason on the probabilistic properties of (a subset of) Caml expressions.

In [13], A. McIver and C. Morgan describe an axiomatic semantics for probabilistic programs written in imperative style. The state-predicates in Hoare logic are replaced by so-called *expectations* which are functions from states to $\mathbb{R}^+$, to be evaluated following the distribution defined by the program. An important aspect of this work is to introduce in the language a non-deterministic (demonic) choice $p \sqcap q$. The probability for a property P to hold after executing $p \sqcap q$ is the minimum of the probabilities that P holds after executing p and after executing q. This operator is used to represent specifications and for defining a refinement relation. In order to adapt our approach to the non-deterministic case, an idea could be to relax the compatibility condition for addition in the definition of a distribution into the weaker condition $\mu(f) + \mu(g) \leq \mu(f + g)$. Developing the corresponding theory still remains to be done. A mechanization of this calculus using the HOL theorem prover is presented in [7]. In this work programs are interpreted as functionals of type $(\alpha \to \mathbb{R}_\infty^+) \to (\alpha \to \mathbb{R}_\infty^+)$ where $\mathbb{R}_\infty^+ \equiv \mathbb{R}^+ \cup \{\infty\}$ and α is the type of states. They propose a so-called *deep-embedding* where the syntax of the language of guarded commands and the weakest-precondition generator are explicitly encoded in the proof assistant, while we use a *shallow* embedding where we directly use the semantics of the language. Their approach allows to measure an arbitrary function with value in $\mathbb{R}^+$ and not only $[0,1]$. We choose to restrict ourselves to $[0,1]$ in order to simplify the formal development in CoQ and because it is sufficient for correctness. Measuring arbitrary function can nevertheless be interesting in some cases. For instance, in the random walk example, one could measure the average of the result of the function (how many flips before we get false). It is possible to represent an element in $\mathbb{R}^+$ with a pair (n, x) with $n \in \mathbb{N}$ and $x \in [0, 1]$ and reuse a large part of our development in order to extend a measure of type $(A \to [0,1]) \to [0,1]$ into a measure of type $(A \to \mathbb{R}^+) \to \mathbb{R}^+$. We may introduce for each $n \in \mathbb{N}$ a function $f_n : A \to [0,1]$ such that $f_n(x) = y$ when $f(x) = (n, y)$ and $f(x) = 0$ otherwise. We have $f = \Sigma_{n=0}^\infty f_n$ and we can define $\mu(f)$ as $\Sigma_{n=0}^\infty \mu(f_n)$ when it exists.

As already said in the introduction, our approach comes actually closer to J. Hurd's thesis, where formal verification of probabilistic programs is handled with the HOL theorem prover. He uses a monadic translation based on a global state with a stream of boolean values. Reasoning on programs required to define within HOL an adequate distribution over this infinite structure, while we only use simple mathematical constructions. It would be interesting to compare more carefully the complexity of proofs of high-level programs in both systems.

7   Conclusion

We have studied the interpretation of probabilistic programs in a functional framework using a monadic interpretation of programs as probability distributions represented by measures.

We have applied this technique for building an environment for reasoning about probabilistic programs in the CoQ proof assistant. We have developed an axiomatization for the set $[0, 1]$ which uses a few primitive operations : bounded addition, multiplication and inverse $(1 - x)$.

We have derived axiomatic rules for estimating the probability that programs satisfy certain properties, following the structure of the program. The fixpoint rule is especially useful for dealing with probabilistic termination of programs. We use these rules for studying a few basic examples such as the computation of a function following a Bernoulli distribution. The development and results presented in this paper have been formally derived and checked in the COQ proof assistant and are available as a contribution [18].

Future works include automatic translation from functional randomized programs to COQ terms representing the corresponding distribution. One possibility could be to use a monadic meta-language in the spirit of [6] on top of the COQ proof assistant. Another possibility is to follow the approach of the WHY tool [20, 21], a generic environment for analysing non-purely functional programs. It automatically generates verification conditions from the specification of pre and post conditions plus a validation (the correctness proof in COQ obtained from the monadic translation of the program).

We also plan to study advanced examples that certainly will require a more sophisticated automation of proofs.

Acknowledgments. We thank A. McIver and C. Morgan for useful comments on an earlier version of this paper. We also thank R. Lassaigne for stimulating discussions on formal proofs for analyzing random programs.

References

1. Ramsey, N., Pfeffer, A.: Stochastic lambda calculus and monads of probability distributions. In Conf. Record of 29th ACM SIGPLAN-SIGACT Symp. on Principles of Programming Languages, POPL 2002. ACM Press (2002) 154–165
2. The Coq Development Team: The Coq Proof Assistant Reference Manual – Version V8.0. (2004) http://coq.inria.fr.
3. Kozen, D.: Semantics of probabilistic programs. J. of Comput. and Syst. Sci. **22**(3) (1981) 328–350
4. Kozen, D.: A probabilistic PDL. In Proc. of 15th Ann. ACM Symp. on Theory of Computing, STOC' 83. ACM Press (1983) 291–297
5. Morgan, C., McIver, A.: pGCL: formal reasoning for random algorithms. South African Computer J. (1999)
6. Park, S., Pfenning, F., Thrun, S.: A probabilistic language based upon sampling functions. In Proc. of 32nd ACM SIGPLAN-SIGACT Symp. on Principles of Programming Languages, POPL 2005. ACM Press (2005) 171–182
7. Hurd, J., McIver, A., Morgan, C.: Probabilistic guarded commands mechanized in HOL. In Cerone, A., Pierro, A.D., eds.: Proc. of 2nd Wksh. on Quantitative Aspects of Programming Languages, QAPL 2004. Volume 112 of Electron. Notes in Theor. Comput. Sci. Elsevier (2005) 95–111
8. Kwiatkowska, M., Norman, G., Parker, D.: Probabilistic symbolic model checking with PRISM: A hybrid approach. J. on Software Tools for Technology Transfer **6**(2) (2004) 128–42
9. Hurd, J.: Formal Verification of Probabilistic Algorithms. PhD thesis, Univ. of Cambridge (2002)

10. Hurd, J.: Verification of the Miller-Rabin probabilistic primality test. J. of Logic and Algebraic Program. **50**(1–2) (2003) 3–21
11. Jones, C.: Probabilistic Non-determinism. PhD thesis, Univ. of Edinburgh (1989)
12. Jones, C., Plotkin, G.: A probabilistic powerdomain of evaluations. In Proc. of 4th Ann. IEEE Symp. on Logic in Computer Science, LICS '89. IEEE Comput. Soc. Press (1989) 186–195
13. McIver, A., Morgan, C.: Abstraction, Refinement and Proof for Probabilistic Systems. Monographs in Computer Science. Springer-Verlag (2005)
14. Moggi, E.: Notions of computation and monads. Inform. and Comput. **93**(1) (1991) 55–92
15. Pfenning, F., Davies, R.: A judgmental reconstruction of modal logic. Math. Struct. in Comput. Sci. **11**(4) (2001) 511–540
16. Geuvers, H., Niqui, M.: Constructive reals in Coq: Axioms and categoricity. In Callaghan, P., Luo, Z., McKinna, J., Pollack, R., eds.: Selected Papers from 1st Int. Wksh. on Types for Proofs and Programs, TYPES 2000. Vol. 2277 of Lect. Notes in Comput. Sci. Springer-Verlag (2002) 79–95
17. Escardó, M., Simpson, A.: A universal characterization of the closed euclidean interval (extended abstract). In Proc. of 16th Ann. IEEE Symp. on Logic in Computer Science, LICS '01. IEEE Comput. Soc. Press (2001) 115–125
18. Paulin-Mohring, C.: A library for reasoning on randomized algorithms in Coq: description of a Coq contribution, Univ. Paris Sud (2006) `http://www.lri.fr/~paulin/ALEA/library.pdf`
19. Hurd, J.: A formal approach to probabilistic termination. In Carreño, V.A., Muñoz, C.A., Tahar, S., eds.: Proc. of 15th Int. Conf. on Theorem Proving in Higher Order Logics, TPHOLs 2002. Vol. 2410 of Lect. Notes in Comput. Sci. Springer-Verlag (2002) 230–245
20. Filliâtre, J.C.: Verification of non-functional programs using interpretations in type theory. J. of Funct. Program. **13**(4) (2003) 709–745
21. Filliâtre, J.C.: The why verification tool. (2002) `http://why.lri.fr/`

Exercises in Quantifier Manipulation

Roland Backhouse [1] and Diethard Michaelis [2]

[1] School of Computer Science and Inform. Techn., University of Nottingham,
Jubilee Campus, Wollaton Road, Nottingham NG8 1BB, England
`rcb@cs.nott.ac.uk`
[2] Beethovenstr. 55, 90513 Zirndorf, Germany
`diethard.michaelis@t-online.de`

Abstract. The Eindhoven quantifier notation is systematic, unlike standard mathematicial notation. This has the major advantage that calculations with quantified expressions become more straightforward because the calculational rules need be given just once for a great variety of different quantifiers.

We demonstrate the ease of calculation with finite quantifications by considering a number of examples. Two are simple warm-up exercises, using boolean equality as the quantifier. Three are taken from books of challenging mathematical problems, and one is a problem concocted by the authors to demonstrate the techniques.

1 Introduction

Quantifications, both logical ($\forall$, $\exists$) and arithmetic (Σ, Π, etc.) abound in program specifications, but the manipulation of quantified expressions is rarely discussed in any detail. (An important exception is [1].) Moreover, many texts (in mathematics and computing) adopt different (unsystematic) notations for different quantifiers, obscuring the commonalities in their properties. Even worse, the dotdotdot ("$\ldots$") notation is often used, leading inevitably to mistakes[1]. In contrast, the "Eindhoven" quantifier notation is a uniform notation for expressing quantifications over an arbitrary abelian monoid. It has been used since the early 1970s [2, 3]. Initially, little or no explanation of the rules for manipulating quantifiers was given, except for some of the most basic (like empty range and range splitting [4]). Backhouse [5] compiled a list of rules for finite quantifications, partly based on the rules given by Knuth for summation [6]; these were recently updated [7] bringing the naming of the rules into line with that used elsewhere.

In this paper, we demonstrate the importance of manipulating quantifiers using a number of exercises drawn from books about challenging mathematical problems. Our calculations lead to straightforward solutions to the problems

---

[1] The website "The most common errors in undergraduate mathematics" `www.math.vanderbilt.edu/~schectex/commerrs` reports "many errors" in the use of dotdotdot notation ("ellipses"). Of course, the error is the teacher's use of the notation, and should not be blamed on the student!

T. Uustalu (Ed.): MPC 2006, LNCS 4014, pp. 69–81, 2006.

and, in one case, to a new theorem. The calculations are goal-directed and, we hope, may be of benefit to teaching the calculational method.

2   Warm-Up Exercises

A standard exercise is to prove that the parity of a sum of a finite bag of integers is odd equivales the number of odd elements is odd. This is a nice warm-up exercise in the use of the quantifier calculus:

$$even.\langle \Sigma k :: n_k \rangle$$

$=$ { $even$ distributes through summation   }

$$\langle \equiv k :: even.n_k \rangle$$

$=$ {   trading, $even.n_k \equiv (odd.n_k \Rightarrow \mathsf{false})$ }

$$\langle \equiv k : odd.n_k : \mathsf{false} \rangle$$

$=$ { $\mathsf{false} \equiv even.1$ }

$$\langle \equiv k : odd.n_k : even.1 \rangle$$

$=$ { $even$ distributes through summation   }

$$even.\langle \Sigma k : odd.n_k : 1 \rangle \ .$$

The calculation uses two quantifiers: the familiar sum (Σ) quantifier, and the unfamiliar equivales ($\equiv$) quantifier. In general, the Eindhoven quantifier notation extends the binary operator, $\oplus$ say, of an abelian monoid to an arbitrary finite bag of values, the bag being defined by a function (the *term*) acting on a set (the *range*). The form of a quantified expression is

$$\langle \oplus bv \in type : range : term \rangle$$

where $\oplus$ is the quantifier, bv is the *dummy* or *bound variable* and *type* is its type, *range* defines a subset of the type of the dummy over which the dummy ranges, and *term* defines a function on the range. The value of the quantification is the result of applying the operator $\oplus$ to all the values generated by evaluating the term at all instances of the dummy in the range.

Strictly, the type of the dummy should always be explicitly stated because the information can be important (as in, for example, the stronger relation between the less-than and at-most orderings on integers compared with their properties on reals). It is, however, information that is often cumbersome to repeat. For this reason, the information is omitted and a convention on the naming of dummies (such as i, j and k denote integer values) is adopted. This means that the most common use of the notation is in the form

$$\langle \oplus bv : range : term \rangle \ .$$

In addition, the *range* is sometimes omitted (again to avoid unnecessary repetition in calculations). In this case the form of the quantification is

$$\langle \bigoplus bv :: term \rangle.$$

Formally, omitting the range is equivalent to a true range:

$$\langle \bigoplus bv :: term \rangle \;=\; \langle \bigoplus bv : \text{true} : term \rangle.$$

A complete set of rules governing the manipulation of quantified expressions is given in [7]. The example calculation has been chosen not only because it uses an unfamiliar quantifier, but also because the steps involve possibly unfamilar rules of manipulation.

In the first and last step, the distributivity of *even* over finite summation is used. This is a consequence of two properties:

$$even.0 \equiv \text{true},$$

(the unit of addition is mapped to the unit of equivales) and[2]

$$even.(m+n) \equiv even.m \equiv even.n$$

(binary addition is mapped to binary equivales). The second step uses the "trading" rule for equivales. There is a trading rule for every quantifier; the one for equivales is like the trading rule for universal quantification. An implication, $P\Rightarrow$, in the term is "traded" into a conjunct, $P\wedge$, in the range. (Although we don't use it here, it is worth pointing out that the trading rule for inequivalence is like the trading rule for existential quantification — a conjunct is traded with a conjunct.)

Note that a special case for an empty bag does not need to be made. Even in this case, all quantifications are well defined; an equivales-quantification over an empty range is true.

It's useful to take this example a little further. Note that $\langle \Sigma k : odd.n_k : 1 \rangle$ is a count of the odd numbers in the bag. Sometimes, we want to count the number of values in a given finite range that satisfy a given property p. The following is useful.

$$even.\langle \Sigma k : p_k : 1 \rangle$$

$=$ {   *even* distributes through summation   }

$$\langle \equiv k : p_k : even.1 \rangle$$

$=$ {   trading, $even.1 \equiv \text{false}$, $(q\Rightarrow\text{false}) \equiv q \equiv \text{false}$ }

$$\langle \equiv k :: p_k \equiv \text{false} \rangle$$

---

[2] Occurrences of the binary equivales symbol " $\equiv$ " and, later, inequivales " $\not\equiv$ " should be read associatively. Occurrences of the equality symbol " $=$ " should be read conjunctionally.

$=$ {   associativity and symmetry   }

$\langle \equiv k :: p_k \rangle \;\equiv\; \langle \equiv k :: \mathsf{false} \rangle$

$=$ { $\mathsf{false} \equiv even.1$, distributivity   }

$\langle \equiv k :: p_k \rangle \;\equiv\; even.\langle \Sigma\, k :: 1 \rangle$.

In summary,

$$even.\langle \Sigma k : p_k : 1 \rangle \;\equiv\; \langle \equiv k :: p_k \rangle \;\equiv\; even.\langle \Sigma k :: 1 \rangle . \tag{1}$$

(In particular, p_k can be instantiated to $odd.n_k$.)

The equivales-quantifier will be used again later. Because it is unfamiliar, we offer the following exercise relating it to the different-from ($\neq$) quantifier (more commonly known as exclusive-or).

The problem is to relate $\langle \equiv k :: p_k \rangle$ to $\langle \neq k :: p_k \rangle$. Noting the distributivity laws: $\neg(p \equiv q) \equiv \neg p \neq \neg q$, and $\neg\mathsf{true} \equiv \mathsf{false}$, negation distributes through an arbitrary finite equivales-quantification turning it into a different-from quantification. So,

$\langle \neq k :: p_k \rangle$

$=$ {   double negation, distributivity   }

$\neg\, \langle \equiv k :: \neg p_k \rangle$

$=$ {   definition of negation   }

$\langle \equiv k :: p_k \equiv \mathsf{false} \rangle \;\equiv\; \mathsf{false}$

$=$ {   associativity and symmetry of equivales   }

$\langle \equiv k :: p_k \rangle \;\equiv\; \langle \equiv k :: \mathsf{false} \rangle \;\equiv\; \mathsf{false}$

$=$ { $\langle \equiv k :: \mathsf{false} \rangle \equiv even.\langle \Sigma\, k :: 1 \rangle$, odd is $\neg even$ }

$\langle \equiv k :: p_k \rangle \;\equiv\; odd.\langle \Sigma\, k :: 1 \rangle$.

We conclude that

$$\langle \neq k :: p_k \rangle \;\equiv\; \langle \equiv k :: p_k \rangle \;\equiv\; odd.\langle \Sigma k :: 1 \rangle . \tag{2}$$

3   Even Numbers of Even Differences

The following exercise was designed by the authors to illustrate manipulations with quantifiers.

Suppose $\{n_k \mid 0 \le k < M\}$ is a bag of integers. Consider the bag of *differences*

$$\{n_j - n_k \mid j < k\}.$$

(For brevity, we assume throughout that the type of dummies j and k is the set of the first M natural numbers.) The question is: how can we evaluate, with minimal effort, whether the number of even differences is even? To resolve this question, we try to simplify the specification:

$$even.\langle \Sigma j,k \ : \ j < k \land even.(n_j - n_k) \ : \ 1\rangle\,.$$

We begin our calculation with a use of the warm-up exercises.

$\quad even.\langle \Sigma j,k \ : \ j < k \land even.(n_j - n_k) \ : \ 1\rangle$

$=\qquad\quad\{\qquad$ (1) with $p := \langle j,k :: even.(n_j - n_k)\rangle\,,$

$\qquad\qquad\qquad$ distributivity of $even$ over summation $\quad\}$

$\quad \langle \equiv j,k : j < k : even.n_j \equiv even.n_k\rangle \ \equiv \ even.\langle \Sigma j,k : j < k : 1\rangle$

$=\qquad\quad\{\qquad$ distributivity of $even$ over summation $\quad\}$

$\quad even.\langle \Sigma j,k : j < k : n_j + n_k\rangle \ \equiv \ even.\langle \Sigma j,k : j < k : \frac{1}{2} + \frac{1}{2}\rangle\,.$

We now calculate the value of $\langle \Sigma j,k : j < k : n_j + n_k\rangle$. ($\langle \Sigma j,k : j < k : 1\rangle$ is easily seen to be the sum of the first M natural numbers, which is well known to be $\frac{1}{2} \times (M-1) \times M$. It is amusing to note, however, that it is a special case of the first summation, as made obvious by the way it has been written — " $\frac{1}{2} + \frac{1}{2}$ " is a particular case of " $n_j + n_k$ ". The calculation below is an attractive way of deriving the standard formula.)

$\quad \langle \Sigma j,k : j < k : n_j + n_k\rangle$

$=\qquad\quad\{\qquad$ aiming to eliminate the awkward range restriction,

$\qquad\qquad\qquad$ we exploit symmetry of addition $\quad\}$

$\quad \frac{1}{2} \times \langle \Sigma j,k : j < k \lor k < j : n_j + n_k\rangle$

$=\qquad\quad\{\qquad j < k \lor k < j \ \equiv \ \neg(j = k)$, range splitting $\quad\}$

$\quad \frac{1}{2} \times (\langle \Sigma j,k :: n_j + n_k\rangle \ - \ \langle \Sigma j,k : j = k : n_j + n_k\rangle)$

$=\qquad\quad\{\qquad$ associativity and symmetry, one-point rule $\quad\}$

$\quad \frac{1}{2} \times (\langle \Sigma j,k :: n_j\rangle \ + \ \langle \Sigma j,k :: n_k\rangle \ - \ \langle \Sigma j :: 2 \times n_j\rangle)$

$=\qquad\quad\{\qquad$ dummy renaming and distributivity $\quad\}$

$\quad \frac{1}{2} \times 2 \times (\langle \Sigma j,k :: n_j\rangle \ - \ \langle \Sigma j :: n_j\rangle)$

$=\qquad\quad\{\qquad$ arithmetic, nesting and

$\qquad\qquad\qquad$ associativity and symmetry $\quad\}$

$\quad \langle \Sigma j \ :: \ \langle \Sigma k :: n_j\rangle \ - \ n_j\rangle$

$=\qquad\quad\{\qquad$ distributivity (of product over addition) $\quad\}$

$\quad \langle \Sigma j \ :: \ n_j \times (\langle \Sigma k :: 1\rangle \ - \ 1)\rangle$

$=\qquad\quad\{\qquad$ range of k is $0 \leq k < M$, distributivity $\quad\}$

$\quad (M-1) \times \langle \Sigma j :: n_j\rangle\,.$

Consequently,

$$even. \langle \Sigma \, j,k \, : \, j < k \, : \, n_j + n_k \rangle \quad \equiv \quad odd.M \ \lor \ even. \langle \Sigma \, j :: n_j \rangle \,.$$

Similarly, we have:

$$even. \langle \Sigma \, j,k \, : \, j < k \, : \, 1 \rangle$$

$$= \qquad \{ \qquad \text{above with } n_j = \tfrac{1}{2} \text{, or standard formula} \quad \}$$

$$even.(\tfrac{1}{2} \times (M{-}1) \times M)$$

$$= \qquad \{ \qquad \text{case analysis on } even.M \quad \}$$

$$even. \lfloor \tfrac{M}{2} \rfloor \,.$$

Substituting, we have determined that

$$even. \langle \Sigma \, j,k \, : \, j < k \land even.(n_j - n_k) \, : \, 1 \rangle$$

$$\equiv \quad odd.M \ \lor \ even. \langle \Sigma j : odd.n_j : 1 \rangle \quad \equiv \quad even. \lfloor \tfrac{M}{2} \rfloor \quad .$$

We conclude that, when M is even, the evenness of the number of even differences is determined by first determining whether the number of odd numbers is
even, and then comparing this boolean for equality with $even. \lfloor \tfrac{M}{2} \rfloor$. That is, we
evaluate:

$$even. \langle \Sigma j : odd.n_j : 1 \rangle \quad \equiv \quad even. \lfloor \tfrac{M}{2} \rfloor \,.$$

In the case that M is odd, the answer is independent of the numbers in the
bag; it is simply

$$even. \lfloor \tfrac{M}{2} \rfloor \,.$$

An interesting feature of this example is that we have chosen to simplify summations rather than to use the equivales quantifier. The crucial step of eliminating
the awkward range restriction, $j < k$, exploits a property of addition that has no
counterpart for equivales. This extra degree of calculational freedom significantly
enhances the elegance of the calculation.

4   1906 Hungarian Contest Problem

Exercise [8, 3.4.8] is a special case of the following.
    Suppose a bag of M numbers is given. Let a and b be both arbitrary
arrangements of the bag. Prove that, if M is odd, the product

$$(a_1 - b_1)(a_2 - b_2)(a_3 - b_3) \ldots (a_M - b_M)$$

is an even number. (In [8, 3.4.8], the bag is the set of numbers 1, 2, $\ldots$, M.)

The calculational solution is as follows.

$$even.\langle \Pi k :: a_k - b_k \rangle$$

$=$ { $even$ distributes through product and summation }

$$\langle \exists k :: even.a_k \equiv even.b_k \rangle$$

$\Leftarrow$ { discussed below }

$$\langle \not\equiv k :: even.a_k \equiv even.b_k \rangle$$

$=$ { (2) }

$$\langle \equiv k :: even.a_k \equiv even.b_k \rangle \;\equiv\; odd.\langle \Sigma k :: 1 \rangle$$

$=$ { associativity and symmetry of equivalence }

$$\langle \equiv k :: even.a_k \rangle \;\equiv\; \langle \equiv k :: even.b_k \rangle \;\equiv\; odd.\langle \Sigma k :: 1 \rangle$$

$=$ { a and b are rearrangements of the same bag }

$$odd.\langle \Sigma k :: 1 \rangle .$$

The second step of this calculation is the most risky because it is a strengthening step. It is suggested by the goal of separating the two operands of the equivalence in the term of the quantification. Formally, the property used is that, for all predicates p,

$$\langle \exists k :: p_k \rangle \;\Leftarrow\; \langle \not\equiv k :: p_k \rangle \tag{3}$$

In words, (3) is read as an inclusive-or is weaker than an exclusive-or. Its truth is established by observing that the contrapositive law, $\langle \forall k :: p_k \rangle \;\Rightarrow\; \langle \equiv k :: p_k \rangle$ for all predicates p, is an immediate consequence of Leibniz's rule. (Substitute **true** for p_k in the right side of the implication.)

A special case of (3) is

$$\langle \exists k :: even.n_k \rangle \;\Leftarrow\; even.\langle \Sigma k :: n_k \rangle \wedge odd.\langle \Sigma k :: 1 \rangle . \tag{4}$$

(Take p_k to be $even.n_k$ and use distributivity of $even$ through summation and (2). The property is better known in the contrapositive form: the sum of an odd number of odd numbers is odd.) In this way, our proof is directly comparable to Zeitz's solution 2 [8, 3.4.8]. The difference is that Zeitz's solution has a "rabbit"[3]: an (implicit) proof by contradiction is used in order to replace multiplication by addition. Our solution replaces disjunction by equivales, but the replacement is suggested directly by the shape of the formulae.

5 Summing Absolute Differences

In this section and the next, we consider two problems taken from [9] that involve sums of absolute differences. We present calculational solutions. Our calculations lead to theorems that are stronger than those stated in [9].

---

[3] Zeitz's solution begins with the words "The crux move: consider the *sum* of the terms".

It is useful to "lift" a binary operator $\oplus$ on numbers to sequences of equal length by defining, for sequences a and c, each of length m,

$$a \oplus c \ = \ \langle i : 0 \le i < m : a_i \oplus c_i \rangle.$$

We extend unary operators to sequences (in particular, the absolute value operator) in the same way. Thus, $|a-c|$ denotes the sequence of absolute differences

$$\langle i : 0 \le i < m : |a_i - c_i| \rangle.$$

Quantifiers are functions from sequences to values. For example, the sum quantifier, "Σ", maps a sequence of numbers to a number. Combined with lifting, this gives the concise notation $\Sigma |a-c|$ for $\langle \Sigma i : 0 \le i < m : |a_i - c_i| \rangle$.

This section's problem is as follows. The numbers 1, 2, 3, ... $2 \times N$ are divided over two sequences a and b, each of length N, in such a way that a is increasing and b is decreasing. Prove that

$$\Sigma |a-b| \ = \ N^2.$$

The first step in the solution is to "disentangle" summation and absolute values. Let a and b be arbitrary equal-length sequences of numbers. Then, denoting maximum by the infix operator "$\uparrow$" and minimum by "$\downarrow$",

$\Sigma |a-b|$

$=$ $\qquad \{ \qquad$ definition of absolute value $\quad \}$

$\Sigma ((a \uparrow b) - (a \downarrow b))$

$=$ $\qquad \{ \qquad$ associativity and symmetry of summation,

$\qquad \qquad \qquad$ distributivity of negation over sum $\quad \}$

$\Sigma (a \uparrow b) - \Sigma (a \downarrow b).$

In summary, for arbitrary sequences a and b of equal length,

$$\Sigma |a-b| \ = \ \Sigma (a \uparrow b) - \Sigma (a \downarrow b). \tag{5}$$

Except for their having equal length, the above calculation makes no assumption about the sequences a or b. We now take into account the fact that a is increasing, b is decreasing, and the sequences have no common elements.

Suppose i and j index elements of the sequences. Then

$a_i \downarrow b_i \ < \ a_j \uparrow b_j$

$=$ $\qquad \{ \qquad$ distributivity of $(\,<x\,)$ over minimum,

$\qquad \qquad \qquad$ and $(\,x<\,)$ over maximum (for any x) $\quad \}$

$a_i < a_j \ \lor \ a_i < b_j \ \lor \ b_i < a_j \ \lor \ b_i < b_j$

$=$ $\qquad \{ \qquad a$ is increasing, b is decreasing $\quad \}$

$$i < j \ \lor \ (a_i < b_j \ \lor \ b_i < a_j) \ \lor \ j < i$$

$$\Leftarrow \qquad \{ \qquad \langle \forall \, k :: a_k \neq b_k \rangle \ . \ \text{I.e.} \ \langle \forall k :: a_k < b_k \ \lor \ b_k < a_k \rangle \qquad \}$$

$$i < j \ \lor \ i = j \ \lor \ j < i$$

$$= \qquad \{ \qquad \text{inequalities} \quad \}$$

true.

The conclusion is that

$$\langle \forall \, i,j :: a_i {\downarrow} b_i \ < \ a_j {\uparrow} b_j \rangle \tag{6}$$

where dummies i and j range over indices of a and b. The significance of (6) is that $\Sigma(a{\uparrow}b)$ is the sum of the N largest elements in the concatenated sequence $a \mathbin{+\!\!+} b$ (where N is the common length of the sequences a and b), and $\Sigma(a{\downarrow}b)$ is the sum of the N smallest elements. Thus, combining (6) with (5), we get the following theorem.

Theorem 1. Suppose $2 {\times} N$ distinct numbers are divided over two sequences a and b, each of length N, in such a way that a is increasing and b is decreasing. Then, $\Sigma |a{-}b|$ is the difference between

− the sum of the N largest
  and
− the sum of the N smallest

of the given numbers.

Applying this theorem to the case that the numbers are 1, 2, 3, ..., $2 {\times} N$, using the well-known formula for the sum of 1, 2, 3, ..., n, we get that $\Sigma |a{-}b|$ is

$$(\tfrac{1}{2} {\times} (2 {\times} N) {\times} (2 {\times} N + 1) - \tfrac{1}{2} {\times} N {\times} (N+1)) - \tfrac{1}{2} {\times} N {\times} (N+1),$$

which simplifies to N^2. (Note that N may be zero.)

Our calculation does not presuppose a knowledge of the answer. The most crucial step is the first one, in which the arithmetic involved in calculating absolute differences is disentangled from summation of a sequence. The symmetry between minimum and maximum in (5) suggests the calculation that follows it.

6   A De Morgan-Like Theorem

For our final exercise, we consider the following problem [9].

An arbitrary set of $m{+}n$ numbers is divided into two arbitrary groups a_1, a_2, ..., a_m and b_1, b_2, ..., b_n, and the numbers in each group arranged in ascending order

$$a_1 < a_2 < \ldots < a_m, \quad b_1 < b_2 < \ldots < b_n.$$

Then the same numbers are again divided into two arbitrary groups c_1, c_2, ..., c_m and d_1, d_2, ..., d_n, and the numbers in each group arranged in ascending order

$$c_1 < c_2 < \ldots < c_m, \quad d_1 < d_2 < \ldots < d_n.$$

Prove the equality

$$|a_1 - c_1| + |a_2 - c_2| + \ldots + |a_m - c_m| \;=\; |b_1 - d_1| + |b_2 - d_2| + \ldots + |b_n - d_n| \quad.$$

Our solution to the problem involves identifying a novel theorem on ascending sequences. We also eliminate the requirement that all the numbers are distinct. This leads to novel applications (omitted here for brevity).

We assume that we are given a finite bag U, the elements of which are (totally) ordered by the relation $\preceq$. If c is a subbag of U, we use $\#c$ to denote its size. The complement of c (in U) is denoted $\bar{c}$. For all i, $0 \leq i < \#c$, the ith element of c in the resulting ordered sequence is denoted by $c.i$. Formally, we have, for all subbags c of U,

$$\langle \forall j,k \; : \; 0 \leq j \leq k < \#c \; : \; c.j \preceq c.k \rangle. \tag{7}$$

When U is a set (i.e. there are no duplicates in the bag), we have the stronger: for all subsets c of U,

$$\langle \forall j,k \; : \; 0 \leq j < \#c \wedge 0 \leq k < \#c \; : \; j < k \equiv c.j \prec c.k \rangle. \tag{8}$$

As in section 5, we "lift" operators to map sequences to sequences. In general, it is not the case that the indexing function $(.i)$, as defined above, distributes through lifted operators. For example, $|a-c|.i$ need not be equal to $|a.i - c.i|$. It is the case, however, for minimum and maximum (with respect to $\preceq$), because they are monotonic. This is important.

We are now in a position to reformulate the problem: An arbitrary bag U of numbers is split into subbags a and $\bar{a}$. The same bag U is split again into b and $\bar{b}$, where $\#a = \#b$. Prove that

$$\Sigma |a - b| \;=\; \Sigma |\bar{a} - \bar{b}|. \tag{9}$$

Before beginning the calculation, we observe two complications:

- In general, the two sums range over different numbers of elements.
- Order (absolute value) and arithmetic (addition and subtraction) are heavily entangled.

The first step is thus to improve the situation:

$$\Sigma |a - b| \;=\; \Sigma |\bar{a} - \bar{b}|$$

$= \qquad \{ \qquad \text{definition of absolute value} \qquad \}$

$$\langle \Sigma i \; :: \; a.i \uparrow b.i - a.i \downarrow b.i \rangle \;=\; \langle \Sigma i \; :: \; \bar{a}.i \uparrow \bar{b}.i - \bar{a}.i \downarrow \bar{b}.i \rangle$$

$= \qquad \{ \qquad \text{for all } i, \; (.i) \text{ distributes through max and min,}$

$\qquad\qquad \text{associativity and symmetry of addition} \qquad \}$

$$\Sigma(a{\uparrow}b) - \Sigma(a{\downarrow}b) = \Sigma(\bar{a}{\uparrow}\bar{b}) - \Sigma(\bar{a}{\downarrow}\bar{b})$$

$$= \qquad \{ \qquad \text{arithmetic} \qquad \}$$

$$\Sigma(a{\uparrow}b) + \Sigma(\bar{a}{\downarrow}\bar{b}) = \Sigma(\bar{a}{\uparrow}\bar{b}) + \Sigma(a{\downarrow}b).$$

This is much better. Both sides have $\#U$ summands, and they differ only by complementation. This suggests a seemingly bold[4] step:

$$\Sigma(a{\uparrow}b) + \Sigma(\bar{a}{\downarrow}\bar{b}) = \Sigma(\bar{a}{\uparrow}\bar{b}) + \Sigma(a{\downarrow}b)$$

$$\Leftarrow \qquad \{ \qquad \Sigma U = \Sigma(a{\uparrow}b) + \Sigma(\overline{a{\uparrow}b}) = \Sigma(\overline{a{\downarrow}b}) + \Sigma(a{\downarrow}b) \qquad \}$$

$$\overline{a{\uparrow}b} = \bar{a}{\downarrow}\bar{b} \ \wedge \ \overline{a{\downarrow}b} = \bar{a}{\uparrow}\bar{b}.$$

We have thus reduced the original problem to establishing the following theorem on increasing sequences.

Theorem 2 ("De Morgan's Rule").   For all equal-length subbags a and b of a totally ordered bag U:

$$\overline{a{\uparrow}b} = \bar{a}{\downarrow}\bar{b} \quad \text{and} \quad \overline{a{\downarrow}b} = \bar{a}{\uparrow}\bar{b}.$$

We first prove the theorem assuming that U is a set, and then show how to extend the proof to bags. Clearly, it suffices to prove just the first conjunct. (The second is obtained from the first by the replacements $a,b := \bar{a},\bar{b}$.)

We have:

$$\overline{a{\uparrow}b} = \bar{a}{\downarrow}\bar{b}$$

$$= \qquad \{ \qquad \#(\overline{a{\uparrow}b}) = \#(\bar{a}{\downarrow}\bar{b}), \text{complementation} \qquad \}$$

$$\langle \forall i,j :: (a{\uparrow}b).i \neq (\bar{a}{\downarrow}\bar{b}).j \rangle$$

$$= \qquad \{ \qquad \text{monotonicity of min and max} \qquad \}$$

$$\langle \forall i,j :: a.i {\uparrow} b.i \neq \bar{a}.j {\downarrow} \bar{b}.j \rangle \ .$$

Now consider arbitrary i and j. We show that $a.i{\uparrow}b.i = \bar{a}.j{\downarrow}\bar{b}.j$ implies false.

$$a.i {\uparrow} b.i = \bar{a}.j {\downarrow} \bar{b}.j$$

$$= \qquad \{ \qquad a.i \neq \bar{a}.j, \ b.i \neq \bar{b}.j \ \text{(because } a \text{ and } b \text{ are sets)} \qquad \}$$

$$(a.i \preceq . b.i = \bar{a}.j \preceq \bar{b}.j)$$

$$\vee \quad (b.i \preceq a.i = \bar{b}.j \preceq \bar{a}.j) \ .$$

By symmetry, it suffices to prove that just one of the two disjuncts implies false. We proceed with the first.

---

[4] The step is actually not that bold. It is suggested by the obvious fact stated in the hint, and the similarity of the expressions in a and b.

$$a.i \preceq b.i = \bar{a}.j \preceq \bar{b}.j$$

$=$ { disentangling a from b }

$$a.i \preceq \bar{a}.j \ \land \ \bar{a}.j = b.i \ \land \ b.i \preceq \bar{b}.j$$

$=$ { a and $\bar{a}$ are disjoint, as are b and $\bar{b}$ }

$$a.i \prec \bar{a}.j \ \land \ \bar{a}.j = b.i \ \land \ b.i \prec \bar{b}.j.$$

The next step is crucial. The property $a.i \prec \bar{a}.j$ implies that $(i+1)+j$ elements of U are less than $\bar{a}.j$; similarly, the property $b.i \prec \bar{b}.j$ implies that $(\#b - (i+1)) + (\#\bar{b} - j)$ elements of U are greater than $b.i$. Formally:

$$a.i \prec \bar{a}.j$$

$=$ { (8) and transitivity of $\prec$ }

$$\langle \forall k : k \leq i : a.k \prec \bar{a}.j \rangle \ \land \ \langle \forall k : k < j : \bar{a}.k \prec \bar{a}.j \rangle$$

$\Rightarrow$ { a and $\bar{a}$ are disjoint subsets of U }

$$\langle \Sigma k : U.k \prec \bar{a}.j : 1 \rangle \ \geq \ (i+1)+j.$$

Similarly,

$$b.i \prec \bar{b}.j$$

$=$ { (8) and transitivity of $\prec$ }

$$\langle \forall k : i < k : b.i \prec b.k \rangle \ \land \ \langle \forall k : j \leq k : b.i \prec \bar{b}.k \rangle$$

$\Rightarrow$ { b and $\bar{b}$ are disjoint subsets of U }

$$\langle \Sigma k : b.i \prec U.k : 1 \rangle \ \geq \ (\#b - (i+1)) + (\#\bar{b} - j).$$

We now combine these two counts with the middle conjunct: $\bar{a}.j = b.i$.

$$a.i \prec \bar{a}.j \ \land \ \bar{a}.j = b.i \ \land \ b.i \prec \bar{b}.j$$

$\Rightarrow$ { above, Leibniz }

$$\langle \Sigma k : U.k \prec b.i \lor b.i \prec U.k : 1 \rangle \ \geq \ (i+1)+j+(\#b - (i+1)) + (\#\bar{b} - j)$$

$=$ { arithmetic, $\#b + \#\bar{b} = \#U$ }

$$\langle \Sigma k : U.k \neq b.i : 1 \rangle \ \geq \ \#U$$

$=$ { $b.i$ is an element of U }

false.

This completes the proof of theorem 2, assuming that U is a set. Given a bag U, this lemma can be applied to the sets of pairs $(U.i, i)$ ordered lexicographically by $(x,i) \succeq (y,j)$ equivales $x \succ y \lor (x = y \land i \geq j)$.

   It is interesting to compare our calculation with the argument given by Savchev and Andreescu [9]. Their argument starts immediately with induction and a subsequent case analysis. Our calculation is driven by heuristic principles, which lead to the discovery of the much more general De Morgan-like theorem. Their argument has 10 lines of displayed formulae (including 16 occurrences of ellipsis dots) and 20 lines of printed text. Ours is much more detailed, but has just 16 calculation steps, and a similar amount of text (including the hints accompanying calculation steps). Their argument assumes that U is a set, and is split into *non-empty* subsets; our calculation assumes that U is a bag, that is split arbitrarily.

7   Conclusion

Manipulating quantified expressions is an important calculational skill. Elsewhere, Knuth, Patashnik and Graham [1] also emphasise its importance and give several examples of non-trivial calculations with the Σ quantifier. We have provided further evidence for the importance of the skill by tackling a number of challenging mathematical exercises.

Acknowledgements. Thanks to Wim Feijen for bringing the problems in [9] to our attention, to Jeremy Weissmann for comments on an earlier presentation of section 5, and to the referees for their detailed and insightful comments.

References

1. Graham, R. L., Knuth, D. E., Patashnik, O.: Concrete Mathematics. Addison Wesley Publ. Co. (1989)
2. Dijkstra, E. W.: Guarded commands, nondeterminacy and formal derivation of programs. Commun. of ACM **18** (1975) 453–457
3. Dijkstra, E. W.: A Discipline of Programming. Prentice Hall (1976)
4. Gries, D.: The Science of Programming. Springer-Verlag (1981)
5. Backhouse, R.: Program Construction and Verification. Prentice Hall (1986)
6. Knuth, D.E.: The Art of Computer Programming. Vol. I: Fundamental Algorithms. Addison-Wesley Publ. Co. (1968)
7. Backhouse, R.: Program Construction. Calculating Implementations From Specifications. John Wiley & Sons (2003)
8. Zeitz, P.: The Art and Craft of Problem Solving. John Wiley & Sons (1999)
9. Savchev, S., Andreescu, T.: Mathematical Miniatures. Vol. 43 of Anneli Lax New Mathematical Library. Math. Assoc. of America (2003)

Improving Saddleback Search: A Lesson in Algorithm Design

Richard S. Bird

Programming Research Group, Oxford University,
Wolfson Building, Parks Road, Oxford, OX1 3QD, UK
bird@comlab.ox.ac.uk

Abstract. Over the past twenty-five years or so Saddleback search has been used as an paradigm of how methods of formal program construction can quickly lead to a simple and effective algorithm for searching an ordered table. In this paper we revisit the problem and show that saddleback search is not in fact the best algorithm when one dimension of the table is much smaller than the other. The paper is structured in the form of a classroom discussion involving a teacher and four very clever students.

The setting is a class on algorithm design. There are four students: Anne, Jack, Mary and Theo.

Teacher: Good morning class. Today I would like you design a function *invert* that takes two arguments, a function f from pairs of natural numbers to natural numbers, and a natural number z. The value *invert* f z is a list of all pairs (x, y) satisfying $f(x, y) = z$. You can assume that f is strictly increasing in each argument, but nothing else.

Jack: That seems an easy problem. Since f is increasing in each argument, we know that $f(x, y) = z$ implies $x \leq z$ and $y \leq z$. Hence we can define *invert* by a simple search of all possible pairs of values:

$$\textit{invert } f\ z = [(x, y) \mid x \leftarrow [0 .. z],\ y \leftarrow [0 .. z],\ f(x, y) = z]$$

Doesn't this solve the problem?

Teacher: Yes it does, but your solution involves $(z + 1)^2$ evaluations of f. Since f may be very expensive to compute, I would like a solution with as few evaluations of f as possible.

Theo: Well, its easy to halve the number of evaluations. Since $f(x, y) \geq x + y$ if f is increasing, the search can be confined to values on or below the diagonal of the square:

$$\textit{invert } f\ z = [(x, y) \mid x \leftarrow [0 .. z],\ y \leftarrow [0 .. z - x],\ f(x, y) = z]$$

Come to think of it, you can replace the two upper bounds by $z - f(0, 0)$ and $z - x - f(0, 0)$. Then if $z < f(0, 0)$ the search terminates at once.

T. Uustalu (Ed.): MPC 2006, LNCS 4014, pp. 82–89, 2006.

Anne: Assuming it doesn't matter in which order the solutions are found, I think you can do better still. Jack's method searches a square of size $z + 1$ from the origin at the bottom left, and proceeds upwards column by column. We can do better if we start at the top-left corner $(0, z)$ of the square. At any stage the search space is constrained to be a rectangle with top-left corner (u, v) and bottom-right corner $(z, 0)$. Let me define

$$find\ (u, v)\ f\ z = [(x, y) \mid x \leftarrow [u .. z],\ y \leftarrow [v, v - 1 .. 0],\ f(x, y) = z]$$

so that *invert* $f\ z = find\ (0, z)\ f\ z$. It is now easy enough to calculate a more efficient implementation of *find*.

First of all, if $u > z$ or $v < 0$, then clearly *find* $(u, v)\ f\ z = [\ ]$. Otherwise, we carry out a case analysis on the value $f(u, v)$. If $f(u, v) < z$, then the rest of column u can be eliminated since $f(u, v') < f(u, v) < z$ for $v' < v$. If $f(u, v) > z$, we can similarly eliminate the rest of row v. Finally, if $f(u, v) = z$, then we can record (u, v) and eliminate the rest of both column u and row v.

Here is the my improved version of *find*:

$$
\begin{aligned}
find\ (u, v)\ f\ z & \\
\mid u > z \lor v < 0 \quad &= \quad [\ ] \\
\mid z' < z \quad &= \quad find\ (u + 1, v)\ f\ z \\
\mid z' = z \quad &= \quad (u, v) : find\ (u + 1, v - 1)\ f\ z \\
\mid z' > z \quad &= \quad find\ (u, v - 1)\ f\ z \\
\textbf{where}\ \ z' &= f(u, v)
\end{aligned}
$$

In the worst case, when *find* traverses the square from the top-left corner to the bottom-right one, it performs $2z + 1$ evaluations of f. In the best case, when *find* proceeds directly to either the bottom or rightmost boundary, it requires only $z + 1$ evaluations.

Theo: You can reduce the search space still further since the initial square with top-left corner $(0, z)$ and bottom-right corner $(z, 0)$ is an overly-generous estimate of where the required values lie. Suppose we first compute m and n, where

$$
\begin{aligned}
m &= maximum\ (filter\ (\lambda y \rightarrow f(0, y) \leq z)\ [0 .. z]) \\
n &= maximum\ (filter\ (\lambda x \rightarrow f(x, 0) \leq z)\ [0 .. z])
\end{aligned}
$$

Then we can define *invert* $f\ z = find\ (0, m)\ f\ z$, where *find* has exactly the same form that Anne gave, except that the first guard becomes $u > n \lor v < 0$. In other words, rather than search a $(z + 1) \times (z + 1)$ square we can get away with searching a $(m + 1) \times (n + 1)$ rectangle.

The crucial point is that we can compute m and n by binary search. Let g be an increasing function on the natural numbers and suppose x, y and z satisfy $g\ x \leq z < g\ y$. To determine the unique value m, where $m = binary\ g\ (x, y)\ z$, in the range $x \leq m < y$ such that $g\ m \leq z < g\ (m + 1)$ we can maintain the invariants $g\ a \leq z < g\ b$ and $x \leq a < b \leq y$. This leads to the program

$$binary\ g\ (a,b)\ z$$
$$|\ a+1 = b\ = a$$
$$|\ g\ m \le z\quad = binary\ g\ (m,b)\ z$$
$$|\ otherwise = binary\ g\ (a,m)\ z$$
$$\textbf{where}\ \ m = (a+b)\ \textbf{div}\ 2$$

Since $a+1 < b \Rightarrow a < m < y$ it follows that neither $g\ x$ nor $g\ y$ are evaluated by the algorithm, so they can be fictitious values. In particular, we have

$$m = binary\ (\lambda y \to f(0,y))\ (-1, z+1)\ z$$
$$n = binary\ (\lambda x \to f(x,0))\ (-1, z+1)\ z$$

where we extend f with fictitious values $f(0,-1) = 0$ and $f(-1,0) = 0$.

This version of *invert* takes about $2 \log z + m + n$ evaluations of f in the worst case, and $2 \log z + min\ (m,n)$ in the best case. Since m or n may be substantially less than z, for example when $f(x,y) = 2^x + 3^y$, we can end up with an algorithm that takes only $O(\log z)$ steps in the worst case.

Teacher: Congratulations, Anne and Theo, you have rediscovered an important search strategy, dubbed *Saddleback Search* by David Gries, see [1, 2, 3]. I imagine Gries called it that because the shape of the three-dimensional plot of f, with the smallest element at the bottom-left, the largest at the top-right, and two wings, is a bit like a saddle. The crucial idea, as Anne has spotted, is to start the search at the tip of one of the wings rather than at the smallest or highest value. In his treatment of the problem, Dijkstra [2] also mentioned the advantage of using a logarithmic search to find the appropriate starting point.

Mary: What happens if we go for a divide and conquer solution? I mean, why don't we look at the middle element of the rectangle first? Surely it is reasonable to investigate the two-dimensional analogue of binary search.

Suppose we have confined the search to a rectangle with top-left corner (u,v) and bottom-right corner (r,s). Instead of looking at $f(u,v)$ why don't we inspect $f(p,q)$ where $p = (u+r)\ \textbf{div}\ 2$ and $q = (v+s)\ \textbf{div}\ 2$? If $f(p,q) < z$, then we can throw away all elements of the lower-left rectangle $((u,q),(p,s))$. Similarly, if $f(p,q) > z$ we can throw away the upper-right rectangle $((p,v),(r,q))$. And if $f(p,q) = z$, then we can throw away both.

I know that this strategy doesn't maintain Anne's property that the search space is always a rectangle; instead we have two rectangles or an L-shape. But we are functional programmers and don't have to confine ourselves to simple loops: a divide and conquer algorithm is as easy for us to implement as an iterative one because both have to be expressed recursively.

Jack: You have to deal with the L-shape though. You can split an L-shape into two rectangles of course. In fact you can do it in two ways, either with a horizontal cut or a vertical one. Let me do a rough calculation. Consider a $m \times n$ rectangle and let $T(m,n)$ denote the number of evaluations of f required to search it. If $m = 0$ or $n = 0$ there is nothing to search. If $m = 1$ or $n = 1$ we have

$$T(1, n) = 1 + T(1, \lceil n/2 \rceil)$$
$$T(m, 1) = 1 + T(\lceil m/2 \rceil, 1)$$

Otherwise, when $m \geq 2$ and $n \geq 2$, we can throw away a rectangle of size at least $\lfloor m/2 \rfloor \times \lfloor n/2 \rfloor$. If we make a horizontal cut, then we are left with two rectangles, one of size $\lfloor m/2 \rfloor \times \lceil n/2 \rceil$ and the other of size $\lceil m/2 \rceil \times n$. Hence

$$T(m, n) = 1 + T(\lfloor m/2 \rfloor, \lceil n/2 \rceil) + T(\lceil m/2 \rceil, n)$$

If we make a vertical cut, then we have

$$T(m, n) = 1 + T(\lceil m/2 \rceil, \lfloor n/2 \rfloor) + T(m, \lceil n/2 \rceil)$$

I don't immediately see the solutions to these recurrence relations.

Theo: If you make both a horizontal and a vertical cut, you are left with three rectangles, so when $m \geq 2$ and $n \geq 2$ we have

$$T(m, n) = 1 + T(\lceil m/2 \rceil, \lfloor n/2 \rfloor) + T(\lceil m/2 \rceil, \lceil n/2 \rceil) + T(\lfloor m/2 \rfloor, \lceil n/2 \rceil)$$

I can solve this recurrence. Set $U(i, j) = T(2^i, 2^j)$, so

$$\begin{aligned} U(i, 0) &= i \\ U(0, j) &= j \\ U(i + 1, j + 1) &= 1 + 3U(i, j) \end{aligned}$$

The solution is $U(i, j) = 3^k(|j - i| + 1/2) - 1/2$ where $k = min\,(i, j)$, as one can check by induction. Hence if $m \leq n$ we have

$$T(m, n) \leq 3^{\log m} \log(2n/m) = m^{1.59} \log(2n/m)$$

That's better than $m + n$ when m is much smaller than n.

Jack: I don't think the three-rectangle solution is as good as the two-rectangle one. Following your approach, Theo, let me set $U(i, j) = T(2^i, 2^j)$. Supposing $i \leq j$ and making a horizontal cut, we have

$$\begin{aligned} U(0, j) &= j \\ U(i + 1, j + 1) &= 1 + U(i, j) + U(i, j + 1) \end{aligned}$$

The solution is $U(i, j) = 2^i(j - i/2 + 1) - 1$, as one can check by induction. Hence

$$T(m, n) \leq m \log(2n/\sqrt{m})$$

If $i \geq j$ we should make a vertical cut rather than a horizontal one; then we get an algorithm with at most $n \log(2m/\sqrt{n})$ evaluations of f. In either case, if one of m or n is much smaller than the other we get a better algorithm than saddleback search.

Anne: While you two have been solving recurrences I have been thinking of a lower bound on the complexity of *invert*. Consider the different possible outputs when we have a $m \times n$ rectangle to search. Suppose there are $A(m,n)$ different possible answers. Each test of $f(x,y)$ against z has three possible outcomes, so the height h of the ternary tree of tests has to satisfy $h \geq \log_3 A(m,n)$. Provided we can estimate $A(m,n)$ this gives us a lower bound on the number of tests that have to be performed. The situation is the same with sorting n items by binary comparisons; there are $n!$ possible outcomes, so any sorting algorithm has to make at least $\log_2 n!$ comparisons in the worst case.

It's easy to estimate $A(m,n)$: each possible list of pairs (x,y) in the range $0 \leq x < n$ and $0 \leq y < m$ with $f(x,y) = z$ is in a one-to-one correspondence with a step shape from the top-left corner of the $m \times n$ rectangle to the bottom-right corner, in which the value z appears at the inner corners of the steps. Of course, this step shape is not necessarily the one traced by the function *find*. The number of such paths is $\binom{m+n}{n}$, so that is the value of $A(m,n)$.

Another way to see this result is to suppose there are k solutions. The value z can appear in k rows in exactly $\binom{m}{k}$ ways, and for each way there are $\binom{n}{k}$ possible choices for the columns. Hence

$$A(m,n) = \sum_{k=0}^{m} \binom{m}{k}\binom{n}{k} = \binom{m+n}{n}$$

since the summation is an instance of Vandermonde's convolution, see [4]. Taking logarithms, we obtain the lower bound

$$\log A(m,n) = \Omega(m\log(1+n/m) + n\log(1+m/n))$$

This estimate shows that when $m = n$ we can't do better than $\Omega(m+n)$ steps. But if $m \leq n$ then $m \leq n\log(1+m/n)$ since $x \leq \log(1+x)$ if $0 \leq x \leq 1$. Thus $A(m,n) = \Omega(m\log(n/m))$. Jack's solution does not quite achieve this bound because he obtains only an $O(m\log(n/\sqrt{m}))$ algorithm in the case $m \leq n$.

Mary: I don't think that Jack's divide and conquer solution is really necessary; there are other ways of using binary search to solve the problem. One is simply to carry out m binary searches, one on each row. That gives an $O(m\log n)$ solution. But I think we can do better and achieve the optimal asymptotic $O(m\log(n/m))$ bound, assuming $m \leq n$.

Suppose, as before, we have confined the search to a rectangle with top-left corner (u,v) and bottom-right corner (r,s). Thus there are $r - u$ columns and $s-v$ rows. Furthermore, assume $v-s \leq r-u$ so there at least as many columns as rows. Suppose we carry out a binary search along the middle row, $q = (v+s)\mathbf{div}\,2$ in order to determine a p such that $f(p,q) \leq z < f(p+1,q)$. If $f(p,q) < z$, then we need continue the search only on the two rectangles $((u,v),(p,q+1))$ and $((p+1,q-1),(r,s))$. If $f(p,q) = z$ we can cut out column p and can continue the search only on the rectangles $((u,v),(p-1,q+1))$ and $((p+1,q-1),(r,s))$. The reasoning is dual if there are more rows than columns. As a result, we can eliminate about half the elements of the array with a logarithmic number of probes.

Here is the algorithm I have in mind: we implement *invert* by

$$invert\ f\ z = find\ (0, m)\ (n, 0)\ f\ z$$
$$\mathbf{where}\quad m = binary\ (\lambda y \to f(0, y))\ (-1, z{+}1)\ z$$
$$n = binary\ (\lambda x \to f(x, 0))\ (-1, z{+}1)\ z$$

where *find* $(u, v)\ (r, s)\ f\ z$, given in Figure 1, searches a rectangle with top-left corner (u, v) and bottom-right corner (r, s):

```
find (u, v) (r, s) f z
  | u > r ∨ v < s = [ ]
  | v−s ≤ r−u    = row (binary (λx → f(x, q)) (u−1, r+1) z)
  | otherwise    = col (binary (λy → f(p, y)) (s−1, v+1) z)
  where
  p     = (u+r) div 2
  q     = (v+s) div 2
  row p = if  f(p, q) = z
          then  (p, q) : find (u, v) (p−1, q+1) f z ++ find (p+1, q−1) (r, s) f z
          else  find (u, v) (p, q+1) f z ++ find (p+1, q−1) (r, s) f z
  col q = if  f(p, q) = z
          then  (p, q) : find (u, v) (p−1, q+1) f z ++ find (p+1, q−1) (r, s) f z
          else  find (u, v) (p−1, q+1) f z ++ find (p+1, q) (r, s) f z
```

Fig. 1. The revised definition of *find*

As to the analysis, again let $T(m, n)$ denote the number of evaluations required to search an $m \times n$ rectangle. Suppose $m \le n$. In the best case, when for example each binary search on a row returns the leftmost or rightmost element, we have $T(m, n) = \log n + T(m/2, n)$ with solution $T(m, n) = O(\log m \times \log n)$. In the worst case, when each binary search returns the middle element, we have $T(m, n) = \log n + 2T(m/2, n/2)$. To solve this, set $U(i, j) = T(2^i, 2^j)$. Then we have

$$U(i, j) = \sum_{k=0}^{i-1} 2^k (j - k) = O(2^i (j - i))$$

Hence $T(m, n) = O(m \log(n/m))$, which is asymptotically optimal by Anne's lower bound.

Teacher: Well done the four of you! It is surprising that in the twenty-five years or so that Saddleback search has been presented as a paradigm of formal program construction, none of the presenters has seemed to notice that it is not asymptotically the best algorithm for searching.

Afterword: The real story behind the paper was that I decided to use saddleback search as an exercise when interviewing candidates for entry to Oxford this year. They were given a two-dimensional array of numbers, increasing along each row and up each column and asked for a systematic way to spot all occurrences of a given number. My aim was to get them to realise that searching from the top-left or bottom-right was a good strategy. But those candidates who had done some computing at school kept wanting to use binary search, either by going for the middle of each row, or for the middle element of the rectangle. Being aware of what Backhouse [1] had written,[1] I steered them away from pursuing this thought. Only afterwards did I wonder whether they might have had a point.

Apart from describing a new algorithm for an old problem, I think that two other methodological aspects are worthy of note. Firstly, formal program calculation is heavily influenced by the available computational structures of the target language. Mary's final program, while not particularly elegant, is simple enough given recursion and list concatenation as basic constructs, but would be more difficult to express given just arrays and loops. Secondly, as algorithm designers fully appreciate, formal program calculation has to be supplemented by insight into possible directions for improving efficiency. Such insight is provided, in part, by solving recurrence relations and determining lower bounds. That is why the paper's subtitle is 'A Lesson in Algorithm Design'.

One of the referees of the paper wrote: "Complexity brings with it its own efficiency overheads, which are so often neglected in the sort of analyses included in the paper. If the author really wants to convince us that his algorithms are better than Gries's, then he should show some concrete evidence. Run the algorithm for specific functions on specific data, and compare the results." The following two tables provide such evidence. Five functions were chosen almost at random:

$$f_0\ (x,y) = 2^y(2x+1) - 1$$
$$f_1\ (x,y) = x2^x + y2^y + 2x + y$$
$$f_2\ (x,y) = 3x + 27y + y^2$$
$$f_3\ (x,y) = x^2 + y^2 + x + y$$
$$f_4\ (x,y) = x + 2^y + y - 1$$

Table 1 lists the exact number of evaluations of f_i required in the computation of *invert* f_i 5000 using Anne's initial version of saddleback search, Theo's version (with binary search to compute the boundaries), and Mary's final version. Table 2 lists absolute running times in seconds under GHCi. The close correspondence with the first table shows that the number of evaluations is a reasonable guide to absolute running time:

The classroom style of the paper may not be to everyone's taste but I quite like it, and it is the third paper in this style that I have written. After it was composed it was road-tested at a meeting of the Oxford Algebra of Programming Group. I would like to thank Ian Bayley, Sharon Curtis, Jeremy Gibbons, Geraint Jones, Clare Martin, and Bruno Oliveira, whose contributions were included in

---

[1] "When first confronted with this problem many students immediately think that binary search is applicable. This betrays a lack of preliminary investigation into the properties of the supplied data." (page 175)

Table 1. Number of evaluations

Algorithm	f_0	f_1	f_2	f_3	f_4
Anne	7501	5011	6668	5068	9989
Theo	2537	38	1749	157	5025
Mary	121	42	445	181	134

Table 2. Absolute running times

Algorithm	f_0	f_1	f_2	f_3	f_4
Anne	0.42	0.40	0.17	0.15	0.54
Theo	0.06	0.01	0.05	0.01	0.15
Mary	0.01	0.01	0.02	0.02	0.01

a second draft. I also thank the referees for pointing out typos and making other suggestions.

References

1. Backhouse, R.: Program Construction and Verification. Int. Series in Computer Science. Prentice Hall (1986)
2. Dijkstra, E. W.: The Saddleback Search. Note EWD-934. (1985) URL `http://www.cs.utexas.edu/users/EWD/index09xx.html`
3. Gries, D.: The Science of Programming. Springer-Verlag (1981)
4. Graham, R. L., Knuth, D. E, Patashnik, O.: Concrete Mathematics. Addison-Wesley (1989)

Loopless Functional Algorithms

Richard S. Bird

Programming Research Group, Oxford University,
Wolfson Building, Parks Road, Oxford, OX1 3QD, UK
bird@comlab.ox.ac.uk

Abstract. A loopless algorithm is a procedure for generating a list of values under two restrictions: the first element should be produced in linear time and each subsequent element in constant time. Loopless algorithms arise in the enumeration of combinatorial patterns such as permutations or subsequences. The elements of the generated list describe transitions that determine how the next combinatorial pattern is to be determined from its predecessor. Loopless algorithms were introduced in a procedural setting, and many clever tricks, such as focus pointers, doubly-linked lists and coroutines, have been used to construct them. This paper explores what a purely functional approach can bring to the subject, and calculates loopless functional versions of the Gray code algorithm, the Koda-Ruskey algorithm for listing the prefixes of a forest, and the Johnson-Trotter algorithm for generating permutations. The functional algorithms are completely different from their procedural counterparts, and rely on nothing more fancy than lists, trees and queues.

1 Introduction

The idea of a loopless algorithm was first introduced by Ehrlich in [2]. Given is an element x of some data type for which it is required to produce an enumeration of certain combinatorial patterns associated with x. For example, if x is a list one might want to enumerate all the permutations or all the subsequences of x. It is supposed that each pattern can be obtained from its predecessor in the enumeration, except the very first, by applying an appropriate *transition*. For permutations one possible kind of transition is a single integer i meaning "swap the item in position i with the item in position $i - 1$". For subsequences a transition i could mean "insert/delete the item at position i". An algorithm for producing a complete list of such transitions is called *loopless* if

- The first transition is produced within $O(n)$ steps, where n is the size of x;
- Each subsequent transition is produced within $O(1)$ steps.

Note that the idea of a loopless algorithm is defined as one of generating the transitions between combinatorial patterns, not the patterns themselves. This is because producing a pattern itself may not be possible within constant time. Clearly, it takes n steps simply to write down a permutation of n items.

Loopless algorithms were formulated in a procedural setting, but it is possible to capture the essential idea in a purely functional one. To do so we make use

T. Uustalu (Ed.): MPC 2006, LNCS 4014, pp. 90–114, 2006.

of the standard Haskell function *unfoldr*. First, recall the Haskell standard type *Maybe*:

$$\textbf{data } Maybe\ a = Nothing \mid Just\ a$$

The function *unfoldr* is defined by

$$unfoldr \qquad :: (b \rightarrow Maybe\ (a, b)) \rightarrow b \rightarrow [a]$$
$$unfoldr\ step\ b = \textbf{case }\ step\ b\ \textbf{of}$$
$$\qquad\qquad Just\ (a, b') \rightarrow a : unfoldr\ step\ b'$$
$$\qquad\qquad Nothing \qquad \rightarrow [\ ]$$

For our purposes, a loopless algorithm is one that is expressed in the form *unfoldr step · prolog*, where *step* takes constant time and *prolog* takes time linear in the size of the input. In a lazy language like Haskell the work done by *prolog* is distributed throughout the computation of *unfoldr step*, and not concentrated at the beginning. Therefore for true looplessness we should really interpret the composition operator (·) as being fully strict, meaning that *prolog* is evaluated fully before *unfoldr step* begins. Although it is not possible to define a general fully-strict composition operator in Haskell, we will take pains to ensure *step* takes constant time under a strict as well as a lazy semantics.

A number of loopless algorithms for generating combinatorial patterns appear in Knuth's web-published drafts of three sections of Volume 4 of *The Art of Computer Programming* [5]. These "pre-fascicles" contain references to much of the literature on looplessness. The loopless algorithms described by Knuth involve subtle programming techniques, including focus pointers, doubly-linked lists, coroutines, and so on. Our aim in this paper is to see what a functional approach can bring to the topic. In particular, we will give loopless functional versions of an algorithm for generating Gray codes, the Koda-Ruskey algorithm for generating the prefixes of a forest, and the Johnson-Trotter algorithm for generating permutations. Bear in mind though that as far as the *total* execution time is concerned, a loopless algorithm may well be less efficient that a non-loopless alternative. To quote from [4]:

> "The extra contortions that we need to go through in order to achieve looplessness are usually ill-advised, because they actually cause the total execution time to be longer than it would be with a more straightforward algorithm. But hey, looplessness carries an academic cachet. So we might as well treat this task as a challenging exercise that might help us to sharpen our algorithmic wits."

Change the penultimate word to 'calculational' and you will appreciate the point of this paper.

2   Warm-Ups

As a first warm-up, consider the function *concat* :: $[[a]] \rightarrow [a]$ that concatenates a list of lists together. One could argue that the standard definition of *concat*, viz $foldr\,(+\!\!+)\,[\,]$, meets the two criteria listed in the Introduction, at least in a lazy functional language like Haskell, but it is instructive to give a definition based on *unfoldr*:

$$
\begin{aligned}
concat = \;&unfoldr\,step \cdot filter\,(not \cdot null)\\
\textbf{where }\;&step\,[\,] &&= Nothing\\
&step\,((x:xs):xss) &&= Just\,(x, consList\,xs\,xss)
\end{aligned}
$$

The subsidiary function *consList* conses only nonempty lists onto a list of lists:

$$consList\,xs\,xss = \textbf{if }\,null\,xs\,\textbf{ then }\,xss\,\textbf{ else }\,xs:xss$$

The function *step* clearly takes constant time. Empty lists have to be filtered out of the input, otherwise this time bound would be violated. For example, consider an input of the form $[[1],[\,],[\,],\dots,[\,],[2]]$ in which there are n empty sequences between the first and last singleton lists. After producing the first element 1, it takes n steps to produce the second element 2 of the final list.

Sea lawyers might claim that the given definition of *concat* is overkill, since the alternative

$$
\begin{aligned}
concat = \;&unfoldr\,step \cdot foldr\,(+\!\!+)\,[\,]\\
\textbf{where }\;&step\,[\,] &&= Nothing\\
&step\,(x:xs) &&= Just\,(x, xs)
\end{aligned}
$$

is also loopless. Here the real work is done in the prolog, *unfoldr step* merely being an elaborate way of writing the identity function on lists. Though a valid criticism for *concat*, the idea of putting all the work into the prolog would not work for functions whose output has length not linear in the size of the input.

As a second warm-up, consider the preorder traversal of a forest of rose trees:

$$\textbf{data }\,Rose\,a = Node\,a\,[Rose\,a]$$

A forest is a list of trees and the preorder traversal of a forest can be cast in the form

$$
\begin{aligned}
preorder &&::\;& [Rose\,a] \rightarrow [a]\\
preorder\,[\,] &&=\;& [\,]\\
preorder\,(Node\,x\,xrs:yrs) &&=\;& x:preorder\,(xrs +\!\!+ yrs)
\end{aligned}
$$

This definition of *preorder* takes time linear in the size of the forest. Furthermore, $preorder = unfoldr\,step$, where

$$
\begin{aligned}
step\,[\,] &&=\;& Nothing\\
step\,(Node\,x\,xrs:yrs) &&=\;& Just\,(x, xrs +\!\!+ yrs)
\end{aligned}
$$

The function *step* is not constant time but we can make it so by processing lists of forests, elements of $[[Rose\,a]]$, instead of forests. The revised definition of *step* reads:

$$
\begin{aligned}
step &&::\;& [[Rose\,a]] \rightarrow Maybe\,(a, [[Rose\,a]])\\
step\,[\,] &&=\;& Nothing\\
step\,((Node\,x\,xrs:yrs):zrss) &&=\;& Just\,(x, consList\,xrs\,(consList\,yrs\,zrss))
\end{aligned}
$$

Now we have *preorder* = *unfoldr step·wrapList*, where *wrapList xrs* = [*xrs*]. This is a loopless algorithm for *preorder*. Of course, it suffers from the same defect as *concat*; since the length of the output is proportional to the size of the input we could equally well have done all the work in the prolog.

For the third and final warm-up consider the inorder traversal of a binary tree:

$$\textbf{data } \textit{Tree } a = \textit{Null} \mid \textit{Fork } (\textit{Tree } a) \, a \, (\textit{Tree } a)$$

The function *inorder* is defined by

$$\textit{inorder Null} \qquad = [\,]$$
$$\textit{inorder } (\textit{Fork } xt \, x \, yt) = \textit{inorder } xt + x : \textit{inorder } yt$$

To convert *inorder* into a loopless algorithm, consider the function *spines* that converts a tree into a list of its spines, namely the list of pairs of labels and spines of right subtrees along the path from the leftmost node to the root. We can use a forest of rose trees for spines and define *spines* by

$$\textit{spines} \qquad\qquad :: \textit{Tree } a \to [\textit{Rose } a]$$
$$\textit{spines Null} \qquad = [\,]$$
$$\textit{spines } (\textit{Fork } xt \, x \, yt) = \textit{spines } xt + [\textit{Node } x \, (\textit{spines } yt)]$$

In the worst case, when all the right subtrees are *Null*, evaluation of *spines* takes quadratic time in the size of the tree. This can be reduced to linear time with the help of a suitable accumulating parameter. Define *addspines* by

$$\textit{addspines } xt \, xrs = \textit{spines } xt + xrs$$

Then *spines xt* = *addspines xt* [ ]. It is straightforward to synthesise the following recursive definition of *addspines*:

$$\textit{addspines Null } xrs \qquad\qquad = xrs$$
$$\textit{addspines } (\textit{Fork } xt \, x \, yt) \, xrs = \textit{addspines } xt \, (\textit{Node } x \, (\textit{addspines } yt \, [\,])) : xrs)$$

The function *addspines* takes linear time in the size of the tree.

The inorder traversal of the binary tree is now given by the preorder traversal of the forest of rose trees. Specifically,

$$\textit{inorder} = \textit{unfoldr step} \cdot \textit{wrapList} \cdot \textit{spines}$$

where *step* was given above. The result is a loopless algorithm for *inorder*.

3 Mixing

Many combinatorial enumeration algorithms involve running up and down one list in between generating successive elements of another list. To capture this idea, consider the following function *mix*:

$$\textit{mix} \qquad\qquad :: [a] \to [a] \to [a]$$
$$\textit{mix } [\,] \, ys \qquad = ys$$
$$\textit{mix } (x : xs) \, ys = ys + x : \textit{mix } xs \, (\textit{reverse } ys)$$

For example, $mix\,[3,4,5,6]\,[0,1,2] = [0,1,2,3,2,1,0,4,0,1,2,5,2,1,0,6,0,1,2]$. Thus mix runs through the second list, generates the next element of the first list, runs backwards through the second list, and so on.

The function mix is associative with $[\,]$ as identity element. The proof of this not totally obvious fact is left to the diligent reader. The given definition of mix mixes 'from the right', but we could equally well have defined a similar version that mixes from the left, as in

$$mixl\ xs\,[\,] \qquad\quad = xs$$
$$mixl\ xs\ (y : ys) = xs + y : mixl\ (reverse\ xs)\ ys$$

Either definition will serve our purpose, and we have chosen the former.

The function $mixall :: [[a]] \to [a]$ is defined by $mixall = foldr\ mix\,[\,]$. Since mix is associative we could just as well have defined $mixall = foldl\ mix\,[\,]$. For a list of length n of lists each of length m, the output of $mixall$ has length $(m+1)^n - 1$, which is exponential in mn, the total length of the input.

As we will see, the function $mixall$ can be used to good effect in the construction of a number of combinatorial algorithms, including Gray codes, the Koda-Ruskey algorithm and the Johnson-Trotter algorithm, all of which generate a list of transitions for enumerating certain combinatorial objects. For example, the function $gray$, where

$$gray\ n = mixall\,[[i] \mid i \leftarrow [n{-}1, n{-}2 \mathbin{..} 0]]$$

returns a list of transitions to change the bits in an n-tuple $(a_{n-1}, a_{n-2}, \ldots, a_0)$ of bits so that the result is the binary Gray code. Transition i means "swap the parity of the bit a_i". In particular,

$$gray\ 4 = [0,1,0,2,0,1,0,3,0,1,0,2,0,1,0]$$

Starting with the pattern 0000, the corresponding Gray code is as follows, reading columns downwards from left to right:

0000	0110	1100	1010
0001	0111	1101	1011
0011	0101	1111	1001
0010	0100	1110	1000

The Gray code example explains why we have chosen to mix from the right: conventionally the least significant bit is on the right, so that is where the action is. We will return to Gray codes later on. Our aim in this section is simply to derive a loopless algorithm for $mixall$.

3.1   Fusion and Fission

It is easy to cast $mixall$ into loopless form: simply take $prolog = foldr\ mix\,[\,]$ and define $step$ so that $unfoldr\ step$ is the identity function on lists. Then we have $mixall = unfoldr\ step \cdot prolog$. But, of course, $prolog$ takes exponential time.

The way to make progress lies in the *fusion* law for *foldr*. Recall that this law states that $f \cdot foldr\ g\ a = foldr\ h\ b$ provided f is strict, $f\ a = b$ and $f \cdot g\ x = h\ x \cdot f$. Fusion is one of the fundamental laws of functional programming. The twist here is that we seek to apply it in the "anti-fusion" or "fission" direction, breaking up a fold into two components.

Suppose we represent elements of $[a]$ by elements of some type $T\ a$ under an abstraction function $abst :: T\ a \to [a]$. Suppose also that $tmix$ is a function with type $tmix :: [a] \to T\ a \to T\ a$ satisfying the condition

$$abst \cdot tmix\ xs = mix\ xs \cdot abst \qquad (1)$$

Provided $T\ a$ contains a constructor *Null* for representing the empty list, so $abst\ Null = [\ ]$, we now have enough ingredients to apply fission, resulting in

$$mixall = abst \cdot foldr\ tmix\ Null$$

If we can arrange that $abst$ takes the form *unfoldr step* for a constant time function *step*, and $prolog = foldr\ tmix\ Null$ takes linear time, then we have a loopless algorithm for *mixall*.

Let us see what information we can derive from (1) by doing a case analysis on xs. First, we calculate

$$abst\ (tmix\ [\ ]\ yt)$$
$$=\quad \{\text{equation (1)}\}$$
$$mix\ [\ ]\ (abst\ yt)$$
$$=\quad \{\text{definition of } mix\ [\ ]\}$$
$$abst\ yt$$

This suggests we define $tmix\ [\ ]\ yt = yt$. Second,

$$abst\ (tmix\ (x : xs)\ yt)$$
$$=\quad \{\text{equation (1)}\}$$
$$mix\ (x : xs)\ (abst\ yt)$$
$$=\quad \{\text{definition of } mix\}$$
$$abst\ yt \mathbin{+\!\!+} x : mix\ xs\ (reverse\ (abst\ yt))$$
$$=\quad \{\text{supposing } ty \text{ is such that } abst\ ty = reverse\ (abst\ yt)\}$$
$$abst\ yt \mathbin{+\!\!+} x : mix\ xs\ (abst\ ty)$$
$$=\quad \{\text{equation (1)}\}$$
$$abst\ yt \mathbin{+\!\!+} x : abst\ (tmix\ xs\ ty)$$

The last expression looks very similar to the recursive case of the inorder traversal of a binary tree. It suggests that we take $T = Tree$, where *Tree* is the type of binary trees defined in the warm-up section, and $abst = inorder$. Supposing $reflect :: Tree\ a \to Tree\ a$ is such that $inorder \cdot reflect = reverse \cdot inorder$, the above calculation gives

$$inorder\ (tmix\ (x : xs)\ yt) = inorder\ yt \mathbin{+\!\!+} x : inorder\ (tmix\ xs\ (reflect\ yt))$$

All this suggests the following definition of *tmix* to satisfy (1):

$$tmix \,[\,] \, yt \qquad = yt$$
$$tmix \,(x : xs) \, yt = Fork \, yt \, x \,(tmix \, xs \,(reflect \, yt))$$

It is easy to define *reflect*:

$$reflect \, Null \qquad\quad = Null$$
$$reflect \,(Fork \, xt \, x \, yt) = Fork \,(reflect \, yt) \, x \,(reflect \, xt)$$

Now we have $mixall = inorder \cdot foldr \, tmix \, Null$.

So far, so good. However, $foldr \, tmix \, Null$ cannot serve as our prolog because it suffers from the same defect as $foldr \, mix \,[\,]$: it takes exponential time in the total length of its input. The reason is that $foldr \, tmix \, Null$ produces a tree of exponential size, so reflecting it takes exponential time.

3.2   Tupling

The way to make progress is to avoid invoking *reflect*. The idea is to tuple the computation of $foldr \, tmix \, Null$ with the computation of $reflect \cdot foldr \, tmix \, Null$, thereby computing both a tree and its reflection without invoking the function *reflect* explicitly.

Two steps are required, the first of which is another application of the fusion law. Suppose we can find a function, *ximt* say, so that

$$reflect \cdot foldr \, tmix \, Null = foldr \, ximt \, Null$$

Given *ximt*, the second step is an application of the *tupling* law for *foldr*, another fundamental law of functional programming. The tupling laws states that

$$fork \,(foldr \, f \, a, foldr \, g \, b) = foldr \, h \,(a, b)$$

where $fork \,(f, g) \, x = (f \, x, g \, x)$ and $h \, x \,(y, z) = (f \, x \, y, g \, x \, z)$. In particular,

$$fork \,(foldr \, tmix \, Null, reflect \cdot foldr \, tmix \, Null) = foldr \, pmix \,(Null, Null)$$

where $pmix \, xs \,(yt, ty) = (tmix \, xs \, yt, ximt \, xs \, ty)$.

Let us see what tupling says about *mixall*. Define $pair \, f \,(x, y) = (f \, x, f \, y)$. Then

$$pair \, inorder \cdot foldr \, pmix \,(Null, Null)$$
$$= \quad \{\text{above expression for } foldr \, pmix \,(Null, Null)\}$$
$$pair \, inorder \cdot fork \,(foldr \, tmix \, Null, reflect \cdot foldr \, tmix \, Null)$$
$$= \quad \{\text{since } pair \, f \cdot fork \,(g, h) = pair \,(f \cdot g, f \cdot h)\}$$
$$pair \,(inorder \cdot foldr \, tmix \, Null, inorder \cdot reflect \cdot foldr \, tmix \, Null)$$
$$= \quad \{\text{since } inorder \cdot reflect = reverse \cdot inorder\}$$
$$pair \,(inorder \cdot foldr \, tmix \, Null, reverse \cdot inorder \cdot foldr \, tmix \, Null)$$
$$= \quad \{\text{as } mixall = inorder \cdot foldr \, tmix \, Null\}$$
$$pair \,(mixall, reverse \cdot mixall)$$

Hence

$$pair\,(mixall, reverse \cdot mixall) = pair\;inorder \cdot foldr\;pmix\,(Null, Null)$$

Returning to the first step, fusion is possible if we can establish the fusion condition

$$reflect \cdot tmix\;xs = ximt\;xs \cdot reflect \qquad (2)$$

Equivalently, $ximt\;xs = reflect \cdot tmix\;xs \cdot reflect$. It is now straightforward to calculate a recursive definition of $ximt$:

$$
\begin{aligned}
ximt\,[\,]\;ty \quad &= ty \\
ximt\,(x : xs)\;ty &= Fork\,(ximt\;xs\,(reflect\;ty))\;x\;ty
\end{aligned}
$$

We can also calculate a direct recursive definition of $pmix$. Under the assumption that $ty = reflect\;yt$, we have

$$
\begin{aligned}
&pmix\,(x : xs)\,(yt, ty) \\
=\quad &\{\text{definition}\} \\
&(tmix\,(x : xs)\;yt, ximt\,(x : xs)\;ty) \\
=\quad &\{\text{definitions}\} \\
&(Fork\;yt\;x\,(tmix\;xs\;ty), Fork\,(ximt\;xs\;yt)\;x\;ty) \\
=\quad &\{\text{with } (zt, tz) = (tmix\;xs\;ty, ximt\;xs\;yt)\} \\
&(Fork\;yt\;x\;zt, Fork\;tz\;x\;ty)
\end{aligned}
$$

Hence

$$
\begin{aligned}
pmix\,[\,]\,(yt, ty) \quad &= (yt, ty) \\
pmix\,(x : xs)\,(yt, ty) &= (Fork\;yt\;x\;zt, Fork\;tz\;x\;ty) \\
&\qquad\textbf{where } (zt, tz) = pmix\;xs\,(ty, yt)
\end{aligned}
$$

Now $foldr\;pmix\,(Null, Null)$ takes linear time in the total length of the input. The resulting pair of trees each have exponential size, but they are constructed in linear time because subtrees are shared and there is no call on $reflect$. In reality we are constructing an acyclic directed graph rather than a tree.

3.3 From Trees to Forests

The next step is to deal with $inorder$. Recall from our warm-up exercises that $inorder = preorder \cdot spines$, where $spines$ converts a binary tree into a forest of rose trees. The loopless algorithm $preorder = unfoldr\;step \cdot wrapList$ was constructed in Sect. 2. Hence

$$pair\,(mixall, reverse \cdot mixall) = pair\,(preorder \cdot spines) \cdot foldr\;pmix\,(Null, Null)$$

The game now is to fuse $pair\;spines$ with $foldr\;pmix\,(Null, Null)$. Specifically, suppose $smix$ satisfies

$$pair\;spines \cdot pmix\;xs = smix\;xs \cdot pair\;spines \qquad (3)$$

Then, since $pair\ spines\ (Null, Null) = ([\,], [\,])$ another application of the fusion law gives

$$pair\ spines \cdot foldr\ pmix\ (Null, Null) = foldr\ smix\ ([\,], [\,])$$

It remains to determine $smix$. It is easy to calculate from (3) that

$$smix\ [\,]\ (yrs, sry) = (yrs, sry)$$

For the recursive case, suppose $(yrs, sry) = pair\ spines\ (yt, ty)$. Then

$$
\begin{aligned}
&smix\ (x : xs)\ (yrs, sry) \\
=\ &\{\text{fusion condition (3)}\} \\
&pair\ spines\ (pmix\ (x : xs)\ (yt, ty)) \\
=\ &\{\text{definition of } pmix, \text{ with } (zt, tz) = pmix\ xs\ (ty, yt)\} \\
&(spines\ (Fork\ yt\ x\ zt), spines\ (Fork\ tz\ x\ ty)) \\
=\ &\{\text{definition of } spines\} \\
&(spines\ yt \mathbin{+\!\!+} [Node\ x\ (spines\ zt)], spines\ tz \mathbin{+\!\!+} [Node\ x\ (spines\ ty)]) \\
=\ &\{\text{with } (zrs, srz) = pair\ spines\ (zt, tz)\} \\
&(yrs \mathbin{+\!\!+} [Node\ x\ zrs], srz \mathbin{+\!\!+} [Node\ x\ sry])
\end{aligned}
$$

Summarising,

$$
\begin{aligned}
smix\ [\,]\ (yrs, sry) &= (yrs, sry) \\
smix\ (x : xs)\ (yrs, sry) &= (yrs \mathbin{+\!\!+} [Node\ x\ zrs], srz \mathbin{+\!\!+} [Node\ x\ sry]) \\
&\mathbf{where}\ (zrs, srz) = smix\ xs\ (sry, yrs)
\end{aligned}
$$

For example, $foldr\ smix\ ([\,], [\,])\ [[1, 2, 3], [4, 5]]$ produces the two forests

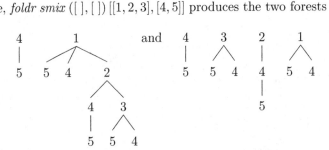

We are nearly there, but unfortunately $foldr\ smix\ ([\,], [\,])$ does not take linear time: adding to the end of a list is not a constant-time operation. And invoking an accumulating parameter won't help. It's time to introduce queues.

3.4   Introducing Queues

First, recall the definition of $step$ from Sect. 2:

$$
\begin{aligned}
step\ [\,] &= Nothing \\
step\ ((Node\ x\ xts : yts) : tss) &= Just\ (x, consList\ xts\ (consList\ yts\ tss))
\end{aligned}
$$

Observe that *step* removes elements from the front of a list. So in order to make *smix* efficient without making *step* inefficient we want a data structure in which both adding to the end of a list and removing an element from the front are constant-time operations. In other words, a queue. Fortunately, Okasaki's implementation of queues [7] provides a type *Queue a* for which the following operations all take constant time:

$$
\begin{aligned}
insert\ &::\ Queue\ a \to a \to Queue\ a \\
remove\ &::\ Queue\ a \to (a, Queue\ a) \\
empty\ &::\ Queue\ a \\
isempty\ &::\ Queue\ a \to Bool
\end{aligned}
$$

To install queues, we need to redeclare the type *Rose a* so that the children of a node constitute a queue of trees rather than a list of trees. The translation is then completely straightforward and the complete code is given in Fig. 1.

$$
\begin{aligned}
\textbf{data}\ Qrose\ a \quad &=\ Qnode\ a\ (Queue\ (Qrose\ a)) \\[4pt]
mixall \quad &::\ [[a]] \to [a] \\
mixall \quad &=\ unfoldr\ step \cdot prolog \\[4pt]
prolog \quad &::\ [[a]] \to [Queue\ (Qrose\ a)] \\
prolog \quad &=\ wrapQueue \cdot fst \cdot foldr\ smix\ (empty, empty) \\[4pt]
smix \quad &::\ [a] \to (Queue\ (Qrose\ a), Queue\ (Qrose\ a)) \to \\
&\qquad (Queue\ (Qrose\ a), Queue\ (Qrose\ a)) \\
smix\ [\,]\ (yrq, qry) \quad &=\ (yrq, qry) \\
smix\ (x : xs)\ (yrq, qry) \quad &=\ (insert\ yrq\ (Qnode\ x\ zrq), insert\ qrz\ (Qnode\ x\ qry)) \\
&\quad \textbf{where}\ (zrq, qrz) = smix\ xs\ (qry, yrq) \\[4pt]
wrapQueue \quad &::\ Queue\ a \to [Queue\ a] \\
wrapQueue\ xq \quad &=\ consQueue\ xq\ [\,] \\
consQueue\ xq\ xqs \quad &=\ \textbf{if}\ isempty\ xq\ \textbf{then}\ xqs\ \textbf{else}\ xq : xqs \\[4pt]
step \quad &::\ [Queue\ (Qrose\ a)] \to Maybe\ (a, [Queue\ (Qrose\ a)]) \\
step\ [\,] \quad &=\ Nothing \\
step\ (xr : xrs) \quad &=\ Just\ (x, consQueue\ yq\ (consQueue\ zq\ xrs)) \\
&\quad \textbf{where}\ (Qnode\ x\ yq, zq) = remove\ xr
\end{aligned}
$$

Fig. 1. A loopless algorithm for *mixall*

So, finally, we have a genuine 24-carat loopless algorithm for *mixall*. As a bonus, we can compute *reverse* · *mixall* by a virtually identical algorithm; the only change is to replace *fst* by *snd* in the definition of *prolog*.

Another way to make *mixall* loopless is to dispense with queues and use cyclic lists instead. Although the result is a somewhat faster algorithm, the derivation requires a number of Knuth's "extra contortions", so details are omitted.

4 The Gray Code

Since $gray = mixall\ [[i] \mid i \leftarrow [n-1, n-2..0]]$ we now have a loopless algorithm for $gray$. But for this example, everything is simplifiable: the two generated forests of rose trees are essentially the same in that they have exactly the same preorder traversals. Therefore we need keep only one and the definition of $prolog$ in Fig. 1 can be replaced by the much simpler

$$prolog\ n\ \ = (wrapQueue \cdot foldr\ smix\ empty)\ [n-1, n-2 .. 0]$$
$$smix\ n\ xrq = insert\ xrq\ (Node\ n\ xrq)$$

In fact there is an even simpler loopless algorithm for $gray$, which dispenses with queues and uses a cyclic list instead, but we won't go into details.

5 The Koda-Ruskey Algorithm

The Koda-Ruskey algorithm is a method for enumerating the prefixes of a given forest of rose trees. An arbitrary prefix of a forest can be obtained by pruning each tree in the forest. A tree is pruned by removing zero or more subtrees. In the literature on this problem the prefixes of a forest are also known as the "principal sub-forests" and the "ideals of a forest poset".

The idea can also be explained in terms of colourings. A colouring consists of marking every node as either Black or White, with the constraint that all descendants of a White node are also coloured White. Thus the nodes coloured Black form a prefix of the given forest.

As part of the problem specification, the enumeration has to be in Gray-code order, meaning that two consecutive colourings have to differ in the colouring of exactly one node. Thus the transition between one colouring and the next can be given by naming a single node, meaning "change the colour of the node". Ingenious loopless algorithms for this problem are described in [6, 4, 5]. Recently, Filliatre and Pottier [3] gave a non-loopless functional algorithm for the problem based on continuations.

It is very easy to give an efficient functional program for prefix colouring. Given a forest in which every node is labelled with a unique label, the following function $koda$ does the job:

$$koda\ \ \ \ :: [Rose\ a] \rightarrow [a]$$
$$koda\ xrs = mixall\ [x : koda\ yrs \mid Node\ x\ yrs \leftarrow xrs]$$

It is surely impossible to improve on this one-liner, certainly in brevity of expression and perhaps also in speed of execution. The algorithm is conceptually quite simple: beginning with an all-White colouring, interleave the individual colourings of the subtrees using the function $mixall$. Each tree is coloured by colouring the root node Black, and again interleaving the colourings of its subtrees. For example, the forest

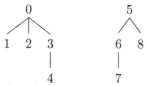

produces the koda sequence

586878 0 878685 3 586878 4 878685 2 586878 4 878685 3 586878 1
878685 3 586878 4 878685 2 586878 4 878685 3 586878

The way to make *koda* loopless is breathtaking in its simplicity and we shall
state the result before deriving it: simply change the function *smix* of Fig. 1 to
a function *kmix* defined by

$$kmix \, (Node \, x \, xrs) \, (yrq, qry)$$
$$= (insert \, yrq \, (Qnode \, x \, zrq), insert \, qrz \, (Qnode \, x \, qry))$$
$$\textbf{where} \, (zrq, qrz) = foldr \, kmix \, (qry, yqr) \, xrs$$

With this change we have $koda = unfoldr \, step \cdot prolog$. The prolog takes time
linear in the size of the given forest, so this is a loopless algorithm.

It is astounding that such a simple change works and, to speak personally for
a moment, it took me over eight months of hard work to find it. For most of that
time I followed a false trail, the instructive details of which are given in Sect. 6.

Having seen the solution, it remains to justify it. First, it is necessary to revisit
the derivation of the loopless program for *mixall*, going back to the point just
before we introduced queues. In effect, we calculated that

$$pair \, (mixall, reverse \cdot mixall) = pair \, preorder \cdot foldr \, smix \, ([\,], [\,])$$

where the definition of *smix* was given by

$$smix \, [\,] \, (yrs, sry) \quad = (yrs, sry)$$
$$smix \, (x : xs) \, (yrs, sry) = (yrs \mathbin{+\mkern-10mu+} [Node \, x \, zrs], srz \mathbin{+\mkern-10mu+} [Node \, x \, sry])$$
$$\textbf{where} \, (zrs, srz) = smix \, xs \, (sry, yrs)$$

In a short while we will need a somewhat messy technical result about the form
of *smix*, which we will call the *substitution lemma*. Suppose we define *amix* and
bmix by the equations

$$amix \, [\,] \, (yrs, sry) \quad = (yrs, sry)$$
$$amix \, (x : xs) \, (yrs, sry) = (yrs \mathbin{+\mkern-10mu+} [Node \, x \, zrs], srz \mathbin{+\mkern-10mu+} [Node \, x \, sry])$$
$$\textbf{where} \, (zrs, srz) = cmix \, xs \, (sry, yrs)$$
$$bmix \, [\,] \, (yrs, sry) \quad = (yrs, sry)$$
$$bmix \, (x : xs) \, (yrs, sry) = (yrs \mathbin{+\mkern-10mu+} [Node \, x \, zrs], srz \mathbin{+\mkern-10mu+} [Node \, x \, sry])$$
$$\textbf{where} \, (zrs, srz) = dmix \, xs \, (sry, yrs)$$

where *cmix* and *dmix* two further functions. Abbreviating *pair preorder* to *pp*,
we claim that

$$pp \, (foldr \, amix \, ([\,], [\,]) \, xss) = pp \, (foldr \, bmix \, ([\,], [\,]) \, xss)$$

for all finite lists xss, provided $pp\,(yrs, sry) = pp\,(yrs', sry')$ implies

$$pp\,(cmix\,xs\,(yrs, sry)) = pp\,(dmix\,xs\,(yrs'\,sry'))$$

for all values of the five variables xs, yrs, sry, yrs' and sry'.

The proof is by induction on the argument xss. Concentrating just on the recursive case $(x : xs) : xss$, let $(yrs, sry) = foldr\,amix\,([\,],[\,])\,xss$. We reason:

$pp\,(amix\,(x : xs)\,(yrs, sry))$
$=$ {definition of $amix$ with $(zrs, srz) = cmix\,xs\,(sry, yrs)$}
  $(preorder\,(yrs + [Node\,x\,zrs]), preorder\,(srz + [Node\,x\,sry]))$
$=$ {property of $preorder$}
  $(preorder\,yrs + x : preorder\,zrs, preorder\,srz + x : preorder\,sry)$

On the right-hand side, let $(yrs', sry') = foldr\,bmix\,([\,],[\,])\,xss$, so

$$pp\,(yrs, sry) = pp\,(yrs', sry')$$

by the induction hypothesis. Reasoning in a similar fashion, we have:

$pp\,(bmix\,(x : xs)\,(yrs', sry'))$
$=$ {definition of $kmix$ with $(zrs', srz') = dmix\,xs\,(sry', yrs')$}
  $(preorder\,(yrs' + [Node\,x\,zrs']), preorder\,(srz' + [Node\,x\,sry']))$
$=$ {property of $preorder$}
  $(preorder\,yrs' + x : preorder\,zrs', preorder\,srz' + x : preorder\,sry')$

The two sides yield identical results under the given assumption.

Let us now return to the definition of $koda$. It is convenient to introduce

$$ruskey \qquad\qquad\qquad :: Rose\,a \rightarrow [a]$$
$$ruskey\,(Node\,x\,xrs) = x : koda\,xrs$$

so that $koda = mixall \cdot map\,ruskey$. A third basic law of functional programming is the fold-map fusion law, which states that $foldr\,f\,e \cdot map\,g = foldr\,(f \cdot g)\,e$. Using this law, we obtain

$$foldr\,smix\,([\,],[\,]) \cdot map\,ruskey = foldr\,kmix\,([\,],[\,])$$

where $kmix = smix \cdot ruskey$. Since $kmix\,(Node\,x\,xrs) = smix\,(x : koda\,xrs)$ by the definition of $ruskey$, we have

$$kmix\,(Node\,x\,xrs)\,(yrs, sry) = (yrs + [Node\,x\,zrs], srz + [Node\,x\,sry])$$
$$\mathbf{where}\,(zrs, srz) = smix\,(koda\,xrs)\,(sry, yrs)$$

We now focus on the function $smix\,(koda\,xrs)$. It is clear that

$$smix\,(koda\,[\,]) = smix\,[\,] = id$$

where id denotes the identity function. In the case of a nonempty list of trees we reason:

$$smix\,(koda\,(xr:xrs))$$
$$=\quad \{\text{definition of }koda\}$$
$$smix\,(mixall\,(ruskey\,xr:map\,ruskey\,xrs))$$
$$=\quad \{\text{definition of }mixall\}$$
$$smix\,(mix\,(ruskey\,xr)\,(mixall\,(map\,ruskey\,xrs)))$$
$$=\quad \{\text{definition of }koda\}$$
$$smix\,(mix\,(ruskey\,xr)\,(koda\,xrs))$$

Here we seem to be stuck. Fortunately help, of a kind, is at hand:

$$pp \cdot smix\,(mix\,xs\,ys) = pp \cdot smix\,xs \cdot smix\,ys \qquad (4)$$

This surprising identity is proved below. It would be certainly be simpler if we had $smix\,(mix\,xs\,ys) = smix\,xs \cdot smix\,ys$, but this identity doesn't hold: each side can produce a different forest. Nevertheless, the preorders are the same and this is just sufficient. Using (4), we can therefore conclude that

$$pp \cdot smix\,(koda\,(xr:xrs)) = pp \cdot kmix\,xr \cdot smix\,(koda\,xrs)$$

Now comes the payoff. Suppose we define $dmix$ by the equations

$$dmix\,[\,] \qquad = id$$
$$dmix\,(xr:xrs) = kmix\,xr \cdot dmix\,xrs$$

An easy proof by induction shows that, with $cmix = smix \cdot koda$ the condition of the substitution lemma holds, namely if $pp\,(yrs, sry) = pp\,(yrs', sry')$ then

$$pp\,(smix\,(koda\,xrs)\,(yrs, sry)) = pp\,(dmix\,xrs\,(yrs'\,sry'))$$

Consequently, we can replace the definition of $kmix$ by

$$kmix\,(Node\,x\,xrs)\,(yrs, sry) = (yrs \mathbin{+\!\!+} [Node\,x\,zrs], srz \mathbin{+\!\!+} [Node\,x\,sry])$$
$$\textbf{where }\,(zrs, srz) = dmix\,xrs\,(sry, yrs)$$

But look again at the two equations defining $dmix$. They are sufficient for us to express $dmix\,xrs$ in terms of $foldr$, for if $f\,[\,] = id$ and $f\,(x:xs) = g\,x \cdot f\,xs$, then $f\,xs\,e = foldr\,g\,e\,xs$ for any e. The proof is a simple consequence of the recursive definition of $foldr$. Hence

$$dmix\,xrs\,(yrs, sry) = foldr\,kmix\,(yrs, sry)\,xrs$$

and, apart from reinstalling queues, we are done.

It remains to prove the magic (4). The crucial fact on which it depends is that mix is associative. This property can be expressed in functional form:

$$mix\,(mix\,xs\,ys) = mix\,xs \cdot mix\,ys$$

In order to exploit it we need to go back and recall all the essential steps in Sect. 3.1 out of which the definition of *smix* was constructed. Specifically, recall the fusion conditions (1), (2) and (3), the definition of *pmix*, and the relationship between *inorder*, *reflect* and *reverse*, all repeated again now for convenience:

$$
\begin{aligned}
inorder \cdot tmix\ xs &= mix\ xs \cdot inorder \\
ximt\ xs &= reflect \cdot tmix\ xs \cdot reflect \\
smix\ xs \cdot pair\ spines &= pair\ spines \cdot pmix\ xs \\
pmix\ xs &= cross\,(tmix\ xs, ximt\ xs) \\
inorder \cdot reflect &= reverse \cdot inorder
\end{aligned}
$$

In the definition of *pmix* we have used $cross\,(f,g)\,(x,y) = (f\ x, g\ y)$ just to be able to express *pmix xs* at the function level.

The proof of (4) is in pieces. We first show that

$$inorder \cdot tmix\,(mix\ xs\ ys) = inorder \cdot tmix\ xs \cdot tmix\ ys$$

Here is the calculation:

$$
\begin{aligned}
&inorder \cdot tmix\,(mix\ xs\ ys) \\
=\ &\{\text{since } inorder \cdot tmix\ xs = mix\ xs \cdot inorder\} \\
&mix\,(mix\ xs\ ys) \cdot inorder \\
=\ &\{\text{associativity of } mix\} \\
&mix\ xs \cdot mix\ ys \cdot inorder \\
=\ &\{\text{since } inorder \cdot tmix\ xs = mix\ xs \cdot inorder\} \\
&inorder \cdot tmix\ xs \cdot tmix\ ys
\end{aligned}
$$

A similar calculation yields

$$inorder \cdot ximt\,(mix\ xs\ ys) = inorder \cdot ximt\ xs \cdot ximt\ ys$$

Next we have

$$pair\ inorder \cdot pmix\,(mix\ xs\ ys) = pair\ inorder \cdot pmix\ xs \cdot pmix\ ys$$

The calculation is:

$$
\begin{aligned}
&pair\ inorder \cdot pmix\,(mix\ xs\ ys) \\
=\ &\{\text{since } pmix\ xs = cross\,(tmix\ xs, ximt\ xs)\} \\
&pair\ inorder \cdot cross\,(tmix\,(mix\ xs\ ys), ximt\,(mix\ xs\ ys)) \\
=\ &\{\text{since } pair\ f \cdot cross\,(g,h) = cross\,(f \cdot g, f \cdot h)\} \\
&cross\,(inorder \cdot tmix\,(mix\ xs\ ys), inorder \cdot ximt\,(mix\ xs\ ys)) \\
=\ &\{\text{first two pieces}\} \\
&cross\,(inorder \cdot tmix\ xs \cdot tmix\ ys, inorder \cdot ximt\ xs \cdot ximt\ ys) \\
=\ &\{\text{since } cross\,(f,g) \cdot cross\,(h,k) = cross(f \cdot h, g \cdot k)\} \\
&pair\ inorder \cdot cross\,(tmix\ xs, ximt\ xs) \cdot cross\,(tmix\ ys, ximt\ ys) \\
=\ &\{\text{definition of } pmix\} \\
&pair\ inorder \cdot pmix\ xs \cdot pmix\ ys
\end{aligned}
$$

Next, we show

$$pp \cdot smix\,(mix\ xs\ ys) \cdot pair\ spines = pp \cdot smix\ xs \cdot smix\ ys \cdot pair\ spines$$

by calculating

$$pp \cdot smix\,(mix\ xs\ ys) \cdot pair\ spines$$

$= \quad \{\text{since } smix\ xs \cdot pair\ spines = pair\ spines \cdot pmix\ xs\}$

$$pp \cdot pair\ spines \cdot pmix\,(mix\ xs\ ys)$$

$= \quad \{\text{since } pair\ f \cdot pair\ g = pair\,(f \cdot g)\}$

$$pair\,(preorder \cdot spines) \cdot pmix\,(mix\ xs\ ys)$$

$= \quad \{\text{since } inorder = preorder \cdot spines\}$

$$pair\ inorder \cdot pmix\,(mix\ xs\ ys)$$

$= \quad \{\text{second step}\}$

$$pair\ inorder \cdot pmix\ xs \cdot pmix\ ys$$

$= \quad \{\text{reversing previous steps}\}$

$$pp \cdot smix\ xs \cdot smix\ ys \cdot pair\ spines$$

Finally, (4) is established from the last identity since *spines* is a bijection: the function *unspines* defined by

$$unspines\,[\,] \qquad\qquad = Null$$
$$unspines\,(ts +\!\!+ [Node\ t\ vs]) = Fork\,(unspines\ ts)\ x\,(unspines\ vs)$$

satisfies *spines* $\cdot$ *unspines* = *id* and *unspines* $\cdot$ *spines* = *id*. Hence, composing both sides with *pair unspines*, and using *pair id* = *id*, we obtain (4).

6   Mixing with Implicit Lists

Before proceeding to our final application, let us first ask the question: What can we say if the argument to *mixall* is not given as a list of explicit lists, but as a list of lists each generated by a loopless algorithm? More precisely, can we define *mixall* $\cdot$ *map loopless* as a loopless algorithm, assuming *loopless* is a loopless algorithm? Note carefully that what is wanted is a prolog that takes time linear in the length of the input, *not* in the length of *concat* $\cdot$ *map loopless*. Without this restriction we can do it easily using the above loopless algorithm for *mixall*. It turns out that such a generalisation seems to be needed for the final application, the Johnson-Trotter algorithm.

In this section we will give a positive answer to the question but only under the following restrictions. Firstly, both *loopless* and *reverse* $\cdot$ *loopless* are given by loopless algorithms:

$$loopless \qquad\quad = unfoldr\ fstep \cdot fprolog$$
$$reverse \cdot loopless = unfoldr\ rstep \cdot rprolog$$

Secondly, $ll = length \cdot loopless$ can be evaluated in constant time. It may be possible to relax these conditions, but we don't know how, so it is a topic for future research.

In order to answer the question, it seems necessary to go back to the very beginning of our story, and derive another loopless algorithm for $mixall$, one in which the use of $reverse$ appears explicitly.

6.1   Another Loopless Program for $mixall$

Recall that $mixall = foldr\ mix\ [\ ]$. If we can find a function, xim say, satisfying the fusion condition

$$reverse \cdot mix\ xs = xim\ xs \cdot reverse \tag{5}$$

then we have $reverse \cdot mixall = foldr\ xim\ [\ ]$. Use of the tupling law then yields

$$fork\ (mixall, reverse \cdot mixall) = foldr\ mixp\ ([\ ], [\ ])$$

where $mixp\ xs\ (ys, sy) = (mix\ xs\ ys, xim\ xs\ sy)$.

Since (5) is equivalent to $xim\ xs = reverse \cdot mix\ xs \cdot reverse$, one definition of xim is easily obtained:

$$
\begin{aligned}
xim\ [\ ]\ sy\ &= sy \\
xim\ (x : xs)\ sy\ &= xim\ xs\ (reverse\ sy) \mathbin{+\!\!+} x : sy
\end{aligned}
$$

We essentially made use of this definition in Sect. 3.1, though on trees rather than lists –see (2). But another definition of xim also does the job. It is easy to see with a parity argument that

$$
\begin{aligned}
reverse\ (mix\ xs\ ys) = \ &\textbf{if}\ even\ (length\ xs)\ \textbf{then}\ mix\ (reverse\ xs)\ (reverse\ ys) \\
&\textbf{else}\ mix\ (reverse\ xs)\ ys
\end{aligned}
$$

Consequently, xim can be defined in the following way to satisfy (5):

$$
\begin{aligned}
xim\ xs\ sy = \ &\textbf{if}\ even\ (length\ xs)\ \textbf{then}\ mix\ (reverse\ xs)\ sy \\
&\textbf{else}\ mix\ (reverse\ xs)\ (reverse\ sy)
\end{aligned}
$$

Unlike the former definition, xim is now expressed as an instance of mix.

With $sy = reverse\ ys$, and using the second definition of xim, we have

$$
\begin{aligned}
mixp\ xs\ (ys, sy) = \ &\textbf{if}\ even\ (length\ xs)\ \textbf{then}\ (mix\ xs\ ys, mix\ sx\ sy) \\
&\textbf{else}\ (mix\ xs\ ys, mix\ sx\ ys) \\
&\textbf{where}\ sx = reverse\ xs
\end{aligned}
$$

At this point, we need to make an observation about mix that we could have made much earlier: the original definition of $mix\ xs\ ys$ gives rise to an inefficient program since ys is reversed at each step. Better is the following version in which ys is reversed only once:

$$mix\ xs\ ys = mixg\ xs\ (ys, reverse\ ys) \tag{6}$$

where
$$mixg\ xs\ (ys, sy) = ys \mathbin{+\!\!+} concat\ (zipWith\ (:)\ xs\ sys)$$
$$\textbf{where}\ sys = sy : ys : sys$$

The definition of $mixg$ makes use of the standard function $zipWith$ and an infinite list of lists. This version is faster than the previous one because the function $reverse$ is invoked only once.

The point about introducing $mixg$ is that we can use it in another expression for $mixp$:

$$mixp\ xs\ (ys, sy) = \textbf{if}\ even\ (length\ xs)\ \textbf{then}\ (mixg\ xs\ (ys, sy), mixg\ sx\ (sy, ys))$$
$$\textbf{else}\ (mixg\ xs\ (ys, sy), mixg\ sx\ (ys, sy))$$
$$\textbf{where}\ sx = reverse\ xs$$

As in the previous development, the next step is to apply fission to the function $foldr\ mixp\ ([\,], [\,])$. However, unlike Sect. 3.1, which used binary trees and inorder traversal as the abstraction function, we will now use forests of rose trees and preorder traversal.

To apply fission we require a function $mixf$ satisfying

$$pair\ preorder \cdot mixf\ xs = mixp\ xs \cdot pair\ preorder \tag{7}$$

Then we obtain

$$foldr\ mixp\ ([\,], [\,]) = pair\ preorder \cdot foldr\ mixf\ ([\,], [\,])$$

We simply state the definition of $mixf$, leaving the verification of (7) to the reader:

$$mixf\ xs\ (yrs, sry) = \textbf{if}\ even\ (length\ xs)$$
$$\textbf{then}\ (mixg\ xs\ (yrs, sry), mixg\ sx\ (sry, yrs))$$
$$\textbf{else}\ (mixg\ xs\ (yrs, sry), mixg\ sx\ (yrs, sry))$$
$$\textbf{where}\ sx = reverse\ xs$$

where $mixg$ is redefined to read

$$mixg\ xs\ (yrs, sry) = yrs \mathbin{+\!\!+} zipWith\ Node\ xs\ sys$$
$$\textbf{where}\ sys = sry : yrs : sys$$

Computation of $mixg\ xs\ (yrs, sry)$ takes time proportional to the length of yrs plus the length of xs, but we can make it take time proportional to xs alone by once again introducing queues. Specifically, the above definition of $mixg$ can be replaced by

$$mixg\ xs\ (yrq, qry) = foldl\ insert\ yrq\ (zipWith\ Qnode\ xs\ sys)$$
$$\textbf{where}\ sys = qry : yrq : sys$$

The function $foldl\ insert$ appends a list of rose trees to a queue of rose trees, taking time proportional to the appended list. The complete program for $mixall$ is given in Fig. 2.

$$\textbf{data}\ Qrose\ a \quad = Qnode\ a\ (Queue\ (Qrose\ a))$$

$$mixall \qquad\qquad = unfoldr\ step \cdot prolog$$

$$prolog \qquad\qquad = wrapQueue \cdot fst \cdot foldr\ mixf\ (empty, empty)$$

$$
\begin{aligned}
mixf\ xs\ (yrq, qry) = \ &\textbf{if}\ even\ (length\ xs)\\
&\textbf{then}\ (mixg\ xs\ (yrq, qry), mixg\ sx\ (qry, yrq))\\
&\textbf{else}\ (mixg\ xs\ (yrq, qry), mixg\ sx\ (yrq, qry))\\
&\textbf{where}\ sx = reverse\ xs
\end{aligned}
$$

$$
\begin{aligned}
mixg\ xs\ (yrq, qry) = \ &foldl\ insert\ yrq\ (zipWith\ Qnode\ xs\ sys)\\
&\textbf{where}\ sys = qry : yrq : sys
\end{aligned}
$$

$$
\begin{aligned}
wrapQueue\ xq \quad &= consQueue\ xq\ [\,]\\
consQueue\ xq\ xqs &= \textbf{if}\ isempty\ xq\ \textbf{then}\ xqs\ \textbf{else}\ xq : xqs
\end{aligned}
$$

$$
\begin{aligned}
step\ [\,] \qquad\quad &= Nothing\\
step\ (xq : xqs) &= Just\ (x, consQueue\ yq\ (consQueue\ zq\ xqs))\\
&\textbf{where}\ (Qnode\ x\ yq, zq) = remove\ xq
\end{aligned}
$$

Fig. 2. A second loopless algorithm for *mixall*

The essential difference between the two loopless programs for *mixall* is that the second one uses *reverse* explicitly (in the definition of *mixf*), while the first one uses it only implicitly. In fact, the second loopless algorithm for *mixall* was the version I derived first. It seems a shame then that the Koda-Ruskey algorithm couldn't be based on it; at least, substantial effort couldn't show me how. I couldn't see how to construct efficiently a forest whose *koda* sequence was the reverse of the *koda* sequence of a given forest.

On the other hand, the second version seems to be necessary to answer the question posed at the outset of this section.

6.2   A Generalised Version

Let us now return to the main point, which is how to make *mixall* · *map loopless* loopless, given

$$
\begin{aligned}
loopless \qquad\qquad &= unfoldr\ fstep \cdot fprolog\\
reverse \cdot loopless &= unfoldr\ rstep \cdot rprolog
\end{aligned}
$$

and a constant time function $ll = length \cdot loopless$.

Here is a reasonably obvious way of modifying the code in Fig. 2 to solve the problem. Start with the list *intro*, defined by

$$intro\ xs = [(ll\ x, fprolog\ x, rprolog\ x)\ |\ x \leftarrow xs]$$

and replace *prolog* by

$$prolog = wrapQueue \cdot fst \cdot foldr\ mixf\ (empty, empty) \cdot intro$$

Elements of *intro* give the length of *loopless x*, and the starting values, *fprolog x* and *rprolog x*, for the unfolding phase for each x in xs. The functions *mixf* and *mixg* are modified to read

$$mixf\,(n, a, b)\,(yrq, qry) = \textbf{if } even\ n$$
$$\textbf{then }\,(mixg\ fstep\ a\,(yrq, qry), mixg\ rstep\ b\,(qry, yrq))$$
$$\textbf{else }\,(mixg\ fstep\ a\,(yrq, qry), mixg\ rstep\ b\,(yrq, qry))$$
$$mixg\ f\ a\,(yrq, qry)\quad = foldl\ insert\ yrq\,(zipWith\ Qnode\,(unfoldr\ f\ a)\ sys)$$
$$\textbf{where } sys = qry : yrq : sys$$

Essentially all we have done is to replace the explicit list xs by *unfoldr fstep a* and *reverse xs* by *unfoldr rstep b*. The problem, of course, is that *mixf* may now take exponential time, and therefore *prolog* may take exponential time.

The solution is to delay evaluation of the unfolding phase, letting *step* do the work. This is what happens implicitly with a lazy functional language but, as we said at the outset, we will not allow ourselves to exploit laziness.

We will need a new data type to represent delayed evaluations, and we take

data *Delay a b*
$$= Hold\,(a \rightarrow Maybe\,(b, a))\ b\ a\,(Queue\,(Delay\ a\ b), Queue\,(Delay\ a\ b))$$

The first argument of *Hold* is a step function used in the unfolding; the second argument is an output value; the third argument is a starting value for the next unfolding; and the final value is a pair of delayed queues.

Now, we replace *mixg* once again by

$$mixg\ f\ a\,(ydq, qdy) = \textbf{case } f\ a\ \textbf{of}$$
$$Nothing\quad \rightarrow ydq$$
$$Just\,(x, b) \rightarrow insert\ ydq\,(Hold\ f\ x\ b\,(ydq, qdy))$$

The function *mixg* takes a step function, a seed and a pair of queues of delayed elements and adds a new delayed element to the end of the first queue.

Finally, we replace *step* by

$$step\,[\,] = Nothing$$
$$step\,(xdq : xdqs)$$
$$= Just\,(x, consQueue\,(mixg\ f\ b\,(qdy, ydq))\,(consQueue\ zdq\ xdqs))$$
$$\textbf{where }\,(Hold\ f\ x\ b\,(ydq, qdy), zdq) = remove\ xdq$$

The revised functions *mixf* and *step* take constant time assuming both *fstep* and *rstep* do. The complete program is summarised in Fig. 3.

7   The Johnson-Trotter Algorithm

The Johnson-Trotter permutation algorithm produces a sequence of all permutations of a given list in which the transition from one permutation to the next is accomplished by a single transposition of adjacent elements. A description of a loopless algorithm for this problem was the main topic of [2].

$$\textbf{data } Delay\ a\ b \qquad = Hold\ (a \rightarrow Maybe\ (b, a))\ b\ a$$
$$(Queue\ (Delay\ a\ b),\ Queue\ (Delay\ a\ b))$$

$$gmixall \qquad = unfoldr\ step \cdot prolog$$

$$prolog \qquad = wrapQueue \cdot fst \cdot foldr\ mixf\ (empty, empty) \cdot intro$$
$$intro\ xs \qquad = [(ll\ x, fprolog\ x, rprolog\ x)\ |\ x \leftarrow xs]$$

$$mixf\ (n, a, b)\ (yrq, qry) = \textbf{if } even\ n$$
$$\textbf{then } (mixg\ fstep\ a\ (yrq, qry), mixg\ rstep\ b\ (qry, yrq))$$
$$\textbf{else } (mixg\ fstep\ a\ (yrq, qry), mixg\ rstep\ b\ (yrq, qry))$$

$$mixg\ f\ a\ (ydq, qdy) \qquad = \textbf{case } f\ a\ \textbf{of}$$
$$Nothing \quad \rightarrow ydq$$
$$Just\ (x, b) \rightarrow insert\ ydq\ (Hold\ f\ x\ b\ (ydq, qdy))$$

$$step\ [\ ] \qquad = Nothing$$
$$step\ (xdq : xdqs) \qquad = Just\ (x, consQueue\ (mixg\ f\ b\ (qdy, ydq))$$
$$(consQueue\ zdq\ xdqs))$$
$$\textbf{where } (Hold\ f\ x\ b\ (ydq, qdy), zdq) = remove\ xdq$$

$$wrapQueue\ xq \qquad = consQueue\ xq\ [\ ]$$
$$consQueue\ xq\ xqs \qquad = \textbf{if } isempty\ xq\ \textbf{then } xqs\ \textbf{else } xq : xqs$$

$$fstep, rstep, ll \qquad = \dots$$
$$fprolog, rprolog \qquad = \dots$$

Fig. 3. *gmixall* - a generalised loopless algorithm for *mixall*

The Johnson-Trotter transitions for a list of length $n > 1$ is defined in terms of the transitions for a list of length $(n - 1)$. Label the elements of the list with positions 0 through $(n - 1)$ and let the list be denoted by $xs \mathbin{+\!\!+} [x]$. Begin with a downward run $[n-1, n-2, \dots, 1]$, where transition i means "interchange the element at position i with the element at position $(i - 1)$". The effect is to move x from the last position to the first, resulting in the final permutation $[x] \mathbin{+\!\!+} xs$. For example, the transitions $[3, 2, 1]$ applied to abcd result in the following three permutations:

abdc   adbc   dabc

Now, suppose the transitions generating the permutations of xs are $[j_1, j_2, \dots]$. Apply the transition $(j_1 + 1)$ to $[x] \mathbin{+\!\!+} xs$. We have to increase j_1 by 1 because xs is now one step to the right of the "runner" x. Next, run x upwards again to the last position by applying the transition sequence $[1, 2, \dots, n - 1]$. This results in a final permutation $ys \mathbin{+\!\!+} [x]$, where ys is the result of applying transition j_1 to xs. For example, the transitions $[3, 1, 2, 3]$ applied to dabc result in four more permutations

dacb   adcb   acdb   acbd

For the next step, apply the second transition j_2 for xs and run x down again. We don't have to modify the transition j_2 after upward runs because the relevant permutation is to the left of x. Continue in the same fashion, interleaving runs of x downwards and upwards, with the transitions for $(n-1)$. Here is the complete list of the permutations of abcd, in which the table is to be read by columns from left to right:

abcd	dacb	cabd	dcba	bcad	dbac
abdc	adcb	cadb	cdba	bcda	bdac
adbc	acdb	cdab	cbda	bdca	badc
dabc	acbd	dcab	cbad	dbca	bacd

The above description codes quite easily in Haskell using the function mix:

$$jtcode \quad :: Int \rightarrow [Int]$$
$$jtcode\, 1 = [\,]$$
$$jtcode\, n = mix\,(bump\, 1\,(jtcode(n-1)))\,[n{-}1, n{-}2\mathbin{.\,.} 1]$$

The function $bump\, k$ adds k to every item in even position (counting from 0):

$$bump\, k\,[\,] \qquad\quad = [\,]$$
$$bump\, k\,[a] \qquad\quad = [a + k]$$
$$bump\, k\,(a : b : ns) = (a + k) : b : bump\, k\, ns$$

Because $mixall$ is the only loopless weapon we have, our task is to express $jtcode$ in terms of $mixall$. To do so we have to generalise the problem slightly and express $code$ in terms of $mixall$, where

$$code\,(k, n) = bump\, k\,(jtcode\, n)$$

In particular, $jtcode\, n = code\,(0, n)$. The first task is to construct a direct recursive definition of $code$. We will omit detailed calculations and sketch only the main steps.

First, it is fairly easy to see that

$$bump\, k\,(xs \mathbin{+\!\!+} y : ys) = \textbf{if}\ even\,(length\, xs)\ \textbf{then}\ bump\, k\, xs \mathbin{+\!\!+} bump\, k\,(y : ys)$$
$$\textbf{else}\ bump\, k\, xs \mathbin{+\!\!+} y : bump\, k\, ys$$

Consequently, we have

$$bump\, k\,(mix\, xs\, ys) = \textbf{if}\ even\,(length\, ys)\ \textbf{then}\ mix\,(bump\, k\, xs)\,(bump\, k\, ys)$$
$$\textbf{else}\ mix\, xs\,(bump\, k\, ys)$$

Finally, after a little calculation, we obtain

$$code\,(k, 1) = [\,]$$
$$code\,(k, n) = \textbf{if}\ odd\, n\ \textbf{then}\ mix\,(code\,(k + 1, n - 1))\,(bumpdown\,(k, n))$$
$$\textbf{else}\ mix\,(code\,(1, n - 1))\,(bumpdown\,(k, n))$$

The function *bumpdown* is defined by

$$bumpdown\,(k, n) = bump\,k\,[n{-}1, n{-}2 .. 1]$$

Assume now that for some suitable definition of *list* we have

$$code = mixall \cdot map\,bumpdown \cdot list$$

We can determine *list* from the definition of *code*. Assuming $n > 1$ is odd, we reason

$\quad code\,(k, n)$
$=\quad$ {definition of *code* in the case $n > 1$ is odd}
$\quad mix\,(code\,(k + 1, n - 1))\,(bumpdown\,(k, n))$
$=\quad$ {assumed form for *code*}
$\quad mix\,((mixall \cdot map\,bumpdown \cdot list)\,(k + 1, n - 1))\,(bumpdown\,(k, n))$
$=\quad$ {since $mix\,(mixall\,xss)\,xs = mixall\,(xss \mathbin{+\!\!+} [xs])$}
$\quad mixall((map\,bumpdown \cdot list)\,(k + 1, n - 1) \mathbin{+\!\!+} [bumpdown\,(k, n)])$
$=\quad$ {definition of *map*}
$\quad (mixall \cdot map\,bumpdown)\,(list\,(k + 1, n - 1) \mathbin{+\!\!+} [(k, n)])$

If n is even, similar reasoning gives

$$code\,(k, n) = (mixall \cdot map\,bumpdown)\,(list\,(1, n - 1) \mathbin{+\!\!+} [(k, n)])$$

Hence we obtain an explicit recursive definition of *list*:

$$list\,(k, 1) = [\,]$$
$$list\,(k, n) = \textbf{if } odd\ n \textbf{ then } list\,(k + 1, n - 1) \mathbin{+\!\!+} [(k, n)]$$
$$\textbf{else } list\,(1, n - 1) \mathbin{+\!\!+} [(k, n)]$$

Evaluation of *list* (k, n) takes $O(n^2)$ steps, but we can reduce it to $O(n)$ steps with the following alternative:

$$list\,(k, 1) = [\,]$$
$$list\,(k, n) = \textbf{if } odd\ n \textbf{ then } zip\,twoones\,[2 .. n{-}2] \mathbin{+\!\!+} [(k + 1, n - 1), (k, n)]$$
$$\textbf{else } zip\,twoones\,[2 .. n{-}2] \mathbin{+\!\!+} [(1, n - 1), (k, n)]$$
$$\textbf{where } twoones = 2 : 1 : twoones$$

The proof that these two definitions of *list* are equivalent is left to the reader. Note that in the case $k = 0$ the two branches of the conditional are the same, so we obtain

$$jtcode = mixall \cdot map\,bumpdown \cdot list$$

where

$$list\,1 = [\,]$$
$$list\,n = zip\,twoones\,[2 .. n{-}2] \mathbin{+\!\!+} [(1, n - 1), (0, n)]$$
$$\textbf{where } twoones = 2 : 1 : twoones$$

This nearly gives us a loopless algorithm for *jtcode*, except that evaluation of the prolog *map bumpdown · list* takes quadratic time under a strict semantics.

Fortunately we have already prepared for the final hurdle: *bumpdown* can itself be cast as a loopless algorithm, so we can invoke the function *gmixall* of the previous section. To make *bumpdown* loopless we use "bump instructions". A bump instruction consists of a *direction* and three integers:

$$\textbf{data } Direction \ = Down \mid DownSkip \mid Up \mid UpSkip$$
$$\textbf{type } BumpInst = (Direction, Int, Int, Int)$$

It is reasonably straightforward to define *fstep, fprolog, rstep* and *rprolog* so that

$$bumpdown \qquad\qquad = unfoldr\ fstep \cdot fprolog$$
$$reverse \cdot bumpdown = unfoldr\ rstep \cdot rprolog$$

We have $fprolog\,(k, n) = (Down, k, n - 1, 1)$ and

$$rprolog\,(k, n) = \textbf{if } even\ n \textbf{ then } (Up, k, 1, n - 1)$$
$$\textbf{else } (UpSkip, k, 1, n - 1)$$

We take $rstep = fstep$ and define *fstep* by

$$
\begin{aligned}
fstep\,(Down, k, m, n) \quad &= \textbf{if } m < n \textbf{ then } Nothing \\
&\quad \textbf{else } Just\,(m + k, (DownSkip, k, m - 1, n)) \\
fstep\,(DownSkip, k, m, n) &= \textbf{if } m < n \textbf{ then } Nothing \\
&\quad \textbf{else } Just\,(m, (Down, k, m - 1, n)) \\
fstep\,(Up, k, m, n) \quad &= \textbf{if } m > n \textbf{ then } Nothing \\
&\quad \textbf{else } Just\,(m + k, (UpSkip, k, m + 1, n)) \\
fstep\,(UpSkip, k, m, n) &= \textbf{if } m > n \textbf{ then } Nothing \\
&\quad \textbf{else } Just\,(m, (Up, k, m + 1, n))
\end{aligned}
$$

Finally, $length\,(bumpdown\,(k, n)) = n - 1$, so $ll = length \cdot bumpdown$ is certainly constant time. Installing these functions in Fig. 3 we obtain

$$jtcode = gmixall \cdot list$$

This is a loopless algorithm for Johnson-Trotter.

Acknowledgements. I would like to thank Sharon Curtis, Jeremy Gibbons, Geraint Jones, Clare Martin, Barney Stratford, and other participants in the Algebra of Programming Group at Oxford for many interesting discussions about loopless algorithms. Thanks are also due to Chris Okasaki for providing the code for queues. A special debt of gratitude is owed to Ralf Hinze for a most enjoyable visit to Oxford, when he was pressured into providing another loopless algorithm for *mixall*, and came up with one that was based on a carefully tuned interpreter for evaluating the basic definition. Finally, the referees provided numerous useful comments and suggestions, all of which led me to completely rewrite several sections. In particular, it was only during the final revision that I spotted that (4) couldn't be cast in the simpler form described in Sect. 5, forcing me to a more elaborate calculation. Any mistakes that remain are, of course, solely my responsibility.

References

1. Bird, R. S.: Introduction to Functional Programming Using Haskell. Prentice Hall (1998)
2. Ehrlich, G.: Loopless algorithms for generating permutations, combinations, and other combinatorial configurations. J. of ACM **20** (1973) 500–513
3. Filliatre, J.-C., and Pottier, F.: Producing all ideals of a forest, functionally. J. of Funct. Program. **13**(5) (2003) 945–956
4. Knuth, D.E.: SPIDERS. A program downloadable from `www-cs-faculty.stanford.edu/~knuth/programs.html` (2001)
5. Knuth, D. E.: The Art of Computer Programming, Vol 4. `www-cs-faculty.stanford.edu/~knuth/` (2004)
6. Koda, Y., Ruskey, R.: A Gray code for the ideals of a forest poset. J. of Algorithms **15** (1993) 324–340
7. Okasaki, C.: Simple and efficient purely functional queues and deques. J. of Funct. Program. **5**(4) (1995) 583–592

Compositional Reasoning for Pointer Structures

Yifeng Chen[1] and J.W. Sanders[2]

[1] Department of Computer Science,
University of Durham, Durham DH1 3LE, UK
[2] Oxford University Computing Laboratory,
Oxford OX1 3QD, UK

Abstract. This paper studies the compositional definition and behaviour of properties that arise in pointer structures. A pointer structure is represented as a (pointer) graph. A pointer property is a set of pointer structures. A parameterised binary combinator is defined that enables important properties (like acyclicity, canonicity and reachability) to be defined in a compositional manner. The technique of parameterising a combinator derives from the definition of parallel-by-merge in 'Unifying Theories of Programming'. It is applied here to the study of disjointness combinators that extend the separating conjunction of Separation Logic. A case study is provided to demonstrate how these ideas are used, in the form of rules of Hoare logic, to verify the correctness of an Object-Oriented program.

1 Introduction

The advances in software engineering due to techniques from Object Orientation (OO), at both the programming and design levels, have revealed a lack of support for the relevant formal reasoning. At stake is our understanding of modularisation and the way it interacts with abstraction, the software engineer's two primary weapons against complexity [11]. Indeed with the use of shared mutable modules, where OO methods currently prevail, an implementation passes addresses and so is based on pointers. The immaturity of the appropriate formal methods is reflected in the largely graphical techniques by which we teach OO design and pointer programming. Much of the effort has been spent on semantic models of OO, with scant regard for modularisation and abstraction. But recent advances in resource-bound logics, and Separation Logic in particular, have made it possible to augment graphical reasoning with program annotations, written using separating conjunction of domain disjointness [11,15].

The present paper is devoted to the study of general disjointness combinators (those useful for reasoning about pointer graphs) and to the means of constructing new combinators from those already existing. Our purpose is to promote the success of Separation Logic further. For example, we obtain a compositional characterisation of general acyclic pointer graphs without assumption on the number (and names) of attributes in each object; and we construct a new combinator (from those existing) to factorise any pointer graph uniquely into garbage and non-garbage parts.

T. Uustalu (Ed.): MPC 2006, LNCS 4014, pp. 115–139, 2006.

The setting for this paper is the general one in which a pointer structure is viewed as a labelled directed graph called a *pointer graph*. For each vertex in such a graph, the outgoing edge with a particular label is unique (i.e. determinism). This reflects the fact that every attribute of each object at an address is linked to the address of a unique object. Here each vertex represents an address (or a constant value as a deadend in the graph), and the outgoing labelled edges from the vertex represent the attribute names of the object stored at the address. The current paper does not deal with 'pure' pointers, which may immediately point to other pointers without doing so via an attribute. This assumption is sometimes made by mentioning 'references' instead of 'pointers'; we simply adhere to the term 'pointer structure' to avoid ambiguity.

The semantic model of Separation Logic consists of a *store* (a mapping from global program variables to their address or constant values) and a *heap* (a mapping from addresses to objects stored there). Such a model directly corresponds to a pointer graph in which the global programs variables become the *immediate* edges from a *root* vertex (see Section 2.2 for more details).

The separating conjunction of Separation Logic is surprisingly effective for combining various pointer structures and has been applied successfully to reasoning about many pointer algorithms [11]. However, the expressiveness of this combinator is still limited. For example, by combining with arbitrary additional pointer structures, arbitrary attributes can be added, but the domain disjointness operator requires that the added attributes be located at only the added addresses. In graph theory, the property of acyclicity is defined as the freedom from cycles, that is, "there exists no cycle contained in (or extendable to) the whole graph". It is because the edges may be added from either vertices lying on the cycle or from other vertices that separating conjunction is inadequate for expressing that property. Fortunately, this property can be easily expressed with an *edge-disjointness operator* that combines two pointer structures if they do not share any address (i.e. entry) and an attribute name (i.e. edge) at that address at the same time. If we already know the rough pointer structure (for example to assume that every address locates only two attributes *left* and *right*), then the acyclicity of such a special structure is expressible inductively in Separation Logic using the separating conjunction. The general acyclicity without such assumptions is, however, not expressible with the separating conjunction.

As is clear from [15], Separation Logic used in that way is low level: to be employed at the level of code, where a state is modelled as the combination of a *store* and a *heap*. For the higher reaches of specification and derivation (where far more abstraction is to be expected), and for formal methods to scale up, more expressive techniques are needed. We need to understand better how to reason in a high-level and compositional manner. But that requires the identification of key properties and the combinators for composition of properties. Separation Logic, by comparison, is based entirely on domain-disjoint composition. This motivates us to explore other possible disjointness combinators and study them in a general framework. Modularisation and abstraction can only be achieved if we employ the right combinators at the right places. It is also important to understand how different combinators are related to each other and how new combinators can be constructed from those existing.

An important influence in our approach has been the **parameterised combinator**, *parallel-by-merge*, that arose from the Unifying Theories of Programming work [6] as a generalisation of the parallel composition from process algebra [5,10]. The merge relation controls the way in which two processes synchronise. In the extreme case it does so by forcing the process behaviours to be disjoint, so that in parallel they do not interact at all; in more typical cases it does so by starting with disjoint copies and then quantifying the manner of interaction [6] (Section 7.2). Chen [3] has defined a more general such combinator, *parallel-via-medium* not restricted to sequential processes. He introduces as parameter a 3-way relation linking two properties by combining their behaviours and producing the composed behaviour via that relation. In the present paper we introduce a special parameterised combinator which checks the consistency between two pointer graphs using a binary-relation parameter before joining them together in one pointer graph.

Graph Logic [2] is designed for reasoning about graph properties. Its basic combinator corresponds to disjoint union (of edges). Separation Logic can be viewed as a special Graph Logic (with additional axioms) in which any graph is deterministic (uniqueness of attributes), and the disjointness combinator maintains determinism by disjoining the sources of the edges.

Compared with Graph Logic, the basic formalism of this paper employs a binary relation as a parameter of the binary modalities. The parameter can be constructed from some basic ones. This difference is analogous to the difference between Propositional Dynamic Logic [4] and Propositional Modal Logic. Such parameterisation is particularly useful in practice as we need combinators of *unique decomposition*, a property not shared by the common basic combinators.

Unique decomposition is the main conceptual innovation of this paper. It turns out to have a wealth of relevant application. A decomposition of a pointer graph into two parts with respect to a combinator is unique if the combined choice of the two disjoint parts is unique. The same intuition applies to the decomposition of properties on pointer graphs. Accordingly, this notion has a simple algebraic characterisation as a distributivity law for combined conjunction. Combinators of unique decomposition play a key role in compositional reasoning. For example, given a unique decomposition, we can always uniquely factorise a pointer-graph property into the weakest left and hand-part one. Unique composition also allows an external safety property to distribute into a structural composition and hence supports compositional reasoning.

None of the common basic combinators is a unique decomposition. For example, the separating conjunction of Separation Logic may arbitrarily decompose a graph as long as the source vertices are separated. Some combinators derivable from more basic combinators are unique decompositions. A typical example is the combinator that separates the garbage part from the non-garbage part. The garbage of a pointer graph contains all edges whose sources are not reachable from a particular root vertex. The separation between the garbage and the rest of a pointer graph is unique. A combinator that represents this kind of separation can be derived from the basic ones. Such creation of new combinators is not supported by Graph Logic, which fixes the axioms of a combinator from the beginning.

We have chosen to present our model algebraically, via its laws, after introducing the model with respect to which the laws are sound. It is largely a matter of taste whether that is replaced by an axiom system in the same style as, for example, separating conjunction.

Further theoretical background of our approach is that of the (canonical) trace model [7]. The idea is that since the behaviour of a pointer program does not depend on the exact location of addresses, and since the programmer is deliberately abstracted from specific addresses in order to make programming simpler, a formal theory should reflect such abstraction and simplicity: the naming of the vertices in a pointer graph must be unimportant. Technically, a pointer model that is sensitive to vertex names is not fully abstract with respect to upper-level reasoning about program correctness. Full abstraction may be achieved by one of two means in upper-level reasoning: by using nondeterminism or by choosing a representative of the equivalence class of isomorphic pointer graphs over which that nondeterminism is permitted. The former approach requires the upper level to allow all possible naming-insensitive isomorphic copies of a pointer graph; the latter leads to canonical models.

In the trace model Hoare and He represent each vertex of the pointer graph by the set of all traces of edge-labelled paths from a root vertex through the vertex. Thus the naming of each vertex, as a set of traces, in a given pointer graph is unique. However it may be complicated. For example the resulting representation of a finite graph may be infinite. As a result Hoare and He's hope for a Hoare-logic axiom system based on their model has remained unrealised.

The canonical model may be simplified by imposing an extra condition on paths, resulting in the so-called *navigation paths* [13]. We might choose to consider only acyclic paths. Or we might consider only shortest paths, an idea on which we elaborate in the present paper by representing each vertex as the lexically smallest of the minimal paths from the root. Other paths can then be recovered from such a canonical representation by navigation from the root. The compositional technique mentioned above is used to provide an abstract definition of canonicity.

The biggest difference between canonical and non-canonical models is the treatment of garbage. Automatic garbage collection is an important feature of most contemporary OO programming languages, and so it is equally important that our model supports it. A canonical pointer graph does not represent garbage and so may be more convenient for OO computation with automatic garbage collection. This is a feature we inherit from path-canonical models. In the Hoare-logical reasoning of our case study, we will assume that the state of the program is canonically represented as a pointer graph.

Section 2 introduces pointer graphs and graph-theoretic properties including canonicity. Section 3 introduces basic properties, the techniques to compose them and the notion of unique decomposition. Section 4 introduces the notion of unique decomposition. Section 5 studies some derived properties and the laws they satisfy; a number of unique decompositions are identified in this section. Section 6 studies assertional reasoning. Section 7 studies a pointer search algorithm.

2 Pointer Graphs and Minimum-Path Canonicity

2.1 Pointer Graphs

A pointer structure in memory can be represented as a directed graph (see Figure 1(a)). Each vertex represents a memory address at which can be stored an object with several attributes. Each attribute is represented as a labelled edge. The entry (i.e. the source) is the address and the exit (i.e. the target) is the value (either address or constant) stored for the attribute. We do not consider isolated vertices and assume that from any address each attribute leads to a unique value.

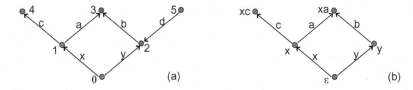

Fig. 1. A pointer graph and its canonical representation

Let A be the set of all atoms including names and constants which are assumed to be totally ordered, C the set of all constants which are assumed to be the smallest atoms in the total order, $S \cong A^*$ the set of all finite sequences on A, and S^3 the set of all triples of such sequences.

We use $a, b, x, y, 1, 2, \cdots$ to denote atoms and $v, u, w, \cdots$ to denote sequences. Let ϵ be the empty sequence, which usually stands for the *root vertex*. For convenience, we do not distinguish an atom and a sequence of length 1. Let $|v|$ be the length of a sequence, $v.u$ sequence concatenation (assuming $\epsilon.w = w.\epsilon = w$), $v \preccurlyeq u$ the prefix order, and $v \sqsubseteq u$ the lexical order after comparing the lengths (i.e. shorter length or the same length but lexically smaller). For example, if we assume the total order of A is alphabetical, then we have $d.e \sqsubseteq a.b.c$, but $a.b.c \sqsubseteq a.c.b$. The front atoms are compared first.

Each triple $(v, w, u) \in S^3$ is called an *edge* from the *entry* v to the *exit* u via *label* w. The denotation of a vertex is a sequence of atoms, because we will use paths (i.e. sequences of atoms) to address vertices in the canonical representation. This will become clear later in the paper.

In this section, we adopt a set representation of graphs. Each graph is a set of edges. A pointer graph is a subset of S^3 in which the label of every edge is an atom, and from an entry there is a unique exit for any specific label:

Definition 1. *A set $G \subseteq S^3$ is a* pointer graph *if, for any $(v, w, u), (v, w, u') \in G$, we have $|w| = 1$ and $u = u'$.*

Let $\Pi(S)$ denote the space of all pointer graphs. We use a triple (v, a, u) to denote an edge labelled with a from vertex v to vertex u. For example, the pointer graph in Figure 1(a) is a set:

$$\{(0, \mathsf{x}, 1), (0, \mathsf{y}, 2), (1, \mathsf{a}, 3), (1, \mathsf{c}, 4), (2, \mathsf{b}, 3), (5, \mathsf{d}, 2)\}$$

in which $A \supseteq \{1, 2, 3, 4, 5, \mathsf{x}, \mathsf{y}, \mathsf{a}, \mathsf{b}, \mathsf{c}, \mathsf{d}\}$. Pointer graphs may contain cycles, sharing of exits, deadends (from which there are no edges), deadheads (to which there are no edges) and so on. These will be formalised later.

The above definition covers any pointer structure. In fact the constants can be incorporated into pointer graphs. Let $C = \{0, 1, 2, \cdots\}$ be the set of all constants. We can add an edge (ϵ, n, n) for each constant n. For example, if n is the value of an attribute x of an object stored at v, then there is an edge (v, x, n) in the set representation. In the reasoning about program states, we assume that every constant is a deadend and every deadend is a constant.

Some common graph-theoretic notions can be defined as follows.

Definition 2. *Let G be a pointer graph. A sequence $w = a_0.a_1 \cdots a_n$ is a path from v to u in G, if there exist $v_1, v_2, \cdots, v_n$ such that $(v, a_0, v_1), (v_n, a_n, u) \in G$ and for any $1 \leqslant i < n$ we have $(v_i, a_i, v_{i+1}) \in G$. A path w is* minimum *if w is a path from ϵ to the vertex w and, if a sequence w' is a path from ϵ to w, then $w \sqsubseteq w'$.*

2.2   Minimum-Path Canonical Representation

A pointer graph can be used to denote a *state* of an OO program. We assume the existence of a root vertex ϵ that denotes the entry point of any memory access by the program. For example, the program may keep the current object in a 'global program variable' this. So there is an edge $(\epsilon, \mathsf{this}, v)$ from the root to the address v of the object. No edge is allowed to reach the root. This requirement is called *rootedness*. So the root vertex is a deadhead. We assume that any constant $c \in C$ is linked to the root, and every constant is a deadend. For example, that the attribute x of an object stored at vertex v has a constant value c is represented as an edge (v, x, c). So the value stored at the exit of any edge is either a constant or an (non-constant) object. An object must have at least one attribute. Thus the constants are the only deadends. There can be infinitely many constants in the set representation of a state, but the rest of the pointer graph must contain a finite number of edges. This property is called *finiteness*. Finally, the observable behaviour of the program does not depend on the exact locations of the addresses (i.e. pointers). Thus, for all pointer graphs with isomorphic structures ignoring the names of the vertices, we adopt a unique naming scheme. We assume that the pointer graph of a program state is always the result of such a naming scheme. This property is called *canonicity*.

A directed graph provides redundant information for representing a pointer structure. There are two possible solutions. One is to introduce nondeterminism at a higher-level to ignore the choice of vertex naming. The other is to identify a representative in each bisimulation class. We follow the latter approach in this paper. The collection of such representatives provides the so-called *canonical* representation. There are different schemes for choosing representatives. Under a particular scheme, the representative for the class of isomorphic pointer graphs is unique.

The canonical representation in [7] identifies each vertex as the set of all traces passing that vertex from a root vertex. So a canonical graph is a set of sets of traces of labels. The naming then becomes unique and dependent on only the topological structure of the pointer graph. Garbage is naturally abstracted from the representation, which is more convenient for OO computation with automatic garbage collection. As the lengths of the traces are unbounded, the representation of a finite graph is a set of infinite sets. This complexity has limited the applicability of the approach. There are several ways to simplify the representation.

- We may identify each vertex as the set of all acyclic navigation paths reaching (instead of passing) the vertex from the root. If the graph is finite, this representation is finite. The method has been taken in several works [13].
- We may further restrict the navigation paths to include only the shortest paths.
- All these representations identify each vertex as a set. In this paper, we further simplify the representation by choosing a minimum path as a representative. The minimum path is the alphabetically smallest path among the shortest paths to a vertex. The order used here is $\sqsubseteq$.

We use the empty sequence ϵ to represent the root of a canonical pointer graph. For example, the canonical representation of Figure 1(a) is shown in Figure 1(b): $\{(\epsilon, x, x), (\epsilon, y, y), (x, c, xc), (x, a, xa), (y, b, xa)\}$. Note that the edge $(5, d, 2)$ in the original graph is ignored as garbage in the canonical representation.

The advantage of the simplified representation is that the resulting model is a normal model. It does not require promotion to a "higher order" representation of vertices.

Definition 3. *A pointer graph G is canonical if, for every edge $(v, a, u) \in G$, the sequences v and u are minimum paths from the root to v and u respectively.*

Every edge of a canonical pointer graph is reachable from the root through a path.

A program state is a combination of rootedness, constants (as the only dead-ends), finiteness and canonicity. The smallest such graph contains the edges from the root to all constants.

Definition 4. *A program state is a canonical pointer graph in which the root ϵ is a deadhead, each constant $c \in C$ is linked from the root via an edge (ϵ, c, c), the constants are deadends and the only deadends of the graph, and the number of edges not from the root to the constants is finite.*

Note that we assume constants are smaller than other names in the total order of atoms. Thus the naming of the constant vertices remains invariant in any program state.

2.3   Comparison with Separation Logic's Store and Heap

The underlying model of Separation Logic [15] consists of two parts: a store and a heap. The store is a mapping from program variables to addresses in the heap. The heap is a mapping from addresses to the values stored. A value can be either an address or a constant. The canonical approaches including that of Hoare and He [7] and that of this paper integrate the store and the heap in one graph. The program variables are represented as the *immediate* edges from the root. Note that no edge leads to the root.

The biggest difference between canonical and non-canonical models is the treatment of garbage. Canonical pointer graphs do not represent garbage and can be more convenient for OO computation with automatic garbage collection.

In an OO program, the update to the state may be through a long path deep in the nested pointer structure. If an update is not directly to a global variable in the store, the distinction between the store and heap will not make the update simpler. In short, the combination of global variables and the state in a pointer graph is conceptually integrated and no more difficult to manipulate for general OO programs.

3   Basic Abstract Properties for Pointer Graphs

The aim of this paper is to support high-level compositional reasoning for pointer graphs. The intention is to define abstract properties like *acyclicity* and *canonicity* as predicates. We start from basic properties first.

3.1   Unary Properties

A unary property P on a pointer graph is a unary predicate $P = P(X)$ where X is a logical variable denoting a pointer graph. We use $\lceil G \rceil \,\hat{=}\, (X = G)$ to denote the lifted property that is true only on the pointer graph G. Conjunction $P \wedge Q$ and negation $\neg P$ are allowed. A property may have sequences as parameters. For example, a property $\lceil \{(v, a, u)\} \rceil$ allowing only one edge has three parameters v, a and u. A parameter can be quantified for a property $\exists v \cdot P$. A property is called constant if it is related to the parameters but not the logical variable X. The property is true for any pointer graph if the combination of the parameters satisfy the property; otherwise it allows no pointer graph. For example, $v \in C$ is a constant property; so are $True$ and $False$. We use P_0, Q_0 to denote arbitrary constant properties. Let $\mathrm{FP}(P_0)$ denote the set of all free parameters in a constant property P_0. For example, $\mathrm{FP}(v \in C) = \{v\}$. Some simple properties are defined in the following table:

$$
\begin{aligned}
True && \text{any graph} \\
False && \text{no graph} \\
Empty &\mathrel{\hat{=}} \lceil\{\,\}\rceil & \text{the empty graph} \\
Edge(v,a,u) &\mathrel{\hat{=}} \lceil\{(v,a,u)\}\rceil & \text{one edge } (v,a,u) \\
EdgeFromTo(v,u) &\mathrel{\hat{=}} \exists a \cdot Edge(v,a,u) & \text{one edge from } v \text{ to } u \\
EdgeFromVia(v,a) &\mathrel{\hat{=}} \exists u \cdot Edge(v,a,u) & \text{one edge from } v \text{ via } a \\
EdgeFrom(v) &\mathrel{\hat{=}} \exists u \cdot EdgeFromTo(v,u) & \text{one edge from } v \\
EdgeTo(u) &\mathrel{\hat{=}} \exists v \cdot EdgeFromTo(v,u) & \text{one edge to } u \\
Edge &\mathrel{\hat{=}} \exists v \cdot EdgeFrom(v) & \text{one edge} \\
CycEdge &\mathrel{\hat{=}} \exists v \cdot (EdgeFrom(v) \wedge EdgeTo(v)) & \text{one cyclic edge} \\
AcycEdge &\mathrel{\hat{=}} Edge \wedge \neg\, CycEdge & \text{one acyclic edge.}
\end{aligned}
$$

3.2 Binary Properties

A binary property r relating two pointer graphs is a binary predicate $r = r(X,Y)$. Again, we allow connectives $r \wedge s$, $\neg r$ and quantifiers $\exists v \cdot r$. Unfortunately, the set union (as a binary property) of two pointer graphs, may not be a pointer graph by violating the uniqueness of exits, even if their set representations are disjoint. Before joining (i.e. taking the union of) two pointer graphs, we need to check their consistency first.

The following table lists a number of binary properties for consideration. Let $A \diamond B \mathrel{\hat{=}} (A \cap B = \emptyset)$ denote the set disjointness, $G^0 \mathrel{\hat{=}} \{(v,w) \mid \exists u \cdot (v,w,u) \in G\}$ be the set of pairs of entries and labels, ${}^{\bullet}G \mathrel{\hat{=}} \{v \mid \exists wu \cdot (v,w,u) \in G\}$ be the set of all entries, and $G^{\bullet} \mathrel{\hat{=}} \{u \mid \exists vw \cdot (v,w,u) \in G\}$ be the set of all exits.

$$
\begin{aligned}
\uplus(X,Y) &\mathrel{\hat{=}} X^0 \diamond Y^0 & \text{entry and label disjointness} \\
\oslash(X,Y) &\mathrel{\hat{=}} ({}^{\bullet}X \diamond {}^{\bullet}Y) & \text{entry disjointness (from sepration logic)} \\
\oslash(X,Y) &\mathrel{\hat{=}} (X^{\bullet} \diamond Y^{\bullet}) & \text{exit disjointness} \\
\otimes(X,Y) &\mathrel{\hat{=}} ({}^{\bullet}X \diamond Y^{\bullet}) & \text{no edge from } Y \text{ to } X \\
\ominus(X,Y) &\mathrel{\hat{=}} (X^{\bullet} \diamond {}^{\bullet}Y) & \text{no edge from } X \text{ to } Y \\
\triangledown(X,Y) &\mathrel{\hat{=}} ({}^{\bullet}X = {}^{\bullet}Y) & \text{entry sharing} \\
\triangle(X,Y) &\mathrel{\hat{=}} (X^{\bullet} = Y^{\bullet}) & \text{exit sharing} \\
\triangleright(X,Y) &\mathrel{\hat{=}} (X^{\bullet} \backslash {}^{\bullet}X = {}^{\bullet}Y \backslash Y^{\bullet}) & \text{sharing deadends of } X \text{ and deadheads of } Y \\
\triangleleft(X,Y) &\mathrel{\hat{=}} ({}^{\bullet}X \backslash X^{\bullet} = Y^{\bullet} \backslash {}^{\bullet}Y) & \text{sharing deadheads of } X \text{ and deadends of } Y.
\end{aligned}
$$

The binary property $\uplus$ provides the basic consistency checking before joining two pointer graphs (in set union). The binary property $\oslash$, implying $\uplus$, corresponds to the operator $*$ in Separation Logic. Other binary properties must be checked together with $\uplus$ to ensure a safe composition. Figure 2 illustrates the decomposition of a pointer graph in Figure 1(a) by different decompositional methods. Note that these are compositions and decompositions of pointer graphs. We will study the composition and decomposition of properties on pointer graphs in the next subsection.

The basic properties satisfy some simple laws.

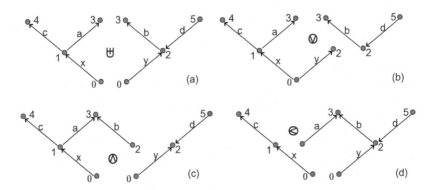

Fig. 2. Comparison of binary properties for composition and decomposition

Law 1. (1) $P \ r \ Empty \Rightarrow P$

(2) $Empty$ is the left and right unit of $\uplus, \oslash, \oslash, \ominus, \ominus$.

(3) $P \bigtriangledown Empty \ = \ P \bigtriangleup Empty \ = \ P \wedge Empty$.

We introduce a notation $\langle P, r, Q \rangle$ for constructing a binary property from two unary properties and a binary one in conjunction:

Definition 5. $\quad \langle P, r, Q \rangle \ \widehat{=} \ P(X) \wedge r(X, Y) \wedge Q(Y)$.

Let P^2 denote $\langle P, true, P \rangle$.

3.3 Parameterised Composition of Unary Properties

We also need operators to compose and decompose higher-level properties. The disjoint composition $P \ r \ Q$ of two unary properties P and Q via a binary property r is a unary property:

Definition 6.

$$P \ r \ Q \ \widehat{=} \ \exists Z_0 Z_1 \cdot (P(Z_0) \wedge Q(Z_1) \wedge r(Z_0, Z_1) \wedge \uplus(Z_0, Z_1) \wedge X = Z_0 \cup Z_1).$$

Each pointer graph allowed by the composition is the union of two graphs allowed by P and Q. Before taking the union, the two graphs must satisfy r and $\uplus$. Because of the compulsory checking of $\uplus$, the resulting composition is always a property only on pointer graphs. Inconsistent properties result in false.

This definition is a special case of parallel-by-merge [6] and parallel-via-medium [3] in particular. The similarity between pointer compositions and parallel compositions has been noticed by many researchers and regarded as a motivation for BI [8]. In parallel-by-merge, the final result is produced by combining the behaviours of the two computations through a 3-way relation, which becomes a parameter of the composition. In the above definition, the binary relation r has a similar role to relate X_1 and X_2, but the final result X is always produced as the set union of X_1 and X_2. The combinator satisfies the following laws.

Law 2. (1) $P \ r \ False = False \ r \ P = False$

(2) $\lceil G \rceil \ r \ \lceil H \rceil = (G \ r \ H) \wedge (G \uplus H) \wedge \lceil G \cup H \rceil$

(3) $P_0 \wedge (P \ r \ Q) = (P_0 \wedge P) \ r \ Q = P \ r \ (P_0 \wedge Q)$

(4) $P \ r \ Q = P \ (\uplus \wedge r) \ Q$

(5) $P \ r \ Q = True \ \langle P, r, Q \rangle \ True$

(6) $(P_1 \vee P_2) \ r \ Q = (P_1 \ r \ Q) \vee (P_2 \ r \ Q)$

(7) $P \ r \ (Q_1 \vee Q_2) = (P \ r \ Q_1) \vee (P \ r \ Q_2)$

(8) $P \ (r_1 \vee r_2) \ Q = (P \ r_1 \ Q) \vee (P \ r_2 \ Q)$

We furthermore assume universal disjunctivity in Law 2(6)(7)(8). The existential quantifier can be viewed as general disjunction and satisfies similar left/right distributivity laws. The combinators $\uplus, \otimes, \oslash, \triangle, \triangledown$ are commutative and associative, while the combinators $\ominus, \oslash, \triangleleft, \triangleright$ are only associative. In general the following theorem holds.

Theorem 1. *If r is commutative (or associative), so is $P \ r \ Q$.*

The general composition $P \ r \ Q$ of unary properties P and Q has a weak inverse operator denoted by $R/_r Q$, which is the weakest predicate A such that $(A \ r \ R) \Rightarrow P$. It can be characterised as a Galois connection:

Definition 7. $A \Rightarrow R/_r Q$ *iff* $(A \ r \ Q) \Rightarrow R$ *for any predicate A.*

The weak inverse satisfies the following laws of Galois connection:

Law 3. (1) $R \Rightarrow ((R \ r \ Q)/_r Q)$ (2) $(R/_r Q) \ r \ Q \Rightarrow R$

(3) $R/_r (P \vee Q) = (R/_r P) \wedge (R/_r Q)$

(4) $(R_1 \wedge R_2)/_r Q = (R_1/_r Q) \wedge (R_2/_r Q)$.

3.4 More Expressiveness Compared to Separation Logic

We informally illustrate that these new combinators are not expressible in general using the separating conjunction of Separation Logic. The following table shows that the relational compositions can be combined to specify any topological structures of two arbitrary acyclic edges in Figure 3. Note that we assume conjunction when placing the combinators together. Both sharing and disjointness can now be specified. Cyclic edges can be treated similarly.

AcycEdge r AcycEdge	(a)	(b)	(c)	(d)	(e)	(f)
$r =$	$\otimes\oslash\ominus\ominus$	$\otimes\triangle$	$\oslash\triangledown$	$\ominus\triangleright$	$\triangle\triangledown$	$\triangleleft\triangleright$

The separating conjunction $(P * Q)$ in Separation Logic corresponds to $P \otimes Q$, which is stronger than our most basic composition $P \uplus Q$. The separating implication $Q \twoheadrightarrow R$ turns out to correspond to $R/_\otimes Q$ (and also $R\backslash_\otimes Q$ for symmetry). For example, the properties $(Edge \uplus True)$ and $(Edge \otimes True)$ are not equivalent. The former allows any non-empty graph (with at least one edge), while the latter allows any graph that contains at least one vertex from which there is only one edge. Separation Logic does not generate the singleton graph property for a graph $Edge(u, a, v) \uplus Edge(u, b, w)$ with only two edges from the same entry vertex u. Replacing $\uplus$ with $\otimes$ would result in false.

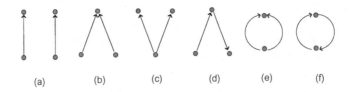

Fig. 3. Topological structures of two arbitrary acyclic edges

4   Unique Decomposition

Sometimes, the decomposition of a pointer graph is unique. For example, for any given pointer graph, we can decompose it into two parts: one part that is reachable from a given vertex v and another part that is not. Such a decomposition is always unique, if we separate edges so that the reachable edges do not lead to the entries of the unreachable edges.

Definition 8. *A binary property* r *is a unique decomposition, if for any pointer graph* G, *there exist pointer graphs* $G_1, G_2 \in \Pi(S)$ *such that* $\lceil G_1 \rceil$ r $\lceil G_2 \rceil =$ $\lceil G \rceil$, *and for any* $G'_1, G'_2 \in \Pi(S)$ *such that* $\lceil G'_1 \rceil$ r $\lceil G'_2 \rceil = \lceil G \rceil$, *we have* $G_1 = G'_1$ *and* $G_2 = G'_2$.

For example, for any pointer graph G, the binary property $\langle \lceil G \rceil, \uplus, True \rangle$ is a unique decomposition, since the choice on the left-hand side is unique. A related notion is that of "precise predicate" [9] for distributivity of conjunction when one side is fixed like the above example. This is only sufficient but not necessary to guarantee unique decompostionality. More interesting examples of unique composition will be discussed in the next section. The following theorem characterises the above notion algebraically.

Theorem 2. *A binary property* r *is a unique decomposition iff, for any pointer graphs* $P_1, P_2, Q_1, Q_2 \in \Pi(S)$, *we have*

$$(P_1 \wedge P_2) \; r \; (Q_1 \wedge Q_2) \; = \; (P_1 \; r \; Q_1) \wedge (P_2 \; r \; Q_2).$$

Proof. This is essentially the equivalence between (relational) determinism of the combined choices on both sides and distributivity of the combinator over conjunction. □

Corollary 3. *If* r *is a unique decomposition, so are*

1. *the converse of* r,
2. *and any binary property* r' *such that* $r' \Rightarrow r$.

5   Derived Abstract Properties

We are now ready to define interesting abstract properties. We use $P{\uparrow} = P \uplus$ *True* to denote arbitrary extension with edges.

5.1   Cones

The following table lists some properties for cone-shaped pointer graphs (i.e. arbitrarily many edges from or to a vertex):

$From(v) \ \widehat{=} \ EdgeFrom(v) \ \triangledown \ True$	edges from v
$To(u) \ \widehat{=} \ EdgeTo(u) \ \triangle \ True$	edges to v
$AtLeastTo(V) \ \widehat{=} \ \forall v \in V \cdot To(v)\!\uparrow$	at least to vertices
$OnlyTo(V) \ \widehat{=} \ \forall v \cdot (To(v)\!\uparrow \ \Rightarrow \ v \in V)$	only to vertices
$ExactlyTo(V) \ \widehat{=} \ AtLeastTo(V) \wedge OnlyTo(V)$	exactly to vertices
$AtLeastFrom(V) \ \widehat{=} \ \forall v \in V \cdot From(v)\!\uparrow$	at least from vertices
$OnlyFrom(V) \ \widehat{=} \ \forall v \cdot (From(v)\!\uparrow \ \Rightarrow \ v \in V)$	only from vertices
$ExactlyFrom(V) \ \widehat{=} \ AtLeastFrom(V) \wedge OnlyFrom(V)$	exactly from vertices.

Theorem 4. *The following binary properties form unique decompositions:*

1. $\langle From(v), \oslash, True \rangle$
2. $\langle To(v), \oslash, True \rangle$.

Note that $\langle From(v), \uplus, True \rangle$ is not a unique decomposition as arbitrary edges from v may be added; neither is $\langle To(v), \uplus, True \rangle$ for a similar reason.

5.2   Cycles, Deadends and Constancy

The following table lists some properties about cycles, deadends and constancy:

$CycEdges \ \widehat{=} \ \exists v \cdot (From(v) \wedge To(v))$	cyclic edges on a vertex
$Cycles \ \widehat{=} \ \neg (AcycEdge \otimes True) \wedge$	every edge in some cycle
$\qquad \neg (AcycEdge \oslash True)$	
$Rooted \ \widehat{=} \ \neg \, To(\epsilon)\!\uparrow$	root vertex as a deadhead
$IsolatedEdges \ \widehat{=} \ \neg \exists v \cdot (To(v)\!\uparrow \wedge From(v)\!\uparrow)$	only deadends and deadheads
$ConstIsDeadend \ \widehat{=} \ True \ \dashv \ AtLeastTo(C)$	any constant is a deadend
$DeadendIsConst \ \widehat{=} \ True \ \dashv \ OnlyTo(C)$	any deadend is a constant
$Const \ \widehat{=} \ True \ \dashv \ ExactlyTo(C)$	constants as only deadends.

where $\dashv \ \widehat{=} \ \langle True, \oslash\triangleright, IsolatedEdges \rangle$. Obviously we have $CycEdge \Rightarrow Cyc\text{-}Edges$ and $CycEdges \Rightarrow Cycles$.

We can always decompose a pointer graph into a part with all the deadends and a part that reaches into the deadend part (and hence not containing any deadend):

Theorem 5. *The binary property $\dashv$ is a unique decomposition.*

For example, a program state requires all constants to be deadends and to be the only deadends.

5.3   Finiteness

The following table defines the property for finiteness:

$Finite(o) \cong Empty$	empty graph
$Finite(n+1) \cong Edge \uplus Finite(n)$	graph with n edges
$Finite \cong \exists n \in \mathbb{N} \cdot Finite(n)$	finite graph.

Finiteness satisfies the following laws:

Law 4.   (1) $Empty \Rightarrow Finite$
(2) $(Edge \uplus Finite) \Rightarrow Finite$
(3) $Finite = Finite \uplus Finite$
(4) $(Finite\ r\ Finite) \Rightarrow Finite$.

5.4   Paths

The following table lists some properties of paths where $w = a_0.a_1. \cdots .a_n$:

$Path(v, w, u) \cong Edge(v, a_o, v_1) \uplus Edge(v_n, a_n, v)$	a path w from v to u
$\quad \uplus\ \biguplus_{i=1}^{n-1} Edge(v_i, a_i, v_{i+1})$	
$Path(v, u) \cong \exists w \cdot Path(v, w, u)$	a path from v to u
$PathFrom(v) \cong \exists u \cdot Path(v, u)$	a path from v
$PathTo(u) \cong \exists v \cdot Path(v, u)$	a path to u
$Cycle \cong \exists v \cdot Path(v, v)$	a cycle
$Acyc \cong \neg(Cycle \uplus True)$	acyclic graph.

For example, The property $PathFrom(v) \oslash PathFrom(v)$ describes two non-overlapping paths from v. The above definitions correspond to their graph-theoretic definitions directly. They also have constructive definitions as recursion, which alternatively becomes the following laws.

Law 5.   (1) $Path(v, (w_1.w_2), u) = Path(v, w_1, w) \oslash Path(w, w_2, u)$
(2) $Path(v, a, u) = Edge(v, a, u)$

The following theorem holds because the exit is unique for any label, and hence the middle vertices visited by a path are determined in a pointer graph.

Theorem 6. *The binary property* $\langle Path(v, w, u), \uplus, True \rangle$ *is a unique decomposition.*

We have $Cycle \Rightarrow Cycles$. $Acyc$ is the least fixpoint of equations Law 6(3)(4), i.e. the least fixpoint in the complete lattice ordered by implication with $False$ as the bottom.

Law 6.   (1) $Acyc = Acyc \oslash Acyc$
(2) $Acyc = Acyc \dashv True$
(3) $Acyc = Empty \vee (AcycEdge \oslash Acyc)$
(4) $Acyc = Empty \vee AcycEdge \vee (Acyc \oslash Acyc)$

The two recursive definitions actually suggest different ways of checking acyclicity: by recursively removing acyclic edges or by decomposing a graph in two with only one-directional links between them.

The separation of an explicit path is unique, reflecting the determinism of the edges in pointer graphs. Decomposing a pointer graph into an acyclic part and a part with only cycles is unique, if the interaction between the two parts is one-directional:

Theorem 7. *The following binary properties form unique decompositions:*

1. $\langle Acyc, \oslash, Cycles \rangle$
2. $\langle Acyc, \ominus, Cycles \rangle$.

Some common acyclic pointer structures can be defined recursively. For example, a list of values (either pointers or constants) can be defined as a (unique) fixpoint:

Definition 9.
$$List(v, [u]^\wedge \alpha) \;\hat{=}\; \exists w \cdot ((Edge(v, \mathtt{data}, u) \uplus Edge(v, \mathtt{next}, w)) \oslash List(w, \alpha))$$
$$List(v, []) \;\hat{=}\; (v = \mathtt{nil}).$$

Note that a list only contains edges labelled as $\mathtt{next}$ or $\mathtt{data}$. The composition $(List(v, \alpha) \oslash True)$ extends the list with new vertices, but it differs from $(List(v, \alpha) \uplus True)$, which allows arbitrary additional edges from the list nodes. A list is acyclic and hence has the unique decompositionality property according to Theorem 7:

Law 7. (1) $IsolatedEdges \Rightarrow Acyc$ (2) $List(v, \alpha) \Rightarrow Acyc$.

5.5   Reachability

The following table lists some properties of path reachability:

$ReachableFrom(v) \;\hat{=}\; \forall u \neq v \cdot (From(u){\uparrow} \;\Rightarrow\; Path(v, u){\uparrow})$
$ReachableFromEdge(v, a) \;\hat{=}\; Empty \vee \exists u \cdot (Edge(v, a, u) \uplus ReachableFrom(u))$.

$ReachableFrom(v)$ is the least fixpoint of the following equation:

Law 8. $ReachableFrom(v) \;=\; Empty \vee From(v) \vee (ReachableFrom(v) \triangleright True)$.

The following table introduces some important binary properties. They will be used for the decomposition of program state in assertion-based reasoning.

$\oslash_v \;\hat{=}\; \langle \neg\, From(v){\uparrow}, \oslash, ReachableFrom(v) \rangle$	reachability dominated decomposition
$\ominus_v \;\hat{=}\; \langle \neg\, From(v){\uparrow}, \ominus, ReachableFrom(v) \rangle$	non-reachability dominated decomposition
$\oslash_{v,a} \;\hat{=}\; \langle \neg\, From(v){\uparrow}, \oslash, ReachableFromEdge(v, a) \rangle$	edge reachability dominated decomposition
$\ominus_{v,a} \;\hat{=}\; \langle \neg\, From(v){\uparrow}, \ominus, ReachableFromEdge(v, a) \rangle$	non-edge reachability dominated decomposition

The separation of a part reachable from a given vertex or a given edge is unique, if the rest of the pointer graph is not accessible from the reachable part.

Theorem 8. *The binary properties* $\ominus_v, \ominus_v, \ominus_{v,a}, \ominus_{v,a}$ *form unique decompositions.*

Thus the binary property $\ominus_\epsilon$ is a unique decomposition. That means the separation is unique between the non-garbage part reachable from the root and the garbage not reachable from the non-garbage part.

The following laws identify some properties which distribute the above unique decompositions:

Law 9. (1) $Acyc = Acyc \; r \; Acyc$
          (2) $Finite = Finite \; r \; Finite$
          (3) $Edge(v,a,u){\uparrow} = True \; r \; Edge(v,a,u){\uparrow}$
          (4) $DeadendIsConst = DeadendIsConst \; r \; DeadendIsConst$
where $r = \ominus_v, \ominus_v, \ominus_{v,a}, \ominus_{v,a}$.

5.6 Canonicity

The following table lists some properties related to canonicity:

$$
\begin{aligned}
MinPath(v,w,u) &\mathrel{\hat{=}} Path(v,w,u){\uparrow} \wedge \\
&\quad \forall w' \cdot (Path(v,w',u){\uparrow} \Rightarrow w \sqsubseteq w') \\
Canonical &\mathrel{\hat{=}} \forall vu \cdot (EdgeFromTo(v,u){\uparrow} \Rightarrow \\
&\quad MinPath(\epsilon,v,v) \wedge MinPath(\epsilon,u,u)) \\
State &\mathrel{\hat{=}} Canonical \wedge Rooted \wedge Const.
\end{aligned}
$$

Any vertex of a canonical pointer graph is reachable from the root. The abstract property allows exactly all the canonical graphs and is the least fixpoint of the equation in Law 10(2). The recursion suggests a method of checking canonicity by removing vertices one after another. The removed vertex (as a sequence) is always the minimum path to the vertex and no other vertex is represented as a smaller sequence. Such a choice of removal never changes the minimum-path representation of other vertices in a canonical graph and always leaves a smaller canonical pointer graph and can be repeated until the graph is emptied. *State* is the property of all states of an OO program (with automatic garbage collection).

Law 10. (1) $Canonical \Rightarrow ReachableFrom(\epsilon)$
           (2) $Canonical = Empty \vee$
                      $\exists v \cdot \; MinPath(\epsilon,v,v)$
                             $\wedge \; \forall u \cdot EdgeTo(u){\uparrow} \Rightarrow u \sqsubseteq v$
                             $\wedge \; (Canonical \oslash To(v)) \oslash From(v)$

6   Reasoning with Hoare Logic

In this section we begin the programme apparently hoped for in [7] of using the canonical model to provide sound laws of Hoare logic for reasoning about programs involving pointers. We exploit the properties defined in the current paper to provide Hoare-logical rules for reasoning about pointer swing.

6.1   Relating Assertions at Different Locations of a Program

The standard technique to link two assertions is to introduce an arbitrary constant: **con** c ⨾ $\{P\}$ **code** $\{Q\}$. The annotation is valid if for any arbitrary constant, the inner annotation $\{P\}$ **code** $\{Q\}$ is valid.

Separation Logic [15] explicitly identifies the pointers as integers. When linking two assertions at different locations of a program, the corresponding pointers must be the same integer. However the naming of the pointers (i.e. the addresses or vertices in a pointer graph) is irrelevant to the external behaviour of a program as long as the pointer graphs in new states of the program are (partly) isomorphic to the original state. In practice, the operating system may move memory blocks during the execution of a program without affecting its behaviour. The model of Separation Logic is not fully abstract on the renaming of vertices.

Some properties, however, are insensitive under such renaming. For example, if the property $Acyc$ is true for a part of the state before a program and the part is not modified by the code, then we can expect $Acyc$ to be true in the state after the program.

In general, if a property does not mention vertices as explicit parameters, it is insensitive under renaming. We use a function to capture such insensitivity by estimating the set of the free *vertex parameters* in a property. Note that we assume every program state to be a canonical pointer graph. The set C is the set of constants in every such graph. The set ϕP estimates the free parameters occurring in a property P.

Definition 10. $\phi P_0 = \mathrm{FP}(P_0) \setminus C$
$\phi True = \{\,\}$
$\phi Edge(v, a, u) = \{v, u\} \setminus C$
$\phi \neg P = \phi P$
$\phi(P \wedge Q) \subseteq (\phi P \cup \phi Q)$
$\phi(\exists v \cdot P) = \phi P \setminus \{v\}$
$\phi(P \; r \; Q) \subseteq \phi P \cup \phi Q$

If a property P has no free vertex parameters i.e. $\phi P = \{\,\}$, then it is insensitive to isomorphic renaming of the vertices. For example, ϕP_0 returns all non-constant free parameters of a constant property, $\phi Acyc = \{\,\}$ but $\phi(v = u) = \{v, u\}$. Note that the above definition is semi-syntactical. For example, it allows us to calculate $\phi(P \wedge \neg P)$ as $\{\,\}$ instead of ϕP. Explicit parameters for labels and paths are not counted. For example, $\phi Path(v, w, u) = \{v, u\}$. Constants are not free vertex parameters as they remain unchanged in our canonical model.

Vertex parameters must not be left free in assertions. When vertices are needed in reasoning, they can be identified through path navigation. We now introduce a notation $\partial v{:}w \cdot P$ to turn a vertex parameter v in P to a path parameter w denoting path reachability from the root to the vertex:

Definition 11. $\partial v{:}w \cdot P \;\; \widehat{=} \;\; \exists v \cdot (Path(\epsilon, w, v)\!\uparrow \,\wedge\, P)$.

The following laws can be used for reasoning about it:

Law 11. (1) $\partial v{:}w \cdot P \,\vee\, \partial v{:}w \cdot Q \;\;=\;\; \partial v{:}w \cdot (P \vee Q)$
         (2) $\partial v{:}w \cdot P \,\wedge\, \partial v{:}w \cdot Q \;\;=\;\; \partial v{:}w \cdot (P \wedge Q)$
         (3) $\partial v{:}w \cdot P \,\wedge\, \partial u{:}w \cdot Q \;\;=\;\; \partial v{:}w\, \partial u{:}w \cdot (v = u \,\wedge\, P \wedge Q)$
         (4) $\partial v{:}w \cdot P \;\;=\;\; \partial v{:}w \cdot P[u/v] \quad (u \notin \phi P)$.

We have $\phi\,(\partial v{:}w \cdot P) \,=\, \phi P \setminus \{v\}$. Law 11(2) holds because, in any pointer graph, the vertex reachable through a specific path is unique.

6.2   A General Rule for Pointer Swing

The behaviour of pointer programs can be characterised as Hoare-logical rules. Note that every assertion P must satisfy $\phi P = \{\,\}$ for insensitivity with respect to renaming of vertices.

    The effect of an assignment statement on the program state is complicated. We start from the most general and accurate rule and then try to identify its less accurate but simpler approximations. For example, a typical assignment in OO languages is $(\texttt{this.x} := \texttt{this.x.a})$ where $\texttt{this}$ points to the current object whose address may vary at runtime. Such manipulation of nested environments is common in OO. If this is represented in the model of Separation Logic, the variable $\texttt{this}$ will be located in the store, while the actual assignment happens in the heap. The separation between the store and the heap is convenient for C-style imperative pointer programming but has not made OO pointer assignments any simpler. Canonical models do not make such a distinction.

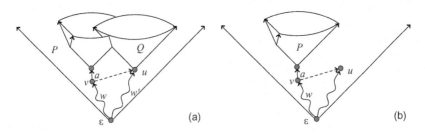

Fig. 4. Pointer swing $w.a := w'$ (accurate and simplified decompositions)

    In general, a pointer assignment has the form: $(w.a := w')$ where w and w' are navigation paths, i.e. sequences of attribute labels. This statement assigns the attribute a of an object stored at program variable w to a value stored at program variable w'. Any garbage is automatically disposed. Figure 4(a) illustrates the operation. The entire cone represents the whole canonical pointer graph, which can be (uniquely) decomposed into three parts for consideration: the smaller right-hand cone that represents the reachable part from u, which vertex is reachable from the root through path w'; the left-hand cone denoting the garbage resulting from this pointer swing as the part reachable from the edge (included) from vertex v with label a but not reachable from u or the root without navigating via v; and the rest of the pointer graph. The properties of the first and the third parts in the state before the assignment are preserved, while the second part is automatically disposed of as garbage. A new edge is established from w to w' via a. Caution is required here. In assignments like $w.a := w.a.b$, the original path $w.a.b$ is lost due to the pointer swing. Fortunately, we can still reach the vertex through the new path $w.a$. The following annotation is valid and captures all the changes:

Rule 1. $\{\partial v{:}w\,\partial u{:}w' \cdot ((P \otimes_{v,a} True) \otimes_u Q)\}$

$\qquad w.a := w'$

$\qquad \{\partial v{:}w\,\partial u{:}(w.a) \cdot ((P \otimes_{v,a} Edge(v,a,u)) \otimes_u Q)\}$

Note that we can strengthen the precondition by replacing $True$ with another property R, which will be ignored in the postcondition for automatic garbage collection. That is equivalent to the strengethening of the precondition in the above annotation for monotonicity.

6.3   Frame Rule of Separation Logic Implied

Rule 1 can be simplified if we do not consider so accurately the result on the right-hand side of the assignment. This may be the result when the value of the right-hand expression is unknown in static analysis. In Figure 4(b), the pointer graph is (uniquely) decomposed into the part of *potential* garbage in the smaller cone, which is reachable from the edge with label a from vertex v but not reachable from the root if not via v and the rest of the pointer graph that satisfies the property P. If an edge can be reached from the root not via v, the edge must not be garbage; on the other hand if it is only reachable from v, whether it is garbage depends on the whether the pointer is changed to somewhere reaching it. In short, as the exact location of the new pointer is ignored in this simplified decomposition, we simply treat the small cone as potential garbage as a whole and obtain the following simplified rule:

Rule 2. $\{\partial v{:}w \cdot (P \otimes_{v,a} True)\}$

$\qquad w.a := exp$

$\qquad \{\partial v{:}w\,\partial u{:}exp \cdot (P \otimes_{v,a} Edge(v,a,u)\!\uparrow)\}$

where exp is an expression and the potential garbage is turned into the arbitrary extension of the new edge $Edge(v,a,u)$. It is an arbitrary extension because some part of the potential garbage might be preserved after the assignment.

The above annotation can be further simplified if we ignore the formation of the new edge (i.e. functionality of code):

Rule 3. $\{\partial v{:}w \cdot (P \otimes_{v,a} True)\}$ **code**$(w.a)$ $\{\partial v{:}w \cdot (P \otimes_{v,a} True)\}$.

where **code**$(w.a)$ is a (terminating) program that only modifies the variable $w.a$. The rule allowing the modification of multiple variables has a similar form.

Let $w = \epsilon$. We then obtain a simpler rule for pointer swing adjacent to the root vertex (corresponding to modification of global variables):

Rule 4. $\{P \otimes_{\epsilon,a} True\}$ **code**(a) $\{P \otimes_{\epsilon,a} True\}$.

Note that the empty path can reach only the root in a canonical pointer graph. If we have shown, with some other rules, that $\{Q\}$ **code**(a) $\{R\}$, then we have $\{Q \wedge (P \otimes_{\epsilon,a} True)\}$ **code**(a) $\{R \wedge (P \otimes_{\epsilon,a} True)\}$. This rule actually corresponds to the frame rule in Separation Logic. Note that the program state is rooted. The unique decomposition ensures that the conjunction of two assertions will pair the corresponding properties for the same part of the pointer graph (see Theorem 8), which has a function similar to the separating conjunction in the frame rule.

7   Example: Searching a Constant in an Acyclic Sub-graph

We consider a simple pointer algorithm under the presence of automatic garbage collection. The purpose of this case study is to demonstrate the compositional reasoning methods at work.

Let this be the variable pointing to the current value (either an object or a constant) in an OO program. As a precondition, the attribute x of the object stores an acyclic sub-graph whose deadends are some constants. The requirement is to find one of the constants in the sub-graph. The nondeterministic algorithm is very simple: if the current value is an object then we choose an attribute and follow the link and repeat the process; if the current value is a constant then the iteration stops:

> **con** $D : \{\,\} \subset D \subseteq C$ ⦂
>
> $\{\partial v{:}\text{this.x} \cdot True \otimes_v (Acyc \dashv ExactlyTo(D \backslash \{v\}))\}$
>
> **do** $[]_{a \in A}$ **exist**$(\text{this.x}.a) \to \text{this.x} := \text{this.x}.a$ **od**
>
> $\{\partial v{:}\text{this.x} \cdot v \in D\}$.

When the pointer this.x moves ahead, cells left behind may be garbage-collected automatically. Note that the above program manipulates pointers entirely within the current object and does not use any temporary global variable immediately associated with the root to point to the sub-graph. In general, relying on global pointer variables is unrealistic in OO programming, because methods may be invoked recursively. That means in the model of Separation Logic, the reasoning for an OO program involves as complicated heap decomposition as that in canonical models. The divide between store and heap does not simplify the reasoning for OO programs in general, as the frame rule cannot be applied for similar partitioning in the heap.

In the precondition of the above program, the set D (introduced as a constant variable in Hoare Logic) is a *non-empty* set of constants. The pre and post conditions are linked via D. The precondition assumes that the reachable part from the vertex at the end of path this.x is acyclic, and either contains constant deadends or is empty when v must be a constant itself such that $D = \{v\}$. The postcondition guarantees to point this.x at one of the constants in D. To reason about the correctness of the above program, we introduce a loop invariant:

$$Inv \; \widehat{=} \; \partial v\text{:this.x} \cdot (True \; \otimes_v \; (Acyc \; \dashv \; \exists E : \{\} \subset E \subseteq D \cdot ExactlyTo(E \backslash \{v\}))).$$

The invariant states that there exists a non-empty subset E of D, the part reachable from the vertex at the end of path this.x is acyclic, and either contains constant deadends or is empty when v must be a constant itself such that $\{v\} = E \subseteq D$. The whole annotation is as follows:

> **con** $D : \{\} \subset D \subseteq C \, \mathring{,}$
>
> $\{ \partial v\text{:this.x} \cdot \; True \; \otimes_v \; (Acyc \; \dashv \; ExactlyTo(D \backslash \{v\})) \}$
>
> $\{ Inv \}$
>
> **do**
>
> $\quad [\![ ]\!]_{a \in A} \; \textbf{exist}(\text{this.x}.a) \; \rightarrow$
>
> $\qquad \{ Inv \wedge \partial v\text{:}(\text{this.x}) \cdot EdgeFromVia(v, a) \!\uparrow \}$
>
> $\qquad \text{this.x} \; := \; \text{this.x}.a \, \mathring{,}$
>
> $\qquad \{ Inv \}$
>
> **od**
>
> $\{ Inv \wedge \partial v\text{:this.x} \cdot (True \; \otimes_v \; Empty)) \}$
>
> $\{ \partial v\text{:this.x} \cdot \; v \in D \}.$

In the above annotation, $EdgeFromVia(v, a) \!\uparrow$ checks the existence of an attribute a from the vertex v. If no such edge exits for any label, the vertex v must be a deadend, and hence the reachable part from v must be empty, and this forces v to be one of the constants in D according to the loop invariant. The loop must terminate as the size of the reachable part is strictly reduced because of acyclicity and finiteness.

Figure 5 illustrate the function of the body of the loop. The outmost cone represents the whole canonical pointer graph reachable from ϵ; the middle-sized cone represents the garbage reachable from v (a vertex reachable through path this.x) but not reachable from either ϵ or u (a vertex initially reachable through path this.x.a) without going via v; the smallest cone is the part reachable from u, which becomes the new location of this.x. Eventually the smallest cone will become empty, and v becomes one of the constants in D. Rule 1 is used for the safety of the assignment statement as the target area of pointer swing must be preserved and not treated as garbage.

In the annotation, the property for the non-reachable part from v is $True$. In fact, it can be any property, as the program modifies only this.x. According to Rule 3, we have

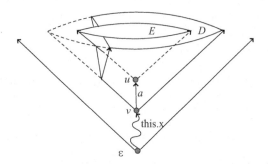

Fig. 5. Pointer swing along the edge a from v

$$\{\partial v\text{:this.x}\cdot(P \ominus_{v,a} True)\}   \textbf{code}(\text{this.x})   \{\partial v\text{:this.x}\cdot(P \ominus_{v,a} True)\},$$

where **code**(this.x) is the searching program that only modifies this.x. The safety rule can be conjoined with the annotation for the program with properties paired according to the unique decomposition. The effect is the same as replacing *True* with P in the program annotation, just as the frame rule does in Separation Logic. Remember that constant property $v \in D$ distributes the decomposition. This explains how unique decomposition achieves the function of the frame rule.

8   Related Work

Separation Logic has been successful in providing (Hoare-logic-style) program annotations [12,15] at the level of abstraction of algorithms operating on data structures consisting of a store and heap. In view of the intricacy of such algorithms, and since software engineers who design and write such algorithms have lacked support for rigorous reasoning, Separation Logic has thus provided a substantial advance. Proof rules for modularised reasoning have been developed: in [11] the vital *frame rule* is given, phrased in terms of the concept of a *precise predicate* that determines which heap cells are accessed (an idea that goes back to [1]). The former has been influential in our Rule 4 for pointer swing and the latter in our concept of unique decomposition (Definition 8 and Theorem 2).

What more might be done so that formal support for reasoning about object-orientated structures draws level with support for reasoning about simpler traditional algorithms expressed in say the guarded-command language? Support must also be provided for the step-wise reasoning about program correctness that allows data representation as well as the algorithm refinement covered by program annotations. For then the assertional method can be used for abstract algorithms whose state is far more general than store-plus-heap, even though that is the form of its ultimate implementation several derivation steps later. Recently a theory of data refinement for the situation in which the invoking program shares store with the module it invokes, has been proposed [9] the interaction between the invoking program's use of space and that of the invoked procedure; for then the resulting notion of refinement is robust against 'allocation-status testing' (i.e. use of memory allocation followed by pointer comparison to tell, though nondeterministically, which cells are used internally by a module).

With such theory in place there is, in principle, nothing to stop us from reasoning about pointer algorithms just as we do for standard algorithms. So what is the reluctance to do so? The only examples we have been able to find are derivational correctness proofs of the Schorr-Waite marking algorithm [17,16]. The reason seems to be that the relevant theory of data refinement has not been complemented by appropriate notation for hierarchical, modularised reasoning. We have seen in this paper the sort of concepts and notations that might be useful, by showing in the example how an algorithm can be verified by annotation at a level of abstraction above that of store-plus-heap. Subsequent steps of data refinement, ending with a pointer program, are by comparison more routine using the techniques of data refinement referred to above.

Another solution to the these limits of Separation Logic has been relational Separation Logic [16]. There a relational calculus has been introduced specifically to support the practice of program derivation, using Hoare quadruples, and shown at work on the Schorr-Waite algorithm. This calculus is strong, due to the strong assumptions it makes concerning the cells that may be accessed by a computation, as indicated by the quadruples' 'pre-relation'. So it seems most useful at the stages of derivation closer to code.

Complementing the direction we have taken is work [14] that provides the predicates appearing in an abstract description with a notion of scope in order to control their access. 'Predicates with scope' move the abstraction into the logical framework, so that the expansion (and contraction) of a predicate definition is controlled by scope. It is hoped that those presented in the present paper and those deriving from Graph Logic [2], enabling Formal Methods to be replayed successfully in the context of OO. But convincing realistic examples are to date lacking.

We have applied the theory to reason about an OO program. From the modelling of program states, we have adopted the approach of the canonical models [7] to achieve full abstraction so that the naming of vertices is unique for pointer structures isomorphic to each other. Subsequent work [13] has simplified that of [7] and we have built upon it here with the minimum-path representation. Note that most techniques of this paper are applicable to either canonical or non-canonical representations.

9 Conclusion

The main technique of this paper has been the general composition of properties over pointer graphs. It has been shown how a binary property can be used as a parameter to combine two unary properties, in such a way that the result satisfies pleasing general laws.

We have also identified nine useful combinators as examples. The separating conjunction (or entry disjointness in our terms) of Separation Logic is one of them and cannot express the other eight combinators. Several combinators may be used together (in conjunction). The necessity of these operators is illustrated in Figure 3 where each topological relationship between two acyclic edges corresponds to the conjunction of specific combinators. The weakest combinator ⊎ clearly behaves differently from entry disjointness. For example, some properties such as general acyclicity (without assumption on the number of attributes in each object) cannot be specified with the entry disjoint combinator, since we sometimes need edge-wise composition instead of vertex-wise composition. This shows the value of our extra combinators over that of Separation Logic.

The combinators of reachability decomposition turn out to be extremely useful in program reasoning: they enable the behaviour of pointer swing to be captured precisely and compositionally using a Hoare triple. Furthermore, garbage can be pinpointed exactly. The rule has simpler but less accurate special cases, one of which is the frame rule in Separation Logic.

The main technical contributions of this paper have been the concept of unique decomposition and the identification of useful candidates for reachability decomposition. The algebraic characterisation of unique decomposition proves to be the key to compositional reasoning in this approach. For example, we have seen that the frame rule in Separation Logic is a consequence of those rules based on the unique decomposition of reachability.

Because the canonical models ignore garbage, the representation we use is most suitable for Java-like languages which support automatic garbage collection. We have followed that route because it is the more challenging one. The integration of program variables and object attributes in one pointer graph is convenient for general OO programming and design, which may involve reasoning for deeply nested environments.

Our solution to linking two canonical states at different locations of a program has been to turn explicit vertex parameters of assertions into path parameters so that every assertion is insensitive to the naming of vertices (important because naming may change dramatically after pointer swing).

We have deliberately chosen to define concepts first and identify their least-fixpoint recursive definitions as laws. This demonstrates that the formalism may be used at different levels of abstraction. The recursive definitions we view as more concrete and closer to actual implementations that check properties.

The choice between algebraic and logical presentations is one of little essence; we have chosen to favour the former and exploit the concept of weak inverse from the theory of Galois connections. The algebraic approach can be axiomatised as can the logical.

Acknowledgement

The authors are grateful for a variety of refereeing comments that helped them to put the contents of the paper in perspective.

References

1. Bornat, R.: Proving pointer programs in Hoare logic. In Backhouse, R. C., Oliveira, J. N., eds.: Proc. of 5th Int. Conf. of Mathematics of Program Construction, MPC '00, Vol. 1837 of Lect. Notes in Comput. Sci. Springer-Verlag (2000) 102–126

2. Cardelli, L., Gardner, P., and Ghelli, G.: A spatial logic for querying graphs. In Widmayer, P. et al., eds.: Proc. of 29th Int. Coll. on Automata, Languages and Programming, ICALP '02, Vol. 2380 of Lect. Notes in Comput. Sci. Springer-Verlag (2002) 597–610

3. Chen, Y.: Generic composition. Formal Aspects of Computing **14**(2) (2002) 108–122

4. Harel, D.: Dynamic logic. In Gabbay, D., Guenthner, F., eds.: Handbook of Philosophical Logic, Vol. II: Extensions of Classical Logic. D. Reidel Publ. Co. (1984) 497–604

5. Hoare, C. A. R.: Communicating Sequential Processes. Prentice Hall (1985)

6. He, J., Hoare, C. A. R.: Unifying Theories of Programming Prentice Hall (1998)

7. He, J., Hoare, C. A. R.: A trace model for pointers and objects. In Guerraoui, R., ed.: Proc. of 13th Europ. Conf. on Object-Oriented Programming, ECOOP '99, Vol. 1628 of Lect. Notes in Comput. Sci. Springer-Verlag (1999) 1–17

8. Ishtiaq, S. S., O'Hearn, P. W.: BI as an assertion language for mutable data structures. In Conf. Record of 28th ACM SIGPLAN-SIGACT Symp. on Principles of Programming Languages, POPL '01. ACM Press (2001) 14–26

9. Mijajlović, I., Torp-Smith, N., O'Hearn, P. W.: Refinement and separation contexts. In Lodaya, K., Mahajan, M., eds.: Proc. of 24th Int. Conf. on Foundations of Software Technology and Theoretical Computer Science, FSTTCS 2004, Vol. 3328 of Lect. Notes in Comput. Sci. Springer-Verlag (2004) 421–433

10. Milner, R.: Communication and Concurrency. Prentice Hall (1989)

11. O'Hearn, P. W., Reynolds, J. C., Yang, H.: Local reasoning about programs that alter data structures. In Fribourg, L., ed.: Proc. of 15th Int. Wksh. on Computer Science Logic, CSL 2001, Vol. 2142 of Lect. Notes in Comput. Sci. Springer-Verlag (2001) 1–19

12. O'Hearn, P. W., Reynolds, J. C., Yang, H.: Separation and information hiding. In Proc. of 31st ACM SIGPLAN-SIGACT Symp. on Principles of Programming Languages, POPL 2004. ACM Press (2004) 268–280

13. Paige, R. F., Ostroff, J. S.: ERC—an object-oriented refinement calculus for Eiffel. Formal Aspects of Computing **16**(1) (2004) 51–79

14. Parkinson, M., Bierman, G.: Separation logic and abstraction. In Proc. of 32nd ACM SIGPLAN-SIGACT Symp. on Principles of Programming Languages, POPL '05. ACM Press (2005) 259–270

15. Reynolds, J. C.: Separation logic: a logic for shared mutable data structures. In: Proc. of 17th IEEE Symp. on Logic in Computer Science, LICS '02. IEEE Comput. Soc. Press (2002) 55–74

16. Yang, H.: Relational separation logic. Submitted to Theor. Comput. Sci.

17. Yang, H.: Verification of the Schorr–Waite graph marking algorithm by refinement. Workshop presentation (2003)

Progress in Deriving Concurrent Programs: Emphasizing the Role of Stable Guards

Brijesh Dongol[1] and Arjan J. Mooij[2,*]

[1] School of Information Technology and Electrical Engineering,
The University of Queensland, Brisbane, Qld. 4072, Australia
brijesh@itee.uq.edu.au

[2] Dept. of Mathematics and Computer Science, Technische Universiteit Eindhoven,
Postbus 513, NL-5600 MB Eindhoven, The Netherlands
A.J.Mooij@tue.nl

Abstract. We present some techniques to obtain smooth derivations of concurrent programs that address both safety and progress in a formal manner. Our techniques form an extension to the calculational method of Feijen and van Gasteren using a UNITY style progress logic. We stress the role of stable guards, and we illustrate the derivation techniques on some examples in which progress plays an essential role.

1 Introduction

In [1], Feijen and van Gasteren describe an elegant programming method for the notoriously hard task of constructing concurrent programs. It is based on the calculational method of sequential program derivation from Dijkstra [2] and the axiomatic theory of Owicki and Gries [3]. The method starts with a specification that includes an abstract program, called the computation proper, and a formalization of the synchronization requirements. By repeatedly adjusting the program, the requirements are established.

Like the theory in [3], the method in [1] does not address progress. As a consequence the derivations emphasize safety, while progress is postponed and addressed in an ad-hoc manner. However, as progress often plays an important role in concurrent programs, proper derivations need to consider it at an early stage. Thereto, Dongol and Goldson [4] provided an extension to the theory in [3], integrating it with the progress logic of Chandy and Misra [5] as described in their UNITY formalism.

In the current work, we explore whether the logic in [4] can be integrated nicely with the method in [1] such that safety and progress are considered equally in derivations. As the logic allows proofs via algebraic manipulation, we head for a calculational style of derivation. The challenge is to be formal and precise, while keeping the complexity of the derivations low. The approach we have taken is to consider some elementary programs, in a search for techniques and heuristics necessary for smooth derivations.

* This author is supported by the NWO under project 016.023.015 "Improving the Quality of Protocol Standards".

In particular, we evaluate how the techniques from [1] affect progress, and we develop a number of lemmas, heuristics and theorems to aid derivations. We also emphasize the role of stable guards in the construction of programs by rephrasing the usual informal definition of individual progress. To experiment with these techniques, we discuss the derivation of two elementary programs in which progress plays an essential role.

Other attempts at progress-based derivations do exist. Apart from a progress logic, Chandy and Misra [5] also present derivations of concurrent programs. With their method, one performs refinements on the original specification until a level of detail is reached where the UNITY program is 'obvious'. Hence, derivations stay within the realms of specifications until the final step, where the specification is transformed to a UNITY program. However, as each specification consists of a list of invariants and leads-to assertions, it is hard to judge the overall structure of the program. Furthermore, it is difficult to decide when there is enough detail in the specification to translate it to a program.

To illustrate the progress logic, Dongol and Goldson [4, 6] started to integrate progress with program derivation, but the presented techniques are undeveloped. A clear methodology is not provided, and the derivations are quite complex and seem to contain arbitrary design decisions.

Overview. In Section 2 we present the necessary background, which includes the logics of safety and progress, and an overview of the method of [1]. Then in Section 3 we present our extensions, which address both progress calculations and program derivations. We present example derivations of an initialization protocol in Section 4 and a mutual exclusion algorithm in Section 5. Finally in Section 6 we conclude this work.

2 Preliminaries

In this section, we summarize various basic theories as far as we use them in the rest of this work. We describe the programming language used and its semantics in Section 2.1, the safety logic in Section 2.2, and the progress logic in Section 2.3. Then, we discuss stability in Section 2.4 and overview safety-based derivations in Section 2.5. In Section 2.6 we describe a technique for avoiding total deadlock.

2.1 Syntax and Semantics

A concurrent program consists of a number of sequential programs, which are called its components, to be executed in parallel by interleaving the atomic statements of the components. We adopt a weakly fair scheduling regime so that in the interleaving, no component is neglected forever. The location between two subsequent atomic statements in a component is referred to as a *control point*. We consider components that communicate via shared variables.

The programming language we use to define each component is based on Dijkstra's Guarded Command Language [2], where statements take the following form:

$$skip \mid x := E \mid \langle S \rangle \mid S_1; S_2 \mid \textbf{if } B_1 \rightarrow S_1 \ [] \ B_2 \rightarrow S_2 \textbf{ fi} \mid \textbf{do } B \rightarrow S \textbf{ od}$$

We refer to skip statements, assignments and guard evaluations as *elementary* statements. In concurrent programs, the **if** statement blocks whenever both B_1 and B_2 evaluate to *false*, and hence it is important for synchronization. In addition, $*[\ S\ ]$ is used as an abbreviation of **do** *true* $\rightarrow S$ **od**.

To use the progress logic of [4], each control point is assigned a label that is unique within the component. We use X_i to refer to the control point with label i in component X, or to the atomic statement at this control point; the particular meaning will be clear from the context. The elementary statements and statement $\langle S \rangle$ are assumed to be atomic, and hence statements are labelled as follows:

$$i: \ skip \ j: \ \mid \ i: \ x := E \ j: \ \mid \ i: \ \langle S \rangle \ j: \ \mid \ i: \ S_1; j: \ S_2 \ k: \ \mid$$
$$i: \textbf{ if } B_1 \rightarrow j_1: \ S_1 \ [] \ B_2 \rightarrow j_2: \ S_2 \textbf{ fi } k: \ \mid \ i: \textbf{ do } B \rightarrow j: S \textbf{ od } k:$$

The non-elementary statements can be decomposed as follows. A coarse-grained atomic statement $i: \ \langle S \rangle \ j:$ consists of an atomic execution of S, eliminating all control points within S. A sequential composition $i: \ S_1; \ j: \ S_2 \ k:$ consists of the two statements $i: \ S_1 \ j:$ and $j: \ S_2 \ k:$. A selection statement $i: \textbf{ if } B_1 \rightarrow j_1: \ S_1 \ [] \ B_2 \rightarrow j_2: \ S_2 \textbf{ fi } k:$ consists of:

1. atomic guard evaluation $i: \ (B_1 \rightarrow j_1: \ [] \ B_2 \rightarrow j_2:)$, where a non-deterministic choice between B_1 and B_2 is made if both guards hold, and
2. statements $j_1: \ S_1 \ k:$ and $j_2: \ S_2 \ k:$

A repetition $i: \textbf{ do } B \rightarrow j: \ S \textbf{ od } k:$ consists of:

1. atomic guard evaluation $i: \ (B \rightarrow j: \ [] \ \neg B \rightarrow k:)$, and
2. statement $j: \ S \ i:$

For each component X, an auxiliary variable pc_X is introduced to model the program counter of component X. Variable pc_X is updated implicitly by each atomic statement to reflect the change in the control state. Auxiliary variables are used as a proof aid, and they may not influence the flow of control.

Control points are annotated with a series of assertions, i.e., predicates on the state of the system. An assertion P at control point X_i is equivalent to a condition $[\ pc_X = i \Rightarrow P\ ]$, where notation $[\ F\ ]$ denotes formula F surrounded by a universal quantifier binding all program variables. At each control point X_i the predicate $pc_X = i$ is implicit. In addition, there is a special predicate *Pre* that describes the initial state of the program, including implicitly that the program counters of the components have their initial value.

Semantics for the labelled elementary statements are provided using both the weakest liberal precondition *wlp* and the weakest precondition *wp* as both partial and total correctness need to be addressed. In the definitions below, we reduce clutter by removing mention of the first label.

Definition 1 (Weakest liberal precondition). *The* weakest liberal precondition (*wlp*) *of a statement S and a predicate P is the weakest predicate that* *needs to hold before executing S, so that each terminating execution of S ends up in a state satisfying P. For the elementary statements it is defined as:*

$$[\ wlp.(skip\ j:).P \qquad\qquad \equiv\ (pc:=j).P\ ]$$
$$[\ wlp.(x:=E\ j:).P \qquad\qquad \equiv\ (x,pc:=E,j).P\ ]$$
$$[\ wlp.(B_1 \rightarrow j_1: [\!] \ B_2 \rightarrow j_2:).P \equiv\ (B_1 \Rightarrow (pc:=j_1).P)\ \wedge$$
$$(B_2 \Rightarrow (pc:=j_2).P)\ ]$$

Definition 2 (Weakest precondition). *The* weakest precondition *(wp) of a statement S and a predicate P is the weakest predicate that needs to hold before executing S, so that S is guaranteed to terminate in a state satisfying P. For the elementary statements it is defined as:*

$$[\ wp.(skip\ j:).P \qquad\qquad \equiv\ (pc:=j).P\ ]$$
$$[\ wp.(x:=E\ j:).P \qquad\qquad \equiv\ (x,pc:=E,j).P\ ]$$
$$[\ wp.(B_1 \rightarrow j_1: [\!] \ B_2 \rightarrow j_2:).P \equiv\ (B_1 \Rightarrow (pc:=j_1).P)\ \wedge$$
$$(B_2 \Rightarrow (pc:=j_2).P)\ \wedge\ (B_1 \vee B_2)\ ]$$

Note that for each statement X_i we have $[\ wlp.X_i.(pc_X \neq i)\ ]$. In particular, notice that guard evaluations and the skip statement have the side effect that they update the program counter. For the typical synchronization statement $S \mathrel{\hat{=}} \langle \textbf{if}\ B \rightarrow skip\ \textbf{fi} \rangle$, we have $[\ wlp.(S\ j:).P \equiv B \Rightarrow (pc:=j).P\ ]$ and $[\ wp.(S\ j:).P \equiv B \wedge (pc:=j).P\ ]$.

2.2   Safety

Safety properties are expressed by assertions. To prove their correctness, we use the Owicki/Gries theory [3] using the nomenclature of [1].

Definition 3 (Correct assertion). *An assertion P in a component is* correct *if it is both*

- locally correct, *i.e., it is established in the component:*
  - *if P is an initial assertion in the component: $[\ Pre \Rightarrow P\ ]$ holds;*
  - *if P is preceded by an atomic statement $\{Q\}\ S$, where Q is a pre-assertion of S, then $[\ Q \Rightarrow wlp.S.P\ ]$ holds.*
- globally correct, *i.e., it is maintained by all other components:*
  - *for each atomic statement $\{Q\}\ S$ in any other component, where Q is a pre-assertion of S, then $[\ P \wedge Q \Rightarrow wlp.S.P\ ]$ holds.*

We note that the last condition for local correctness (also in [4]) may not be appropriate for the atomic evaluation of multiple guards. However, since it gives no problems in our study, we only suggest as an alternative the condition $[\ Q \Rightarrow wlp.S.(pc_X = j \Rightarrow P)\ ]$ if P occurs at control point X_j.

2.3   Progress

To prove progress properties of a program, we use the progress logic from [5] as described in [4]. It is based on the **un** relation, which captures the temporal [7] notion of 'unless', which is also known as 'weak until'. Expression P **un** Q denotes that P continues to hold until Q becomes *true*, but it does not guarantee that Q will become *true*.

Definition 4 (Unless). *For predicates P and Q, condition P* **un** *Q holds in an annotated program if*

$$[\ P \wedge \neg Q \wedge U\ \Rightarrow\ wlp.S.(P \vee Q)\ ]$$

holds for all atomic statements {U} S.

Progress conditions are typically expressed using the leads-to relation $\rightsquigarrow$, which is related to temporal logic using $(P \rightsquigarrow Q) \equiv \Box(P \Rightarrow \Diamond Q)$. Expression $P \rightsquigarrow Q$ for a program denotes that whenever an execution of the program reaches a state that satisfies P, each continuation of the execution will eventually reach a state that satisfies Q.

Definition 5 (Leads-to). *For any predicates P and Q, condition $P \rightsquigarrow Q$ holds in an annotated program if $P \rightsquigarrow Q$ can be derived by a finite number of applications of the following rules:*

- Immediate progress rule: $P \rightsquigarrow Q$ *holds in an annotated program whenever P* **un** *Q holds in the program and there exists an atomic statement X_i such that $[\ P \wedge \neg Q\ \Rightarrow\ pc_X = i\ \wedge\ wp.X_i.Q\ ]$ holds.*
- Transitivity rule: $P \rightsquigarrow Q$ *holds if there exists a predicate R such that $P \rightsquigarrow R$ and $R \rightsquigarrow Q$.*
- Disjunction rule: $P \rightsquigarrow Q$ *holds if there exist predicates R.i such that $[\ P \equiv (\exists i:: R.i)\ ]$ and $(\forall i:: R.i \rightsquigarrow Q)$.*

The rule of immediate progress, which is the base rule of progress, consists of two parts. The first part is P **un** Q which requires that each statement in the annotated program either preserves P or establishes Q. To ensure that Q eventually holds, the second part requires that there exists an atomic statement, say X_i, such that $P \wedge \neg Q$ implies that control is at X_i and X_i is guaranteed to terminate and establish Q.

A number of useful lemmas about $\rightsquigarrow$ can be found in [5, 4]. In particular we will use:

Lemma 1 (Properties of $\rightsquigarrow$). *For predicates P and Q, the following hold:*

(Implication) $\quad (P \rightsquigarrow Q)\ \Leftarrow\ [\ P \Rightarrow Q\ ]$

(Induction) $\quad (P \rightsquigarrow Q)\ \Leftarrow\ (\forall m:: P \wedge M = m\ \rightsquigarrow\ (P \wedge M \prec m) \vee Q),$
provided m is a fresh variable and $\prec$ is a well-founded order on the type of M, which is an expression over program variables.

2.4   Stability

A special instance of the **un** relation is P **un** *false*, for any predicate P. It corresponds to the notion that P is stable, i.e., it is maintained by each atomic statement. Note that a stable predicate does not need to be *true* initially.

Definition 6 (Stable). *A predicate P is stable under component X, if for each atomic statement X_i with pre-assertion U, $[\ P \wedge U\ \Rightarrow\ wlp.X_i.P\ ]$ holds. A predicate P is stable in a program, if it is stable under all components.*

In particular, stability of $P \wedge Q$ follows from stability of both P and Q, but not vice versa. The assumption that evaluating a series of guards is a single atomic statement, may be too demanding for an implementation. The following lemma from [1] shows a technique that exploits stability to relieve this assumption.

Lemma 2 (Guard disjunction lemma). *Any program fragment*

$$\textbf{if } B \vee C \rightarrow S \textbf{ fi}$$

in a component can be implemented (without impairing total correctness) as

$$\textbf{if } B \rightarrow S \; [\!] \; C \rightarrow S \textbf{ fi}$$

where the atomicity of guard evaluation is just per single guard, if (at least) one of the disjuncts B or C is stable under all other components.

2.5   Safety Derivations

In this section we summarize the programming method of [1]. Program development starts by expressing the program's specification in terms of a preliminary program and some queried assertions. A queried assertion is an assertion that has not yet been proved correct, and it is marked with a '**?**' before it. The derivation process consists of turning each of these into a correct assertion. When all assertions (which include those from the specification) are correct, the developed program is correct with respect to the specification. There are three main ways to make an assertion correct:

- strengthen the annotation;
- introduce new statements; and
- modify an existing statement.

Introducing a new statement, or modifying an existing one may turn all assertions into queried assertions again. Fortunately, this does not happen upon strengthening the annotation, which means we are freely able to add conjuncts to existing assertions. This occurs often enough that we allow multiple assertions (co-assertions) to be placed at a single control point which denotes their conjunction. Hence, annotations $\{P\}\{Q\}$ and $\{P \wedge Q\}$ are equivalent. An important result in [1] is that correctness of each co-assertion may be proved independently. Introducing a new assertion maintains correctness of previous assertions, and typically the weakest possible strengthening that serves the goal is calculated.

2.6   Avoiding Total Deadlock

In [8] a technique to guarantee the absence of total deadlock is described (see also [9]). In a setting with program counters, it can be reformulated as follows. To establish a condition $[\ pc_X = j \wedge pc_Y = k \ \Rightarrow \ Q\ ]$, where X and Y are components, j and k are labels, and Q is some predicate, it is sufficient to ensure that Q is (locally) established by each atomic statement that can terminate at control point X_j or Y_k. If the statement at X_j and the statement at Y_k are **if** statements, absence of total deadlock corresponds to the case that Q is the disjunction of the guards of these two statements.

3   Derivation Techniques

In this section, we describe the techniques we have developed for progress-based derivations. We describe some properties of progress claims and lemmas for preserving progress in Section 3.1. The notion of weakest immediate progress is described in Section 3.2. Then we address the role of stability in establishing individual progress in Section 3.3. To aid readability, we postpone our proofs to the appendix, however, an interested reader can refer to the proof to gain a better understanding of the theory.

3.1   Maintenance of Progress

To aid our proofs and derivations, we have developed the following important rules. These give formal justification to strengthening and weakening predicates in proofs, which are frequently demanded in derivations.

Lemma 3 (Monotonicity). *For predicates P, Q and R, the following hold:*

- **un** *is monotonic (or isotonic) in its second argument, i.e.,*

$$(P \text{ un } Q) \wedge [\, Q \Rightarrow R \,] \quad \Rightarrow \quad (P \text{ un } R)$$

- $\leadsto$ *is anti-monotonic (or antitonic) in its first argument, i.e.,*

$$[\, P \Rightarrow Q \,] \wedge (Q \leadsto R) \quad \Rightarrow \quad (P \leadsto R)$$

- $\leadsto$ *is monotonic (or isotonic) in its second argument, i.e.,*

$$(P \leadsto Q) \wedge [\, Q \Rightarrow R \,] \quad \Rightarrow \quad (P \leadsto R)$$

Lemma 4 (Contradiction). *For predicates P and Q, the following holds:*

$$(P \wedge \neg Q \leadsto Q) \quad \equiv \quad (P \leadsto Q)$$

For derivations, it is of utmost importance to know how progress is maintained by modifications of the program under construction. Informally speaking, we can imagine that a progress condition $P \leadsto Q$ cannot be endangered by statements at control points that cannot be reached from any state that satisfies P. However, the notion of reachability does not really help if at least one program counter does not occur in expression P, or if the components contain repetitions.

Remark 1. Using our experiences we prescribe as a heuristic that progress can be better addressed from the end of a program towards its start.

In what follows, we investigate a stronger approach to this issue, viz. when the *proof* of a progress property is maintained. We use $\mathcal{A} \models P \leadsto Q$ to denote that condition $P \leadsto Q$ holds for annotated program $\mathcal{A}$, where the annotation may include queried assertions.

Theorem 5 (Immediate Progress Preservation). *Let* $\mathcal{A}$ *be a program, and* P *and* Q *be predicates. Suppose* $\mathcal{A} \models P \rightsquigarrow Q$ *holds and some proof of it is based on a certain set of instances of immediate progress. Then for any program* $\mathcal{B}$ *in which these instances of immediate progress are valid,* $\mathcal{B} \models P \rightsquigarrow Q$ *holds.*

This theorem suggests an approach in which all applied instances of immediate progress are stored. Correctness of the proved progress properties is maintained by preserving all instances of immediate progress. However, although such a list of immediate progress instances avoids checking all previous proofs after any change to the program, maintaining such a list easily becomes a burden. Fortunately, within our derivations, the immediate progress instances are usually such that they can hardly be falsified upon modifying the program. To address the few cases in which they can be falsified, we will explicitly require dedicated constraints.

Corollary 6 (Annotation Strengthening). *Let* $\mathcal{A}$ *be a program and* P, Q, U *and* V *be predicates. Suppose* $\mathcal{A} \models P \rightsquigarrow Q$ *holds and* $[\, V \Rightarrow U \,]$. *If* $\mathcal{B}$ *is a program that is obtained from* $\mathcal{A}$ *by replacing an assertion* U *in* $\mathcal{A}$ *by assertion* V *in* $\mathcal{B}$, *then* $\mathcal{B} \models P \rightsquigarrow Q$.

This corollary allows us to strengthen the annotation of a program without having to worry about the program's progress properties. Adding co-assertions to the program is also justified as that is just strengthening the annotation.

An important technique in the method of [1] is strengthening the guard of a selection statement, as it maintains correctness of the (safety) assertions. However, as remarked in [1], both strengthening and weakening a guard can endanger progress. In our derivations, we will not strengthen or weaken any guard. Instead we will only *refine* them when necessary, i.e., we gradually impose more (logical) structure on it.

3.2   Weakest Immediate Progress

Following [2, 1], we have come to realise the importance of the *wlp* in safety-based program derivation. In this section, we search for a similar notion in progress-based derivations. As immediate progress forms the base of $\rightsquigarrow$, the following is a frequently occurring pattern in derivations.

$$P \rightsquigarrow R$$
$$\Leftarrow \quad \{ \, Q \rightsquigarrow R \text{ by immediate progress of statement } X_i \, \}$$
$$P \rightsquigarrow Q$$

We investigate a systematic way to compute a predicate Q such that $Q \rightsquigarrow R$ holds by the immediate progress rule for a given statement X_i. Since $\rightsquigarrow$ is monotonic in its second argument, we want to obtain a weakest suitable Q which we will refer to as the weakest immediate-progress (*wip*) condition of X_i.

The second part of the immediate progress rule of X_i gives the following requirement on Q (after trading):

$$[\, Q \Rightarrow R \lor (pc_X = i \land wp.X_i.R) \,] \tag{1}$$

The first part of the immediate progress rule is Q **un** R, which gives the following requirement for each atomic statement $\{U\}\ S$ in the program:

$$[\ Q\ \Rightarrow\ R\ \vee\ \neg U\ \vee\ wlp.S.(Q \vee R)\ ] \tag{2}$$

Conjunct $pc_X = i$ in (1) restricts the statements in component X that need to be considered for (2) to X_i. Moreover (1) implies (2) for statement X_i as $[\ wp.X_i.R\ \Rightarrow\ wlp.X_i.(Q \vee R)\ ]$.

In general, (2) gives rise to a fixed point computation for the weakest solution of Q in these equations (see [10]). Note that each approximation of Q contains a disjunct R, which corresponds to a kind of 0-step immediate progress, i.e., $[\ Q \Rightarrow R\ ]$. This disjunct ensures that the above proof step is an equivalence, using monotonicity of $\leadsto$. In many derivations, this disjunct is not important and we just leave it out.

3.3   Individual Progress

Individual progress ensures that it is impossible to be blocked at any statement forever. In particular, it excludes individual starvation and deadlock, but it does not guarantee termination of repetitions.

As the control points before and after each atomic statement are different, individual progress is guaranteed if $pc_X = i \leadsto pc_X \neq i$ for each statement X_i. This condition can be simplified using the contradiction lemma with $P := true$ and $Q := (pc_X \neq i)$, yielding for each statement X_i:

$$true\ \leadsto\ pc_X \neq i.$$

Thanks to weak fairness, this condition holds trivially for each non-blocking statement X_i. In contrast, upon introducing a blocking statement X_i, we will immediately introduce this condition as a proof obligation.

Individual progress of a selection statement is guaranteed if "eventually one of its guards becomes stably $true$". When constructing programs, it is easier to rephrase this into: "eventually a stable disjunct of one of its guards becomes $true$". This is formalized in the following lemma.

Lemma 7 (Stable Termination). *For any atomic statement X_i and predicate T, condition $true \leadsto pc_X \neq i$ follows from condition*

$$true\ \leadsto\ pc_X \neq i \vee T$$

provided that

– $[\ T\ \Rightarrow\ wp.X_i.(pc_X \neq i)\ ]$ *and*
– T *is stable in all components different from* X.

Notice that due to the monotonicity of $\leadsto$, this rule is even an equivalence.

For blocking statement X_i, application of the implication rule to prove this condition would yield $[\ pc_X = i \Rightarrow T\ ]$, which defeats the purpose of blocking. As suggested by the ground rule of progress in [1], the other components must have the potential to establish condition T. Therefore it is common to apply induction, often based on their program counters with a well-founded order based on the reverse execution order. In the case where there is just one other component, say Y, we obtain:

$$(\forall j:: pc_Y = j \rightsquigarrow pc_X \neq i \vee pc_Y \prec j \vee T).$$

Notice that due to the monotonicity of $\rightsquigarrow$, induction is an equivalence.

Remark 2. In the case that a component is a loop, we break the circular execution order by choosing an appropriate base. As a heuristic, good bases are control points of statements preceding a blocking statement.

For the many statements in component Y that establish T or that are guaranteed to terminate in a control point with a smaller label according to $\prec$, the above condition can immediately be discharged.

Lemma 8 (Ordering). *For any statement Y_j such that condition $[\ pc_Y = j \Rightarrow wp.Y_j.(pc_Y \prec j \vee T)\ ]$ holds, the following condition is guaranteed:*

$$pc_Y = j \rightsquigarrow pc_Y \prec j \vee T.$$

If the base control point according to $\prec$ contains a statement, we typically exploit the ordering lemma by ensuring that this statement establishes T.

4   Initialization Protocol

As a first example, we consider the initialization protocol for two components from [11]. The protocol ensures that both components have executed their initialization code before the rest of the program is executed. [1] presents a derivation that first emphasizes safety, and afterwards progress is ensured in an ad-hoc manner. The alternative design in [4] addresses progress in a formal way, but it is not calculational.

4.1   Specification

The starting point is the specification below, which consists of the computation proper and the synchronization requirements to be established.

Component X:	Component Y:
0: init.X	0: init.Y
1: $\{?\ pc_Y \neq 0\}$	1: $\{?\ pc_X \neq 0\}$

Statement init.X denotes the (terminating) contribution of component X to the initialization of the system. All variables that will be used for synchronization are fresh, and hence init.X is treated as a skip statement. The queried assertion in component X expresses that init.Y has terminated. In addition to these visible requirements, no precondition may be imposed on the synchronization variables.

4.2   Derivation

We are heading for a symmetric solution, and hence our discussions focus on only one of the components, say X. The derivation starts by considering the sole queried assertion, viz. $pc_Y \neq 0$. Since pc_Y cannot be accessed by component X, its local correctness must be established by a guarded skip. For the guard we introduce a fresh variable b_X and obtain $b_X \Rightarrow pc_Y \neq 0$ as required pre-assertion. Global correctness of assertion $pc_Y \neq 0$ is guaranteed by the shape of the program. Thus we obtain the following program:

Component X:	Component Y:
0: init.X ;	0: init.Y ;
2: $\{?\ b_X \Rightarrow pc_Y \neq 0\}$	2: $\{?\ b_Y \Rightarrow pc_X \neq 0\}$
$\langle$**if** $b_X \rightarrow$ skip **fi**$\rangle$	$\langle$**if** $b_Y \rightarrow$ skip **fi**$\rangle$
1: $\{pc_Y \neq 0\}$	1: $\{pc_X \neq 0\}$

Upon introducing blocking statement X_2, for individual progress we require

$$true \ \rightsquigarrow \ pc_X \neq 2.$$

To prove this, we want to apply the stable termination lemma for a condition T that implies b_X. As we would like to obtain the weakest possible proof obligation, we choose $T := b_X$. Hence, the proof obligation becomes

$$true \ \rightsquigarrow \ pc_X \neq 2 \lor b_X$$

provided we require the following constraint:

$$b_X \text{ is stable under component } Y \qquad (I_1)$$

Since component Y needs to establish b_X, we apply induction on pc_Y with a well-founded order $\prec$ that corresponds to the reverse execution order:

$$(\forall j :: pc_Y = j \ \rightsquigarrow \ pc_X \neq 2 \lor pc_Y \prec j \lor b_X) \qquad (I_2)$$

We prove this condition by case analysis on j. Thanks to the ordering lemma, we will not consider the above proof obligation for labels j such that statement Y_j is guaranteed to terminate. Following our heuristic (see Remark 1), we start to consider label 1.

case $j = 1$.

$\qquad pc_Y = 1 \ \rightsquigarrow \ pc_X \neq 2 \lor pc_Y \prec 1 \lor b_X$

$\equiv \qquad \{1 \text{ is the base of } \prec\}$

$\qquad pc_Y = 1 \ \rightsquigarrow \ pc_X \neq 2 \lor b_X$

$\Leftarrow \qquad \{wip \text{ calculation of } Y_1 \text{ is impossible}\}\{wip \text{ calculation of } X_2 \text{ does not}$
$\qquad \qquad \text{help, see below}\}\{\text{lemma 1: implication}\}$

$\qquad pc_Y = 1 \ \Rightarrow \ pc_X \neq 2 \lor b_X$

$\Leftarrow \qquad \{\text{logic}\}$

$\qquad pc_Y = 1 \ \Rightarrow \ b_X$

For the *wip* calculation of X_2, the intermediate predicate for requirement (1) must imply $pc_X \neq 2 \vee b_X \vee (pc_X = 2 \wedge wp.X_2.(pc_X \neq 2 \vee b_X))$, which simplifies to $pc_X \neq 2 \vee b_X$. This is useless as it is not weaker than the original.

Condition $pc_Y = 1 \Rightarrow b_X$ obtained from the proof above guarantees the absence of individual deadlock of component X upon termination of component Y. We will treat it as a queried assertion b_X at Y_1 and deal with its correctness immediately as additional statements may need to be introduced. Global correctness of the assertion is guaranteed as b_X is not yet modified in X. Local correctness can be established by inserting an assignment $b_X := true$ just before Y_1 (see the program below). Note that this assignment does not endanger correctness of the annotation, and it does not need to be considered for the progress requirement thanks to the ordering lemma.

Component X:	Component Y:
0: init.X ;	0: init.Y ;
2: $\{? \; b_X \Rightarrow pc_Y \neq 0\}$ $\langle$ if $b_X \rightarrow$ skip fi$\rangle$;	2: $\{? \; b_Y \Rightarrow pc_X \neq 0\}$ $\langle$ if $b_Y \rightarrow$ skip fi$\rangle$;
3: $\{pc_Y \neq 0\}$ $\quad b_Y := true$	3: $\{pc_X \neq 0\}$ $\quad b_X := true$
1: $\{pc_Y \neq 0\}\{b_Y\}$	1: $\{pc_X \neq 0\}\{b_X\}$

I_1: b_X is stable under component Y

? I_2: $(\forall j:: pc_Y = j \rightsquigarrow pc_X \neq 2 \vee pc_Y \prec j \vee b_X)$

case $j = 2$.
$$pc_Y = 2 \;\rightsquigarrow\; pc_X \neq 2 \vee pc_Y \prec 2 \vee b_X$$
$\equiv \quad$ {formal weakening by lemma 4: contradiction}
$$pc_X = 2 \wedge pc_Y = 2 \wedge \neg b_X \;\rightsquigarrow\; pc_X \neq 2 \vee pc_Y \prec 2 \vee b_X$$
$\Leftarrow \quad$ {*wip* calculation of Y_2, use stability of b_Y under X}
$$pc_X = 2 \wedge pc_Y = 2 \wedge \neg b_X \;\rightsquigarrow\; pc_Y = 2 \wedge b_Y$$
$\Leftarrow \quad$ {lemma 1: implication}{logic}
$$pc_X = 2 \wedge pc_Y = 2 \;\Rightarrow\; b_X \vee b_Y \qquad\qquad (I_3)$$

This condition guarantees the absence of total deadlock as when both X and Y are at their blocking statement, at least one of their guards is *true*. The instance of immediate progress used in this proof follows as $[\; b_Y \Rightarrow wp.Y_2.(pc_Y \prec 2) \;]$ holds. Since we will not strengthen any guard, this condition and hence the instance of immediate progress cannot be endangered later on. Note that without the first formal weakening step, the last condition would be $pc_Y = 2 \Rightarrow b_Y$, which is obviously too strong.

To ensure correctness of condition I_3, we want to apply the technique in [8]. The consequent of the implication can be established by an assignment $b_X := true$ or $b_Y := true$ just before X_2. Both preserve the stability constraint, but $b_X := true$ defeats the purpose of X_2. Thus we introduce an assignment $b_Y := true$ just before X_2 (see the program below). This assignment does not endanger the correctness of the annotation.

Component X:	Component Y:
0: init.X ;	0: init.Y ;
4: $b_Y := true$;	4: $b_X := true$;
2: $\{? \ b_X \ \Rightarrow \ pc_Y \neq 0\}$	2: $\{? \ b_Y \ \Rightarrow \ pc_Y \neq 0\}$
$\langle$**if** $b_X \rightarrow$ **skip fi**$\rangle$;	$\langle$**if** $b_Y \rightarrow$ **skip fi**$\rangle$;
3: $\{pc_Y \neq 0\}$	3: $\{pc_X \neq 0\}$
$b_Y := true$	$b_X := true$
1: $\{pc_Y \neq 0\}\{b_Y\}$	1: $\{pc_X \neq 0\}\{b_X\}$

I_1: b_X is stable under component Y
I_2: $(\forall j:: pc_Y = j \ \rightsquigarrow \ pc_X \neq 2 \ \vee \ pc_Y \prec j \ \vee \ b_X)$
I_3: $pc_X = 2 \ \wedge \ pc_Y = 2 \ \Rightarrow \ b_X \ \vee \ b_Y$

So far, we have introduced assignments to b_X and b_Y to guarantee progress. The remaining queried assertion addresses safety. Its global correctness is already guaranteed by the shape of the program. To avoid returning to the original problem, local correctness can be established by an assignment $b_X := false$. However, it may not be inserted just before X_2, due to our way of establishing condition I_3. Hence, we also require this assertion at X_4, and insert the assignment just before X_4 at a control point X_5.

This new assignment can only endanger assertion b_X at Y_1. Thereto we require a co-assertion $pc_X \neq 5$, which is correct although its proof requires some annotation that we simply copy from [4, 1] (see the program below).

Component X:	Component Y:
0: init.X ;	0: init.Y ;
5: $b_X := false$;	5: $b_Y := false$;
4: $\{b_X \ \Rightarrow \ pc_Y \notin \{0,5\}\}$	4: $\{b_Y \ \Rightarrow \ pc_X \notin \{0,5\}\}$
$b_Y := true$;	$b_X := true$;
2: $\{b_X \ \Rightarrow \ pc_Y \notin \{0,5\}\}$	2: $\{b_Y \ \Rightarrow \ pc_X \notin \{0,5\}\}$
$\langle$**if** $b_X \rightarrow$ **skip fi**$\rangle$;	$\langle$**if** $b_Y \rightarrow$ **skip fi**$\rangle$;
3: $\{pc_Y \notin \{0,5\}\}$	3: $\{pc_X \notin \{0,5\}\}$
$b_Y := true$	$b_X := true$
1: $\{pc_Y \notin \{0,5\}\}\{b_Y\}$	1: $\{pc_X \notin \{0,5\}\}\{b_X\}$

I_1: b_X is stable under component Y
I_2: $(\forall j:: pc_Y = j \ \rightsquigarrow \ pc_X \neq 2 \ \vee \ pc_Y \prec j \ \vee \ b_X)$
I_3: $pc_X = 2 \ \wedge \ pc_Y = 2 \ \Rightarrow \ b_X \ \vee \ b_Y$

After eliminating the annotation, we obtain the following program:

Component X:	Component Y:
init.X ;	init.Y ;
$b_X := false$;	$b_Y := false$;
$b_Y := true$;	$b_X := true$;
$\langle$**if** $b_X \rightarrow$ **skip fi**$\rangle$;	$\langle$**if** $b_Y \rightarrow$ **skip fi**$\rangle$;
$b_Y := true$	$b_X := true$

5   Peterson's Mutual Exclusion Algorithm

The next example we consider is Peterson's mutual exclusion algorithm for two components [12]. The derivation in [1] first emphasizes safety based on the safe choice algorithm, and afterwards progress is ensured in an ad-hoc manner. In the alternative derivation in [13] the first emphasis is on progress based on an ad-hoc formalization. The derivation in [14] starts to formalize progress based on an auxiliary notion of overtaking.

5.1   Specification

The starting point is the following specification:

Component X:	Component Y:
$*[$	$*[$
0: **if** $true \rightarrow$	0: **if** $true \rightarrow$
1: nncs.X	1: nncs.Y
$[]$ $true \rightarrow$	$[]$ $true \rightarrow$
2: tncs.X	2: tncs.Y
fi ;	**fi** ;
3: $\{?\ pc_Y \neq 3\}$	3: $\{?\ pc_X \neq 3\}$
cs.X	cs.Y
$]$	$]$

Statement cs.X denotes the critical section of component X, and it is guaranteed to terminate. The non-critical section is not guaranteed to terminate, which is modelled by splitting it into a non-terminating case nncs.X and a terminating case tncs.X. For the required synchronization no statements may be introduced within the corresponding non-deterministic **if** statement. All variables that will be used for synchronization are fresh, and hence we treat cs.X and tncs.X as skip statements, and nncs.X as a statement $\langle$**if** $false \rightarrow$ skip **fi**$\rangle$. The queried assertion expresses mutual exclusion of the critical sections.

To simplify the modelling of the non-critical section, it is tempting to use a single atomic statement

$$\langle\textbf{if}\quad true \rightarrow \text{nncs}.X$$
$$[]\quad true \rightarrow \text{tncs}.X$$
$$\textbf{fi}\rangle$$

Regarding the wlp this model is equivalent to nncs.X, and regarding the wp this model is equivalent to tncs.X. However, as the interleaving execution model requires that atomic statements either completely block or completely terminate, this model of a non-critical section is invalid.

5.2   Derivation

We are heading for a symmetric solution, and hence we focus on only component X. The derivation can only start by considering the sole queried assertion, viz. $pc_Y \neq 3$ at X_3. Since pc_Y cannot be accessed by component X, the way to establish its local correctness is to introduce a guarded skip, say at a new control point X_4. For its guard we introduce a fresh variable b_X and we require as pre-assertion $b_X \Rightarrow pc_Y \neq 3$. This is also sufficient for global correctness, in particular under statement Y_4 using its analogous pre-assertion $b_Y \Rightarrow pc_X \neq 3$. Thus we obtain the following program:

Component X:	Component Y:
$*\lceil$	$*\lceil$
0: **if** $true \to$	0: **if** $true \to$
1: nncs.X	1: nncs.Y
$]$ $true \to$	$]$ $true \to$
2: tncs.X	2: tncs.Y
fi ;	**fi** ;
4: $\{?\ b_X \Rightarrow pc_Y \neq 3\}$	4: $\{?\ b_Y \Rightarrow pc_X \neq 3\}$
$\langle$**if** $b_X \to$ skip **fi**$\rangle$;	$\langle$**if** $b_Y \to$ skip **fi**$\rangle$;
3: $\{pc_Y \neq 3\}$	3: $\{pc_X \neq 3\}$
cs.X	cs.Y
$\rceil$	$\rceil$

Upon introducing a blocking statement X_4, for individual progress we require:

$$true \rightsquigarrow pc_X \neq 4.$$

To prove this, we want to apply the stable termination lemma for a condition T that implies b_X. It turns out that choosing b_X for T gives a stability requirement on b_X that is too restrictive. To obtain more manipulative freedom, we introduce fresh variables s_X and r_X, substitute guard b_X by the more generic guard $s_X \vee r_X$, and choose s_X for T. Note that a similar substitution could have been performed in our derivation of the initialization protocol, but it would not have been useful. Thus the current proof obligation becomes

$$true \rightsquigarrow pc_X \neq 4 \vee s_X$$

provided we require the following constraint:

$$s_X \text{ is stable under component } Y \qquad (P_1)$$

Since component Y needs to establish s_X, we apply induction on pc_Y:

$$(\forall j :: pc_Y = j \rightsquigarrow pc_X \neq 4 \vee pc_Y \prec j \vee s_X) \qquad (P_2)$$

We choose a well-founded order $\prec$ that corresponds to the reverse execution order. Since the component is a loop, following Remark 2 we should choose the statement preceding Y_4 as a base. In the current program, this happens to be part of the non-critical section, which hardly allows manipulation. Thus we insert before Y_4 a new control point, say Y_5, containing a skip statement and use it as a base.

We prove condition P_2 by case analysis on j. Using the ordering lemma, the base case $j = 5$ follows from the constraint:

$$[\ wp.Y_5.s_X\ ] \qquad (P_3)$$

which can be established by modifying the skip statement at Y_5 to $s_X := true$. In what follows, we exploit the ordering lemma to only consider labels j such that statement j is not guaranteed to terminate.

case $j = 1$.

$$pc_Y = 1 \;\rightsquigarrow\; pc_X \neq 4 \vee pc_Y \prec 1 \vee s_X$$

$\equiv$ {formal weakening by lemma 4: contradiction}

$$pc_X = 4 \wedge pc_Y = 1 \wedge \neg s_X \;\rightsquigarrow\; pc_X \neq 4 \vee pc_Y \prec 1 \vee s_X$$

$\Leftarrow$ {*wip* calculation of Y_1 does not help}{*wip* calculation of X_4:
   first attempt $pc_X = 4 \wedge (s_X \vee r_X)$ could be endangered by Y
   since r_X is not stable; add conjunct $pc_Y = 1$ using [$wlp.Y_1.false$]}

$$pc_X = 4 \wedge pc_Y = 1 \wedge \neg s_X \;\rightsquigarrow\; pc_X = 4 \wedge pc_Y = 1 \wedge (s_X \vee r_X)$$

$\Leftarrow$ {lemma 1: implication}{logic}

$$pc_Y = 1 \;\Rightarrow\; r_X$$

We require an assertion r_X at Y_1, since it is unreasonable at X_4. The instance
of immediate progress follows from conditions [$wlp.Y_1.false$] and [$s_X \vee r_X \Rightarrow$
$wp.X_4.(pc_X \neq 4)$]. Since we will not modify any guard, they cannot be endangered later on.

case $j = 4$.

$$pc_Y = 4 \;\rightsquigarrow\; pc_X \neq 4 \vee pc_Y \prec 4 \vee s_X$$

$\equiv$ {formal weakening by lemma 4: contradiction}

$$pc_X = 4 \wedge pc_Y = 4 \wedge \neg s_X \;\rightsquigarrow\; pc_X \neq 4 \vee pc_Y \prec 4 \vee s_X$$

$\Leftarrow$ {*wip* calculation of Y_4: first attempt $pc_Y = 4 \wedge (s_Y \vee r_Y)$ could be
   endangered by X; add conjunct $pc_X = 4$ using [$wlp.X_4.(pc_X \neq 4)$]}

$$pc_X = 4 \wedge pc_Y = 4 \wedge \neg s_X \;\rightsquigarrow\; pc_X = 4 \wedge pc_Y = 4 \wedge (s_Y \vee r_Y)$$

$\Leftarrow$ {lemma 1: implication}{logic}

$$pc_X = 4 \wedge pc_Y = 4 \;\Rightarrow\; s_X \vee (s_Y \vee r_Y) \tag{P_4}$$

The instance of immediate progress follows from tautology [$wlp.X_4.(pc_X \neq 4)$]
and condition [$s_Y \vee r_Y \Rightarrow wp.Y_4.(pc_Y \prec 4)$]. Since we will not strengthen
any guard, it cannot be endangered later on. Correctness of condition P_4 is
guaranteed using the technique of [8] thanks to statements X_5 and Y_5. Thus we
obtain the following program:

Component X:		Component Y:	
$*[$		$*[$	
0:	**if** $true \rightarrow$	0:	**if** $true \rightarrow$
1:	$\{?\ r_Y\}$	1:	$\{?\ r_X\}$
	$nncs.X$		$nncs.Y$
$[]$	$true \rightarrow$	$[]$	$true \rightarrow$
2:	$tncs.X$	2:	$tncs.Y$
	fi ;		**fi** ;
5:	$s_Y := true$;	5:	$s_X := true$;
4:	$\{?\ (s_X \vee r_X) \Rightarrow pc_Y \neq 3\}$	4:	$\{?\ (s_Y \vee r_Y) \Rightarrow pc_X \neq 3\}$
	$\langle$**if** $s_X \vee r_X \rightarrow$ skip **fi**$\rangle$;		$\langle$**if** $s_Y \vee r_Y \rightarrow$ skip **fi**$\rangle$;
3:	$\{pc_Y \neq 3\}$	3:	$\{pc_X \neq 3\}$
	$cs.X$		$cs.Y$
$]$		$]$	

P_1: s_X is stable under component Y
P_2: $(\forall j :: pc_Y = j \;\rightsquigarrow\; pc_X \neq 4 \vee pc_Y \prec j \vee s_X)$
P_3: [$wp.Y_5.s_X$]
P_4: $pc_X = 4 \wedge pc_Y = 4 \;\Rightarrow\; s_X \vee (s_Y \vee r_Y)$

What remains is to ensure that the queried assertions become correct. We first consider queried assertion $(s_X \vee r_X) \Rightarrow pc_Y \neq 3$ at X_4. We split this assertion according to the disjuncts in the antecedent into the two assertions

(i) $s_X \Rightarrow pc_Y \neq 3$ and
(ii) $r_X \Rightarrow pc_Y \neq 3$

The simplest way to establish local correctness of (i) is to falsify its antecedent. We choose to modify the assignment at control point X_5 to $s_Y, s_X := true, false$. Note that this assignment does not endanger the correctness of the annotation. Global correctness of (i) at X_4 can only be endangered by statement Y_4. To avoid this, we require $pc_X = 4 \wedge pc_Y = 4 \wedge (s_Y \vee r_Y) \Rightarrow \neg s_X$, or equivalently $pc_X = 4 \wedge pc_Y = 4 \Rightarrow \neg s_X \vee (\neg s_Y \wedge \neg r_Y)$. To make this condition more homogenous, we split off term $\neg r_Y$ and require it as an assertion at X_4 since it would not make sense at Y_4. The remaining condition $pc_X = 4 \wedge pc_Y = 4 \Rightarrow \neg s_X \vee \neg s_Y$ is added as a requirement on the program.

Correctness of this condition is guaranteed using the technique from [8] via new assignments X_5 and Y_5. Using assertion $\neg r_Y$ at X_4, this condition and condition P_4 can be combined into condition

$$pc_X = 4 \wedge pc_Y = 4 \Rightarrow s_X \neq s_Y \qquad (P_5)$$

Assertion (ii) at X_4 is equivalent to assertion $pc_Y = 3 \Rightarrow \neg r_X$ at X_4. To make it more similar to required assertion $\neg r_X$ at Y_4, we strengthen it into a queried assertion $\neg r_X$ at Y_3. Note that this strategy is not useful for assertion (i), because local correctness would be hindered by the required stability of s_X under Y. Thus we obtain the following program:

Component X:	Component Y:
$*\lceil$	$*\lceil$
0: **if** $true \rightarrow$	0: **if** $true \rightarrow$
1: $\{?\ r_Y\}$	1: $\{?\ r_X\}$
nncs.X	nncs.Y
⫿ $true \rightarrow$	⫿ $true \rightarrow$
2: tncs.X	2: tncs.Y
fi ;	**fi** ;
5: $s_X, s_Y := false, true$;	5: $s_Y, s_X := false, true$;
4: $\{s_X \Rightarrow pc_Y \neq 3\}\{?\ \neg r_Y\}$	4: $\{s_Y \Rightarrow pc_X \neq 3\}\{?\ \neg r_X\}$
$\langle$**if** $s_X \vee r_X \rightarrow$ skip **fi**$\rangle$;	$\langle$**if** $s_Y \vee r_Y \rightarrow$ skip **fi**$\rangle$;
3: $\{pc_Y \neq 3\}\{?\ \neg r_Y\}$	3: $\{pc_X \neq 3\}\{?\ \neg r_X\}$
cs.X	cs.Y
$\rfloor$	$\rfloor$

P_1: s_X is stable under component Y
P_2: $(\forall j :: pc_Y = j \rightsquigarrow pc_X \neq 4 \vee pc_Y \prec j \vee s_X)$
P_3: $[\ wp.Y_5.s_X\ ]$
P_5: $pc_X = 4 \wedge pc_Y = 4 \Rightarrow s_X \neq s_Y$

Notice that nncs.X, the case that the non-critical section does not terminate, has hardly played a role so far, and that the only occurrences of variable r_Y in the annotation are in some assertions of component X. In absence of nncs.X (and the queried assertion at X_1), variable r_Y can even be replaced by *false*.

What remains to be done is to find places for assignments that establish the assertions about r_Y. Since we have applied [8] to establish P_5, we cannot insert any assignment between X_5 and X_4 and hence we insert an assignment $r_Y := false$ just before X_5. The only suitable place for an assignment $r_Y := true$ is just before X_0. Correctness of the queried assertions follows by topology. Hence, we get the following program:

Component X:		Component Y:	
$*[$		$*[$	
7:	$r_Y := true$;	7:	$r_X := true$;
0:	**if** $true \rightarrow$	0:	**if** $true \rightarrow$
1:	$\{r_Y\}$	1:	$\{r_X\}$
	nncs.X		nncs.Y
	$[]$ $true \rightarrow$		$[]$ $true \rightarrow$
2:	tncs.X	2:	tncs.Y
	fi ;		**fi** ;
6:	$r_Y := false$;	6:	$r_X := false$;
5:	$s_Y, s_X := true, false$;	5:	$s_X, s_Y := true, false$;
4:	$\{s_X \Rightarrow pc_Y \neq 3\}\{\neg r_Y\}$	4:	$\{s_Y \Rightarrow pc_X \neq 3\}\{\neg r_X\}$
	$\langle$**if** $s_X \vee r_X \rightarrow$ skip **fi**$\rangle$;		$\langle$**if** $s_Y \vee r_Y \rightarrow$ skip **fi**$\rangle$;
3:	$\{pc_Y \neq 3\}\{\neg r_Y\}$	3:	$\{pc_X \neq 3\}\{\neg r_X\}$
	cs.X		cs.Y
$]$		$]$	

P_1: s_X is stable under component Y
P_2: $(\forall j:: pc_Y = j \leadsto pc_X \neq 4 \vee pc_Y \prec j \vee s_X)$
P_3: $[\ wp.Y_5.s_X\ ]$
P_5: $pc_X = 4 \wedge pc_Y = 4 \Rightarrow s_X \neq s_Y$

Note that variable r_X is not used to enclose a critical section, but to enclose a possibly non-terminating non-critical section. What remains is to implement the assignments to s_X and s_Y, since they are too coarse-grained. Since $s_X \neq s_Y$ is maintained by the program, we propose to introduce a variable v and implement variable s_X as $v = Y$. Thus we obtain the program in below, where we have abbreviated the non-atomic non-critical section into ncs.

Component X:	Component Y:
$*[$ $r_Y := true$;	$*[$ $r_X := true$;
ncs.X ;	ncs.Y ;
$r_Y := false$;	$r_X := false$;
$v := X$;	$v := Y$;
$\langle$**if** $v = Y \vee r_X \rightarrow$ skip **fi**$\rangle$;	$\langle$**if** $v = X \vee r_Y \rightarrow$ skip **fi**$\rangle$;
cs.X	cs.Y
$]$	$]$

Strictly speaking, the guard of the guarded skip is too coarse-grained for an implementation, since it contains more than one shared variable. However, since one of the disjuncts is stable (by construction), it can be implemented using the guard disjunction lemma.

6   Conclusions and Further Work

We have presented techniques for the derivation of concurrent programs, paying equal attention to safety and progress. The techniques extend the calculational method of [1]. While constructing a program, the program text is repeatedly adapted as guided by the open proof obligations. We have investigated what transformations maintain the proved progress conditions.

Our main theorem in this respect is the immediate progress preservation theorem. Straightforward application of this theorem requires maintaining a list of immediate progress conditions. Although this is similar to maintaining the proved assertions for safety, we have not yet developed a convenient notational device. The reason is that we have shown that most of these progress conditions cannot be endangered by the program modifications that we allow. Nevertheless we consider notations an important piece of further work.

We have used a notion of weakest immediate progress to calculate the weakest condition required for progress, similar to weakest preconditions. Our derivations rely on the stable termination lemma, which emphasizes stable guards. Individual progress of a statement is usually said to be guaranteed if "eventually one of its guards becomes stably true", but our experiments suggest rephrasing it into: "eventually a stable disjunct of one of its guards becomes true".

We have illustrated these techniques by deriving an initialization protocol and a mutual exclusion algorithm. Thanks to the ordering lemma, many proof obligations for progress could be discharged trivially. It is further work to address programs that consist of more than two components.

Acknowledgements. The authors would like to thank Robert Colvin, Ian Hayes and the anonymous referees for their comments on earlier versions of this work.

References

1. Feijen, W., van Gasteren, A.: On a Method of Multiprogramming. Springer-Verlag (1999)
2. Dijkstra, E.: A Discipline of Programming. Prentice Hall (1976)
3. Owicki, S., Gries, D.: An axiomatic proof technique for parallel programs I. Acta Inform. **6** (1976) 319–340
4. Dongol, B., Goldson, D.: Extending the theory of Owicki and Gries with a logic of progress. Logical Methods in Comput. Sci. **2**(1) (2006) 1–25
5. Chandy, K., Misra, J.: Parallel Program Design: A Foundation. Addison-Wesley Longman Publ. Co. (1988)
6. Goldson, D., Dongol, B.: Concurrent program design in the extended theory of Owicki and Gries. In Proc. of 11th Computing, Australasian Theory Symp., CATS 2005. Vol. 41 of Confs. in Research and Practice in Inform. Techn., Australian Comput. Soc. (2005) 41–50
7. Manna, Z., Pnueli, P.: Temporal Verification of Reactive and Concurrent Systems: Specification. Springer-Verlag (1992)
8. Feijen, W.: A method for avoiding total deadlock, courtesy Diethard Michaelis. Personal note WF284 (2005)

9. Mooij, A.: Formal derivations of non-blocking multiprograms. Computer Science Report 02-13, Techn. Univ. Eindhoven (2002) Master's Thesis under supervision of W.H.J. Feijen

10. Jutla, C., Knapp, E., Rao, J.: A predicate transformer approach to semantics of parallel programs. In Proc. of 8th Ann. ACM Symp. on Principles of Distributed Computing, PODC '89. ACM Press (1989) 249–263

11. Misra, J.: Phase synchronization. Inform. Process. Lett. **38**(2) (1991) 101–105

12. Peterson, G.: Myths about the mutual exclusion problem. Inform. Process. Lett. **12** (1981) 115–116

13. van der Sommen, F., Feijen, W., van Gasteren, A.: Peterson's mutual exclusion algorithm revisited. Sci. of Comput. Program. **29**(3) (1997) 327–334

14. van der Sommen, F.: When mutual exclusion rules out overtaking. Personal note FvdS39 (2003)

Appendix: Proofs for Section 3

Lemma (Monotonicity). *For predicates P, Q and R, the following hold:*

- **un** *is monotonic (or isotonic) in its second argument, i.e.,*

$$(P \text{ } \mathbf{un} \text{ } Q) \wedge [\, Q \Rightarrow R \,] \quad \Rightarrow \quad (P \text{ } \mathbf{un} \text{ } R)$$

- $\rightsquigarrow$ *is anti-monotonic (or antitonic) in its first argument, i.e.,*

$$[\, P \Rightarrow Q \,] \wedge (Q \rightsquigarrow R) \quad \Rightarrow \quad (P \rightsquigarrow R)$$

- $\rightsquigarrow$ *is monotonic (or isotonic) in its second argument, i.e.,*

$$(P \rightsquigarrow Q) \wedge [\, Q \Rightarrow R \,] \quad \Rightarrow \quad (P \rightsquigarrow R)$$

Proof.
Monotonicity of **un** follows from monotonicity of wlp.

Anti-monotonicity of $\rightsquigarrow$:
$$P \rightsquigarrow R$$
$$\Leftarrow \quad \{\text{transitivity}\}$$
$$(P \rightsquigarrow Q) \wedge (Q \rightsquigarrow R)$$
$$\Leftarrow \quad \{\text{implication}\}$$
$$[\, P \Rightarrow Q \,] \wedge (Q \rightsquigarrow R)$$

Monotonicity of $\rightsquigarrow$:
$$P \rightsquigarrow R$$
$$\Leftarrow \quad \{\text{transitivity}\}$$
$$(P \rightsquigarrow Q) \wedge (Q \rightsquigarrow R)$$
$$\Leftarrow \quad \{\text{implication}\}$$
$$(P \rightsquigarrow Q) \wedge [\, Q \Rightarrow R \,]$$

□

Lemma (Contradiction). *For predicates P and Q, the following holds:*

$$(P \wedge \neg Q \rightsquigarrow Q) \quad \equiv \quad (P \rightsquigarrow Q)$$

Proof.

Part $\Rightarrow$:
$$P \rightsquigarrow Q$$
$$\Leftarrow \quad \{\text{disjunction}\}$$
$$(P \wedge Q \rightsquigarrow Q) \wedge (P \wedge \neg Q \rightsquigarrow Q)$$
$$\equiv \quad \{\text{implication}\}$$
$$P \wedge \neg Q \rightsquigarrow Q$$

Part $\Leftarrow$:
$$P \wedge \neg Q \rightsquigarrow Q$$
$$\Leftarrow \quad \{\text{anti-monotonicity}\}$$
$$P \rightsquigarrow Q$$

□

Theorem (Immediate Progress Preservation). *Let $\mathcal{A}$ be a program, and P and Q be predicates. Suppose $\mathcal{A} \models P \rightsquigarrow Q$ holds and some proof of it is based on a certain set of instances of immediate progress. Then for any program $\mathcal{B}$ in which these instances of immediate progress are valid, $\mathcal{B} \models P \rightsquigarrow Q$ holds.*

Proof. By the definition of $\rightsquigarrow$, any proof of $\mathcal{A} \models P \rightsquigarrow Q$ consists of a finite number of applications of immediate progress, transitivity and disjunction. Given a proof of $\mathcal{A} \models P \rightsquigarrow Q$ such that $\mathcal{B}$ preserves each instance of immediate progress in this proof, we show that this proof can be mimicked for $\mathcal{B}$. Thereto we apply induction on the structure of the proof for $\mathcal{A}$:

- Immediate progress: Suppose $\mathcal{A} \models P \rightsquigarrow Q$ is an instance of immediate progress:

$$\mathcal{B} \models P \rightsquigarrow Q$$
$$\Leftarrow \quad \{\mathcal{B} \text{ preserves instances of immediate progress}\}$$
$$\mathcal{A} \models P \rightsquigarrow Q$$

- Transitivity: Suppose $\mathcal{A} \models P \rightsquigarrow Q$ is proved using $\mathcal{A} \models (P \rightsquigarrow R) \wedge (R \rightsquigarrow Q)$, for some intermediate predicate R:

$$\mathcal{B} \models P \rightsquigarrow Q$$
$$\Leftarrow \quad \{\text{By transitivity}\}$$
$$\mathcal{B} \models (P \rightsquigarrow R) \wedge (R \rightsquigarrow Q)$$
$$\equiv \quad \{\text{By logic}\}$$
$$(\mathcal{B} \models P \rightsquigarrow R) \wedge (\mathcal{B} \models R \rightsquigarrow Q)$$
$$\Leftarrow \quad \{\text{Induction hypothesis (twice)}\}$$
$$(\mathcal{A} \models P \rightsquigarrow R) \wedge (\mathcal{A} \models R \rightsquigarrow Q)$$
$$\equiv \quad \{\text{By logic}\}$$
$$\mathcal{A} \models (P \rightsquigarrow R) \wedge (R \rightsquigarrow Q)$$

- Disjunction: Suppose $[\, P \equiv (\exists i :: R.i) \,]$, for some predicates $R.i$, and $\mathcal{A} \models (\exists i :: R.i) \rightsquigarrow Q$ is proved using $\mathcal{A} \models (\forall i :: R.i \rightsquigarrow Q)$:

$$\mathcal{B} \models (\exists i :: R.i) \rightsquigarrow Q$$
$$\Leftarrow \quad \{\text{By disjunction}\}$$
$$\mathcal{B} \models (\forall i :: R.i \rightsquigarrow Q)$$
$$\equiv \quad \{\text{By logic}\}$$
$$(\forall i :: \mathcal{B} \models R.i \rightsquigarrow Q)$$
$$\Leftarrow \quad \{\text{Induction hypothesis}\}$$
$$(\forall i :: \mathcal{A} \models R.i \rightsquigarrow Q)$$
$$\equiv \quad \{\text{By logic}\}$$
$$\mathcal{A} \models (\forall i :: R.i \rightsquigarrow Q) \qquad \qquad \square$$

Corollary (Annotation Strengthening). *Let $\mathcal{A}$ be a program and P, Q, U and V be predicates. Suppose $\mathcal{A} \models P \rightsquigarrow Q$ holds and $[\, V \Rightarrow U \,]$. If $\mathcal{B}$ is a program that is obtained from $\mathcal{A}$ by replacing an assertion U in $\mathcal{A}$ by assertion V in $\mathcal{B}$, then $\mathcal{B} \models P \rightsquigarrow Q$.*

Proof. Thanks to the immediate progress preservation theorem, it is sufficient to show that the instances of immediate progress are preserved. This is the case since strengthening U into V only weakens the individual proof obligations. $\quad \square$

Lemma (Stable Termination). *For any atomic statement X_i and predicate T, condition true $\rightsquigarrow$ $pc_X \neq i$ follows from condition*

$$true \;\rightsquigarrow\; pc_X \neq i \vee T$$

provided that

− $[\, T \;\Rightarrow\; wp.X_i.(pc_X \neq i) \,]$ *and*
− T *is stable in all components different from X.*

Proof.

> $true \rightsquigarrow pc_X \neq i$
> $\Leftarrow$ { *wip* calculation of X_i: for X_i we get $pc_X \neq i \vee (pc_X = i \wedge T)$,
> and the **un** requirements of the other components follow from
> the stability of T}
> $true \;\rightsquigarrow\; pc_X \neq i \vee (pc_X = i \wedge T)$
> $\equiv$ {logic}
> $true \;\rightsquigarrow\; pc_X \neq i \vee T$ $\hfill \square$

Fission for Program Comprehension

Jeremy Gibbons

Oxford University Computing Laboratory,
Wolfson Building, Parks Road, Oxford OX1 3QD, UK
jeremy.gibbons@comlab.ox.ac.uk

Abstract. *Fusion* is a program transformation that combines adjacent computations, flattening structure and improving efficiency at the cost of clarity. *Fission* is the same transformation, in reverse: creating structure, ex nihilo. We explore the use of fission for *program comprehension*, that is, for reconstructing the design of a program from its implementation. We illustrate through rational reconstructions of the designs for three different C programs that count the words in a text file.

1 Introduction

Program *fusion* is a meaning-preserving transformation that combines two adjacent computations into one. Those computations might be independent; for example, computing the mean of a sequence of numbers involves both summing and counting the elements of the sequence, and these two independent loops may be fused into one, returning a pair. Alternatively, the computations might be consecutive; for example, testing for membership of a collection can be expressed as comparisons against every element of the collection, then disjoining the results, and these two consecutive loops may be fused into one.

Program fusion is usually seen as an efficiency-improving transformation, perhaps at the cost of comprehensibility. A clear and simple version of a program is developed first, as a composition of strongly coherent but loosely coupled components; for example, membership in terms of comparisons and distributed disjunction, or mean in terms of sum and count. That modular structure might incur unnecessary runtime costs: either in building up an intermediate data structure, only to take it apart straight away, or in making two traversals of a data structure when only one is required. Fusion laws show how to combine components, breaking down the modular structure and the redundant manipulations it entails.

Program *fission* uses the same properties of programs as fusion does, but in the opposite direction. Starting from a complex monolithic optimized program, one constructs a simpler, more modular 'specification' or 'prototype', identifying the components from which the complex program might have been assembled. This construction might be for the first time, for a program that was never properly designed or whose structure has evolved over time from an initial design that has not been kept up to date; or it might be a matter of reconstructing a lost design. Either way, it can be used for *program comprehension*, that is, for understanding the behaviour of an undocumented unit of code.

T. Uustalu (Ed.): MPC 2006, LNCS 4014, pp. 162–179, 2006.

Program fission is harder than program fusion, because it entails *entropy reduction*: the introduction of structure, rather than its elimination. It is a fundamental phenomenon of physical systems that entropy increases in a closed system: in order to prevent the inevitable increase in disorder over time, it is necessary to inject some energy into the system. A similar phenomenon seems to arise in logical systems such as software; witness tales of 'software rot', for example [1].

Program fission is one approach among many to the problem of *software reverse-engineering*, or the reconstruction of lost or out-of-date documentation for legacy systems. This whole area has been described as being 'about as easy as reconstructing a pig from a sausage' [2]. Indeed, as we shall see, it is harder even than that: a given sausage can have only one explanation, but a given program might have multiple explanations. By analogy, you might not even know that it is a pig you should be reconstructing from your sausage.

2   Notation

We will make use of a Haskell-like notation, for the sake of familiarity; we will also use a number of functions from the Haskell standard library, but we will explain them as we introduce them. However, we will make greater use of sum and product types and less use of currying than is usual in the Haskell language or libraries.

2.1   Sums and Products

We use $\alpha \times \beta$ for the product type with first component of type α and second of type β (normally written '(α, β)' in Haskell); the projection functions *fst, snd* are as expected. We write '$f \times g$' for the map operation on pairs, applying f to the first component and g to the second, and '$f \vartriangle g$' for the 'fork' operation, taking x to $(f\ x, g\ x)$. The function *twist* $:: \alpha \times \beta \to \beta \times \alpha$ twists a pair. The unit type is 1 (normally written '()' in Haskell). We also use $\alpha + \beta$ for the sum type (normally written '*Either* $\alpha\ \beta$' in Haskell). In the special case that $\alpha = 1$, we use the injections *Nothing* $:: 1 + \beta$ and *Just* $:: \beta \to 1 + \beta$ as in Haskell.

2.2   Datatypes

We will have need of both 'cons lists' (constructed by prefixing elements) and 'snoc lists' (constructed by suffixing). We extend Haskell's neutral notation involving a plain colon for constructing a non-empty list, and use '$\cdot$:' for prefixing to a cons list and ':$\cdot$' for suffixing to a snoc list. The type $[\alpha]$ denotes cons lists with elements of type α, and $\langle \alpha \rangle$ denotes snoc lists. However, we will resort to using the conventional notation '[]' for the empty list and '[a]' for a singleton list in what follows, trusting to context to disambiguate which kind of list is meant. We will also use a datatype *Nat* of Peano numbers, with *Zero* $::$ *Nat* and *Succ* $::$ *Nat* $\to$ *Nat*.

2.3 Folds

The natural pattern of computation over cons lists, the so-called universal arrow induced by the datatype definition, is called *foldr* in the Haskell library; it consumes list elements, starting at the end of the list. We use the same name here, but give it a slightly different type by uncurrying the binary operator.

$$foldr :: (\alpha \times \beta \to \beta) \to \beta \to [\alpha] \to \beta$$
$$foldr\ f\ e\ [\,]\quad\ = e$$
$$foldr\ f\ e\ (a :: x) = f\ (a, foldr\ f\ e\ x)$$

In contrast, the natural pattern of computation over snoc lists consumes list elements starting from the beginning of the list, since that is how snoc lists are constructed.

$$folds :: (\beta \times \alpha \to \beta) \to \beta \to \langle\alpha\rangle \to \beta$$
$$folds\ f\ e\ [\,]\quad\ = e$$
$$folds\ f\ e\ (x :\cdot a) = f\ (folds\ f\ e\ x, a)$$

The Haskell standard library also provides a variant of *foldr*, which uses an accumulating parameter [3] and consumes the list elements from left to right rather than right to left. Again, we adapt its type.

$$foldl :: (\beta \times \alpha \to \beta) \to \beta \to [\alpha] \to \beta$$
$$foldl\ f\ e\ [\,]\quad\ = e$$
$$foldl\ f\ e\ (a :: x) = foldl\ f\ (f\ (e, a))\ x$$

Note that, apart from the variety of lists, the types of *foldl* and *folds* are identical. Indeed, if we introduce the function *snoc2cons* :: $\langle\alpha\rangle \to [\alpha]$ to convert from one list type to another, preserving ordering, then for finite cons lists x, it is not difficult to show that

$$folds\ f\ e\ x = foldl\ f\ e\ (snoc2cons\ x)$$

The proof is essentially the same as for Bird and Wadler's *Third Duality Theorem* [4] for *foldl* and *foldr*. (For infinite x, the above result holds only for certain non-strict f.)

2.4 Unfolds

The categorical dual of a fold on lists, which collapses a list to a value, is an unfold, which grows a list from a value. The Haskell standard library provides essentially the right definition for us.

$$unfoldr :: (\beta \to 1 + (\alpha \times \beta)) \to \beta \to [\alpha]$$
$$unfoldr\ f\ b = \textbf{case}\ f\ b\ \textbf{of}$$
$$Nothing\quad \to [\,]$$
$$Just\ (a, b') \to a :: unfoldr\ f\ b'$$

Here is an analogous operation for growing natural numbers:

$$unfoldn :: (\beta \rightarrow 1 + \beta) \rightarrow \beta \rightarrow Nat$$
$$unfoldn\ f\ b = \textbf{case}\ f\ b\ \textbf{of}$$
$$Nothing \rightarrow Zero$$
$$Just\ b' \quad \rightarrow Succ\ (unfoldn\ f\ b')$$

2.5   Paramorphisms and Hylomorphisms

Meertens [5] presents a generalization of folds called *paramorphisms*, which correspond to the primitive recursive definitions. Practically, these are characterized by having available, as well as the results of recursive calls, the data substructures on which those calls were made. We will use the paramorphism operator for snoc lists:

$$paras :: ((\beta \times \langle\alpha\rangle) \times \alpha \rightarrow \beta) \rightarrow \beta \rightarrow \langle\alpha\rangle \rightarrow \beta$$
$$paras\ f\ e\ [\,] \qquad = e$$
$$paras\ f\ e\ (x :\cdot a) = f\ ((paras\ f\ e\ x, x), a)$$

Meijer, Fokkinga and Paterson [6] introduce what they call a *hylomorphism*, which is the composition of an unfold (to generate a data structure) and a fold (to consume that data structure). We use the cons list instance:

$$hylor :: (\alpha \rightarrow 1 + (\beta \times \alpha)) \rightarrow (\beta \times \gamma \rightarrow \gamma) \rightarrow \gamma \rightarrow \alpha \rightarrow \gamma$$
$$hylor\ g\ f\ e = foldr\ f\ e \circ unfoldr\ g$$

The crucial fact about hylomorphisms is that the intermediate data structure is a virtual data structure [7]: it determines the shape of the computation, but need not actually be constructed, and (under certain mild strictness conditions) may be *deforested* [8]. In our case, this gives:

$$hylor\ g\ f\ e\ a = \textbf{case}\ g\ a\ \textbf{of}$$
$$Nothing \qquad \rightarrow e$$
$$Just\ (b, a') \rightarrow f\ (b, hylor\ g\ f\ e\ a')$$

2.6   Fusion

Each of the various recursion patterns introduced above enjoys a crucial property called *fusion*, whereby an adjacent computation can be absorbed. We will use the fusion laws for *folds*:

$$h \circ folds\ f\ e = folds\ g\ (h\ e) \quad \Leftarrow \quad h \circ f = g \circ (h \times id)$$

and for *paras*:

$$h \circ paras\ f\ e = paras\ g\ (h\ e) \quad \Leftarrow \quad h \circ f = g \circ ((h \times id) \times id)$$

To be precise, each of these fusion laws has mild side conditions concerning strictness, but we elide them here because they do not affect subsequent calculations.

For more details, including proofs of the fusion laws from universal properties of the recursion patterns, see for example [9].

2.7   Functors

Finally, many datatypes form *functors*, operations on types with a corresponding 'map' operation on functions:

$$fmap :: Functor\ f \Rightarrow (\alpha \to \beta) \to f\ \alpha \to f\ \beta$$

We will use this just for the 'maybe' functor taking α to $1 + \alpha$.

3   Counting Words

We will use as an illustration in this paper the Unix word count utility wc, a now-standard example in the program comprehension literature. The program shown in Figure 1 is taken from Kernighan and Ritchie's classic book on the C programming language [10], and counts the characters, words and lines in a text file. In fact, it is really only the word counting aspect of this program that

```
#include <stdio.h>
#define IN   1  /* inside a word */
#define OUT  0  /* outside a word */

/* count lines, words, and characters in input */
main()
{
    int c, nl, nw, nc, state;
    state = OUT;
    nl = nw = nc = 0;
    while ((c = getchar()) != EOF) {
        ++nc;
        if (c == '\n')
            ++nl;
        if (c == ' ' || c == '\n' || c == '\t')
            state = OUT;
        else if (state == OUT) {
            state = IN;
            ++nw;
        }
    }
    printf("%d %d %d\n", nl, nw, nc);
}
```

Fig. 1. Kernighan and Ritchie's wc program

has interesting structure; counting the characters is simply computing the length of the text, and counting the lines is implemented as counting the newline characters, which is the length of the text filtered for newlines. So we will actually start with the program in Figure 2, which counts only the words. This might

```
#include <stdio.h>
#define IN   1   /* inside a word */
#define OUT  0   /* outside a word */

int blank(int c) {
  return ( c==' ' || c=='\n' || c=='\t');
}

/* count words in input */
main()
{
    int c, nw, state;
    state = OUT;
    nw = 0;
    while ((c = getchar()) != EOF) {
        if (blank(c))
            state = OUT;
        else if (state == OUT) {
            state = IN;
            ++nw;
        }
    }
    printf("%d\n", nw);
}
```

Fig. 2. The word-counting slice of Kernighan and Ritchie's wc program

be considered as the first step in re-engineering a specification from the original program, by *slicing* that program into three independent aspects [11, 12]. (Indeed, slicing is a fission transformation, reversing the fusion of independent but similarly-structured computations.)

We argue that the C program in Figure 2 is 'obviously' equivalent to the following functional program. The imperative loop has been converted to a tail-recursive function.

$$wc_1 :: [Char] \rightarrow Integer$$
$$wc_1 = fst \circ foldl\ step_1\ (0, False)$$

$$step_1\ ((n, b),\quad c) \mid blank\ c = (n, False)$$
$$step_1\ ((n, True), c)\qquad = (n, True)$$
$$step_1\ ((n, False), c)\qquad = (n + 1, True)$$
$$blank\ c = (c == '\ ') \vee (c == '\n') \vee (c == '\t')$$

Characters come from a string argument rather than standard input, and the count is returned as an integer result rather than printed to standard output. In a fuller study of program comprehension, one would make this equivalence between imperative and functional programming more explicit; but for our purposes — namely, illustrating program fission — we will take the functional program wc_1 as the starting point.

In the remainder of this paper, we reconstruct a number of different implementations wc_2, wc_3... of wc_1. They will all be extensionally equal, possibly modulo different representations of lists, but will have different structures and hence different 'explanations'. We refer to this common behaviour collectively as wc.

4   Directionality

The first observation we make about program wc_1 is that tail recursion — here, in the form of a *foldl* — is somewhat alien to a lazy functional programmer, although — in the form of a `while` loop — it comes quite naturally to an imperative programmer. Program wc_1 would be more comprehensible if it were expressed in a less alien idiom.

With the benefit of understanding of the purpose of the program, namely that it counts words, we could reasonably argue that it does not matter whether we scan the input from left to right or vice versa. We could therefore refactor wc as follows:

$$wc_2 = fst \circ foldr\ step_2\ (0, False)$$
$$step_2 = step_1 \circ twist$$

However, there are two counter-arguments. The first is that, although this refactoring seems reasonable, its formal justification is not so obvious. In particular, it is not the case that the uses of *foldl* in wc_1 and *foldr* in wc_2 are equal: a text that starts with a non-blank but ends with a blank will yield different boolean state values in different directions, even though the number of words is the same both ways. The second counter-argument is that this step depends on understanding the purpose of the program, which is exactly what is unavailable in a program comprehension exercise.

So we take an alternative approach: adapt the underlying data structure to reflect more closely the pattern of computation. After all, we introduced the list type into the problem in the first place: it was not present in the C program. Specifically, the left-to-right traversal in the C program is the natural pattern of computation on snoc lists rather than on cons lists. Therefore, in place of the tail-recursive *foldl* pattern for cons lists, we use the naturally recursive fold on snoc lists:

$$folds :: (\beta \times \alpha \to \beta) \to \beta \to \langle \alpha \rangle \to \beta$$

We therefore make the following refactoring instead.

$$wc_3 :: \langle Char \rangle \to Integer$$
$$wc_3 = fst \circ folds\ step_1\ (0, False)$$

We might elevate this step to a general principle of program comprehension: *consider carefully the data structures used, because they determine the pattern of computation.* This strengthens the case for functional programming as a medium for program comprehension; functional programming encourages the definition of tailor-made datatypes, rather than shoe-horning a problem into one of a fixed collection of general-purpose but sometimes ill-fitting datatypes.

5 Extracting Length

Now, it seems reasonable (although still an invention) that wc involves $length$ somehow; in particular, wc is $length$ after some initial computation. It is evident that wc_3 is counting something, because the result that is returned is constructed from an initial zero that is occasionally incremented. Perhaps we could elevate this observation to a second principle of program comprehension: *if a program returns a count, investigate what it is counting.*

Returning to the program, we name the generator of things to be counted *words* — without any justification as yet, but what's in a name?

$$wc_4 = length \circ words_4$$

Since wc_4 should equal wc_3, in order to deduce a definition of $words_4$, we need to extract a factor of $length$ from the definition of wc_3. Extracting this factor from the *fst* is straightforward, since, by the pair calculus,

$$fst \circ f = length \circ fst \circ g \; \Leftarrow \; f = (length \times id) \circ g$$

That is, extracting a factor of $length$ from wc_3 amounts to extracting a factor of $length \times id$ from $folds \; step_1 \; (0, False)$.

Now we can use fission — fusion in reverse — to deduce e and $glue_4$ (the latter another name chosen with hindsight) such that

$$folds \; step_1 \; (0, False) = (length \times id) \circ folds \; glue_4 \; e$$

For the seed, this requires $(length \times id) \; e = (0, False)$, and so $e = ([\,], False)$. For the binary operator, it requires

$$(length \times id) \circ glue_4 = step_1 \circ ((length \times id) \times id)$$

This equation characterizes a data refinement relation between $glue_4$ and $step_1$, where $glue_4$ is the abstract operation, $step_1$ the concrete operation, and $length \times id$ the abstraction function. Informally, where $glue_4$ trades in sequences, $step_1$ trades in their lengths. Normally, however, one uses a data refinement relationship to derive a concrete implementation from an abstract one; here, of course, we need to go in the opposite direction.

That is, where $step_1$ trades in numbers, we need to construct a function $glue_4$ that trades in their 'unlengths', or sequences of those lengths. Of course, 'unlength' is not a function; there are many sequences of a given length. As a consequence, the data refinement relationship does not completely determine $glue_4$. We need to exercise some creativity in inventing suitable sequences of given lengths. Ockham's Razor suggests that we should use as little creativity as possible in inventing such sequences. This corresponds in our physical analogy with entropy to minimizing the energy injected into the system. Moreover, one might expect that the less creative we are at any given step in a re-engineering exercise, the more freedom there is in later steps (and the less likely we are to lead ourselves into a dead end).

For example, the first clause of the definition of $step_1$ entails that, when c is blank, $glue_4\ ((ws, b), c)$ should be a pair $(ws', False)$ such that ws and ws' have the same length. The least creative way to achieve this is naturally to let $ws' = ws$.

$$glue_4\ ((ws, b), c)\ |\ blank\ c = (ws, False)$$

For the second clause, when c is non-blank, we require $glue_4\ ((ws, True), c)$ to be a pair $(ws', True)$ where ws should again be the same length ws'. We could do the same thing again, equating the two sequences, but in fact there is an even less creative way of proceeding. We note that the physical theory of information states that it requires energy to erase data as well as to invent it. Therefore, we look for a way to use c, combining it with ws while maintaining the latter's length. This is straightforward to do, if ws is a sequence of sequences of characters, provided that it is non-empty: we suffix c to the last sequence in ws. Fortunately, it is an invariant of the fold in wc_3 that when the boolean component of the pair is $True$, the integer component is greater than zero, so our abstract value ws will be a non-empty sequence.

$$glue_4\ ((ws \mathbin{:\cdot} w, True), c) = (ws \mathbin{:\cdot} (w \mathbin{:\cdot} c), True)$$

Finally, for the third clause, again we assume that c is non-blank, and we require $glue_4\ ((ws, False), c)$ to be a pair $(ws', False)$ where ws' is one longer than ws. The least creative way to extend the sequence of strings ws by one string, using the given data c, is to suffix c as an additional singleton string.

$$glue_4\ ((ws, False), c) = (ws \mathbin{:\cdot} [c], True)$$

Assembling these three cases, we have

$$
\begin{aligned}
glue_4\ ((ws, b), c)\ |\ blank\ c &= (ws, False) \\
glue_4\ ((ws \mathbin{:\cdot} w, True), c) &= (ws \mathbin{:\cdot} (w \mathbin{:\cdot} c), True) \\
glue_4\ ((ws, False), c) &= (ws \mathbin{:\cdot} [c], True)
\end{aligned}
$$

And to rewind the reasoning that led us here: if we let

$$words_4 = fst \circ folds\ glue_4\ ([\,], False)$$

then indeed the composition

$$wc_4 = length \circ words_4$$

computes the words in a text, and proceeds to count them.

6   Mind the Gap

In Section 5, we used an argument based on entropy to suggest that, when introducing structure in order to satisfy a fusion law, one should both invent and discard as little information as possible. We stuck to this principle for the second and third clauses of the function $glue_4$, but wavered a little in our resolve when it came to the first clause. The function $words_4$ does discard some information that might be preserved: it conflates different blank characters, such as spaces and newlines, and it also fails to keep track of how many blanks separate words. Therefore, $words_4$ is not invertible. How would the development have proceeded if we had stuck to our principle, and found a way to preserve blank characters?

In the case that c is blank, we wanted $glue_4$ $((ws, b), c)$ to return a pair $(ws', False)$ such that ws and ws' have the same length. We chose to let $ws' = ws$, but this required us to discard c. We can preserve c while maintaining the length of the first component of the pair, provided that that first component is non-empty:

$$glue\ ((ws \mathbin{:\cdot} w, b), c) \mid blank\ c = (ws \mathbin{:\cdot} (w \mathbin{:\cdot} c), False)$$

In effect, this corresponds to representing each word in the input as a non-empty sequence of non-blanks followed by a (possibly-empty, in the case of the last word) sequence of blanks. However, there is nowhere to keep the c while preserving the length of an empty first component — because this representation does not capture blanks at the start of the input. We therefore augment the state, the result of $words$, to represent also the possibly-empty sequence of blanks at the start of the input.

$$words_5 :: \langle Char \rangle \to \langle Char \rangle \times \langle\langle Char \rangle\rangle$$
$$words_5 = fst \circ folds\ glue_5\ (([\,], [\,]), False)$$
$$wc_5 = (length \circ snd) \circ words_5$$

$$glue_5\ (((wb, [\,]), b), c) \qquad\ \ \mid blank\ c = ((wb \mathbin{:\cdot} c, [\,]), False)$$
$$glue_5\ (((wb, ws \mathbin{:\cdot} w), b), c) \mid blank\ c = ((wb, ws \mathbin{:\cdot} (w \mathbin{:\cdot} c)), False)$$
$$glue_5\ (((wb, ws \mathbin{:\cdot} w), True), c) \qquad\ = ((wb, ws \mathbin{:\cdot} (w \mathbin{:\cdot} c)), True)$$
$$glue_5\ (((wb, ws), False), c) \qquad\quad = ((wb, ws \mathbin{:\cdot} [c]), True)$$

Note now that the boolean component of the state is redundant, as it can be determined from the remaining components.

7 A Different Starting Point

The Kernighan and Ritchie C programs above maintain in their main loops, in addition to the counts which are the point of the exercise and will eventually be printed out, a boolean variable **state** indicating whether, if the next character to be read is a non-blank, it will start a new word. One might start with a different program: one that dispenses with this boolean variable, but uses instead a two-character window onto the text to determine which non-blank characters start words. Such a program is shown in Figure 3. We omit the definition of **blank**, since it is identical to the one given earlier. In this section, we subject this new program to the same kind of reasoning as before, to determine whether it could be considered as having 'the same explanation' but with a different implementation, or whether it really arose from a different design.

The program in Figure 3 maintains the invariant that the variable **d** records the character before the 'current' character **c** (except initially, when it acts as

```c
#include <stdio.h>

/* count words in input */
main()
{
  int c, d, nw;
  nw = 0;
  d = ' ';
  c = getchar();
  while (c != EOF) {
    if (!blank(c) && blank(d)) {
      ++nw;
    }
    d = c; c = getchar();
  }
  printf("%d\n", nw);
}
```

Fig. 3. A different wc program, with a two-character window

a space character). This is an instance of the general paramorphism pattern, whereby the treatment of each element depends not just on the treatment of previous elements, but also on those previous elements themselves.

$$wc_6 = paras\ step_6\ 0$$
$$step_6\ ((n, x), c) \qquad | \ blank\ c = n$$
$$step_6\ ((n, x :\cdot d), c) \ | \ blank\ d = n + 1$$
$$step_6\ ((n, x :\cdot d), c) \qquad\qquad = n$$
$$step_6\ ((n, []), c) \qquad\qquad = n + 1$$

Note that the use of the paramorphism pattern encodes the invariant that $n = wc_6\ x$ in every application $step_6\ ((n, x), c)$. It therefore explicitly captures the invariant about the value of variable d, which must therefore be comprehended from the code. It also provides a separate initial boundary condition to remove the need for the 'virtual' space character before the first 'real' character.

As before, we try to write this as the composition of $length$ with some simpler function, using paramorphism fission. Clearly, the seed of the paramorphism has to be $[]$, the only sequence with length 0. For the operator, the fusion condition is that

$$length \circ glue_7 = step_6 \circ ((length \times id) \times id)$$

If we can construct a function $glue_7$ satisfying this condition, then $length$ fuses with $paras\ glue_7\ []$ to give wc_6.

For the first clause, when c is blank, apparently $glue_7$ should simply return the first of its three argument components.

$$glue_7\ ((ws, x), c) \ | \ blank\ c = ws$$

For the second clause, when c is non-blank, the initial segment $x :\!\cdot d$ of characters seen so far is non-empty, and the previous character d is blank, we should return a sequence one longer than the first argument component ws. The obvious thing to do is to suffix a new element to ws, and the least creative data-preserving way of doing that is to suffix $[c]$.

$$glue_7 \ ((ws, x :\!\cdot d), c) \mid blank \ d \ = \ ws :\!\cdot [c]$$

For the third clause, when c is non-blank, the initial segment $x :\!\cdot d$ is non-empty, and d is also non-blank, we should return a sequence the same length as the first argument component ws. Returning ws unchanged loses the data c. A less creative way would be to preserve c by combining it with data in ws, provided the latter is non-empty. Fortunately, it is an invariant that in this circumstance ws is non-empty.

$$glue_7 \ ((ws :\!\cdot w, x :\!\cdot d), c) \ = \ ws :\!\cdot (w :\!\cdot c)$$

For the fourth and final clause, when c is non-blank but the initial segment of the list is empty, we need to extend the sequence by a single element. The least creative type-correct way to do this is make a singleton string from c.

$$glue_7 \ ((ws, [\,]), c) \ = \ ws :\!\cdot [c]$$

Summing up, we have deduced the following definition of $glue_7$:

$$
\begin{aligned}
glue_7 \ ((ws, x), c) \qquad & \mid blank \ c \ = \ ws \\
glue_7 \ ((ws, x :\!\cdot d), c) \mid & blank \ d \ = \ ws :\!\cdot [c] \\
glue_7 \ ((ws :\!\cdot w, x :\!\cdot d), c) \quad & = \ ws :\!\cdot (w :\!\cdot c) \\
glue_7 \ ((ws, [\,]), c) \qquad & = \ ws :\!\cdot [c]
\end{aligned}
$$

We then define

$$
\begin{aligned}
wc_7 \ \ & = \ length \circ words_7 \\
words_7 & = \ paras \ glue_7 \ [\,]
\end{aligned}
$$

Using paramorphism fusion, the $length$ combines with the paramorphism, yielding the earlier program wc_6. Moreover, $words_7$ does indeed yield the individual words in the text.

8   Nested Loops

All the C programs for the wordcount problem that we have seen so far have a single loop, with additional hidden state to determine the behaviour of the loop body. A different way of solving the problem is to use nested loops, in effect using the program counter instead of that hidden state. One such program is shown in Figure 4. In this program, the variable c always contains the next character in the text, or the EOF character at the end of the text. The outer loop runs indefinitely. The first inner loop skips blanks. If this first inner loop reaches the end of the text, control breaks out of the outer loop and the program

```
#include <stdio.h>

main() {
    int c=getchar(), nw=0;
    while (1) {
        while (c != EOF && blank(c))
            c=getchar();
        if (c == EOF)
            break;
        nw++;
        while (c != EOF && !blank(c))
            c=getchar();
    }
    printf("%d\n", nw);
}
```

Fig. 4. A wc program with nested loops

quits. Otherwise, the first inner loop terminated because it reached a non-blank character; the number of words is incremented, and the rest of that word skipped.

We claim that this program has the following 'obvious' functional equivalent.

$$wc_8\ x = \textbf{let}\ y = dropWhile\ blank\ x\ \textbf{in}$$
$$\textbf{if}\ null\ y\ \textbf{then}\ 0$$
$$\textbf{else}\ 1 + wc_8\ (dropWhile\ (not \circ blank)\ y)$$

where $null$ is the predicate that returns $True$ precisely of the empty list, and $dropWhile::(\alpha \rightarrow Bool) \rightarrow [\alpha] \rightarrow [\alpha]$ takes a predicate p and a list x and discards the longest prefix of x all of whose elements satisfy p. (Strictly speaking, getting to this program entails the elimination of the accumulating parameter that is the word count.) This program matches the pattern of a list hylomorphism:

$$wc_9 :: [Char] \rightarrow Integer$$
$$wc_9 = hylor\ word_9\ plus_9\ 0$$
$$plus_9\ (w, n) = 1 + n$$
$$word_9\ x = \textbf{let}\ y = dropWhile\ blank\ x\ \textbf{in}$$
$$\textbf{if}\ null\ y\ \textbf{then}\ Nothing$$
$$\textbf{else}\ Just\ ((), dropWhile\ (not \circ blank)\ y)$$

Of course, a hylomorphism fissions automatically into a fold after an unfold:

$$wc_{10} = foldr\ plus_9\ 0 \circ unfoldr\ word_9$$

And as expected, the fold phase is just $length$, and counts the items generated by the unfold phase; these items are all units, but there is precisely one of them for each word.

We might apply the principle of least creativity again, preserving those non-blank elements of y discarded by $word_9$:

$$word_{11}\ x = \textbf{let}\ y = dropWhile\ blank\ x\ \textbf{in}$$
$$\textbf{if}\ null\ y\ \textbf{then}\ Nothing$$
$$\textbf{else}\ \ Just\ (span\ (not \circ blank)\ y)$$

Here, $span :: (\alpha \to Bool) \to [\alpha] \to [\alpha] \times [\alpha]$ is a generalization of $dropWhile$: it takes a predicate p and a list x and returns a pair of lists (y, z) such that $y + z = x$ and $y = dropWhile\ p\ x$.

When $hylor\ word_{11}\ plus_9\ 0$ is fissioned, we get:

$$wc_{11} = foldr\ plus_9\ 0 \circ unfoldr\ word_{11}$$

Here, the unfold phase really is just *words* again.

It might seem curious that we have reverted to cons lists for the virtual data structure of the hylomorphism, rather than continuing to work with snoc lists. But of course, the virtual data structure of a hylomorphism merely encapsulates the pattern of recursion, and hylomorphisms for cons lists and snoc lists are entirely equivalent.

9   Counting Revisited

Let us return our attention to the recursive equivalent of the program with nested loops from Figure 4:

$$wc_8\ x = \textbf{let}\ y = dropWhile\ blank\ x\ \textbf{in}$$
$$\textbf{if}\ null\ y\ \textbf{then}\ 0$$
$$\textbf{else}\ \ 1 + wc_8\ (dropWhile\ (not \circ blank)\ y)$$

Our reconstruction in Section 8 started from the observation that this recursive program is an instance of the hylomorphism pattern on lists. However, the list algebra involved in this hylomorphism is a very special one, namely the initial algebra of natural numbers. This leads to another explanation of the same program.

We adapt the type of the function, so that it returns a recursively-constructed natural number rather than a built-in integer.

$$wc_{12}\ \ :: [Char] \to Nat$$
$$wc_{12}\ x = \textbf{let}\ y = dropWhile\ blank\ x\ \textbf{in}$$
$$\textbf{if}\ null\ y\ \textbf{then}\ Zero$$
$$\textbf{else}\ \ Succ\ (wc_{12}\ (dropWhile\ (not \circ blank)\ y))$$

Now we see immediately that this is a straightforward instance of *unfoldn*:

$$wc_{13} = unfoldn\ dropWord_{13}$$
$$dropWord_{13}\ x = \textbf{let}\ y = dropWhile\ blank\ x\ \textbf{in}$$
$$\textbf{if}\ null\ y\ \textbf{then}\ Nothing$$
$$\textbf{else}\ \ Just\ (dropWhile\ (not \circ blank)\ y)$$

In fact, this observation is an instance of a more general rule about the composition of *length* and an unfold to lists:

$$length \circ unfoldr\ f = nat2int \circ unfoldn\ (fmap\ snd \circ f)$$

where *nat2int* :: *Nat* → *Integer* coerces from recursively-constructed naturals to built-in integers. This law could be phrased as a principle of counting: rather than enumerating a list of things, then computing the length of that list, one can more directly count the number of times the operation 'discard a thing' can be performed.

Unfolds to the naturals are surprisingly common, despite the unfamiliarity of the operator *unfoldn* itself. The law above suggests that they capture many counting problems. Gibbons [13] shows that *unfoldn* is essentially the minimization operator from recursive function theory, the additional operator needed to progress from the primitive recursive to the general recursive functions, or equivalently from `for` to `while` loops. For example, integer division is an unfold to naturals, since dividing by m is the same as computing the number of times m can be subtracted without the difference becoming negative. Elsewhere [14] we have argued that even unfolds to lists are underappreciated; we believe that argument applies a fortiori to unfolds to other datatypes such as the naturals.

10   Discussion

The reconstruction of specifications from programs is an important part of a larger endeavour called *software renovation*. This field addresses the difficult problem of maintaining legacy software when its design documentation is inadequate or unavailable. In order to modify undocumented software, one essentially is forced to spend some effort in comprehending the existing system (unless one is prepared to use trial and error, making random changes and hoping for a useful result), *reverse engineering* a higher-level design from a lower-level implementation. Nelson [15] presents a useful, if brief and rather old, survey of reverse engineering and program comprehension terminology.

Program comprehension has applications beyond software maintenance, too; it is also a useful educational tool. Linger's classic text on structured programming [16, Chapter 5] presents as a pedagogic exercise a significant case study of reconstructing a top-down design for an unstructured and undocumented program. Dromey [17], Knuth [18], and Deimel and Naveda [19] argue for the benefits of program comprehension, and more generally *program reading*, in helping students learn to program.

There has been other work on using program comprehension techniques to reintroduce recursion (for example, [20]), but this tends to focus on the earlier stage of simply introducing recursion, which we have glossed over; the later stage of subsequently investigating the structure of that recursion is largely unexplored. The most relevant work in this direction is by Oliveira, who inspired our work. One presentation [21] presents calculations in both VDM-SL and a pointfree functional style, and focusses on the 'BMF transformation' between the two notations; later work [12] sticks to the pointfree style, and places a stronger emphasis on slicing. Neither paper uses fission to extract the *length* factor, and curiously, both derive the paramorphism wc_6 from Kernighan and Ritchie's original program rather than from our alternative starting point in Figure 3, arguably straying from reverse engineering into re-engineering.

The view we have taken in this paper is that the essence of a design is expressed in terms of higher-order recursion patterns. A similar view underlies our and others' arguments [13, 22] that the different designs for sorting algorithms embodied by insertion sort, merge sort, quick sort and so on arise from using different patterns of recursion. If one accepts the claim that design patterns in object-oriented programming correspond to recursion patterns in generic functional programming [23, 24], then this is further support for Johnson's slogan that 'patterns document architectures' [25].

An advantage of using a formal linguistic vehicle such as functional programming for expressing patterns, rather than the informal prose and pictures that are traditional in the patterns community [26], is that those patterns and the programs that exhibit them may be manipulated and reasoned about mathematically [24]. In particular, well-known *fusion laws* can be used to flatten the structure imposed by a pattern, for efficiency; in this paper, we have used those laws in reverse as *fission laws* in order to recover lost structure. The term 'program fission' has been mentioned before [27], but in the context of partitioning data- rather than control structures.

We have examined three different C programs for counting the words in a text file, and attempted to reverse engineer designs from these implementations. Naturally, different implementations of a program arise from different designs for those implementations; but it is reasonable to ask how divergent those designs are: how much of the development is shared, and how late in the process do the evolutionary forks appear? In fact, we have shown that the three different wordcount programs might all have arisen from the same high-level design, namely the composition *length ∘ words*. The differences between the three programs are explained in terms of different strategies for implementing *words*: as a fold, a paramorphism, or an unfold — the first two of which are inductive, the last coinductive. However, the coinductive design lends itself to an alternative explanation of the problem, in terms of counting rather than enumeration, which might be considered a second high-level design.

We leave as future work a closer study of the translation from imperative programs (such as in Figure 2) into what we have called their 'obvious' functional equivalents (such as the program wc_1). It would also be interesting to prove the equivalence of the various specifications $wc_4, wc_7, wc_{11}, wc_{13}$ that we have reconstructed; presumably, it would be simpler than proving the equivalence of the lower-level programs from which they were obtained.

Acknowledgements. This paper was inspired by a discussion with José Nuno Oliveira at the 59th meeting of IFIP Working Group 2.1 in Nottingham in September 2004. The use of the Unix wc utility as a standard benchmark example in the program comprehension community appears to be due to Gallagher and Lyle [28], although we learnt about it from Oliveira [21]. Our approach has been informed by Oliveira's 'Program Understanding and Re-engineering' project [29].

We are indebted to a number of people who have helped to improve this paper. We are grateful to the participants at the PURe workshop in Minho in October 2005, especially to José Nuno Oliveira for the invitation to speak, and to Alcino Cunha for the realisation that our program wc_8 is really an unfold to the naturals. Members of the Algebra of Programming research group at Oxford, IFIP Working Group 2.1, the *Datatype-Generic Programming* project at Oxford and Nottingham, and the anonymous *Mathematics of Program Construction* referees, made a number of insightful comments; the quip about not even knowing it is a pig you should reconstruct is due to Geraint Jones. The code is formatted with Ralf Hinze and Andres Löh's wonderful lhs2TEX translator.

References

1. Raymond, E.S., ed.: The New Hacker's Dictionary. MIT Press (1991)
2. Eastwood, A.: It's a hard sell—and hard work too (software re-engineering). Computing Canada **18**(22) (1992) 35
3. Bird, R.S.: The promotion and accumulation strategies in transformational programming. ACM Trans. on Program. Lang. and Syst. **6**(4) (1984) 487–504 // Addendum in **7**(3) (1985) 490–492
4. Bird, R.S., Wadler, P.L.: An Introduction to Functional Programming. Prentice Hall (1988)
5. Meertens, L.: Paramorphisms. Formal Aspects of Comput **4**(5) (1992) 413–424
6. Meijer, E., Fokkinga, M., Paterson, R.: Functional programming with bananas, lenses, envelopes and barbed wire. In Hughes, J., ed.: Proc. 5th ACM Conf. on Functional Programming Languages and Computer Architecture, FPCA '91. Vol. 523 of Lect. Notes in Comput. Science. Springer-Verlag (1991) 124–144
7. Swierstra, S. D., de Moor, O.: Virtual data structures. In Möller, B., Partsch, H., Schumann, S., eds.: IFIP TC2/WG2.1 State-of-the-Art Report on Formal Program Development. Vol. 755 of Lect. Notes in Comput. Sci. Springer-Verlag (1993) 355–371
8. Wadler, P.: Deforestation: Transforming programs to eliminate trees. Theor. Comput. Sci. **73** (1990) 231–248
9. Gibbons, J.: Calculating functional programs. In Backhouse, R., Crole, R., Gibbons, J., eds.: Revised Lectures from Int. Summer School and Wksh. on Algebraic and Coalgebraic Methods in the Mathematics of Program Construction, ACMMPC 2000. Vol. 2297 of Lect. Notes in Comput. Sci. Springer-Verlag (2002) 148–203
10. Kernighan, B.W., Ritchie, D.M.: The C Programming Language. Prentice Hall (1988)
11. Weiser, M.: Program slicing. IEEE Trans. on Softw. Engin. **10**(4) (1984) 352–357
12. Villavicencio, G., Oliveira, J.N.: Reverse program calculation supported by code slicing. In: Proc. of 8th Working Conf. on Reverse Engineering, WCRE '01. IEEE (2001) 35–48
13. Gibbons, J.: Origami programming. In Gibbons, J., de Moor, O., eds.: The Fun of Programming. Cornerstones in Computing. Palgrave (2003) 41–60

14. Gibbons, J., Jones, G.: The under-appreciated unfold. In Proc. of 3rd ACM SIGPLAN Int. Conf. on Functional Programming, ICFP '88. ACM Press (1998) 273–279

15. Nelson, M.L.: A survey of reverse engineering and program comprehension. Techn. Report cs.SE/0503068, arXiv.org (1996)

16. Linger, R.C., Mills, H.D., Witt, B.I.: Structured Programming: Theory and Practice. Addison-Wesley (1979)

17. Dromey, R.G.: How to Solve It by Computer. Prentice Hall (1982)

18. Knuth, D.E.: Literate programming. Computer J. **27**(2) (1984) 97–111

19. Deimel, L.E., Naveda, J.F.: Reading computer programs: Instructor's guide and exercises. Techn. Report CMU/SEI-90-EM-3. Software Engineering Inst., Carnegie-Mellon University (1990)

20. Ward, M.P., Bennett, K.H.: Recursion removal/introduction by formal transformation: An aid to program development and program comprehension. Computer J. **42**(8) (1999) 650–673

21. Oliveira, J.N.: Bagatelle in C arranged for VDM SoLo. J. of Univ. Comput. Sci. **7**(8) (2001) 754–781

22. Augusteijn, L.: Sorting morphisms. In Swierstra, S.D., Henriques, P.R., Oliveira, J.N., eds.: Revised Lectures from 3rd Int. School on Advanced Functional Programming, AFP '98. Vol. 1608 of Lect. Notes in Comput. Sci. (1999) 1–27

23. Gibbons, J.: Patterns in datatype-generic programming. In Striegnitz, J., Davis, K., eds.: Multiparadigm Programming 2003: Joint Proc. of 3rd Int. Wksh. on Multiparadigm Programming with Object-Oriented Languages, MPOOL'03, and 1st Int. Wksh. on Declarative Programming in the Context of Object-Oriented Languages (PD-COOL'03) Vol. 27 of NIC Series. John von Neumann Institute for Computing (NIC) (2003) 277–289

24. Gibbons, J.: Design patterns as higher-order datatype-generic programs. Submitted for publication (2006)

25. Johnson, R.: Documenting frameworks using patterns. In Proc. of 7th Ann. Conf. on Object-Oriented Programming Systems, Languages and Applications, OOPSLA '92. ACM Press (1992) 63–76

26. Gamma, E., Helm, R., Johnson, R., Vlissides, J.: Design Patterns: Elements of Reusable Object-Oriented Software. Addison-Wesley (1995)

27. Bobeff, G., Noyé, J.: Molding components using program specialization techniques. In Bosch, J., Szyperski, C., Weck, W., eds.: Proc. of 8th Int. Wksh. on Component-Oriented Programming, WCOP '03 (2003)

28. Gallagher, K.B., Lyle, J.R.: Using program slicing in software maintenance. IEEE Trans. on Softw. Engin. **17**(8) (1991) 751–761

29. PURe research group: Program understanding and re-engineering: Calculi and applications. Web site (1999-2005) http://wiki.di.uminho.pt/wiki/bin/view/PURe/

"Scrap Your Boilerplate" Revolutions

Ralf Hinze and Andres Löh

Institut für Informatik III, Universität Bonn
Römerstraße 164, 53117 Bonn, Germany
{ralf, loeh}@informatik.uni-bonn.de

Abstract. Generic programming allows you to write a function once, and use it many times at different types. Traditionally, generic functions are defined by induction on the structure of types. "Scrap your boilerplate" (SYB) is a radically different approach that dispatches on the structure of values. In previous work, we have shown how to reconcile both approaches using the concept of generic views: many generic functions can be based either on the classical sum-of-products view or on the view that underlies SYB, the so-called 'spine' view. One distinct advantage of the spine view is its generality: it is applicable to a large class of data types, including generalised algebraic data types. Its main weakness roots in the value-orientation: one can only define generic functions that consume data (*show*) but not ones that produce data (*read*). Furthermore, functions that abstract over type constructors (*map*, *reduce*) are out of reach. In this paper, we show how to overcome both limitations. The main technical contributions are the 'type spine' view and the 'lifted spine' view.

1 Introduction

A generic function is one that the programmer writes once, but which is used over many different data types. The folklore examples are pretty printing, parsing, mapping functions, reductions, and so on. There is an impressive body of work on generic programming [1,2,3]. The approaches differ wildly in syntax, expressiveness and ease of use. However, they all share a common structure. In general, support for generic programming consists of two essential ingredients: a way to write overloaded functions, and independently, a way to access the structure of values in a uniform way.

Overloading is essential as almost every generic function exhibits type-specific behaviour: Haskell's pretty printer, for instance, displays pairs and lists using a special mix-fix notation.

A uniform mechanism for accessing the structure of values is essential to program the 'generic part' of a generic function: a generic pretty printer works for all data types including types that the programmer is yet to define. Consequently, the pretty printer has to treat elements of these types in a uniform way: in Haskell, for instance, they are displayed using prefix notation.

The two ingredients are orthogonal concepts, and for both, there is a choice. In Haskell, overloaded functions can be expressed

T. Uustalu (Ed.): MPC 2006, LNCS 4014, pp. 180–208, 2006.

- using the class system [4,5],
- using a type-safe cast operation [6,3],
- by reflecting the type structure onto the value level [7,8],
- by specialisation [1,9],
- or by a combination of the above [10].

Each approach has certain advantages and disadvantages. Nonetheless, they are mostly interchangeable and of similar expressiveness. For the purposes of this paper, we pick the third alternative, type reflection, as it is the most perspicuous.

The structural view, on the other hand, has a much larger impact: it affects the set of data types we can represent, the class of functions we can write and potentially the efficiency of these functions. For instance,

- PolyP [1] views data types as fixed points of regular functors,
- Generic Haskell [2] uses a sum-of-products view.

"Scrap your boilerplate" (SYB) [3] was originally introduced as a combinator library for generic programming, so it seemed to lack the structural view on data types. In a previous paper [11], we have revealed this structure:

- SYB [3] builds upon the so-called 'spine' view.

The spine view treats data uniformly as constructor applications; it is, in a sense, *value-oriented*. This is in contrast to the classical views of PolyP and Generic Haskell, which can be characterised as *type-oriented*. One distinct advantage of the spine view is its generality: it is applicable to a large class of data types, including *generalised algebraic data types* (GADTs) [12,13]. The reason for the wide applicability is simple: a data type definition describes how to construct data, the spine view captures just this. Its main weakness also roots in the value-orientation: one can only define generic functions that consume data (*show*) but not ones that produce data (*read*). Again, the reason for the limitation is simple: a uniform view on individual constructor applications is useful if you have data in your hands, but it is of no help if you want to construct data. Furthermore, functions that abstract over type constructors (*map*, *reduce*) are out of reach, because type constructors comprise no values.

In this paper, we show how to overcome both limitations. The main technical contributions are the 'type spine' view for defining generic producers and the 'lifted spine' view, which renders it possible to define generic functions that abstract over type constructors.

The rest of the paper is structured as follows. In Section 2 we review the SYB approach to generic programming. We introduce the spine view and explain how to define generic consumers such as *show*. Section 3 introduces a variant of the spine view, the 'type spine' view, that allows us to write generic producers such as *read*. Section 4 then broadens the scope of SYB to generic functions that abstract over type constructors. In particular, we show how to implement classic generic functions such as *map*. Finally, Section 5 reviews related work and Section 6 concludes. For reference, Appendix A defines the helper functions that are used in the main body of the paper.

2 Recap: "Scrap Your Boilerplate" Reloaded

This section summarises the essentials ideas of the SYB approach to generic programming. The material is based on the paper " 'Scrap Your Boilerplate' Reloaded" [11]. Readers familiar with our previous work may wish to skim through Sections 2.1 and 2.2 and proceed with Section 2.3.

As noted in the introduction, support for generic programming consists of two essential ingredients: a way to write overloaded functions and a way to access the structure of values in a uniform way. Section 2.1 introduces *type reflection*, the mechanism we use to implement overloaded functions. This choice is entirely independent of the paper's main theme and has been taken with clarity in mind. Section 2.2 then reveals the generic view SYB builds upon.

2.1   Overloaded Functions

Assume that you want to define a pretty printer, such as Haskell's *show* function, that works for a family of types including characters, integers, lists and pairs. The *show* function cannot be assigned the polymorphic type $\alpha \to String$, as *show* is not insensitive to what type its argument is. Quite on the contrary, the particular algorithm *show* invokes depends on the type: characters, for instance, are displayed differently from lists.

An obvious idea is to pass the pretty printer an additional argument that *represents* the type of the value that we wish to convert to its string representation. As a first try, we could assign the pretty printer the type $Type \to \alpha \to String$ where *Type* is the type of type representations. Unfortunately, this is too simple-minded: the parametricity theorem [14] implies that a function of this type must necessarily ignore its second parameter. This argument breaks down, however, if we additionally parameterise *Type* by the type it represents. The signature of the pretty printer then becomes $Type\ \alpha \to \alpha \to String$.

The idea is that an element of type $Type\ \tau$ is a representation of the type τ. Using a *generalised algebraic data type* [12,13], we can define *Type* directly in Haskell.

```
data Type :: * → * where
    Char :: Type Char
    Int  :: Type Int
    List :: Type α → Type [α]
    Pair :: Type α → Type β → Type (α, β)
```

Each type has a unique representation: the type *Int* is represented by the constructor *Int*, the type $(String, Int)$ is represented by *Pair (List Char) Int*. For any given τ in our family of types, $Type\ \tau$ comprises exactly one element; $Type\ \tau$ is a so-called *singleton type*.

In the sequel, we shall often need to annotate an expression with its type representation. We introduce a special type for this purpose.[1]

infixl 1 :
data $Typed\ \alpha = (:)\{\,val :: \alpha,\ type :: Type\ \alpha\,\}$

The **data** definition defines a single two-argument constructor, named ':', which is usually written infix. Using Haskell's record notation we additionally introduce two projection functions *val* and *type*. Thus, $4711 : Int$ is an element of $Typed\ Int$ and $(47, \texttt{"hello"}) : Pair\ Int\ (List\ Char)$ is an element of $Typed\ (Int, String)$. It is important to note the difference between $x : t$ and $x :: \tau$. The former expression constructs a pair consisting of a value x and a representation t of its type. The latter expression is Haskell syntax for 'x has type τ'.

Given these prerequisites, we can define the desired family of pretty printers. For concreteness, we re-implement Haskell's *showsPrec* function (the Int argument of *showsPrec* specifies the operator precedence of the enclosing context; $ShowS$ is shorthand for $String \rightarrow String$, Hughes' efficient sequence type [15]).

$$
\begin{aligned}
&showsPrec :: Int \rightarrow Typed\ \alpha \rightarrow ShowS \\
&showsPrec\ d\ (c : Char) \qquad = showsPrec_{Char}\quad d\ c \\
&showsPrec\ d\ (n : Int) \qquad\quad = showsPrec_{Int}\qquad d\ n \\
&showsPrec\ d\ (s : List\ Char) = showsPrec_{String}\ d\ s \\
&showsPrec\ d\ (xs : List\ a) \quad = showsList\ [\,shows\ (x : a)\ |\ x \leftarrow xs\,] \\
&showsPrec\ d\ ((x, y) : Pair\ a\ b) \\
&\quad = showChar\ {'}({'} \cdot shows\ (x : a) \cdot showChar\ {'},{'} \\
&\qquad\qquad\quad \cdot shows\ (y : b) \cdot showChar\ {'}){'}
\end{aligned}
$$

The function *showsPrec* makes heavy use of type annotations; its type $Int \rightarrow Typed\ \alpha \rightarrow ShowS$ is essentially an uncurried version of $Int \rightarrow Type\ \alpha \rightarrow \alpha \rightarrow ShowS$. Even though *showsPrec* has a polymorphic type, each equation implements a more specific case as dictated by the type representation. For example, the first equation has type $Int \rightarrow Typed\ Char \rightarrow ShowS$. This is typical of functions on GADTs.

Let us consider each equation in turn. The first three equations delegate the work to tailor-made functions, $showsPrec_{Char}$, $showsPrec_{Int}$ and $showsPrec_{String}$, which are provided from somewhere. Lists are shown using *showsList*, defined in Appendix A, which produces a comma-separated sequence of elements between square brackets. Note that strings, lists of characters, are treated differently: they are shown in double quotes by virtue of the third equation. Finally, pairs are enclosed in parentheses, the two elements being separated by a comma.

The function *showsPrec* is defined by explicit case analysis on the type representation. This is typical of an overloaded function, but not compulsory: the

---

[1] The operator ':' is predefined in Haskell for constructing lists. However, since we use type annotations much more frequently than lists, we use ':' for the former and *Nil* and *Cons* for the latter purpose. Furthermore, we agree upon that the pattern $x : t$ is matched from *right to left*: first the type representation t is matched, then the associated value x.

wrapper functions *shows* and *show*, defined below, are given by simple abstractions.

$$shows \quad :: \; Typed \; \alpha \rightarrow ShowS$$
$$shows \quad = showsPrec \; 0$$
$$show \quad :: \; Typed \; \alpha \rightarrow String$$
$$show \; x = shows \; x \; ""$$

Note that *shows* and *showsPrec* are mutually recursive.

An overloaded function is a single entity that incorporates a family of functions where each member implements some type-specific behaviour. If we wish to extend the pretty printer to other data types we have to add new constructors to the *Type* data type and new equations to *showsPrec*. As an example, consider the data type of binary trees.

data *Tree* α = *Empty* | *Node* (*Tree* α) α (*Tree* α)

To be able to show binary trees, we add *Tree* to the type of type representations

Tree :: *Type* $\alpha \rightarrow$ *Type* (*Tree* α)

and extend *showsPrec* by suitable equations

$$showsPrec \; d \; (Empty : Tree \; a) = showString \; "Empty"$$
$$showsPrec \; d \; (Node \; l \; x \; r : Tree \; a)$$
$$= showParen \; (d > 10) \; (showString \; "Node" \bullet showsPrec \; 11 \; (l : Tree \; a)$$
$$\bullet \; showsPrec \; 11 \; (x : a)$$
$$\bullet \; showsPrec \; 11 \; (r : Tree \; a))$$

The predefined function *showParen* b puts its argument in parentheses if b is *True*. The operator '$\bullet$' separates two elements by a space, see Appendix A.

2.2   Generic Functions

Using type reflection we can program an *overloaded function* that works for all types of a given family. Let us now broaden the scope of *showsPrec*, *shows* and *show* so that they work for *all* data types including types that the programmer is yet to define. For emphasis, we call such functions *generic functions*.

We have seen in the previous section that whenever we define a new data type, we add a constructor of the same name to the type of type representations and we add corresponding equations to *all* overloaded functions that are defined by explicit case analysis. While the extension of *Type* is cheap and easy (a compiler could do this for us), the extension of all overloaded functions is laborious and difficult (can you imagine a compiler doing that?). In this section we shall develop a scheme so that it suffices to extend *Type* by a new constructor and to extend a *single* overloaded function. The remaining functions adapt themselves.

To achieve this goal we need to find a way to treat elements of a data type in a general, uniform way. Consider an arbitrary element of some data type. It is always of the form $C \; e_1 \; \cdots \; e_n$, a constructor applied to some values. For instance, an element of *Tree Int* is either *Empty* or of the form *Node l a r*. The idea is to make this applicative structure visible and accessible: to this end we mark the constructor using *Con* and each function application using '$\diamond$'. Additionally, we annotate the constructor arguments with their types and the constructor itself with information on its syntax. As an example, *Empty* becomes *Con empty* and *Node l a r* becomes *Con node*$\diamond$*(l: Tree Int)*$\diamond$*(a:Int)*$\diamond$*(r:Tree Int)* where *empty* and *node* are the tree constructors augmented with additional information. The functions *Con* and '$\diamond$' are themselves constructors of a data type called *Spine*.

infixl 0 $\diamond$

data *Spine* :: $* \to *$ **where**
    Con :: *Constr* $\alpha \to$ *Spine* α
    ($\diamond$) :: *Spine* $(\alpha \to \beta) \to$ *Typed* $\alpha \to$ *Spine* β

The type is called *Spine* because its elements represent the possibly partial spine of a constructor application. The following table illustrates the stepwise construction of a spine.

    node :: *Constr* (*Tree Int* $\to$ *Int* $\to$ *Tree Int* $\to$ *Tree Int*)
    Con node :: *Spine* (*Tree Int* $\to$ *Int* $\to$ *Tree Int* $\to$ *Tree Int*)
    Con node $\diamond$ (*l* : **Tree Int**) :: *Spine* (*Int* $\to$ *Tree Int* $\to$ *Tree Int*)
    Con node $\diamond$ (*l* : **Tree Int**) $\diamond$ (*a* : **Int**) :: *Spine* (*Tree Int* $\to$ *Tree Int*)
    Con node $\diamond$ (*l* : **Tree Int**) $\diamond$ (*a* : **Int**) $\diamond$ (*r* : **Tree Int**) :: *Spine* (*Tree Int*)

Note that the type variable α does not appear in the result type of '$\diamond$': it is existentially quantified.[2] This is the reason why we annotate the second argument with its type. Otherwise, we wouldn't be able to use it as an argument of an overloaded function, see below.

Elements of type *Constr* α comprise an element of type α, namely the original data constructor, plus some additional information about its syntax: for the purposes of this paper we confine ourselves to the name of the constructor.

    data *Constr* $\alpha = Constr\{\, constr :: \alpha, name :: String\,\}$

Given a value of type *Spine* α, we can easily recover the original value of type α by undoing the conversion step.

    fromSpine :: *Spine* $\alpha \to \alpha$
    fromSpine (*Con c*) = *constr c*
    fromSpine (*f* $\diamond$ *x*) = (*fromSpine f*) (*val x*)

The function *fromSpine* is parametrically polymorphic: it works independently of the type in question as it simply replaces *Con* with the original constructor and '$\diamond$' with function application.

---

[2] All type variables in Haskell are universally quantified. However, $\forall \alpha.\sigma \to \tau$ is isomorphic to $(\exists \alpha.\sigma) \to \tau$ provided α does not appear free in τ, which is where the term 'existential type' comes from.

The inverse of *fromSpine* is not polymorphic; rather, it is an overloaded function of type *Typed* $\alpha \to$ *Spine* α. Its definition, however, follows a trivial pattern (so trivial that the definition could be easily generated by a compiler): if the data type contains a constructor C with signature

$$C :: \tau_1 \to \cdots \to \tau_n \to \tau_0$$

then the equation for *toSpine* takes the form

$$toSpine \ (C \ x_1 \ \ldots \ x_n : t_0) = Con \ c \ \diamond \ (x_1 : t_1) \ \diamond \cdots \diamond \ (x_n : t_n)$$

where c is the annotated version of C and t_i is the type representation of τ_i. As an example, here is the definition of *toSpine* for binary trees:

$$
\begin{aligned}
&toSpine :: Typed \ \alpha \to Spine \ \alpha \\
&toSpine \ (Empty : Tree \ a) \quad = Con \ empty \\
&toSpine \ (Node \ l \ x \ r : Tree \ a) = Con \ node \ \diamond \ (l : Tree \ a) \ \diamond \ (x : a) \ \diamond \ (r : Tree \ a)
\end{aligned}
$$

The smart constructors *empty* and *node* are given by

$$
\begin{aligned}
&empty \ :: \ Constr \ (Tree \ \alpha) \\
&empty \ = \ Constr\{ constr = Empty, name = \texttt{"Empty"}\} \\
&node \ \ :: \ Constr \ (Tree \ \alpha \to \alpha \to Tree \ \alpha \to Tree \ \alpha) \\
&node \ \ = \ Constr\{ constr = Node, \ \ name = \texttt{"Node"}\}
\end{aligned}
$$

It is easy to see that *fromSpine* (*toSpine* $(x : t)$) = x. The converse, however, is not true as the *Spine* type is not restricted to constructor applications: for instance, *fromSpine* (*Con copy* $\diamond$ (*Empty* : *Tree Int*)) = *Empty* where *copy* is the annotated identity, $Constr\{ constr = \lambda x \to x, name = \texttt{"copy"}\}$.

With all the machinery in place we can now turn *showsPrec* into a truly generic function. The idea is to add a catch-all case that takes care of all the remaining type cases in a uniform manner.

$$
\begin{aligned}
&showsPrec \ d \ x = showParen \ (arity \ x > 0 \land d > 10) \ (shows_- \ (toSpine \ x)) \\
&shows_- :: Spine \ \alpha \to ShowS \\
&shows_- \ (Con \ c) = showString \ (name \ c) \\
&shows_- \ (f \ \diamond \ x) \ \ = shows_- \ f \bullet showsPrec \ 11 \ x
\end{aligned}
$$

The catch-all case displays its argument x using prefix notation. It first converts x into a spine, which the helper function *shows_-* then traverses. Note that in the last equation of *shows_-* the variable x is of type *Typed* α; at this point we require the type information so that we can call *showsPrec* recursively. The *Tree* instance of *showsPrec* is subsumed by this general pattern, so the two *Tree* equations can be safely removed.

The function *arity* used above computes the arity of a data constructor. Its implementation follows the same definitional scheme as *showsPrec*:

$$
\begin{aligned}
&arity \ :: \ Typed \ \alpha \to Int \\
&arity \ = \ arity_- \cdot toSpine
\end{aligned}
$$

$$arity_- :: Spine\ \alpha \rightarrow Int$$
$$arity_-\ (Con\ c) = 0$$
$$arity_-\ (f \diamond x)\ \ = arity_-\ f + 1$$

Interestingly, *arity* exhibits no type-specific behaviour; it is completely generic.

Now, why are we in a better situation than before? When we introduce a new data type such as, say, *XML*, we still have to extend the representation type with a constructor $XML :: Type\ XML$ and provide cases for the data constructors of *XML* in the *toSpine* function. However, this has to be done only once per data type, and it is so simple that it could easily be done automatically. The code for the generic functions (of which there can be many) is completely unaffected by the addition of a new data type. As a further plus, the generic functions are unaffected by changes to a given data type (unless they include code that is specific to the data type). Only the function *toSpine* must be adapted to the new definition (and possibly the type representation if the kind of the data type changes).

2.3   Discussion

The key to genericity is a uniform view on data. In the previous section we have introduced the spine view, which views data as constructor applications. Of course, this is not the only generic view. PolyP [1], for instance, views data types as fixed points of regular functors; Generic Haskell [2] uses a sum-of-products view. These two approaches can be characterised as *type-oriented*: they provide a uniform view on all elements of a data type. By contrast, the spine view is *value-oriented*: it provides a uniform view on single elements.

The spine view is particularly easy to use: the generic part of a generic function only has to consider two cases: *Con* and '$\diamond$'. By contrast, Generic Haskell distinguishes three cases, PolyP even six.

A further advantage of the spine view is its generality: it is applicable to a large class of data types. Nested data types [16], for instance, pose no problems: the type of perfect binary trees [17]

data $Perfect\ \alpha = Zero\ \alpha\ |\ Succ\ (Perfect\ (\alpha, \alpha))$

gives rise to the following two equations for *toSpine*:

$$toSpine\ (Zero\ x : Perfect\ a) = Con\ zero \diamond (x : a)$$
$$toSpine\ (Succ\ x : Perfect\ a) = Con\ succ \diamond (x : Perfect\ (Pair\ a\ a))$$

The equations follow exactly the general scheme introduced in Section 2.2. The scheme is even applicable to *generalised algebraic data types*. Consider as an example a typed representation of expressions.

data $Expr :: * \rightarrow *$ **where**
  $Num :: Int \rightarrow Expr\ Int$
  $Plus\ :: Expr\ Int \rightarrow Expr\ Int \rightarrow Expr\ Int$

$$Eq \quad :: Expr\ Int \to Expr\ Int \to Expr\ Bool$$
$$If \quad :: Expr\ Bool \to Expr\ \alpha \to Expr\ \alpha \to Expr\ \alpha$$

The relevant equations for *toSpine* are

$$toSpine\ (Num\ i : Expr\ Int) \quad = Con\ num \diamond (i : Int)$$
$$toSpine\ (Plus\ e_1\ e_2 : Expr\ Int) = Con\ plus \diamond (e_1 : Expr\ Int) \diamond (e_2 : Expr\ Int)$$
$$toSpine\ (Eq\ e_1\ e_2 : Expr\ Bool) = Con\ eq \diamond (e_1 : Expr\ Int) \diamond (e_2 : Expr\ Int)$$
$$toSpine\ (If\ e_1\ e_2\ e_3 : Expr\ a)$$
$$= Con\ if \diamond (e_1 : Expr\ Bool) \diamond (e_2 : Expr\ a) \diamond (e_3 : Expr\ a)$$

Given this definition we can apply *show* to values of type *Expr* without further ado. Note in this respect that the Glasgow Haskell Compiler (GHC) currently does not support **deriving** (*Show*) for GADTs. We can also turn *Type* itself into a representable type (recall that *Type* is a GADT). One may be tempted to consider this an intellectual curiosity, but it is not. The possibility to reflect *Type* is vital for implementing dynamic values.

data *Dynamic* :: * **where**
    Dyn :: *Typed* $\alpha \to Dynamic$

Note that the type variable α does not appear in the result type: it is effectively existentially quantified. However, since α is accompanied by a representation of its type, we can define a suitable *toSpine* instance.

$$Dynamic :: Type\ Dynamic$$
$$Type \qquad :: Type\ \alpha \to Type\ (Type\ \alpha)$$
$$Typed \qquad :: Type\ \alpha \to Type\ (Typed\ \alpha)$$
$$toSpine\ (Dyn\ x : Dynamic) \ = Con\ dyn \diamond (x : Typed\ (type\ x))$$
$$toSpine\ ((x : t) : Typed\ a) \quad = Con\ hastype \diamond (x : t) \diamond (t : Type\ t) \quad \text{-- } t = a$$
$$toSpine\ (Char : Type\ Char) = Con\ char$$
$$\ldots$$

It is important to note that the first instance does *not* follow the general pattern for *toSpine*. This points out the only limitation of the spine view: it can, in general, not cope with existentially quantified types. Consider, as an example, the following extension of the expression data type:

$$Apply :: Expr\ (\alpha \to \beta) \to Expr\ \alpha \to Expr\ \beta$$

The equation for *toSpine*

$$toSpine\ (Apply\ f\ x : Expr\ b)$$
$$= Con\ apply \diamond (f : Expr\ (a \to b)) \diamond (x : Expr\ a) \quad \text{-- not legal Haskell}$$

is not legal Haskell, as *a*, the representation of α, appears free on the right-hand side. The only way out of this dilemma is to augment *x* by a representation of its type, as in *Dynamic*.[3]

---

[3] Type-theoretically, we have to turn the existential quantifier $\exists \alpha . \tau$ into an intensional quantifier $\exists \alpha . Type\ \alpha \times \tau$. This is analogous to the difference between parametrically polymorphic functions of type $\forall \alpha . \tau$ and overloaded functions of type $\forall \alpha . Type\ \alpha \to \tau$.

To make a long story short: a data declaration describes how to construct data; the spine view captures just this. Consequently, it is applicable to almost every data type declaration. The classic views are much more restricted: Generic Haskell's sum-of-products view is only applicable to Haskell 98 types excluding GADTs and existential types; PolyP is even restricted to fixed points of regular functors excluding nested data types and higher-order kinded types.

On the other hand, the classic views provide more information as they represent the complete data type, not just a single constructor application. The spine view effectively restricts the class of functions we can write: one can only define generic functions that consume data (such as *show*) but not ones that produce data (such as *read*). The uniform view on individual constructor applications is useful if you have data in your hands, but it is of no help if you want to construct data. We make this more precise in the following section.

Furthermore, functions that abstract over type constructors (such as *map* and *reduce*) are out of reach for SYB. The latter deficiency is somewhat ironic as these functions are the classic examples of generics. In the following two sections we show how to overcome both limitations.

3   Extension I: The Type Spine View

A *generic consumer* is a function of type $Type\ \alpha \to \alpha \to \tau$ ($\cong Typed\ \alpha \to \tau$), where the type we abstract over occurs in an argument position (and possibly in the result type τ). We have seen in the previous section that the generic part of a consumer follows the general pattern below.

```
consume :: Type α → α → τ
...
consume a x  = consume_ (toSpine (x : a))
consume_  :: Spine α → τ
consume_ ... = ...
```

The element x is converted to the spine representation, over which the helper function *consume_* then recurses. By duality, we would expect that a generic producer of type $Type\ \alpha \to \tau \to \alpha$, where α appears in the result type *but not* in τ, takes on the following form.

```
produce :: Type α → τ → α
...
produce a t  = fromSpine (produce_ t)
produce_  :: τ → Spine α   -- does not work
produce_ ... = ...
```

The helper function *produce_* generates an element in spine representation, which *fromSpine* converts back. Unfortunately, this approach does not work. The formal reason is that *toSpine* and *fromSpine* are different beasts: *toSpine* is an overloaded function, while *fromSpine* is parametrically polymorphic. If it were possible to define $produce_- :: \forall \alpha.\tau \to Spine\ \alpha$, then the composition $fromSpine \cdot produce_-$ would yield a parametrically polymorphic function of type $\forall \alpha.\tau \to \alpha$, which is the type of an unsafe cast operation. And, indeed, a closer inspection of the catch-all case reveals that a, the type representation of α, does not appear on the right-hand side. However, as we already know a truly polymorphic function cannot exhibit type-specific behaviour.

Of course, this does not mean that we cannot define a function of type $Type\ \alpha \to \tau \to \alpha$. We just require additional information about the data type, information that the spine view does not provide. Consider in this respect the syntactic form of a GADT (eg $Type$ itself or $Expr$ in Section 2.3): a data type is essentially a sequence of signatures. This motivates the following definitions.

type $Datatype\ \alpha = [\,Signature\ \alpha\,]$

infixl 0 □

data $Signature :: * \to *$ **where**

    Sig $:: Constr\ \alpha \to Signature\ \alpha$

    (□) $:: Signature\ (\alpha \to \beta) \to Type\ \alpha \to Signature\ \beta$

The type $Signature$ is almost identical to the $Spine$ type, except for the second argument of '□', which is of type $Type\ \alpha$ rather than $Typed\ \alpha$. Thus, an element of type $Signature$ contains the types of the constructor arguments, but not the arguments themselves. For that reason, $Datatype$ is called the *type spine view*.

This view is similar to the sum-of-products view: the list encodes the sum, the constructor '□' corresponds to a product and Sig is like the unit element. To be able to use the type spine view, we additionally require an overloaded function that maps a type representation to an element of type $Datatype\ \alpha$.

$datatype :: Type\ \alpha \to Datatype\ \alpha$
$datatype\ (Char)$ $= [\,Sig\ (char\ c)\ |\ c \leftarrow [\,minBound \mathrel{..} maxBound\,]\,]$
$datatype\ (Int)$ $= [\,Sig\ (int\ i)\ |\ i \leftarrow [\,minBound \mathrel{..} maxBound\,]\,]$
$datatype\ (List\ a)$ $= [\,Sig\ nil, Sig\ cons\ □\ a\ □\ List\ a\,]$
$datatype\ (Pair\ a\ b) = [\,Sig\ pair\ □\ a\ □\ b\,]$

$char$ $:: Char \to Constr\ Char$
$char\ c = Constr\{\,constr = c, name = show_{Char}\ c\,\}$

int $:: Int \to Constr\ Int$
$int\ i\ = Constr\{\,constr = i, name = show_{Int}\ \ i\,\}$

Here, nil, $cons$ and $pair$ are the annotated versions of Nil, $Cons$ and '(,)'. As an aside, the first two equations produce rather long lists; they are only practical in a lazy setting. The function $datatype$ plays the same role for producers as $toSpine$ plays for $consumers$.

The first example of a generic producer is a simple test-data generator. The function $generate\ a\ d$ yields all terms of the data type α up to a given finite depth d.

$generate :: Type\ \alpha \to Int \to [\,\alpha\,]$
$generate\ a\ 0$ $= [\,]$

$$generate \ a \ (d+1) \ = \ concat \ [generate_- \ s \ d \ | \ s \leftarrow datatype \ a]$$
$$generate_- :: Signature \ \alpha \rightarrow Int \rightarrow [\alpha]$$
$$generate_- \ (Sig \ c) \ d = [constr \ c]$$
$$generate_- \ (s \ \Box \ a) \ d = [f \ x \ | \ f \leftarrow generate_- \ s \ d, x \leftarrow generate \ a \ d]$$

The helper function *generate*_ constructs all terms that conform to a given signature. The right-hand side of the second equation essentially computes the cartesian product of *generate*_ *s d* and *generate a d*. Here is a short interactive session that illustrates the use of *generate* (we assume a suitable *Bool* instance of *datatype*).

Main⟩ generate (List Bool) 3
$[[\ ], [False], [False, False], [False, True], [True], [True, False], [True, True]]$
Main⟩ generate (List (List Bool)) 3
$[[\ ], [[\ ]], [[\ ], [\ ]], [[False]], [[False], [\ ]], [[True]], [[True], [\ ]]]$

As a second example, let us define a generic parser. For concreteness, we re-implement Haskell's *readsPrec* function (again, the *Int* argument specifies the operator precedence of the enclosing context; *ReadS* abbreviates *String* $\rightarrow$ $[(\alpha, String)]$, the type of backtracking parsers [18]).

$$readsPrec :: Type \ \alpha \rightarrow Int \rightarrow ReadS \ \alpha$$
$$readsPrec \ (Char) \qquad d = readsPrec_{Char} \ d$$
$$readsPrec \ (Int) \qquad d = readsPrec_{Int} \ d$$
$$readsPrec \ (List \ Char) \ d = readsPrec_{String} \ d$$
$$readsPrec \ (List \ a) \qquad d = readsList \ (reads \ a)$$
$$readsPrec \ (Pair \ a \ b) \quad d$$
$$= readParen \ False \ (\lambda s_0 \rightarrow [((x, y), s_5) \ | \ ("(", s_1) \leftarrow lex \qquad s_0,$$
$$(x, \quad s_2) \leftarrow reads \ a \ s_1,$$
$$(",", s_3) \leftarrow lex \qquad s_2,$$
$$(y, \quad s_4) \leftarrow reads \ b \ s_3,$$
$$(")", s_5) \leftarrow lex \qquad s_4])$$
$$readsPrec \ a \qquad\qquad d$$
$$= alt \ [readParen \ (arity' \ s > 0 \land d > 10) \ (reads_- \ s) \ | \ s \leftarrow datatype \ a]$$

The overall structure is similar to that of *showsPrec*. The first three equations delegate the work to tailor-made parsers. Given a parser for elements, *readsList*, defined in Appendix A, parses a list of elements. Pairs are read using the usual mix-fix notation. The predefined function *readParen b* takes care of optional ($b = False$) or mandatory ($b = True$) parentheses. The catch-all case implements the generic part: constructors in prefix notation. Parentheses are mandatory if the constructor has at least one argument and the operator precedence of the enclosing context exceeds 10 (the precedence of function application is 11). The parser for α is the alternation of all parsers for the individual constructors of α (*alt* is defined in Appendix A). The auxiliary function *reads*_ parses a single constructor application.

$$reads_- :: Signature\ \alpha \rightarrow ReadS\ \alpha$$
$$reads_-\ (Sig\ c)\ s_0 = [(constr\ c, s_1) \mid (t, s_1) \leftarrow lex\ s_0, name\ c == t]$$
$$reads_-\ (s\ \square\ a)\ s_0 = [(f\ x, s_2) \mid (f, s_1) \leftarrow reads_-\ s\ s_0,$$
$$(x, s_2) \leftarrow readsPrec\ a\ 11\ s_1]$$

Finally, *arity'* determines the arity of a constructor.

$$arity' :: Signature\ \alpha \rightarrow Int$$
$$arity'\ (Sig\ c) = 0$$
$$arity'\ (s\ \square\ a) = arity'\ s + 1$$

As for *showsPrec*, we can define suitable wrapper functions that simplify the use of the generic parser.

$$reads :: Type\ \alpha \rightarrow ReadS\ \alpha$$
$$reads\ a\ = readsPrec\ a\ 0$$
$$read\ :: Type\ \alpha \rightarrow String \rightarrow \alpha$$
$$read\ a\ s = \textbf{case}\ [x \mid (x, t) \leftarrow reads\ a\ s, ("", "") \leftarrow lex\ t]\ \textbf{of}$$
$$[x] \rightarrow x$$
$$[]\ \ \rightarrow error\ \texttt{"read: no parse"}$$
$$\_\ \ \rightarrow error\ \texttt{"read: ambiguous parse"}$$

From the code of *generate* and *readsPrec* we can abstract a general definitional scheme for generic producers.

$$produce :: Type\ \alpha \rightarrow \tau \rightarrow \alpha$$
$$\ldots$$
$$produce\ a\ t\ = \ldots[\ldots produce_-\ s\ t \ldots \mid s \leftarrow datatype\ a]$$
$$produce_-\ :: Signature\ \alpha \rightarrow \tau \rightarrow \alpha$$
$$produce_-\ \ldots = \ldots$$

The generic case is a two-step procedure: the list comprehension processes the list of constructors; the helper function *produce_* takes care of a single constructor.

The type spine view is complementary to the spine view, but independent of it. The latter is used for generic producers, the former for generic consumers (or transformers). This is in contrast to Generic Haskell's sum-of-products view or PolyP's fixed point view where a single view serves both purposes.

The type spine view shares the major advantage of the spine view: it is applicable to a large class of data types. Nested data types such as the type of perfect binary trees can be handled easily:

$$datatype\ (Perfect\ a) = [Sig\ zero\ \square\ a, Sig\ succ\ \square\ Perfect\ (Pair\ a\ a)]$$

The scheme can even be extended to generalised algebraic data types. Since *Datatype* α is a homogeneous list, we have to partition the constructors according to their result types. Re-consider the expression data type of Section 2.3. We have three different result types, *Expr Bool*, *Expr Int* and *Expr* α, and consequently three equations for *datatype*.

datatype (*Expr Bool*)
  = [*Sig eq* □ *Expr Int* □ *Expr Int*,
     Sig if □ *Expr Bool* □ *Expr Bool* □ *Expr Bool*]
datatype (*Expr Int*)
  = [*Sig num* □ *Int*,
     Sig plus □ *Expr Int* □ *Expr Int*,
     Sig if □ *Expr Bool* □ *Expr Int* □ *Expr Int*]
datatype (*Expr a*)
  = [*Sig if* □ *Expr Bool* □ *Expr a* □ *Expr a*]

The equations are ordered from specific to general; each right-hand side lists all the constructors that have the given result type *or* a more general one. Consequently, the *If* constructor, which has a polymorphic result type, appears in every list. Given this declaration we can easily generate well-typed expressions (for reasons of space we have modified *generate Int* so that only 0 is produced):

Main⟩ **let** *gen a d* = *putStrLn* (*show* (*generate a d* : *List a*))
Main⟩ *gen* (*Expr Int*) 4
[*Num* 0, *Plus* (*Num* 0) (*Num* 0), *Plus* (*Num* 0) (*Plus* (*Num* 0) (*Num* 0)), *Plus* (*Plus* (*Num* 0) (*Num* 0)) (*Num* 0), *Plus* (*Plus* (*Num* 0) (*Num* 0)) (*Plus* (*Num* 0) (*Num* 0)), *If* (*Eq* (*Num* 0) (*Num* 0)) (*Num* 0) (*Num* 0), *If* (*Eq* (*Num* 0) (*Num* 0)) (*Num* 0) (*Plus* (*Num* 0) (*Num* 0)), *If* (*Eq* (*Num* 0) (*Num* 0)) (*Plus* (*Num* 0) (*Num* 0)) (*Num* 0), *If* (*Eq* (*Num* 0) (*Num* 0)) (*Plus* (*Num* 0) (*Num* 0)) (*Plus* (*Num* 0) (*Num* 0))]
Main⟩ *gen* (*Expr Bool*) 4
[*Eq* (*Num* 0) (*Num* 0), *Eq* (*Num* 0) (*Plus* (*Num* 0) (*Num* 0)), *Eq* (*Plus* (*Num* 0) (*Num* 0)) (*Num* 0), *Eq* (*Plus* (*Num* 0) (*Num* 0)) (*Plus* (*Num* 0) (*Num* 0)), *If* (*Eq* (*Num* 0) (*Num* 0)) (*Eq* (*Num* 0) (*Num* 0)) (*Eq* (*Num* 0) (*Num* 0))]
Main⟩ *gen* (*Expr Char*) 4
[]

The last call shows that there are no character expressions of depth 4.

In general, for each constructor C with signature

$$C :: \tau_1 \rightarrow \cdots \rightarrow \tau_n \rightarrow \tau_0$$

we add an element of the form

$$Sig\ c \ \square\ t_1 \ \square \cdots \square\ t_n$$

to each right-hand side of *datatype* (*t*) provided τ_0 is more general than τ.

4   Extension II: The Lifted Spine View

The generic functions of the previous two sections abstract over a type. For instance, *shows* generalises functions of type

$$Char \rightarrow ShowS, \quad String \rightarrow ShowS, \quad [[Int]] \rightarrow ShowS$$

to a single generic function of type

$$Type\ \alpha \rightarrow \alpha \rightarrow ShowS \qquad\qquad \cong Typed\ \alpha \rightarrow ShowS$$

A generic function may also abstract over a type constructor of higher kind. Take, as an example, the function *size* that counts the number of elements contained in some data structure. This function generalises functions of type

$$[\alpha] \rightarrow Int, \quad Tree\ \alpha \rightarrow Int, \quad [Tree\ \alpha] \rightarrow Int$$

to a single generic function of type

$$Type'\ \varphi \rightarrow \varphi\ \alpha \rightarrow Int \qquad\qquad \cong Typed'\ \varphi\ \alpha \rightarrow Int$$

where $Type'$ is a representation type for types of kind $* \rightarrow *$ and $Typed'$ is a suitable type for annotating values with these representations.

The original spine view is not appropriate in this context as it cannot capture type abstractions. To illustrate, consider a variant of *Tree* whose inner nodes are annotated with an integer, say, a balance factor.

data $BalTree\ \alpha = Empty \mid Node\ Int\ (BalTree\ \alpha)\ \alpha\ (BalTree\ \alpha)$

If we call the generic function on a value of type $BalTree\ Int$, then the two integer components are handled in a uniform way. This is fine for generic functions on types, but not acceptable for generic functions on type constructors. For instance, a generic version of *sum* must consider the label of type $\alpha = Int$, but ignore the balance factor of type Int. In the Sections 4.1 and 4.2 we introduce suitable variants of *Type* and *Spine* that can be used to define the latter brand of generic functions.

4.1   Lifted Types

To represent type constructors of kind $* \rightarrow *$ we introduce a new tailor-made representation type.

data $Type' :: (* \rightarrow *) \rightarrow *$ **where**
  $List :: Type'\ []$
  $Tree :: Type'\ Tree$

infixl 1 $:'$
data $Typed'\ \varphi\ \alpha = (:')\{\ val' :: \varphi\ \alpha,\ type' :: Type'\ \varphi\}$

The type is only inhabited by two constructors since the other data types listed in *Type* have kinds different from $* \rightarrow *$.

An overloaded version of *size* is now straightforward to define.

$size :: Typed'\ \varphi\ \alpha \rightarrow Int$
$size\ (Nil :'\ List) \qquad = 0$

$$size\ (Cons\ x\ xs\ :'\ List)\ = 1 + size\ (xs\ :'\ List)$$
$$size\ (Empty\ :'\ Tree)\qquad = 0$$
$$size\ (Node\ l\ x\ r\ :'\ Tree) = size\ (l\ :'\ Tree) + 1 + size\ (r\ :'\ Tree)$$

Unfortunately, the overloaded function *size* is not as flexible as *shows*. If we have some compound data structure x, say, a list of trees of integers, then we can simply call *shows* $(x : List\ (Tree\ Int))$. We cannot, however, use *size* to count the total number of integers, simply because the new versions of *List* and *Tree* take no arguments.

There is one further problem, which is more fundamental. Computing the size of a compound data structure is inherently ambiguous: in the example above, shall we count the number of integers, the number of trees or the number of lists? Formally, we have to solve the type equation $\varphi\ \tau = List\ (Tree\ Int)$. The equation has, in fact, not three but four principal solutions: $\varphi = \Lambda\alpha \to \alpha$ and $\tau = List\ (Tree\ Int)$, $\varphi = \Lambda\alpha \to List\ \alpha$ and $\tau = Tree\ Int$, $\varphi = \Lambda\alpha \to List\ (Tree\ \alpha)$ and $\tau = Int$, and $\varphi = \Lambda\alpha \to List\ (Tree\ Int)$ and τ arbitrary. How can we represent these different container types? One possibility is to lift the type constructors [9] so that they become members of *Type'* and to include *Id*, the identity type, as a representation of the type variable α:

$$Id\qquad :: Type'\ Id$$
$$Char'\ :: Type'\ Char'$$
$$Int'\quad :: Type'\ Int'$$
$$List'\quad :: Type'\ \varphi \to Type'\ (List'\ \varphi)$$
$$Pair'\quad :: Type'\ \varphi \to Type'\ \psi \to Type'\ (Pair'\ \varphi\ \psi)$$
$$Tree'\quad :: Type'\ \varphi \to Type'\ (Tree'\ \varphi)$$

The type *List'*, for instance, is the lifted variant of *List*: it takes a type constructor of kind $* \to *$ to a type constructor of kind $* \to *$. Using the lifted types we can specify the four different container types as follows: $List'\ (Tree'\ Id)$, $List'\ Id$, Id and $List'\ (Tree'\ Int')$. Essentially, we replace the types by their lifted counterparts and the type variable α by *Id*. Note that the above constructors of *Type'* are *exactly identical* to those of *Type* except for the kinds.

It remains to define *Id* and the lifted versions of the type constructors.

newtype $Id\qquad \chi = In_{Id}\quad \{\,out_{Id}\quad :: \chi\qquad \}$
newtype $Char'\ \chi = In_{Char'}\{\,out_{Char'} :: Char\,\}$
newtype $Int'\quad \chi = In_{Int'}\ \{\,out_{Int'}\quad :: Int\quad \}$
data $List'\ \alpha'\qquad \chi = Nil' \mid Cons'\ (\alpha'\ \chi)\ (List'\ \alpha'\ \chi)$
data $Pair'\ \alpha'\ \beta'\ \chi = Pair'\ (\alpha'\ \chi)\ (\beta'\ \chi)$
data $Tree'\ \alpha'\qquad \chi = Empty' \mid Node'\ (Tree'\ \alpha'\ \chi)\ (\alpha'\ \chi)\ (Tree'\ \alpha'\ \chi)$

The lifted variants of the nullary type constructors *Int* and *Char* simply ignore the additional argument χ. The **data** definitions follow a simple scheme: each data constructor C with signature

$$C :: \tau_1 \to \cdots \to \tau_n \to \tau_0$$

is replaced by a polymorphic data constructor C' with signature

$$C' :: \forall \chi.\tau_1' \; \chi \to \cdots \to \tau_n' \; \chi \to \tau_0' \; \chi$$

where τ_i' is the lifted variant of τ_i.

The function *size* can be easily extended to *Id* and to the lifted types.

$$
\begin{array}{ll}
size \; (x :' \; Id) & = 1 \\
size \; (c :' \; Char') & = 0 \\
size \; (i :' \; Int') & = 0 \\
size \; (Nil' :' \; List' \; a') & = 0 \\
size \; (Cons' \; x \; xs :' \; List' \; a') = size \; (x :' \; a') + size \; (xs :' \; List' \; a') \\
size \; (Empty' :' \; Tree' \; a') & = 0 \\
size \; (Node' \; l \; x \; r :' \; Tree' \; a') \\
\quad = size \; (l :' \; Tree' \; a') + size \; (x :' \; a') + size \; (r :' \; Tree' \; a')
\end{array}
$$

The instances are similar to the ones for the unlifted types except that *size* is now also called recursively for components of type α'.

Unfortunately, in Haskell, *size* no longer works on the original data types: we cannot call, for instance, $size \; (x :' \; List' \; (Tree' \; Id))$ where x is is a list of trees of integers, since $List' \; (Tree' \; Id) \; Int$ is different from $[\, Tree \; Int\,]$. We address this problem later in Section 4.3 after we have introduced the lifted spine view.

4.2   Lifted Spine View

A constructor of a lifted type has the signature $\forall \chi.\tau_1' \; \chi \to \cdots \to \tau_n' \; \chi \to \tau_0' \; \chi$ where the type variable χ marks the parametric components. We can write the signature more perspicuously as $\forall \chi.(\tau_1' \overset{.}{\to} \cdots \overset{.}{\to} \tau_n' \overset{.}{\to} \tau_0') \; \chi$, using the lifted function space:

infixr $\overset{.}{\to}$
newtype $(\varphi \overset{.}{\to} \psi) \; \chi = Fun\{ app :: \varphi \; \chi \to \psi \; \chi\}$

For technical reasons, '$\overset{.}{\to}$' must be defined by a **newtype** rather than a **type** declaration.[4] As an example, here are variants of *Nil'* and *Cons'*:

$$
\begin{array}{ll}
nil' & :: \forall \chi.\forall \alpha'.(List' \; \alpha') \; \chi \\
nil' & = Nil' \\
cons' & :: \forall \chi.\forall \alpha'.(\alpha' \overset{.}{\to} List' \; \alpha' \overset{.}{\to} List' \; \alpha') \; \chi \\
cons' & = Fun \; (\lambda x \to Fun \; (\lambda xs \to Cons' \; x \; xs))
\end{array}
$$

Now, an element of a lifted type can always be put into the applicative form $c' \; `app` \; e_1 \; `app` \cdots `app` \; e_n$. As in the first-order case we can make this structure visible and accessible by marking the constructor and the function applications.

---

[4] In Haskell, types introduced by **type** declarations cannot be partially applied.

data $Spine' :: (* \to *) \to * \to *$ **where**
$\quad Con' :: (\forall \chi.\varphi\ \chi) \to Spine'\ \varphi\ \alpha$
$\quad (\diamond') \ :: Spine'\ (\varphi \overset{.}{\to} \psi)\ \alpha \to Typed'\ \varphi\ \alpha \to Spine'\ \psi\ \alpha$

The structure of $Spine'$ is very similar to that of $Spine$ except that we are now working in a higher realm: Con' takes a *polymorphic function* of type $\forall\chi.\varphi\ \chi$ to an element of $Spine'\ \varphi$; the constructor '$\diamond'$' applies an element of type $Spine'\ (\varphi \overset{.}{\to} \psi)$ to a $Typed'\ \varphi$ yielding an element of type $Spine'\ \psi$.

Turning to the conversion functions, $fromSpine'$ is again *polymorphic*.

$fromSpine' :: Spine'\ \varphi\ \alpha \to \varphi\ \alpha$
$fromSpine'\ (Con'\ c) = c$
$fromSpine'\ (f \diamond' x) \ = fromSpine'\ f\ `app`\ val'\ x$

Its inverse is an *overloaded* function that follows a similar pattern as $toSpine$: each constructor C' with signature

$$C' :: \forall\chi.\tau_1'\ \chi \to \cdots \to \tau_n'\ \chi \to \tau_0'\ \chi$$

gives rise to an equation of the form

$$toSpine'\ (C'\ x_1\ \ldots\ x_n :'\ t_0') = Con\ c' \diamond (x_1 : t_1') \diamond \cdots \diamond (x_n : t_n')$$

where c' is the variant of C' that uses the lifted function space and t_i' is the type representation of the lifted type τ_i'. As an example, here is the instance for lifted lists.

$toSpine' :: Typed'\ \varphi\ \alpha \to Spine'\ \varphi\ \alpha$
$toSpine'\ (Nil' :'\ List'\ a') \qquad\quad = Con'\ nil'$
$toSpine'\ (Cons'\ x\ xs :'\ List'\ a') = Con'\ cons' \diamond' (x :'\ a') \diamond' (xs :'\ List'\ a')$

The equations are surprisingly close to those of $toSpine$; pretty much the only difference is that $toSpine'$ works on lifted types.

The $Spine'$ data type provides the generic view that allows us to implement the 'generic part' of a generic function. The following declarations make the concept of a generic view explicit.[5]

infixr $5 \rightarrowtail$
infixl $5 \leftarrowtail$
type $\varphi \rightarrowtail \psi = \forall\alpha.\varphi\ \alpha \to \psi\ \alpha$
type $\varphi \leftarrowtail \psi = \forall\alpha.\psi\ \alpha \to \varphi\ \alpha$
data $View' :: (* \to *) \to *$ **where**
$\quad View' :: Type'\ \psi \to (\varphi \rightarrowtail \psi) \to (\varphi \leftarrowtail \psi) \to View'\ \varphi$

A view consists of three ingredients: a so-called *structure type* that provides a uniform view on the original type and two functions that convert to and fro. In our case, the structure view of φ is simply $Spine'\ \varphi$.

---

[5] It is also possible to introduce an explicit view for the spine data type. We have not done so mainly for reasons of space.

$Spine' :: Type' \; \varphi \to Type' \; (Spine' \; \varphi)$
$spineView :: Type' \; \varphi \to View' \; \varphi$
$spineView \; a' = View' \; (Spine' \; a') \; (\lambda x \to toSpine' \; (x :' a')) \; fromSpine'$

Similar to the spine view, we have $fromSpine' \; (toSpine' \; (x :' t')) = x$; the converse, however, does not hold.

Given these prerequisites we can finally turn $size$ into a generic function.

$size \; (x :' Spine' \; a') = size_- \; x$
$size \; (x :' a') \qquad = \textbf{case } spineView \; a' \textbf{ of}$
$\qquad\qquad\qquad\qquad\quad View' \; b' \; from \; to \to size \; (from \; x :' b')$

The catch-all case applies the spine view: the argument x is converted to the structure type, on which $size$ is called recursively. Currently, the structure type is always of the form $Spine' \; \varphi$ (this will change in the next section), so the first equation applies, which in turn delegates the work to the helper function $size_-$.

$size_- :: Spine' \; \varphi \; \alpha \to Int$
$size_- \; (Con' \; c) = 0$
$size_- \; (f \; \diamond' \; x) \quad = size_- \; f + size \; x$

The implementation of $size_-$ is entirely straightforward: it traverses the spine summing up the sizes of the constructors arguments. It is worth noting that the catch-all case of $size$ subsumes all the previous instances except the one for Id, as we cannot provide a $toSpine'$ instance for the identity type. In other words, the generic programmer has to take care of essentially three cases: Id, Con' and '$\diamond'$'.

As a second example, here is an implementation of the generic mapping function:

$map :: Type' \; \varphi \to (\alpha \to \beta) \to (\varphi \; \alpha \to \varphi \; \beta)$
$map \; Id \qquad\qquad m = In_{Id} \cdot m \cdot out_{Id}$
$map \; (Spine' \; a') \; m = map_- \; m$
$map \; a' \qquad\qquad m = \textbf{case } spineView \; a' \textbf{ of}$
$\qquad\qquad\qquad\qquad\qquad View' \; b' \; from \; to \to to \cdot map \; b' \; m \cdot from$

$map_- :: (\alpha \to \beta) \to (Spine' \; \varphi \; \alpha \to Spine' \; \varphi \; \beta)$
$map_- \; m \; (Con' \; c) \qquad = Con' \; c$
$map_- \; m \; (f \; \diamond' \; (x :' a')) = map_- \; m \; f \; \diamond' \; (map \; a' \; m \; x :' a')$

The definition is stunningly simple: the argument function m is applied in the Id case; the helper function map_- applies map to each argument of the constructor. Note that the mapping function is of type $Type' \; \varphi \to (\alpha \to \beta) \to (\varphi \; \alpha \to \varphi \; \beta)$ rather than $(\alpha \to \beta) \to (Typed' \; \varphi \; \alpha \to \varphi \; \beta)$. Both variants are commensurate, so picking one is just a matter of personal taste.

4.3   Bridging the Gap

We have noted in Section 4.1 that the generic size function does not work on the original, unlifted types as they are different from the lifted ones. However, both are closely related: if τ' is the lifted variant of τ, then τ' Id is isomorphic to τ [9]. Even more, τ' Id and τ can share the same run-time representation, since Id is defined by a **newtype** declaration and since the lifted data type τ' has exactly the same structure as the original data type τ.

As an example, the functions $fromList\ In_{Id}$ and $toList\ out_{Id}$ exhibit the isomorphism between $[\,]$ and $List'\ Id$.

$$fromList :: (\alpha \rightarrow \alpha'\ \chi) \rightarrow ([\alpha] \rightarrow List'\ \alpha'\ \chi)$$
$$fromList\ from\ Nil \qquad = Nil'$$
$$fromList\ from\ (Cons\ x\ xs) = Cons'\ (from\ x)\ (fromList\ from\ xs)$$
$$toList \quad :: (\alpha'\ \chi \rightarrow \alpha) \rightarrow (List'\ \alpha'\ \chi \rightarrow [\alpha])$$
$$toList\ to\ Nil' \qquad = Nil$$
$$toList\ to\ (Cons'\ x\ xs) = Cons\ (to\ x)\ (toList\ to\ xs)$$

Operationally, if the types τ' Id and τ have the same run-time representation, then $fromList\ In_{Id}$ and $toList\ out_{Id}$ are identity functions (the Haskell Report [19] guarantees this for In_{Id} and out_{Id}).

We can use the isomorphism to broaden the scope of generic functions to unlifted types. To this end we simply re-use the view mechanism (the equation below must be inserted before the catch-all case).

$$spineView\ List = View'\ (List'\ Id)\ (fromList\ In_{Id})\ (toList\ out_{Id})$$

The following interactive session illustrates the use of $size$.

$Main\rangle$ **let** $ts = [\,tree\ [0\mathinner{.\,.}i :: Int]\mid i \leftarrow [0\mathinner{.\,.}9]\,]$
$Main\rangle$ $size\ (ts :'\ List)$
10
$Main\rangle$ $size\ (fromList\ (fromTree\ In_{Id})\ ts :'\ List'\ (Tree'\ Id))$
55
$Main\rangle$ $size\ (fromList\ In_{Id}\ ts :'\ List'\ Id)$
10
$Main\rangle$ $size\ (In_{Id}\ ts :'\ Id)$
1
$Main\rangle$ $size\ (fromList\ (fromTree\ In_{Int'})\ ts :'\ List'\ (Tree'\ Int'))$
0

With the help of the conversion functions we can implement each of the four different views on a list of trees of integers. Since Haskell employs a kinded first-order unification of types [20], the calls almost always involve a change on the value level. The type equation $\varphi\ \tau = List\ (Tree\ Int)$ is solved setting $\varphi = List$ and $\tau = Tree\ Int$, that is, Haskell picks one of the four higher-order unifiers. Only in this particular case we need not change the representation of values: $size\ (ts :'\ List)$ implements the intended call. In the other cases, $List\ (Tree\ Int)$ must be rearranged so that the unification with $\varphi\ \tau$ yields the desired choice.

4.4 Discussion

The lifted spine view is almost as general as the original spine view: it is applicable to all data types that are definable in Haskell 98. In particular, nested data types can be handled with ease. As an example, for the data type $Perfect$, see Section 2.3, we introduce a lifted variant

> **data** $Perfect'\ \alpha'\ \chi = Zero'\ (\alpha'\ \chi)\ |\ Succ'\ (Perfect'\ (Pair'\ \alpha'\ \alpha')\ \chi)$
>
> $Perfect\ ::\ Type'\ Perfect$
> $Perfect'\ ::\ Type'\ \varphi \to Type'\ (Perfect'\ \varphi)$
>
> $toSpine'\ (Zero'\ x :'\ Perfect'\ a') = Con'\ zero'\ \Diamond'\ (x :'\ a')$
> $toSpine'\ (Succ'\ x :'\ Perfect'\ a') = Con'\ succ'\ \Diamond'\ (x :'\ Perfect'\ (Pair'\ a'\ a'))$

and functions that convert between the lifted and the unlifted variant.

> $spineView\ (Perfect)$
> $\quad = View'\ (Perfect'\ Id)\ (fromPerfect\ In_{Id})\ (toPerfect\ out_{Id})$
>
> $fromPerfect :: (\alpha \to \alpha'\ \chi) \to (Perfect\ \alpha \to Perfect'\ \alpha'\ \chi)$
> $fromPerfect\ from\ (Zero\ x) = Zero'\ (from\ x)$
> $fromPerfect\ from\ (Succ\ x) = Succ'\ (fromPerfect\ (fromPair\ from\ from)\ x)$
>
> $toPerfect\quad :: (\alpha'\ \chi \to \alpha) \to (Perfect'\ \alpha'\ \chi \to Perfect\ \alpha)$
> $toPerfect\ to\ (Zero'\ x) = Zero\ (to\ x)$
> $toPerfect\ to\ (Succ'\ x) = Succ\ (toPerfect\ (toPair\ to\ to)\ x)$

The following interactive session shows some examples involving perfect trees.

> $Main\rangle\ \ size\ (Succ\ (Zero\ (1,2)) :'\ Perfect)$
> 2
> $Main\rangle\ \ map\ (Perfect)\ (+1)\ (Succ\ (Zero\ (1,2)))$
> $Succ\ (Zero\ (2,3))$

We have seen in Section 2.3 that the spine view is also applicable to *generalised algebraic data types*. This does not hold for the lifted spine view, as it is not possible to generalise *map* or *reduce* to GADTs. Consider the expression data type of Section 2.3. Though $Expr$ is parameterised, it is not a container type: an element of $Expr\ Int$, for instance, is an expression that evaluates to an integer; it is not a data structure that contains integers. This means, in particular, that we cannot define a mapping function $(\alpha \to \beta) \to (Expr\ \alpha \to Expr\ \beta)$: How could we possibly turn expressions of type $Expr\ \alpha$ into expression of type $Expr\ \beta$? The type $Expr\ \beta$ might not even be inhabited: there are, for instance, no terms of type $Expr\ String$. Since the type argument of $Expr$ is not related to any component, $Expr$ is also called a *phantom type* [21].

It is instructive to see where the attempt to generalise *map* or *reduce* to GADTs fails technically. We can, in fact, define a lifted version of the $Expr$ type (we confine ourselves to one constructor).

> **data** $Expr' :: (* \to *) \to * \to *$ **where**
> $\quad Num' :: Int'\ \chi \to Expr'\ Int'\ \chi$

However, we cannot establish an isomorphism between $Expr$ and $Expr'\ Id$: the following code simply does not type-check.

$fromExpr :: (\alpha \to \alpha'\ \chi) \to (Expr\ \alpha \to Expr'\ \alpha'\ \chi)$
$fromExpr\ from\ (Num\ i) = Num'\ (In_{Int'}\ i)$ -- wrong: does not type-check

The isomorphism between τ and $\tau'\ Id$ only holds for Haskell 98 types.

In the preceding section we have seen two examples of generic consumers (or transformers). As in the first-order case generic producers are out of reach and for exactly the same reason: $fromSpine'$ is a polymorphic function while $toSpine'$ is overloaded. Of course, the solution to the problem suggests itself: we must also lift the type spine view to type constructors of kind $* \to *$. In a sense, the spine view really comprises two views: one for consumers (and transformers) and one for pure producers.

Up to now we have confined ourselves to generic functions that abstract over types of kind $*$ or $* \to *$. An obvious question is whether the approach can be generalised to *kind indices* of arbitrary kinds. The answer is an emphatic "Yes!". Let us briefly sketch the main steps, for a formal treatment see Hinze's earlier work [9]. Assume that $\kappa = \kappa_1 \to \cdots \to \kappa_n \to *$ is the kind of the type index. We first introduce a suitable type representation and lift the data types to kind κ by adding n type arguments of kind $\kappa_1, \ldots, \kappa_n$. Types and lifted types are related as follows: τ is isomorphic to $\tau'\ Out_1\ \ldots\ Out_n$ where Out_i is the *projection type* that corresponds to the i-th argument of κ. The spine representation must be lifted accordingly. The generic programmer then has to consider two cases for the spine view and additionally n cases, one for each of the n projection types $Out_1, \ldots, Out_n$.

Introducing lifted types for each possible type index sounds like a lot of work. Note, however, that the declarations can be generated completely mechanically (a compiler could do this easily). Furthermore, generic functions that are indexed by higher-order kinds, for instance, $(* \to *) \to * \to * \to *$ are rare. In practice, most generic functions are indexed by a first-order kind such as $*$ or $* \to *$.

5   Related Work

Scrap your boilerplate. The SYB approach has been developed by Lämmel and Peyton Jones in a series of papers [3,22,5]. The original approach is *combinator-based*: the user writes generic functions by combining a few generic primitives. The first paper [3] introduces two main combinators: a type-safe cast for defining ad-hoc cases and a generic recursion operator, called *gfoldl*, for implementing the generic part. It turns out that *gfoldl* is essentially the catamorphism of the *Spine* data type [11]: *gfoldl* equals the catamorphism composed with *toSpine*. The second paper [22] adds a function called *gunfold* to the set of predefined combinators, which is required for defining generic producers. The name suggests that the new combinator is the anamorphism of the *Spine* type, but it is not: *gunfold* is actually the catamorphism of *Signature*, introduced in Section 3.

view(s)	representation of overloaded functions			
	type reflection	type classes	type-safe cast	specialisation
none	ITA [25, 7, 26–28]	–	–	–
fixed point	Reloaded [11]	PolyP [29, 30]	–	PolyP [1]
sum-of-products	LIGD [8, 21]	DTC [31], GC [32], GM [10]	–	GH [33, 2, 34, 35]
spine	Reloaded [11], this paper	SYB [5], Reloaded [36]	SYB [3, 22]	–

Fig. 1. Generic programming: the design space

Relating approaches to generic programming. There is a wealth of material on the subject of generic programming. The tutorials [23,2,24] provide an excellent overview of the field. We have noted in the introduction that support for generic programming consists of two essential ingredients: a way to write overloaded functions, and independently, a way to access the structure of values in a uniform way. The different approaches to generic programming can be faithfully classified along these two dimensions. Figure 1 provides an overview of the design space. The two ingredients are largely independent of each other and for each there are various choices. Overloaded functions can be expressed using

- *type reflection:* This is the approach we have used in this paper. Its origins can be traced back to the work on intensional type analysis [25,7,26,27,28] (ITA). ITA is intensively used in typed intermediate languages, in particular, for optimising purely polymorphic functions. Type reflection avoids the duplication of features: a type case, for instance, boils down to an ordinary **case** expression. Cheney and Hinze [8] present a library for generics and dynamics (LIGD) that uses an *encoding* of type representations in Haskell 98 augmented by existential types.
- *type classes* [4]*:* Type classes are Haskell's major innovation for supporting ad-hoc polymorphism. A type class declaration corresponds to the type signature of an overloaded value—or rather, to a collection of type signatures. An instance declaration is related to a type case of an overloaded value. For a handful of built-in classes Haskell provides support for genericity: by attaching a **deriving** clause to a **data** declaration the Haskell compiler automatically generates an appropriate instance of the class. *Derivable type classes* (DTC) generalise this feature to arbitrary user-defined classes. A similar, but more expressive variant is implemented in Generic Clean [32] (GC). Clean's type classes are indexed by kind so that a single generic function can be applied to type constructors of different kinds. A pure Haskell 98

implementation of generics (GM) is described by Hinze [10]. The implementation builds upon a class-based encoding of the type *Type* of type representations.

– *type-safe cast* [6]: A cast operation converts a value from one type to another, provided the two types are identical at run-time. A cast can be seen as a type-case with exactly one branch. The original SYB paper [3] is based on casts.
– *specialisation* [9]: This implementation technique transforms an overloaded function into a family of polymorphic functions (*dictionary translation*). While the other techniques can be used to write a library for generics, specialisation is mainly used for implementing full-fledged generic programming systems such as PolyP [1] or *Generic Haskell* [35], that are set up as preprocessors or compilers.

The approaches differ mostly in syntax and style, but less in expressiveness— except perhaps for specialisation, which cannot cope with higher-order generic functions. The second dimension, the generic view, has a much larger impact: we have seen that it affects the set of data types we can represent, the class of functions we can write and potentially the efficiency of these functions.

– *no view*: Haskell has a *nominal type system*: each **data** declaration introduces a new type that is incompatible with all the existing types. Two types are equal if and only if they have the same name. By contrast, in a *structural type system* two types are equal if they have the same structure. In a language with a structural type system there is no need for a generic view; a generic function can be defined exhaustively by induction on the structure of types. The type systems that underly ITA are structural.
– *fixed point view*: PolyP [1] views data types as fixed points of regular functors, which are in turn represented as lifted sums of products. This view is quite limited in applicability: only data types of kind $* \to *$ that are regular can be represented, excluding nested data types and higher-order kinded data types. Its particular strength is that recursion patterns such as cata- or anamorphisms can be expressed generically, because each data type is viewed as a fixed point, and the points of recursion are visible. The original implementation of PolyP is set up as a preprocessor that translates PolyP code into Haskell. A later version [29] embeds PolyP program into Haskell augmented by multiple parameter type classes with functional dependencies [37]. Oliveira and Gibbons [30] present a lightweight variant of PolyP that works within Haskell 98.
– *sum-of-products view*: Generic Haskell [2,34,35] (GH) builds upon this view. It is applicable to all data types definable in Haskell 98. Generic Haskell is a full-fledged implementation of generics based on ideas by Hinze [33,38] that features generic functions, generic types and various extensions such as default cases and constructor cases [39]. Generic Haskell supports the definition of functions that work for all types of all kinds, such as, for example, a generalised mapping function.

- *spine views:* The spine view treats data uniformly as constructor applications. The different spine views have been extensively discussed in Sections 2.3, 3 and 4.4.

6   Conclusion

The SYB approach to generic programming was originally presented as an implementation of *strategic programming* in Haskell. Strategic programming [40] is an idiom for processing and querying complex, compound data such as, for example, abstract syntax trees. Because of this background and because of the particular presentation as a combinator library, the approach seemed to be tied to generic consumers indexed by types of kind $*$. This paper makes the following contributions revealing the full potential of the SYB approach.

- The 'type spine' view allows us to implement generic producers in the same elegant manner as generic consumers that build upon the spine view. The type spine view can be seen as the hidden structure that underlies the *gunfold* combinator.
- Functions that abstract over type constructors can be handled using the technique of *lifting*. Previously, these functions were thought to be out of reach for the SYB approach. For reasons of space, we have confined ourselves to type indices of kind $* \to *$. Lifting, however, works for indices of arbitrary kinds.

Using one of the different spine views one can program almost all of the standard examples of generic functions.

The spine views are attractive for at least two reasons: they are easy to use and they are widely applicable. The generic programmer only has to consider two cases plus one case for each argument of the type index (that is, n additional cases for indices of kind $\kappa_1 \to \cdots \to \kappa_n \to *$). The spine view and the type spine view cover almost all data types *including* generalised algebraic data types, but excluding existential types. For principal reasons, the lifted spine view is more restricted: generic functions that abstract over type constructors can be instantiated to arbitrary *container types* but not to *phantom types* (GADTs).

We have left a couple of topics for future work. The overloading technique used in this paper, type reflection, hinders in its present form the formulation of the approach as a re-usable library: the encoding of overloaded functions using explicit type arguments requires the extensibility of the *Type* data type and of functions such as *toSpine*. Using the concepts of open data types and open functions [41] this limitation can be overcome. We plan to build an industrial-strength library based on this extension. Type reflection has at least one distinct advantage over a class-based approach: we expect that it is much easier to prove algebraic properties of generic functions in this setting. We believe that the work of Reig [42] could be recast using our approach, leading to shorter and more concise proofs.

Acknowledgements

We would like to thank Jeremy Gibbons for correcting the English. Special thanks are due to Stefan Holdermans and to the anonymous referees of MPC for many suggestions regarding style and presentation. Andres Löh would like to thank Tarmo Uustalu for pointing him to the question of how to write generic functions that work on GADTs and for several enlightening discussions on the topic.

References

1. Jansson, P., Jeuring, J.: PolyP—a polytypic programming language extension. In: Conference Record 24th ACM SIGPLAN-SIGACT Symposium on Principles of Programming Languages (POPL'97), Paris, France, ACM Press (1997) 470–482
2. Hinze, R., Jeuring, J.: Generic Haskell: Practice and theory. In Backhouse, R., Gibbons, J., eds.: Generic Programming: Advanced Lectures. Volume 2793 of Lecture Notes in Computer Science. Springer-Verlag (2003) 1–56
3. Peyton Jones, S., Lämmel, R.: Scrap your boilerplate: a practical approach to generic programming. In: Proceedings of the ACM SIGPLAN Workshop on Types in Language Design and Implementation (TLDI 2003), New Orleans. (2003) 26–37
4. Hall, C.V., Hammond, K., Peyton Jones, S.L., Wadler, P.L.: Type classes in Haskell. ACM Transactions on Programming Languages and Systems 18(2) (1996) 109–138
5. Lämmel, R., Peyton Jones, S.: Scrap your boilerplate with class: extensible generic functions. In Pierce, B., ed.: Proceedings of the 2005 International Conference on Functional Programming, Tallinn, Estonia, September 26–28, 2005. (2005)
6. Weirich, S.: Type-safe cast: functional pearl. In: Proceedings of the ACM SIGPLAN International Conference on Functional Programming (ICFP '00). Volume (35)9 of ACM SIGPLAN Notices., N.Y., ACM Press (2000) 58–67
7. Crary, K., Weirich, S., Morrisett, G.: Intensional polymorphism in type-erasure semantics. In: Proceedings of the ACM SIGPLAN International Conference on Functional Programming (ICFP '98), Baltimore, MD. Volume (34)1 of ACM SIGPLAN Notices., ACM Press (1999) 301–312
8. Cheney, J., Hinze, R.: A lightweight implementation of generics and dynamics. In Chakravarty, M.M., ed.: Proceedings of the 2002 ACM SIGPLAN Haskell Workshop, ACM Press (2002) 90–104
9. Hinze, R.: A new approach to generic functional programming. In Reps, T.W., ed.: Proceedings of the 27th Annual ACM SIGPLAN-SIGACT Symposium on Principles of Programming Languages (POPL'00), Boston, Massachusetts, January 19-21. (2000) 119–132
10. Hinze, R.: Generics for the masses. In Fisher, K., ed.: Proceedings of the 2004 International Conference on Functional Programming, Snowbird, Utah, September 19–22, 2004, ACM Press (2004) 236–243
11. Hinze, R., Löh, A., Oliveira, B.C.d.S.: "Scrap Your Boilerplate" reloaded. In Wadler, P., Hagiya, M., eds.: Proceedings of the Eighth International Symposium on Functional and Logic Programming (FLOPS 2006), 24-26 April 2006, Fuji Susono, Japan. Lecture Notes in Computer Science, Springer-Verlag (2006)

12. Xi, H., Chen, C., Chen, G.: Guarded recursive datatype constructors. In: Proceedings of the ACM SIGPLAN-SIGACT symposium on Principles of Programming Languages (POPL 2003), ACM Press (2003) 224–235

13. Peyton Jones, S., Washburn, G., Weirich, S.: Wobbly types: Type inference for generalised algebraic data types. Technical Report MS-CIS-05-26, University of Pennsylvania (2004)

14. Wadler, P.: Theorems for free! In: The Fourth International Conference on Functional Programming Languages and Computer Architecture (FPCA'89), London, UK, Addison-Wesley Publishing Company (1989) 347–359

15. Hughes, R.J.M.: A novel representation of lists and its application to the function "reverse". Information Processing Letters **22**(3) (1986) 141–144

16. Bird, R., Meertens, L.: Nested datatypes. In Jeuring, J., ed.: Fourth International Conference on Mathematics of Program Construction, MPC'98, Marstrand, Sweden. Volume 1422 of Lecture Notes in Computer Science., Springer-Verlag (1998) 52–67

17. Hinze, R.: Functional Pearl: Perfect trees and bit-reversal permutations. Journal of Functional Programming **10**(3) (2000) 305–317

18. Hutton, G.: Higher-order functions for parsing. Journal of Functional Programming **2**(3) (1992) 323–343

19. Peyton Jones, S.: Haskell 98 Language and Libraries. Cambridge University Press (2003)

20. Jones, M.P.: A system of constructor classes: overloading and implicit higher-order polymorphism. Journal of Functional Programming **5**(1) (1995) 1–35

21. Hinze, R.: Fun with phantom types. In Gibbons, J., de Moor, O., eds.: The Fun of Programming. Palgrave Macmillan (2003) 245–262 ISBN 1-4039-0772-2 hardback, ISBN 0-333-99285-7 paperback.

22. Lämmel, R., Peyton Jones, S.: Scrap more boilerplate: reflection, zips, and generalised casts. In Fisher, K., ed.: Proceedings of the 2004 International Conference on Functional Programming, Snowbird, Utah, September 19–22, 2004. (2004) 244–255

23. Backhouse, R., Jansson, P., Jeuring, J., Meertens, L.: Generic Programming — An Introduction —. In Swierstra, S.D., Henriques, P.R., Oliveira, J.N., eds.: 3rd International Summer School on Advanced Functional Programming, Braga, Portugal. Volume 1608 of Lecture Notes in Computer Science. Springer-Verlag, Berlin (1999) 28–115

24. Hinze, R., Jeuring, J.: Generic Haskell: Applications. In Backhouse, R., Gibbons, J., eds.: Generic Programming: Advanced Lectures. Volume 2793 of Lecture Notes in Computer Science. Springer-Verlag (2003) 57–97

25. Harper, R., Morrisett, G.: Compiling polymorphism using intensional type analysis. In: 22nd Symposium on Principles of Programming Languages, POPL '95. (1995) 130–141

26. Crary, K., Weirich, S.: Flexible type analysis. In: Proceedings ICFP 1999: International Conference on Functional Programming, ACM Press (1999) 233–248

27. Trifonov, V., Saha, B., Shao, Z.: Fully reflexive intensional type analysis. In: Proceedings ICFP 2000: International Conference on Functional Programming, ACM Press (2000) 82–93

28. Weirich, S.: Encoding intensional type analysis. In: European Symposium on Programming. Volume 2028 of LNCS., Springer-Verlag (2001) 92–106

29. Norell, U., Jansson, P.: Polytypic programming in Haskell. In Trinder, P., Michaelson, G., Peña, R., eds.: Implementation of Functional Languages: 15th International Workshop, IFL 2003, Edinburgh, UK, September 8-11, 2003. (2003) 168–184

30. Oliveira, B.C., Gibbons, J.: Typecase: A design pattern for type-indexed functions. In Leijen, D., ed.: Proceedings of the 2005 ACM SIGPLAN workshop on Haskell, Tallinn, Estonia. (2005) 98–109
31. Hinze, R., Peyton Jones, S.: Derivable type classes. In Hutton, G., ed.: Proceedings of the 2000 ACM SIGPLAN Haskell Workshop. Volume 41.1 of Electronic Notes in Theoretical Computer Science., Elsevier Science (2001) The preliminary proceedings appeared as a University of Nottingham technical report.
32. Alimarine, A., Plasmeijer, R.: A generic programming extension for Clean. In Arts, T., Mohnen, M., eds.: Proceedings of the 13th International workshop on the Implementation of Functional Languages, IFL'01, Älvsjö, Sweden (2001) 257–278
33. Hinze, R.: Polytypic values possess polykinded types. Science of Computer Programming **43** (2002) 129–159
34. Löh, A.: Exploring Generic Haskell. PhD thesis, Utrecht University (2004)
35. Löh, A., Jeuring, J.: The Generic Haskell user's guide, version 1.42 - Coral release. Technical Report UU-CS-2005-004, Universiteit Utrecht (2005)
36. Hinze, R., Löh, A., Oliveira, B.C.: "Scrap Your Boilerplate" reloaded. Technical Report IAI-TR-2006-2, Institut für Informatik III, Universität Bonn (2006)
37. Jones, M.P.: Type classes with functional dependencies. In Smolka, G., ed.: Proceedings of the 9th European Symposium on Programming, ESOP 2000, Berlin, Germany. Volume 1782 of Lecture Notes in Computer Science., Springer-Verlag (2000) 230–244
38. Hinze, R., Jeuring, J., Löh, A.: Type-indexed data types. Science of Computer Programming **51** (2004) 117–151
39. Clarke, D., Löh, A.: Generic Haskell, specifically. In Gibbons, J., Jeuring, J., eds.: Proceedings of the IFIP TC2 Working Conference on Generic Programming, Schloss Dagstuhl, Kluwer Academic Publishers (2002) 21–48
40. Visser, E.: Language independent traversals for program transformation. In Jeuring, J., ed.: Proceedings of the 2nd Workshop on Generic Programming, Ponte de Lima, Portugal. (2000) 86–104 The proceedings appeared as a technical report of Universiteit Utrecht, UU-CS-2000-19.
41. Hinze, R., Löh, A.: Open data types and open functions. Technical Report IAI-TR-2006-3, Institut für Informatik III, Universität Bonn (2006)
42. Reig, F.: Generic proofs for combinator-based generic programs. In Loidl, H.W., ed.: Trends in Functional Programming. Volume 5. Intellect (2006)
43. Braun, W., Rem, M.: A logarithmic implementation of flexible arrays. Memorandum MR83/4, Eindhoven University of Technology (1983)

A   Library

The function *tree* turns a list of elements into a balanced binary tree, a so-called *Braun tree* [43].

$$tree :: [\alpha] \to Tree\ \alpha$$
$$tree\ x$$
$$\qquad |\ null\ x \qquad\qquad = Empty$$
$$\qquad |\ otherwise \qquad = Node\ (tree\ x_1)\ a\ (tree\ x_2)$$
$$\qquad \textbf{where}\ (x_1, a : x_2) = splitAt\ (length\ x\ `div`\ 2)\ x$$

The type *ShowS* is Haskell's type of pretty printers. The operator '•' separates two elements of this type by a space.

$$(\bullet) :: ShowS \rightarrow ShowS \rightarrow ShowS$$
$$s_1 \bullet s_2 = s_1 \cdot showChar \text{ ' ' } \cdot s_2$$

The function *showsList* produces a comma-separated sequence of elements between square brackets.

$$showsList :: [ShowS] \rightarrow ShowS$$
$$showsList\ Nil \qquad\quad = showString \text{ "[]"}$$
$$showsList\ (Cons\ x\ xs) = showChar \text{ '['} \cdot x$$
$$\qquad\qquad\qquad\quad \cdot\ foldr\ (\cdot)\ id\ [showChar \text{ ','} \cdot s \mid s \leftarrow xs]$$
$$\qquad\qquad\qquad\quad \cdot\ showChar \text{ ']'}$$

The type *ReadS* is Haskell's parser type. The function *alt* implements the alternation of a list of parsers.

$$alt :: [ReadS\ \alpha] \rightarrow ReadS\ \alpha$$
$$alt\ rs = \lambda s \rightarrow concatMap\ (\lambda r \rightarrow r\ s)\ rs$$

Give a parser for elements, *readsList* parses a list of elements written as a comma-separated sequence between square brackets.

$$readsList :: ReadS\ \alpha \rightarrow ReadS\ [\alpha]$$
$$readsList\ r = readParen\ False\ (\lambda s \rightarrow [x \mid (\text{"["}, s_1) \leftarrow lex\ s, x \leftarrow readl\ s_1])$$
$$\textbf{where}\ readl\ s = [([\,], \quad s_1) \mid (\text{"]"}, s_1) \leftarrow lex \qquad s]$$
$$\qquad\qquad\quad +\!\!+\ [(x : xs, s_2) \mid (x, \quad s_1) \leftarrow r \qquad s,$$
$$\qquad\qquad\qquad\qquad\qquad\quad (xs, \quad s_2) \leftarrow readl'\ s_1]$$
$$\qquad\quad readl'\ s = [([\,], \quad s_1) \mid (\text{"]"}, s_1) \leftarrow lex \qquad s]$$
$$\qquad\qquad\qquad +\!\!+\ [(x : xs, s_3) \mid (\text{","}, s_1) \leftarrow lex \qquad s,$$
$$\qquad\qquad\qquad\qquad\qquad\quad (x, \quad s_2) \leftarrow r \qquad s_1,$$
$$\qquad\qquad\qquad\qquad\qquad\quad (xs, \quad s_3) \leftarrow readl'\ s_2]$$

Generic Views on Data Types

Stefan Holdermans[1], Johan Jeuring[1], Andres Löh[2], and Alexey Rodriguez[1]

[1] Department of Information and Computing Sciences, Utrecht University
P.O. Box 80.089, 3508 TB Utrecht, The Netherlands
{stefan, johanj, alexey}@cs.uu.nl
[2] Institut für Informatik III, Universität Bonn
Römerstraße 164, 53117 Bonn, Germany
loeh@informatik.uni-bonn.de

Abstract. A generic function is defined by induction on the structure of types. The structure of a data type can be defined in several ways. For example, in PolyP a pattern functor gives the structure of a data type viewed as a fixed point, and in Generic Haskell a structural representation type gives an isomorphic type view of a data type in terms of sums of products. Depending on this generic view on the structure of data types, some generic functions are easier, more difficult, or even impossible to define. Furthermore, the efficiency of some generic functions can be improved by choosing a different view. This paper introduces generic views on data types and shows why they are useful. Furthermore, it shows how generic views have been added to Generic Haskell, an extension of the functional programming language Haskell that supports the construction of generic functions. The separation between inductive definitions on type structure and generic views allows us to combine many approaches to generic programming in a single framework.

1 Introduction

A generic function is defined by induction on the structure of types. Several approaches to generic programming [1, 2, 3, 4, 5] have been developed in the last decade. These approaches have their commonalities and differences:

- All the approaches provide either a facility for defining a function by induction on the structure of types, or a set of basic, compiler generated, generic functions which are used as combinators in the construction of generic functions. The compiler generated functions, however, are also defined by induction on the structure of types.
- All the approaches differ on how they *view* data types. There are various ways in which the inductive structure of data types can be defined, and each approach to generic programming chooses a different one.

This paper introduces *generic views* on data types. Using generic views it is possible to define generic functions for different views on data types. Generic views provide a framework in which the different approaches to generic programming can be used and compared.

T. Uustalu (Ed.): MPC 2006, LNCS 4014, pp. 209–234, 2006.

The inductive structure of types. Different approaches to generic programming view the structure of types differently:

- In PolyP [1] a data type is viewed as the fixed point of a pattern functor that has kind $* \to * \to *$. Viewing a data type as a fixed point of a pattern functor allows us to define recursive combinators such as the catamorphism and anamorphism [6], and functions that return the direct recursive children of a constructor [7]. A downside of this view on data types is that PolyP can only handle regular data types of kind $* \to *$.
- In Generic Haskell [2, 8, 9], a data type is described in terms of a top-level sums of products structural representation type. Generic functions in Generic Haskell are defined on possibly nested data types of any kind. However, because the recursive structure of data types is invisible in Generic Haskell, it is hard to define the catamorphism and children functions in a natural way, for example.
- In the 'Scrap your boilerplate' [3, 10] approach the generic fold is the central steering concept. The generic fold views a value of a data type as either a constructor, or as an application of a (partially applied) constructor to a value. Using the generic fold it is easy to define traversal combinators on data types, which can, for example, be specialized to update small parts of a value of a large data structure. A disadvantage of the boilerplate approach is that some generic functions, such as the equality and zipping functions, are harder to define. Furthermore, the approach does not naturally generalize to type-indexed data types [11, 9]. We can translate the boilerplate approach to the level of data types by defining a particular generic view.

Other approaches to representing data types can be found in the Constructor Calculus [4], and in the work of De Moor and Hoogendijk [5].

Generic views on data types. An approach to generic programming essentially consists of two components: a facility to define recursive functions on a specific set of types, called view types, and a view on the inductive structure of data types, which maps data types onto view types. We call such a view on the structure of types a *generic view* (or just *view*) on data types. Wadler [12] also defines views on data types. The difference between Wadler's views and generic views is that the former constitute a method for viewing a single data type in different ways, whereas the latter describes how the structure of a large class of data types is viewed.

Each of the above generic views on data types has its advantages and disadvantages. Some views allow the definition of generic functions that are impossible or hard to define in other approaches, other views allow the definition of more efficient generic functions. This paper

- identifies the concept of generic views as an important building block of an implementation for generic programming;
- shows that different choices of generic views have significant influence on the class of generic functions that can be expressed;
- clearly defines what constitutes a generic view, and discusses how generic views have been added to Generic Haskell;

– provides a common framework which can be used to compare different approaches to generic programming.

Views add expressiveness to a generic programming language. Generic functions still work for arbitrary data types that can be expressed in the view, but the choice between different views allows us to define more generic functions.

Organization. This paper is organized as follows. Section 2 briefly introduces generic programming in Generic Haskell. Section 3 shows by means of examples why generic views on data types are useful, and how they increase the expressiveness of a generic programming language. Section 4 formally defines a generic view. For some of the examples of Section 3, we give the formal definition. Section 5 discusses how views have been added to the Generic Haskell compiler. Section 6 gives related work and conclusions.

2   Introduction to Generic Programming in Generic Haskell

This section introduces generic programming in Generic Haskell. The introduction will be brief, for more information see [13, 11, 9]. Generic Haskell has slightly changed in the last couple of years, and we will use the version described in Löh's thesis 'Exploring Generic Haskell' [9] (EGH) in this paper, which to a large extent has been implemented in the Coral release [8].

2.1   Type-Indexed Functions

A type-indexed function takes an explicit type argument, and can have behavior that depends on the type argument. For example, suppose the unit type Unit, sum type +, and product type × are defined as follows,

data Unit $= Unit$
data $a + b = Inl\ a \mid Inr\ b$
data $a \times b = a \times b$.

We use infix types + and × and an infix value constructor × here to ease the presentation. The type-indexed function *collect* collects values from a data structure. We define function *collect* on the unit type, sums and products, integers, and characters as follows:

$$
\begin{array}{llll}
collect\langle\text{Unit}\rangle & Unit & = [\,] \\
collect\langle\alpha + \beta\rangle & (Inl\ a) & = collect\langle\alpha\rangle\ a \\
collect\langle\alpha + \beta\rangle & (Inr\ b) & = collect\langle\beta\rangle\ b \\
collect\langle\alpha \times \beta\rangle & (a \times b) & = collect\langle\alpha\rangle\ a \mathbin{+\!\!+} collect\langle\beta\rangle\ b \\
collect\langle\text{Int}\rangle & n & = [\,] \\
collect\langle\text{Char}\rangle & c & = [\,].
\end{array}
$$

The type signature of *collect* is as follows:

$$collect\langle a :: * \mid c :: *\rangle :: (collect\langle a \mid c\rangle) \Rightarrow a \rightarrow [\,c\,].$$

The type of *collect* is parameterized over two type variables. The first type variable, a, appearing to the left of the vertical bar, is a generic type variable, and represents the type of the type argument of *collect*. Type variable c, appearing to the right of a vertical bar, is called a non-generic (or parametric) type variable. Such non-generic variables appear in type-indexed functions that are parametrically polymorphic with respect to some type variables. The collect function is parametrically polymorphic in the element type of its list result. It always returns the empty list, but we will show below how to adapt it so that it collects values from a data structure. Since it always returns the empty list there is no need, but also no desire, to fix the type of the list elements. The type context $(collect\langle a \mid c\rangle) \Rightarrow$ appears in the type because *collect* is called recursively on sums and products, which means that, for example, if we want an instance of *collect* on the type $\alpha + \beta$, we need instances of *collect* on the types α and β. Thus *collect depends on* itself. The theory of dependencies and type signatures of generic functions is an integral part of dependency-style Generic Haskell.

The type signature of *collect* can be instantiated for specific cases, including cases omitted in the definition as we shall see later, by the Generic Haskell compiler, yielding, for example, the types

$$collect\langle \text{Unit}\rangle :: \forall c . \text{Unit} \rightarrow [c]$$
$$collect\langle [\alpha]\rangle \ :: \forall c \ a . (collect\langle \alpha\rangle :: a \rightarrow [c]) \Rightarrow [a] \rightarrow [c]$$

for the cases of the unit type and lists, respectively. The latter type can be read as "given a function $collect\langle \alpha\rangle$ of type $a \rightarrow [c]$, the expression $collect\langle [\alpha]\rangle$ is of type $[a] \rightarrow [c]$".

Depending on the situation, the function $collect\langle \alpha\rangle$ can be automatically inferred by the compiler, or it can be user specified using *local redefinitions*. For example, if we only want to collect the positive numbers from a list, we write:

let $collect\langle \alpha\rangle \ x = $ **if** $x > 0$ **then** $[x]$ **else** $[\,]$
in $collect\langle [\alpha]\rangle$,

which has type $Num \ a \Rightarrow [a] \rightarrow [a]$. Generally, we use a *local redefinition* to locally modify the behavior of a generic function. Some generic functions such as *collect* only reveal their full power in the context of local redefinitions.

2.2   Default Cases

Suppose we wish to use function *collect* to collect the variables of the data type Term, which represents lambda terms:

data Term   = *Var* Variable | *Abs* Variable Term | *App* Term Term
newtype Variable = *V* String.

We cannot use local redefinitions as we did for the list case, because this would require that the data type Term is parameterized over the type of variables. Instead, we write function *varcollect* making use of *default cases*:

$varcollect\langle\text{Variable}\rangle\ v = [v]$
$varcollect$ **extends** $collect$
   where $collect$ **as** $varcollect$.

The first line defines the Variable case of $varcollect$. The next two lines copy the definition of $collect$ and rename its dependency on $collect$ to $varcollect$. The use of a default case is equivalent to manually copying the definition of $collect$, replacing the calls to $collect$ with calls to $varcollect$, and adding the case for Variable. The more specific behavior of $varcollect$ is reflected in its type signature:

$$varcollect\langle a :: * \rangle :: (varcollect\langle a\rangle) \Rightarrow a \rightarrow [\text{Variable}].$$

2.3 View Types

A type-indexed function such as $collect$ does not only work on the types that appear as its type indices. To see why $collect$ is in fact *generic* and works on arbitrary data types, we give a mapping from data types to view types such as units, sums and products. It suffices to define a function on view types (and primitive or abstract types such as Int and Char) in order to obtain a function that can be applied to values of arbitrary data types. If there is no specific case for a type in the definition of a generic function, generic behavior is derived automatically by the compiler by exploiting the structural representation.

For example, the definition of the function $collect$ generically derived for lists coincides with the following specific definition:

$$collect\langle[\alpha]\rangle\ []\quad\ = []$$
$$collect\langle[\alpha]\rangle\ (x : xs) = collect\langle\alpha\rangle\ x \mathbin{+\!\!+} collect\langle[\alpha]\rangle\ xs.$$

To obtain this instance, the compiler needs to know the structural representation of lists, and how to convert between lists and their structural representation. We will describe these components in the remainder of this section.

The structural representation (or structure type) of types is expressed in terms of units, sums, products, and base types such as integers, characters, etc. For example, for the list and tree data types defined by

data List $a\quad = Nil \mid Cons\ a\ (\text{List}\ a)$
data Tree $a\ b = Tip\ a \mid Node\ (\text{Tree}\ a\ b)\ b\ (\text{Tree}\ a\ b)$

we obtain the following structural representations:

type List$^\circ$ $a\quad = \text{Unit} + a \times \text{List}\ a$
type Tree$^\circ$ $a\ b = a + \text{Tree}\ a\ b \times b \times \text{Tree}\ a\ b,$

where we assume that $\times$ binds stronger than $+$, and both type constructors associate to the right. Note that the representation of a recursive type is not recursive, and refers to the recursive type itself. The representation of a type in Generic Haskell only represents the structure of the top level of the type.

If two types are isomorphic, the corresponding isomorphisms, also called embedding-projection pairs, can be stored as a pair of functions converting back and forth:

data EP a b $= EP\{ from :: (a \to b), to :: (b \to a) \}$.

A type T and its structural representation type T° are isomorphic, witnessed by a value $conv_T :: $ EP T T°. For example, for the list data type we have that $conv_{\mathrm{List}} = EP$ $from_{\mathrm{List}}$ to_{List}, where $from_{\mathrm{List}}$ and to_{List} are defined by

$$
\begin{aligned}
&from_{\mathrm{List}} && :: \forall a . \text{List } a \to \text{List}^\circ a \\
&from_{\mathrm{List}} \; Nil && = Inl \; Unit \\
&from_{\mathrm{List}} \; (Cons \; x \; xs) && = Inr \; (x \times xs) \\
\\
&to_{\mathrm{List}} && :: \forall a . \text{List}^\circ a \to \text{List } a \\
&to_{\mathrm{List}} \; (Inl \; Unit) && = Nil \\
&to_{\mathrm{List}} \; (Inr \; (x \times xs)) && = Cons \; x \; xs.
\end{aligned}
$$

The definitions of the embedding-projection pairs are automatically generated by the Generic Haskell compiler for all data types that appear in a program.

Using structural representation types and embedding-projection pairs, a call to a generic function on a data type T is reduced to a call on type T°. Hence, if the generic function is defined for view types such as Unit, +, and ×, we do not need cases for specific data types such as List or Tree anymore. For primitive types such as Int, Float, IO or →, no structure is available. Therefore, for a generic function to work on these types, a specific case is necessary.

2.4   Specializing Generic Functions

In this section we sketch how Generic Haskell specializes a generic function. Assume that *collect*, the collect function from Section 2.1, is called on the type argument Bool. No case is given for Bool, so Generic Haskell considers the structural representation for Bool. The data type Bool and its structural representation are given by

data Bool $=$ *False* | *True*,
type Bool$^\circ$ $=$ Unit $+$ Unit.

We reduce a call of *collect*⟨Bool⟩ to a call *collect*⟨Bool$^\circ$⟩. The translation of the latter function to Haskell code, using the cases of *collect* for view types, is quite simple and described elsewhere (EGH,[2]). The call *collect*⟨Bool$^\circ$⟩ is of type Bool$^\circ \to [c]$, whereas *collect*⟨Bool⟩ is of type Bool $\to [c]$. So to express the call of *collect*⟨Bool⟩ in terms of the the call of *collect*⟨Bool$^\circ$⟩, we have to lift the isomorphism between Bool and its representation to the type of the generic function *collect*.

Given an embedding-projection pair between a type D and its structure type D°, we can use the generic function *bimap* to lift the isomorphism to arbitrarily complex types. Recall that *collect* is defined in such a way that it returns the empty list for every data type, and only becomes useful when locally redefined.

Similarly, *bimap* defines the identity embedding-projection pair for each data type generically. A remarkable fact is that *bimap* can be defined on function types. We give the cases for Unit, +, and → as an example (see, for example, EGH for a complete definition):

$bimap\langle a_1 :: *, a_2 :: * \rangle :: (bimap\langle a_1, a_2 \rangle) \Rightarrow$ EP $a_1\ a_2$
$bimap\langle \text{Unit} \rangle\quad = EP\ id\ id$
$bimap\langle \alpha + \beta \rangle\ =$
 let $from_+$ $(Inl\ a)$ $= Inl\ (from\ bimap\langle\alpha\rangle\ a)$
  $from_+$ $(Inr\ b)$ $= Inr\ (from\ bimap\langle\beta\rangle\ b)$
  to_+ $(Inl\ a)$ $= Inl\ (to\quad bimap\langle\alpha\rangle\ a)$
  to_+ $(Inr\ b)$ $= Inr\ (to\quad bimap\langle\beta\rangle\ b)$
 in $EP\ from_+\ to_+$
$bimap\langle \alpha \to \beta \rangle\ =$
 let $from_\to\ c = from\ bimap\langle\beta\rangle \cdot c \cdot to\quad bimap\langle\alpha\rangle$
  $to_\to\quad c = to\quad bimap\langle\beta\rangle \cdot c \cdot from\ bimap\langle\alpha\rangle$
 in $EP\ from_\to\ to_\to.$

Using local redefinition, we can plug in an embedding-projection pair in *bimap* to lift the isomorphism between Bool and its representation to the type of the generic function *collect*.

$$collect\langle \text{Bool} \rangle = \textbf{let } bimap\langle\alpha\rangle = ep_{\text{Bool}} \textbf{ in } to\ (bimap\langle\alpha \to [c]\rangle)\ collect\langle\text{Bool}^\circ\rangle.$$

The details of why this works are omitted here. It is, however, important to realize that for generic functions that both consume and produce values of the type argument's type, both components of the embedding projection pair will be applied: a value of the original type D is transformed into D° to be in suitable form to be passed to the function that works on the structural representation. Because the function also returns something containing values of type D°, these values are then converted back to type D. This is the reason why the embedding-projection pair should contain an isomorphism. If it does not, a value could change simply by the conversion functions that are applied, making it highly difficult to define, for example, the generic identity function.

3 Views

We have explained how Generic Haskell defines a structural representation type plus an embedding-projection pair for any Haskell data type. A type-indexed function is generic because the embedding-projection pair is applied to the type arguments by the compiler as needed. Other approaches to generic programming use different, but still fixed representations of data types. In this section, we argue that different views improve the expressiveness of a generic programming system, because not every view is equally suitable for every generic function. In Section 4 we will give a formal definition of generic views.

3.1 Fixed Points

Consider the data type Term, introduced in Section 2.2, and the function
subterms that, given a term, produces the immediate subterms.

$$
\begin{array}{ll}
subterms & :: \text{Term} \rightarrow [\text{Term}] \\
subterms\ (Var\ x) & = [\,] \\
subterms\ (Abs\ x\ t) & = [t] \\
subterms\ (App\ t\ u) & = [t, u]
\end{array}
$$

This function is an instance of a more general pattern. The function *subtrees*,
for example, produces the immediate subtrees of an external binary search
tree.

$$
\begin{array}{ll}
subtrees :: \forall a\ b\ .\ \text{Tree}\ a\ b \rightarrow [\text{Tree}\ a\ b] \\
subtrees\ (Tip\ a) & = [\,] \\
subtrees\ (Node\ l\ b\ r) & = [l, r]
\end{array}
$$

Given a recursive data type's value, both *subterms* and *subtrees* retrieve the
immediate children corresponding to the recursion points in the data type's definition. Since the general pattern is clear, we would like to be able to express
it as a generic function. However, Generic Haskell does not allow us to define
such a function directly, due to the fact that the structure over which generic
functions are inductively defined does not expose the recursive occurrences in a
data type's definition.

Generic Haskell's precursor, PolyP, does give access to these recursive calls,
enabling the definition of a generic function that collects the immediate recursive
children of a value [7]. Generic functions in PolyP, however, are limited in the
sense that they can only be applied to regular[1] data types of kind $* \rightarrow *$. In
particular, this precludes nested and mutually recursive data types.

Interestingly, it is possible to write a program in Generic Haskell that produces
the immediate children of a value, but it requires some extra effort from the user
of the program. If regular recursive data types are expressed using an explicit
type-level fixed point operator:

$$
\begin{array}{ll}
\textbf{data}\ \text{Fix}\ f & = In\ (f\ (\text{Fix}\ f)) \\
\textbf{data}\ \text{TermBase}\ r & = VarBase\ \text{Variable} \mid AbsBase\ \text{Variable}\ r \mid AppBase\ r\ r \\
\textbf{type}\ \text{Term}' & = \text{Fix TermBase} \\
\textbf{data}\ \text{TreeBase}\ a\ b\ r & = TipBase\ a \mid NodeBase\ r\ b\ r \\
\textbf{type}\ \text{Tree}'\ a\ b & = \text{Fix (TreeBase}\ a\ b),
\end{array}
$$

then the generic function *children* can be defined with a single case for Fix.

$$
\begin{array}{l}
children\langle a :: *\rangle :: (\forall c\ .\ collect\langle a \mid c\rangle) \Rightarrow a \rightarrow [a] \\
children\langle\text{Fix}\ \varphi\rangle\ (In\ r) = \textbf{let}\ collect\langle\alpha\rangle\ x = [x]\ \textbf{in}\ collect\langle\varphi\ \alpha\rangle\ r
\end{array}
$$

---

[1] A data type is *regular* if it does not contain function spaces, and if the arguments of
the type constructor on the left- and right-hand sides in its definition are the same.
So the data type *Flip* defined by **data** *Flip a b = MkFlip a (Flip b a)* is not regular.

The *children* function depends on the collect function *collect*[2] defined in Section 2. The local redefinition fixes the type of the produced list and adapts the collect function to construct singleton lists from the recursive components in a fixed point's value. The function *collect* ensures that these singletons are concatenated to produce the result list.

Although this approach works fine, there is an obvious downside. The programmer needs to redefine her recursive data types in terms of Fix. Whenever she wants to use *children* to compute the recursive components of a value of any of the original recursive types, say Term or Tree, a user-defined bidirectional mapping from the original types to the fixed points, Term' and Tree', has to be applied.

With a *fixed-point view*, the compiler becomes capable of deriving the fixed point for any regular recursive data type and will generate and apply the required mappings automatically. The structure of a data type is then no longer perceived as a sum of products, but as the fixed point of a sum of products. The only thing we have to change in the definition of *children* to make use of the new view is to add the name of the view to the type signature:

$$children\langle a :: * \textbf{ viewed } \mathsf{Fix}\rangle :: (\forall c\,.\,collect\langle a \mid c\rangle) \Rightarrow a \rightarrow [a].$$

The definition of *children* is unchanged. For example, $children\langle[\text{Int}]\rangle\;[1,2,3]$ yields $[[2,3]]$. The user of the function does not have to worry about defining types in terms of Fix any longer: the translation happens behind the scenes.

Another well-known function that can be defined using the fixed-point view is the *catamorphism* [14]. In the definition of *cata* we use a type-indexed type AlgebraOf, which returns the algebra of a data type: a function from the pattern functor of the data type to the result type. The details of this definition can be found in EGH, and in the forthcoming release of Generic Haskell with views.

3.2   Balanced Sums of Products

Traditionally, Generic Haskell views the structure of data types using nested right-deep binary sums and products. The choice for such a view is rather arbitrary. A nested left-deep view or a balanced view may be just as suitable. However, the chosen view has some impact on the behavior of certain generic programs. The generic function *enc*, for instance, encodes values of data types as lists of bits.

data Bit = *Off* | *On*
$$enc\langle a :: *\rangle :: (enc\langle a\rangle) \Rightarrow a \rightarrow [\text{Bit}]$$
$$enc\langle\text{Unit}\rangle\;\;Unit\;\;\;\; = [\,]$$
$$enc\langle\alpha + \beta\rangle\;(Inl\;a) = Off : enc\langle\alpha\rangle\;a$$
$$enc\langle\alpha + \beta\rangle\;(Inr\;b) = On : enc\langle\beta\rangle\;b$$

---

[2] One might be tempted to write $collect\langle a \mid a\rangle$ for the dependency, but this produces incorrect type signatures for some specializations of *children*. The reason is that the non-generic variable of *collect* must have kind $*$, which in general does not hold since variable a can have any arbitrary kind.

$$enc\langle \alpha \times \beta \rangle \ (a \times b) = enc\langle \alpha \rangle \ a \mathbin{+\!\!+} enc\langle \beta \rangle \ b$$
$$enc\langle \mathrm{Int} \rangle \quad n \qquad = encInt \ n$$
$$enc\langle \mathrm{Char} \rangle \ c \qquad = encChar \ c$$

Here, $encInt$ and $encChar$ denote primitive encoders for integers and characters, respectively. The interesting cases are the ones for sums where a bit is emitted for every choice that is made between a pair of constructors. In the case for products the encodings of the constituent parts are concatenated.

Applying a nested right-deep view to the type $Compass$ of directions

data $Compass \ = North \mid East \mid South \mid West,$

gives the structure

type $Compass^\circ \ = \mathrm{Unit} + (\mathrm{Unit} + (\mathrm{Unit} + \mathrm{Unit})).$

Using this structure, encoding a value with enc takes one bit at best ($North$) and three bits at worst ($West$). In contrast, a balanced view Bal on the structure, i.e.,

type $Compass^\circ_B = (\mathrm{Unit} + \mathrm{Unit}) + (\mathrm{Unit} + \mathrm{Unit}),$

requires only two bits for any value of $Compass$.

In general, encoding requires $O(n)$ bits on average when a nested structure representation is applied, and $O(\log n)$ bits when a balanced representation is used. All we have to do (next to implementing a balanced view Bal) is to change the type signature of enc accordingly:

$$enc\langle a :: * \textbf{ viewed } \mathsf{Bal} \rangle :: (enc\langle a \rangle) \Rightarrow a \to [\mathrm{Bit}].$$

3.3   List-Like Sums and Products

Suppose we have a generic function $show$ which is of type

$$show\langle a :: * \rangle :: (show\langle a \rangle) \Rightarrow a \to \mathrm{String}$$

and produces a human-readable string representation of a value. We want to write a function $showP$ that shows only a part of a value. The part that is shown is determined by a path of type

type $\mathrm{Path} = [\mathrm{Int}].$

Non-empty lists of type Path select a part of the value to print. For instance, $[1]$ selects the second field of the top-level constructor, and $[1,0]$ selects the first field of the top-level constructor thereof. The function has type

$$showP\langle a :: * \rangle :: (show\langle a \rangle, showP\langle a \rangle) \Rightarrow \mathrm{Path} \to a \to \mathrm{String}.$$

The motivation for $showP$ comes from the Proxima editor [15], where there is a need to generically handle paths to selections in arbitrary documents. Let us look at the definition of $showP$ on products:

$$showP\langle \alpha \times \beta \rangle \ (0 : p) \ (a \times b) = \textbf{if } null \ p \textbf{ then } show\langle \alpha \rangle \ a \textbf{ else } showP\langle \alpha \rangle \ p \ a.$$

If the first path element is 0, the left component is selected. The encoding in binary products is such that the left component is always a field of the constructor, and not an encoding of multiple fields. We can therefore test if the remainder of the path is empty: if this is the case, we show the complete field using *show*; otherwise, we show the part of the field that is selected by the tail of the current path.

$$showP\langle \alpha \times \beta \rangle \ (n : p) \ (a \times b) = showP\langle \beta \rangle \ (n - 1 : p) \ b$$

If the first path element is not 0, we can decrease it by one and show a part of the right component, containing the remaining fields.

There are several problems with this approach. Consider the following data type and its structural representation:

> **data** Con012 *a b* = *Con0* | *Con1 a* | *Con2 a b*
> **type** Con012° *a b* = Unit + *a*   + *a* × *b*.

Using the standard view of Generic Haskell a product structure is only created if there are at least two fields. If there is only one field, such as for *Con1*, the single field (here *a*) is the representation. Obviously, we then cannot use the product case of the generic function to make sure that 0 is the topmost element of the path.

We could add a check to the sum case of the function, detecting the size of the underlying product structure by calling another generic function, or by modifying the type of *showP* to pass additional information around. However, consider a data type Rename and its structural representation:

> **data** Rename = *R Original*
> **type** Rename° = *Original*.

The structural representation does not even contain a sum structure. Although it is possible to write *showP* in the standard view, it is extremely tiresome to do so. The same functionality has to be distributed over a multitude of different cases, simply because the structural encoding is so irregular, and we cannot rely on sum and product structure to be present in any case.

A list-like view List on data types can help. For this purpose we introduce a data type without constructors and without values (except bottom).

> **data** Zero

The type Zero plays the role of a neutral element for sums in the same way as Unit does for products. The above definition is not Haskell 98, but is supported by GHC and can be simulated in Haskell 98.

In our list-like view, the left component of a sum always encodes a single constructor, and the right component of a sum is either another sum or Zero. For products, the left component is always a single field, and the right component is either another product or Unit. In particular, there is always a sum and a product structure. The data type Con012 is encoded as follows:

> **type** Con012$_L^\circ$ *a b* = Unit + *a* × Unit + *a* × *b* × Unit + Zero.

Now, we can define *showP* easily:

$$showP\langle a :: * \textbf{ viewed List}\rangle :: (show\langle a\rangle, showP\langle a\rangle) \Rightarrow \text{Path} \to a \to \text{String}$$

$showP\langle\text{Unit}\rangle$	$\_$	$Unit$	$= error$ `"illegal path"`
$showP\langle\alpha \times \beta\rangle\ (0 : p)$	$(a \times b)$	$= showP\langle\alpha\rangle$	$p\ \ a$
$showP\langle\alpha \times \beta\rangle\ (n : p)$	$(a \times b)$	$= showP\langle\beta\rangle\ (n - 1 : p)\ b$	
$showP\langle\text{Zero}\rangle$	$\_$	$\_$	$= error$ `"cannot happen"`
$showP\langle\alpha + \beta\rangle\ []$	x	$= show\langle\alpha + \beta\rangle\ x$	
$showP\langle\alpha + \beta\rangle\ p$	$(Inl\ a)$	$= showP\langle\alpha\rangle\ p\ a$	
$showP\langle\alpha + \beta\rangle\ p$	$(Inr\ b)$	$= showP\langle\beta\rangle\ p\ b.$	

We have moved the check for the empty path to the sum case. We can do this because we know that every data type has a sum structure in the list-like view.

3.4 Boilerplate Approach

In the 'Scrap Your Boilerplate' approach, Lämmel and Peyton Jones present a design pattern for writing programs that traverse data structures [3, 10]. These traversals are defined using a relatively small library that comprises two types of generic combinators: recursive traversals and type extensions. Generic functions are defined in terms of these library functions, and not by induction on the structure of types. The library functions, however, do use a particular view on data types. This section discusses this view, dubbed Boilerplate, and shows how to implement a traversal function based on this view. The emulation of the boilerplate approach in Generic Haskell is useful for comparing different approaches to generic programming, but it turns out to be less convenient to use than the original boilerplate library due to the lack of higher-order generic functions.

In the boilerplate approach all traversals are instances of a general scheme imposed by a left-associative generic fold over constructor applications. So a type is viewed as a sum of products, where a product is either a nullary constructor, or the application of a constructor(-application) to a type. To emulate the behavior of the generic fold, the product constructor $\times$ in the Boilerplate view is left associative as well. The right component of a product is always a single field, and the left component is either another product or Unit, similar to the List view from Section 3.3.

For example, the Boilerplate view representations of the types of lists and trees are given by:

$$\textbf{type } \text{List}^{\circ}_{BP}\ a \quad = \text{Unit} + (\text{Unit} \times a) \times \text{List } a$$
$$\textbf{type } \text{Tree}^{\circ}_{BP}\ a\ b = \text{Unit} \times a + ((\text{Unit} \times \text{Tree } a\ b) \times b) \times \text{Tree } a\ b.$$

Besides generic traversals such as the generic fold, the Boilerplate view makes use of type extensions. A type extension extends the type of a function such that it works on many types instead of a single type. To emulate type extensions, we have to be able to distinguish types by name. Therefore we use a type-indexed function equipped with cases for specific types. The remaining cases – that is, the extension – are provided in a definition on a view that does not operate on the structure of types. For this purpose, we use the identity view (Id), which merely wraps a data type in the Id data type:

data Id $a = Id\ a$.

For example, consider the function *addPrefixVar* that adds prefixes to variables:

$addPrefixVar$ :: Variable $\rightarrow$ Variable
$addPrefixVar\ (V\ x) = V\ (\texttt{"gh\_"} +\!\!+ x)$,

this function is extended as follows to work on any type:

$addPrefix\langle a :: * \textbf{ viewed } \text{Id}\rangle :: a \rightarrow a$
$addPrefix\langle\text{Variable}\rangle\ x\qquad = addPrefixVar\ x$
$addPrefix\langle\text{Id }\alpha\rangle\qquad (Id\ x) = Id\ x$.

The Generic Haskell specialization algorithm chooses the Variable arm when *addPrefix* is applied to that type. For all other types, the last arm is selected.

The definitions of the traversal combinators rely on the list-like character of the Boilerplate view. For example, the *gmapT* combinator applies a transformation argument to the immediate children of a node, traversing it in a right to left fashion. The transformation argument is a type-extended function, which in our approach is modeled by a type-indexed function.

We implement type-extended arguments to combinators as type-indexed functions bound to the combinator's name followed by the *Par* suffix. For example, the *gmapT* combinator has the following definition (omitting the dependencies in the type, these can easily be inferred from the function definition):

$gmapT\langle a :: * \textbf{ viewed } \text{Boilerplate}\rangle :: a \rightarrow a$
$gmapT\langle\text{Unit}\rangle\quad Unit\quad = Unit$
$gmapT\langle\alpha + \beta\rangle\ (Inl\ a) = Inl\ (gmapT\langle\alpha\rangle\ a)$
$gmapT\langle\alpha + \beta\rangle\ (Inr\ b) = Inr\ (gmapT\langle\beta\rangle\ b)$
$gmapT\langle\alpha \times \beta\rangle\ (a \times b) = gmapT\langle\alpha\rangle\ a \times gmapTPar\langle\beta\rangle\ b$.

The default definition of the transformation argument is the identity:

$gmapTPar\langle a :: * \textbf{ viewed } \text{Id}\rangle :: a \rightarrow a$
$gmapTPar\langle\text{Id }\alpha\rangle\ (Id\ x) = Id\ x$.

The *everywhere* combinator applies a transformation to all nodes in a tree, traversing it in a bottom-up fashion. It is defined in terms of the simple non-recursive one-layer traversal combinator *gmapT*, or rather in terms of *gmapTInst*, an instance of *gmapT* where the parameter *gmapTPar* is instantiated with *everywhere*.

$everywhere\langle a :: * \textbf{ viewed } \text{Id}\rangle :: a \rightarrow a$
$everywhere\langle\text{Id }\alpha\rangle\ (Id\ x) = Id\ (everywherePar\langle\alpha\rangle\ (gmapTInst\langle\alpha\rangle\ x))$
$everywherePar\langle a :: * \textbf{ viewed } \text{Id}\rangle :: a \rightarrow a$
$everywherePar\langle\text{Id }\alpha\rangle\ (Id\ x) = Id\ x$

The first function transforms the children by means of a call to *gmapTInst* and then applies the transformation argument *everywherePar* to the result. The generic function *gmapTInst* is the defunctionalized equivalent of the application of *gmapT* to *everywhere*:

> *gmapTInst*⟨a :: ∗ **viewed** Boilerplate⟩ :: $a \rightarrow a$
> *gmapTInst* **extends** *gmapT*
>   **where** *gmapT*   **as** *gmapTInst*
>   *gmapTPar* **as** *everywhere*.

Function *gmapTInst* is defined by means of a *default case*: it behaves as *gmapT* except that the dependency on *gmapTPar* is changed to one on *everywhere*.

It is now trivial to write a function that adds prefixes generically by 'applying' *everywhere* to *addPrefix*.

> *genAddPrefix*⟨a :: ∗⟩ :: $a \rightarrow a$
> *genAddPrefix* **extends** *everywhere*
>   **where** *everywhere*   **as** *genAddPrefix*
>   *everywherePar* **as** *addPrefix*.

Note that the *gmapT* case for products only recurses on the left component of a product. Since the Boilerplate view guarantees that all fields of a constructor are encoded as right components of products, it is easy to verify that *gmapT* does indeed define a non-recursive traversal. This simple non-recursive scheme allows us to derive several rich recursive traversal strategies from a single base combinator. These strategies are written using default cases.

The type-extension operators used in the Boilerplate approach can be defined using type-indexed functions on the Id view. First class type-indexed functions are not supported in Generic Haskell. We emulate application of generic combinators to type-extension operators using defunctionalization techniques [16]. Defunctionalization is a standard technique to transform higher-order programs into first-order equivalents.

Because Generic Haskell lacks higher-order generic functions, these and other Scrap Your Boilerplate examples are better expressed using the standard view instead of the Boilerplate view. We believe, however, that an encoding of the Boilerplate approach within the view formalism can help to better compare it with other approaches, and improve the overall understanding of different generic programming techniques.

Hinze, Löh and Oliveira [17] define a generic boilerplate view using generalized algebraic data types. The view uses run-time representations of types and higher order functions, and is hence closer to the original Boilerplate approach. It follows that this view represents boilerplate functions more faithfully. Generic Haskell does not use run-time representations of types, so we cannot use the same approach.

4   Generic Views, Formally

The previous section shows why generic views are useful. This section formally defines generic views, and presents the formal definition of the standard view. The definition of the fixed-point view can be found in the technical report [18]. The other views mentioned in the previous section can also be defined using the formalism introduced in this section.

4.1   Notation

Throughout this section, we often use the following notation to denote repetition:

$$\{X_i\}^{i \in 1..n} \equiv X_1 \dots X_n$$
$$\{X_i\}_{;}^{i \in 1..n} \equiv X_1; \dots; X_n$$

If not explicitly mentioned otherwise, such repetitions can be empty, i.e., n can be 0. We sometimes omit the range of the variable if it is irrelevant or clear from the context.

4.2   Syntax

Programs. Figure 1 shows the syntax of programs in the core language. This language is a rather standard functional language. A program consists of zero or more type declarations and a single expression: the main function.

Types and kinds. The syntax of the type and kind language is shown in Figure 2. New types are introduced by means of **data** declarations. Such a declaration associates a type constructor with zero or more data constructors, each of which has zero or more fields. The *parameterized types* are explained below.

Generic programming extensions. To facilitate generic programming, the core language should be extended with parameterized type patterns and type-indexed functions with dependencies, and adapted with the facility to specify a view in the signature of a generic function.

Programs

$P ::= \{D_i; \}^i\ e$ type declarations and main expression

Value declarations

$d ::= x = e$ function declaration

Patterns

$p ::= x$ variable pattern
$\quad |\ (C\ \{p_i\}^i)$ constructor pattern

Expressions

$e ::= x$ variable
$\quad |\ C$ data constructor
$\quad |\ \lambda x\ .\ e$ abstraction
$\quad |\ (e_1\ e_2)$ application
$\quad |\ \textbf{case}\ e_0\ \textbf{of}\ \{p_i \rightarrow e_i\}^i_;$ case
$\quad |\ (\textbf{fix}\ e)$ fixed point
$\quad |\ \textbf{let}\ \{d_i\}^i_;\ \textbf{in}\ e$ let

Fig. 1. Syntax of the expression language

Types

$$t ::= a \qquad \text{type variable}$$
$$| \quad T \qquad \text{type constructor}$$
$$| \quad (t_1 \; t_2) \quad \text{type application}$$
$$| \quad \forall a :: \kappa . t \;\; \text{universal quantification}$$

Type declarations

$$D ::= \textbf{data} \; T = \{ \Lambda a_i :: \kappa_i \; . \; \}^i \; \{ C_j \; \{ t_{j,k} \}^k \}^j_|$$
algebraic data type

Parameterized types

$$u ::= \{ \Lambda a_i :: \kappa_i \; . \; \}^i \; t \;\; \text{type-level abstraction}$$

Kinds

$$\kappa ::= * \qquad\qquad \text{kind of proper types}$$
$$| \quad \kappa_1 \to \kappa_2 \;\; \text{function kind}$$

Fig. 2. Syntax of types and kinds

Kind environments

$$K ::= \varepsilon \qquad\qquad\quad \text{empty kind environment}$$
$$| \quad K, a :: \kappa \;\; \text{type-variable binding}$$
$$| \quad K, T :: \kappa \;\; \text{type-constructor binding}$$

Type environments

$$\Gamma ::= \varepsilon \qquad\qquad \text{empty type environment}$$
$$| \quad \Gamma, x :: t \;\; \text{variable binding}$$
$$| \quad \Gamma, C :: t \;\; \text{data-constructor binding}$$

Fig. 3. Syntax of environments

Structure types in Haskell are declared as **type** synonyms. Type synonyms are not supported in the core language. Therefore, to describe structure types, the language contains *parameterized types*, which are essentially a nesting of type-level lambda abstractions around a type of kind $*$. Parameterized types are only used in view definitions, they cannot appear in a core-language program.

Rules. The well-formedness rules for programs, types and kinds, the kinding rules for types and the typing rules for expressions are standard. The operational semantics of the core language is omitted. More information about the core language can be found elsewhere (EGH,[19]).

4.3   Definitions

Using the notion of parameterized types, we can formalize the observation that a view comprises a collection of view types and algorithms for the generation of structure types and conversion functions. In the following definitions we will use kind environments and type environments; their syntax is defined in Figure 3.

Definition 1 (Generic View). *A generic view* $\mathcal{V}$ *consists of a collection of bindings for view types,*

$$\text{viewtypes}_{\mathcal{V}} \equiv K; \Gamma,$$

a partial mapping from types to structure types,

$$\mathcal{V}[\![D_0]\!]^{\text{str}} \equiv u; \{ D_i \}^{i \in 1..n},$$

and, for each type in the domain of this mapping, conversions between values and structure values,

$$\mathcal{V}[\![D_0]\!]^{\text{conv}} \equiv e_{\text{from}}; e_{\text{to}}.$$

Notice that we allow the mapping from types to structure types to generate zero or more additional declarations for supporting data types. The types introduced by these declarations can be used for the generation of structure types. This is used in the fixed-point view, for example.

For a view to be useful for generic programming, we require it to have three essential properties. First, the mapping from types to structure types should preserve kinds.

Definition 2 (Kind Preservation). *A generic view $\mathcal{V}$ with*

$$\text{viewtypes}_{\mathcal{V}} \equiv K_{\mathcal{V}}; \Gamma_{\mathcal{V}}$$

is kind preserving *if for each well-formed declaration D_0 of a type constructor T such that $K \vdash T :: \kappa$, for which a structure type u can be derived,*

$$\mathcal{V}[\![D_0]\!]^{\text{str}} \equiv u; \{D_i\}^{i \in 1..n},$$

it follows that under kind environment K'

$$K' \equiv K, K_{\mathcal{V}} \{, T_i :: \kappa_i\}^{i \in 1..n},$$

containing K, $K_{\mathcal{V}}$, and all the kinds of the D_i declarations, the supporting type declarations D_i are well-formed and the structure type u has the same kind κ as the original type T,

$$K' \vdash u :: \kappa.$$

Furthermore, the conversion functions derived from a type declaration should be well-typed and indeed convert between values of the original type and values of the structure type, which is captured by the following definition.

Definition 3 (Well-typed Conversion). *A view $\mathcal{V}$ with*

$$\text{viewtypes}_{\mathcal{V}} \equiv K_{\mathcal{V}}; \Gamma_{\mathcal{V}}$$

generates well-typed conversions *if, for each well-formed declaration D_0 of a type constructor T of kind $\{\kappa_i \rightarrow\}^{i \in 1..\ell} *$, for which a structure type t can be derived,*

$$\mathcal{V}[\![D_0]\!]^{\text{str}} \equiv \{\Lambda a_i :: \kappa_i \ . \ \}^{i \in 1..\ell} t; \{D_i\}^{i \in 1..n},$$

it follows that the corresponding conversion functions e_{from} and e_{to},

$$\mathcal{V}[\![D_0]\!]^{\text{conv}} \equiv e_{\text{from}}; e_{\text{to}},$$

take values of the original data type T to values of the structure type t and vice versa,

$$K'; \Gamma' \vdash e_{\text{from}} :: \{\forall a_i :: \kappa_i . \}^{i \in 1..\ell} \ T \ \{a_i\}^{i \in 1..\ell} \rightarrow t$$
$$K'; \Gamma' \vdash e_{\text{to}} \quad :: \{\forall a_i :: \kappa_i . \}^{i \in 1..\ell} \ t \rightarrow T \ \{a_i\}^{i \in 1..\ell}$$

under environments K' as in Definition 2 and Γ' containing the view bindings $\Gamma_{\mathcal{V}}$ and the types of the constructors from D_0 and all D_i.

$$\boxed{\mathcal{S}[\![D_0]\!]^{\mathrm{str}} \equiv u; \{D_i\}_,^i}$$

$$\dfrac{\mathcal{S}[\![\{C_j\ \{t_{j,k}\}^k\}_|^j]\!]^{\mathrm{str}} \equiv t}{\mathcal{S}[\![\mathbf{data}\ T = \{\Lambda a_i :: \kappa_i\ .\ \}^i\ \{C_j\ \{t_{j,k}\}^k\}_|^j]\!]^{\mathrm{str}} \equiv \{\Lambda a_i :: \kappa_i\ .\ \}^i\ t; \varepsilon}$$

Fig. 4. Representation of data types in the standard view

Finally, the conversion functions from structure values to values should form the inverses of the corresponding functions in the opposite direction:

Definition 4 (Well-behaved Conversion). *A generic view $\mathcal{V}$ produces well-behaved conversions if, for each well-formed declaration D of a type constructor T, conversion functions e_{from} and e_{to} are generated,*

$$\mathcal{V}[\![D]\!]^{\mathrm{conv}} \equiv e_{\mathrm{from}}; e_{\mathrm{to}},$$

such that e_{to} is the left inverse of e_{from} with respect to function composition:

$$e_{\mathrm{to}}\ (e_{\mathrm{from}}\ v)\ \ \text{evaluates to } v$$

for each value v of type T.

(Note that, for a well-behaved conversion pair, the function that takes values to structure values is injective; thus, a structure type should have at least as many elements as the corresponding original type.) Why do we want a generic view to have well-behaved conversions? Assume function *gid* is a generic identity function that is defined as a recursive function that traverses and copies the structure. To prove that this function is an identity, we have to ensure that the conversions that are applied during the traversal are well-behaved and do not modify the value.

Only views that possess all three of the discussed properties are considered valid:

Definition 5 (Validity). *A generic view is* valid *if it is kind preserving and generates well-typed, well-behaved conversions.*

We claim the validity of the standard, fixed point, balanced, list-like and boiler-plate views.

The validity of a view has two important consequences. First, well-behaved conversions allow us to prove properties like the property for the generic iden-tity function given after Definition 4. Second, let us recall from Section 5.2 that a generic function call using a new data type can be reduced to a call using the structural representation of the data type. This reduction is achieved by means of a wrapper that uses the structural representation and embedding-projection specified in the view. The theorem states that the generated wrapper is type-correct:

$$\boxed{\mathcal{S}[\![\{C_j \ \{t_{j,k}\}^k\}_|^j]\!]^{\text{str}} \ \equiv t}$$

$$\overline{\mathcal{S}[\![\varepsilon]\!]^{\text{str}} \ \equiv \text{Zero}} \quad \text{(str-std-1)} \qquad \overline{\mathcal{S}[\![C]\!]^{\text{str}} \ \equiv \text{Unit}} \quad \text{(str-std-2)}$$

$$\overline{\mathcal{S}[\![C \ t]\!]^{\text{str}} \ \equiv t} \quad \text{(str-std-3)}$$

$$\frac{n \in 2.. \qquad \mathcal{S}[\![C \ \{t_k\}^{k\in 2..n}]\!]^{\text{str}} \ \equiv t_2'}{\mathcal{S}[\![C \ \{t_k\}^{k\in 1..n}]\!]^{\text{str}} \ \equiv \text{Prod} \ t_1 \ t_2'} \quad \text{(str-std-4)}$$

$$\frac{m \in 2.. }{}$$
$$\frac{\mathcal{S}[\![\{C_j \ \{t_{j,k}\}^{k\in 1..n_j}\}_|^{j\in 2..m}]\!]^{\text{str}} \ \equiv t_2 \qquad \mathcal{S}[\![C_1 \ \{t_{1,k}\}^{k\in 1..n_1}]\!]^{\text{str}} \ \equiv t_1}{\mathcal{S}[\![\{C_j \ \{t_{j,k}\}^{k\in 1..n_j}\}_|^{j\in 1..m}]\!]^{\text{str}} \ \equiv \text{Sum} \ t_1 \ t_2} \quad \text{(str-std-5)}$$

Fig. 5. Representation of constructors in the standard view

$$\boxed{\mathcal{S}[\![D]\!]^{\text{conv}} \ \equiv e_{\text{from}}; \ e_{\text{to}}}$$

$$\mathcal{S}[\![\{C_j \ \{t_{j,k}\}^k\}_|^j]\!]^{\text{conv}} \ \equiv \{p_{\text{from},j}\}_|^j; \ \{p_{\text{to},j}\}_|^j$$
$$\frac{e_{\text{from}} \equiv \lambda x \ . \ \textbf{case} \ x \ \textbf{of} \ \{p_{\text{from},j} \rightarrow p_{\text{to},j}\}_|^j \qquad e_{\text{to}} \equiv \lambda x \ . \ \textbf{case} \ x \ \textbf{of} \ \{p_{\text{to},j} \rightarrow p_{\text{from},j}\}_|^j}{\mathcal{S}[\![\textbf{data} \ T = \{\Lambda a_i :: \kappa_i \ . \ \}^i \ \{C_j \ \{t_{j,k}\}^k\}_|^j]\!]^{\text{conv}} \ \equiv e_{\text{from}}; \ e_{\text{to}}}$$

Fig. 6. Conversions for data types in the standard view

Theorem 1. *Let $\mathcal{V}$ be a view with*

$$\mathcal{V}[\![D_0]\!]^{\text{str}} \equiv u; \ \{D_i\}^{i\in 1..n},$$
$$\mathcal{V}[\![D_0]\!]^{\text{conv}} \equiv e_{\text{from}}; \ e_{\text{to}}.$$

For a type-indexed function x of arity $\langle r \mid s \rangle$, where all types γ_j in non-generic positions of x are of kind $*$, the declaration

let $\{bimap\langle \beta_i \rangle = EP \ e_{\text{from}} \ e_{\text{to}}\}^{i\in 1..r}_;$
$\quad \{bimap\langle \gamma_j \rangle = EP \ id \ id\}^{j\in 1..s}$
in *to bimap*$\langle \text{base} \ (x\langle\{\beta_i\}^{i\in 1..r} \mid \{\gamma_j\}^{j\in 1..s}\rangle)\rangle \ x\langle u\rangle$

has the same type as $x\langle T \ \{\alpha_j\}^{j\in 1..n}\rangle$. Here base *$(f)$ returns the* base type *(see EGH) of f, i.e., the type specified for the generic function.*

We will use the above declaration as the translation (or specialization) of

$$x\langle T \ \{\alpha_j\}^{j\in 1..n} \ \text{viewed} \ \mathcal{V}\rangle.$$

The proof of this theorem (which is very similar to the proof of Theorem 11.1 in EGH) uses the facts that a valid view preserves kinds, and has well-typed conversions. Well-behavedness of the conversions is not necessary for proving the theorem.

4.4   The Standard View

We describe the three components of a generic view for the standard Generic Haskell view $\mathcal{S}$ of data types

View types. The view types of the standard view are given by the declarations

> **data** Zero =
> **data** Unit = *Unit*
> **data** Sum = $\Lambda a :: * . \Lambda b :: * . $ *Inl a | Inr b*
> **data** Prod = $\Lambda a :: * . \Lambda b :: * . a \times b.$

These types represent nullary sums, nullary products, binary sums, and binary products, respectively. It is easy to convert these definitions into bindings in the environments Γ and K.

Generating structure types. The algorithm that generates structural representations for data types is expressed by judgements of the forms

$$\mathcal{S}[\![D_0]\!]^{\text{str}} \equiv u; \{D_i\}^{i \in 1..n},$$
$$\mathcal{S}[\![\{C_j \{t_{j,k}\}^{k \in 1..n_j}\}^{j \in 1..m}_|]\!]^{\text{str}} \equiv t.$$

The former express how type declarations are mapped to parameterized types and lists of supporting declarations; the latter express how a type is derived from a list of constructors. The rules are shown in Figures 4 and 5.

Type declarations are handled by the rule in Figure 4. The type parameters of a declared type constructor are directly copied to the resulting structure type. Notice that the standard view does not need auxiliary declarations.

For constructors, we distinguish five cases. The first rule, (str-std-1), represents empty constructor lists with Zero. The next three cases handle singleton lists of constructors. Fieldless constructors are, by rule (str-std-2), represented by nullary products. Rule (str-std-3) represents a unary constructors by the type of its field. If a constructor has two or more fields, rule (str-std-4) generates a product type and recurses. Finally, lists that contain two or more constructors are represented by a recursively built sum (str-std-5).

Generating conversions. The rules for generating conversion functions are shown in Figures 6 and 7 and are of the forms

$$\mathcal{S}[\![D_0]\!]^{\text{conv}} \equiv e_{\text{from}}; e_{\text{to}}$$
$$\mathcal{S}[\![\{C_j \{t_{j,k}\}^k\}^j_|]\!]^{\text{conv}} \equiv \{p_{\text{from},j}\}^j_|; \{p_{\text{to},j}\}^j_|,$$

i.e., type declarations give rise to pairs of conversion functions, while lists of data constructors give rise to pairs of patterns.

$$\boxed{\mathcal{S}[\![\{C_j \ \{t_{j,k}\}^k\}^j_|]\!]^{\text{conv}} \equiv \{p_{\text{from},j}\}^j_|; \{p_{\text{to},j}\}^j_|}$$

$$\overline{\mathcal{S}[\![\varepsilon]\!]^{\text{conv}} \equiv \varepsilon;\varepsilon} \quad \text{(conv-std-1)} \qquad \overline{\mathcal{S}[\![C]\!]^{\text{conv}} \equiv C; \mathit{Unit}} \quad \text{(conv-std-2)}$$

$$\overline{\mathcal{S}[\![C \ t]\!]^{\text{conv}} \equiv C \ x; x} \quad \text{(conv-std-3)}$$

$$\frac{n \in 2.. \quad \{x_1 \not\equiv x_k\}^{k\in 2..n} \quad \mathcal{S}[\![C \ \{t_k\}^{k\in 2..n}]\!]^{\text{conv}} \equiv C \ \{x_k\}^{k\in 2..n}; p_{\text{to}}}{\mathcal{S}[\![C \ \{t_k\}^{k\in 1..n}]\!]^{\text{conv}} \equiv C \ \{x_k\}^{k\in 1..n}; x_1 \times p_{\text{to}}} \quad \text{(conv-std-4)}$$

$$\frac{\mathcal{S}[\![C_1 \ \{t_{1,k}\}^{k\in 1..n_1}]\!]^{\text{conv}} \equiv p_{\text{from},1}; p_{\text{to},1} \quad m \in 2.. \quad \mathcal{S}[\![\{C_j \ \{t_{j,k}\}^{k\in 1..n_j}\}^{j\in 2..m}_|]\!]^{\text{conv}} \equiv \{p_{\text{from},j}\}^{j\in 2..m}_|; \{p_{\text{to},j}\}^{j\in 2..m}_|}{\mathcal{S}[\![\{C_j \ \{t_{j,k}\}^{k\in 1..n_j}\}^{j\in 1..m}_|]\!]^{\text{conv}} \equiv \{p_{\text{from},j}\}^{j\in 1..m}_|; \mathit{Inl} \ p_{\text{to},1} \ \{| \ \mathit{Inr} \ p_{\text{to},j}\}^{j\in 2..m}} \quad \text{(conv-std-5)}$$

Fig. 7. Conversions for constructors in the standard view

The rule in Figure 6 constructs a 'from' function that matches values of the original type against a list of patterns. If a value matches a certain pattern, a structure value is produced by using a complementary pattern; here, we make use of the fact that the pattern language is just a subset of the expression language. A 'to' function is created by inverting the patterns. The pairs of pattern lists are generated using the rules for constructor lists. These rules are analogous to the rules for generating structure types from constructor lists.

If there are no constructors, there are no patterns either (conv-std-1). Rule (conv-std-2) associates a single constructor with the value *Unit*. Rule (conv-std-3) associates unary constructors with variables that correspond to their field values. If a constructor has two or more fields, rule (conv-std-4) associates the corresponding variables to product patterns. Finally, if the list of constructors has two or more elements, rule (conv-std-5) applies; it prefixes the patterns with the injection constructors *Inl* and *Inr*.

5 Generic Views in the Generic Haskell Compiler

The latest version of the Generic Haskell compiler that implements views can be downloaded via svn: `https://svn.cs.uu.nl:12443/repos/Generic-Haskell/branches/GenericViews`. We have implemented (an extension of) the standard view, the fixed-point view and the list-like sums and products view. The next release of Generic Haskell will come with all the views mentioned in this paper: in addition to the views already implemented, the balanced sums and products view, and the identity and boilerplate views. In the previous version of the

Generic Haskell compiler [8] we do not really use the standard view as presented here, but additionally use representation data types Con and Lab to encode information about constructors and record field labels in the data type. The presence of these data types makes it possible to write functions such as *show* and *read* that produce or consume a representation of a value and therefore rely on the names of constructors and labels.

Since there is no reason to assume that the six views given in this paper are the only useful views, we have considered developing a special-purpose language for specifying views in user programs. We have decided not to do this for three reasons:

– We expect that these views suffice for most purposes and users.
– A generic view consists of a set of view types, a function that generates structure types, and a function that generates conversion functions, and it follows that such a special-purpose language for specifying views would be a complete programming language in itself.
– To add a new view to Generic Haskell, the compiler has to be modified. Although this might sound scary, in practice it is rather simple.

The next section describes how a view is added to the Generic Haskell compiler.

5.1 Adding a View to the Generic Haskell Compiler

A new view is added to the Generic Haskell compiler by implementing a module that contains a view declaration with the following type:

$$(\text{Name}, \text{TDecl} \rightarrow \text{Maybe} (\text{LamType}, [\text{TDecl}], \text{Expr}, \text{Expr}, [\text{TDecl}])).$$

A view consists of a name, and a function that can be called on the abstract representation of a type synonym or a data type (a TDecl) to produce a parameterized structure representation type (a LamType), supporting type declarations (first [TDecl]) and an embedding-projection pair (two Expr's). Views that apply to a subset of the Haskell data types can be implemented by returning *Nothing* on data type definitions that are outside of the view domain. Note that the result of the view-generating function directly corresponds to the maps $\mathcal{V}[\![\cdot]\!]^{\text{str}}$ and $\mathcal{V}[\![\cdot]\!]^{\text{conv}}$. The collection viewtypes$_{\mathcal{V}}$ of bindings that are required by the view must be added to the Generic Haskell Prelude, i.e., they must be available for the Generic Haskell compiler to parse.

The need for the second list of type declarations is better explained with an example. Consider the application of the *children* function (Section 3) to the Tree data type. This function definition uses the fixed-point view structure type of Tree. That is, the type Fix applied to the supporting type TreeBase, which is the base functor of Tree. This structure type is not yet enough. The definition of *children* applies *collect* to the base functor of the data type. Because *collect* is defined on the standard view, we need to generate a standard structure type for TreeBase, a pair of standard embedding projections and supporting declarations. In short, if we need a fixed-point view on Tree, we also need a standard view on TreeBase. This is achieved by returning TreeBase in the second declaration list when generating the view components for Tree. This list, which is a subset of the list of supporting declarations, is recursively processed by view-generating functions. The implementation keeps track of additional information to determine which view-generating functions should be called on these declarations, and to avoid non-termination in certain cases.

The validity of a view can only be checked to a certain extent. The compiler can verify the kind preservation and well-typed conversion properties of the view: for each structural representation and embedding-projection pair generated, kind and type checking is performed. The well-behavedness of the conversion cannot be verified by the compiler, since verifying that the composition of two arbitrary functions is the identity is an undecidable problem. This property remains a proof obligation for the implementor of the view.

A view implementor has to deal with some additional implementation details that slightly complicate views, but that are not of direct concern for this paper. The interested reader can find more implementation information in the source distribution of Generic Haskell extended with views, in particular in the file /src/views/README and the view modules in the same directory.

5.2 Specialization

The specialization mechanism is independent of the actual view, see Theorem 1. For other views than the standard view, different structural representations and embedding-projection pairs are used, but the specialization procedure remains exactly the same. The only thing that has changed in the implementation of specialization within the Generic Haskell compiler is that all the references to structural representation types and embedding-projection pairs point to the view that is specified for the function in question.

6   Conclusions, and Related Work

We have shown that generic views on data types can make generic functions both easier to write and more efficient. Generic views add expressiveness to a generic programming language. Furthermore, generic views allow us to use different generic programming styles in a single framework.

Although there are a multitude of approaches for generic programming, the idea to use multiple views on data types in a single approach is, to the best of our knowledge, original. Using our approach to views we can express many different approaches to generic programming in a single framework. Our framework does have a limitation though: a structure type is created from a single data type declaration at a time. This poses no problems for views that transform only the top level representation of a data type, consider for instance type List° in Section 2.3. Views that deeply transform representations, however, face limitations: the fixed-point view, for example, transforms the recursive occurrences of a single recursive data type, and hence it cannot handle mutually recursive ones. This is not a fundamental problem: we could have adapted the framework to allow for this. However, since we know of no existing approach to generic programming that would need this extra complexity we have refrained from doing so.

The name "generic view" is derived from Wadler's proposal to introduce views in (a predecessor of) Haskell [12]. Using one of these views, a single Haskell data type can be analyzed in a different way, by introducing additional constructors by which a value can be constructed, and on which pattern matching can be performed. A view is essentially like the introduction of an additional data type, together with the definition of conversion functions between values from the original type and values of the view type. These conversions are then transparently applied by the compiler where necessary.

Generic views are different in that they define a representation and conversions for many types at the same time. Moreover, the representation types need not be new data types, but can be built from existing data types. Wadler's views have the advantage that they can be added to the Haskell programming language relatively easily, allowing every programmer to add her own views. On the other hand, generic views have to be added to a generic programming system, such as the Generic Haskell compiler, following the guidelines described in the previous sections. However, we expect that the views we describe in this paper are sufficient for most purposes and users, and we do not assume a user will frequently want to add a new view to the Generic Haskell compiler.

Both views and generic views require that the definition of a new view goes along with a proof obligation for the programmer that cannot easily be captured in a language like Haskell. The conversion between the original type and the view type (structure type in our framework), be it a single pair of functions such as in Wadler's proposal, or a type-indexed family of functions such as for generic views, must really witness isomorphisms, otherwise unexpected results may occur.

Since Wadler's views proposal, several variations of views have been given [20, 21, 22]. Our approach is closest to Wadler's proposal in that we also require the existence of an isomorphism between the original type and the view type (structure type). Views have also been proposed in the context of XML and databases [23, 24]. Generic views as proposed in [25] are used to automatically convert between two given views. The generic view concept as introduced in this paper does not seem to have been investigated in this field.

The idea of using different sets of data types for inductive definitions of type-indexed functions is common in the world of dependent types [26, 27]. This corresponds to the idea of having views that work on different subsets of the Haskell data types. However, in the approaches we have seen there is no automatic conversion between syntactically definable data types as offered by the dependently typed programming language into representations as defined by the view or universe.

Acknowledgements. Our thanks go to a number of anonymous referees and Daan Leijen for several helpful comments. This research has partly been funded by the Netherlands Organization for Scientific Research (NWO) (project Generic Haskell, nr. 612.069.000).

References

1. Jansson, P., Jeuring, J.: PolyP — a polytypic programming language extension. In: Conference Record of POPL '97: The 24th ACM SIGPLAN-SIGACT Symposium on Principles of Programming Languages, ACM Press (1997) 470–482
2. Hinze, R.: Polytypic values possess polykinded types. Science of Computer Programming **43**(2-3) (2002) 129–159
3. Lämmel, R., Jones, S.P.: Scrap your boilerplate: a practical approach to generic programming. ACM SIGPLAN Notices **38**(3) (2003) 26–37 Proceedings ACM SIGPLAN Workshop on Types in Language Design and Implementation (TLDI 2003).
4. Jay, C.B.: Distinguishing data structures and functions: the constructor calculus and functorial types. In Abramsky, S., ed.: Typed Lambda Calculi and Applications: 5th International Conference TLCA 2001. Volume 2044 of LNCS., Springer-Verlag (2001) 217–239
5. Hoogendijk, P., de Moor, O.: Container types categorically. Journal of Functional Programming **10**(2) (2000) 191–225
6. Meijer, E., Fokkinga, M., Paterson, R.: Functional programming with bananas, lenses, envelopes, and barbed wire. In Hughes, J., ed.: Functional Programming Languages and Computer Architecture, FPCA 1991. Volume 523 of LNCS., Springer-Verlag (1991) 124–144
7. Jansson, P., Jeuring, J.: A framework for polytypic programming on terms, with an application to rewriting. In Jeuring, J., ed.: Workshop on Generic Programming 2000, Ponte de Lima, Portugal, July 2000. (2000) 33–45 Utrecht Technical Report UU-CS-2000-19.
8. Löh, A., Jeuring, J., Clarke, D., Hinze, R., Rodriguez, A., de Wit, J.: The Generic Haskell user's guide, version 1.42 (Coral). Technical Report UU-CS-2005-004, Institute of Information and Computing Sciences, Utrecht University (2005)
9. Löh, A.: Exploring Generic Haskell. PhD thesis, Utrecht University (September 2004)
10. Lämmel, R., Peyton Jones, S.: Scrap more boilerplate: reflection, zips, and generalised casts. In: Proceedings of the ACM SIGPLAN International Conference on Functional Programming, ICFP 2004, ACM Press (2004) 244–255
11. Hinze, R., Jeuring, J.: Generic Haskell: applications. In: Generic Programming, Advanced Lectures. Volume 2793 of LNCS., Springer-Verlag (2003) 57–97
12. Wadler, P.: Views: a way for pattern matching to cohabit with data abstraction. In: Conference Record of POPL '87: The 14th ACM SIGPLAN-SIGACT Symposium on Principles of Programming Languages. (1987)
13. Hinze, R., Jeuring, J.: Generic Haskell: practice and theory. In: Generic Programming, Advanced Lectures. Volume 2793 of LNCS., Springer-Verlag (2003) 1–56
14. Malcolm, G.: Data structures and program transformation. Science of Computer Programming **14** (1990) 255–279
15. Schrage, M.: Proxima, a presentation-oriented editor for structured documents. PhD thesis, Utrecht University (October 2004)
16. Reynolds, J.C.: Definitional interpreters for higher-order programming languages. In: ACM '72: Proceedings of the ACM annual conference, New York, NY, USA, ACM Press (1972) 717–740
17. Hinze, R., Löh, A., Oliveira, B.C.d.S.: "Scrap Your Boilerplate" Reloaded. In: Proceedings of the Eighth International Symposium on Functional and Logic Programming (FLOPS 2006). Volume 3945 of LNCS., Springer-Verlag (2006)

18. Holdermans, S., Jeuring, J., Löh, A., Rodriguez, A.: Generic views on data types. Technical Report UU-CS-2006-020, Department of Information and Computing Sciences, Utrecht University (2006)
19. Holdermans, S.: Generic views. Master's thesis, Institute of Information and Computing Sciences, Utrecht University (2005)
20. Burton, F.W., Cameron, R.D.: Pattern matching with abstract data types. Journal of Functional Programming 3(2) (1993) 117–190
21. Okasaki, C.: Views for Standard ML. In: SIGPLAN Workshop on ML. (1998) 14–23
22. Burton, F.W., Meijer, E., Sansom, P., Thompson, S., Wadler, P.: Views: an extension to Haskell pattern matching. Available from http://www.haskell.org/development/views.html (1996)
23. Abiteboul, S.: On views and XML. In: Proceedings of the 18th ACM SIGACT-SIGMOD-SIGART Symposium on Principles of Database Systems, ACM Press (1999) 1–9
24. Ohori, A., Tajima, K.: A polymorphic calculus for views and object sharing. In: Proceedings of the 13th ACM SIGACT-SIGMOD-SIGART Symposium on Principles of Database Systems. (1994) 255–266
25. Souza dos Santos, C., Abiteboul, S., Delobel, C.: Virtual schemas and bases. In: Proceedings of the International Conference on Extensive Data Base Technology (EDBT'94), Cambridge, UK, Springer-Verlag (1994) 81–94
26. Altenkirch, T., McBride, C.: Generic programming within dependently typed programming. In Gibbons, J., Jeuring, J., eds.: Generic Programming: IFIP TC2/WG2.1 Working Conference on Generic Programming July 11–12, 2002, Dagstuhl, Germany. Number 115 in International Federation for Information Processing, Kluwer Academic Publishers (2003) 1–20
27. Benke, M., Dybjer, P., Jansson, P.: Universes for generic programs and proofs in dependent type theory. Nordic Journal of Computing 10(4) (2003) 265–289

Recursion Schemes for Dynamic Programming

Jevgeni Kabanov and Varmo Vene

Dept. of Computer Science, University of Tartu,
J. Liivi 2, EE-50409 Tartu, Estonia
ekabanov@gmail.com, varmo@cs.ut.ee

Abstract. Dynamic programming is an algorithm design technique, which allows to improve efficiency by avoiding re-computation of identical subtasks. We present a new recursion combinator, dynamorphism, which captures the dynamic programming recursion pattern with memoization and identify some simple conditions when functions defined by structured general recursion can be redefined as a dynamorphism. The applicability of the new recursion combinator is demonstrated on classical dynamic programming algorithms: Fibonacci numbers, binary partitions, edit distance and longest common subsequence.

1 Introduction

Solutions for many problems admit a simple recursive description where the original problem is split to some subproblems, these are solved recursively and then combined to a final solution. The corresponding program can then straightforwardly expressed as a hylomorphism [9], where the decomposition of a problem is represented by some functor coalgebra and the forming of a final result by an algebra of the same functor. However, if the problem description contains identical subproblems such a naive implementation is very inefficient as these subproblems are solved independently from each other over and over again. This kind of unnecessary re-computation can often be avoided using dynamic programming techniques.

In this paper we study dynamic programming in the setting of categorical approach to recursive datatypes and constructive algorithmics [2, 7, 8, 5]. We introduce a new recursion combinator, which captures the dynamic programming recursion pattern. It is a generalization of the combinator for a course-of-value iteration, histomorphism [10, 12], and uses annotated tree-like intermediate structure to tabulate previously computed values, hence avoiding re-computation on identical subarguments. Like hylomorphism, it is parametrized by a coalgebra and an algebra but for different (albeit related) functors. We show that given a hylomorphism if its coalgebra satisfies a simple equation it can be redefined in terms of the new combinator involving a related coalgebra and reusing the algebra of the hylomorphism. The applicability of the new recursion operator is demonstrated on classical dynamic programming algorithms: Fibonacci numbers, binary partitions, edit distance and longest common subsequence.

T. Uustalu (Ed.): MPC 2006, LNCS 4014, pp. 235–252, 2006.

The rest of the paper is organized as follows. Section 2 presents the setting and summarizes the basic theory of recursive datatypes and recursion combinators. Section 3 introduces two recursion combinators for dynamic programming, histomorphism and dynamorphism, and studies their properties. Section 4 provides four concrete examples from dynamic programming that can be expressed as dynamorphisms. Finally, Section 5 concludes by pointing out some directions for further work.

2   Categorical Datatypes and Recursion Combinators

In this section we briefly review the basic notions of categorical approach to recursive datatypes and its application to program calculation. For a more comprehensive and excellent introduction of the subject see e.g. [3, 6].

2.1   Preliminaries

Throughout the work we assume that the category we're dealing with is $\mathcal{CPO}$ category of (pointed) complete partial orders with a least element $\bot$ (*cpos*) and continuous partial functions between them. A function $f : A \to B$ is said to be *strict* if $f(\bot) = \bot$, i.e. it preserves the least element. The final object in $\mathcal{CPO}$ is given by the singleton set $\{\bot\}$ and is denoted by $\mathbf{1}$. The subcategory of $\mathcal{CPO}$ where all functions are strict is denoted by $\mathcal{CPO}_\bot$.

A recursive type is defined categorically using a functor fixpoint. That is given an endofunctor $\mathsf{F} : \mathcal{C} \to \mathcal{C}$ we get the recursive type $\mu\mathsf{F}$ as the solution of the equation $\mu\mathsf{F} \simeq \mathsf{F}\mu\mathsf{F}$. This equation is solvable in $\mathcal{CPO}$ for *locally continuous* functors. We assume that the type signature is given by a combination of following basic functors: Id (identity), $\underline{\mathsf{A}}$ (constant), $\times$ (product) and $+$ (separated sum). The product bifunctor $A \times B$ is given by the Cartesian product. We denote projections by $\mathsf{outl} : A \times B \to A$ and $\mathsf{outr} : A \times B \to B$. The pairing of $f : C \to A$ and $g : C \to B$, i.e. the unique morphism $h : C \to A \times B$ such that $\mathsf{outl} \circ h = f$ and $\mathsf{outr} \circ h = g$, is written $\langle f, g \rangle$. The separated sum bifunctor $A + B$ is given by the disjoint union, with injections denoted by $\mathsf{inl} : A \to A + B$ and $\mathsf{inr} : B \to A + B$. The case analysis of $f : A \to C$ and $g : B \to C$, i.e. the unique strict $h : A + B \to C$ such that $h \circ \mathsf{inl} = f$ and $h \circ \mathsf{inr} = g$, is written $[f, g]$. In the examples, we often use also pattern matching for case analysis.

We shall also use type functors which are attained by taking a fixpoint over bifunctors (e.g. functor List that lifts set of values to set of lists of values). The functors attainable by a combination of described functors are called *regular functors* and are locally continuous in $\mathcal{CPO}$.

2.2   Catamorphisms

Let $\mathsf{F} : \mathcal{C} \to \mathcal{C}$ be a functor. An F-*algebra* is a pair consisting of an object A (called the carrier) and an arrow $\varphi : \mathsf{F}A \to A$. A homomorphism between algebras $\varphi : \mathsf{F}A \to A$ and $\psi : \mathsf{F}B \to B$ is an arrow $f : A \to B$ such that $f \circ \varphi = \psi \circ \mathsf{F}f$. F-algebras and their homomorphisms form a category $\mathcal{A}lg(\mathsf{F})$

where composition and identities are inherited from the base category $\mathcal{C}$. An initial F-algebra $in_F : F\mu F \to \mu F$ is the one from which a unique homomorphism exists to any other F-algebra $\varphi : FA \to A$. This unique morphism is called *catamorphism* or *fold* and is denoted by $(\!|\varphi|\!)_F : \mu F \to A$.

An initial algebra $in_F : F\mu F \to \mu F$ (if it exists) is necessarily isomorphism (we denote its inverse by $out_F : \mu F \to F\mu F$), hence its carrier μF is a solution of recursive domain equation $X \simeq FX$. Unfortunately, in $\mathcal{CPO}$ initial algebras do not exist, but just weakly initial ones, i.e. the uniqueness of the outgoing homomorphism is missing. On the other hand, a locally continuous functor F, which preserves strictness, has an initial algebra in $\mathcal{CPO}_\bot$. Moreover, the catamorphism combinator can be extended to $\mathcal{CPO}$ by defining: for any F-algebra $\varphi : FA \to A$, the catamorphism $(\!|\varphi|\!)_F$ is a least arrow $f : \mu F \to A$ making the following diagram commute:

$$
\begin{array}{ccc}
F\mu F & \xrightarrow{\ in\ } & \mu F \\
{\scriptstyle Ff}\downarrow & & \downarrow{\scriptstyle f} \\
FA & \xrightarrow{\ \varphi\ } & A
\end{array}
$$

i.e. the least homomorphism from in_F to φ.

Catamorphisms comes equipped with the following properties:

- **Cancellation:** For any F-algebra $\varphi : FA \to A$

$$(\!|\varphi|\!)_F = \varphi \circ F(\!|\varphi|\!)_F \circ out_F \qquad \text{(cata-cancellation)}$$

- **Reflection**

$$id_{\mu F} = (\!|in_F|\!)_F \qquad \text{(cata-reflection)}$$

- **Fusion:** For any F-algebras $\varphi : FA \to A$, $\psi : FB \to B$ and a morphism $f : A \to B$

$$f \text{ is strict} \wedge f \circ \varphi = \psi \circ Ff \ \Rightarrow\ f \circ (\!|\varphi|\!)_F = (\!|\psi|\!)_F \qquad \text{(cata-fusion)}$$

Catamorphisms capture structural recursion over inductive types.

2.3 Anamorphisms

The notion of a coalgebra is dual to the one of an algebra. Let $F : \mathcal{C} \to \mathcal{C}$ be a functor. An F-*coalgebra* is a pair consisting of an object A and an arrow $\psi : A \to FA$. A homomorphism between coalgebras $\psi : A \to FA$ and $\varphi : B \to FB$ is an arrow $f : A \to B$ such that $\varphi \circ f = Ff \circ \psi$. F-coalgebras and their homomorphisms form a category $\mathcal{C}o\mathcal{A}lg(F)$ where composition and identities are inherited from the base category $\mathcal{C}$. A final F-coalgebra is the one to which a unique homomorphism exists from any other F-coalgebra $\psi : A \to FA$. This unique morphism is called *anamorphism* or *unfold* and is denoted by $[\!(\psi)\!]_F : A \to \mu F$.

In general, carriers of an initial F-algebra and a final F-coalgebra are different. However, in $\mathcal{CPO}$ the inverse of an initial F-algebra $\mathrm{out}_F : \mu F \to F\mu F$ is a final F-coalgebra. Hence, for any F-coalgebra $\psi : A \to FA$, the anamorphism $[\![\psi]\!]$ is defined as a unique arrow $f : A \to \mu F$ making the following diagram commute:

$$
\begin{array}{ccc}
A & \xrightarrow{\psi} & FA \\
{\scriptstyle f}\downarrow & & \downarrow{\scriptstyle Ff} \\
\mu F & \xrightarrow{\mathrm{out}_F} & F\mu F
\end{array}
$$

Anamorphisms come equipped with the following properties:

– **Cancellation:** For any F-coalgebra $\psi : A \to FA$

$$[\![\psi]\!]_F = \mathrm{in}_F \circ F[\![\psi]\!]_F \circ \psi \qquad \text{(ana-cancellation)}$$

– **Reflection**

$$id_{\mu F} = [\![\mathrm{out}_F]\!]_F \qquad \text{(ana-reflection)}$$

– **Fusion:** For any F-coalgebras $\psi : A \to FA$, $\varphi : B \to FB$ and a morphism $f : A \to B$

$$\varphi \circ f = Ff \circ \psi \;\Rightarrow\; [\![\varphi]\!]_F \circ f = [\![\psi]\!]_F \qquad \text{(ana-fusion)}$$

Anamorphisms capture structural corecursion over coinductive types.

2.4 Hylomorphisms

As in $\mathcal{CPO}$ inductive and coinductive types coincide we can also define a concept that captures general recursion. Given an F-coalgebra $\psi : A \to FA$ and an F-algebra $\varphi : FB \to B$, a *hylomorphism* denoted by $\mathrm{hylo}(\varphi, \psi)_F$ is the least arrow $f : A \to B$ that makes the following diagram commute:

$$
\begin{array}{ccc}
FA & \xleftarrow{\psi} & A \\
{\scriptstyle Ff}\downarrow & & \downarrow{\scriptstyle f} \\
FB & \xrightarrow{\varphi} & B
\end{array}
$$

Equivalently, a hylomorphism is a composition of an anamorphism with a catamorphism:

$$\mathrm{hylo}(\varphi, \psi)_F = (\!(\varphi)\!)_F \circ [\![\psi]\!]_F \qquad \text{(hylo-definition)}$$

Hylomorphisms capture general recursion by producing a virtual intermediate structure and then collapsing it. The intermediate structure represents the function *call-tree* that would be otherwise produced on the stack.

Hylomorphisms come equipped with the following properties:

- **Cancellation:** For any F-algebra $\varphi : FB \to B$ and F-coalgebra $\psi : A \to FA$

$$\mathsf{hylo}(\varphi, \psi)_\mathsf{F} = \varphi \circ \mathsf{Fhylo}(\varphi, \psi)_\mathsf{F} \circ \psi \qquad \text{(hylo-cancellation)}$$

- **Cata-Fusion:** For any F-algebra $\varphi : FB \to B$, $\phi : FC \to C$, F-coalgebra $\psi : A \to FA$ and a morphism $f : B \to C$

$$f \text{ is strict} \wedge f \circ \varphi = \phi \circ Ff \ \Rightarrow \ f \circ \mathsf{hylo}(\varphi, \psi)_\mathsf{F} = \mathsf{hylo}(\phi, \psi)_\mathsf{F}$$
$$\text{(hylo-cata-fusion)}$$

- **Ana-Fusion:** For any F-coalgebras $\psi : FA \to A$, $\xi : FB \to B$, F-algebra $\varphi : FC \to C$ and a morphism $f : A \to B$

$$\xi \circ f = Ff \circ \psi \ \Rightarrow \ \mathsf{hylo}(\varphi, \xi)_\mathsf{F} \circ f = \mathsf{hylo}(\varphi, \psi)_\mathsf{F} \qquad \text{(hylo-ana-fusion)}$$

- **Hylo-Shift:** For any F-coalgebra $\psi : A \to FA$, G-algebra $\phi : B \to GB$ and a natural transformation $\tau : \mathsf{F} \overset{\cdot}{\to} \mathsf{G}$

$$\mathsf{hylo}(\varphi \circ \tau_B, \psi)_\mathsf{F} = \mathsf{hylo}(\varphi, \tau_A \circ \psi)_\mathsf{G} \qquad \text{(hylo-shift)}$$

Further on, subscripts will be omitted for brevity when obvious from the context.

3   Combinators for Dynamic Programming

Dynamic programming is a programming technique that can be applied to some algorithms redefining them with better performance (and specially smaller complexity in terms of the input). The application of dynamic programming requires that the problem would have: a) optimal substructure, and b) overlapping subproblems.

Optimal substructure (also known as the *principle of optimality* [1]) in this context means that to solve the problem we can break it into subproblems, solve them recursively and then combine the results to solve the original problem. Overlapping here means that the subproblem results are recomputed several times, since the same sub-subproblems appear in different subproblems.

In such a case the dynamic programming method suggests to use memoization to reuse the overlapping subproblem computation results and thus reduce the complexity of the algorithm.

Note that every function expressible as a hylomorphism already has an optimal substructure, so we can apply dynamic programming technique knowing only that a hylomorphism has overlapping subproblems. Note also that in case of a hylomorphism overlapping subproblems will mean that some parts of the intermediate structure will be equal (though we do not use this fact in the paper, it helps to understand the problem background).

3.1 Histomorphisms

The simplest instance of dynamic programming problem is provided by a course-of-value iteration. As an example consider the Fibonacci function which can be specified as follows:

$$fibo(0) = 0$$
$$fibo(1) = 1$$
$$fibo(n + 2) = fibo(n + 1) + fibo(n).$$

These equations give us the definition for the function as a hylomorphism (see the next section). However this definition is of exponential complexity in terms of its input. In [10], Uustalu and Vene defined a recursion combinator called *histomorphism* which solves the problem by internally using an auxiliary tree-like structure to capture the memoization of previously computed values on substructures.

For a given endofunctor F and an object A, define a new endofunctor $F_A^\times$ as follows:

$$F_A^\times(X) = A \times FX$$
$$F_A^\times(f) = id \times Ff$$

The $F_A^\times$-functor represents one level of the structure μF with an extra annotation. Next we define a recursive type based on this functor:[1]

$$\tilde{F}(A) = \mu F_A^\times$$
$$\tilde{F}(f) = [\![\langle f \circ \varepsilon, \theta \rangle]\!]_{F_A^\times}$$

where natural transformations $\varepsilon_A = \mathsf{outl} \circ \mathsf{out} : \tilde{F}(A) \to A$ and $\theta_A = \mathsf{outr} \circ \mathsf{out} :$ $\tilde{F}(A) \to F\tilde{F}(A)$ are projections of the final coalgebra $\mathsf{out}_{F_A^\times} = \langle \varepsilon_A, \theta_A \rangle : \tilde{F}(A) \to A \times F\tilde{F}(A)$.

Intuitively, the recursive type $\tilde{F}(A)$ is a datatype of F-branching trees, where every node is annotated by values of type A. In a special case, when annotations are empty, it's isomorphic to the original recursive type, i.e. $\tilde{F}(1) \simeq \mu F$. The function $\varepsilon_A : \tilde{F}(A) \to A$ gives the value of the annotation in the root node and $\theta_A : \tilde{F}(A) \to F\tilde{F}(A)$ returns "subtrees" of the given tree.

Often, these annotated trees are constructed using anamorphisms in the form $[\![\langle f, \psi \rangle]\!]_{F_A^\times} : A \to \tilde{F}B$, where $\psi : A \to FA$ is an F-coalgebra and $f : A \to B$ is an arrow for computing an annotation of a node. Later we make use following properties of this anamorphism:

$$\varepsilon_A \circ [\![\langle f, \psi \rangle]\!] = f \qquad\qquad\qquad (\varepsilon\text{-cancellation})$$
$$\theta_A \circ [\![\langle f, \psi \rangle]\!] = F[\![\langle f, \psi \rangle]\!] \circ \psi \qquad\quad (\theta\text{-cancellation})$$
$$[\![\langle f, \psi \rangle]\!] = \tilde{F}f \circ [\![\langle id, \psi \rangle]\!] \qquad\quad (\text{map-build-fusion})$$

---

[1] In [10], the functor $\tilde{F}$ is defined as $\tilde{F}(A) = \nu F_A^\times$. However, in our setting inductive and coinductive types coincide, hence the definition uses the least fixed point.

The first two equations are obvious. The third one can be shown by using *ana-fusion* law, i.e., we need to show that $h = [\![\langle id, \psi \rangle]\!]$ is a coalgebra homomorphism:

$$
\begin{array}{ccc}
B \times \mathsf{F}A & \xleftarrow{\ \langle f,\psi \rangle\ } & A \\[2pt]
{\scriptstyle id \times \mathsf{F}h} \downarrow & & \downarrow {\scriptstyle h} \\[2pt]
B \times \mathsf{F}\tilde{\mathsf{F}}A & \xleftarrow{\ \langle f \circ \varepsilon,\theta \rangle\ } & \tilde{\mathsf{F}}A
\end{array}
$$

As the following simple calculation shows, this is indeed the case:

$$
\begin{aligned}
\langle f \circ \varepsilon, \theta \rangle \circ [\![\langle id, \psi \rangle]\!] &= (f \times id) \circ \mathsf{out} \circ [\![\langle id, \psi \rangle]\!] \\
&= (f \times id) \circ (id \times \mathsf{F}[\![\langle id, \psi \rangle]\!]) \circ \langle id, \psi \rangle \\
&= (id \times \mathsf{F}[\![\langle id, \psi \rangle]\!]) \circ \langle f, \psi \rangle
\end{aligned}
$$

Definition 1. *(histomorphism)*
Let $\varphi : \mathsf{F}\tilde{\mathsf{F}}A \to A$ be an $\mathsf{F}\tilde{\mathsf{F}}$-algebra. A histomorphism, *denoted by* $\mathsf{histo}(\varphi)$, *is the least function* $f : \mu\mathsf{F} \to A$ *making the following diagram commute:*

$$
\begin{array}{ccc}
\mathsf{F}\mu\mathsf{F} & \xrightarrow{\ \text{in}\ } & \mu\mathsf{F} \\[2pt]
{\scriptstyle \mathsf{F}[\![\langle f,\text{out} \rangle]\!]} \downarrow & & \downarrow {\scriptstyle f} \\[2pt]
\mathsf{F}\tilde{\mathsf{F}}A & \xrightarrow{\ \varphi\ } & A
\end{array}
$$

Informally the definition of the histomorphism tells that its value on the given argument is computed by first building an annotated F-branching tree and then using an F$\tilde{\mathsf{F}}$-algebra to give the final result. The annotated tree is generated using an anamorphism, which gets the immediate subargument as the initial seed. On every step, the anamorphism computes (recursively) the value of the histomorphism on the current seed, and also a new seed by taking a "predecessor" of the current one. Thus, all nodes in the tree contain the recursively computed value of the histomorphism on the corresponding substructure of the argument. The given F$\tilde{\mathsf{F}}$-algebra can use these values to produce a final result. Note that the annotated tree is recalculated on every recursive call, hence the definition above corresponds to the naive (exponential) algorithm of computing course-of-value iterative functions.

In the case of natural numbers, the base functor is $\mathsf{F}X = 1 + X$ and annotated trees are of type $\tilde{\mathsf{F}}(A) = \mu X.A \times (1 + X)$, i.e. non-empty lists. The Fibonacci function can be defined as a histomorphism $\textit{fibo} = \mathsf{histo}(\varphi)$, where the F$\tilde{\mathsf{F}}$-coalgebra is defined as follows:

$$
\varphi\,(\mathsf{inl}\ \bot) = \quad 0
$$

$$
\varphi\,(\mathsf{inr}\ x) =
\begin{cases}
1 & \text{if } \theta(x) = \mathsf{inl}\ \bot \\
\varepsilon(x) + \varepsilon(y) & \text{if } \theta(x) = \mathsf{inr}\ y
\end{cases}
$$

Histomorphisms come equipped the following properties:

- **Cancellation:** For any $F\tilde{F}$-algebra $\varphi : F\tilde{F}A \to A$

$$\mathsf{histo}(\varphi) \circ \mathsf{in} = \varphi \circ F[\![\langle \mathsf{histo}(\varphi), \mathsf{out} \rangle]\!]) \qquad \text{(histo-cancellation)}$$

- **Reflection**

$$id = \mathsf{histo}(\mathsf{in} \circ F\varepsilon) \qquad \text{(histo-reflection)}$$

- **Fusion:** For any $F\tilde{F}$-algebras $\varphi, \psi : F\tilde{F}A \to A$ and an arrow $f : A \to B$

$$f \text{ is strict} \wedge f \circ \varphi = \psi \circ F\tilde{F}f \;\Rightarrow\; f \circ \mathsf{histo}(\varphi) = \mathsf{histo}(\psi) \quad \text{(histo-fusion)}$$

As noted above, the recursive definition of a histomorphism corresponds to the exponential algorithm. In [10], Uustalu and Vene show that every histomorphism can be defined in terms of a catamorphism and this alternative definition gives a more efficient algorithm for computing histomorphisms.

Proposition 1. *Let* $\varphi : F\tilde{F}A \to A$ *be an* $F\tilde{F}$*-algebra, then*

$$\mathsf{histo}(\varphi) = \varepsilon_A \circ (\![\mathsf{in} \circ \langle \varphi, id \rangle]\!]) \qquad \text{(histo-as-cata)}$$

The equation can be illustrated by the following diagram where the catamorphism $(\![\mathsf{in} \circ \langle \varphi, id \rangle]\!])$ is denoted by f:

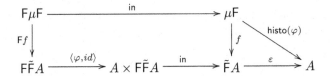

Instead of computing a value of the histomorphism directly, the catamorphism f builds an F-branching tree, which contains values of the histomorphism on corresponding subarguments and, in particular, the final value in its root node. The tree is constructed "bottom-up" by first recursively building subtrees for the immediate subarguments, which are then combined by the $F\tilde{F}$-algebra to get the value of the histomorphism on the current argument and the resulting tree. Since the building of the annotated tree is done by one pass over the argument structure, the equation gives a linear algorithm for computing histomorphisms.

3.2   Dynamorphisms

Although histomorphism is enough for the Fibonacci function, it is not so for some other classic dynamic programming algorithms like edit distance. This is due to histomorphism capturing structural (course-of-value) recursion, which requires that the recursion pattern of the algorithm follows that of its input. Next we will define a combinator that will lift this restriction and allow to capture all generally recursive dynamic algorithms.

Definition 2. *(dynamorphism)*
Let $\psi : A \to \mathsf{F}A$ be an F-coalgebra and $\varphi : \mathsf{F}\tilde{\mathsf{F}}B \to B$ be an $\mathsf{F}\tilde{\mathsf{F}}$-algebra. A dynamorphism *denoted by* $\mathsf{dyna}(\varphi, \psi)_\mathsf{F}$ *is the least arrow* $f : A \to B$ *that makes the following diagram commute:*

$$
\begin{array}{ccc}
\mathsf{F}A & \xleftarrow{\;\;\psi\;\;} & A \\
{\scriptstyle \mathsf{F}[\langle f, \psi\rangle]}\big\downarrow & & \big\downarrow {\scriptstyle f} \\
\mathsf{F}\tilde{\mathsf{F}}B & \xrightarrow{\;\;\varphi\;\;} & B
\end{array}
$$

Proposition 2. *Let* $\psi : A \to \mathsf{F}A$ *be an* F-*coalgebra and* $\varphi : \mathsf{F}\tilde{\mathsf{F}}B \to B$ *be an* $\mathsf{F}\tilde{\mathsf{F}}$-*algebra, then*

$$\mathsf{dyna}(\varphi, \psi)_\mathsf{F} = \mathsf{histo}(\varphi)_\mathsf{F} \circ [\![\psi]\!]_\mathsf{F} \qquad\qquad \text{(dyna-definition)}$$

Proof. We will use the fusion law of least fixed points [9]:

$$\mathcal{G} \text{ is strict} \wedge \mathcal{F} \circ \mathcal{G} = \mathcal{G} \circ \mathcal{H} \implies \mathsf{fix}\,\mathcal{F} = \mathcal{G}(\mathsf{fix}\,\mathcal{H})$$

In our case we have:
$$
\begin{aligned}
\mathcal{F}(f) &= \varphi \circ \mathsf{F}[\![\langle f, \psi\rangle]\!] \circ \psi \\
\mathcal{G}(g) &= g \circ [\![\psi]\!] \\
\mathcal{H}(h) &= \varphi \circ \mathsf{F}[\![\langle h, \mathsf{out}\rangle]\!] \circ \mathsf{out}
\end{aligned}
$$

i.e. $\mathsf{dyna}(\varphi, \psi) = \mathsf{fix}\,\mathcal{F}$ and $\mathsf{histo}(\varphi) = \mathsf{fix}\,\mathcal{H}$.

Obviously $\mathcal{G}$ is strict. Thus, we need to show that for any $h : \mu\mathsf{F} \to B$

$$(\mathcal{F} \circ \mathcal{G})(h) = (\mathcal{G} \circ \mathcal{H})(h)$$

The left and right hand side of the equation simplify as follows:

$$
\begin{aligned}
(\mathcal{F} \circ \mathcal{G})(h) &= \mathcal{F}(h \circ [\![\psi]\!]) \\
&= \varphi \circ \mathsf{F}[\![\langle h \circ [\![\psi]\!], \psi\rangle]\!] \circ \psi \\
(\mathcal{G} \circ \mathcal{H})(h) &= \mathcal{G}(\varphi \circ \mathsf{F}[\![\langle h, \mathsf{out}\rangle]\!] \circ \mathsf{out}) \\
&= \varphi \circ \mathsf{F}[\![\langle h, \mathsf{out}\rangle]\!] \circ \mathsf{out} \circ [\![\psi]\!] \\
&= \varphi \circ \mathsf{F}([\![\langle h, \mathsf{out}\rangle]\!] \circ [\![\psi]\!]) \circ \psi
\end{aligned}
$$

Here, the last equality holds because of *ana-cancellation*.

Hence, it suffices to show that $[\![\langle h, \mathsf{out}\rangle]\!] \circ [\![\psi]\!] = [\![\langle h \circ [\![\psi]\!], \psi\rangle]\!]$. For this we can use *ana-fusion* law because $[\![\psi]\!]$ is an $\mathsf{F}_B^\times$-coalgebra homomorphism:

$$
\begin{array}{ccc}
B \times \mathsf{F}A & \xleftarrow{\;\langle h \circ [\![\psi]\!], \psi\rangle\;} & A \\
{\scriptstyle id \times \mathsf{F}[\![\psi]\!]}\big\downarrow & & \big\downarrow {\scriptstyle [\![\psi]\!]} \\
B \times \mathsf{F}\mu\mathsf{F} & \xleftarrow{\;\langle h, \mathsf{out}\rangle\;} & \mu\mathsf{F}
\end{array}
$$

The equality on the first component of the product is obvious and the equality on the second component holds by *ana-cancellation*. $\qquad\square$

Dynamorphisms come equipped with the following properties:

- **Cancellation:** For any coalgebra $\psi : A \to FA$ and algebra $\varphi : F\tilde{F}B \to B$

$$\mathsf{dyna}(\varphi, \psi)_\mathsf{F} = \varphi \circ \mathsf{F}[\![\langle \mathsf{dyna}(\varphi, \psi)_\mathsf{F}, \psi \rangle]\!]_{\mathsf{F}^\times} \circ \psi \qquad \text{(dyna-cancellation)}$$

- **Histo-Fusion:** For any algebras $\varphi : F\tilde{F}A \to A$, $\psi : F\tilde{F}B \to B$ and an arrow $f : A \to B$

$$f \text{ is strict} \wedge f \circ \varphi = \psi \circ \tilde{F}f \;\Rightarrow\; f \circ \mathsf{dyna}(\varphi, \xi)_\mathsf{F} = \mathsf{dyna}(\psi, \xi)_\mathsf{F}$$
$$\text{(dyna-histo-fusion)}$$

- **Ana-Fusion:** For any coalgebras $\psi : A \to FA$, $\xi : B \to FB$, algebra $\varphi : F\tilde{F}C \to C$ and morphism $f : A \to B$

$$\xi \circ f = Ff \circ \psi \;\Rightarrow\; \mathsf{dyna}(\varphi, \xi)_\mathsf{F} \circ f = \mathsf{dyna}(\varphi, \psi)_\mathsf{F} \qquad \text{(dyna-ana-fusion)}$$

- **Histo-as-Dyna:** For any algebra $\varphi : F\tilde{F}B \to B$

$$\mathsf{histo}(\varphi)_\mathsf{F} = \mathsf{dyna}(\varphi, \mathsf{out})_\mathsf{F} \qquad \text{(histo-as-dyna)}$$

- **Ana-as-Dyna:** For any coalgebra $\psi : A \to FA$

$$[\![\psi]\!]_\mathsf{F} = \mathsf{dyna}(\mathsf{in} \circ F\varepsilon, \psi)_\mathsf{F} \qquad \text{(ana-as-dyna)}$$

Although the recursive form of dynamorphism is more comfortable to reason about it adds an exponential complexity penalty to the function, therefore we use *histo-as-cata* to define a dynamorphism in terms of a corresponding hylomorphism.

Proposition 3. *Let* $\psi : FA \to A$ *be an* F*-coalgebra and* $\varphi : F\tilde{F}B \to B$ *be an* $F\tilde{F}$*-algebra, then*

$$\mathsf{dyna}(\varphi, \psi) = \varepsilon_B \circ \mathsf{hylo}(\mathsf{in} \circ \langle \varphi, id \rangle, \psi) \qquad \text{(dyna-as-hylo)}$$

Proof. Follows trivially from *histo-as-cata*, *dyna-definition* and *hylo-definition*. □

Thanks to *dyna-as-hylo* we can now define dynamorphisms which will recursively reuse the annotated structure instead of rebuilding it every time some annotation is needed ("bottom-up" approach versus "top-down"), thus getting an efficient algorithm for their computation. Now we could define effectively the Fibonacci function and others as dynamorphisms (and indeed we do so in the next section), but first we bring in one more property that connects together a hylomorphism function definition with a dynamorphism function definition through a natural transformation.

Theorem 1. *Let* F *and* G *be endofunctors,* $\psi : A \to GA$ *and* $\xi : A \to FA$ *coalgebras,* $\varphi : GB \to B$ *an algebra, and* $\sigma : F\tilde{F} \dot{\to} G$ *a natural transformation. Then*

$$\psi = \sigma_A \circ \theta \circ [\![\langle id, \xi \rangle]\!]_{\mathsf{F}^\times}$$
$$\implies \mathsf{hylo}(\varphi, \psi)_\mathsf{G} = \mathsf{dyna}(\varphi \circ \sigma_B, \xi)_\mathsf{F} \qquad \text{(rec-compression)}$$

Proof. First note that by *θ-cancellation* the premiss of the implication is equivalent to

$$\psi = \sigma_A \circ \mathsf{F}[\![\langle id, \xi \rangle]\!]_{\mathsf{F}\times} \circ \xi$$

Now, consider the following diagram:

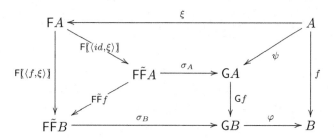

Here, the square on right corresponds to the hylomorphism and the outer square to the dynamorphism. The upper square corresponds to the left hand side of the implication and the lower square is the naturality square of σ, thus both commute. As the triangle on the left also commutes (due to *map-build-fusion*), it is easy to see that the whole square commutes whenever the square on right does (and vice versa), hence the corresponding sets of functions coincide and their minimal elements, the dynamorphism and the hylomorphism respectively, are equal.   □

The *rec-compression* law expresses a property stating that when the coalgebras in hylomorphism and dynamorphism are connected by a natural transformation then we can reuse the algebra in both function definitions.

Intuitively this is the case since dynamic programming technique changes only the recursion structure of the algorithm and there is no need to update the actual calculating part of the algorithm. The required relation between the coalgebras expresses an intuitive fact that the order of recursion in dynamic algorithm must proceed in such a way that the needed subtask solutions are always (if indirectly) available. The natural transformation plays the role of projection that restores one level of the original recursive structure by projecting the annotated values from the depths of the new annotated recursive structure.

4   Examples

In this section we review four classical dynamic algorithms: Fibonacci numbers, binary partitioning of numbers, edit distance and longest common subsequence. In each case we first define it as a hylomorphism and then as a dynamorphism reusing the algebra as shown in *rec-compression* law.

4.1   Fibonacci Numbers

The first algorithm we present is that of Fibonacci numbers, which is a very well known algorithm commonly used for illustrating the dynamic programming technique. Though it is a bit too simple (being the only example we consider that can be expressed as a histomorphism) it is nevertheless useful to illustrate the mechanics of the transformation from a hylomorphism to a dynamorphism definition.

Since we already defined the algorithm in the previous section we start with the hylomorphism definition $fibo = \mathsf{hylo}(\varphi, \psi)_\mathsf{G}$, where $\mathsf{G}(X) = 1 + 1 + X^2$ and $\psi : \mathbb{N} \to \mathsf{GN}$, $\varphi : \mathsf{GN} \to \mathbb{N}$ are defined below:

$$
\begin{aligned}
\psi\,(0) &= \mathrm{inj}_1 \perp \\
\psi\,(1) &= \mathrm{inj}_2 \perp \\
\psi\,(n) &= \mathrm{inj}_3\,(n-1,\, n-2)
\end{aligned}
$$

$$
\begin{aligned}
\varphi\,(\mathrm{inj}_1 \perp) &= 0 \\
\varphi\,(\mathrm{inj}_2 \perp) &= 1 \\
\varphi\,(\mathrm{inj}_3\,(n_1, n_2)) &= n_1 + n_2
\end{aligned}
$$

As one can see the intermediate structure hylomorphism is using is that of binary trees which size is exponential in relation to the size of input. It is also clearly visible that the coalgebra ψ defines the exact shape of the intermediate structure producing dependencies for every argument. So $\psi(0)$ and $\psi(1)$ does not have any dependencies (since their value is constant) and any other natural number n dependencies are $n-1$ and $n-2$.

Next we define Fibonacci as a dynamorphism $fibo = \mathsf{dyna}(\varphi \circ \sigma, \xi)_\mathsf{F}$ making use of *rec-compression* law. We use the fact that natural numbers have a natural order and it is obvious that both dependencies ($n-1$ and $n-2$) comes one after another in this order. Therefore we can use the base functor for natural numbers $\mathsf{F}(X) = 1 + X$ and define the coalgebra $\xi : \mathbb{N} \to \mathsf{FN}$ as follows:

$$
\begin{aligned}
\xi\,(0) &= \mathrm{inl} \perp \\
\xi\,(n) &= \mathrm{inr}\,(n-1)
\end{aligned}
$$

We derive the definition of $\sigma : \mathsf{F\tilde{F}} \to \mathsf{G}$, by making sure, that the premiss of *rec-compression* law is satisfied. For the case $n = 0$ note that

$$
(\theta \circ [\![\langle id, \xi \rangle]\!])\,(0) = \mathrm{inl} \perp
$$

Hence, for the case $n = 0$, we have to define $\sigma\,(\mathrm{inl} \perp) = \mathrm{inj}_1 \perp$. If $n > 0$, we have that

$$
(\theta \circ [\![\langle id, \xi \rangle]\!])\,(n) = (\mathrm{inr} \circ [\![\langle id, \xi \rangle]\!])\,(n-1)
$$

Now, in the case of $n = 1$, we get

$$
\begin{aligned}
(\theta \circ [\![\langle id, \xi \rangle]\!])\,(1) &= \mathrm{inr}\,x, \text{ where } x = [\![\langle id, \xi \rangle]\!]\,(0) \\
&= \mathrm{inr}\,x, \text{ where } \langle \varepsilon, \theta \rangle(x) = (0,\ \mathrm{inl} \perp)
\end{aligned}
$$

In the case of $n > 1$, we get

$$
\begin{aligned}
(\theta \circ [\![\langle id, \xi \rangle]\!])\,(n) &= \mathrm{inr}\,x, \text{ where } x = [\![\langle id, \xi \rangle]\!]\,(n-1) \\
&= \mathrm{inr}\,x, \text{ where } \langle \varepsilon, \theta \rangle(x) = (n-1,\ \mathrm{inr}\,y) \\
&\qquad \text{and} \quad y = [\![\langle id, \xi \rangle]\!]\,(n-2)
\end{aligned}
$$

Hence, we can define $\sigma : \mathsf{F}\tilde{\mathsf{F}} \overset{.}{\to} \mathsf{G}$ as follows:

$$\sigma \ (\mathrm{inl} \perp) = \quad \mathrm{inj}_1 \perp$$

$$\sigma \ (\mathrm{inr} \ x) = \begin{cases} \mathrm{inj}_2 \perp & \text{if } \theta(x) = \mathrm{inl} \perp \\ \mathrm{inj}_3(\varepsilon(x), \varepsilon(y)) & \text{if } \theta(x) = \mathrm{inr} \ y \end{cases}$$

Note, that the composite algebra $\varphi \circ \sigma : \mathsf{F}\tilde{\mathsf{F}}\mathbb{N} \to \mathbb{N}$ is equivalent to that of used in the previous section to define Fibonacci as a histomorphism. Moreover, as the coalgebra $\xi : \mathbb{N} \to \mathsf{F}\mathbb{N}$ is the final coalgebra of functor $\mathsf{F}(X) = 1 + X$, the dynamorphism we derived is in fact the very same histomorphism.

4.2   Binary Partitions

Binary partitioning of a number is representing this number as a sum of powers of 2. The number of binary partitions for a number n is the number of unique ways to partitions this number (ignoring the order) into powers of 2.

The function can be defined by the following equations:

$$\mathrm{bp}(0) = 1$$

$$\mathrm{bp}(n) = \begin{cases} \mathrm{bp}(n-1), \text{ if } n \text{ is odd} \\ \mathrm{bp}(n-1) + \mathrm{bp}(n/2), \text{ if } n \text{ is even} \end{cases}$$

Defining the function as a hylomorphism is quite straightforward. The intermediate structure in this case is a tree with maximal branching factor of two, i.e., $\mathrm{bp} = \mathrm{hylo}(\varphi, \psi)_\mathsf{G}$, where $\mathsf{G}(X) = 1 + X + X^2$ and $\psi : \mathbb{N} \to \mathsf{G}\mathbb{N}$, $\varphi : \mathsf{G}\mathbb{N} \to \mathbb{N}$ are defined below:

$$\psi \ (0) \qquad = \quad \mathrm{inj}_1 \perp$$

$$\psi \ (n) \qquad = \begin{cases} \mathrm{inj}_2(n-1) & \text{if } n \text{ is odd} \\ \mathrm{inj}_3(n-1, n/2) & \text{if } n \text{ is even} \end{cases}$$

$$\begin{aligned} \varphi \ (\mathrm{inj}_1 \perp) \quad &= 1 \\ \varphi \ (\mathrm{inj}_2 \ n) \quad &= n \\ \varphi \ (\mathrm{inj}_3 \ (n_1, \ n_2)) &= n_1 + n_2 \end{aligned}$$

To transform the function to a dynamorphism we notice that again $\psi(n)$ functionally depends on the previous numbers only. However, as the dependencies have dynamic depth, we need to know the size of the intermediate structure. Hence we choose the intermediate structure to be a list of natural numbers, i.e., the base functor is $\mathsf{F}(X) = 1 + \mathbb{N} \times X$ and define coalgebra $\xi : \mathbb{N} \to \mathsf{F}\mathbb{N}$ as follows:

$$\begin{aligned} \xi \ (0) &= \mathrm{inl} \perp \\ \xi \ (n) &= \mathrm{inr} \ (n, \ n-1) \end{aligned}$$

Similarly to Fibonacci function, we derive the definition of $\sigma : \mathsf{F}\tilde{\mathsf{F}} \overset{.}{\to} \mathsf{G}$, by making sure, that the premiss of *rec-compression* law is satisfied. For the case $n = 0$ we obviously have to define $\sigma \ (\mathrm{inl} \perp) = \mathrm{inj}_1 \perp$. If $n > 0$, we notice that

$$(\theta \circ \llbracket \langle id, \xi \rangle \rrbracket)(n) = \text{inr}(n, \ \llbracket \langle id, \xi \rangle \rrbracket \, (n-1))$$

Therefore, if n is odd, we can use ε-*cancellation* $\varepsilon(\llbracket \langle id, \xi \rangle \rrbracket)(n-1) = n-1$ to conclude that $\sigma \, (\text{inr}(n, x)) = \text{inj}_2(\varepsilon(x))$.

If n is even, we need not only the annotation in the root node but also in the node which corresponds to $n/2$. For this, we define a partial function $\pi : \tilde{\mathsf{F}}A \to \tilde{\mathsf{F}}A$ by $\pi(x) = y$, if $\theta(x) = \text{inr}(m, y)$, and denote by π^k its k-fold composition. Using induction over natural numbers, we can show that for $k \leqslant n$

$$(\varepsilon \circ \pi^k \circ \llbracket \langle id, \xi \rangle \rrbracket)(n) = n - k$$

Indeed, the base case $k = 0$ is trivial. For the case $k > 0$ we have

$$\begin{aligned}(\varepsilon \circ \pi^k \circ \llbracket \langle id, \xi \rangle \rrbracket)(n) &= (\varepsilon \circ \pi^{k-1} \circ \pi \circ \llbracket \langle id, \xi \rangle \rrbracket), (n) \\ &= (\varepsilon \circ \pi^{k-1} \llbracket \langle id, \xi \rangle \rrbracket)(n-1) \\ &= n - 1 - (k-1) = n - k\end{aligned}$$

Now, since the annotated tree we can access is generated by $\llbracket \langle id, \xi \rangle \rrbracket \, (n-1)$, we need to take $k = n - n/2 - 1 = n/2 - 1$. Therefore, we can define the natural transformation $\sigma : \mathsf{F}\tilde{\mathsf{F}} \dot\to \mathsf{G}$ as follows:

$$\sigma \, (\text{inl} \perp) \ = \ \text{inj}_1 \perp$$

$$\sigma \, (\text{inr} \, (n, x)) = \begin{cases} \text{inj}_2(\varepsilon(x)) & \text{if } n \text{ is odd} \\ \text{inj}_3(\varepsilon(x), \varepsilon(\pi^{n/2-1}(x))) & \text{if } n \text{ is even} \end{cases}$$

Note that even though the definition $\text{bp} = \text{dyna}(\varphi \circ \sigma, \xi)_\mathsf{F}$ uses structural recursion it *cannot* be defined by a single histomorphism. This is due to the need to know the size of the intermediate structure built so far (one can define it though as a composition of a histomorphism and a projection).

4.3   Edit Distance

Edit distance is a classical dynamic programming algorithm that measures the measure of "distance" or "difference" between two strings (i.e. lists of characters List_C). The algorithm can be defined as follows:

$$\begin{aligned}editDist([], bs) &= \#bs \\ editDist(as, []) &= \#as \\ editDist(a{:}as, b{:}bs) &= \min \, (\end{aligned}$$

$$\begin{aligned}&editDist(as, b{:}bs) + 1, \\ &editDist(a{:}as, bs) + 1, \\ &editDist(as, bs) + (\text{if } a = b \text{ then } 0 \text{ else } 1))\end{aligned}$$

Here $\#as$ denotes the length of the list as.

The definition above translates fairly straightforwardly to a hylomorphism $editDist = \mathsf{hylo}(\varphi, \psi)_\mathsf{G}$, where $\mathsf{G}(X) = \mathsf{List}_C + C^2 \times X^3$ and $\psi : \mathsf{List}_C^2 \to \mathsf{GList}_C^2$, $\varphi : \mathsf{G}\mathbb{N} \to \mathbb{N}$ are defined below:

$$\psi\,([\,], \, bs) \qquad = \mathsf{inl}\, bs$$
$$\psi\,(as, \, [\,]) \qquad = \mathsf{inl}\, as$$
$$\psi\,(a{:}as, \, b{:}bs) = \mathsf{inr}\,((a, b), \, (as, b{:}bs), \, (a{:}as, bs), \, (as, bs))$$

$$\varphi\,(\mathsf{inl}\, as) \qquad = \#as$$
$$\varphi\,(\mathsf{inr}\,((a, b), \, x_1, \, x_2, \, x_3))$$
$$\qquad = \min\,(x_1 + 1, \, x_2 + 1, \, x_3 + (\text{if } a = b \text{ then } 0 \text{ else } 1))$$

However translating this definition to a dynamorphism is not as simple. Typically a matrix is used to accumulate and look up values in the dynamic version of edit distance algorithm. Matrix however is not an inductive structure and thus cannot be used as the intermediate structure in the dynamorphism. So instead of using a matrix we use a *walk-through* of a matrix—a list of values from the matrix ordered predictably, e.g. row by row or column by column or wavefront way. This list is indeed inductive and also corresponds in some way to the recursion used in the edit distance algorithm to walk through and fill in the matrix. In our case we choose to order row by row (or column by column, depending how you imagine the matrix).

However, taking such a list for the intermediate structure brings in another problem—now to project a value from the previous row or column (which we need in this case) and to build the list recursively we need to know at least one input string in our coalgebra and its length in the natural transformation. As these are constant throughout the computation, we give them as an additional parameter to ξ and σ denoted by subscript. So,

$$editDist\,(s_1, s_2) = \mathsf{dyna}(\varphi \circ \sigma_{\#s_1}, \, \xi_{s_1})_\mathsf{F}\,(s_1, s_2),$$

where $\mathsf{F}(X) = (\mathsf{List}_C)^2 \times (1 + X)$ and $\xi_{s_1} : \mathsf{List}_C^2 \to \mathsf{FList}_C^2$, $\sigma_n : \mathsf{F}\tilde{\mathsf{F}} \overset{\cdot}{\to} \mathsf{G}$ are defined below:

$$\xi_{cs}\,([\,], [\,]) \qquad\qquad = (([\,], [\,]), \, \mathsf{inl}\,\bot)$$
$$\xi_{cs}\,([\,], b{:}bs) \qquad\quad = (([\,], b{:}bs), \, \mathsf{inr}\,(cs, bs))$$
$$\xi_{cs}\,(a{:}as, bs) \qquad\quad = ((a{:}as, bs), \, \mathsf{inr}\,(as, bs))$$

$$\sigma_n\,((as, bs), \, \mathsf{inl}\,\bot) \qquad = \mathsf{inl}\,[\,]$$
$$\sigma_n\,(([\,], bs), \, \mathsf{inr}\, x) \qquad = \mathsf{inl}\,\, bs$$
$$\sigma_n\,((as, [\,]), \, \mathsf{inr}\, x) \qquad = \mathsf{inl}\,\, as$$
$$\sigma_n\,((a{:}as, b{:}bs), \, \mathsf{inr}\, x) = \mathsf{inr}\,((a, b), \, \varepsilon\,(x), \, \varepsilon\,(\pi^n\, x), \, \varepsilon\,(\pi^{n+1}\, x))$$

While the definition of σ_n could be derived similarly to the previous examples, we do not present the derivation here, as it gets quite complicated.

Note that since the base functor F of edit distance differs from that of binary partitions the partial function $\pi : \tilde{\mathsf{F}}A \to \tilde{\mathsf{F}}A$ is defined here by $\pi(x) = y$, if $\theta(x) = (s, \mathsf{inr}(m, y))$, which is also the definition used in the next example.

4.4   Longest Common Subsequence

Longest common subsequence is another well-known dynamic programming algorithm. It finds the longest character subsequence that is common to both input strings. It can be defined as follows:

$$lcs([], bs) = []$$
$$lcs(as, []) = []$$
$$lcs(a{:}as, b{:}bs) = \text{if } a = b \text{ then } a{:}lcs(as, bs)$$
$$\text{else (if } \#lcs(a{:}as, bs) > \#lcs(as, b{:}bs)$$
$$\text{then } lcs(a{:}as, bs)$$
$$\text{else } lcs(as, b{:}bs))$$

The hylomorphism definition comes straight from the above.

$$G(X) = 1 + C^2 \times X^3$$
$$lcs = \mathsf{hylo}(\varphi, \psi)_G$$

$$\psi\ ([], bs) = \mathsf{inl}\ \bot$$
$$\psi\ (as, []) = \mathsf{inl}\ \bot$$
$$\psi\ (a{:}as, b{:}bs) = \mathsf{inr}\ ((a, b),\ (as, b{:}bs),\ (a{:}as, bs),\ (as, bs))$$

$$\varphi\ (\mathsf{inl}\ \bot) = []$$
$$\varphi\ (\mathsf{inr}\ ((a, b), x_1, x_2, x_3))$$
$$= \text{if } a = b \text{ then } a{:}x_3 \text{ else (if } \#x_1 > \#x_2 \text{ then } x_1 \text{ else } x_2)$$

When defining the dynamorphism version we have the same problems as with edit distance and we solve them the same way.

$$F(X) = (\mathsf{List}_C)^2 \times (1 + X)$$
$$lcs(s_1, s_2) = \mathsf{dyna}(\varphi \circ \sigma_{\#s_1}, \xi_{s_1})_F\ (s_1, s_2)$$

$$\xi_{cs}\ ([], []) = (([], []), \mathsf{inl}\ \bot)$$
$$\xi_{cs}\ ([], b{:}bs) = (([], b{:}bs), \mathsf{inr}\ (cs, bs))$$
$$\xi_{cs}\ (a{:}as, b{:}bs) = ((a{:}as, b{:}bs), \mathsf{inr}\ (as, b{:}bs))$$

$$\sigma_n\ ((as, bs), \mathsf{inl}\ \bot) = \mathsf{inl}\ \bot$$
$$\sigma_n\ (([], bs), \mathsf{inr}\ x) = \mathsf{inl}\ \bot$$
$$\sigma_n\ ((as, []), \mathsf{inr}\ x) = \mathsf{inl}\ \bot$$
$$\sigma_n\ ((a{:}as, b{:}bs), \mathsf{inr}\ x) = \mathsf{inr}\ ((a, b),\ \varepsilon\ (x),\ \varepsilon\ (\pi^n\ x),\ \varepsilon\ (\pi^{n+1}\ x))$$

5   Conclusions and Future Work

We have shown that the dynamic programming recursion pattern can be captured by a generic recursion combinator, dynamorphism, which avoids the recomputing of identical substructures. We have identified a simple condition when a function defined by a hylomorphism can be redefined as a dynamorphism. While the transformation is not automatic, it requires of guessing a coalgebra, it allows to reuse some parts of original definition, namely the algebra. Moreover, after the coalgebra is given, the another required component of the new definition, a natural transformation, can often be derived without further guessing.

In all our examples, the intermediate structure used by dynamorphisms was linear, i.e. some form of lists. Of course, this is to be expected, as one of the requirements of dynamic programming is the existence of partial order among the value dependencies, which we have sorted topologically to get a linear order. While our formulation allows arbitrary tree-shaped intermediate structures, it's not clear whether this generality is really useful. Additional restrictions on the shape of the intermediate structure might provide necessary information for deriving instead of guessing the corresponding coalgebra. This is an important area of further work.

It is known that histomorphism is an instance of comonadic recursion [11] and that the latter can be generalized in a recursive coalgebra setting [4]. What is the exact relationship between dynamorphisms and comonadic recursive coalgebras is another interesting topic to study.

Acknowledgments. We are grateful to our anonymous referees for their constructive criticism and suggestions. We are also grateful to Jeremy Gibbons for first pointing out that dynamic programming might provide relevant examples of histomorphisms, and to Tarmo Uustalu for technical discussions. This work was partially supported by Estonian Science Foundation grants No. 5567 and No. 6713.

References

1. Bellman, R.: Dynamic Programming. Princeton Univ. Press, Princeton, NJ (1957)
2. Bird, R.S.: An introduction to the theory of lists. In Broy, M., ed.: Logic of Programming and Calculi of Discrete Design. Vol. 36 of NATO ASI Series F. Springer-Verlag, Berlin (1987) 3–42
3. Bird, R., de Moor, O.: Algebra of Programming. Vol. 100 of Prentice Hall Int. Series in Computer Science. Prentice Hall, London (1997)
4. Capretta, V., Uustalu, T., Vene, V.: Recursive coalgebras from comonads. Inform. and Comput. **204**(4) (2006) 437–468
5. Fokkinga, M.: Law and Order in Algorithmics. PhD thesis. Dept. of Informatics, Univ. of Twente (1992)
6. Gibbons, J.: Calculating functional programs. In Backhouse, R.C., Crole, R.L., Gibbons, J., eds.: Revised Lectures from Int. Summer School and Wksh. on Algebraic and Coalgebraic Methods in the Mathematics of Program Construction. Vol. 2297 of Lect. Notes in Comput. Sci., Springer-Verlag, Berlin (2000) 149–202
7. Hagino, T.: A Categorical Programming Language. PhD thesis CST-47-87. Laboratory for Foundations of Computer Science, Dept. of Computer Science, Univ. of Edinburgh (1987)
8. Malcolm, G.: Data structures and program transformation. Sci. of Comput. Program. **14**(2–3) (1990) 255–279

9. Meijer, E., Fokkinga, M., Paterson, R.: Functional programming with bananas, lenses, envelopes and barbed wire. In Hughes, J., ed.: Proc. of 5th ACM Conf. on Functional Programming Languages and Computer Architecture, FPCA '91. Vol. 523 of Lect. Notes in Comput. Sci. Springer-Verlag, Berlin (1991) 124–144

10. Uustalu, T., Vene, V.: Primitive (co)recursion and course-of-value (co)iteration, categorically. Informatica **10**(1) (1999) 5–26

11. Uustalu, T., Vene, V., Pardo, A.: Recursion schemes from comonads. Nordic J. of Computing **8**(3) (2001) 366–390

12. Vene, V.: Categorical Programming with Inductive and Coinductive Types. PhD thesis. Vol. 23 of Diss. Math. Univ. Tartuensis. Dept. of Computer Science, Univ. of Tartu (2000)

Bimonadic Semantics for Basic Pattern Matching Calculi

Wolfram Kahl, Jacques Carette, and Xiaoheng Ji

Department of Computing and Software, McMaster University,
Hamilton, Ontario, Canada L8S 4K1
kahl@cas.mcmaster.ca, carette@cas.mcmaster.ca

Abstract. The pattern matching calculi introduced by the first author are a refinement of the λ-calculus that integrates mechanisms appropriate for fine-grained modelling of non-strict pattern matching.

While related work in the literature only uses a single monad, typically Maybe, for matchings, we present an axiomatic approach to semantics of these pattern matching calculi using two monads, one for expressions and one for matchings.

Although these two monads only need to be relatively lightly coupled, this semantics implies soundness of all core PMC rules, and is a useful tool for exploration of the design space for pattern matching calculi.

Using lifting and Maybe monads, we obtain standard Haskell semantics, and by adding another level of Maybe to both, we obtain a denotational semantics of the "matching failure as exceptions" approach of Erwig and Peyton Jones. Using list-like monads opens up interesting extensions in the direction of functional-logic programming.

1   Introduction

Although (pure) functional programming in general is very accessible to equational reasoning, the addition of pattern-matching function definitions introduces non-equations looking like equations, for example the second line in

```
isEmptyList (x : xs) = False
isEmptyList ys       = True
```

The operational semantics of such definitions employs the *functional rewriting strategy* defined over several pages by Plasmeijer and van Eekelen [17] or, essentially equivalently, in the section on `case` expressions in the Haskell report [16]. This implies that syntactic use of the definitions of a program in reasoning about that program has to take into account that complex strategy, and loses the simplicity of equational reasoning.

The pattern matching calculus (PMC) introduced by Kahl [11] remedies this situation. It separates pattern matching aspects into a separate syntactic category of "matchings", not unlike groups of "case branches `p -> e`" considered by Harrison *et al.* [7], but with an additional "argument supply" constructor

---

T. Uustalu (Ed.): MPC 2006, LNCS 4014, pp. 253–273, 2006.

that rationalises and generalises the pattern guards proposed by Erwig and Peyton Jones [4]. PMC is equipped with a confluent (second-order) rewriting system, thereby enabling equational reasoning starting from the definitions of a program. The rewriting system directly gives a normalisation strategy [11].

PMC allows straightforward internalisation of pattern matching definitions without the ballast of having to introduce the new variables necessary as case arguments (the syntax will be explained in detail in Sect. 2):

$$isEmptyList = \{\!| (x:xs) \mapsto \uparrow\mathsf{False}\!\upharpoonright \ |\ ys \mapsto \uparrow\mathsf{True}\!\upharpoonright |\!\}$$

Application to the empty list $[]$ induces the following reduction sequence:

$$
\begin{aligned}
isEmptyList\ [] \ \longrightarrow\ & \{\!| (x:xs) \mapsto \uparrow\mathsf{False}\!\upharpoonright \ |\ ys \mapsto \uparrow\mathsf{True}\!\upharpoonright |\!\}\ []\\
\longrightarrow\ & \{\!| []\,\triangleright((x:xs) \mapsto \uparrow\mathsf{False}\!\upharpoonright \ |\ ys \mapsto \uparrow\mathsf{True}\!\upharpoonright) |\!\}\\
\longrightarrow\ & \{\!| []\,\triangleright(x:xs) \mapsto \uparrow\mathsf{False}\!\upharpoonright \ |\ []\,\triangleright ys \mapsto \uparrow\mathsf{True}\!\upharpoonright |\!\}\\
\longrightarrow\ & \{\!| \lightning\ |\ []\,\triangleright ys \mapsto \uparrow\mathsf{True}\!\upharpoonright |\!\}\\
\longrightarrow\ & \{\!| []\,\triangleright ys \mapsto \uparrow\mathsf{True}\!\upharpoonright |\!\}\\
\longrightarrow\ & \{\!| \uparrow\mathsf{True}\!\upharpoonright |\!\}\\
\longrightarrow\ & \mathsf{True}
\end{aligned}
$$

There is also a "conservative embedding" of the λ-calculus into PMC: Application is the same, and abstraction translates into a one-alternative variable-pattern matching:

$$\lambda\,v\,.\,e \ \ := \ \ \{\!| v \mapsto \uparrow e\!\upharpoonright |\!\}$$

With this definition, β-reduction can be emulated by a three-step reduction sequence in PMC (the reduction rules are listed in Fig. 2 and explained in App. A):

$$
\begin{aligned}
(\lambda\,v\,.\,e)\,a \ \ =\ \ & \{\!| v \mapsto \uparrow e\!\upharpoonright |\!\}\ a\\
\xrightarrow[(\{\!| |\!\}@)]{}\ & \{\!| a\,\triangleright v \mapsto \uparrow e\!\upharpoonright |\!\}\\
\xrightarrow[(\triangleright v)]{}\ & \{\!| \uparrow e\!\upharpoonright[v\backslash a] |\!\}\\
=\ \ & \{\!| \uparrow e[v\backslash a]\!\upharpoonright |\!\}\\
\xrightarrow[(\{\!| \uparrow \upharpoonright |\!\})]{}\ & e[v\backslash a]
\end{aligned}
$$

β-normal forms translate into PMC normal forms, and PMC reduction sequences starting from translations of λ-terms essentially correspond to β-reduction sequences, so the embedding is faithful.

Pattern guards extend Boolean guards with the ability to bind additional variables; Peyton Jones' standard example is:

```
clunky env v1 v2 |  Just r1 <- lookup env v1
              , Just r2 <- lookup env v2   = r1 + r2
              | otherwise                  = v1 + v2
```

This directly translates into PMC, with a slightly different structure (with appropriate conventions, we could omit more parentheses):

$$clunky = \{\!| \; env \mapsto v_1 \mapsto v_2 \mapsto ((lookup \; env \; v_1 \rhd \mathsf{Just}(r_1) \mapsto$$
$$lookup \; env \; v_2 \rhd \mathsf{Just}(r_2) \mapsto \lceil r_1 + r_2 \rceil)$$
$$[\!] \; \lceil v_1 + v_2 \rceil)$$
$$|\!\}$$

PMC is really a family of calculi based on a common core syntax: starting from the rewriting system corresponding to Haskell evaluation or the standard functional strategy and *exchanging a single rule*, we obtain a system that corresponds to Erwig and Peyton Jones's proposal [4] to treat pattern matching failure as an exception that can be caught in the same *or in another* case expression.

In this paper, we provide a *semantic* basis for the exploration of these and further pattern matching calculi by giving a compositional monadic semantics for the core PMC syntax. The interesting aspect is that the two syntactic categories of PMC correspond to two separate monads that are, in general, only relatively lightly coupled. As we fundamentally use the separate notions of "computation" in each syntactic category, it is very natural to use a monadic formalism, and from there to continue using a categorical setting throughout for our semantics. It has been suggested to us that using a metalanguage like that of [15] could clarify our presentation; while we agree with this, we do not yet know how to model the necessary "pointwise extensions" we need (see Sect. 4.1) in the metalanguage. Thus we have opted to stay with a purely categorical presentation.

The main contributions of this paper are the clean separation of concerns between the (monadic) semantics of *expressions* and of *matchings*, the crucial observation that the interpretation of function types must be different for matchings and expressions, and a clean isolation of the design choices available when considering pattern-matching semantics. Another important technical ingredient was the need to create appropriate "pointwise extensions" of operations in the base monads to function types — something routinely done in mathematics but seldom done in statically typed programming languages.[1]

After presenting and explaining the abstract syntax of simply typed PMC in the next section, we fix some category-theoretical notation and terminology in Sect. 3.1 before defining the bimonadic PMC semantics in Sect. 4. In Sect. 5 we give the soundness theorem for the core reduction rules from [11] (listed in Appendix A) with respect to our semantics without further constraints on the two monads, and explain the core of its proof steps. We then start an exploration of possible bimonadic constellations for alternative interpretations of PMC in Sect. 6.

2   Abstract Syntax

PMC has two major syntactic categories, *expressions* and *matchings*. These are defined by mutual recursion.

---

[1] Maple^{TM} and Mathematica^{TM} both overload arithmetic operators so that $f + g$ means pointwise addition, but both of these languages are dynamically typed.

When considering the analogy to functional programs, only *expressions* of the pattern matching calculus correspond to expressions of functional languages.

Matchings can be seen as a generalisation of (groups of) case alternatives. Matchings can expose patterns to be matched against arguments; we say such matchings are *waiting for argument supply*, and give them function types. Complete case expressions correspond to expressions formed from matchings that already have an argument supplied to their outermost patterns; matchings that have arguments supplied to all their open patterns are called *saturated*. Argument supply to patterns is separated from performing pattern matching itself; depending on the outcomes of the involved pattern matchings, saturated matchings can *succeed* and then *return* an expression, or they can *fail*.

Patterns form a separate, auxiliary syntactic category that will be used to construct pattern matchings.

In this paper, we will consider a class of simply-typed pattern matching calculi with common syntax; the abstract syntax of these calculi is defined by the following grammar:

Pat	$::=$ Var	variable
	$\mid$ Constr(Pat, ..., Pat)	constructor pattern
Expr	$::=$ Var	variable
	$\mid$ Constr(Expr, ..., Expr)	constructor application
	$\mid$ Expr Expr	function application
	$\mid \{\!\mid$ Match $\mid\!\}$	(function) extraction
	$\mid$ fix$_{\mathsf{Type}}$	fixed-point combinator
	$\mid \oslash_{\mathsf{Type}}$	empty expression
Match	$::= \lceil$ Expr $\rceil$	lifting
	$\mid \nleftarrow_{\mathsf{Type}}$	failure
	$\mid$ Pat $\Mapsto$ Match	pattern matching
	$\mid$ Expr $\triangleright$ Match	argument supply
	$\mid$ Match $\mid$ Match	alternative

Since this syntax has a number of unusual aspects, we explain the intuition behind it in more detail below.

Throughout this paper, we will use the following conventions for meta-level variables:

- α. α_i, β, ... are types; τ, τ_i are constructed types.
- v, v_i, w_i, x, x_i, y, y_i are variables; c, d are constructors.
- p, p_1, p_2, ..., q are patterns; m, m_1, m_2, ... are matchings,
- a, b, e, e_1, e_2, ..., f are expressions,
- i, k, n are natural numbers,

Types are generated from data type constructors and the function type constructor. Technically, we assume a family $(\mathsf{TConstr}_k)_{k \in \mathbb{N}}$ of disjoint countable sets of data type constructors of arity k, and types are generated by:

Type	$::=$ TConstr$_k$(Type$_1$, ..., Type$_k$)	constructed types
	$\mid$ Type $\rightarrow$ Type	function types

For the sake of simplicity, we do not consider polymorphism in this paper, so there are no type variables, and therefore no concept of principal types; each well-typed expression or matching has exactly one type.

We then assume that the set of constructors is organised as a family of disjoint countable sets $\mathsf{Constr}_{\alpha_1 \times \cdots \times \alpha_n \to \tau}$ for all types $\alpha_1, \ldots, \alpha_n, \tau$.

We also assume that the set of (expression) variables is organised as a family of disjoint countable sets

$$\mathsf{Var} = \biguplus_{\alpha \in \mathsf{Type}} \mathsf{Var}_\alpha$$

and a function $\mathsf{type} : \mathsf{Var} \to \mathsf{Type}$ to be given such that $v \in \mathsf{Var}_{\mathsf{type}\ v}$ for each variable $v \in \mathsf{Var}$. Type judgements then need no context.

For the purpose of our examples, all literals, like numbers and characters, are assumed to be constructors of appropriate types, and are used only in zero-ary constructions (which are written without parentheses). Constructors will, as usual, be used to build both patterns and expressions. Indeed, one might consider Pat as a subset of Expr.

Typing judgements expressing that pattern p, expression e, respectively matching m are well-typed of type α are written in the following way:

$$\underset{\mathsf{P}}{\vdash}\ p : \alpha \qquad\qquad \underset{\mathsf{E}}{\vdash}\ e : \alpha \qquad\qquad \underset{\mathsf{M}}{\vdash}\ m : \alpha$$

Patterns are built from variables and constructor applications. All variables occurring in a pattern are *free* in that pattern; for every pattern $p : \mathsf{Pat}$, we denote its set of free variables by $\mathsf{FV}(p)$. In the following, we silently restrict *all* patterns to be *linear*, i.e., not to contain more than one occurrence of any variable. The pattern typing rules are as follows:

$$\underset{\mathsf{P}}{\vdash}\ v : \mathsf{type}\ v \qquad\qquad \frac{c \in \mathsf{Constr}_{\alpha_1 \times \cdots \times \alpha_n \to \alpha} \qquad \underset{\mathsf{P}}{\vdash}\ p_1 : \alpha_1 \quad \cdots \quad \underset{\mathsf{P}}{\vdash}\ p_n : \alpha_n}{\underset{\mathsf{P}}{\vdash}\ c(p_1, \ldots, p_n) : \alpha}$$

Expressions are the syntactic category that embodies the term construction aspects; besides variables, constructor application and function application, we also have the following special kinds of expressions: Every matching m gives rise to the *(function) extraction* $\{\!| m |\!\}$. If the type of matching m is a function type, then $\{\!| m |\!\}$ extracts a function from m. If m is not a pattern matching again, then it can either succeed or fail; if it succeeds, then $\{\!| m |\!\}$ extracts the value(s) "returned" by m; otherwise, $\{\!| m |\!\}$ extracts "nothing", which can also be expressed as the expression $\oslash$, which is henceforth called the *empty expression*.

We use this somewhat uncommitted name "empty expression" since we shall consider two interpretations of $\oslash$:

- It can be a "manifestly undefined" expression equivalent to non-termination, following the common view that divergence is semantically equivalent to run-time errors.
- It can be a special "error" value, propagating matching failure considered as an "exception" through the syntactic category of expressions.

None of the expression constructors binds any variables; we overload the $\mathsf{FV}(\_)$ notation and use it to denote the set of free variables $\mathsf{FV}(e)$ for an expression $e : \mathsf{Expr}$. Expressions are typed according to the following rules:

$$
\vdash_{\mathsf{E}} v : \mathsf{type}\ v \qquad \vdash_{\mathsf{E}} \mathsf{fix}_\alpha : (\alpha \to \alpha) \to \alpha \qquad \vdash_{\mathsf{E}} \oslash : \alpha \qquad \frac{\vdash_{\mathsf{M}} m : \alpha}{\vdash_{\mathsf{E}} \{\!| m |\!\} : \alpha}
$$

$$
\frac{c \in \mathsf{Constr}_{\alpha_1 \times \cdots \times \alpha_n \to \alpha} \qquad \vdash_{\mathsf{E}} e_1 : \alpha_1 \quad \cdots \quad \vdash_{\mathsf{E}} e_n : \alpha_n}{\vdash_{\mathsf{E}} c(e_1, \ldots, e_n) : \alpha} \qquad \frac{\vdash_{\mathsf{E}} e_1 : \alpha \to \beta \qquad \vdash_{\mathsf{E}} e_2 : \alpha}{\vdash_{\mathsf{E}} (e_1\ e_2) : \beta}
$$

Matchings are the syntactic category that embodies the pattern analysis aspects:

- For an expression $e : \mathsf{Expr}$, the *lifting* or *expression embedding* $\lceil \mathsf{Expr} \rceil$ can be seen as the matching that always succeeds and attempts to lift the result e into the enclosing expression, so we propose to read it "*lift e*".
- Failure $\maltese$ is the matching that always fails.
- The *pattern matching* $p \Mapsto m$ waits for supply of one argument more than m; this pattern matching can be understood as succeeding on instances of the (linear) pattern $p : \mathsf{Pat}$ and then continuing to behave as the resulting instance of the matching $m : \mathsf{Match}$. It roughly corresponds to a single **case** alternative in languages with **case** expressions, or to pattern-binding λ-abstractions.
- *argument supply* $a \triangleright m$ is the matching-level incarnation of function application, with the argument on the left and the matching it is supplied to on the right. It saturates the first argument m is waiting for. "$a \triangleright m$" can be read "*a into m*" or "*a feeds m*". The inclusion of argument supply into the calculus is an important source of flexibility. By separating the aspects of traversing the boundary between expressions and matchings, and matching patterns against the right arguments, the design of the reduction system is made more modular.
- the *alternative* $m_1 \mid m_2$ combines the possible matching results of m_1 and m_2 in some way that can usefully be understood as "alternative". In instances corresponding to conventional functional programming, it has to be understood sequentially: $m_1 \mid m_2$ then behaves like m_1 until this fails, and then (and only then) it behaves like m_2.

The typing rules for matchings are again straight-forward:

$$
\vdash_{\mathsf{M}} \maltese : \alpha \qquad\qquad \frac{\vdash_{\mathsf{P}} p : \alpha \qquad \vdash_{\mathsf{M}} m : \beta}{\vdash_{\mathsf{M}} (p \Mapsto m) : \alpha \to \beta}
$$

$$
\frac{\vdash_{\mathsf{E}} e : \alpha \qquad \vdash_{\mathsf{M}} m : \alpha \to \beta}{\vdash_{\mathsf{M}} (e \triangleright m) : \beta} \qquad \frac{\vdash_{\mathsf{E}} e : \alpha}{\vdash_{\mathsf{M}} \lceil e \rceil : \alpha} \qquad \frac{\vdash_{\mathsf{M}} m_1 : \alpha \qquad \vdash_{\mathsf{M}} m_2 : \alpha}{\vdash_{\mathsf{M}} (m_1 \mid m_2) : \alpha}
$$

Pattern matching $p \mapsto m$ binds all variables occurring in p, so $\mathsf{FV}(p \mapsto m) = \mathsf{FV}(m) - \mathsf{FV}(p)$, letting $\mathsf{FV}(m)$ denote the set of free variables of a matching m. Pattern matching is the only variable binder in this calculus — taking this into account, the definitions of free variables, bound variables, and substitution are as usual. Note that there are no "matching variables"; variables can only occur as patterns or as expressions.

We will omit the parentheses in matchings of the shape $a \triangleright (p \mapsto m)$ since there is only one way to parse $a \triangleright p \mapsto m$ in PMC.

As-Patterns and Irrefutable Patterns

Several "more advanced" pattern matching facilities have been proposed in the literature; Haskell98 defines two of those, namely as-patterns and irrefutable patterns. Both are defined via syntactic translations in the Haskell98 report. For as-patterns, the following translation is used:

$$\mathsf{case}\ v\ \mathsf{of}\{x@p \to e;\ \_ \to e'\} \qquad = \qquad \mathsf{case}\ v\ \mathsf{of}\{p \to (\lambda x \to e)\ v;\ \_ \to e'\}$$

In PMC, we can arrange this slightly more economically, thanks to the possibility to have sequential matchings — in Haskell with pattern guards, the same approach would be possible:

$$x@p \mapsto m \qquad = \qquad x \mapsto x \triangleright p \mapsto m$$

Although irrefutable patterns appear to be much more intricate, the Haskell98 report formally defines these using a straight-forward translation:

$$
\begin{aligned}
&\mathsf{case}\ v\ \mathsf{of}\{\tilde{}p \to e;\ \_ \to e'\} \\
&= (\lambda x_1 \ldots x_n \to e)\ (\mathsf{case}\ v\ \mathsf{of}\{p \to x_1\})\ \ldots\ (\mathsf{case}\ v\ \mathsf{of}\{p \to x_n\}) \\
&\qquad \text{where } x_1, \ldots, x_n \text{ are all the variables in } p
\end{aligned}
$$

Non-strictness implies that matching (with potential failure) is only performed when evaluation of e requires one of the x_i. We can follow the same approach:

$$
\begin{aligned}
\tilde{}p \mapsto m\ =\ &y \mapsto (y \triangleright p \mapsto x_1) \triangleright x_1 \mapsto \ldots (y \triangleright p \mapsto x_n) \triangleright x_n \mapsto m \\
&\text{where } x_1, \ldots, x_n \text{ are all the variables in } p \text{ and } y \text{ is a new variable.}
\end{aligned}
$$

The above two translations could be used as reduction rules. Another option is to restrict ourselves to a core calculus where only variables can be arguments of constructors in patterns; then the above two translations turn into expansion rules and we can consider as-patterns and irrefutable patterns as syntactic sugar. This approach also requires an expansion rule for nested patterns, considering them as just an abbreviation for sequential matchings:

$$
\begin{aligned}
c(p_1, \ldots, p_n) \mapsto m\ \ :=\ \ &c(y_1, \ldots, y_n) \mapsto y_1 \triangleright p_1 \mapsto \cdots y_n \triangleright p_n \mapsto m \\
&\text{where } y_1, \ldots, y_n \text{ are distinct new variables.}
\end{aligned}
$$

With this, pattern semantics becomes slightly easier to formulate, but nothing else really changes.

3 PMC Monads

We will define the semantics for PMC in an abstract categorical setting; we assume some "standard" familiarity with category theory basics (some more details are supplied in the appendix). We quickly introduce the notations we need in Sect. 3.1, then characterise the bi-monadic setting for PMC-semantics in Sect. 3.2, and also explain some simple instances of this setting.

3.1 Summary of Categorical Notation

We will define the semantics for PMC in an abstract categorical setting; in this section we assume some "standard" familiarity with category theory basics, and quickly introduce the notations we need.

We write $f : a \to b$ for a morphism with *source* object a and *target* object b. The identity on object a is id_a, and composition of morphisms $f : a \to b$ and $g : b \to c$ is written $f \mathbin{;} g$.

We assume a choice $\times$ of binary products with projections $\mathsf{fst}_{a,b} : a \times b \to a$ and $\mathsf{snd}_{a,b} : a \times b \to b$, and morphism pairing $\langle f, g \rangle : c \to a \times b$ for morphisms $f : c \to a$ and $g : c \to b$. We will denote by $\mathsf{term}_a : a \to \mathbb{1}$ the unique morphism into the terminal object $\mathbb{1}$.

As we restrict ourselves to cartesian closed categories, for every two objects a and b, there are an exponential object (for "functions from a to b") written $[a \to b]$, a "function application" morphism $\mathsf{eval}_{[a \to b]} : [a \to b] \times a \to b$, and a currying operation Λ that maps every morphism $f : c \times a \to b$ to the unique morphism $\Lambda f : c \to [a \to b]$ such that $(\Lambda f \times \mathrm{id}_a) \mathbin{;} \mathsf{eval}_{[a \to b]} = f$.

We essentially follow Barr and Wells [1] in adopting the following notations: we write $\Pi i : \mathcal{I} \bullet a(i)$ for the indexed (but not necessarily ordered) product over the *finite* index set $\mathcal{I}$, with component $a(i)$ for index i; the projection to the sub-product indexed by elements of a subset $\mathcal{J} \subseteq \mathcal{I}$ is

$$\mathsf{proj}^a_{I \succ J} : (\Pi i : \mathcal{I} \bullet a(i)) \to (\Pi i : \mathcal{J} \bullet a(i)) \ .$$

We identify singleton products with their components: $(\Pi i : \{j\} \bullet a(i)) = a(j)$.

We will follow category theoretic usage in writing both the object mapping and the morphism mapping of a functor as an application of the functor name so that for a functor H and a morphism $f : a \to b$ we have $H f : H a \to H b$.

A *monad* is a triple $(M, \mathsf{return}^M, \mathsf{join}^M)$ consisting of a functor M together with two natural transformations which, for readability, we also present as polymorphic morphisms:

$$\begin{array}{llll} \mathsf{return}^M : \mathrm{id} \to M & , \text{ i.e.,} & \mathsf{return}^M_a : a \to M\, a \\ \mathsf{join}^M \ \ : M \mathbin{;} M \to M & , \text{ i.e.,} & \mathsf{join}^M_a \ \ : M\,(M\,a) \to M\,a \end{array}$$

Every monad M gives rise to a so-called Kleisli category; it has return^M morphisms as identities, and for arrows $f : a \to M\, b$ and $g : b \to M\, c$, composition is defined as:

$$\begin{array}{l} f \odot_{\mathsf{M}} g \ : \ a \to M\, c \\ f \odot_{\mathsf{M}} g = f \mathbin{;} M\, g \mathbin{;} \mathsf{join}^M_c \end{array}$$

An *additive monad* in addition has two natural transformations

$$\mathsf{zero}^M : \mathbb{1} \to M \qquad\text{, i.e.,} \qquad \mathsf{zero}^M_a : \mathbb{1} \to M\ a$$
$$\mathsf{plus}^M : M \times M \to M \text{, i.e.,} \qquad \mathsf{plus}^M_a : M\ a \times M\ a \to M\ a$$

with zero^M being (up to the canonical isomorphisms) a right and left unit for plus^M, and plus^M associative.

As Moggi explains in [15], we need *strong monads* for being able to deal with expressions with more than one free variable; a strong monad M has a natural transformation

$$\mathsf{strengthL}^M_{a,b} : a \times M\ b \to M\ (a \times b)$$

called *tensorial strength* satisfying several properties. Using the isomorphism ($\mathsf{swap}_{a,b}$ from $a \times b$ to $b \times a$), we can define the "swapped version" $\mathsf{strengthR}^M_{a,b} :$ $M\ a \times b \to M\ (a \times b)$. This allows us to define

$$\otimes_M : (M\ a \times M\ b) \to M(a \times b)\ ,$$

as well as an n-ary version, denoted $\bigotimes_M$, defined via folding over ordered tuples.

3.2   The Bi-monadic Setting

We need a monad E for the expression semantics, and an additive monad M for the matching semantics, so we have zero^M and plus^M. In addition, there should be two natural transformations

$$\mathsf{extract} : M \to E \text{, i.e.,} \qquad \mathsf{extract}_a : M\ a \to E\ a$$
$$\mathsf{lift} : E \to M \text{, i.e.,} \qquad \mathsf{lift}_a : E\ a \to M\ a$$

satisfying the following additional laws:

$$\mathsf{lift}\mathbin{\mathsf{;}}\mathsf{extract} = \mathsf{id}_E \qquad\text{, i.e.,} \qquad \mathsf{lift}_a\mathbin{\mathsf{;}}\mathsf{extract}_a = \mathsf{id}_{E\ a} \qquad (\mathsf{lift}\mathbin{\mathsf{;}}\mathsf{extract})$$
$$\mathsf{return}^E\mathbin{\mathsf{;}}\mathsf{lift} = \mathsf{return}^M \text{, i.e.,} \qquad \mathsf{return}^E_a\mathbin{\mathsf{;}}\mathsf{lift}_a = \mathsf{return}^M_a \qquad (\mathsf{return}^E\mathbin{\mathsf{;}}\mathsf{lift})$$

The law ($\mathsf{lift}\mathbin{\mathsf{;}}\mathsf{extract}$) ensures that lift_a is injective; a further consequences of these laws is:

$$\mathsf{return}^M_a\mathbin{\mathsf{;}}\mathsf{extract}_a = \mathsf{return}^E_a\mathbin{\mathsf{;}}\mathsf{lift}_a\mathbin{\mathsf{;}}\mathsf{extract}_a = \mathsf{return}^E_a\ .$$

Although it is tempting to demand that lift and $\mathsf{extract}$ should be monad homomorphisms, i.e., not only preserve return, but also join, we have not found it necessary to make that assumption for proving that the core PMC reduction rules are sound with respect to the semantics given in Sect. 4.

Two particularly simple patterns of binmonadic settings will cover most of the examples discussed in Sect. 6:

Setting 3.2.1 (M = E)
We can use the same monad in both rôles of matching monad and expression monad, with identical natural transformations for $\mathsf{extract}$ and lift. Such a setting trivially satisfies the laws ($\mathsf{lift}\mathbin{\mathsf{;}}\mathsf{extract}$) and ($\mathsf{return}^E\mathbin{\mathsf{;}}\mathsf{lift}$).

Setting 3.2.2 ($M = E + \mathbb{1}$)

More interesting is the case where the image of zero_a^M is disjoint from the image of lift_a.

On the first class of settings we consider, the matching monad M is the monad coproduct [13] of the expression monad E and the constant monad $\mathbb{1}$. This gives us as the two monad coproduct injections the natural transformations $\mathsf{lift} : E \to M$ and $\mathsf{zero}^M : \mathbb{1} \to M$; since these commute by definition with return and join, the law ($\mathsf{return}^E \mathbin{;} \mathsf{lift}$) is automatically satisfied.

For any choice of monad homomorphism $\mathsf{empty}^E : \mathbb{1} \to E$, we then define $\mathsf{extract} : M \to E$ as the mediating morphism $\mathsf{extract} := [\mathsf{id}_E, \mathsf{empty}^E]$, and from the coproduct definition we immediately obtain ($\mathsf{lift} \mathbin{;} \mathsf{extract}$).

For the additive part of M, we still need to define $\mathsf{plus}^M : M \times M \to M$. To be able to essentially follow the additive pattern of the Maybe monad, we restrict ourselves to cases where there is a distribution isomorphism $\mathsf{distrL}_{E,\mathbb{1}}$ from $M \times M = (E + \mathbb{1}) \times M$ to $(E \times M) + (\mathbb{1} \times M)$, so we can define:

$$\mathsf{plus}^M = \mathsf{distrL}_{E,\mathbb{1}} \mathbin{;} [\mathsf{fst}_{E,M}, \mathsf{snd}_{\mathbb{1},M}]$$

4   Monadic **PMC** Semantics

The semantics in this section is very much influenced by previous work, more specifically [14, 15, 9].

4.1   Type Semantics

The interpretation of function types is different for matchings and expressions. Therefore, for defining type semantics in the setting of the two monads E and M, we will use $K \in \{E, M\}$ as a meta-variable to unify treatment of expression and matching semantics.

For each of our two syntactic categories of expressions and matchings, we will define below *two* different type semantics (both parameterised with a monad K) for each type α:

- the "raw" type semantics $[\![\alpha]\!]_K$, and
- the "standard" type semantics $[\![\alpha]\!]^K$.

As a mnemonic rule, one could remember that "superscript semantics" $[\![\alpha]\!]^K = K [\![\alpha]\!]_K$ is, in a generalised way, "in" the monad, while subscript $[\![\alpha]\!]_K$ semantics only "involves" the monad, where "involving" means that the type typically is a container of items "in" the monad.

Constructed Types

For each constructed type τ, the type semantics is obtained from the raw type semantics by application of the corresponding monad:

$$[\![\tau]\!]^K = K [\![\tau]\!]_K \ ,$$

and the "raw" semantics $[\![\tau]\!]_K$ is the direct sum (over all constructors producing this type) of the direct products of the corresponding constructor argument types.[2] Since constructor applications take expressions as arguments, these argument types have to be wrapped in the expression semantics monad E — the raw semantics of constructed types τ does indeed not depend on K.

$$[\![\tau]\!]_K = \biguplus_{n \in \mathbb{N}, (c : \alpha_1 \times \cdots \times \alpha_n \to \tau) \in \mathsf{Constr}} [\![\overline{\alpha}]\!]_E$$

where we use $[\![\overline{\alpha}]\!]_E$ to denote

$$[\![\alpha_1]\!]^E \times \cdots \times [\![\alpha_n]\!]^E$$

A constructor $c : \alpha_1 \times \cdots \times \alpha_n \to \tau$ is then interpreted by the corresponding *constructor injection* $c^E : [\![\overline{\alpha}]\!]_E \to [\![\tau]\!]_E$ together with the corresponding *destructor morphism*:

$$\widetilde{c}^E : [\![\tau]\!]_E \to M\left([\![\overline{\alpha}]\!]_E\right)$$

such that $c^E \text{\textsemicolon} \widetilde{c}^E = \mathsf{return}^M_{[\![\overline{\alpha}]\!]_E}$ and, if $c \neq d$, with $d : \beta_1 \times \cdots \times \beta_n \to \tau_d$, then:

$$d^E \text{\textsemicolon} \widetilde{c}^E = \mathsf{term}^{\mathcal{C}}_{[\![\overline{\beta}]\!]_E} \text{\textsemicolon} \mathsf{zero}^M_{[\![\overline{\alpha}]\!]_E}$$

Function Types
Now consider the raw semantics of function types. Since *all* application constructs of the PMC syntax (constructor application, function application, and argument supply) take *expressions* as arguments, the argument type in the K-semantics will always be the *expression* type semantics of the argument type β. The result type however depends on the context, and will therefore be the (raw) K-semantics of the result type γ:

$$[\![\beta \to \gamma]\!]_K = [[\![\beta]\!]^E \to [\![\gamma]\!]_K]$$

$$[\![\beta \to \gamma]\!]^K = [[\![\beta]\!]^E \to [\![\gamma]\!]^K]$$

In order to ease analysis of our semantics, we provide essentially full type information, but this tends to blow up our notation. We therefore incorporates the function type semantics pattern into a variant notation for eval:

$$\mathsf{Eval}^K_{\beta,\gamma} \;:\; [\![\beta \to \gamma]\!]^K \times [\![\beta]\!]^E \;\to\; [\![\gamma]\!]^K$$

$$\mathsf{Eval}^K_{\beta,\gamma} := \mathsf{eval}_{[[\![\beta]\!]^E \to [\![\gamma]\!]^K]}$$

---

[2] Since, normally, only finite sets of constructors are considered, practical applications only require finite sums to exist in the underlying category.

Point-Wise Extension Combinators

Since the semantics of function types is not directly monadic, we need a generalisation of Kleisli composition: If $f : q \to \mathsf{K}\, r$ and $g : r \to [\![\alpha]\!]^{\mathsf{K}}$, then $(f \boxdot_{\alpha}^{\mathsf{K}} g) : q \to [\![\alpha]\!]^{\mathsf{K}}$ is defined by:

$$f \boxdot_{\tau}^{\mathsf{K}} g = f \odot_{\mathsf{K}} g$$

$$f \boxdot_{\beta \to \gamma}^{\mathsf{K}} g = \Lambda\left(((f \times \mathrm{id}_{[\![\beta]\!]^{\mathsf{E}}}) \mathbin{;} \mathsf{strengthR}_{r,[\![\beta]\!]}^{\mathsf{K}}) \boxdot_{\gamma}^{\mathsf{K}} ((g \times \mathrm{id}_{[\![\beta]\!]^{\mathsf{E}}}) \mathbin{;} \mathsf{Eval}_{\beta,\gamma}^{\mathsf{K}}) \right)$$

This behaves "mostly like" Kleisli composition: we have $(f \mathbin{;} g) \boxdot_{\alpha}^{\mathsf{K}} h = f \mathbin{;} (g \boxdot_{\alpha}^{\mathsf{K}} h)$, so we can omit those parentheses, and we also have $\mathsf{return}_r^{\mathsf{K}} \boxdot_{\alpha}^{\mathsf{K}} g = g$.

Because of the way we treat of function types, we shall frequently need a construction that corresponds to "point-wise extension to function types" of the composition $f \mathbin{;} t_{[\![\tau]\!]}$ of a morphism $f : q \to [\![\tau]\!]^{\mathsf{K}}$ with a transformation $t : \mathsf{K} \to \mathsf{H}$. For this purpose, we define a following "generalised composition" operation inductively over the function type structure.

If $f : q \to [\![\alpha]\!]^{\mathsf{K}}$, then $\left[_{q}\, f\, \boxed{;}^{\alpha}\, t\, \right] : q \to [\![\alpha]\!]^{\mathsf{H}}$ is defined by:[3]

$$\left[_{q}\, f\, \boxed{;}^{\tau}\quad t\, \right] = f \mathbin{;} t_{[\![\tau]\!]}$$

$$\left[_{q}\, f\, \boxed{;}^{\beta \to \gamma}\, t\, \right] = \Lambda\left[_{q \times [\![\beta]\!]^{\mathsf{E}}}\, (f \times \mathrm{id}_{[\![\beta]\!]^{\mathsf{E}}}) \mathbin{;} \mathsf{Eval}_{\beta,\gamma}^{\mathsf{K}}\, \boxed{;}^{\gamma}\, t\, \right]$$

This even works for $\mathsf{K} = \mathbb{1}$ since the constant functor $\mathbb{1}$ is trivially a strong monad; in this case all f arguments are morphisms to the terminal object $\mathbb{1}$.

Similarly, we need a "pointwise extension" of $\mathsf{plus}^{\mathsf{M}}$ to function types: For two morphisms $g_1, g_2 : q \to [\![\alpha]\!]^{\mathsf{M}}$, we define $g_1 \boxplus_{\alpha} g_2 : q \to [\![\alpha]\!]^{\mathsf{M}}$ as:

$$g_1 \boxplus_{\tau} g_2 = \langle g_1, g_2 \rangle \mathbin{;} \mathsf{plus}^{\mathsf{M}} \qquad g_1 \boxplus_{\beta \to \gamma} g_2 = \Lambda\begin{pmatrix} (g_1 \times \mathrm{id}_{[\![\beta]\!]^{\mathsf{E}}}) \mathbin{;} \mathsf{Eval}_{\beta,\gamma}^{\mathsf{M}} \\ \boxplus_{\gamma} \\ (g_2 \times \mathrm{id}_{[\![\beta]\!]^{\mathsf{E}}}) \mathbin{;} \mathsf{Eval}_{\beta,\gamma}^{\mathsf{M}} \end{pmatrix}$$

The following properties enable high-level reasoning using the point-wise extension combinators defined above; the proofs can be found in [10]:

$$\left(\left[_{q}\, f\, \boxed{;}^{\beta \to \gamma}\, t\, \right] \times g\right) \mathbin{;} \mathsf{Eval}_{\beta,\gamma}^{\mathsf{H}} = \left[_{q \times r}\, (f \times g) \mathbin{;} \mathsf{Eval}_{\beta,\gamma}^{\mathsf{K}}\, \boxed{;}^{\gamma}\, t\, \right]$$

$$f \mathbin{;} \left[_{r}\, g\, \boxed{;}^{\alpha}\, t\, \right] = \left[_{q}\, f \mathbin{;} g\, \boxed{;}^{\alpha}\, t\, \right]$$

$$\left[_{q}\, \left[_{q}\, f\, \boxed{;}^{\alpha}\, t\, \right]\, \boxed{;}^{\alpha}\, u\, \right] = \left[_{q}\, f\, \boxed{;}^{\alpha}\, t \mathbin{;} u\, \right]$$

$$f \mathbin{;} (g_1 \boxplus_{\alpha} g_2) = f \mathbin{;} g_1 \boxplus_{\alpha} f \mathbin{;} g_2$$

$$((g_1 \boxplus_{\beta \to \gamma} g_2) \times h) \mathbin{;} \mathsf{Eval}_{\beta,\gamma}^{\mathsf{H}} = ((g_1 \times h) \mathbin{;} \mathsf{Eval}_{\beta,\gamma}^{\mathsf{H}}) \boxplus_{\gamma} ((g_2 \times h) \mathbin{;} \mathsf{Eval}_{\beta,\gamma}^{\mathsf{H}})$$

---

[3] Note that the transformation t has to be mentioned in $\left[_{q}\, f\, \boxed{;}^{\alpha}\, t\, \right]$ without type argument, since it will be instantiated as $t_a : \mathsf{K}\, a \to \mathsf{H}\, a$ at different types a.
Also note that we put the subscript q not close to the box, but after the opening parenthesis, since q is the type "before f".

4.2 Organisation of the Semantic Functions

While in strict languages, in the rewriting semantics only values can be substituted for variables, and analogously only values need to be bound to variables by the valuations in the denotational semantics, we are here targeting non-strict languages, where the operational semantics can substitute arbitrary expressions for variables, and therefore, analogously, the type of the denotational variable semantics has to coincide with that of the expression semantics. The object associated with a variable is therefore the E-image of the object that interprets the variable's type.

Pattern semantics:

$$[\![p]\!]_\alpha^P \qquad\quad : [\![\alpha]\!]^E \to M\,(FV(p)^E)$$

$$[\![v]\!]^P \qquad\quad = \mathsf{return}^M_{vE}$$

$$[\![c(p_1,\ldots,p_n)]\!]_\tau^P = \mathsf{lift}_{[\![\tau]\!]} \odot_M \widetilde{c}^E \odot_M \left(([\![p_1]\!]^P \times \cdots \times [\![p_n]\!]^P); \bigotimes\right)$$

> for $c : \alpha_1 \times \cdots \times \alpha_n \to \tau$.
> The target type here is isomorphic to $M\,(\Pi v : FV(p) \bullet [\![\mathsf{type}(v)]\!]^E)$; for the sake of conciseness we consider these two types as identified.

Expression semantics:

$$[\![e]\!]_{\mathcal{V},\alpha}^E \qquad\quad : \mathcal{V}^E \to [\![\alpha]\!]^E$$

$$[\![v]\!]_{\mathcal{V}}^E \qquad\quad = \mathsf{proj}_{\mathcal{V} \succ \{v\}}^E$$

$$[\![c(e_1,\ldots,e_n)]\!]_{\mathcal{V}}^E = \langle [\![e_1]\!]_{\mathcal{V}}^E,\ldots,[\![e_n]\!]_{\mathcal{V}}^E \rangle; c^E; \mathsf{return}_{[\![\alpha]\!]E}^E$$

$$[\![f\ a]\!]_{\mathcal{V},\gamma}^E \qquad = \langle [\![f]\!]_{\mathcal{V},\beta\to\gamma}^E, [\![a]\!]_{\mathcal{V},\beta}^E \rangle; \mathsf{Eval}_{\beta,\gamma}^E$$

$$[\![\{\!|\,m\,|\!\}]\!]_{\mathcal{V},\alpha}^E \qquad = \left[_{\mathcal{V}E}\,[\![m]\!]_{\mathcal{V},\alpha}^M\,\boxed{;}^\alpha\,\mathsf{extract}\,\right]$$

$$[\![\varnothing_\alpha]\!]_{\mathcal{V}}^E \qquad = \left[_{\mathcal{V}E}\,\mathsf{term}_{\mathcal{V}E}^{\mathcal{C}}\,\boxed{;}^\alpha\,\mathsf{zero}^M; \mathsf{extract}\,\right]$$

Matching semantics:

$$[\![m]\!]_{\mathcal{V},\alpha}^M \qquad\quad : \mathcal{V}^E \to [\![\alpha]\!]^M$$

$$[\![\mathbb{1}\,e\mathbb{1}]\!]_{\mathcal{V},\alpha}^M \qquad = \left[_{\mathcal{V}E}\,[\![e]\!]_{\mathcal{V}}^E\,\boxed{;}^\alpha\,\mathsf{lift}\,\right]$$

$$[\![\mathord{\not\Leftarrow}_\alpha]\!]_{\mathcal{V},\alpha}^M \qquad = \left[_{\mathcal{V}E}\,\mathsf{term}_{\mathcal{V}E}^{\mathcal{C}}\,\boxed{;}^\alpha\,\mathsf{zero}^M\,\right]$$

$$[\![a \vartriangleright m]\!]_{\mathcal{V},\gamma}^M \qquad = \langle [\![m]\!]_{\mathcal{V},\beta\to\gamma}^M, [\![a]\!]_{\mathcal{V},\beta}^E \rangle; \mathsf{Eval}_{\beta,\gamma}^M$$

$$[\![m_1 \mid m_2]\!]_{\mathcal{V},\alpha}^M \qquad = [\![m_1]\!]_{\mathcal{V},\alpha}^M \boxplus_\alpha [\![m_2]\!]_{\mathcal{V},\alpha}^M$$

$$[\![p \mapsto m]\!]_{\mathcal{V},\beta\to\gamma}^M = \Lambda\left((\mathsf{proj}_{\mathcal{V} \succ \mathcal{U}}^E \times [\![p]\!]_\beta^P)\,;\,\mathsf{strengthL}_{\mathcal{U}E,FV(p)E}^M\,\boxdot_\gamma^M\,[\![m]\!]_{\mathcal{U}\oplus FV(p),\gamma}^M\right)$$

> where $\mathcal{U} = \mathcal{V} \setminus FV(p)$, and a product rearrangement morphism is again omitted

---

Fig. 1. PMC semantics

For the sake of conciseness and readability, we abbreviate the object corresponding to the type of a variable v by

$$v^E := [\![\text{type}(v)]\!]^E$$

and also introduce similar notation for each set $\mathcal{V}$ of variables:

$$\mathcal{V}^E := \Pi v : \mathcal{V} \bullet [\![\text{type}(v)]\!]^E$$

Since we want the reduction rules to translate into semantic equations, both sides of a rule always have to be interpreted in a compatible way; since the reduction rules do not preserve all free variables, we have to externally impose a source object for the semantic morphisms.

Therefore, given a variable set $\mathcal{V}$, we define the semantics of an expression e of type α with $\text{FV}(e) \subseteq \mathcal{V}$ as a morphism from the product corresponding to the variable set $\mathcal{V}$ to the object corresponding to α:

$$[\![e]\!]^E_{\mathcal{V},\alpha} : \mathcal{V}^E \to [\![\alpha]\!]^E$$

(When the type α is clear from the context, we write $[\![e]\!]^E_{\mathcal{V}}$ instead of $[\![e]\!]^E_{\mathcal{V},\alpha}$, and analogously for the other semantics functions.)

For each matching m of type α, we define its semantics as a morphism in the Kleisli category for M from the variables to the result type:

$$[\![m]\!]^M_{\mathcal{V},\alpha} : \mathcal{V}^E \to [\![\alpha]\!]^M$$

Finally, to each pattern p of type α, we associate a morphism in the Kleisli category of M from the object used for expression semantics of type α to the object corresponding to the set of free variables of the pattern:

$$[\![p]\!]^P_\alpha : [\![\alpha]\!]^E \to M\ (\text{FV}(p)^E)$$

Constructor pattern semantics have to be "strict" as can be seen from the first occurrence of $\odot_M$ in the corresponding clause in Fig. 1.

The definitions for all three semantics functions are listed in Fig. 1.

5   Soundness of the Core Reduction Rules

For the core reduction rules of PMC listed in Fig. 2 (see [11] and Appendix A for more explanation), we prove the following soundness result in appendix [10]:

Theorem 5.1 All core reduction rules listed in Fig. 2 are sound at arbitrary types.   □

Here is a quick summary of which assumptions were crucial for the proofs to succeed; the detailed proofs, to be found in [10], mostly proceed at the level of the semantics definitions of Fig. 1, thanks to the properties of the "pointwise extensions" operators $\boxed{;}^\alpha$ and $\boxplus_\alpha$ listed in Sect. 4.1.

$$\begin{array}{llll}
\text{↯} \mid m \xrightarrow[M]{} m & (\text{↯}\mid) & e \rhd (m_1 \mid m_2) \xrightarrow[M]{} (e \rhd m_1) \mid (e \rhd m_2) & (\rhd\mid) \\[2mm]
\{\!\mid\!\text{↯}\!\mid\!\} \xrightarrow[E]{} \oslash & (\{\!\mid\!\text{↯}\!\mid\!\}) & \{\!\mid\!\lceil e \rceil\!\mid\!\} \xrightarrow[E]{} e & (\{\!\mid\!\lceil\rceil\!\mid\!\}) \\[2mm]
\oslash\, e \xrightarrow[E]{} \oslash & (\oslash@) & \{\!\mid\! m \!\mid\!\}\, a \xrightarrow[E]{} \{\!\mid\! a \rhd m \!\mid\!\} & (\{\!\mid\!\mid\!\}@) \\[2mm]
e \rhd \text{↯} \xrightarrow[M]{} \text{↯} & (\rhd\text{↯}) & a \rhd \lceil e \rceil \xrightarrow[M]{} \lceil e\, a \rceil & (\rhd\lceil\rceil) \\[2mm]
& & a \rhd v \mapsto m \xrightarrow[M]{} m[v\backslash a] & (\rhd v)
\end{array}$$

$$d(e_1,\ldots,e_k) \rhd c(p_1,\ldots,p_n) \mapsto m \xrightarrow[M]{} \text{↯} \qquad \text{if } c \neq d \text{ or } k \neq n \qquad (d \rhd c)$$

$$c(e_1,\ldots,e_n) \rhd c(p_1,\ldots,p_n) \mapsto m \xrightarrow[M]{} e_1 \rhd p_1 \mapsto \cdots e_n \rhd p_n \mapsto m \qquad (c \rhd c)$$

$$\text{if } \mathsf{FV}(c(e_1,\ldots,e_n)) \cap \mathsf{FV}(c(p_1,\ldots,p_n)) = \{\}$$

Fig. 2. PMC core reduction rules

- $(\text{↯}\mid)$ relies on zero_τ^M being a left-unit for plus_τ^M.
- $(\rhd\mid)$ relies crucially on the type-dependent, recursive definition of $\boxplus$.
- $(\{\!\mid\!\text{↯}\!\mid\!\})$ relies on compositionality for $\boxed{;}^\alpha$.
- $(\{\!\mid\!\lceil\rceil\!\mid\!\})$ is because $\mathsf{lift}_\tau\text{;}\mathsf{extract}_\tau = \mathsf{id}_\tau$
- $(\{\!\mid\!\mid\!\}@)$ and $(\rhd\lceil\rceil)$ are both a reflection of the symmetry of the rules for supply and application, as well as commutativity of $\boxplus$ and Eval.
- $(\oslash@)$ and $(\rhd\text{↯})$ rely on the same properties as $(\{\!\mid\!\mid\!\}@)$ and $(\rhd\lceil\rceil)$, but also on the definition of $\oslash$ and ↯ at function types, which reflect their being defined "pointwise".
- $(\rhd v)$ corresponds to β-reduction in λ-calculi, and relies on standard categorical and monadic properties.
- $(c \rhd c)$ relies crucially on the fact that $c^{\mathsf{E}}\text{;}\widetilde{c}^{\mathsf{E}} = \mathsf{return}^M_{\mathsf{E}\,[\![\alpha]\!]_\mathsf{E} \to [\![\tau]\!]}$, as well on $\mathsf{return}^M_a\text{;}\mathsf{extract}_a = \mathsf{return}^\mathsf{E}_a$, and on $\varLambda$ being able to curry multiple variables.
- $(d \rhd c)$ relies on $d^{\mathsf{E}}\text{;}\widetilde{c}^{\mathsf{E}} = \mathsf{term}^\mathcal{C}_{[\![\beta]\!]_\mathsf{E}}\text{;}\mathsf{zero}^M_{[\![\alpha]\!]_\mathsf{E}}$ for $d \neq c$, and on propagation of zero^M by strength.

6   Using Different Monad Instances

Depending on the choice of monads E and M, additional rules become sound. In deterministic functional programming, we have a rule that turns expression matchings into left-zeros for alternative, and so essentially prohibits backtracking (and non-deterministic choice):

$$\lceil e \rceil \mid m \xrightarrow[M]{} \lceil e \rceil \qquad (\lceil\rceil\mid)$$

For the case where an empty expression is matched against a constructor pattern, [11] offers two different right-hand sides:

- The first rule corresponds to interpreting the empty expression as equivalent to non-termination, as usual in Haskell:

$$\oslash \triangleright c(p_1, \ldots, p_n) \mapsto m \quad \xrightarrow[\mathsf{M}]{} \quad \mathord{\uparrow}\oslash\mathord{\uparrow} \qquad\qquad (\oslash \triangleright c \to \oslash)$$

- The second rule corresponds to interpreting the empty expression as propagating the exception of matching failure as in the approach proposed in [4], this rule "resurrects" that failure:

$$\oslash \triangleright c(p_1, \ldots, p_n) \mapsto m \quad \xrightarrow[\mathsf{M}]{} \quad \mbox{\Lightning} \qquad\qquad (\oslash \triangleright c \to \mbox{\Lightning})$$

For each of the resulting rule sets, we now show a monadic setting making all the rules sound, and then go on to explore more general monads.

Haskell uses a non-strict cpo semantics where all objects have a least element undefined, but morphisms need not preserve this least element. Therefore, the essential building block of Haskell semantics is the "Haskell monad" H, which we define to be the lifting monad $\mathsf{H} := (\_)^\perp$ over an appropriate cartesian closed category (CCC) of cpo's.

6.1   Haskell

For standard Haskell semantics, we choose the above Haskell monad as the expression monad $\mathsf{E} := \mathsf{H}$, and complete this to a bimonadic setting as in Setting 3.2.2 with $\mathsf{M} = \mathsf{E} + \mathbb{1}$, choosing $\mathsf{empty}^\mathsf{E} : \mathbb{1} \to \mathsf{E}$ so that it maps failure to $\perp$.

This corresponds to the approaches used by Tullsen [19] and Harrison *et al.* [7, 8] which all essentially employ the Maybe monad for this kind of purpose.

This setting also makes the rules $(\mathord{\uparrow}\mathord{\uparrow}\,|)$ and $(\oslash \triangleright c \to \oslash)$ sound — which proves that $\mathsf{PMC}_\oslash$ as defined in [11] appropriately implements the semantics of Haskell.

6.2   Matching Failure as Exception

To achieve a semantics that is consistent with [4], and treats matching failure as exception that can be caught by other matching alternatives, $\oslash$ needs to be a zero for the expression monad E, which can chose as $\mathsf{E} = \mathsf{H} + \mathbb{1}$. If we complete this via Setting 3.2.1 with $\mathsf{M} = \mathsf{E}$, then this equates the semantics of $\mbox{\Lightning}$ and $\mathord{\uparrow}\oslash\mathord{\uparrow}$, and makes rule $(\oslash \triangleright c \to \mbox{\Lightning})$ sound. But it also has as consequence that the rule $(\mathord{\uparrow}\mathord{\uparrow}\,|)$, which corresponds to (deterministic) functional programming, introduces inconsistencies, e.g.:

$$\oslash = \{\!|\mathord{\uparrow}\oslash\mathord{\uparrow}|\!\} = \{\!|\mathord{\uparrow}\oslash\mathord{\uparrow}\,|\,142\mathord{\uparrow}|\!\} \stackrel{!}{=} \{\!|\mbox{\Lightning}\,|\,142\mathord{\uparrow}|\!\} = \{\!|142\mathord{\uparrow}|\!\} = 42$$

So this semantics informs us that in this case, we should not use the general rule $(\mathord{\uparrow}\mathord{\uparrow}\,|)$, but only restricted rules, e.g. $\mathord{\uparrow}c(e_q, \ldots, e_n)\mathord{\uparrow}\,|\,m \quad \xrightarrow[\mathsf{M}]{} \quad \mathord{\uparrow}c(e_q, \ldots, e_n)\mathord{\uparrow}$.

6.3   Functional-Logic Programming

Lazy functional-logic programming (FLP) extends lazy-functional programming with logic variables and non-deterministic choice and the ability that any expression evaluates to "multiple values". This kind of choice can be modelled for example using a list monad, a tree monad, or the LogicT monad of Kiselyov *et al.* [12].

By using this kind of monad both for M, where choice originates in PMC, and, following Setting 3.2.1 with E = M, also for the expression monad, to which it needs to propagate in FLP, we obtain an appropriate semantics for the fragment of FLP that can be expressed with the syntax of PMC as presented here. The pointwise extension behaviour of alternative in our semantics actually exactly corresponds to the way choice is treated in the functional-logic programming language Curry [5, 6]. (To obtain the full expressive power of FLP, we need to extend the pattern syntax with the third alternative of call-by-value variables — the details are beyond the scope of the present paper.)

6.4   Choice

A particularly interesting situation arises when the list monad is chosen for M, but just partiality for E. Then we get all possible matches, yet we must then return only a single valid result. This can be very useful in some situations where we have either an intrinsic measurement of "better" choices, or where choice is inevitable but inessential. The same algorithm, Gaussian Elimination, can serve as an example of both of these situations. [3] shows how for many different domains, there is an intrinsic notion of "better than" for the purposes of pivot choice. On the other hand, [18] shows that either multi-valuedness or non-determinism are necessary ingredients even for single-valued functions (like Gaussian Elimination) if one wishes to be fully abstract, in other words representation-independent. Correspondingly, the "better than" notions of [3] are generally representation-dependent. Having a convenient programming language where we can disentangle these issues would clearly be beneficial. We believe that this could allow versions of some numerical algorithms, in the style of [2], to be made even more generic.

7   Conclusion and Outlook

Using a monad, most typically Maybe, for the semantics of pattern matching in Haskell-like languages has been proposed previously [19, 7, 8].

Since PMC offers a finer-grained, more systematic separation of pattern matching aspects from other expression evaluation aspects, choosing to interpret the two syntactic categories with separate monads is an obvious choice — the alternative of using a monad transformer deserves further exploration.

From this starting point, defining a general, monadic semantics for PMC required the resolution of two fine technical points:

- the necessity to use different definitions of the function type semantics for expressions and matchings, and
- the necessity to provide the corresponding "pointwise extensions" to the operations in the base monads.

As a result, assuming only remarkably light coupling of the two monads through the laws assumed for extract and lift, establishes the soundness of all the core reduction rules of the two PMC calculi defined in [11], which is all their common rules except the rule $(\uparrow\uparrow\mathbf{|})$ expressing that the first success of a matching will be its only result, and therefore obviously would exclude monads with a non-determinism or backtracking component from being used for matching semantics.

By not including such an assumption, we keep our bi-monadic PMC semantics open to uses also in functional-logic programming, which is one of the topics we plan to explore in more depth in the future, and we are extending our current prototype Haskell implementation of PMC reduction and of the semantics presented in the paper to serve as a test-bed for exploration in this direction.

It is also quite intriguing that by just taking two List monads, one gets "all" answers out of programs written as pure functions, if the patterns turned out to be overlapping. Generalising this further, to say tree monads, is definitely worth exploring.

Finally we would like to use the given semantics as justification for transformation rules that are useful for compilation of non-strict pattern matching.

Acknowledgements. We would like to thank the anonymous referees for their valuable comments.

Wolfram Kahl and Xiaoheng Xi were supported by the National Science and Engineering Research Council (NSERC), Canada.

References

1. Barr, M., Wells, C.: Category Theory for Computing Science. 3rd edn. Centre de recherches mathématiques (CRM), Université de Montréal (1999)
2. Carette, J., Kiselyov, O.: Multi-stage programming with functors and monads: eliminating abstraction overhead from generic code. In Glück, R., Lowry, M. R., eds.: Proc. of 4th Int. Conf. on Generative Programming and Component Engineering, GPCE 2005. Vol. 3676 of Lect. Notes in Comput. Sci. Springer-Verlag (2005) 256–274
3. Carette, J.: Gaussian elimination: a case study in efficient genericity with Meta-OCaml. Sci. of Comput. Program. (to appear)
4. Erwig, M., Peyton Jones, S.: Pattern guards and transformational patterns. In Proc. of 2000 ACM SIGPLAN Haskell Wksh., Haskell 2000. Electron. Notes in Theor. Comput. Sci. **41**(1) (2001) 27 pp.
5. Hanus, M.: A unified computation model for declarative programming. In Proc. of 1997 APPIA-GULP-PRODE Joint Conf. on Declarative Programming. (1997) 9–24
6. Hanus, M. et al.: Curry—an integrated functional logic language, version 0.8.2 (2006) http://www.informatik.uni-kiel.de/~{}curry/report.html.

7. Harrison, W. L., Sheard, T., Hook, J.: Fine control of demand in Haskell. In Boiten, E. A., Möller, B., eds.: Proc. of 6th Int. Conf. on Mathematics of Program Construction, MPC 2002. Vol. 2386 of Lect. Notes in Comput. Sci. Springer-Verlag (2002) 68–93

8. Harrison, W. L., Kieburtz, R. B.: The logic of demand in Haskell. J. of Funct. Program. **15**(6) (2005) 837–891

9. Jung, A., Fiore, M., Moggi, E., O'Hearn, P., Riecke, J., Rosolini, G., Stark, I.: Domains and denotational semantics: history, accomplishments and open problems. Bull. of EATCS **59** (1996) 227–256

10. Kahl, W., Carette, J., Ji, X.: Bimonadic semantics for basic pattern matching calculi. SQRL Report 33. Software Quality Research Laboratory, McMaster Univ., (2003) Available from `http://sqrl.mcmaster.ca/sqrl_reports.html`.

11. Kahl, W.: Basic pattern matching calculi: a fresh view on matching failure. In Kameyama, Y., Stuckey, P., eds.: Proc. of 7th Int. Symp. on Functional and Logic Programming, FLOPS 2004. Vol. 2998 of Lect. Notes in Comput. Sci. Springer-Verlag (2004) 276–290

12. Kiselyov, O., Shan, C.-c., Friedman, D. P., Sabry, A.: Backtracking, interleaving, and terminating monad transformers. In Proc. of 10th Int. Conf. on Functional Programming, ICFP 2005. ACM Press (2005) 192–203

13. Lüth, C., Ghani, N.: Composing monads using coproducts. In Proc. of 7th Int. Conf. on Functional Programming, ICFP 2002. ACM Press (2002) 133–144

14. Moggi, E.: A modular approach to denotational semantics. In Pitt, D. H. et al., eds.: Proc. of 4th Int. Conf. on Category Theory and Computer Science, CTCS '91. Vol. 530 of Lect. Notes in Comput. Sci. Springer-Verlag (1991) 138–139

15. Moggi, E.: Notions of computation and monads. Inform. and Comput. **93** (1991) 55–92

16. Peyton Jones, S. et al.: The Revised Haskell 98 Report. Cambridge Univ. Press (2003) Also available from `http://haskell.org/`.

17. Plasmeijer, R., van Eekelen, M.: Functional Programming and Parallel Graph Rewriting. Int. Computer Science Series. Addison-Wesley (1993)

18. Tucker, J. V., Zucker, J. I.: Abstract versus concrete computation on metric partial algebras. ACM Trans. Comput. Logic **5**(4) (2004) 611–668

19. Tullsen, M.: First class patterns. In Pontelli, E., Santos Costa, V., eds.: Proc. of 2nd Int. Wksh. on Practical Aspects of Declarative Languages, PADL 2000. Vol. 1753 of Lect. Notes in Comput. Sci. Springer-Verlag (2000) 1–15

A PMC Core Reduction Rules

Here, we repeat from [11] the set of rules that implement the usual pattern matching semantics of non-strict functional programming languages by allowing corresponding reduction of PMC expressions as they arise from translating functional programs. In particular, we do not include extensionality rules.

Formally, we define separate *redex reduction* relations for expressions and matchings:

$$\xrightarrow[E]{} : \mathsf{Expr} \leftrightarrow \mathsf{Expr} \ , \qquad \text{and} \qquad \xrightarrow[M]{} : \mathsf{Match} \leftrightarrow \mathsf{Match} \ .$$

These are the smallest relations including the rules listed below. The resulting rewriting system contains a mix of first-order rules, rule schemata, and second-order rules; the first author described a direct confluence proof mechanised in

Isabelle and a deterministic normalising strategy (via reduction to strong head normal form) in [11].

A.1 Failure and Returning

Failure is the (left) unit for $|$:

$$\xi \mid m \quad \xrightarrow[M]{} \quad m \qquad\qquad (\xi\,|)$$

A matching abstraction where all alternatives fail can be understood as representing an ill-defined case — this is reduced to the "empty expression":

$$\{\!\{\xi\}\!\} \quad \xrightarrow[E]{} \quad \oslash \qquad\qquad (\{\!\{\xi\}\!\})$$

Matching abstractions built from expression matchings are equivalent to the contained expression:

$$\{\!\{ 1e\!\restriction\}\!\} \quad \xrightarrow[E]{} \quad e \qquad\qquad (\{\!\{1\!\restriction\}\!\})$$

A.2 Application and Argument Supply

Application of a matching abstraction reduces to argument supply inside the abstraction:

$$\{\!\{ m \}\!\}\, a \quad \xrightarrow[E]{} \quad \{\!\{ a \triangleright m \}\!\} \qquad\qquad (\{\!\{ \}\!\}@)$$

Argument supply to an expression matching reduces to function application inside the expression matching:

$$a \triangleright 1e\!\restriction \quad \xrightarrow[M]{} \quad 1e\,a\!\restriction \qquad\qquad (\triangleright 1\!\restriction)$$

No matter which of our two interpretations of the empty expression we choose, it absorbs arguments when used as function in an application:

$$\oslash\, e \quad \xrightarrow[E]{} \quad \oslash \qquad\qquad (\oslash @)$$

Analogously, failure absorbs argument supply:

$$e \triangleright \xi \quad \xrightarrow[M]{} \quad \xi \qquad\qquad (\triangleright\xi)$$

Argument supply distributes into alternatives:

$$e \triangleright (m_1 \mid m_2) \quad \xrightarrow[M]{} \quad (e \triangleright m_1) \mid (e \triangleright m_2) \qquad\qquad (\triangleright|)$$

A.3   Pattern Matching

Everything matches a variable pattern; this matching gives rise to substitution:

$$a \triangleright v \Mapsto m \quad \xrightarrow[\mathsf{M}]{} \quad m[v \backslash a] \qquad\qquad (\triangleright v)$$

Matching constructors match, and the proviso in the following rule can always be ensured via α-conversion (for this rule to make sense, linearity of patterns is important):

$$c(e_1, \ldots, e_n) \triangleright c(p_1, \ldots, p_n) \Mapsto m \quad \xrightarrow[\mathsf{M}]{} \quad e_1 \triangleright p_1 \Mapsto \cdots e_n \triangleright p_n \Mapsto m$$
$$\text{if } \mathsf{FV}(c(e_1, \ldots, e_n)) \cap \mathsf{FV}(c(p_1, \ldots, p_n)) = \{\} \qquad\qquad (c \triangleright c)$$

Matching of different constructors fails:

$$d(e_1, \ldots, e_k) \triangleright c(p_1, \ldots, p_n) \Mapsto m \quad \xrightarrow[\mathsf{M}]{} \quad \lightning \qquad\qquad \text{if } c \neq d \text{ or } k \neq n (d \triangleright c)$$

Nondeterministic Folds

Clare E. Martin and Sharon A. Curtis

Department of Computing, Oxford Brookes University,
Wheatley Campus, Oxford OX33 1HX, UK
cemartin@brookes.ac.uk, sharoncurtis@brookes.ac.uk

Abstract. The *map* and *fold* operators are both key elements of every functional programmer's toolkit. In this paper we examine the corresponding concepts in the domain of multirelations, which can be used to model both angelic and demonic nondeterminism.

1 Introduction

The *map* and *fold* operators of functional programming are both standard tools for capturing common patterns of recursion among list processing functions, and their relational equivalents are now widely used for the same purpose in specifications [Bi98, BdM97]. A less well-known fact is that both these operators also have predicate transformer equivalents which have not previously been used for program derivation. One reason for this lack of attention is that the operators do not take on a very familiar form in this context. Another reason is that the class of problems that require the expressive power of predicate transformers, as opposed to relations, is quite restricted. A third factor is that, apart from a few exceptions such as [W94], predicate transformers have traditionally been associated with the derivation of imperative, rather than functional programs. The first contribution of this paper is to show how, when viewed in the equivalent model of multirelations, the *map* and *fold* operators do look familiar, and this is illustrated by a number of concrete examples. The second contribution is to show how the laws associated with such operators can be used to transform specifications at this level.

Multirelations were introduced in [Rew03] as an alternative to predicate transformers for reasoning about specifications that contain both angelic and demonic nondeterminism. Angelic nondeterminism occurs when the choice is made by an 'angel': it is assumed that the angel will choose the best possible outcome. Demonic nondeterminism occurs when the choice is made by a 'demon': no assumption can be made about the choice made by the demon, so we must be prepared for the worst possible outcome. Ordinary relations can only be used to describe one of these kinds of nondeterminism at a time, but several convincing examples in [MCR04] show how well-suited multirelations are for expressing both. In our view, the primary advantage of multirelations over predicate transformers is that they model programs forwards rather than backwards. So, instead of mapping postconditions to preconditions, they can be used to relate inputs, or initial states, to outputs, or final states.

T. Uustalu (Ed.): MPC 2006, LNCS 4014, pp. 274–298, 2006.

The close relationship between multirelations and predicate transformers can be expressed as an isomorphism of categories. This is useful for translating some well-established properties of the category of predicate transformers to multirelations. In particular, we will show that functors like *map* have a unique extension from relations to multirelations, as do initial algebras. It is this property of initial algebras that yields the definition of *foldr* on multirelations, together with its associated fusion law. The datatype of lists will be used to illustrate these concepts, but the principle can be applied to any inductive datatype.

The structure of the paper is as follows. Section 2 contains an introduction to multirelations, summarizing the main concepts and definitions from [MCR04]. Section 3 introduces some operations on multirelations, including *map*, *foldr* and *foldl*, and includes several illustrative examples. Section 4 describes one application in depth: that of a voting system, Section 5 gives the theory that underpins the definitions of Section 3, and Section 6 is the conclusion.

2   Multirelations

Multirelations are to relations what multifunctions (relations) are to functions: that is to say, they are relations whose target type is a powerset type. A multirelation represents a specification if and only if it is up-closed:

Definition 2.1 (up-closed multirelation). *An* up-closed multirelation M *with source A and target B is a subset of the cartesian product $A \times \mathbb{P}\,B$ such that for all $x \in A$ and $X,\ Y \subseteq B$,*

$$x\ M\ X \wedge X \subseteq Y \Rightarrow x\ M\ Y$$

The types of all relations and up-closed multirelations with source A and target B are denoted by $A \leftrightarrow B$ and $A \rightrightarrows B$ respectively. Note that we will abbreviate "up-closed multirelation" to "multirelation".

Multirelations model program behaviour in a different way from ordinary relations. A relation R relates two values x and y, written $x\ R\ y$, if and only if the corresponding program can terminate with output y given input x. However, a multirelation M relates two values x and *post*, written $x\ M\ post$, if and only if the corresponding program can terminate with an output value that satisfies the predicate *post* given input x. In addition, if *post'* is another postcondition such that *post* $\subseteq$ *post'*, then clearly any output value that satisfies *post* must also satisfy *post'*, which is reflected by the up-closure property.

The choice between various postconditions is interpreted as angelic: the angel chooses which predicate to guarantee, and the demon chooses how to satisfy that predicate.

Example 2.1. Let *Int* denote the type of all integers, $M : Int \rightrightarrows Int$, and suppose that for all $x : Int$ and $X : \mathbb{P}\,Int$

$$x\ M\ X \Leftrightarrow (\{x\} \subseteq X \vee \{x-1, x+1\} \subseteq X)$$

then two of the postconditions that the angel can choose between are $\{x\}$ and $\{x - 1, x + 1\}$. If he chooses the latter, then the choice of output value is determined by the demon.   □

2.1   Strongest Postconditions

In the above example, the two postconditions $\{x\}$ and $\{x - 1, x + 1\}$ are the strongest ones that the angel can choose between, in the following sense:

Definition 2.2 (strongest postcondition). *Let* $M : A \rightrightarrows B$, $x \in A$ *and* $post \subseteq B$. *Then post is a* strongest postcondition *of M with respect to x if and only if*

1. $x \; M \; post$
2. $(\forall \, post' : x \; M \; post' : post' \not\subseteq post)$

In general, we shall refer to the set of all strongest postconditions of a multirelation M with respect to an initial state x by $sp(x, M)$. The values in this set can represent the choices of guarantee offered to the angel, as the examples below illustrate, but this is not always the case. An example to demonstrate that strongest postconditions do not necessarily correspond to angelic choices is included in the appendix. Note that the strongest postconditions of a multirelation may not exist. For instance, consider abort, defined by

$$x \; \mathsf{abort} \; X \Leftrightarrow \mathit{False}$$

Example 2.2. Each type A has identity $\in_A : A \rightrightarrows A$, where $\in_A$ (sometimes denoted by id_A) represents the set membership relation on subsets of A. So, given an input value $x \in A$, the only strongest postcondition it can achieve is $\{x\}$, which means that the value x is output. This specification is guaranteed to establish all postconditions that are satisfied by x itself.   □

Example 2.3. For each pair of types A, B, and each value $b \in B$, the constant specification *const* $b : A \rightrightarrows B$ is defined by

$$const \; b = A \times \uparrow \{b\}$$

where $\uparrow X = \{Y \mid X \subseteq Y\}$. Here, the strongest postcondition that is satisfied for any input value is $\{b\}$, ensuring that the value b is output.   □

Example 2.4. Consider the multirelation $A \times \uparrow \{1, 2\}$, for some source type A. Here the strongest postcondition for any input value is $\{1, 2\}$, so the angel has no choice and must select the postcondition $\{1, 2\}$, giving the demon the choice between output values 1 and 2. This is an example of demonic nondeterminism.   □

Example 2.5. In contrast, now consider the multirelation $A \times (\uparrow \{1\} \cup \uparrow \{2\})$, for some source type A. Here the strongest postconditions for any input value are $\{1\}$ and $\{2\}$, so the angel can always choose between output values 1 and 2, with no choice available for the demon. This is an example of angelic nondeterminism.   □

Example 2.6. Suppose that the angel is offered a fixed amount of money, which he can either keep or gamble to win double or nothing. This choice can be modelled by the multirelation $choose : \mathbb{N} \rightrightarrows \mathbb{N}$ where for all $x : \mathbb{N}$, $X : \mathbb{P}\,\mathbb{N}$

$$x \; choose \; X \Leftrightarrow \{x\} \subseteq X \vee \{0, 2x\} \subseteq X$$

The strongest postconditions of *choose* with respect to input value x are $\{x\}$ and $\{0, 2x\}$. If the angel chooses the former, then the demon will have no choice and x will be output, but in the latter case the demon can choose between output values 0 or $2x$.   □

It can be dangerous to rely solely on strongest postconditions for intuition about arbitrary multirelations, since not all multirelations have them, but there is a large class for which it is safe to do so, as characterised by the following definition:

Definition 2.3. *Let* $M : A \rightrightarrows B$. *Then* M *is* representable *if, for all* $x : A$, $X : \mathbb{P}\,B$

$$x \; M \; X \Leftrightarrow (\exists \, Y : Y \in sp(x, M) : Y \subseteq X)$$

All of the examples above are representable in this sense.

3 Operations

We will now introduce some operations on multirelations, some of which will be familiar to readers of [MCR04], and the rest of which are new.

3.1 Composition

Multirelations cannot be composed using ordinary relational composition for obvious type reasons. Instead, composition is defined as follows:

Definition 3.1 (composition). *The* composition *of two multirelations* $M : A \rightrightarrows B$, $N : B \rightrightarrows C$ *is denoted by* $M \,\fatsemi\, N : A \rightrightarrows C$ *where for all* $x : A$, $X : \mathbb{P}\,C$

$$x \; (M \,\fatsemi\, N) \; X \;\; \Leftrightarrow \;\; (\exists \, Y : x \; M \; Y : (\forall \, y : y \in Y : y \; N \; X))$$

So, given input value x, the angel can only guarantee that $M \,\fatsemi\, N$ will output a value that satisfies X if he can ensure that M will establish some intermediate postcondition Y and if he can also guarantee that N will establish X given any value in Y.

The composition operator is associative, with identity id_A for each A, and preserves up-closure. An alternative formulation of its definition that can be useful in calculations involving representable multirelations is given below.

Lemma 3.1. *Let* $M : A \rightrightarrows B$ *be representable, and let* $N : B \rightrightarrows C$, *then for all* $x : A$, $X : \mathbb{P}\,C$

$$x \; (M \,\fatsemi\, N) \; X \;\; \Leftrightarrow \;\; (\exists \, Z : Z \in sp(x, M) : (\forall \, z : z \in Z : z \; N \; X))$$

The proof of this lemma is omitted.

When working with folds, it is frequently useful to be able to insert an additional value when composing one multirelation with another. This composition-like operator captures that idea:

Definition 3.2. *For any* $z : C$ *and multirelations* $M : A \rightrightarrows B$ *and* $N : (C \times B) \rightrightarrows D$, *the* composition with z of M and N *is denoted by* $M \mathbin{\overset{\circ}{\underset{9_z}{}}} N : A \rightrightarrows D$ *where for all* $x : A$, $X : \mathbb{P} D$

$$x \left(M \mathbin{\overset{\circ}{\underset{9_z}{}}} N \right) X \;\Leftrightarrow\; (\exists\, Y : x \; M \; Y : (\forall\, y : y \in Y : (z, y) \; N \; X))$$

The operator $\overset{\circ}{\underset{9}{}}_{\_}$ behaves very much like $\overset{\circ}{\underset{9}{}}$ does: it has associative properties which include

$$M \mathbin{\overset{\circ}{\underset{9_z}{}}} (N \mathbin{\overset{\circ}{\underset{9}{}}} S) = (M \mathbin{\overset{\circ}{\underset{9_z}{}}} N) \mathbin{\overset{\circ}{\underset{9}{}}} S$$
$$M \mathbin{\overset{\circ}{\underset{9}{}}} (N \mathbin{\overset{\circ}{\underset{9_z}{}}} S) = (M \mathbin{\overset{\circ}{\underset{9}{}}} N) \mathbin{\overset{\circ}{\underset{9_z}{}}} S$$
$$M \mathbin{\overset{\circ}{\underset{9_y}{}}} (N \mathbin{\overset{\circ}{\underset{9_z}{}}} S) = (M \mathbin{\overset{\circ}{\underset{9_y}{}}} N) \mathbin{\overset{\circ}{\underset{9_z}{}}} S$$

for all suitably-typed values and multirelations.

3.2   Lifting

Another pair of operators that are useful in program specifications are the following well-known functions for lifting relations to multirelations [BvW98]. The notation used here is the same as that used for the closely related operators of propositional dynamic logic [FL79].

Definition 3.3. *For any relation* $R : A \leftrightarrow B$, *its* angelic lifting $\langle R \rangle : A \rightrightarrows B$ *is defined for all* $x : A$, $X : \mathbb{P} B$ *by*

$$x \; \langle R \rangle \; X \;\Leftrightarrow\; (\exists\, y : x \; R \; y : y \in X)$$

Definition 3.4. *For any relation* $R : A \leftrightarrow B$, *its* demonic lifting $[R] : A \rightrightarrows B$ *is defined for all* $x : A$, $X : \mathbb{P} B$ *by*

$$x \; [R] \; X \;\Leftrightarrow\; (\forall\, y : x \; R \; y : y \in X)$$

Both lifting operators distribute through composition and if R is a total function, then the two liftings coincide. A multirelation is said to be *angelic* (*demonic*) if it is the angelic (demonic) lifting of some relation. Notice that a demonic multirelation has only one strongest postcondition for any initial state, which is to be expected since it contains no angelic choice. In contrast, an angelic one may have many strongest postconditions, but each one must be a singleton set since it contains no demonic choice. One property of angelic multirelations that will be required in Section 5 is given by the following lemma, where ; denotes composition of ordinary relations.

Lemma 3.2. *Let* $R : A \leftrightarrow B$ *and* $M : B \rightrightarrows C$, *then*

$$\langle R \rangle \mathbin{\overset{\circ}{\underset{9}{}}} M = R \,;\, M$$

Proof

Let $x \in A$ and $X \in \mathbb{P}\, C$, then

$$x \; (\langle R \rangle \mathbin{\mathring{,}} M) \; X$$
$$\Leftrightarrow \quad \{\text{Definition of } \mathbin{\mathring{,}}\}$$
$$(\exists \, Y : x \; \langle R \rangle \; Y : (\forall \, y \in Y : y \; M \; X))$$
$$\Leftrightarrow \quad \{\text{Definition of } \langle \; \rangle \text{ and logic}\}$$
$$(\exists \, y : x \; R \; y : y \; M \; X)$$
$$\Leftrightarrow \quad \{\text{Definition of } \mathbin{;}\}$$
$$x \; (R \mathbin{;} M) \; X \qquad\qquad\qquad\qquad\qquad\qquad \square$$

3.3   Sums and Products

Sums are defined in exactly the same way for relations and multirelations:

Definition 3.5 (sum). *The* sum *of $M : A \rightrightarrows C$ and $N : B \rightrightarrows D$ is defined for all $x : A$, $y : B$ and $X + Y : \mathbb{P}(C + D)$ by*

$$(x, 0) \; (M \mathbin{+\!\!+} N) \; (X + Y) \Leftrightarrow x \, M \, X$$
$$(y, 1) \; (M \mathbin{+\!\!+} N) \; (X + Y) \Leftrightarrow y \, N \, Y$$

where $C + D$ denotes the disjoint sum $(C \times \{0\}) \cup (D \times \{1\})$ of sets C and D.

So this specification simply tests the tag component of its input and then behaves like M or N accordingly. Once again, the strongest postconditions of $M \mathbin{+\!\!+} N$ are closely related to those of M and N:

$$sp((x, 0), M \mathbin{+\!\!+} N) = \{X \times \{0\} \mid X \in sp(x, M)\}$$
$$sp((y, 1), M \mathbin{+\!\!+} N) = \{Y \times \{1\} \mid Y \in sp(y, N)\}$$

It follows that the sum of two representable multirelations is also representable.

The *product* operator can be used to model the simultaneous execution of programs [BB95]. It is not exactly like that for relations, and instead has the following definition:

Definition 3.6 (product). *The* product *of two multirelations $M : A \rightrightarrows C$ and $N : B \rightrightarrows D$ is defined for all $x : A$, $y : B$ and $Z : \mathbb{P}(C \times D)$ by*

$$(x, y) \; (M \mathbin{\text{\textasteriskcentered}} N) \; Z \Leftrightarrow (\exists \, X, Y : x \; M \; X \wedge y \; N \; Y \wedge X \times Y \subseteq Z)$$

where $C \times D$ denotes the cartesian product of the sets C and D.

Not surprisingly, there is a very simple relationship between the strongest postcondition of $M \mathbin{\text{\textasteriskcentered}} N$ and those of M and N individually:

$$sp((x, y), M \mathbin{\text{\textasteriskcentered}} N) = \{X \times Y \mid X \in sp(x, M) \wedge Y \in sp(y, N)\}$$

It follows that the product of two representable multirelations is itself representable.

The following example illustrates how this operator can be used.

Example 3.1. Consider a sealed bid auction, where two parties simultaneously submit bids for an item. The bidding process of a single bidder can be modelled by a relation $bid : \mathbb{N} \leftrightarrow \mathbb{N}$ where the input value to bid is the amount of money that the bidder has, and the output is the amount that they choose to bid. Assuming that a bidder can never make a bid that exceeds the amount of money they have available, the definition of bid is simply

$$bid = \; \geq$$

A sealed bid auction between two opposing bidders can be modelled by

$$auction = \langle bid \rangle \divideontimes [bid]$$

The set of strongest postconditions of *auction* for each input value $(x, y) : \mathbb{N} \times \mathbb{N}$ is then given by

$$\{ \{w\} \times 0..y \mid 0 \leq w \leq x \}$$

where $0..y$ denotes the set $\{u \mid 0 \leq u \leq y\}$. So, unsurprisingly, the angel can only guarantee to win the auction if he has more money than the demon initially. A more interesting variation on this theme will be developed in Section 4.   □

3.4   Map

The *map* operator of functional programming, which applies a function to each element of a list has the following analogue for multirelations:

Definition 3.7 (map). *Let* $M : A \rightrightarrows B$, *then* map M *is defined (using the Haskell syntax for lists) for all* $x : A$, $xs : [A]$ *and* $Z : \mathbb{P}[B]$ *by*

$$[\,] \; (map \; M) \; Z \Leftrightarrow [\,] \in Z$$
$$(x : xs) \; (map \; M) \; Z \Leftrightarrow (\exists \, Y, YS : x \; M \; Y \wedge xs \; (map \; M) \; YS \; \wedge$$
$$(\forall \, y, ys : y \in Y \wedge ys \in YS \Rightarrow (y : ys) \in Z))$$

So *map* M behaves like the identity when its input is the empty list, but its behaviour on non-empty lists is more easily understood by considering strongest postconditions: for all $x : A$, $xs : [A]$,

$$sp(x : xs, map \; M) = \{ consall(Y, YS) \mid Y \in sp(x, M) \wedge YS \in sp(xs, map \; M) \}$$

where $consall(Y, YS) = \{y : ys \mid y \in Y \wedge ys \in YS\}$.

The following example shows how this operator can be used.

Example 3.2. Consider an elected body of representatives (each member belonging to one of two political parties) participating in a legislative debate. After the debate, each representative must vote on the proposed legislation, and suppose the type *Ballot* = {*For, Against, Abstain*} represents all possible choices of votes. Each representative's voting intentions can be described as a multirelation *castvote* : *Representative* $\rightrightarrows$ *Ballot*.

If the disciplinarians in the angelic party have perfect control over their representatives, then any result can be guaranteed, in other words for any angelic representative a and $X : \mathbb{P}\, Ballot$,

$$a \ castvote \ X \Leftrightarrow X \neq \varnothing$$

Here, the requirement that $X \neq \varnothing$ reflects the compulsion on representatives to vote. This specification has a number of strongest postconditions that a can choose between: $\{For\}$, $\{Against\}$ and $\{Abstain\}$.

Now suppose voter d is from the opposition, then we have no control over his ballot: for all $X : \mathbb{P}\, Ballot$,

$$d \ castvote \ X \Leftrightarrow X = Ballot$$

This specification has a single strongest postcondition, namely the set of all valid ballots.

If all the representatives are represented by a list, their combined behaviour can be specified by

$$allvotes \ : \ [Representative] \rightrightarrows [Ballot]$$
$$allvotes = map \ castvote$$

Then the result of the debate is specified by:

$$debateresult \ : \ [Representative] \rightrightarrows \{For, Against, Draw\}$$
$$debateresult = allvotes \, \mathbin{\substack{\circ\\9}} \langle (remove \ Abstain); \ majority \rangle$$

where *remove* is the function that removes all of the specified element from a list, and *majority* is the function that returns the majority of elements in a list, if one, and otherwise returns a draw. □

3.5   Folds

The *fold* operators of functional programming, which capture a more general pattern of recursion than *map*, have analogues for multirelations. Here is the multirelational *foldr*:

Definition 3.8 (foldr). *For all $M : A \times B \rightrightarrows B$ and $N : 1 \rightrightarrows B$, we have that foldr $M\ N : [A] \rightrightarrows B$, and for all $X : \mathbb{P}\, B$,*

$$[\,](foldr \ M \ N)X \Leftrightarrow X \in ran \ N$$
$$(x : xs)(foldr \ M \ N)X \Leftrightarrow xs((foldr \ M \ N)\mathbin{\substack{\circ\\9x}} M)X$$

So if the initial state is the empty list, the guarantees of *foldr $M\ N$* are the same as those of N. If the initial state is of the form $x : xs$, then the guarantees are more complicated. Informally, it may help to remember that

$$[x_1, x_2, \ldots, x_n](foldr \ M \ N)X \quad \Leftrightarrow \quad X \in ran \ (N \mathbin{\substack{\circ\\9x_n}} M \ldots \mathbin{\substack{\circ\\9x_2}} M \mathbin{\substack{\circ\\9x_1}} M)$$

The strongest postconditions for a *foldr* are also defined recursively. For all $x : A$ and $xs : [A]$, we have that

$$sp(x : xs, foldr\ M\ N) = \{\cap\{sp((x, z), M \mid z \in Z\} \mid Z \in sp(xs, foldr\ M\ N)\}$$

The following example illustrates the use of *foldr*:

Example 3.3. Consider a version of the game of Nim where there is a pile of matches and a stack of positively numbered cards. The top card is removed from the stack at the start of each round, and the number shown on the card is the number of matches then removed from the pile. The players then each remove either one or two matches in turn. The last round of the game occurs when the last card is removed from the stack. If either player removes the last match on this round, then that player loses.

Let the operation to represent the removal of matches in accordance with the number at the top of the stack be called *cardremove*, and let *move* represent a valid move for either player, then

$$cardremove : Nat \times Int \to Int \quad move : Int \leftrightarrow Int$$
$$cardremove\ (w, x) = x - w \quad\quad x\ move\ y \Leftrightarrow y = x - 1 \vee y = x - 2$$

Then, assuming that the angel goes first, the angelic and demonic liftings can be used to define a round as:

$$round\ :\ Nat \times Int \rightrightarrows Int$$
$$round = \langle cardremove \rangle \ {}^{\circ}_{9}\ \langle move \rangle \ {}^{\circ}_{9}\ [move]$$

Now if we assume that the list of cards is consumed from right to left we can define the moves in the game of $nim : Int \to ([Nat] \rightrightarrows Int)$ recursively as follows: let $x : Int$ and $(w : ws) : [Nat]$ denote the starting pile of matches and cards respectively, then for all $X : \mathbb{P}Int$

$$[\ ] \quad\quad (nim\ x)\ X \Leftrightarrow x \in X$$

$$(w : ws)\ (nim\ x)\ X \Leftrightarrow$$
$$(\exists\ Y : ws\ (nim\ x)\ Y \wedge (\forall\ y : y \in Y : (w, y)\ round\ X))$$

Equivalently, this definition can be written more concisely as a *foldr*:

$$nim\ x = foldr\ round\ (const\ x) \quad\quad\quad\quad\quad \square$$

It is sometimes more convenient to model problems using non-empty lists. The *foldr*$^+$ is intended for just such situations, and it is defined in a very similar way to *foldr*:

Definition 3.9 (foldr$^+$). *For all $M : A \times B \rightrightarrows B$ and $N : A \rightrightarrows B$, we have that foldr$^+$ M $N : [A] \rightrightarrows B$, and for all $X : \mathbb{P} B$,*

$$[x](foldr^+\ M\ N)X \Leftrightarrow x\ N\ X$$
$$(x : y : xs)(foldr^+\ M\ N)X \Leftrightarrow (y : xs)((foldr^+\ M\ N)\ {}^{\circ}_{9_x}\ M)X$$

As in functional programming, there are also *foldl* and *foldl*$^+$ operators, which process elements of the list starting from the left-hand end:

Definition 3.10 (foldl). *For all* $M : A \times B \rightrightarrows B$ *and* $N : 1 \rightrightarrows B$, *we have that* $foldl\ M\ N : [A] \rightrightarrows B$, *and for all* $X : \mathbb{P}\,B$,

$$[\ ](foldl\ M\ N)X \Leftrightarrow X \in ran\ N$$
$$(x : xs)(foldl\ M\ N)X \Leftrightarrow xs((foldl\ M\ (N \ {}_{9}^{o}{}_x\ M))X$$

Definition 3.11 (foldl$^+$). *For all* $M : A \times B \rightrightarrows B$ *and* $N : A \rightrightarrows B$, *we have that* $foldl^+\ M\ N : [A] \rightrightarrows B$, *and for all* $X : \mathbb{P}\,B$,

$$[x](foldl^+\ M\ N)X \Leftrightarrow x\ N\ X$$
$$(x : y : xs)(foldl^+\ M\ N)X \Leftrightarrow (y : xs)((foldl^+\ M\ (N \ {}_{9}^{o}{}_x\ M))X$$

Informally, the *foldl* operator can be thought of in the following way:

$$[x_1, x_2, \ldots, x_n](foldl\ M\ N)X \quad \Leftrightarrow \quad X \in ran\ (N \ {}_{9}^{o}{}_{x_1}\ M \ {}_{9}^{o}{}_{x_2} \ldots M \ {}_{9}^{o}{}_{x_n}\ M)$$

Example 3.4. Consider a gambling opportunity where a customer (the angel) is presented with a series of monetary options $[x_1, x_2, \ldots, x_n]$. The customer can either choose to accept the first amount offered (x_1), or can gamble by the second amount (x_2) to receive a payout of either $x_1 - x_2$ or $x_1 + x_2$, depending on what the demon chooses. He may then choose to stick, or to gamble by a further amount (x_3) to receive one of the payoffs $x_1 - x_2 - x_3$, $x_1 - x_2 + x_3$, $x_1 + x_2 - x_3$ or $x_1 + x_2 + x_3$, and so on. The multirelation $M : [Nat] \rightrightarrows Int$ that describes this situation can be written informally as:

$$[x_1, x_2, \ldots, x_n]\ M\ X$$
$$\Leftrightarrow$$
$$\{x_1\} \subseteq X \quad \vee$$
$$\{x_1 - x_2, x_1 + x_2\} \subseteq X \quad \vee$$
$$\{x_1 - x_2 - x_3, x_1 + x_2 - x_3, x_1 - x_2 + x_3, x_1 + x_2 + x_3\} \subseteq X \quad \vee \ldots$$

for all $X : \mathbb{P}Int$. More formally, M can be defined as a fold:

$$M = foldl^+\ gamble\ \in$$

where $gamble : Int \times Int \rightrightarrows Int$ is defined for all $x, y : Int$, and $X : \mathbb{P}Int$ by

$$(y, x)\ gamble\ X \Leftrightarrow x \in X \vee \{x - y, x + y\} \subseteq X \qquad \square$$

In functional programming, there are duality theorems for fold operators, which state under which conditions a *foldl* may be expressed as a *foldr*. There is also a duality theorem for multirelations:

Theorem 3.1. *Let* $M : A \times B \rightrightarrows B$ *and* $N : 1 \rightrightarrows B$. *If for all* $Q : 1 \rightrightarrows B$ *and* $x, y : A$ *we have that* $Q \ {}_{9}^{o}{}_x\ M \ {}_{9}^{o}{}_y\ M = Q \ {}_{9}^{o}{}_y\ M \ {}_{9}^{o}{}_x\ M$, *then*

$$foldl\ M\ N = foldr\ M\ N$$

The proof of this theorem is omitted. It can be proved in the same way as the corresponding proof of the second duality theorem in [Bi98], and given this hint, the proof is straightforward.

4   Case Study: A Series of Elections

This example is inspired by voting systems.

There is to be an election. Two candidates (one from the angelic party, and one from the demonic) are standing, and only one is to be elected. Unlike some election systems which elect a candidate in a single mass voting event, the election of this candidate is split over several regions (so we will have a type *Region*). Each region has its own election on the election date for that region, thus declaring that region's preference, and the results from all the regional elections are combined in some way to select the eventual overall winner.

This being politics, money is heavily involved (you'd be cynical too if you did multirelational proofs). Each candidate has a certain amount of money to spend on the election overall: the angel has an amount a, and the demon has an amount d, for some $a, d : Money$, where $Money = \mathbb{R}^{\geq 0}$. In this system, it is assumed that the total number of votes a candidate obtains in a region is directly proportional to the money he spends in that region. Thus if the angelic candidate spends more than the demonic candidate in a region, the angelic candidate wins that region. (If you prefer to be less cynical about it, you may imagine that the two candidates can count on a roughly equal amount of voting support from their staunch supporters, and the money spent simply woos the floating voters, resulting in the same observation.)

We can represent a candidate's tally of how he is doing so far, by a pair of type $\{Region\} \times Money$, representing the set of regions the candidate has won so far, and the amount of money he has left. Considering this data for both candidates suggests a suitable type for representing the results so far:

$$Results = (\{Region\} \times Money) \times (\{Region\} \times Money)$$

We will use the convention that the pair on the left represents the angelic candidate's results, and the pair on the right the demonic candidate's results.

Thus initially, before any of the regions have had their elections, the results so far are described by this multirelation:

$$initially \ : \ \mathbf{1} \Rightarrow Results$$
$$initially \ = \ const \ ((\{ \ \}, a) \ , \ (\{ \ \}, d))$$

A candidate makes preparations for a regional election by choosing how much money to spend in that region.

$$Spend \ : \ \{Region\} \times Money \leftrightarrow (\{Region\} \times Money) \times Money$$
$$\forall \, m, s : Money, \ rs : \{Region\} \ : \ (rs, m) \ Spend \ ((rs, m), s) \quad \Leftrightarrow \quad 0 \leq s \leq m$$

A region's preferred candidate is determined by seeing which candidate spent the most money:

$$declare \ (r, (((rs_a, m_a), s_a), ((rs_d, m_d), s_d)))$$
$$= \ ((rs_a \cup \{r\}, m_a - s_a), (rs_d, m_d - s_d)), \quad \text{if } s_a > s_d$$
$$= \ ((rs_a, m_a - s_a), (rs_d \cup \{r\}, m_d - s_d)), \quad \text{otherwise}$$

Note that if the monies spent are equal, the region is given to the demonic candidate. This is because in that case, the vote will be so close that the angel certainly can't guarantee winning that region.

We are now in a position to define a multirelation *Election* representing an election for a single region:

$$Election \; : \; (Region \times Results) \rightrightarrows Results$$
$$Election \; = \; (id \mathbin{\$} (\langle Spend \rangle \mathbin{\$} [Spend])) \mathbin{\S} \langle declare \rangle$$

The $\langle Spend \rangle \mathbin{\$} [Spend]$ illustrates the spending decisions of the angel and demon being made in parallel, before the results are declared for that region and added to the tallies so far.

Assuming that the regions are listed in chronological order according to the date of their elections, then the whole series of elections can be suitably described by a *foldl*:

$$ElectionSeries \; : \; [Region] \rightrightarrows Results$$
$$ElectionSeries \; = \; foldl \; Election \; initially$$

The angelic guarantees of the multirelation *ElectionSeries* thus represent possible predicates that the angel can ensure, given a list of regions, his own pot of money, and the demon's.

As for whether the angel actually wins the election or not, that all depends on how the results from all the elections are combined to produce an overall result. One way to do it would be to give a region a weighting (e.g. according to population size), and add up the weightings of the regions won by each candidate, and compare to see which candidate has the most. We will consider a simpler version, where the candidate who wins the most regions is also the overall winner.

4.1 "Will Sufficient Money Buy the Election?"

Although we are interested in knowing whether the angelic candidate wins a majority of the regions, it turns out to be more useful to consider a generalisation: that of whether the angel can guarantee winning at least w regions, for various values of w. So we define, for $st : Results$

$$Wins_w(st) \; \Leftrightarrow \; \#angelwins(st) \geq w$$
$$\text{where} \quad angelwins((rs_a, m_a), (rs_d, m_d)) \; = \; \#rs_a$$

and where $\#$ denotes the size or length of a list or set.

Thus we are interested for what values of w it is the case that

$$rs \; ElectionSeries \; Wins_w$$

Experiments with assorted angelic and demonic pots of money along with small region lists suggest that whilst the angel can always guarantee winning at least 0 of the regions, for $w > 1$ the angel can guarantee winning w of the regions rs if the angel has more money than $(\#rs)d/(\#rs + 1 - w)$.

The intuition behind this suggests that if the demon wants to prevent the angel winning w regions, then the demon must win $\#rs + 1 - w$ regions. If the angel is unlucky then the demon will concentrate his money on the $\#rs + 1 - w$ regions on which the angel spends the least money, thus spending $d/(\#rs + 1 - w)$ on each of those regions. Thus the angel needs to maximise spending in the weakest regions, which can best be achieved by spreading money as evenly as possible across the regions, thus spending $a/(\#rs)$ in each region. Thus the angel will only have a guarantee if $a/(\#rs) > d/(\#rs+1-w)$. But can we prove it formally using multirelations?

The above suggests that what we should aim to prove is

$$(w \geq 0) \vee (1 \leq w \leq \#rs \; \wedge \; (\#rs + 1 - w)a > (\#rs)d \;) \tag{1}$$
$$\Rightarrow \quad rs \; ElectionSeries \; Wins_w \tag{2}$$

for all $a, d : Money$, $w : \mathbb{N}$ and $rs : [Region]$.

4.2   "Can We Prove It?"

When a *fold* is involved, an inductive proof is indicated. If the above suggestion is taken as an inductive hypothesis, this means the inductive hypothesis is in the form

$$P(w, rs) \Rightarrow rs(foldl \; Election \; initially) \, Wins_w$$

and this is problematic, for the same reason that *foldl* proofs are awkward in standard functional programming: as soon as we start on the inductive case, we run into a problem:

$$(r : rs)(foldl \; Election \; initially) \, Wins_w$$
$$\Leftrightarrow \quad \{\text{definition of } foldl\}$$
$$rs(foldl \; Election \; (initially \, \S_r \; Election)) \, Wins_w$$

As the inductive hypothesis does not involve *initially* $\S_r$ *Election*, it cannot be used.

Using *foldr* instead doesn't help, even though we can express *ElectionSeries* using *foldr* with the list of regions rs in reverse chronological order, and there is no difficulty manipulating the expression into a form where the inductive hypothesis can be used, like this:

$$(r : rs)(foldr \; Election \; initially) \, Wins_w$$
$$\Leftrightarrow \quad \{\text{definition of } foldr\}$$
$$rs((foldr \; Election \; initially) \, \S_r \; Election) \, Wins_w$$
$$\Leftrightarrow \quad \{\text{definition of } \S_r\}$$
$$\exists \, Y : rs(foldr \; Election \; initially) Y : (\forall \, st : st \in Y : (r, st) Election \, Wins_w)$$

Trying to go any further is difficult. It relies on demonstrating the existence of a predicate Y which is true after all regions but one have had their elections. It is difficult to see what Y could be, especially since it is not obvious how much money the demon has left by this stage and whether this is a sufficiently small amount to allow the angel to win the final election.

Going back to *foldl*, we need to use the standard functional programmer's trick for *foldl* inductions, and generalise the inductive hypothesis. We require something of the form

$$Sufficient(w, rs, Q) \Rightarrow rs(\mathit{foldl\ Election\ Q})\mathit{Wins}_w \qquad (3)$$

for $Q : 1 \rightrightarrows \mathit{Results}$. We will impose conditions on Q: it must be representable and contain at least one non-empty predicate for the angel to choose from.

Note that the predicate *Sufficient* must involve the initialising multirelation Q in some way - after all, if Q initialised the angel with 7 regions to his credit before the elections in rs had even begun, this would severely affect the w for which the angel can guarantee Wins_w!

The predicate *Sufficient* must somehow express that the angel can guarantee that after performing Q, the angel has sufficient money relative to the demon. We give a definition of *Sufficient* in terms of the range of Q that illustrates a standard form of predicate to use when doing multirelational inductive proofs with *foldl*:

$$Sufficient(w, rs, Q) \Rightarrow \mathit{MoneyEnough}_{w,rs} \in ran\ Q$$

where

$$
\begin{aligned}
\mathit{MoneyEnough}_{w,rs}(st) \Leftrightarrow (w \leq{} &\#aw(st)\ \vee \\
&(1 \leq w - \#aw(st) \leq \#rs\ \wedge \\
&(\#rs + 1 + \#aw(st) - w)am(st) > (\#rs)dm(st)\ ))
\end{aligned}
$$

where aw, am and dm are abbreviations for the obvious functions *angelwins*, *angelmoney* and *demonmoney* on type *Results*.

4.3   "Yes!"

We are now in a position to prove (3), and this will imply (2) by substituting *initially* for Q.

Proof

The full proof is too lengthy for this paper, but we will sketch the proof, which uses induction over rs with hypothesis (3).

Case $(rs = [\ ])$:

This is straightforward when considering the guarantees Q provides in terms of the strongest postconditions of Q.

Case $(r : rs)$:

$$(r : rs)(\mathit{foldl\ Election\ Q})\mathit{Wins}_w$$

$\Leftrightarrow$ {definition of *foldl*}

    $rs(foldl\ Election\ (Q \mathbin{\mathring{\,}}_r Election))\, Wins_w$

$\Leftarrow$ {inductive hypothesis, claim}

    $Sufficient(w, rs, Q \mathbin{\mathring{\,}}_r Election)$

$\Leftrightarrow$ {definition of *Sufficient*}

    $MoneyEnough_{w,rs} \in ran\ (Q \mathbin{\mathring{\,}}_r Election)$

$\Leftrightarrow$ {definition of $\mathbin{\mathring{\,}}_-$}

    $\exists\, Y : Y \in ran\ Q : (\forall\, st : st \in Y : (r, st)Election\ MoneyEnough_{w,rs})$

$\Leftarrow$ {claim}

    $\exists\, Y : Y \in sp(1, Q) : (\forall\, st : st \in Y : MoneyEnough_{w,r:rs}(st))$

$\Leftrightarrow$ {strongest postconditions, Q representable}

    $MoneyEnough_{w,r:rs} \in ran\ Q$

$\Leftrightarrow$ {definition of *Sufficient*}

    $Sufficient(w, r : rs, Q)$

The first claim is that $Q \mathbin{\mathring{\,}}_r Election$ is representable and non-empty if Q is too. When Q is of a form such that its strongest postconditions can be indexed by choices made by the angel and demon (as is the multirelation *initially* that we want to use), the proof is fiddly but straightforward.

For the second claim, it suffices to prove that

$$MoneyEnough_{w,r:rs}(st) \Rightarrow (r, st)Election\ MoneyEnough_{w,rs}$$

This can be shown by choosing a particular strongest postcondition P from $sp((r, st), Election)$, and showing that when $MoneyEnough_{w,r:rs}(st)$, it is the case that $P \Rightarrow MoneyEnough_{w,rs}$.

The strongest postconditions for *Elections* are characterised by the angel's choices of how much to spend at that election, and the choice of P corresponding to the choice of $angelmoney(st)/(\#rs + 1)$ (which might be guessed from the above discussion) allows (4) to be proved with careful detailed predicate calculus calculations (omitted).   □

4.4   Further Notes

We can use the duality theorem for multirelations (Theorem 3.1), to express *ElectionSeries* as a *foldr* too

$$ElectionSeries\ =\ foldr\ Election\ initially$$

since it is the case that

Proposition 4.1. *For all* $Q : 1 \rightrightarrows Results$ *and* $x, y : Region$, *it is the case that*

$$Q \mathbin{\mathring{\,}}_x Election \mathbin{\mathring{\,}}_y Election = Q \mathbin{\mathring{\,}}_y Election \mathbin{\mathring{\,}}_x Election$$

Proof

The details of this proof are omitted, to spare the reader much tedious predicate calculus, but here is a proof sketch:

It is sufficient to prove that for all $st : Results$ and $X : \{Results\}$,

$$(x, st)(Election \,\substack{\circ\\\circ}_y\, Election)X \Leftrightarrow (y, st)(Election \,\substack{\circ\\\circ}_x\, Election)X$$

One side of the above is expanded using the strongest postconditions for the representable multirelation *Election* (see Lemma 3.1), and it is demonstrated that this is symmetrical in x and y. Note that this necessitates election results being represented as sets of regions won so far, rather than a list, otherwise the guarantees of the two above multirelations are different.   □

The choice of postconditions in the proof provides advice for these sorts of elections: if you have a lot more money than your opponent does, then your best chance of guaranteeing a win comes from spreading it out evenly over the regions. However, if you have less money than your opponent, the best chance of defeating your opponent comes from concentrating your money in fewer regions.

5   Initial Algebras and Folds

This section describes the theoretical concepts that underly the definitions of the operations given in Section 3. In particular, it will be shown that functors (like *map*) and initial algebras (like *foldr*) have a unique extension from relations to multirelations. These results are well-known properties of predicate transformers [GMdM94, deM92] which are isomorphic to multirelations [Rew03], but it is instructive to rework some of the proofs directly for multirelations because they turn out quite differently. For instance, the extension of initial algebras is much simpler to derive for multirelations.

There are at least two well established ways to extend both functors and initial algebras from total functions to relations: via Kleisli categories [Fo94] and using span categories [CK84, FrS93]. The same is true of multirelations, but this paper restricts attention to the latter method because it has the advantage that it produces a unique extension of a functor which is itself a weak kind of functor. The version of this method described in this section is based on the factorisation of multirelations into an angelic part followed by a demonic part.

It is beyond the scope of this paper to explain the details of categorical concepts, see [BaW90] for example, for an introduction to category theory. The notation $p \,;\, q$ will be used for the composite of each pair of arrows with compatible types $p : A \to B$ and $q : B \to C$, and id_A is the identity arrow on object A. Function application will be denoted by juxtaposition.

5.1   Order-Enriched Categories

Both relations and multirelations will be modelled using *order-enriched* categories, which are those with a partial order defined on homsets with respect to which the categorical composition is monotonic.

The order-enriched category of relations, **Rel**, is defined as follows. The objects of **Rel** are sets, arrows are relations, composition is defined by ; and the identity arrow for each set A is the identity function id_A. The order on arrows in **Rel** is subset inclusion.

The order-enriched category of up-closed multirelations, **Mul**, is defined as follows. The objects of **Mul** are sets, arrows are up-closed multirelations, composition is defined by $\S$, and the identity arrow for each set A is the set membership relation $\in_A$. The order on arrows in **Mul** is subset inclusion.

The collection of all angelic and demonic multirelations each form subcategories of **Mul** which we will call **Ang** and **Dem** respectively. Both of the lifting functions of Definitions 3.3 can be thought of as functors that define an isomorphism between **Rel** and each of these subcategories.

5.2   Undoing the Demon's Handiwork

Order-enriched categories accommodate a greater range of constructs than ordinary categories because all of the standard definitions can be weakened by substituting inequality for equality. An example of such a definition is that of a *map* [CK84, FrS93] which is a weak analogue of the concept of an isomorphism. (It is unfortunate that the word *map* is used elsewhere in this paper for a very different purpose, but since both are standard it is hoped that the meaning will be clear from the context.)

Definition 5.1 (categorical map). *Let $(\mathcal{C}, \subseteq)$ be an order-enriched category. An arrow $m : A \to B$ is a map if and only if it has an comap $m^* : B \to A$ such that both*

$$id_A \subseteq m \,;\, m^* \text{ and } m^* \,;\, m \subseteq id_B. \tag{4}$$

It is immediate from the following shunting rule that every map uniquely determines its comap and vice versa. Let $M : A \to B$, $N : D \to C$, $r : B \to C$ and $s : A \to D$ in an order-enriched category $(\mathcal{C}, \subseteq)$, where r and s are maps, then

$$M \,;\, r \subseteq s \,;\, N \quad \Leftrightarrow \quad s^* \,;\, M \subseteq N \,;\, r^* \tag{5}$$

In **Mul** the maps are precisely the demonic multirelations, Every demonic multirelation $[R]$ has comap $\langle R^\circ \rangle$, and conversely, it can be shown that every map is demonic. So the concept of a map gives a succinct algebraic characterisation of demonic multirelations, and dually, comaps characterise angelic multirelations.

Intuitively, a comap can be thought of as the angelic multirelation that allows the angel to choose to undo the choices made by its corresponding demonic map.

Furthermore, the * operator can be considered as a (contravariant) functor that defines an isomorphism between the categories **Dem** and **Ang**. In future, demonic multirelations will be written in lowercase, by analogy with the common convention for total functions, which are the maps in the category of relations.

5.3   Factorisation

Just as every ordinary relation can be factorised into an inverse function followed by a function, every multirelation can be factorised into an angelic part followed by a demonic part: let $M : A \rightrightarrows B$, then since $[\ni_B] = \; \subseteq_B$

$$M$$
$$= \quad \{\text{up-closure}\}$$
$$M \,; [\ni_B]$$
$$= \quad \{\text{Lemma 3.2}\}$$
$$\langle M \rangle \, \mathbin{\raise1pt\hbox{$\stackrel{\circ}{\scriptscriptstyle 9}$}} \, [\ni_B]$$

This is not the only way to construct a factorisation of this kind, for example, let C be the subset of $A \times \mathbb{P} B$ corresponding to M, and $outl : C \to A$, $outr : C \to \mathbb{P} B$ be the projection functions, and let $^\circ$ denote relational converse, then

$$M$$
$$= \quad \{\text{definition of } ;\}$$
$$outl^\circ \,; outr$$
$$= \quad \{\text{calculation above}\}$$
$$\langle outl^\circ \,; outr \rangle \, \mathbin{\raise1pt\hbox{$\stackrel{\circ}{\scriptscriptstyle 9}$}} \, [\ni_B]$$
$$= \quad \{\text{lifting distributes through composition}\}$$
$$\langle outl^\circ \rangle \, \mathbin{\raise1pt\hbox{$\stackrel{\circ}{\scriptscriptstyle 9}$}} \, \langle outr \rangle \, \mathbin{\raise1pt\hbox{$\stackrel{\circ}{\scriptscriptstyle 9}$}} \, [\ni_B]$$
$$= \quad \{\text{lifting operators agree on total functions}\}$$
$$\langle outl^\circ \rangle \, \mathbin{\raise1pt\hbox{$\stackrel{\circ}{\scriptscriptstyle 9}$}} \, [outr] \, \mathbin{\raise1pt\hbox{$\stackrel{\circ}{\scriptscriptstyle 9}$}} \, [\ni_B]$$
$$= \quad \{\text{demonic lifting is a functor}\}$$
$$\langle outl^\circ \rangle \, \mathbin{\raise1pt\hbox{$\stackrel{\circ}{\scriptscriptstyle 9}$}} \, [outr \,; \ni_B]$$

This factorisation appears to be quite different from the previous one, but the two are related in a sense that is captured by the following definition:

Definition 5.2 (unique map factorisation). *Let* $(\mathcal{C}, \subseteq)$ *be an order-enriched category. Then* $\mathcal{C}$ *has* unique map factorisation *if, for every arrow* $M : A \to B$, *there exists a pair of maps* $t : C \to A$ *and* $u : C \to B$ *such that*

$$M = t^* \,; u$$

and for any other pair of maps r and s, r^* ; $s \subseteq M$ if and only if there exists a map h such that h ; $t \subseteq r$ and $s \subseteq h$; u.

The proof of this uniqueness property of multirelations is included in the appendix. Factorisation is useful because it provides a mechanism for extending the definitions of functors like *map* to multirelations, but unfortunately the result is not guaranteed to be a functor itself. Instead, it is necessary to introduce a weak analogue of the notion of a relator.

5.4   Relators

Recall the following definition from, for example [BdM97].

Definition 5.3 (relator). *A relator is defined to be a monotonic functor.*

It is easy to check that every relator F preserves comaps, which is to say that for all maps r,

$$F(r^*) = (Fr)^*$$

This property motivates the following weaker notion.

Definition 5.4 (uprelator). *Let $(\mathcal{C}, \subseteq)$ be an order-enriched category. An uprelator $F : \mathcal{C} \to \mathcal{C}$ is a monotonic graph morphism such that for all arrows M, N and maps r,*

$$F\, id_A = id_{FA}$$
$$F(M\,;\,N) \subseteq FM\,;\,FN$$
$$F(r^*) = (Fr)^*$$

So whereas relators distribute through composition, uprelators do not necessarily do so. The product is an example of such an operator, since for instance if magic is defined by x magic $X \Leftrightarrow True$ then

$$(id \divideontimes \text{magic}) \mathbin{\substack{\circ\\\circ}} (\text{abort} \divideontimes \text{abort}) \neq (id \mathbin{\substack{\circ\\\circ}} \text{abort}) \divideontimes (\text{magic} \mathbin{\substack{\circ\\\circ}} \text{abort})$$

It will be assumed that relators and uprelators bind more tightly than any other operations, and since there is no difference between $F(r^*)$ and $(Fr)^*$, the notation Fr^* will be used from now on to mean either. Note that the last clause in the definition of an uprelator is equivalent to saying that for all arrows M, N and maps r,

$$F(M\,;\,r) = FM\,;\,Fr \qquad \text{and} \qquad F(r^*\,;\,N) = Fr^*\,;\,FN \tag{6}$$

If $\mathcal{C}$ is a category with unique map factorisation and *Map $\mathcal{C}$* is the subcategory of all maps in $\mathcal{C}$, then every relator $F : Map\ \mathcal{C} \to Map\ \mathcal{C}$ has a well-defined extension to an uprelator $\widehat{F} : \mathcal{C} \to \mathcal{C}$ defined for all r^* ; s by

$$\widehat{F}\,(r^*\,;\,s) = (Fr)^*\,;\,Fs \tag{7}$$

So every relator $F : \mathbf{Rel} \to \mathbf{Rel}$ can be extended to an uprelator $\mathbb{F} : \mathbf{Mul} \to \mathbf{Mul}$ by the above method via the lifting functors: for all $M : A \rightrightarrows B$,

$$\mathbb{F}\,M = \langle F\,M \rangle \mathbin{\substack{\circ\\\circ}} [F \ni_B] \tag{8}$$

The unique map factorisation property guarantees that this is an uprelator and the following lemma ensures that it is the only one that coincides with F on relations.

Lemma 5.1. *If C is a category with unique map factorisation and two uprelators $F, G : C \to C$ agree on maps, that is $F\,m = G\,m$ for all maps m, then $F = G$.*

The proof of this lemma is in the appendix. It shows that the behaviour of every uprelator on multirelations is uniquely determined by its behaviour on relations. For example, the *product*, *sum* and *map* uprelators of Section 3 were derived via equation (8) from their counterparts on relations.

It is natural to consider whether it is really worth using these categorical concepts to formulate definitions like *map* when they could probably have been guessed quite easily without them. One reason for doing so is that each operator defined by equation (8) is guaranteed to be an uprelator, and so, for example, it preserves the refinement ordering and obeys the laws of equation (6). Moreover, each such operator is known to be the only one that agrees with its analogue for relations. It can also be shown that if a relator F satisfies any law that is expressed as a natural transformation, then its extension $\hat{\mathsf{F}}$ will inherit a weaker form of the law, but it is beyond the scope of this paper to include such laws. Similar arguments can be used to justify the use of initial algebras to formulate the definition of *fold*. Perhaps most importantly, they give a generic definition of *fold*, so it is valid across all regular datatypes.

5.5   Initial Algebras

The definition given below generalises the standard one slightly by using uprelators instead of functors.

Definition 5.5 (initial algebra). *Let F be an uprelator from some order-enriched category C to itself. By definition, an F-algebra is an arrow of type $FA \to A$ for some A. An F-algebra $\tau : FT \to T$ is initial if, for each F-algebra $p : FA \to A$ there exists an arrow $(\!| p |\!) : T \to A$ that satisfies the equivalence*

$$(\tau \,;\, q = F\,q \,;\, p) \;\equiv\; (q = (\!| p |\!))$$

Arrows of the form $(\!| p |\!)$ are called *catamorphisms* and correspond to the familiar fold and reduce operators.

It has been known for some time that initial algebras are preserved under the extension of functors from total functions to relations [EW67]. More recently, it was shown that the extension of functors from relations to predicate transformers transforms initial algebras into final coalgebras [deM92]. The restatement of this result for multirelations uses only initial algebras and is given below:

Lemma 5.2. *Let F : **Rel** $\to$ **Rel** be a relator with initial algebra $\tau : FT \to T$. Then $\mathbb{F} : **Mul** \to **Mul**$ is an uprelator with initial algebra $\langle \tau \rangle$.*

Proof

Let $K : T \rightrightarrows A$ and $H : \mathsf{F} A \rightrightarrows A$, then

$$\langle \tau \rangle \, \mathring{}_{9} \, K = \mathbb{F} K \, \mathring{}_{9} \, H$$

$\equiv$ {Definition of $\mathbb{F}$ (8)}

$$\langle \tau \rangle \, \mathring{}_{9} \, K = \langle \mathsf{F} K \rangle \, \mathring{}_{9} \, [\mathsf{F} \ni] \, \mathring{}_{9} \, H$$

$\equiv$ {Lemma 3.2}

$$\tau \, ; K = \mathsf{F} K \, ; ([\mathsf{F} \ni] \, \mathring{}_{9} \, H)$$

$\equiv$ {Definition 5.5}

$$K = (\![\, [\mathsf{F} \ni] \, \mathring{}_{9} \, H \,]\!)$$

$\square$

This proof is much shorter than its counterpart for predicate transformers and the corresponding fold operator is also more useful because it has a more familiar form, as we saw in Definition 3.8, which stated that a *foldr* is a catamorphism of the initial algebra associated with the uprelator $\mathsf{F}_A : \mathbf{Mul} \to \mathbf{Mul}$, defined by

$$\mathsf{F}_A(B) = 1 \mathbin{\#} (A \mathbin{*} B)$$
$$\mathsf{F}_A(M) = id_1 \mathbin{\#} (id_B \mathbin{*} M)$$

The fusion law below is a fairly immediate consequence of Definition 5.5. Unfortunately, it is less succint than usual because of the relaxation of the condition that F should be a relator.

Lemma 5.3 (fusion). *Let* $\mathsf{F} : \mathbf{Mul} \to \mathbf{Mul}$ *be an uprelator, and let* $M : \mathsf{F} A \rightrightarrows A$, $N : A \rightrightarrows B$ *and* $P : \mathsf{F} B \rightrightarrows B$, *then*

$$(M \, \mathring{}_{9} \, N = \mathsf{F} N \, \mathring{}_{9} \, P \ \wedge \ \mathsf{F}((\![M]\!) \, \mathring{}_{9} \, N) = \mathsf{F}(\![M]\!) \, \mathring{}_{9} \, \mathsf{F} N) \Rightarrow (\![M]\!) \, \mathring{}_{9} \, N = (\![P]\!)$$

Clearly, if F is a functor then the second part of the antecedent above can be dropped. By equation (6) this is also true if M is angelic or N is demonic. A more concrete example of this law, in the context of lists, is given in the following section,

5.6   Fusion for Lists

The fusion laws associated with the definition of *foldr* on relations have been widely used in the derivation of functional programs [BdM97], and ultimately the same might be true of the corresponding laws for multirelations. Unfortunately, the law given below is less succint than its analogue on relations because the product operator is an uprelator, rather than a relator, and so an extra condition is necessary. Nevertheless, it is still much easier to apply than its counterpart for predicate transformers.

Lemma 5.4 (fusion). *Let* $M : A \times B \rightrightarrows B$, $M' : A \times B' \rightrightarrows B'$, $N : 1 \rightrightarrows B$, $N' : 1 \rightrightarrows B'$, *and* $K : B \rightrightarrows B'$, *then*

$$N \mathbin{\substack{\circ \\ 9}} K = N' \wedge M \mathbin{\substack{\circ \\ 9}} K = (id_A \mathbin{\ast} K) \mathbin{\substack{\circ \\ 9}} M'$$

$$\wedge$$

$$(\forall R, S : R \mathbin{\ast} (S \mathbin{\substack{\circ \\ 9}} K) \supseteq (R \mathbin{\ast} S) \mathbin{\substack{\circ \\ 9}} (id_A \mathbin{\ast} K))$$

$$\Rightarrow$$

$$(fold\ M\ N) \mathbin{\substack{\circ \\ 9}} K = fold\ M'\ N'$$

The statement of this law for non-empty lists is identical apart from the types of N and N'. Although the quantified expression above looks rather cumbersome, it can be dropped completely if M and N are angelic or K is demonic. This fact is used in the statement of the following special case of the fusion law.

Lemma 5.5 (map fusion). *Let* $M : A \times B \rightrightarrows B$, $N : 1 \rightrightarrows B$ *and* $K : A' \rightrightarrows A$, *then if* K *is angelic or* M *and* N *are demonic,*

$$map\ K \mathbin{\substack{\circ \\ 9}} fold\ M\ N = fold\ (K \mathbin{\ast} id \mathbin{\substack{\circ \\ 9}} M)\ N$$

6   Conclusions

This paper has introduced *map* and *fold* operators for multirelations, illustrated with examples of their use in modelling and proofs. These operators have been shown to be canonical, in the sense that they are the only ones that agree with their counterparts for relations and functions. Both operators had been defined previously in the equivalent framework of predicate transformers, but they did not take on such a familiar form in that context, and the uniqueness proofs did not work out so simply. The datatype of lists has been used for illustration in this paper, but the generic nature of the definitions means that they are equally applicable to any other regular datatype, such as trees.

We have also presented some theorems showing some of the properties of maps and folds. One topic for future work is the meticulous cataloguing of the various laws of multirelations, including further exploration of those concerning the *map* and *fold* operators. In particular, it would be interesting to see whether any other well-known theorems of *foldr* translate to multirelations in the same way as the duality theorem of [Bi98] and the fusion laws of [BdM97]. The definition of *unfold* also remains to be derived, possibly through the use of Kleisli categories [Fo94]. But perhaps the most pressing concern is to discover more applications of multirelations, like the voting example considered here, in order to demosntrate their potential value. There are areas which could benefit from the application of multirelations, including security, voting systems, transmission protocols, resource-sharing protocols and games.

References

[BvW98]   Back, R.-J., von Wright, J.: Refinement Calculus: A Systematic Introduction. Graduate Texts in Computer Science. Springer-Verlag (1998)

[Bi98]   Bird, R. S.: Introduction to Functional Programming. Prentice Hall (1998)

[BdM97]   Bird, R. S., de Moor, O.: Algebra of Programming. Prentice Hall (1997)
[BB95]   Back, R.-J., Butler, M. J.: Exploring summation and product operators
           in the refinement calculus. In Möller, B., ed.: Proc. of 3rd Int. Conf.
           on Mathematics of Program Construction, MPC ' 95, Vol. 947 of Lect.
           Notes in Comput. Sci. Springer-Verlag (1995) 128–158
[BaW90]   Barr, M., Wells, C.: Category Theory for Computing Science. Prentice-
           Hall (1990)
[BF02]   Brams, S. J., Fishburn, P. C.: Voting procedures. In Arrow, K. J., Sen,
           A. K., Suzumura, K., eds.: Handbook of Social Choice and Welfare,
           Vol. 1. North-Holland (2002) 173–206
[CK84]   Carboni, A., Kasangian, S.: Bicategories of spans and relations. J. of
           Pure and Appl. Algebra **33** (1984) 259–267.
[DaP02]   Davey, B. A., Priestley, H. A.: Introduction to Lattices and Order. 2nd
           edn. Cambridge University Press (2002)
[DiS90]   Dijkstra, E. W., Scholten, C. S: Predicate Calculus and Program Seman-
           tics. Springer-Verlag (1990)
[EW67]   Eilenberg, S., Wright, J. B.: Automata in general algebras. Inform. and
           Control **11**(4) (1967) 452–470
[FL79]   Fischer, M. J., Ladner, R. E.: Propositional logic of regular programs.
           J. of Comput. and Syst. Sci. **18** (1979) 194–211
[Fo94]   Fokkinga, M. M.: Monadic maps and folds for arbitrary datatypes. Mem-
           oranda Informatica 94-28. University of Twente (1994)
[FrS93]   Freyd, P., Ščedrov, A.: Categories, Allegories. Vol. 39 of North-Holland
           Math. Library. North-Holland (1990)
[GMdM94]   Gardiner, P. H. B., Martin, C. E. and de Moor, O.: An algebraic con-
           struction of predicate transformers. Sci. of Comput. Program. **22**(1–2)
           (1994) 21–44.
[MCR04]   Martin, C. E., Curtis, S. A. and Rewitzky, I.: Modelling nondeterminism.
           In Kozen, D., Shankland, C.: Proc. of 7th Int. Conf. on Mathematics of
           Program Construction, MPC 2004. Vol. 3125 of Lect. Notes in Comput.
           Sci. Springer-Verlag (2004) 228–251.
[deM92]   de Moor, O.: Inductive data types for predicate transformers. Inform.
           Process. Lett. **43**(3) (1992) 113–117
[Rew03]   Rewitzky, I.: Binary multirelations. In de Swart, H., Orlowska, E.,
           Schmidt, G., Roubens M., eds.: Revised Papers from COST Action 274
           TARSKI on Theory and Application of Relational Structures as Knowl-
           edge Instruments. Vol. 2929 of Lect. Notes in Comput. Sci. Springer-
           Verlag (2003) 256–271
[W94]   Ward, N. T. E.: A Refinement Calculus for Nondeterministic Expres-
           sions. PhD thesis. Univ. of Queensland (1994)

Appendix

The following example shows that strongest postconditions do not necessarily
correspond to angelic choices.

Example 6.1. Let $M : Int \rightrightarrows Int$ be defined for all $x : Int$, $X : \mathbb{P}\,Int$, by

$$x \; M \; X \Leftrightarrow (\exists\, y : x < y : up \; y \subseteq X)$$

where $up\ y = \{n : Int \mid y \leq n\}$. This multirelation can model a game where the angel chooses a number greater than the input value x and the demon then outputs any number that is at least as large as the one chosen by the angel. The choices offered to the angel are among an infinite sequence $up\,(x + 1)$, $up\,(x + 2),\ldots$ of postconditions, each stronger than its predecessor. This multirelation has no strongest postconditions because it is always possible to find a postcondition that is stronger than any other given postcondition.   □

This is not the only multirelation with no strongest postconditions, since for example abort has none either. So it follows that a multirelation is not uniquely determined by its set of strongest postconditions.

Just after Definition 5.2 it was claimed that **Mul** has unique map factorisation.

Proof. First suppose that $r : D \rightrightarrows A$, $s : D \rightrightarrows B$, $t : C \rightrightarrows A$, $u : C \rightrightarrows B$ and $h : D \rightrightarrows C$ are demonic multirelations such that

$$h \mathbin{⨾} t \subseteq r \text{ and } s \subseteq h \mathbin{⨾} u \qquad (9)$$

then we can calculate that

$$
\begin{aligned}
& h \mathbin{⨾} t \subseteq r \text{ and } s \subseteq h \mathbin{⨾} u \\
\equiv\ & \{^* \text{ is a contravariant functor}\} \\
& r^* \subseteq t^* \mathbin{⨾} h^* \text{ and } s \subseteq h \mathbin{⨾} u \\
\Rightarrow\ & \{\text{Monotonicity of } \mathbin{⨾}\} \\
& r^* \mathbin{⨾} s \subseteq t^* \mathbin{⨾} h^* \mathbin{⨾} h \mathbin{⨾} u \\
\Rightarrow\ & \{\text{Definition of map (4)}\} \\
& r^* \mathbin{⨾} s \subseteq t^* \mathbin{⨾} u
\end{aligned}
$$

Notice that nothing in the above calculation depends on multirelations, and so it is true in any order-enriched category. For the converse, suppose that

$$r^* \mathbin{⨾} s \subseteq t^* \mathbin{⨾} u$$

then by the shunting rule (5), we have that

$$r^* \subseteq t^* \mathbin{⨾} u \mathbin{⨾} s^*$$

Since comaps are angelic, by Lemma 6.1 below, there exists h^* such that

$$
\begin{aligned}
& r^* \subseteq t^* \mathbin{⨾} h^* \text{ and } h^* \subseteq u \mathbin{⨾} s^* \\
\equiv\ & \{^* \text{ is a contravariant functor and shunting (5)}\} \\
& h \mathbin{⨾} t \subseteq r \text{ and } s \subseteq h \mathbin{⨾} u
\end{aligned}
$$

as required.   □

Lemma 6.1. *Let* $R : A \leftrightarrow C$, $S : A \leftrightarrow B$ *and* $M\ B \rightrightarrows C$ *then*

$$\langle R \rangle \subseteq \langle S \rangle \mathbin{\mathring{\,;}} M$$
$$\Rightarrow \exists H : B \leftrightarrow C :$$
$$\langle R \rangle \subseteq \langle S \rangle \mathbin{\mathring{\,;}} \langle H \rangle \ and \ \langle H \rangle \subseteq M$$

Proof

$$\langle R \rangle$$
$= \quad \{\in ; \{\ \}^{\circ} = id\}$
$$\langle R ; \in ; \{\ \}^{\circ} \rangle$$
$= \quad \{\text{Definition of } \langle\ \rangle\}$
$$\langle \langle R \rangle ; \{\ \}^{\circ} \rangle$$
$\subseteq \quad \{\text{Assumption and monotonicity of } \langle\ \rangle\}$
$$\langle (\langle S \rangle \mathbin{\mathring{\,;}} M) ; \{\ \}^{\circ} \rangle$$
$= \quad \{\text{Lemma 3.2 and associativity of } ;\}$
$$\langle S ; M ; \{\ \}^{\circ} \rangle$$
$= \quad \{\langle\ \rangle \text{ distributes through composition}\}$
$$\langle S \rangle \mathbin{\mathring{\,;}} \langle M ; \{\ \}^{\circ} \rangle$$

which establishes the result since $\langle \{\ \}^{\circ} \rangle \subseteq [\ni]$ and so

$$\langle M ; \{\ \}^{\circ} \rangle \subseteq \langle M \rangle \mathbin{\mathring{\,;}} [\ni] = M \qquad\qquad \square$$

Lemma 5.1

Proof. *$r^* ; s$ is a map factorisation of M, then*

    $F\ M$
$= \quad \{\textit{map factorisation}\}$
    $F\ (r^* ; s)$
$= \quad \{(6)\}$
    $F\ r^* ; F\ s$
$= \quad \{F \textit{ and } G \textit{ agree on maps (and hence comaps)}\}$
    $G\ r^* ; G\ s$
$= \quad \{(6)\}$
    $G\ (r^* ; s)$
$= \quad \{\textit{map factorisation}\}$
    $G\ M$ $\qquad\qquad\qquad\qquad\qquad \square$

A Datastructure for Iterated Powers

Ralph Matthes

Institut de Recherche en Informatique de Toulouse (IRIT),
C. N. R. S. et Université Paul Sabatier (Toulouse III),
118 route de Narbonne, F-31062 Toulouse Cedex 9, France
matthes@irit.fr

Abstract. Bushes are considered as the first example of a truly nested datatype, i. e., a family of datatypes indexed over all types where a constructor argument not only calls this family with a changing index but even with an index that involves the family itself. For the time being, no induction principles for these datatypes are known. However, the author has introduced with Abel and Uustalu (TCS 333(1–2), pp. 3–66, 2005) iteration schemes that guarantee to define only terminating functions on those datatypes.

The article uses a generalization of Bushes to n-fold self-application and shows how to define elements of these types that have a number of data entries that is obtained by iterated raising to the power of n. Moreover, the data entries are just all the n-branching trees up to a certain height.

The real question is how to extract this list of trees from that complicated data structure and to prove this extraction correct. Here, we use the "refined conventional iteration" from the cited article for the extraction and describe a verification that has been formally verified inside Coq with its predicative notion of set.

1 Introduction

Assume, we had a type transformation Bsh_3 that yields for every type A an abstract datatype Bsh_3A with just two datatype constructors

$$bnil_3 : Bsh_3A \ ,$$
$$bcons_3 : A \to (Bsh_3)^3A \to Bsh_3A \ .$$

As is usual, we write $F^nA := \underbrace{F(\ldots(F\,A)\ldots)}_{n\times}$ for F any type transformation.

With these constructors, Bsh_3 becomes a "nested datatype" in the sense of Bird and Meertens [7]: These are families of datatypes indexed over types (hence type transformations) where arguments of constructors of the family member with index A may refer to some other members of the family. A classical example are the powerlists that precisely represent perfect binary leaf trees: a powerlist over A is either an element of A or a powerlist over $A \times A$. In $bcons_3$, we even refer to the member with index $(Bsh_3)^2A$ that itself refers to Bsh_3. We would like to call such families truly nested datatypes.

T. Uustalu (Ed.): MPC 2006, LNCS 4014, pp. 299–315, 2006.
© Springer-Verlag Berlin Heidelberg 2006

Definition 1. *A truly nested datatype is a nested datatype with a call to the family name within a type argument of an argument of one of the datatype constructors.*

The treatment to come is not confined to truly nested datatypes but shows that even those complicated nested datatypes can be treated in a framework that guarantees termination of all programs.

The paper [7] considers an example, namely the analogous bushes with exponent 2 instead of our 3. There is not yet a well-established tradition in truly nested datatypes, and Bird and Paterson [8] study a family $Host$ just for demonstration purposes although they discuss an extended de Bruijn representation of lambda terms via true nesting elsewhere [9]. They also appear naturally in Hinze's account of generalized *trie* data structures [13]. But these works do not consider termination guarantees for the programs that traverse these data structures.

Type theory is well aware of termination questions. However, truly nested datatypes are not accepted as inductive definitions in the theorem prover Coq [23] since they are considered to violate the condition of strict positivity [6, Section 14.1.2.1]. This is certainly accepted due to the fact that there are not yet type-theoretical formulations of the reasoning principles for the proposed means of structured programming for these datatypes [8, 12, 17].

At least, there are already systems that guarantee termination of all functions that follow some type discipline in their recursive calls: With Abel and Uustalu [2, 3, 4], the author has proposed a number of iteration principles that can be used with truly nested datatypes and guarantee termination (strong normalization of the respective extension of Girard's system F^ω of higher-order polymorphism [10]). These iteration schemes can all be simulated already within F^ω and hence are available through encodings in Coq – with the universe Set taken to be impredicative, as it used to be in versions prior to 8.0. But impredicativity is still an option for the Coq system, and so the essential parts of the journal article [4] were implemented and verified in Coq in form of a student project with the author [22]. Here, we aim at something different. Although there is still no direct support for reasoning on truly nested datatypes in Coq, we may construct some of their more interesting elements and reason about what they contain.

Let us construct elements of $Bsh_3\,Tri$ with Tri the datatype of ternary unlabelled finite trees, hence just with the constructors

$$L : Tri \ ,$$
$$N : Tri \to Tri \to Tri \to Tri \ .$$

The function $mkTriBsh_3 : nat \to Bsh_3\,Tri$ shall take a natural number m and yield a bush that contains all the elements of Tri of height less than m. For this, we need a more general function $mkTriBsh_3'$ that takes a natural number m and a function argument f of type $Tri \to A$ for some type A and yields an element of $Bsh_3\,A$, in other words:

$$mkTriBsh_3' : nat \to \forall A.\,(Tri \to A) \to Bsh_3\,A \ .$$

The expression $\forall A.\,(Tri \rightarrow A) \rightarrow Bsh_3\,A$ is again a type, i.e., a member of Coq's Set, only if Set is impredicative. Otherwise, it is a construction of the framework (in Coq, an element of $Type$). We define $mkTriBsh_3'$ as the fixpoint F of the following structural recursion on nat (this is even plain iteration):

$$F\,0\,f := bnil_3\ ,$$
$$F(S m)f := bcons_3\,(f\,L)\,(Fm(\lambda t_1.Fm(\lambda t_2.Fm(\lambda t_3.f(Nt_1t_2t_3)))))\ .$$

Finally, set (implicitly taking $A := Tri$)

$$mkTriBsh_3\,m := mkTriBsh_3'\,m(\lambda x.x)\ .$$

Type-correctness can be seen as follows: If $t_1, t_2, t_3 : Tri$, then $f(Nt_1t_2t_3) : A$, hence $\lambda t_3.f(Nt_1t_2t_3) : Tri \rightarrow A$ which qualifies as functional argument for $mkTriBsh_3'\,m$. By induction hypothesis, we have $Fm(\lambda t_3.f(Nt_1t_2t_3)) : Bsh_3\,A$. The next step shows that in fact we have a polymorphic recursion here: The universally quantified type changes during the recursion. $\lambda t_2.Fm(\lambda t_3.f(Nt_1t_2t_3)) :$ $Tri \rightarrow Bsh_3\,A$ has $Bsh_3\,A$ in place of A, hence the recursive call with Fm yields an element of $Bsh_3(Bsh_3\,A)$. Moving up the hierarchy once more, we arrive at

$$Fm(\lambda t_1.Fm(\lambda t_2.Fm(\lambda t_3.f(Nt_1t_2t_3)))) : (Bsh_3)^3 A\ ,$$

which is a good second argument to $bcons_3$.

We would now like to argue that $mkTriBsh_3\,3$ contains precisely the Tri-elements of height less than 3, moreover that they do not occur several times. In essence, we would like to read off the bush the following list (drawn from the Coq development [18]):

```
L :: N L L L
  :: N L L (N L L L)
    :: N L (N L L L) L
      :: N L (N L L L) (N L L L)
        :: N (N L L L) L L
          :: N (N L L L) L (N L L L)
            :: N (N L L L) (N L L L) L
              :: N (N L L L) (N L L L) (N L L L) :: nil.
```

Therefore, there is the need for a function $toListBsh_3$ that transforms any element of Bsh_3A into a (finite) list over A. This cannot be done without the assumption that Bsh_3A has only elements that enter through $bnil_3$ and $bcons_3$. Unfortunately, we cannot say that Bsh_3A is the least set with some closure properties since we relate different instances of Bsh_3 – this is the problem with nested datatypes. The article [8] gives a semantics of nested datatypes within functor categories. Nested datatypes are then initial algebras for an endofunctor on a category of endofunctors. In order to have a better operational view and a termination guarantee through mere typing, Abel and the author introduced in [2] a system of iteration that depends not on an endofunctor on a functor category but just a rank-2 type transformer F with a *monotonicity witness* – a term of a type that expresses monotonicity of F. In the journal version [4] this has been turned into the system $It^\omega_\le$ (Section 6 of *loc. cit.*) of which we will show only the iterator with superscript $\kappa 1$ (we omit those superscripts altogether): Whenever F is a transformation of type transformations, then μF is a type transformation (the nested datatype associated with F). There is only one generic constructor *in* for the elements of μF for all those F's:

$$in : \forall F \forall A.\, F\,(\mu F)\, A \to \mu F\, A \ .$$

(If F happens to be a sum type, *in* represents a product of constructors, one for every summand.) In our case $Bsh_3 := \mu(BshF_3)$ with

$$BshF_3 := \lambda X \lambda A.\, 1 + A \times X(X(XA)) \ ,$$

and in particular, $in : (1 + A \times (Bsh_3)^3 A) \to Bsh_3 A$ whose type is isomorphic with the product of the types assigned to $bnil_3$ and $bcons_3$.

This is well-established tradition. The new contribution is the elimination rule that needs the following abbreviation for type transformations X, G (already present in [11]):

$$X \le G := \forall A \forall B.\, (A \to B) \to XA \to GB \ .$$

The more straightforward notion would have been

$$X \subseteq G := \forall A.\, XA \to GA \ .$$

It is important to base monotonicity of rank-2 type transformers on $\le$ instead of $\subseteq$, since otherwise truly nested datatypes will not be covered, see [4, Section 5.4].[1]

Monotonicity of a type transformation is thus expressed by $X \le X$. The notion of monotonicity for rank-2 type transformers F is defined analogously, but one level higher: The type construction $mon_2\, F$ (inhabiting $Type$ in Coq) is defined to be

$$mon_2\, F := \forall X \forall G.\, X \le G \to FX \le FG \ .$$

System $It^\omega_\le$ assumes a binary function symbol $It_=$ such that for every type transformation G, we have: If m has type $mon_2\, F$ and s has type $FG \subseteq G$, then $It_=(m, s)$ has type $\mu F \le G$. More pictorially:

$$\frac{\Gamma \vdash m : mon_2\, F \qquad \Gamma \vdash s : FG \subseteq G}{\Gamma \vdash It_=(m, s) : \mu F \le G}$$

There is no condition on F (except being transformation of type transformations) or G. The monotonicity witness m need not be closed, it may even be a variable

---

[1] One can pass from $X \subseteq G$ to $X \le G$ if X or G is monotone – certainly a standard assumption in any category-theoretic treatment when type constructors are interpreted as functors.

occurring in the typing context Γ. Certainly, the *step term* s corresponds to the morphism part of the F-algebra G – were this system based on category theory.

The computation rule is

$$It_{=}(m, s)f(in\,t) \longrightarrow s\,(m\,It_{=}(m, s)\,f\,t) \ .$$

Here $f : A \to B$ (from the definition of $\leq$) and $t : F(\mu F)A$, while X in the type of m is instantiated with μF. Hence, the terms on both sides of the rule have type GB. The major result of [2] has been that system F^{ω}, extended with these rules, is still strongly normalizing and hence yields total functions. This counts among the results on *type-based termination*: It is just the type of m that ensures that the recursive calls to $It_{=}(m, s)$ cannot go wrong: m dispatches the argument t (and the type-changing parameter f) to the iteratively defined function $It_{=}(m, s)$. (Note that applications are implicitly parenthesized to the left, hence there is no subterm $It_{=}(m, s)\,f\,t$ in the term to the right-hand side.)

The unavoidable disadvantage of this iteration scheme is that we cannot directly define a function $toListBsh_3 : Bsh_3 \subseteq list$. But we can define $toListBsh'_3 : Bsh_3 \leq list$ as $It_{=}(m, s)$ with the terms m and s, described as follows:

Assume $X \leq G$ and $A \to B$. We have to produce a term inhabiting

$$BshF_3XA \to BshF_3GB \ \equiv\ 1 + A \times X(X(XA)) \to 1 + B \times G(G(GB)) \ .$$

Trivially, we get from 1 to 1 and from A to B. So, we concentrate on

$$X(X(XA)) \to G(G(GB)) \ .$$

But this just requires three applications of the hypothesis $X \leq G$ to the hypothesis $A \to B$, thus illuminating the use of $\leq$ in place of $\subseteq$. Since this construction is the canonical one for $BshF_3$, let $bshf_3$ be a name for that monotonicity witness m.

For $s : BshF_3\,list \subseteq list$, the type nearly suggests the program: Assume a type A and an argument $t : 1 + A \times list(list(list A))$. We have to produce an element of $list A$. We do case analysis on the sum argument. In the left case, just return nil, in the right case, decompose the argument into $a : A$ and $b : list^3 A$. The first element of the list we output is a, and then $flatten(flatten\,b)$, with the usual operation $flatten : list^2 A \to list A$ that concatenates the argument lists.

With the computation rule, we get the following operational equations (we abbreviate $toListBsh'_3 := It_{=}(bsh f_3, s)$ by toL):

$$toL\,f\,bnil_3 = nil \ ,$$
$$toL\,f\,(bcons_3\,a\,b) = f\,a :: flatten(flatten(toL(toL(toL\,f))\,b)) \ .$$

The function parameter f is replaced by $toListBsh'_3(toListBsh'_3 f)$ in the outermost recursive call. The essential difficulty with truly nested datatypes is that the recursive function is used as a whole (for unspecified bush arguments in our case since the second argument is missing!) in the changing parameter f.

Setting that parameter to the identity, we arrive at the desired function $toListBsh_3$. Using a fuller specification that already uniquely determines the result, we will verify in general that $toListBsh_3(mkTriBsh_3\,m)$ always yields the list of all ternary trees with height less than m. And we will generalize this from 3-bushes to n-bushes.

Outline of the paper. After this lengthy introduction that gently introduced many of the needed concepts – in particular the iteration principle that we use throughout to read off lists from our bushes – we informally prove the statement on $mkTriBsh_3$. In section 3, the bushes are generalized to n-fold nesting, and such n-bushes are constructed in detail for the n-ary trees of a given maximum height, thus with an iterated power of entries. In section 4, a mathematical description of the structure of the verification of these n-bushes is given. There is sufficient detail so that everybody could do the proof without having any further ideas. But there is also a full development in the theorem prover Coq, commented in Section 5. It discusses the fine points while the development itself is available on the author's home page [18]. Future work and some further questions are addressed in Section 6.

2   Intuitive Verification

One can program the list of all ternary trees with height less than m by plain iteration on m without making reference to Bsh_3. Given $a : A$ and $s : A \to A$, we use the notation $[a; s]$ for the function $f : nat \to A$ that is defined by iteration as $f\,0 := a$ and $f\,(m+1) := s\,(f\,m)$. For example, $mkTriBsh'_3 = [a_B; s_B]$ with $a_B\,f := bnil_3$ and, for $v : \forall A.(Tri \to A) \to Bsh_3 A$ and $f : Tri \to A$,

$$s_B\,v\,f := bcons_3\,(f\,L)\,(v_{Bsh_3^2 A}(\lambda t_1.v_{Bsh_3 A}(\lambda t_2.v_A\,(\lambda t_3.f(Nt_1t_2t_3)))))\ .$$

(The indices to v are here just for information about the instantiation of the parameter A.)

The question arises how one could find this term s_B. Unfortunately, this cannot be answered fully here, but a motivation can be given.

Define $mkTriList : nat \to list\,Tri$ as $mkTriList := [a_L; s_L]$ with $a_L := nil$ and for $l : list\,Tri$

$$s_L\,l := L :: flatten\Big(flatten\Big(map\Big(\lambda t_1.map(\lambda t_2.map(\lambda t_3.\,Nt_1t_2t_3)l)l\Big)l\Big)\Big)\ .$$

Then $mkTriList\,0 = nil$, and $mkTriList(m+1) = s_L(mkTriList\,m)$.

The construction of s_L is explained as follows: If l contains all the ternary trees of height less than m, then all ternary trees of height less than $m+1$ are obtained by taking just a leaf L or by taking a node N with three trees from l. With t_1, t_2 from l fixed, $map(\lambda t_3.\,Nt_1t_2t_3)l$ builds the list of all $Nt_1t_2t_3$ with t_3 in l. The next step yields the list of these lists where t_2 runs through l, and, finally, the list of lists of lists when t_1 runs through l is obtained. Flattening twice and adding just L yields the result.

Hence, the problem is fully specified by $mkTriList$.

Theorem 1. *For all $m : nat$, $toListBsh_3(mkTriBsh_3\,m) = mkTriList\,m$.*

We cannot hope for a direct verification of this theorem by induction on m since $mkTriBsh_3'(m+1)(\lambda x.x)$ refers to instances of $mkTriBsh_3'\,m\,f$ with f not the identity.

Hence, the theorem has to be generalized for those arguments.

Lemma 1. *For all $m : nat, A, B, f : Tri \to A, g : A \to B$ holds*

$$toListBsh_3'\,g\,(mkTriBsh_3'\,m\,f) = map(g \circ f)(mkTriList\,m)\ .$$

The first idea here is to use the *fusion law* for natural numbers in order to express the right-hand side as a single iteration. To recall, fusion says that $f \circ [a; s] = [a'; s']$ if $a' = f\,a$ and $s' \circ f = f \circ s$ (to be proven by a simple induction over the natural numbers argument).

Let us define $mkTriListMap : nat \to \forall A.(Tri \to A) \to list\,A$ by

$$mkTriListMap\,m\,f := map\,f\,(mkTriList\,m)\ .$$

We will not be able to fix the parameter f in our intended application of the fusion law. Instead, we consider

$$map' : list\,Tri \to \forall A.\,(Tri \to A) \to list\,A\ ,$$

defined by $map'\,l\,f := map\,f\,l$. Thus, $mkTriListMap = map' \circ mkTriList$. Fusion will tell us that $mkTriListMap = [a_M; s_M]$ if $a_M = map'\,a_L$ and

$$s_M \circ map' = map' \circ s_L\ .$$

For the first equation, just set $a_M\,f := map'\,a_L\,f = map\,f\,nil = nil$. The second equation with arguments $l : list\,Tri, f : Tri \to A$ requires

$$s_M(\lambda f.\,map\,f\,l)f = map\,f\,(s_L\,l)\ .$$

We want to calculate the right-hand side of this equation. Here, we need categorical laws for map and $flatten$, namely the second functor law for map, i.e., that map commutes with composition, and naturality of $flatten$ as a transformation from $list^2$ to $list$: For all appropriate f, l,

$$flatten(map(map\,f)l) = map\,f(flatten\,l)\ .$$

With these, the right-hand side $map\,f\,(s_L\,l)$ above becomes

$$fL :: flatten\Big(flatten\Big(map\Big(\lambda t_1.map(\lambda t_2.map(\lambda t_3.\,f(Nt_1t_2t_3))l)l\Big)l\Big)\Big)\ .$$

Now, it is easy to find the definition of $s_M\,v\,f$ with $v : \forall A.\,(Tri \to A) \to list\,A$ that satisfies the equation:

$$s_M\,v\,f := fL :: flatten(flatten(v(\lambda t_1.v(\lambda t_2.v(\lambda t_3.\,f(Nt_1t_2t_3))))))\ .$$

Note that these arguments will need a good deal of extensionality: If two functions are pointwise equal, they are equal. This principle does not hold in intensional type theory. But this does not mean that our reasoning becomes wrong. There is only much more work to do, namely to show that the contexts in which we want to replace one function by "another" that is extensionally equal, only depend on the extension, i.e., on the values of the function. Details are in the Coq development [18], further discussion is to be found in Section 5.

Proving Lemma 1 now means showing

$$toListBsh'_3\, g\, (mkTriBsh'_3\, m\, f) = [a_M; s_M]\, m(g \circ f) \ .$$

With this specialized argument $g \circ f$ to $[a_M; s_M]\, m$, the author sees no hope for further program transformation that might have suggested the recursive definition of $mkTriBsh'_3$. However, the verification is now a plain induction on m that, in intensional type theory, also needs that $[a_M; s_M]\, m\, f$ only depends on the extension of f.

3   Programming the n-Bushes

The number $\sharp_3 m$ of ternary trees of height strictly less than m is given by

$$\begin{aligned}
\sharp_3 0 \quad &:= 0 \ , \\
\sharp_3(m+1) &:= (\sharp_3 m)^3 + 1 \ .
\end{aligned}$$

We get the sequence $(\sharp_3 m)_m$ of iterated third powers (plus 1): 0, 1, 2, 9, 730, 389017001, ... Hence, we now know that we can define elements of $Bsh_3\, Tri$ with $\sharp_3 m$ entries by unfolding m steps of the recursive definition of $mkTriBsh'_3$. We could now sort of generalize this by defining elements of $Bsh_3 A$ with $\sharp_3 m$ elements, described as the values of a function $f : nat \to A$ at the arguments $0, 1, \ldots, \sharp_3 m - 1$. However, for space reasons, this will only be part of the implementation [18] and not pursued further in this article.

But we do generalize in a second direction: The exponent 3 is quite immaterial to the ideas and is replaced by an arbitrary n. Defining and reasoning with arbitrary n is then a challenge for metaprogramming.

Definition 2 (power of type transformation). *Let X be a type transformation. Then $X^0 := \lambda A.A$ and $X^{k+1} := \lambda A.X(X^k A)$.*

Note that we put the "new" X on the outside. For the mathematician, this is immaterial. For our intended verification with Coq, this seems to be an important decision, to be discussed after Definition 5.

Definition 3 (n-bushes). *The rank-2 type transformation is*

$$BshF_n := \lambda X \lambda A.\, 1 + A \times X^n A$$

and its fixed point is $Bsh_n := \mu(BshF_n)$ (using the μ of the introduction that does not require any property of its argument).

Definition 4 (datatype constructors). $bnil_n := in(inl\langle\rangle)$ *with inl the left injection into the sum and* $bcons_n := \lambda a \lambda b. in(inr\langle a, b\rangle)$ *with inr the right injection and pairing operation* $\langle\cdot,\cdot\rangle$.

The parameter n will be fixed throughout (we do not relate Bsh_n and Bsh_m).

This time, we start with the bush decomposition function. Since we cannot argue with dots and braces that are given numbers of repetitions, we have to define the building blocks by iteration on k and then use them with $k := n$.

Definition 5 (iterated flattening). *Define* $flat_k : \forall A. list^k A \to listA$ *by iteration on* k *as follows:*

$$flat_0\, a \quad := a :: nil\ ,$$
$$flat_{k+1}\, l := flatten(map\, flat_k\, l)\ .$$

Remark. The much easier right-hand side $flatten(flat_k\, l)$ would require in the verification that $list(list^k A) = list^k(listA)$ is known to the type-checker which it is not, due to our decision in Definition 2. With some effort due to extensionality problems (also see Section 5), it can be shown nevertheless for every l, that $flat_2\, l = flatten\, l$ and $flat_3\, l = flatten(flatten\, l)$.[2] We used this last term up to now, but $toListBsh'_3$ will now only formally be different but not extensionally.

Definition 6 (lifting $\leq$ to the k-th power). *For type transformations* X, G *and* $i : X \leq G$ *define* $POW_k\, i : X^k \leq G^k$ *by iteration on* k:

$$POW_0\, i \quad := \lambda f.\, f\ ,$$
$$POW_{k+1}\, i := \lambda f.\, i(POW_k\, i\, f)\ .$$

Definition 7 (monotonicity witness). *Define* $bshf_n : mon_2(BshF_n)$ *in analogy with* $bshf_3$ *in the introduction: Assume* $i : X \leq G$, $f : A \to B$ *and* $t : BshF_n XA$. *Produce a term of type* $BshF_n GB$. *For this, do case analysis on* t. *If it is a left injection from 1, then inject this into the left. If it is the right injection of a pair of a term* $a : A$ *and a term* $b : X^n A$, *then inject the following pair into the right: It consists of* fa *and* $POW_n\, i\, f\, b$.

Definition 8 (listifying). *Define* $toListBsh'_n : Bsh_n \leq list$ *analogously to* $toListBsh'_3$ *in the introduction:* $toListBsh'_n := It_=(bshf_n, s)$ *with step term* $s : BshF_n\, list \subseteq list$ *just as before, but with* $flat_n\, b$ *instead of flattening* b *twice.*

We see that the earlier definition for $n = 3$ is only a special case modulo the remark after Definition 5. As usual, set $toListBsh_n := toListBsh'_n(\lambda x.x)$.

Lemma 2 (properties of $toListBsh'_n$). *The operational equations are*

$$toListBsh'_n\, f\, bnil_n = nil\quad and$$

$$toListBsh'_n\, f(bcons_n\, a\, b) = fa :: flat_n(POW_n\, toListBsh'_n\, f\, b)\ .$$

---

[2] The general statement $flat_{k+1}\, l = flatten^k\, l$ does not type-check. Using heterogeneous equality alluded to in Section 5, one can work around this problem so that a single proof is obtained which can be instantiated to every concrete number k.

Proof. Unfold the definitions and use the operational rule for the iterator.   □

The last three definitions only concerned the *analysis* of bushes. Now, we prepare for their definition.

Evidently, the number of n-ary unlabelled trees with height less than m is $\sharp_n m$, defined as follows:

Definition 9 (generalized $\sharp_n m$).

$$\begin{aligned}
\sharp_n 0 &:= 0 \ , \\
\sharp_n(m+1) &:= (\sharp_n m)^n + 1 \ .
\end{aligned}$$

The datatype of the n-ary unlabelled trees will be called $Tree_n$, with datatype constructors $L_n : Tree_n$ and $N_n : vec_n \to Tree_n$. Here (recall that we fix n throughout), vec_k shall represent the k-tuples of $Tree_n$, with datatype constructors

$$\begin{aligned}
vnil &: vec_0 \ , \\
vcons &: Tree_n \to \forall k.\, vec_k \to vec_{k+1} \ .
\end{aligned}$$

First, we generalize $mkTriList := [a_L; s_L] : nat \to list\, Tri$ to

$$mkTreeList_n := [a_{Ln}; s_{Ln}] : nat \to list\, Tree_n$$

with

$$\begin{aligned}
a_{Ln} &:= nil : list\, Tree_n \ , \\
s_{Ln} &:= \lambda l.\, L_n :: flat_n(\mathcal{L}\, l\, n\, N_n). : list\, Tree_n \to list\, Tree_n \ .
\end{aligned}$$

Here, we use the functional

$$\mathcal{L} : list\, Tree_n \to \forall k.\, (vec_k \to Tree_n) \to list^k Tree_n \ ,$$

defined by plain iteration on k as

$$\begin{aligned}
\mathcal{L}\, l\, 0\, f &:= f\, vnil \ , \\
\mathcal{L}\, l\, (k+1)\, f &:= map\Big(\lambda t.\, \mathcal{L}\, l\, k\, (f \circ (vcons\, t\, k))\Big) l \ .
\end{aligned}$$

Define for $t_1, t_2, t_3 : Tree_3$ the abbreviation

$$N_3' t_1 t_2 t_3 := N'(vcons\, t_1\, 2\, (vcons\, t_2\, 1\, (vcons\, t_3\, 0\, vnil))) : Tree_3 \ .$$

Definition unfolding yields

$$s_{L3}\, l = L_3 :: flat_3\Big(map\big(\lambda t_1.map(\lambda t_2.map(\lambda t_3.\, N_3' t_1 t_2 t_3)l)l\big)l\Big) \ .$$

Consequently, up to the remark after Definition 5 and to the isomorphism between Tri and $Tree_3$, we get back our previous s_L.

Again, the function $mkTreeList_n$ fully specifies what we expect from our bush-making function $mkTreeBsh_n : nat \to Bsh_n\, Tree_n$:

$$\forall m.\, toListBsh_n(mkTreeBsh_n\, m) = mkTreeList_n\, m \ .$$

Certainly, one could hope for a proof that this specification really meets our intuition, in the sense that it implies certain properties (a looser specification) such as the correct number of elements and that the elements are of the required maximum height. We shall be satisfied if our definition of $mkTreeBsh_n$ validates the specification above.

As usual, we define a more general function

$$mkTreeBsh'_n : nat \to \forall A. (Tree_n \to A) \to Bsh_n A$$

as $mkTreeBsh'_n := [a_{Bn}; s_{Bn}]$ and set

$$mkTreeBsh_n \, m := mkTreeBsh'_n \, m \, (\lambda x.x) \ .$$

For $v : \forall A. (Tree_n \to A) \to Bsh_n A$ and $f : Tree_n \to A$, define:

$$a_{Bn} \, f := bnil_3 \ ,$$
$$s_{Bn} \, v \, f := bcons_3(f \, L_n)(\mathcal{B} \, v \, n \, (f \circ N_n)) \ ,$$

where the functional

$$\mathcal{B} : (\forall A. (Tree_n \to A) \to Bsh_n A) \to \forall k \forall A. (vec_k \to A) \to Bsh^k_n A$$

is defined by plain iteration on k:

$$\mathcal{B} \, v \, 0 \, f := f \, vnil \ ,$$
$$\mathcal{B} \, v \, (k+1) \, f := v_{Bsh^k_n A}(\lambda t. \, \mathcal{B} \, v \, k \, (f \circ (vcons \, t \, k))) \ .$$

With these definitions, the case $n = 3$ is as follows:

$$s_{B3} \, v \, f = bcons_3 \, (f \, L_n) \, (v_{Bsh^2_3 A}(\lambda t_1.v_{Bsh_3 A}(\lambda t_2.v_A \, (\lambda t_3.f(N'_n t_1 t_2 t_3))))) \ ,$$

which is s_B up to the isomorphism between $Tree_3$ and Tri.

As is usual for nested datatypes, a statement for $mkTreeBsh'_n$ instead of $mkTreeBsh_n$ has to be proved:

Theorem 2 (soundness for general n). *For all numbers m, types A, B and functions $f : Tree_n \to A$, $g : A \to B$,*

$$toListBsh'_n \, g \, (mkTreeBsh'_n \, m \, f) = map(g \circ f)(mkTreeList_n \, m) \ .$$

The proof of the theorem occupies the next section.

4   Verification

Remember that we fixed some n. Theorem 2 will be shown by induction on m. So let $T \, m$ stand for its statement with m fixed. Due to the repeated (n times) use of our function $mkTreeBsh'_n \, m$ in the recursive call for $m+1$ (replacing the formal parameter v of s_{Bn}, there will also be n intermediate steps of a proposition $P \, m \, k$, given in Definition 10. From $T \, m$, we will successively prove $P \, m \, 0, \ldots, P \, m \, n$ and then be able to deduce $T(m+1)$, hence achieve the induction step of the theorem.

Definition 10 (Proposition). *Let* $P\,m\,k$ *be the following statement: For all types* A, B, *functions* $f_0 : vec_k \to Tree_n$, $f : Tree_n \to A$, $g : A \to B$,

$$flat_k(POW_k\,toListBsh'_n\,g\,(\mathcal{B}\,(mkTreeBsh'_n\,m)\,k\,(f \circ f_0))) =$$
$$map(g \circ f)(flat_k(\mathcal{L}\,(mkTriList_n\,m)\,k\,f_0)).$$

Lemma 3 (Theorem implies Proposition). *For all* m, *if* $T\,m$ *holds, then also for all* k, $P\,m\,k$ *holds.*

Proof. We fix m and assume $T\,m$ holds. Prove by induction on k that $P\,m\,k$ holds. The case $k = 0$ goes by unfolding of the definitions. For the inductive step we assume that $P\,m\,k$ holds and want to show $P\,m\,(k+1)$. This starts with simple unfolding of definitions. Then $T\,m$ is used with

$$\lambda t.\,\mathcal{B}\,(mkTreeBsh'_n\,m)\,k\,(f \circ f_0 \circ (vconst\,t\,k))$$

in place of f and $POW_k\,toListBsh'_n\,g$ in place of g. Then, the second functor law for map applies. Now, we may apply the induction hypothesis, namely that $P\,m\,k$ holds. Interestingly, this happens in the function argument of map (and the function f_0 for which the induction hypothesis is used will vary with that argument). In extensional mathematics, this is innocuous, but for the actual verification this requires further thought, see the next section. Once again, we have to use the second functor law for map and then naturality of $flatten$ (also used in Section 2; it can be proven by induction on lists and also needs that $map\,f$ is a homomorphism for list concatenation "++" which is in turn an easy induction). With this exception, we did not need any "free theorems" [24] in this verification. The free theorems say that every function of type $\forall A.\,X\,A \to G\,A$ with X, G functors, is natural in the sense of category theory. This is a very extensional view that would not be well supported by Coq.

Back to the proof: A further application of the second functor law for map suffices. Having the precise proof here does not seem necessary with this detailed description of the kind of reasoning that is needed.   □

The proof of Theorem 2 is then by induction on m: For $m = 0$ just calculate. The induction step is nearly an immediate application of the previous lemma with $k := n$, as announced earlier.

5   Implementation

The complete development in Coq can be found on the author's web page [18].

How does the presentation in this paper match with the implementation in Coq? Firstly, the current presentation lives in F^ω with type dependency on indices n and k added. If we regard n as a fixed constant, then this type dependency already disappears. Then, the induction over k can be reduced just to a step-by-step consideration of the cases $k := 0, \ldots, n$. Moreover, we adopted the raw syntax of the Curry-style typing. Hence, we might see ourselves precisely in the situation of the paper [4]. Hence, through the translations into F^ω given there, the programs can be found even in plain F^ω which is a subsystem of Coq's calculus of inductive constructions as long as *Set* is kept impredicative. Therefore, we know that these functions are all terminating despite their highly unconventional call structure. So good for the programs. Secondly, we never use in any way the universally quantified types in places where we speak about ordinary types. In other words, we do not use the full comprehension of impredicative *Set*. Thus, we may use (and have used) the new Coq 8.0 with predicative *Set* but cannot rely on the built-in equality any longer. The nested datatypes we used in this paper come just from a module parameter of a module type that has typed parameters for:

- the fixed point μ of rank-2 type constructors,
- the datatype constructor *in* and
- the iterator $It_=(\cdot, \cdot)$.

In addition, there is the hypothesis that $It_=(m, s)f(in\, t) = s(m\, It_=(m, s)\, f\, t)$, with $=$ not the built-in decidable convertibility relation but Leibniz equality that is animated by a rewriting mechanism in Coq. There is no implementation whatsoever. We just provide a name for a hypothetical implementation of this module type.

And there is no built-in termination guarantee. So, all the calculations have to be triggered by tactics that rewrite with equations. This will certainly have bad consequences if one wants to study types that depend on results computed from these iterators: The type-checker will not invoke the reductions, and rewritten arguments will no longer be feasible for these dependencies since equality can only be *expressed* between terms of types that are convertible (with respect to that built-in decidable convertibility relation). Fortunately, Coq also supports a heterogeneous equality that will not prove any equality between terms of types that are not provably equal, but where those equalities can at least be expressed. And as soon as they have been expressed, one may work on them by rewriting types with user-defined rewrite rules such as our computation rule for $It_=$. If this succeeds, one may finally also establish Leibniz equality. This heterogeneous equality has been introduced by McBride under the name "John Major Equality" [19] (see also [6, Section 8.2.7]), and there are even extensions of that idea that try to integrate extensional reasoning into intensional type theory [21].

Namely, rewriting has another defect: rewriting cannot be done under a λ-abstraction. Otherwise, the system would be extensional, and currently known extensional type theories have undecidable type-checking. Coq is definitely not based on extensional type theory, but many functionals do not distinguish between only extensionally equal argument functions. For example, *map f l* depends only on the extension of f. This is to say that whenever for all x, $fx = gx$, then $map\, f\, l = map\, g\, l$ for all l. This principle is easily proven by induction on lists l and used in the proof of Lemma 3. Much harder would be to show a similar extensionality of $toListBsh'_n\, f\, b$ for the argument f. One would need an induction principle for the n-bushes b that does not seem to exist yet. In a sense, it is not surprising that we do not need such extensionality for the proof of Lemma 3: the expression on the right-hand side of proposition $P\,m\,k$ only depends on the extension of f and g (due to the property of map just mentioned). So, if $P\,m\,k$ is true, then there should be no concern with extensionality of this kind because we can always pass to the other side in course of the induction proof.

To sum up this last discussion: We cannot assume that extensionally equal functions are equal, but our proofs only would have liked to apply extensionality in situations where those functions were arguments to a functional that is indifferent to intensional differences, as long as the extensions coincide. I would like to call those functionals *extensional* as well.

It should also be mentioned that we used the vectors from the Coq standard library Bvector that has a family of vectors for any type parameter. This explains why $Tree_n$ can be defined in Coq. Other attempts did not work, in particular a definition of the type of N_n as an iterated implication or the type of the argument of N_n as an iterated product.

6   Future Work and Conclusions

Is there a fusion law that would help in establishing Lemma 1 or even Theorem 2? The crucial problem is the splitting into f and g.

Generic programming [5] aims at descriptions of algorithms that exist for every datatype which follows a certain grammar of datatype functors. For nested datatypes, there are the "hofunctors" [8, 17]. Generic Haskell [14, 16] goes further up the hierarchy and allows all finite kinds. Since it generates a Haskell program after having inspected which datatypes are really used, it could perhaps be extended to support the shallow metaprogramming we undertook in this paper. Then Generic Haskell would be a generic extension even of DependentML [25]. Can the function $toListBsh'_n$ be obtained by generic programming?

In general, container types are now quite well understood [15]. Here, we speak about higher containers with true nesting that could and should be seen as strictly positive.[3] The authors of [1] speculate that their framework of Martin-Löf categories should also be useful in this more general setting (they excluded nested datatypes in that article). Will this shed some light on programming with truly nested datatypes?

It would be desirable to see a closer relationship with continuations since our examples worked on function arguments that first only produced elements of type A but climbed up the powers of $Bsh_n A$ in course of the recursion. One should be able to learn considerably from the approaches to program with these first-class higher-order functions.

What exactly is gained if one knows that a certain object is of type $Bsh_n A$ for some specific n and A? The powerlists mentioned in the introduction ensure that one has 2^i elements for some i. With n-bushes, this is by no means the

---

[3] Non-strict positivity is only concerned with appearences of the function space constructor in the type. Our framework does not exclude that at all, but we do not yet have interesting examples of nested datatypes which crucially contain $\rightarrow$.

case: One can construct easily elements of Bsh_n nat that contain exactly the first i numbers, for any i (this is also contained in the Coq development [18]). What we have seen is that only a recursion of height m is needed to get $\natural_n m$ elements and that one can precisely control what they are. Is this the maximum number? A theorem would require a precise computational model for its formulation.

For the moment, our contribution could perhaps more be understood as an adventure in types [20] - more precisely in truly nested container types.

And this adventure is only a beginning in the following sense: Although generic programs sometimes generate truly nested datatypes [13], they are seen as not yet proven useful. This might well be the case, but also the support by type-theoretic systems is still missing for them. Especially with these intricate iteration schemes, one would like to know – at least – that the programs terminate on finite input. Haskell does provide a programming environment, but no guarantees of that sort. In this article, we could reason about elements of truly nested datatypes since they were parameterized by datatypes as simple as the natural numbers. If the only purpose for generating such an n-bush were to flatten it immediately afterwards into a list, this would not justify our efforts. Once arrived in the realm of n-bushes, we would like to transform them – again with termination guarantees for those transformations. And we would like to reason about these transformations in a theorem prover that has decidable type-checking. The principles underlying such a reasoning have yet to be found. Then, truly nested datatypes like the n-bushes may start to prove their usefulness even if an adventure in types is not intended.

Acknowledgements. The questions that led to this paper were brought up by the student project of Dolma Rodriguez [22]. I am especially thankful to her for her program that computes a powerlist of height n with elements $1, \ldots, 2^n$, the linear 2-bush and the 2-bushes with a number of entries that iterates squares. And many thanks to Jan Johannsen who suggested to me to study the relation with the n-branching unlabelled trees of height less than m.

References

1. Abbott, M., Altenkirch, T., Ghani, N.: Containers: Constructing strictly positive types. Theor. Comput. Sci. **342**(1) (2005) 3–27
2. Abel, A., Matthes, R.: (Co-)iteration for higher-order nested datatypes. In Geuvers, H., Wiedijk, F., eds.: Selected Papers from 2nd Int. Wksh. on Types for Proofs and Programs, TYPES 2002. Vol. 2646 of Lect. Notes in Comput. Sci. Springer-Verlag (2003) 1–20
3. Abel, A., Matthes, R., Uustalu, T.: Generalized iteration and coiteration for higher-order nested datatypes. In Gordon, A., ed.: Proc. of 6th Int. Conf. on Foundations of Software Science and Computational Structures, FoSSaCS 2003. Vol. 2620 of Lect. Notes in Comput. Sci. Springer-Verlag (2003) 54–68
4. Abel, A., Matthes, R., Uustalu, T.: Iteration and coiteration schemes for higher-order and nested datatypes. Theor. Comput. Sci. **333**(1–2) (2005) 3–66

5. Backhouse, R., Jansson, P., Jeuring, J., Meertens, L.: Generic programming—an introduction. In Swierstra, S. D., Henriques, P. R., Oliveira, J. N., eds.: Revised Lectures from 3rd Int. School on Advanced Functional Programming, AFP '98. Vol. 1608 of Lect. Notes in Comput. Sci. Springer-Verlag (1999) 28–115

6. Bertot, Y., Castéran, P.: Interactive Theorem Proving and Program Development. Coq'Art: The Calculus of Inductive Constructions. Springer-Verlag (2004)

7. Bird, R., Meertens, L.: Nested datatypes. In Jeuring, J., ed.: Proc. of 4th Int. Conf. on Mathematics of Program Construction, MPC '98. Vol. 1422 of Lect. Notes in Comput. Sci. Springer-Verlag (1998) 52–67

8. Bird, R., Paterson, R.: Generalised folds for nested datatypes. Formal Aspects of Comput. **11**(2) (1999) 200–222

9. Bird, R. S., Paterson, R.: De Bruijn notation as a nested datatype. J. of Functional Programming **9**(1) (1999) 77–91

10. Girard, J.-Y.: Interprétation fonctionnelle et élimination des coupures dans l'arithmétique d'ordre supérieur. Doctorat d'État. Université de Paris VII (1972)

11. Hinze, R.: Polytypic values possess polykinded types. In Backhouse, R. C., Oliveira, J. N., eds.: Proc. of 5th Int. Conf. on Mathematics of Program Construction, MPC 2000. Vol 1837 of Lect. Notes in Comput. Sci. Springer-Verlag (2000) 2–27

12. Hinze, R.: Efficient generalized folds. In Jeuring, J., ed.: Proc. of 2nd Wksh. on Generic Programming, WGP 2000. Univ. Utrecht (2000)

13. Hinze, R.: Generalizing generalized tries. J. of Funct. Program. **10**(4) (2000) 327–351

14. Hinze, R., Jeuring, J.: Generic Haskell: practice and theory. In Backhouse, R., Gibbons, J., eds.: Advanced Lectures from Generic Programming. Vol. 2793 of Lect. Notes in Comput. Sci. Springer-Verlag (2003) 1–56

15. Hoogendijk, P. F., de Moor, O.: Container types categorically. J. of Funct. Program. **10**(2) (2000) 91–225

16. Löh, A.: Exploring Generic Haskell. Proefschrift (PhD thesis). Institute for Programming Research and Algorithmics, Universiteit Utrecht (2004) 331 pages.

17. Martin, C., Gibbons, J., Bayley, I.: Disciplined, efficient, generalised folds for nested datatypes. Formal Aspects of Comput. **16**(1) (2004) 19–35

18. Matthes, R.: Coq development for "A Datastructure for Iterated Powers". http://www.irit.fr/~Ralph.Matthes/Coq/MPC06/ (2006)

19. McBride, C.: Elimination with a motive. In Callaghan, P., Luo, Z., McKinna, J., Pollack, R., eds.: Selected Papers from 1st Int. Wksh. on Types for Proofs and Programs, TYPES 2000. Vol. 2277 of Lect. Notes in Comput. Sci. Springer-Verlag (2002), 197–216

20. Okasaki, C.: From fast exponentiation to square matrices: an adventure in types. In Proc. of 4th ACM SIGPLAN Int. Conf. on Functional Programming, ICFP '99. ACM Press (1999) 28–35

21. Oury, N.: Extensionality in the calculus of constructions. In Hurd, J., Melham, T. F., eds.: Proc. of 18th Int. Conf. on Theorem Proving in Higher Order Logics, TPHOLs 2005. Vol. 3603 of Lect. Notes in Comput. Sci. Springer-Verlag (2005), 278–293

22. Rodriguez, D.: Verification of (co)iteration schemes for nested datatypes in Coq. Student project, Inst. für Informatik, LMU München (2006)   Available from http://www.tcs.ifi.lmu.de/~rodrigue/project.html

23. The Coq Development Team: The Coq Proof Assistant Reference Manual Version 8.0. Project LogiCal, INRIA (2005) System available from `http://coq.inria.fr/`
24. Wadler, P.: Theorems for free! In Proc. of 4th Int. Conf. on Functional Programming Languages and Computer Architecture, FPCA '89. ACM Press (1989), 347–359
25. Xi, H.: Dependent Types in Practical Programming. PhD thesis, Carnegie Mellon University (1998)

Continuous Action System Refinement

Larissa Meinicke and Ian J. Hayes

School of Information Technology and Electrical Engineering,
The University of Queensland, Brisbane, Qld. 4072, Australia
{larissa, ianh}@itee.uq.edu.au

Abstract. Action systems are a framework for reasoning about discrete reactive systems. Back, Petre and Porres have extended these action systems to *continuous action systems*, which can be used to model hybrid systems. In this paper we define a refinement relation, and develop practical data refinement rules for continuous action systems.

The meaning of continuous action systems is expressed in terms of a mapping from continuous action systems to action systems. First, we present a new mapping from continuous action systems to action systems, such that Back's definition of trace refinement is correct with respect to it. Second, we present a stream semantics that is compatible with the trace semantics, but is preferable to it because it is more general. Although action system trace refinement rules are applicable to continuous action systems with a stream semantics, they are not complete. Finally, we introduce a new data refinement rule that is valid with respect to the stream semantics and can be used to prove refinements that are not possible in the trace semantics, and we analyse the completeness of our new rule in conjunction with the existing trace refinement rules.

1 Introduction

Action systems [4, 5] can be used to model discrete systems. Back, Petre and Porres extended action systems to *continuous action systems*, so that they could be used to model hybrid systems [1]. A hybrid system is one in which both continuous and discrete behaviour are modelled. In continuous action systems, variables are modelled as continuous timed streams and a special variable that represents the current time is introduced. Discrete (instantaneous) actions are used to update the continuous timed streams.

In the work of Back et al. [1], the behaviour of a continuous action system is defined in terms of an equivalent action system. This means that the definition of action system trace refinement [2] may be applied to continuous action systems. With respect to the definition of trace refinement, there are problems with the mapping from continuous action systems to action systems given by Back et al. [1]:

- It allows aborting action systems to be refined by ones that modify past behaviours.
- It requires the future values of output streams after every action to be preserved by refinement.

T. Uustalu (Ed.): MPC 2006, LNCS 4014, pp. 316–337, 2006.

The first problem allows a continuous action system to be refined by one that we consider to not faithfully preserve the behaviour of the continuous action system with respect to the intended interpretation. The second problem overly restricts allowable refinements. We provide a variation on their mapping from continuous action systems that addresses these problems.

Even though the new mapping avoids these problems the definition of action system trace refinement [2] is still overly restrictive because it requires the timing of actions to be preserved by refinement. To overcome this problem we introduce the notion of stream semantics. In our stream semantics, the behaviour of a continuous action system is expressed in terms of the set of continuous timed streams that it generates. We formally define stream semantics for continuous action systems in terms of their trace semantics, and compare trace and stream semantics. We find that trace refinement implies stream refinement, but that the converse does not hold. As a result, we argue that stream semantics should be used instead of the trace semantics because it is more general.

Practical refinement rules (simulation and cosimulation rules) exist for proving trace refinements between action systems [2]. Since trace refinement implies stream refinement, we may use these to prove stream refinements between continuous action systems. However, because stream semantics are more general than trace semantics, the trace refinement rules alone are incomplete for continuous action systems with a stream semantics. We introduce a new data refinement rule for continuous action systems that is able to prove refinements that are valid in the stream—but not the trace—model. For a subclass of continuous action systems, we demonstrate that our new rule in conjunction with the standard data refinement rules are as complete for continuous action system stream refinement as the action system data refinement rules are for standard action system trace refinement.

The following three sections contain background information relevant to the paper: the structure and semantics of action systems is described in Sections 2 and 3, Sect. 4 describes continuous action systems and their interpretation as action systems. In Sections 5, 6 and 7 we examine the semantics of continuous action systems in detail: an alternative mapping from continuous action systems to action systems is defined, a stream semantics for continuous action systems is given, and we perform a comparison between the stream and trace semantics. In Sect. 8 an algebra for reasoning about the semantics of continuous action systems is constructed and used to develop a new stream data refinement rule, and we discuss the completeness of the data refinement rules.

2   Action Systems

An action system [4, 5] is of the form:

$$|[\, \textbf{var}\ x_1 : X_1;\ ...;\ x_n : X_n;\ S_0;\ \textbf{do}\ S\ \textbf{od}]\,|{:}< z_1 : Z_1, ..., z_m : Z_m >$$

where each x_i is a local variable, and each z_j is a global variable. S_0 is an *initialisation action* that initialises the local variables without modifying the global variables. S is an *action* that operates on the combined local and global state space. The following syntax is used to represent commands used in actions.

$$S ::= \{g\} \mid [g] \mid x := e \mid S_1;\ S_2 \mid S_1 \sqcap S_2 \mid \sqcap i : T \bullet S_i \mid S^{\omega} \mid S^* \mid S^{\infty}$$

Here g is a predicate, x is a variable in the state space, and e is an expression on the state space. The semantics of our actions are described using conjunctive *predicate transformers*. A predicate transformer is a function from predicates on the output state space Γ to predicates on the input state space Σ. Given a predicate transformer $S : (\Gamma \to \mathbb{B}) \to (\Sigma \to \mathbb{B})$ and a predicate q, $S.q$ returns the weakest precondition of S to achieve q. The conjugate of $S.q$ is written $\overline{S}.q$, and is defined as $\neg S.(\neg q)$. Informally, $\overline{S}.q$ specifies the set of states from which S may possibly achieve q (but is not necessarily guaranteed to achieve q). A predicate transformer S, is conjunctive if it distributes over nonempty meets, i.e., if $S.(\bigwedge i : I \bullet q_i) = (\bigwedge i : I \bullet S.q_i)$. Conjunctivity implies monotonicity. A predicate transformer S_2 is said to be a refinement of S_1 if, for all predicates q, the weakest precondition of S_2 to achieve q is implied by the weakest precondition of S_1 to achieve q:

$$S_1 \sqsubseteq S_2 \triangleq \forall q \bullet S_1.q \Rightarrow S_2.q$$

More detailed information about predicate transformers and program refinement can be found elsewhere [3, 13, 9].

Assertion :	$(\{g\}).q$	$g \wedge q$
Coercion :	$([g]).q$	$g \Rightarrow q$
Assignment :	$(x := e).q$	$q[x \setminus e]$
Sequential composition :	$(S_1;\ S_2).q$	$S_1.(S_2.q)$
Nondeterministic choice :	$(S_1 \sqcap S_2).q$	$S_1.q \wedge S_2.q$
General nondet. choice :	$(\sqcap i : T \bullet S_i).q$	$\bigwedge i : T \bullet S_i.q$
Strong iteration :	$(S^{\omega}).q$	$(\mu\, T \bullet S;\ T \sqcap \mathbf{skip}).q$
Weak iteration :	$(S^*).q$	$(\nu\, T \bullet S;\ T \sqcap \mathbf{skip}).q$
Infinite iteration :	$(S^{\infty}).q$	$(\mu\, T \bullet S;\ T).q$
skip :	$\mathbf{skip}$	$[true]$
magic :	$\mathbf{magic}$	$[false]$
abort :	$\mathbf{abort}$	$\{false\}$

Fig. 1. Predicate transformer semantics of actions

In Fig. 1 we give a semantics for commands in which we identify a command with its predicate transformer. Assignment, assertion, coercion, nondeterministic choice, and sequential composition have the usual definitions. The unary operators $(^*, {}^{\omega}, {}^{\infty})$ have the highest precedence, followed by ";", and then "$\sqcap$". We use the iteration constructs of Back and von Wright [6, 3]. Informally, weak iteration S^* performs the operation S any finite number of times. Strong iteration S^{ω}

either performs S any finite or any infinite number of times. Infinite iteration S^∞ performs S an infinite number of times. Strong and infinite iteration are defined using the least fixed point operators, while weak iteration is defined using the greatest fixed point operator. **skip** has no effect on the state. In terms of the refinement lattice, the least predicate transformer is **abort**, while the greatest predicate transformer is **magic**. **abort** is not guaranteed to terminate or produce any particular output. Infinite iterations of predicate transformers are considered to be aborting: for example, $\mathbf{skip}^\infty = \mathbf{skip}^\omega = \mathbf{abort}$. **magic** is miraculous, it can achieve everything, but it cannot be implemented.

We refer to the state space of an action system $\mathbf{A}$ as Σ_A, which is a mapping from the names of variables in $\mathbf{A}$, to the types of the variables (in each $\sigma : \Sigma_A$ each variable name must be mapped to a value in the corresponding type for that variable). The local and global parts of this space are referred to as $local.\Sigma_A$ and $global.\Sigma_A$ respectively, where $local.\Sigma_A$ and $global.\Sigma_A$ must have disjoint domains. For any state $\sigma : \Sigma_A$, we have that

$$local.\sigma \triangleq dom.(local.\Sigma_A) \lhd \sigma$$
$$global.\sigma \triangleq dom.(global.\Sigma_A) \lhd \sigma$$

where "$\lhd$" represents domain restriction. Given an action system $\mathbf{A}$, we refer to the initialisation action of $\mathbf{A}$ as A_0 and the action as A. The guard of action A is denoted by $g.A$, and $t.A$ denotes the states from which action A terminates,

$$g.A \triangleq \neg A.False$$
$$t.A \triangleq A.True$$

We write $A = g_1 \rightarrow S_1 \ [\!] \ ... \ [\!] \ g_m \rightarrow S_m$, to mean that $A = [g_1]; S_1 \sqcap ... \sqcap [g_m]; S_m$, where each g_i is a predicate and each S_i is a predicate transformer. For an action A of this form, we also refer to each predicate transformer "$[g_i]; S_i$" as an action (an action can be viewed as a nondeterministic choice between a finite set of actions). If all predicate transformers S_i are non-miraculous for $A = g_1 \rightarrow S_1 \ [\!] \ ... \ [\!] \ g_m \rightarrow S_m$, then $g.A$ is simply $\bigvee i \bullet g_i$, and $t.A$ is $\bigwedge i \bullet t.([g_i]; S_i)$.

3   Action System Trace Semantics

Back and von Wright have given a semantics for action systems in terms of traces [2]. The trace semantics of an action system $\mathbf{A}$ is given in terms of sets of *behaviours* that $\mathbf{A}$ may produce, $beh.\mathbf{A} : \mathbb{P}(seq.\Sigma_A)$. Each behaviour is a finite or infinite sequence of states from Σ_A (the state space of $\mathbf{A}$) that may be either terminating, nonterminating, or aborting. Each behaviour $b : beh.\mathbf{A}$ must satisfy the following conditions:

- The first state of b must be reachable by executing A_0 from a global initial state.
- For every pair of adjacent states in b, the second state must be reachable from the first by action A.

– For every state in b other than the final (for infinite behaviours there is no final state), $g.A$ and $t.A$ must hold.
– If b is finite then either $\neg g.A$ or $\neg t.A$ must hold in the final state.

A behaviour is defined to be terminating if it is finite and $\neg g.A$ holds in its final state; it is aborting if it is finite and its last final state satisfies $\neg t.A$, it is nonterminating if it is neither terminating or aborting.

$$term.b \triangleq finite.b \wedge last.b \in \neg g.A \tag{1}$$
$$aborting.b \triangleq finite.b \wedge last.b \in \neg t.A \tag{2}$$
$$nonterm.b \triangleq \neg finite.b \tag{3}$$

Note that action systems are reactive, hence their behaviour differs from that of predicate transformers. In reactive systems, the behaviour of the system up until an aborting action is executed is preserved. This means that nonterminating reactive systems that don't contain aborting actions generate behaviours of infinite length, while nonterminating predicate transformers are considered to be aborting.

An action system $\mathbf{A}$ is refined by another action system $\mathbf{C}$, if the globally visible behaviour of $\mathbf{C}$ is permitted by $\mathbf{A}$. In standard action systems, the globally visible view of a behaviour b is a *trace* $tr.b$ of type $seq.(global.\Sigma_A)$. A trace of a behaviour is simply the behaviour with all finite sequences of *stuttering* steps and local states removed: a stuttering step is a step which does not modify the global state. Formally, the trace refinement relation $\sqsubseteq_{tr}$ between two action systems $\mathbf{A}$ and $\mathbf{C}$ is defined as follows [2]

$$\mathbf{A} \sqsubseteq_{tr} \mathbf{C} \triangleq \forall b_C : beh.\mathbf{C} \bullet (\exists b_A : beh.\mathbf{A} \bullet b_A \preceq_{tr} b_C)$$

where $b_A \preceq_{tr} b_C$ if, neither $tr.b_A$ nor $tr.b_C$ is aborting and $tr.b_A = tr.b_C$, or $tr.b_A$ is aborting and is a prefix of the sequence $tr.b_C$.

4   Continuous Action Systems

Continuous action systems have the same form as action systems, however all variables are represented as timed streams. For some type VAL we define the set of all timed streams on VAL, $Stream.VAL$, as the set of total functions from $Time$ to VAL:

$$Stream \triangleq \lambda VAL \bullet Time \rightarrow VAL$$

where $Time$ is defined to be the set of non-negative real numbers. For any $s : Stream.VAL$, and time interval I, we refer to the stream s over time interval I as $s \downarrow I$. We write $s \ll s'$ to mean that s is a stream prefix of s'.

An implicit variable τ of type $Time$ is used to refer to the current time. Actions that are performed on the continuous state space are atomic and they take no time to execute: time is allowed to pass between the execution of actions. Actions are constrained such that they cannot change the past: they are only allowed to change future values of timed streams. The initialisation command and the action may refer to the implicit variable τ however they may not update it. This variable is implicitly initialised and updated.

Given a variable x and an expression on the state space, the future update statement $x :- e$ [1] is defined as

$$x :- e \;\triangleq\; x := \lambda\, t \bullet \text{ if } t < \tau \text{ then } x.t \text{ else } e.t$$

This assignment statement is used instead of ":=" in order to ensure that actions do not change the past. We express nondeterministic future assignment as

$$x :\in E \;\triangleq\; \sqcap e : E \bullet x :- e$$

where E is a set of expressions on the state.

Any discrete (non-stream) variable, may be given a stream interpretation. For example a variable x of type $\mathbb{N}$ may be interpreted as a variable of type $Stream.\mathbb{N}$, the occurrence of x in expressions may be replaced by $x.\tau$, and assignments $x := v$ can be taken to mean $x :- (\lambda t : Time \bullet v)$. In later examples, for brevity, we define some continuous action system variables to be of discrete types.

The meaning of a continuous action system is expressed by Back et al. [1] using an equivalent action system.

Definition 1 (actSysOLD). *Given a continuous action system* **CA**, *with local variables* $x_i : Stream.X_i$ *for* $i \in [1..n]$, *global variables* $z_j : Stream.Z_j$ *for* $j \in [1..m]$, *initialisation action* A_0, *and action* A, *actSysOLD.***CA** *is defined as*

$$\begin{aligned}
&|[\,\textbf{var}\ \tau : Time, x_1 : Stream.X_1;\ ...;\ x_n : Stream.X_n; \\
&\qquad \tau := 0;\ A_0;\ N;\ \textbf{do}\ A;\ N\ \textbf{od} \\
&\,]|:< z_1 : Stream.Z_1, ..., z_m : Stream.Z_m >
\end{aligned}$$

where

$$N \;\triangleq\; (\tau := next.(g.A).\tau)$$

$$next.gg.t \;\triangleq\; \begin{cases} min\{t' \mid t' \geq t \land gg.t'\}, & \text{if } (\exists\, t' \bullet t' \geq t \land gg.t') \\ t, & \text{otherwise} \end{cases}$$

In this mapping the variable τ is introduced, and initialised to zero. After the execution of each action τ is advanced to the earliest time the action will be enabled, if such a time exists; τ is not modified if no more commands will ever be enabled, or if a command is currently enabled. Although a continuous action system **CA** may map to a terminating action system, continuous action systems themselves have no termination time. Termination of $actSys.$**CA** merely signifies that from the termination time onwards, the stream variables evolve according to their last assignment.

Apart from satisfying these constraints, continuous action systems are not allowed to contain Zeno-behaviour: only a finite number of iterations are allowed in a finite period of time.

5   Continuous Action System Trace Semantics

Given the mapping from continuous action systems to action systems (Definition 1), we consider the definition of trace refinement to be invalid and overly restrictive for continuous action systems. We interpret it to be invalid because it allows aborting action systems to be refined incorrectly by action systems that modify past behaviours.

Continuous action systems should not modify past values of streams. This means that a behaviour that aborts at time t should not be refined by one that produces different output streams in the interval $[0..t)$, nor should it be refined by one that aborts at an earlier time. However, in Fig. 2 we can see that **CJ** is a trace refinement of **CI**: from initial state $y = y_0$, **CI** produces global trace $\langle y_0, f \rangle$, and then aborts, while **CJ** produces global output trace $\langle y_0, f, f \downarrow [0..1) ^\frown g \downarrow [1..\infty) \rangle$. (Where "$^\frown$" is the stream concatenation operator.) **CI** aborts at time 2. **CJ** does not abort, however, it produces a different output stream in the interval $[0..2)$. This problem arises because the time of program abortion is irrelevant to the definition of trace refinement.

$$\mathbf{CI} \triangleq$$
| [**var** $n : \mathbb{N}$;
   $n := 0$;
   do $(\tau = n = 0) \rightarrow y :- f;\ n := n + 2$
   | $(\tau = n = 2) \rightarrow abort$
   od
] | :< $y : Stream.\mathbb{N}$ >

$$\mathbf{CJ} \triangleq$$
| [**var** $n : \mathbb{N}$;
   $n := 0$;
   do $(\tau = n = 0) \rightarrow y :- f;\ n := n + 1$
   | $(\tau = n = 1) \rightarrow$
     $y :- g;\ n := n + 2$
   | $(\tau = n = 3) \rightarrow n := n + 1$
   od
] | :< $y : Stream.\mathbb{N}$ >

Fig. 2. Continuous action systems **CI** and **CJ**. f and g are functions of type $Stream.\mathbb{N}$.

We also consider the definition of trace refinement to be overly restrictive because the global stream variables are defined over all time: therefore the traces that describe the visible behaviour of the action system include information about the future values of output streams after each action. Since the future values of output streams may be modified by further actions, they should not have to be preserved by refinements. For example, we have that **CE** and **CF** (Fig. 3) produce the same overall output stream for y but, according to mapping $actSysOLD$ (Definition 1), they are not trace equivalent: **CE** is not a valid trace refinement of **CF**, although **CF** is a valid trace refinement of **CE**. After each action, the set of possible future values of the streams are not the same, even though both of these programs produce the same output streams. (Both systems produce the same global stream $y = f$.) From initial state $y = y_0$, **CE** produces the set of global traces of the form $\langle y_0, g_1, g_2, g_3... \rangle$, where $\forall i : \mathbb{N} \bullet g_i \downarrow [0..i] = f \downarrow [0..i]$, while **CF** produces the global trace $\langle y_0, f, f, f, ... \rangle$.

$\mathbf{CE} \triangleq$	$\mathbf{CF} \triangleq$
$\vert [\, \mathbf{var}\ n : \mathbb{N};$	$\vert [\, \mathbf{var}\ n : \mathbb{N};$
$\quad n := 0;$	$\quad n := 0;$
$\quad \mathbf{do}\ (\tau = n) \rightarrow$	$\quad \mathbf{do}\ (\tau = n) \rightarrow$
$\qquad n := n + 1;$	$\qquad n := n + 1;$
$\qquad y :\in \{g : Stream.\mathbb{N} \mid g {\downarrow} [0..n] = f {\downarrow} [0..n]\}$	$\qquad y :-f$
$\quad \mathbf{od}$	$\quad \mathbf{od}$
$]\vert :< y : Stream.\mathbb{N} >$	$]\vert :< y : Stream.\mathbb{N} >$

Fig. 3. Continuous action systems **CE** and **CF**. f is a function of type $Stream.\mathbb{N}$.

A simple modification to the mapping from continuous action systems to action systems alleviates these problems. In our modification the global variables are redefined as partial streams: they are used to describe the output streams that have already been produced (and cannot be modified by further actions). Future values of global variables are stored as local variables. At the end of an action, if no future actions will be enabled then the global variables are defined over all time; if future actions are enabled then the global variables are defined over the half-open interval $[0..\tau)$. A half-open interval is used in this last case because future actions may change the values of variables at time τ.

We define $Stream^*.VAL$ to be the set of all partial streams on VAL defined over both half-open and closed intervals, and $Stream^\omega.VAL$ to be set of all partial and total streams on VAL.

$$Stream^* \triangleq \lambda\ VAL \bullet$$
$$\{s : Time \nrightarrow VAL \mid \exists\, r : \mathbb{R} \bullet (dom.s = [0..r) \vee dom.s = [0..r])\}$$
$$Stream^\omega \triangleq \lambda\ VAL \bullet Stream.VAL \cup Stream^*.VAL$$

Definition 2 (actSys). *Given a continuous action system* **CA**, *with local variables* $x_i : Stream.X_i$ *for* $i \in [1..n]$, *global variables* $z_j : Stream.Z_j$ *for* $j \in [1..m]$, *initialisation action* A_0, *and action* A, *let* $z \triangleq \langle z_1, ..., z_m \rangle$, $z' \triangleq \langle z'_1, ..., z'_m \rangle$. *We define* $actSys.\mathbf{CA}$ *as*

$$\vert [\, \mathbf{var}\ \tau : Time;\ x_1 : Stream.X_1;\ ...;\ x_n : Stream.X_n;$$
$$z'_1 : Stream.Z_1;\ ...;\ z'_m : Stream.Z_m;$$
$$\tau := 0;\ A_0[z \setminus z'];\ M;$$
$$\mathbf{do}\ A[z \setminus z'];\ M\ \mathbf{od}$$
$$]\vert :< z_1 : Stream^\omega.Z_1, ..., z_m : Stream^\omega.Z_m >$$

where

$$M \triangleq \tau := next.(g.A[z \setminus z']).\tau;$$
$$z_1 := znext.(g.A[z \setminus z']).z'_1.\tau;\ ...;\ z_m := znext.(g.A[z \setminus z']).z'_m.\tau$$

$$next.gg.t \triangleq \begin{cases} min\{t' \mid t' \geq t \wedge gg.t'\}, & \text{if } (\exists\, t' \bullet t' \geq t \wedge gg.t') \\ t, & otherwise \end{cases}$$

$$znext.gg.z'.t \triangleq \begin{cases} z' {\downarrow} [0..t), & \text{if } gg.t \\ z' & otherwise \end{cases}$$

As before, the variable τ is introduced, and initialized to zero, and after the execution of each action τ is advanced to the earliest time an action will be enabled, if such a time exists. For each global variable z_j, a new local variable $z_j' : Stream.Z_j$ is introduced. This variable is used in actions A_0 and A instead of z_j. Each global variable z_j is redefined to be of type $Stream^\omega.Z_j$. After each action the global variables are updated so that they are defined either: over all time if no further actions are enabled, or just up until the current time if future actions are enabled.

Using our new mapping $actSys$, it is trivial to show that **CJ** is not a trace refinement of **CI** (Fig. 2). **CI** produces global trace $\langle f \downarrow [0..0), f \downarrow [0..2) \rangle$, while **CJ** produces global trace $\langle f \downarrow [0..0), f \downarrow [0..1), f \downarrow [0..1) \frown g \downarrow [1..\infty) \rangle$. We are also able to prove that continuous action systems **CE** and **CF** (Figure 3) are trace equivalent. We have that

$$
\begin{array}{ll}
\mathbf{E} \triangleq actSys.\mathbf{CE} = & \mathbf{F} \triangleq actSys.\mathbf{CF} = \\
|[\ \mathbf{var}\ \tau : Time, n : \mathbb{N}, y' : Stream.\mathbb{N}; & |[\ \mathbf{var}\ \tau : Time, n : \mathbb{N}, y' : Stream.\mathbb{N}; \\
\quad \tau, n, y := 0, 0, y' \downarrow [0..0); & \quad \tau, n, y := 0, 0, y' \downarrow [0..0); \\
\quad \mathbf{do}\ (\tau = n) \rightarrow & \quad \mathbf{do}\ (\tau = n) \rightarrow \\
\qquad n := n + 1; & \qquad n := n + 1; \\
\qquad y' :\in \{g : Stream.\mathbb{N}\ | & \qquad y' :- f; \\
\qquad\qquad g \downarrow [0..n] = f \downarrow [0..n]\}; & \qquad \tau, y := n, y' \downarrow [0..n] \\
\qquad \tau, y := n, y' \downarrow [0..n) & \quad \mathbf{od} \\
\quad \mathbf{od} & \ ]|:< y : Stream^\omega.\mathbb{N} > \\
\ ]|:< y : Stream^\omega.\mathbb{N} > &
\end{array}
$$

where we have simplified expressions *next* and *znext*. It can be seen that both **E** and **F** produce the nonterminating global trace $\langle f \downarrow [0..0), f \downarrow [0..1), f \downarrow [0..2), ... \rangle$, hence they are trace equivalent.

The parallel composition operator that Back et al. [1] defined for continuous action systems is performed at the continuous action system level (before mapping the continuous action systems to action systems), and hence it remains the same despite our modifications to the action system mapping $actSysOLD$.

6   Continuous Action System Stream Semantics

Trace refinement is valid with respect to our new mapping $actSys$ (Definition 2) from continuous action systems to action systems, however it is still overly restrictive: this is because trace refinement requires the timing of actions to be preserved by refinement. This information should not have to be preserved, because it does not influence the set of global output streams that may be produced. In this section we define a stream semantics for continuous action systems that overcomes this problem. The stream semantics that we construct is a better choice of semantics than the trace model because it is more general.

Instead of using discrete traces over the continuous state variables to describe continuous action system semantics, we may describe its semantics in terms of the continuous timed streams that are generated by the program. We can express this alternative semantics in terms of the trace semantics of action systems. We define the set of streams that may be produced by a continuous action system **CA** as $behStreams.(actSys.\mathbf{CA})$, where

$$behStreams.\mathbf{A} \triangleq \{b : beh.\mathbf{A} \bullet behStream.b\} \tag{4}$$

$$behStream.b \triangleq (\lambda\, var : (dom.\Sigma_A - \tau) \bullet \lim getSeq.b.var) \tag{5}$$

$$getSeq.b.var \triangleq \begin{cases} (\lambda\, i : dom.b \bullet b.i.var \downarrow [0..b.i.\tau)) \\ \qquad \frown \langle last.b.var \downarrow Time \rangle, & \text{if } term.b \\ (\lambda\, i : dom.b \bullet b.i.var \downarrow [0..b.i.\tau)), \text{ otherwise} \end{cases} \tag{6}$$

Each stream is defined as the limit of a sequence of partial streams. (Back et al. [1] observed that the streams produced by continuous action systems could be defined in this way, although they did not specify that aborted sequences should be treated in the way we have done, nor do they define a refinement relation on sets of streams.) If the non-Zeno property holds (as assumed), then the limit of the sequence of partial streams $getSeq.b.var$ is defined over all time if b is not aborting, and is defined up until the time of abortion if b is aborting. Aborted behaviours produce partial timed streams that have an open interval at the end. Aborted streams do not define the value of the stream at the time of abortion because refinements may modify this value. Given a continuous action system **CA** and $s : behStream.(actSys.\mathbf{CA})$,

$$aborting.s \triangleq \exists\, r : Time \bullet (\forall\, var : dom.s \bullet dom.(s.var) = [0..r)) \tag{7}$$

The global behaviour of a stream $s : behStreams.\mathbf{CA}$ is referred to as $tr.s$, where

$$tr.s \triangleq global.s \tag{8}$$

If this semantics is adopted then a suitable notion of stream refinement, $\sqsubseteq_{str}$, between continuous action systems may be defined. Given two continuous action systems **CA** and **CB**, we say that **CB** is a stream refinement of **CA** if $actSys.\mathbf{CA} \sqsubseteq_{str} actSys.\mathbf{CB}$, where

$$\mathbf{A} \sqsubseteq_{str} \mathbf{B} \triangleq \forall\, s_B : behStreams.\mathbf{B} \bullet (\exists\, s_A : behStreams.\mathbf{A} \bullet s_A \preceq_{str} s_B) \tag{9}$$

where

$$s_A \preceq_{str} s_B \triangleq \begin{cases} tr.s_A \ll tr.s_B, & \text{if } aborting.(s_A) \\ tr.s_A = tr.s_B & \text{if } \neg aborting.(s_A) \end{cases}$$

Since our stream semantics is derived from the trace semantics, this definition of refinement is equivalent to the following: given action systems **A** and **B**,

$$\mathbf{A} \sqsubseteq_{str} \mathbf{B} \triangleq \forall\, b_B : beh.\mathbf{B} \bullet (\exists\, b_A : beh.\mathbf{A} \bullet behStream.b_A \preceq_{str} behStream.b_B) \tag{10}$$

This definition of refinement is used in later proofs. We write $\mathbf{CA} \sqsubseteq_{str} \mathbf{CB}$ to mean that **CA** is stream equivalent to **CB**.

7   Correspondence Between Trace and Stream Semantics

Simple refinement rules exist for proving trace refinements between action systems. It would be useful if we could use these to prove stream refinements between continuous action systems. In this section, we show that if a refinement is valid using trace semantics then it is also valid using stream semantics.

Lemma 3. *For any continuous action system* **CA**, *and* $b : beh.(actSys.\mathbf{CA})$, *we have that: aborting.b* $\Leftrightarrow$ *aborting.(behStream.b).*

Proof. This follows from the definition of *aborting* for behaviours (2) and streams (7), the definitions of *behStream* (5), and *actSys* (Definition 2)), and the non-Zeno property for continuous action systems.   □

Lemma 4. *For any continuous action system* **CA**, *and* $b : beh.(actSys.\mathbf{CA})$,

$$tr.(behStream.b) = trStream.(tr.b)$$

where

$$trStream.(tr.b) \triangleq \lambda\, var : dom.(global.\Sigma_A) \bullet \lim(\lambda\, i : dom.(tr.b) \bullet (tr.b).i.var)$$

Proof. This follows directly from *behStream* (5), *tr* for both behaviours and streams (8), and *actSys* (Definition 2).   □

Lemma 5. *For continuous action systems* **CA** *and* **CB** *with the same global state space, and* $b_A : beh.(actSys.\mathbf{CA})$, $b_B : beh.(actSys.\mathbf{CB})$,

$$(b_A \preceq_{\mathrm{tr}} b_B) \Rightarrow (behStream.b_A \preceq_{\mathrm{str}} behStream.b_B)$$

Proof. We prove this by cases.

Case 1: *aborting.*b_A
$(b_A \preceq_{\mathrm{tr}} b_B)$
$\Rightarrow$ (Definition $\preceq_{\mathrm{tr}}$ and *aborting.*b_A)
    $\exists\, n : dom.b_B \bullet (\forall\, var : dom.(global.\Sigma_A) \bullet last.b_A.var = b_B.n.var)$
$\Leftrightarrow$ (*actSys* (Definition 2) and *aborting.*b_A)
    $\exists\, n : dom.b_B \bullet (\forall\, var : dom.(global.\Sigma_A) \bullet$
        $last.b_A.var \downarrow [0..last.b_A.\tau) = b_B.n.var \downarrow [0..b_B.n.\tau))$
$\Leftrightarrow$ (*getSeq* (6))
    $\exists\, n : dom.b_B \bullet (\forall\, var : dom.(global.\Sigma_A) \bullet$
        $\lim getSeq.b_A.var = b_B.n.var \downarrow [0..last.b_B.\tau))$
$\Rightarrow$ (*actSys* (Definition 2) and *getSeq* (6). Note that from *actSys* and the constraints on continuous action systems, we have that actions cannot change the past.)
    $\forall\, var : dom.(global.\Sigma_A) \bullet \lim getSeq.b_A.var \ll \lim getSeq.b_B.var$
$\Leftrightarrow$ (*behStream* (5) and *tr* (8))
    $tr.(behStream.b_A) \ll tr.(behStream.b_B)$
$\Leftrightarrow$ (*aborting.*b_A and Lemma 3)
    $tr.(behStream.b_A) \ll tr.(behStream.b_B) \wedge aborting.(behStream.b_A)$
$\Leftrightarrow$ ($\preceq_{\mathrm{str}}$)
    $behStream.b_A \preceq_{\mathrm{str}} behStream.b_B$

Case 2: $\neg aborting.b_A$

$(b_A \preceq_{\mathrm{tr}} b_B)$
$\Leftrightarrow$ (Definition $\preceq_{\mathrm{tr}}$ and $\neg aborting.b_A$)
$tr.b_A = tr.b_B$
$\Rightarrow$ (Lemma 4)
$tr.(behStream.b_A) = tr.(behStream.b_B)$
$\Leftrightarrow$ ($\neg aborting.b_A$ and Lemma 3)
$tr.(behStream.b_A) = tr.(behStream.b_B) \wedge \neg aborting.(behStream.b_A)$
$\Leftrightarrow$ ($\preceq_{\mathrm{str}}$)
$behStream.b_A \preceq_{\mathrm{str}} behStream.b_B$

$\square$

Theorem 6. *For all continuous action systems* **CA** *and* **CB**,

$$(actSys.\mathbf{CA} \sqsubseteq_{\mathrm{tr}} actSys.\mathbf{CB}) \Rightarrow (actSys.\mathbf{CA} \sqsubseteq_{\mathrm{str}} actSys.\mathbf{CB})$$

Proof. We have that,

$b_B \in beh.(actSys.\mathbf{CB})$
$\Rightarrow (actSys.\mathbf{CA} \sqsubseteq_{\mathrm{tr}} actSys.\mathbf{CB})$
$\exists\, b_A \in beh.(actSys.\mathbf{CA}) \bullet b_A \preceq_{\mathrm{tr}} b_B$
$\Rightarrow$ (Lemma 5)
$\exists\, b_A \in beh.(actSys.\mathbf{CA}) \bullet behStream.b_A \preceq_{\mathrm{str}} behStream.b_B$

Hence, by the definition of stream refinement (10), $actSys.\mathbf{CA} \sqsubseteq_{\mathrm{str}} actSys.$
$\mathbf{CB}$. $\square$

The converse does not hold. That is, it is not true for all continuous action systems **CA** and **CB** that

$$(actSys.\mathbf{CA} \sqsubseteq_{\mathrm{str}} actSys.\mathbf{CB}) \Rightarrow (actSys.\mathbf{CA} \sqsubseteq_{\mathrm{tr}} actSys.\mathbf{CB})$$

For example we have that **CM** and **CN** (Fig. 4) are stream equivalent, but not trace equivalent. In **CN**, the action from **CM** has been decomposed into two steps. Both **CM** and **CN** produce global output stream f, however, **CM** produces global trace $\langle f \downarrow [0..0), f \downarrow [0..1), f \downarrow [0..2), ...\rangle$, while **CN** produces global trace $\langle f \downarrow [0..0), f \downarrow [0..0.5), f \downarrow [0..1), f \downarrow [0..1.5), ...\rangle$. Both traces are not aborting, but they are not equal. However, their limits are the same.

8 Data Refinement

As mentioned in the previous section, trace refinement is incomplete for continuous action systems with a stream semantics: that is, there exist valid stream refinements that are considered to be invalid in the trace model. In this section we derive a new simulation rule for proving stream refinements between continuous action systems. This rule can be used to prove refinements that are valid in the stream semantics, but may not be valid in the trace semantics. We then analyse the completeness of our new rule in conjunction with the action system data refinement rules. For our proofs we make use of algebraic properties of action systems.

$\text{CM} \triangleq$
$|[\ \textbf{var}\ n : \mathbb{R};$
$\quad n := 0;$
$\quad \textbf{do}\ \tau = n \rightarrow z :\in \{g : Stream \mid f \downarrow [0..\tau + 1] = g \downarrow [0..\tau + 1]\};$
$\qquad\qquad n := n + 1$
$\quad \textbf{od}$
$]|:< z : Stream.\mathbb{N} >$

$\text{CN} \triangleq$
$|[\ \textbf{var}\ n : \mathbb{R}, b : \mathbb{B};$
$\quad n, b := 0, true;$
$\quad \textbf{do}\ \tau = n \wedge b \rightarrow z :\in \{g : Stream \mid f \downarrow [0..\tau + 1] = g \downarrow [0..\tau + 1]\};$
$\qquad\qquad n, b := n + \frac{1}{2}, false$
$\quad [\!]\ \tau = n \wedge \neg b \rightarrow n, b := n + \frac{1}{2}, true$
$\quad \textbf{od}$
$]|:< z : Stream.\mathbb{N} >$

Fig. 4. Continuous action systems **CM** and **CN**. f is a function of type $Stream.\mathbb{N}$.

8.1 An Algebra for Continuous Action Systems

Algebraic theories are frequently used for reasoning about iterative program constructs: for example, Back and von Wright [6] have used results from fixed point theory to derive transformation rules for loop constructs, Hayes has used a similar approach to reason about execution paths in programs [11], and iterative real-time programming constructs [10], Cohen [7] and Kozen [12] performed early work on the Kleene algebra with tests. Here we define an algebra to describe sets of behaviours, and develop transformation rules for manipulating these sets of behaviours. These rules are used to derive a refinement rule for continuous action systems. Our algebra is closest to the concrete predicate transformer algebra of Back and von Wright [6][1] (the approach taken by Cohen [7] is and Kozen [12] is abstract-algebraic).

Behaviour Set Primitives and Composition Operators. Given a state space Σ, we use the primitives in Fig. 5 to describe sets of traces of type Σ. $\langle\!\langle A_0 \rangle\!\rangle$ defines a set of traces of length one such that the first value in the trace is reachable by A_0 from any global state. $\langle\!\langle A \rangle\!\rangle$ defines a set of traces of length two, where the first element may be any possible state, and the second element is reachable from the first by executing action A (recall from Sect. 2 that $\overline{A_0}$ is the conjugate of A_0). Note that if A aborts, then every possible state is reachable from any initial state, hence $\langle\!\langle \textbf{abort} \rangle\!\rangle$ equals $\{\langle \sigma_1, \sigma_2 \rangle : seq.\Sigma \mid true\}$. A coercion primitive $[g]$ produces a set of traces of length one where the first value in a trace is any input from the state space that satisfies g. $\{g\}$ produces the set of all non-empty traces such that the first element of each trace does not satisfy

---

[1] Note that von Wright [14] later showed how to work with loop refinement in an abstract-algebraic setting.

Initialisation Action :	$\langle\!\langle A_0 \rangle\!\rangle$	$\{\langle\sigma_1\rangle : seq.\Sigma \mid$
		$(\exists\,\sigma_0 : global.\Sigma \bullet \overline{A_0}.(\lambda\,\sigma \bullet \sigma = \sigma_1).\sigma_0)\}$
Action :	$\langle\!\mid A \mid\!\rangle$	$\{\langle\sigma_1, \sigma_2\rangle : seq.\Sigma \mid \overline{A}.(\lambda\,\sigma \bullet \sigma = \sigma_2).\sigma_1\}$
Coercion :	$[g]$	$\{\langle\sigma_1\rangle : seq.\Sigma \mid g.\sigma_1\}$
Assertion :	$\{g\}$	$\{s : seq.\Sigma \mid \neg g.(first.s)\} \cup \{\langle\sigma_1\rangle : seq.\Sigma \mid g.\sigma_1\}$
Bottom :	**abort**	$\{false\}$
Top :	**magic**	$[false]$
Skip :	**skip**	$[true]$

Fig. 5. Trace set primitives. A_0 is an initialisation action, A is an action, and g is a predicate.

Nondeterministic choice :	$X \sqcap Y$	$X \cup Y$
General nondet. choice :	$\sqcap i : T \bullet X_i$	$\bigcup i : T \bullet X_i$
Sequential composition :	$X;\ Y$	$\{b : X \mid \neg finite.b\}\cup$
		$\{b, b' : seq.\Sigma, s : \Sigma \mid b \,^\frown \langle s\rangle \in X \,\wedge$
		$\langle s\rangle \,^\frown b' \in Y \bullet b \,^\frown \langle s\rangle \,^\frown b'\}$
Strong iteration :	Y^ω	$(\mu\,X \bullet Y;\ X \sqcap \mathbf{skip})$
Weak iteration :	Y^*	$(\nu\,X \bullet Y;\ X \sqcap \mathbf{skip})$
Infinite iteration :	Y^∞	$(\mu\,X \bullet Y;\ X)$

Fig. 6. Trace set composition operators

g, combined with the set of all traces of length one such that the first element of each trace satisfies g. The bottom set of traces is **abort**, which is the set of all possible traces, while the top set of traces is **magic**, which defines the empty set of traces. Note that **abort** is not equal to $\langle\!\mid \mathbf{abort} \mid\!\rangle$. Much of the notation we use here is overloaded, i.e., assertions are represented the same way for both actions and sets of traces. The meaning of statements should be clear from the context.

The trace set composition operations are defined in Fig. 6. We reuse the definition of *weak*, *strong* and *infinite* iteration used by Back and von Wright [6, 3]. The definition of *weak* iteration is equivalent to the Kleene star iterator of Kozen and Cohen [12, 7][2]. Informally, Y^* produces the set of traces that are constructed by sequentially composing Y any finite number of times, Y^∞ produces the set of traces that are constructed by sequentially composing Y an infinite number of times, and Y^ω produces the trace set $Y^* \cup Y^\infty$. Note that for programs represented using the predicate transformer semantics from Sect. 2, we have that nonterminating behaviour is equivalent to **abort**; here this is not the case, nontermination generates traces of infinite length. In this sense the meaning of our infinite iteration operator is most similar to that used by Hayes [10]. (Cohen has also constructed an infinite iteration operator (Y^∞) that is applicable to trace-based models [8].)

The set of trace sets satisfies all the properties of an an idempotent semiring under ("$\sqcap$", "; ", **magic**, **skip**), except that X; **magic** $\neq$ **magic** does not hold

---

[2] This equivalence is described by the Kleene star equivalence property.

in general if X does not terminate. Additionally, the trace composition operators satisfy the following properties.

Theorem 7. *The following properties hold for both conjunctive predicate transformer semantics and the semantics of sets of traces.*

$$X^\omega = X;\ X^\omega \sqcap \mathbf{skip}\ and\ X^\omega = X^\omega;\ X \sqcap \mathbf{skip} \qquad \text{(unfold strong iteration)}$$
$$X^* = X;\ X^* \sqcap \mathbf{skip}\ and\ X^* = X^*;\ X \sqcap \mathbf{skip} \qquad \text{(unfold weak iteration)}$$
$$X^\infty = X;\ X^\infty \qquad \text{(unfold infinite iteration)}$$
$$X^\omega = X^* \sqcap X^\infty \qquad \text{(decompose strong iteration)}$$
$$X^\infty = X^\omega;\ \mathbf{magic} \qquad \text{(infinite iteration equivalence)}$$
$$X^* = \sqcap i : \mathbb{N} \bullet X^i \qquad \text{(Kleene star equivalence)}$$
$$X;\ (Y;\ X)^\omega = (X;\ Y)^\omega;\ X \qquad \text{(leapfrog)}$$
$$(X \sqcap Y)^\omega = X^\omega;\ (Y;\ X^\omega)^\omega \qquad \text{(decomposition)}$$
$$[g1] \sqcap [g2] = [g1 \vee g2] \qquad \text{(guard disjunction)}$$
$$[g1];\ [g2] = [g1 \wedge g2] \qquad \text{(guard conjunction)}$$

Here $X^0 = \mathbf{skip}$ and $X^{i+1} = X;\ X^i$ for $i \in \mathbb{N}$.

All of the properties in Theorem 7, apart from *Kleene star equivalence*, have been verified by by Back et al. to be correct for conjunctive predicate transformers [6, 3]: they are also applicable to sets of traces. The *Kleene star equivalence* property may be simply verified for both conjunctive predicate transformers and sets of traces. (Induction rules also exist, however they are not required except to prove Theorem 7).

Theorem 8. *The following properties hold for sets of traces:*

$$\langle\!\langle\ [g];\ A\ \rangle\!\rangle = [g];\ \langle\!\langle\ A\ \rangle\!\rangle \qquad \text{(shift guard)}$$
$$\langle\!\langle\ A \sqcap A'\ \rangle\!\rangle = \langle\!\langle\ A\ \rangle\!\rangle \sqcap \langle\!\langle\ A'\ \rangle\!\rangle \qquad \text{(shift nondet. choice)}$$
$$\langle\!\langle\ \sqcap i : T \bullet A_i\ \rangle\!\rangle = \sqcap i : T \bullet \langle\!\langle\ A_i\ \rangle\!\rangle \qquad \text{(shift general nondet. choice)}$$

Lemma 9. *Given action A such that A^ω is terminating, i.e., $A^\omega.True = True$,*

$$\langle\!\langle\ A\ \rangle\!\rangle^\omega = \langle\!\langle\ A\ \rangle\!\rangle^*\ and\ A^\omega = A^*$$

Proof. If A^ω is terminating $A^\infty = \mathbf{magic}$ (from Theorem 7 (*infinite iteration equivalence*)), and so from Theorem 7 (*decompose strong iteration*) we have that $A^\omega = A^* \sqcap \mathbf{magic} = \mathbf{A^*}$. A similar argument applies for $\langle\!\langle\ A\ \rangle\!\rangle^\omega$. □

Defining Action System Behaviours. The behaviours of an action system may then be expressed using our primitives and composition operators as follows.

$$beh.\mathbf{A} \triangleq \langle\!\langle A_0 \rangle\!\rangle;\ ([t.A];\ \langle\!\langle\ A\ \rangle\!\rangle)^\omega;\ [\neg g.A \vee \neg t.A] \qquad (11)$$

We express guarded loops using iteration constructs in the same way as Back and von Wright [6].

For action systems with trace semantics, it well known that we can merge together two actions A and B as long as B is a stuttering action, without changing the set of global traces that are produced by the action system. For continuous action systems (using stream semantics) we are also able to merge together two actions A and B as long as B does not abort (B may be non-stuttering), without changing the set of streams that are produced by the action system. It is this property that enables us to introduce a new data refinement rule for continuous action systems. We write $X =_{\text{str}} Y$, where X and Y are set of traces, to mean that $behStreams.X = behStreams.Y$.

Lemma 10. *For action A, initialisation action A_0, and terminating action B, we have that*

$$\langle\!| A \,|\!\rangle; \langle\!| B \,|\!\rangle =_{\text{str}} \langle\!| A; B \,|\!\rangle \text{ and } \langle\!\langle A_0 \rangle\!\rangle; \langle\!| B \,|\!\rangle =_{\text{str}} \langle\!\langle A_0; B \rangle\!\rangle$$

Proof. We show that if B is not aborting then $\langle\!| A \,|\!\rangle; \langle\!| B \,|\!\rangle =_{\text{str}} \langle\!| A; B \,|\!\rangle$. The proof of $\langle\!\langle A_0 \rangle\!\rangle; \langle\!| B \,|\!\rangle =_{\text{str}} \langle\!\langle A_0; B \rangle\!\rangle$ is similar. From the definition of the behaviour set primitives and sequential composition we have that

$$\langle\!| A; B \,|\!\rangle = \{\langle \sigma_1, \sigma_3 \rangle \mid \overline{(A; B)}.(\lambda \sigma \bullet \sigma = \sigma_3).\sigma_1\}$$
$$\langle\!| A \,|\!\rangle; \langle\!| B \,|\!\rangle = \{\langle \sigma_1, \sigma_2, \sigma_3 \rangle \mid \overline{A}.(\lambda \sigma \bullet \sigma = \sigma_2).\sigma_1 \wedge \overline{B}.(\lambda \sigma \bullet \sigma = \sigma_3).\sigma_2\}$$

And from the definition of predicate transformer sequential composition and conjugates, we have

$$\overline{(A; B)}.(\lambda \sigma \bullet \sigma = \sigma_3).\sigma_1 \Leftrightarrow \exists \sigma_2 \bullet \overline{A}.(\lambda \sigma \bullet \sigma = \sigma_2).\sigma_1 \wedge \overline{B}.(\lambda \sigma \bullet \sigma = \sigma_3).\sigma_2$$

Hence $\langle \sigma_1, \sigma_2, \sigma_3 \rangle \in \langle\!| A \,|\!\rangle; \langle\!| B \,|\!\rangle$, iff $\langle \sigma_1, \sigma_3 \rangle \in \langle\!| A; B \,|\!\rangle$. Since all traces from $\langle\!| A \,|\!\rangle; \langle\!| B \,|\!\rangle$ and $\langle\!| A; B \,|\!\rangle$ are finite, and each trace b from either $\langle\!| A \,|\!\rangle; \langle\!| B \,|\!\rangle$ or $\langle\!| A; B \,|\!\rangle$, has a corresponding trace b' from the other set in which $last.b' = last.b$, from $behStream$ (5) we have that $behStream.b = behStream.b'$, and hence (from the definition of stream refinement (10)), $\langle\!| A \,|\!\rangle; \langle\!| B \,|\!\rangle =_{\text{str}} \langle\!| A; B \,|\!\rangle$. $\square$

Lemma 11. $\langle\!| \text{ skip } |\!\rangle =_{\text{str}} \text{skip}$, *where the first occurrence of* **skip** *is a predicate transformer, and the second occurrence is a set of traces.*

Lemma 12. *Given terminating action A,*
$$\langle\!| A \,|\!\rangle^* =_{\text{str}} \langle\!| A^* \,|\!\rangle$$

Proof.

$$\langle\!| A \,|\!\rangle^*$$
$=$ (Theorem 7 (*Kleene star equivalence*))
$$\sqcap i : \mathbb{N} \bullet \langle\!| A \,|\!\rangle^i$$
$=_{\text{str}}$ (Lemma 10 and 11)
$$\sqcap i : \mathbb{N} \bullet \langle\!| A^i \,|\!\rangle$$
$=$ (Theorem 8 (*shift general nondet. choice*))
$$\langle\!| \sqcap i : \mathbb{N} \bullet A^i \,|\!\rangle$$
$=$ $\langle\!| A^* \,|\!\rangle$

8.2 Stream Refinement Rules

In this section we derive new stream data refinement rules for continuous action systems using the rules developed in the previous section. First we construct an equivalence rule, that shows how possibly non-stuttering actions may be merged with other actions in a continuous action system without changing the output streams that are generated by it. We then combine this rule with existing action system trace refinement rules to generate new useful stream refinement rules.

Given a continuous action system $\mathbf{CA}$, let $\mathbf{A} = actSys.\mathbf{CA}$. For an action decomposition $A = A_\natural \sqcap A_\sharp$, we define action system $\mathbf{A}_{(A_\natural, A_\sharp)}$ as follows.

$$\mathbf{A}_{(A_\natural, A_\sharp)} \triangleq |[\, \mathbf{var}\ x : X;\ A_0;\ DO_{(A_\natural, A_\sharp)};\ \mathbf{do}\ A_\sharp;\ DO_{(A_\natural, A_\sharp)}\ \mathbf{od}\,]|{:}< z : Z >$$

where the local and global variables are the same as those of $\mathbf{CA}$. Program $DO_{(A_\natural, A_\sharp)}$ may perform action $A_\natural$ for as long as it is enabled and an aborting action isn't enabled, and it may terminate when either the guard of $A_\sharp$ holds or the guard of $A_\natural$ ceases to hold:

$$DO_{(A_\natural, A_\sharp)} \triangleq ([t.A];\ A_\natural)^\omega;\ [\neg g.A_\natural \vee g.A_\sharp]$$

Theorem 13 (Stream Equivalence). *If* $DO_{(A_\natural, A_\sharp)}$ *is terminating (note that this implies that* $A_\natural$ *must not be aborting), we have that*

$$\mathbf{A}\ \sqsubseteq_{\mathrm{str}}\ \mathbf{A}_{(A_\natural, A_\sharp)}$$

Proof. We show that $beh.\mathbf{A}$ is stream equivalent to $beh.\mathbf{A}_{(A_\natural, A_\sharp)}$.

$beh.\mathbf{A}_{(A_\natural, A_\sharp)}$

$=$ (11)

$\langle\!\langle A_0;\ DO_{(A_\natural, A_\sharp)} \rangle\!\rangle;\ ([t.(A_\sharp;\ DO_{(A_\natural, A_\sharp)})];\ \langle\!\langle A_\sharp;\ DO_{(A_\natural, A_\sharp)} \rangle\!\rangle)^\omega;$
$[\neg g.(A_\sharp;\ DO_{(A_\natural, A_\sharp)}) \vee \neg t.(A_\sharp;\ DO_{(A_\natural, A_\sharp)})]$

$=$ $\langle\!\langle A_0;\ DO_{(A_\natural, A_\sharp)} \rangle\!\rangle;\ ([t.A_\sharp];\ \langle\!\langle A_\sharp;\ DO_{(A_\natural, A_\sharp)} \rangle\!\rangle)^\omega;\ [\neg g.A_\sharp \vee \neg t.A_\sharp]$

$=$ $(DO_{(A_\natural, A_\sharp)}$ is terminating, and Lemma 9)

$\langle\!\langle A_0;\ ([t.A];\ A_\natural)^*;\ [\neg g.A_\natural \vee g.A_\sharp] \rangle\!\rangle;$
$([t.A_\sharp];\ \langle\!\langle A_\sharp;\ ([t.A];\ A_\natural)^*;\ [\neg g.A_\natural \vee g.A_\sharp] \rangle\!\rangle)^\omega;\ [\neg g.A_\sharp \vee \neg t.A_\sharp]$

$=_{\mathrm{str}}$ (Lemmas 10 and 12, Theorem 8 *(shift guard)*, and
Theorem 7 *(guard conjunction)*)

$\langle\!\langle A_0 \rangle\!\rangle;\ \langle\!\langle [t.A];\ A_\natural \rangle\!\rangle^*;\ [\neg g.A_\natural \vee g.A_\sharp];$
$([t.A_\sharp \wedge g.A_\sharp];\ \langle\!\langle A_\sharp \rangle\!\rangle;\ \langle\!\langle [t.A];\ A_\natural \rangle\!\rangle^*;\ [\neg g.A_\natural \vee g.A_\sharp])^\omega;\ [\neg g.A_\sharp \vee \neg t.A_\sharp]$

$=$ (Theorem 7 *(leapfrog)*)

$\langle\!\langle A_0 \rangle\!\rangle;\ \langle\!\langle [t.A];\ A_\natural \rangle\!\rangle^*;\ ([\neg g.A_\natural \vee g.A_\sharp];\ [t.A_\sharp \wedge g.A_\sharp];\ \langle\!\langle A_\sharp \rangle\!\rangle;\ \langle\!\langle [t.A];\ A_\natural \rangle\!\rangle^*)^\omega;$
$[\neg g.A_\natural \vee g.A_\sharp];\ [\neg g.A_\sharp \vee \neg t.A_\sharp]$

$=$ (Theorem 7 *(guard conjunction)*, $\neg g.A = \neg g.A_\natural \wedge \neg g.A_\sharp$, $\neg t.A_\sharp \Rightarrow g.A_\sharp$)

$\langle\!\langle A_0 \rangle\!\rangle;\ \langle\!\langle [t.A];\ A_\natural \rangle\!\rangle^*;\ ([t.A_\sharp \wedge g.A_\sharp];\ \langle\!\langle A_\sharp \rangle\!\rangle;\ \langle\!\langle [t.A];\ A_\natural \rangle\!\rangle^*)^\omega;\ [\neg g.A \vee \neg t.A_\sharp]$

$=$ $(DO_{(A_\natural, A_\sharp)}$ is terminating, Lemma 9 and Theorem 8 *(shift guard)*)

$\langle\!\langle A_0 \rangle\!\rangle;\ ([t.A];\ \langle\!\langle A_\natural \rangle\!\rangle)^\omega;\ ([t.A_\sharp];\ \langle\!\langle A_\sharp \rangle\!\rangle;\ ([t.A];\ \langle\!\langle A_\natural \rangle\!\rangle)^\omega)^\omega;\ [\neg g.A \vee \neg t.A_\sharp]$

$=$ (Theorem 7 *(decomposition)*)

$\langle\!\langle A_0 \rangle\!\rangle;\ ([t.A];\ \langle\!\langle A_\natural \rangle\!\rangle \sqcap [t.A_\sharp];\ \langle\!\langle A_\sharp \rangle\!\rangle)^\omega;\ [\neg g.A \vee \neg t.A_\sharp]$

$=$ (Theorem 8 *(shift nondet. choice)*, $t.A = t.A_\natural \wedge t.A_\sharp$ and $t.A_\natural = true$)

$\langle\!\langle A_0 \rangle\!\rangle;\ ([t.A];\ \langle\!\langle A_\natural \sqcap A_\sharp \rangle\!\rangle)^\omega;\ [\neg g.A \vee \neg t.A]$

$=$ (11)

$beh.\mathbf{A}$ □

Since trace refinement implies stream refinement (Theorem 6), we are able to combine the stream equivalence rule (Theorem 13) with standard action system trace refinement rules in order to generate new stream refinement rules. From the standard trace simulation rule for action systems [2] we have that $\mathbf{A}$ is refined by $\mathbf{B}$ if there exists a *valid* representation program *rep* such that

$$A_0; \; rep \sqsubseteq B_0$$
$$A; \; rep \sqsubseteq rep; \; B$$
$$g.A \wedge t.A \Rightarrow rep.gB$$

We say that a representation program is valid if it does not modify the global state and it is non-miraculous.

Theorem 14 (Stream Simulation). *For any continuous action systems* $\mathbf{CA}$ *and* $\mathbf{CB}$ *with the same global state space, let* $\mathbf{A}$ *be actsys.*$\mathbf{CA}$ *and* $\mathbf{B}$ *be actsys.*$\mathbf{CB}$. *If there exists a decomposition* $A = A_\sharp \sqcap A_\natural$ *and* $B = B_\sharp \sqcap B_\natural$ *such that programs* $DO_{(A_\natural, A_\sharp)}$ *and* $DO_{(B_\natural, B_\sharp)}$ *terminate and there exists a valid representation program rep, such that*

$$A_0; \; DO_{(A_\natural, A_\sharp)}; \; rep \sqsubseteq B_0; \; DO_{(B_\natural, B_\sharp)} \tag{12}$$
$$A_\sharp; \; DO_{(A_\natural, A_\sharp)}; \; rep \sqsubseteq rep; \; B_\sharp; \; DO_{(B_\natural, B_\sharp)} \tag{13}$$
$$g.A_\sharp \wedge t.A_\sharp \Rightarrow rep.(gB_\sharp) \tag{14}$$

then $\mathbf{CA} \sqsubseteq_{\mathrm{str}} \mathbf{CB}$.

Proof. This follows directly from Theorems 13 and 6, and the standard action system simulation rule. □

A corresponding stream cosimulation rule exists. The stream simulation rule may be used to prove refinements (using stream semantics) that are not possible using the standard simulation and cosimulation rules. We demonstrate this by showing that $\mathbf{CN}$ is a valid refinement of $\mathbf{CM}$ (Fig. 4). Recall from Sect. 7 that in $\mathbf{CM}$, one action from $\mathbf{CN}$ has been decomposed into two separate actions.

Example. $\mathbf{CM} \sqsubseteq_{\mathrm{str}} \mathbf{CN}$ (Figure 4)

Proof. Let $\mathbf{M}$ and $\mathbf{N}$ be $actSys.\mathbf{CM}$ and $actSys.\mathbf{CN}$, respectively. Then
$M_0 = n, \tau := 0, 0; \; z := z' \downarrow [0..0)$
$N_0 = n, b, \tau := 0, true, 0; \; z := z' \downarrow [0..0)$
The proof obligations of the stream simulation rules can easily be shown to hold given the following action decompositions (proof steps elided). Program *intr* introduces the local variable b.
$rep \triangleq intr; \; b := true$
$M_\sharp \triangleq [\tau = n]; \; z' :\in \{g : Stream.\mathbb{N} \mid f \downarrow [0..\tau + 1] = g \downarrow [0..\tau + 1]\};$
$\qquad n := n + 1; \; \tau := n; \; z := z' \downarrow [0..\tau)$
$M_\natural \triangleq \mathbf{magic}$
$N_\sharp \triangleq [\tau = n \wedge b]; \; z' :\in \{g : Stream.\mathbb{N} \mid f \downarrow [0..\tau + 1] = g \downarrow [0..\tau + 1]\}$
$\qquad n, b := n + \frac{1}{2}, false; \; \tau := n; \; z := z' \downarrow [0..\tau)$
$N_\natural \triangleq [\tau = n \wedge \neg b]; \; n, b := n + \frac{1}{2}, true; \; \tau := n; \; z := z' \downarrow [0..\tau)$

We have that
$$DO_{(M_\natural, M_\sharp)} \triangleq \mathbf{skip}$$
$$DO_{(N_\natural, N_\sharp)} \triangleq [\tau = n \wedge \neg b]; \ n, b := n + \tfrac{1}{2}, true; \ \tau := n; \ z := z' \downarrow [0..\tau)$$
$$\sqcap [(\tau = n) \Rightarrow b]$$
□

8.3   Completeness of Data Refinement Rules

A set of rules is complete with respect to a chosen semantics if all valid refinements in the semantics can be proven using the specified rules. As mentioned earlier, the standard action system data refinement rules alone are incomplete with respect to the stream semantics for continuous action systems. Here we prove a completeness result for our new stream refinement rules in conjunction with the action system data refinement rules, with respect to our stream semantics.

For any continuous action system **CA** such that $actSys.\mathbf{CA}$ is nonterminating, and **CA** only contains terminating actions, we show that it is possible to use our new stream refinement rules to convert $actSys.\mathbf{CA}$ to a stream equivalent canonical form $can.(actSys.\mathbf{CA})$. For any two such continuous action systems, **CA** and **CB**, we show that both trace and stream refinement are equivalent for $can.(actSys.\mathbf{CA})$ and $can.(actSys.\mathbf{CB})$. This means that, for this case, the usual completeness results for action system data refinement apply.

Using our new stream simulation rule (Theorem 14), we can show that any continuous actions system **CA** is stream equivalent to

$$\mathbf{CA_{check}} \triangleq$$
$$|[\ \mathbf{var}\ x : Stream.X, check : Time;$$
$$CA_0; \ check := 0; \ CHECK;$$
$$\mathbf{do}\ CA;\ CHECK\ \|\ check = \tau \rightarrow check := check + p\ \mathbf{od}$$
$$]|:< z : Stream^\omega >$$

where

$$CHECK \triangleq$$
$$\mathbf{if}\ (\exists t : Time \bullet t \geq \tau \wedge (g.CA).t) \rightarrow skip$$
$$\|\ \neg(\exists t : Time \bullet t \geq \tau \wedge (g.CA).t) \rightarrow check := -1$$
$$\mathbf{fi}$$

$check$ is a fresh variable and p is a defined non-zero time period. (It is assumed that x and z are the local and global variables of **CA** respectively.) The action "$[check = \tau]; \ check := check + p$" occurs every p seconds until the action system terminates or aborts:

$$\mathbf{A_{check}} \triangleq actSys.\mathbf{CA_{check}} =$$
$$|[\ \mathbf{var}\ \tau : Time, x : Stream.X, z' : Stream.Z, check : Time;$$
$$(\tau := 0;\ CA_0;\ check := 0;\ CHECK)[z \setminus z'];\ M;$$
$$\mathbf{do}\ (CA;\ CHECK)[z \setminus z'];\ M\ \|\ check = \tau \rightarrow check := check + p;\ M\ \mathbf{od}$$
$$]|:< z : Stream^\omega.Z >$$

For a continuous action system **CA** such that action CA terminates and $actSys.\mathbf{CA}$ is nonterminating, we define the canonical form of $actSys.\mathbf{CA}$, $can.(actSys.\mathbf{CA})$, to be

$$|[\textbf{ var } \tau : Time, x : Stream.X, z' : Stream.Z, check : Time;$$
$$A_{check_0}; \; DO_{(A_{check_\natural}, A_{check_\sharp})};$$
$$\textbf{do } A_{check_\sharp}; \; DO_{(A_{check_\natural}, A_{check_\sharp})} \textbf{ od} \tag{15}$$
$$]|:< z : Stream^\omega.Z >$$

where

$$A_{check_\sharp} \triangleq [check = \tau]; \; check := check + p; \; M$$
$$A_{check_\natural} \triangleq (CA; \; CHECK)[z \setminus z']; \; M$$

The action of $can.(actSys.\textbf{CA})$ occurs every p seconds. It performs all the actions in actSys.$\textbf{CA}$ that occur between τ and $\tau + p$. The variable $check$ is used to regulate the period of the actions. For any two non-aborting, nonterminating action systems in canonical form, the timing of their actions is the same.

Lemma 15. *Given continuous action system* $\textbf{CA}$ *such that action CA is terminating,*

$$can.(actSys.\textbf{CA}) =_{\text{str}} actSys.\textbf{CA}$$

Proof. The stream equivalence rule (Theorem 13) can be used to verify that $actSys.\textbf{CA}_{\textbf{check}}$ is equivalent to $can.(actSys.\textbf{CA})$ (note that because action CA is terminating, $A_{check_\natural}$ is terminating). Theorem 14 can be used to prove the equivalence between $\textbf{CA}_{\textbf{check}}$ and $\textbf{CA}$. □

Lemma 16. *For any two continuous action systems* $\textbf{CA}$ *and* $\textbf{CB}$ *such that actions CA and CB are terminating and actSys.$\textbf{CA}$ and actSys.$\textbf{CB}$ are nonterminating,*

$$(can.(actSys.\textbf{CA}) \sqsubseteq_{\text{str}} can.(actSys.\textbf{CB})) = (can.(actSys.\textbf{CA}) \sqsubseteq_{\text{tr}} can.(actSys.\textbf{CB}))$$

Proof.

1. $(can.(actSys.\textbf{CA}) \sqsubseteq_{\text{str}} can.(actSys.\textbf{CB})) \Rightarrow$
   $(can.(actSys.\textbf{CA}) \sqsubseteq_{\text{tr}} can.(actSys.\textbf{CB}))$
   This follows from the fact that the semantics of continuous action systems are trace extending ($actSys$ (Definition 2)), and that actions in $can.(actSys.\textbf{CA})$ and $can.(actSys.\textbf{CB})$ occur at the same regular interval for all time.
2. $(can.(actSys.\textbf{CA}) \sqsubseteq_{\text{tr}} can.(actSys.\textbf{CB})) \Rightarrow$
   $(can.(actSys.\textbf{CA}) \sqsubseteq_{\text{str}} can.(actSys.\textbf{CB}))$
   There exists a continuous action system $\textbf{CA}_{\textbf{can}}$ such that $actSys.\textbf{CA}_{\textbf{can}} = can.(actSys.\textbf{CA})$, so implication in this direction follows from Theorem 6.

□

Theorem 17. *For any two continuous action systems* $\textbf{CA}$ *and* $\textbf{CB}$ *such that actions CA and CB are terminating,*

$$(actSys.\textbf{CA} \sqsubseteq_{\text{str}} actSys.\textbf{CB}) = (can.(actSys.\textbf{CA}) \sqsubseteq_{\text{tr}} can.(actSys.\textbf{CB}))$$

Proof. This follows from Lemma 15 and Lemma 16.   □

This theorem demonstrates that, for a restricted class of continuous action systems (those that do not contain aborting behaviours, and that are associated with nonterminating action systems), our new stream refinement rules in conjunction with the action system trace refinement rules are as complete with respect to our stream semantics, as the action system trace refinement rules are with respect to the trace semantics. For action systems with neither infinite stuttering nor terminating behaviours, Back and von Wright have proved that any trace refinement can be proved by a combination of backward and forward simulation [2].

9   Conclusion

We have identified how the mapping from continuous action systems to action systems may be adjusted such that action system trace semantics are valid for continuous action systems, and we have defined a stream semantics that is complementary to the trace semantics, but is more general. Our results indicate that action system data refinement rules are applicable to continuous action systems with stream semantics, but they are not complete. Subsequently, we constructed and verified a new stream refinement rule that is capable of proving stream refinements that are not possible in the more restrictive trace semantics. For a certain subclass of continuous action systems we have shown that our new stream refinement rule, in conjunction with the existing action system data refinement rules, are as complete (with respect to our stream semantics) as the data refinement rules are for action systems with trace semantics. This work enables the continuous action systems formalism to be used to reason about the derivation of hybrid systems.

Acknowledgements. This research was supported by Australian Research Council (ARC) Discovery Grant DP0558408, *Analysing and generating fault-tolerant real-time systems.* We would like to thank Robert Colvin for feedback on earlier drafts of this paper, and the anonymous referees for their suggested improvements.

References

1. Back, R.-J., Petre, L., Porres, I.: Generalizing action systems to hybrid systems. In Joseph, M., ed.: Proc. of 6th Int. Symp. on Formal Techniques in Real-Time and Fault-Tolerant Systems, FTRTFT 2000. Vol. 1926 of Lect. Notes in Comput. Sci. Springer-Verlag (2000) 202–213
2. Back, R.-J., von Wright, J.: Trace refinement of action systems. In Jonsson, B., Parrow, J.: Proc. of 5th Int. Conf. on Concurrency Theory, CONCUR '94. Vol. 836 of Lect. Notes in Comput. Sci. Springer-Verlag (1994) 367–384
3. Back, R.-J., von Wright, J.: Refinement Calculus: A Systematic Introduction. Springer-Verlag (1998)

4. Back, R.-J., Kurki-Suonio, R.: Decentralization of process nets with centralized control. In Proc. of 2nd ACM SIGACT-SIGOPS Symp. on Principles of Distributed Computing, PODC '83. ACM Press (1983) 131–142
5. Back, R.-J., Kurki-Suonio, R.: Distributed cooperation with action systems. ACM Trans. on Program. Lang. and Syst. **10**(4) (1988) 513–554
6. Back, R.-J., von Wright, J.: Reasoning algebraically about loops. Acta Inform. **36**(4) (1999) 295–334
7. Cohen, E.: Hypotheses in Kleene algebra. Techn. Report TM-ARH-023814. Belcore (1994)
8. Cohen, E.: Separation and reduction. In Backhouse, R. C., Oliveira, J. N., eds.: Proc. of 5th Int. Conf. on Mathematics of Program Construction, MPC 2000. Vol. 1837 of Lect. Notes in Comput. Sci. Springer-Verlag (2000)
9. Dijkstra, E. W.: A Discipline of Programming. Prentice Hall (1976)
10. Hayes, I. J.: Reasoning about real-time repetitions: Terminating and non-terminating. Sci. of Comput. Program. **43**(2–3) (2002) 161–192
11. Hayes, I. J.: Programs as paths: An approach to timing constraint analysis. In Dong, J. S., Woodcock, J., eds.: Proc. of 5th Int. Conf. on Formal Engineering Methods, ICFEM 2003. Vol. 2885 of Lect. Notes in Comput. Sci. Springer-Verlag (2003) 1–15
12. Kozen, D.: Kleene algebra with tests. ACM Trans. on Program. Lang. and Syst. **19**(3) (1997) 427–443
13. Morgan, C.: Programming from Specifications. 2nd edn. Prentice Hall (1994)
14. von Wright, J.: From Kleene algebra to refinement algebra. In Boiten, E. A., Möller, B., eds.: Proc. of 6th Int. Conf. on Mathematics of Program Construction, MPC 2002. Vol. 2386 of Lect. Notes in Comput. Sci. Springer-Verlag (2002) 233–262

The Linear Algebra of UTP

Bernhard Möller

Institut für Informatik, Universität Augsburg,
Universitätsstraße 14, D-86135 Augsburg, Germany
moeller@informatik.uni-augsburg.de

Abstract. We show that the well-known algebra of matrices over a semiring can be used to reason conveniently about predicates as used in the Unifying Theories of Programming (UTP). This allows a simplified treatment of the designs of Hoare and He and the prescriptions of Dunne. In addition we connect the matrix approach with the theory of test and condition semirings and the modal operators diamond and box. This allows direct re-use of the results and proof techniques of Kleene algebra with tests for UTP as well as a connection to traditional wp/wlp semantics. Finally, we show that matrices of predicate transformers allow an even more streamlined treatment and removal of a restricting assumption on the underlying semirings.

1 Introduction

In the Unifying Theories of Programming (UTP) [5] the termination behaviour of programs is modelled using two special variables ok and ok' that express whether a program has been started and has terminated, respectively. Programs are identified with predicates that relate the initial values v of variables with their final values v'; moreover, ok and ok' may occur freely in such predicates.

The aim of the present paper is to present a calculationally more workable form of the theory of predicates and designs that does no longer mention the "unobservable" variables ok and ok'; in fact it is even completely variable-free and hence, in particular, does not need to work with substitutions. This makes calculations not only simpler, but also safer. Truly hiding the unobservables is important, since their unchecked use can lead to inconsistencies and paradoxes such as the Dead Variable Paradox.

The remainder of this paper is organised as follows. Section 2 presents the basic idea of the matrix model of UTP predicates, while Section 3 deals with the special predicate class of UTP designs. In Section 4 we abstract from the concrete case of predicates over program variables to that of matrices over semirings; next to greater generality this yields a more compact notation. In Section 5 designs are discussed in this more general setting, while Section 6 gives an algebraic formulation of the healthiness conditions that distinguish designs. Designs were introduced to model total correctness, in particular, non-miraculous programs. Section 7 deals with another subclass of UTP predicates, the prescriptions, that model the view of general correctness and may show miraculous behaviour.

T. Uustalu (Ed.): MPC 2006, LNCS 4014, pp. 338–358, 2006.

Section 8 contains a more detailed treatment of conditions, i.e., predicates that only depend on input values of variables, and the related concept of tests in semirings. This allows direct re-use of the results and proof techniques of Kleene algebra with tests for UTP. Sections 9 and 10 employ tests and conditions to establish the link with traditional wlp/wp semantics. However, at a certain point the connection is not as smooth as one may wish. This is remedied in Section 11 using "higher-level" predicate transformers. Section 12 presents a brief conclusion.

To keep the overall structure of the paper clearer, some technicalities are deferred an appendix.

2   A Matrix View of UTP

Our main aim is to get rid of explicit uses of the special variables ok and ok'. We achieve this by recording, for each combination of possible values of these two variables, the residual predicate that depends only on the proper program variables. To emphasise the dependence of a general UTP predicate on ok and ok' we use the notation $R(ok, ok')$. The basic idea of our matrix calculus is now to represent R by a 2×2-matrix. The rows are indexed by the values of ok and the columns by those of ok'; the entries are the residual predicates in which ok and ok' do not occur, i.e.,

$$R = \begin{pmatrix} R(\mathit{false}, \mathit{false}) & R(\mathit{false}, \mathit{true}) \\ R(\mathit{true}, \mathit{false}) & R(\mathit{true}, \mathit{true}) \end{pmatrix} .$$

In this view, a predicate P not depending on ok and ok' corresponds to the constant matrix

$$\begin{pmatrix} P & P \\ P & P \end{pmatrix} .$$

The matrix representation may seem a complication at first. But let us look at sequential composition of UTP predicates, defined as

$$R \,;\, S \Leftrightarrow_{df} \exists\, ok_0, v_0 : R[ok_0, v_0/ok', v'] \,\wedge\, S[ok_0, v_0/ok, v] \,,$$

where v (also with index or prime) stands for the list of all proper program variables. We emphasise again the dependence on ok and ok'. To this end we also split the existential quantifier into the parts concerning the unobservables and the proper variables; afterwards the proper part can be folded into a composition of its own:

$$(R \,;\, S)(ok, ok') \Leftrightarrow_{df} \exists\, ok_0 : \exists\, v_0 : R(ok, ok_0)[v_0/v'] \,\wedge\, S(ok_0, ok')[v_0/v]$$
$$\Leftrightarrow \quad \exists\, ok_0 : R(ok, ok_0) \,;\, S(ok_0, ok') \,.$$

This now has a convenient matrix interpretation. As in graph algorithms such as Warshall's, we can view $\exists\, ok_0$ as summation over all possible values of ok_0 and ; as elementwise multiplication. With this interpretation the above formula gives just the entries for the product of the matrices R and S, i.e., $R \,;\, S = R \cdot S$.

The advantage of this view is that composition can now be treated in a completely component-free manner and existential quantification and substitution disappear. Moreover, the pseudo-variables ok and ok' need no longer be mentioned explicitly at all. If for some reason we need to reason about them explicitly, we can represent them as

$$ok = \begin{pmatrix} false & false \\ true & true \end{pmatrix}, \qquad ok' = \begin{pmatrix} false & true \\ false & true \end{pmatrix}.$$

Next to composition, the matrix algebra supports the Boolean operations: negation, conjunction and disjunction all are defined componentwise. Setting $R \Rightarrow S \Leftrightarrow_{df} R \vee S = S$, also implication works componentwise.

3 Designs

As a subclass of the general UTP predicates, Hoare and He introduce *designs*, that reflect an assumption/commitment style of specification, of the form

$$P \vdash Q \Leftrightarrow_{df} ok \wedge P \Rightarrow ok' \wedge Q,$$

where ok and ok' are not allowed to occur in P or Q. The informal meaning is: if a computation allowed by the design has started in a state that satisfies the precondition P it will eventually terminate in a state that satisfies the postcondition Q. By plugging in the possible combinations of the values of ok and ok' we obtain the matrix representation

$$P \vdash Q = \begin{pmatrix} true & true \\ \overline{P} & \overline{P} \vee Q \end{pmatrix}. \tag{1}$$

To show a first example of the matrix calculus at work, let us derive this representation algebraically:

$$
\begin{aligned}
& ok \wedge P \Rightarrow ok' \wedge Q \\
=~ & \begin{pmatrix} false & false \\ true & true \end{pmatrix} \wedge \begin{pmatrix} P & P \\ P & P \end{pmatrix} \Rightarrow \begin{pmatrix} false & true \\ false & true \end{pmatrix} \wedge \begin{pmatrix} Q & Q \\ Q & Q \end{pmatrix} \\
=~ & \begin{pmatrix} false & false \\ P & P \end{pmatrix} \vee \begin{pmatrix} false & Q \\ false & Q \end{pmatrix} \\
=~ & \begin{pmatrix} true & true \\ \overline{P} & \overline{P} \end{pmatrix} \vee \begin{pmatrix} false & Q \\ false & Q \end{pmatrix} \\
=~ & \begin{pmatrix} true & true \\ \overline{P} & \overline{P} \vee Q \end{pmatrix}.
\end{aligned}
$$

We defer further calculations till we obtain a more compact notation in the next section.

4 Abstracting to Semirings

Again, as in certain graph algorithms, it is useful to base the treatment not on the concrete model of matrices over predicates but on matrices over semirings.

Semirings provide the basic operations of choice and sequential composition under the notations $+$ and $\cdot$ as well as a basic set of algebraic laws for these. A *weak semiring* is a structure $(S, +, \cdot, 0, 1)$ such that

- $(S, +, 0)$ is a commutative monoid,
- $(S, \cdot, 1)$ is a monoid,
- operation $\cdot$ distributes over $+$ in both arguments
- and 0 is a left annihilator, i.e., $0 \cdot a = 0$.

A *semiring* is a weak semiring in which 0 is also a right annihilator, i.e., $a \cdot 0 = 0$. Sometimes for emphasis we write "full semiring" instead of just "semiring".

A (weak) semiring is *idempotent* if $+$ is idempotent, i.e., $a + a = a$. In this case the relation $a \leq b \Leftrightarrow_{df} a + b = b$ is a partial order, called the *natural order* on S. It has 0 as its least element. Moreover, $+$ and $\cdot$ are isotone w.r.t. $\leq$ and $a + b$ is the least upper bound or join of a and b w.r.t. $\leq$.

A (weak) idempotent semiring is *Boolean* if it also has a greatest-lower-bound or meet operation $\wedge$, such that $+$ and $\wedge$ distribute over each other, and a complement operation $\bar{}$ that satisfies de Morgan's laws as well as $a \wedge \bar{a} = 0$ and $a + \bar{a} = \top$, where $\top = \bar{0}$ is the greatest element. In other words, a Boolean semiring is a Boolean algebra with a sequential composition operation. To save parentheses we use the convention that $\wedge$ binds tighter than $+$ but equally tight as $\cdot$ does. We will freely use the implication operator $a \rightarrow b =_{df} \bar{a} + b$ and its standard laws. We use $\wedge$ rather than $\sqcap$ for the meet to avoid a clash of notation between semiring theory and the theory of UTP. To disambiguate the formulas we use a larger $\bigwedge$ for meta-logical conjunction.

An important property is multiplicative idempotence of $\top$:

$$\top \cdot \top = \top. \tag{2}$$

The direction ($\leq$) is trivial, since $\top$ is the greatest element. The converse direction follows by neutrality and isotonicity: $\top = \top \cdot 1 \leq \top \cdot \top$.

From now on we assume S to be a full idempotent Boolean semiring.

In the previous section we have already used the Boolean semiring of UTP predicates with ; as composition. Another important semiring is REL(M), the algebra of binary relations under union and composition over a set M, of which the predicates form a special instance.

Many other examples exist but will not be used here except for the matrix semiring. Let $(S, +, \cdot, 0, 1)$ be a semiring and M be a finite set. Then the set $S^{M \times M}$ of functions from $M \times M$ to S can be viewed as the set of $|M| \times |M|$ matrices with indices in M and elements in S. Consider the structure $\mathrm{MAT}(M, S) = (S^{M \times M}, +, \cdot, \mathbf{0}, \mathbf{1})$ where $+$ and $\cdot$ are the usual operations of matrix addition and multiplication, and $\mathbf{0}$ and $\mathbf{1}$ are the zero and unit matrices. Then $\mathrm{MAT}(M, S)$ again forms a semiring, the *matrix semiring* over M and S. $\mathrm{MAT}(M, S)$ is idempotent if S is. In this case, the natural order is the componentwise one. If S is Boolean, so is $\mathrm{MAT}(M, S)$, with componentwise meet.

Taking S to be the two-element Boolean semiring of truth values yields the usual Boolean matrix representation of REL(M) as $\mathrm{MAT}(M, S)$ in terms of adjacency matrices.

For abstractly representing predicates that depend on two Boolean variables ok and ok' we use 2×2-matrices with elements from a Boolean semiring S as entries. The element 1 represents the predicate $skip \Leftrightarrow_{df} v = v'$. We will use the identifiers $false$, $skip$ and $true$ instead of 0, 1 and $\top$ when appropriate.

For convenience we define

$$ok =_{df} \begin{pmatrix} 0 & 0 \\ \top & \top \end{pmatrix}, \qquad ok' =_{df} \begin{pmatrix} 0 & \top \\ 0 & \top \end{pmatrix}.$$

5   The Algebra of Designs

Generalising formula (1), we set for elements $a, b \in S$ of a Boolean semiring S

$$a \vdash b =_{df} \begin{pmatrix} \top & \top \\ \bar{a} & \bar{a} + b \end{pmatrix}, \tag{3}$$

with $+$ now playing the role of disjunction or choice.

We want to calculate the behaviour of designs under $+$ and $\cdot$. First,

$$(a \vdash b) + (c \vdash d) = \begin{pmatrix} \top & \top \\ \bar{a} & \bar{a} + b \end{pmatrix} + \begin{pmatrix} \top & \top \\ \bar{c} & \bar{c} + d \end{pmatrix} =$$
$$\begin{pmatrix} \top & \top \\ \bar{a} + \bar{c} & \bar{a} + b + \bar{c} + d \end{pmatrix} = \begin{pmatrix} \top & \top \\ \overline{(c \wedge a)} & \overline{(c \wedge a)} + b + d \end{pmatrix} = (c \wedge a) \vdash (b + d) .$$

In particular, the design $\top \vdash 0$, which is the same as $\overline{ok}$, is a neutral element w.r.t. $+$. Moreover, we obtain

$$(a \vdash b) \le (c \vdash d) \;\Leftrightarrow\; (a \vdash b) + (c \vdash d) = (c \vdash d) \;\Leftrightarrow\; (c \le a) \wedge (c \wedge b \le d) \tag{4}$$

and

$$(a \vdash b) = (c \vdash d) \;\Leftrightarrow\; a = c \wedge \bar{a} + b = \bar{c} + d \;\Leftrightarrow\; a = c \wedge (a \wedge b = c \wedge d) . \tag{5}$$

For composition we obtain, using (2),

$$(a \vdash b) \cdot (c \vdash d)$$
$$= \begin{pmatrix} \top & \top \\ \bar{a} & \bar{a} + b \end{pmatrix} \cdot \begin{pmatrix} \top & \top \\ \bar{c} & \bar{c} + d \end{pmatrix}$$
$$= \begin{pmatrix} \top \cdot \top + \top \cdot \bar{c} & \top \cdot \top + \top \cdot (\bar{c} + d) \\ \bar{a} \cdot \top + (\bar{a} + b) \cdot \bar{c} & \bar{a} \cdot \top + (\bar{a} + b) \cdot (\bar{c} + d) \end{pmatrix}$$
$$= \begin{pmatrix} \top & \top \\ \bar{a} \cdot \top + \bar{a} \cdot \bar{c} + b \cdot \bar{c} & \bar{a} \cdot \top + \bar{a} \cdot (\bar{c} + d) + b \cdot \bar{c} + b \cdot d \end{pmatrix}$$
$$= \begin{pmatrix} \top & \top \\ \bar{a} \cdot \top + b \cdot \bar{c} & \bar{a} \cdot \top + b \cdot \bar{c} + b \cdot d \end{pmatrix}$$
$$= \begin{pmatrix} \top & \top \\ \overline{\overline{\bar{a} \cdot \top} \wedge \overline{b \cdot \bar{c}}} & \overline{\overline{\bar{a} \cdot \top} \wedge \overline{b \cdot \bar{c}}} + b \cdot d \end{pmatrix}$$
$$= (\overline{\bar{a} \cdot \top} \wedge \overline{b \cdot \bar{c}}) \vdash (b \cdot d) .$$

Summarised,

$$(a \vdash b) \cdot (c \vdash d) = (\overline{\overline{a} \cdot \top} \wedge \overline{b \cdot \overline{c}}) \vdash (b \cdot d) . \tag{6}$$

In particular, within the set of designs both $\overline{ok} = \top \vdash 0$ and $true =_{df} \begin{pmatrix} \top & \top \\ \top & \top \end{pmatrix}$ are left zeros and $\mathbb{I} =_{df} \top \vdash 1$ is a left-neutral element w.r.t. composition.

6   Healthiness Conditions

In [5] the UTP predicates are classified according to certain *healthiness conditions*. In matrix terminology, designs are characterised by two properties:

(H1) The first row must be constantly $\top$.
(H2) Both rows must be increasing w.r.t $\leq$.

Clearly every design of the form (3) satisfies (H1) and (H2). Conversely, if $a \leq b$ then $\begin{pmatrix} \top & \top \\ a & b \end{pmatrix} = \begin{pmatrix} \top & \top \\ a & a+b \end{pmatrix} = \overline{a} \vdash b$, so that $\begin{pmatrix} \top & \top \\ a & b \end{pmatrix}$ is a design.

Clearly, matrix A satisfies (H1) iff $A = \begin{pmatrix} \top & \top \\ 0 & 0 \end{pmatrix} + A = ok \to A$ (see also Theorem 3.1.4 in [5]).

This type of characterisation by a fixpoint property is particularly useful if the underlying Boolean semiring (and hence the matrix semiring over it) is even a complete lattice, since Tarski's fixpoint theorem then implies that the set of all (H1) predicates forms a complete sublattice.

Next we show how the fixpoint characterisation of (H2) given in Example 4.1.21(1) of [5] can be derived in a systematic way in our matrix calculus. First we observe that

$$\begin{pmatrix} a & b \\ c & d \end{pmatrix} \text{ satisfies (H2)} \Leftrightarrow a+b = b \wedge c+d = d \Leftrightarrow \begin{pmatrix} a & b \\ c & d \end{pmatrix} = \begin{pmatrix} a & a+b \\ c & c+d \end{pmatrix} .$$

So if we manage to generate the latter matrix from the original one by an isotone function defined in terms of the algebra we are done.

In linear algebra this type of transformation is known as a *shearing* and can be described by the multiplication

$$\begin{pmatrix} a & a+b \\ c & c+d \end{pmatrix} = \begin{pmatrix} a & b \\ c & d \end{pmatrix} \cdot \begin{pmatrix} 1 & 1 \\ 0 & 1 \end{pmatrix} .$$

The shearing matrix can be decomposed as follows:

$$\begin{pmatrix} 1 & 1 \\ 0 & 1 \end{pmatrix} = \begin{pmatrix} \top & \top \\ 0 & \top \end{pmatrix} \wedge \begin{pmatrix} 1 & 1 \\ 1 & 1 \end{pmatrix} = (\top \vdash \top) \wedge \begin{pmatrix} 1 & 1 \\ 1 & 1 \end{pmatrix} .$$

Therefore we have the following result.

Lemma 6.1. *A satisfies (H2) iff* $A = A \cdot B$ *where*

$$B = (\top \vdash \top) \wedge \begin{pmatrix} 1 & 1 \\ 1 & 1 \end{pmatrix} .$$

This is indeed a fixpoint characterisation with an isotone generating function, and so the set of all (H2)-matrices forms a complete lattice (provided the underlying semiring S is complete).

The further healthiness conditions (H3) and (H4) serve to characterise the designs for which $\top \vdash 0$ and $\top \vdash 1$ are also a right zero and a right-neutral element w.r.t. $\cdot$, respectively. They are directly given as algebraic conditions:

(H3) $A \cdot \mathbb{I} = A$.
(H4) $A \cdot \textit{true} = \textit{true}$.

By distributivity and associativity it is immediate that each of the classes (H3) and (H4) is closed under addition and composition.

We only work these properties out for the case where A is a design. Here it is easier to work directly with the matrices than going through the composition formula for designs. For (H3) we calculate

$$(a \vdash b) \cdot \mathbb{I} \;=\; \begin{pmatrix} \top & \top \\ \overline{a} & \overline{a} + b \end{pmatrix} \cdot \begin{pmatrix} \top & \top \\ 0 & 1 \end{pmatrix} \;=\; \begin{pmatrix} \top & \top \\ \overline{a} \cdot \top & \overline{a} \cdot \top + \overline{a} + b \end{pmatrix},$$

so that $a \vdash b$ satisfies (H3) iff $\overline{a} \cdot \top = \overline{a} \Leftrightarrow \overline{a} \cdot \top \leq \overline{a}$.

This means that $\overline{a}$ has to be a *right ideal* (in UTP also known as a *condition*). In the semiring REL of relations this is equivalent to a itself being a right ideal, since by Schröder's law

$$\overline{a} \cdot \top \leq \overline{a} \;\Leftrightarrow\; a \cdot \top^{\smile} \leq a \;\Leftrightarrow\; a \cdot \top \leq a.$$

In general semirings this need not be the case.

Following [3], we call matrices satisfying (H3) *normal*. For normal designs we obtain the simplified composition formula (see also Theorem 3.2.4 in [5])

$$(a \vdash b) \cdot (c \vdash d) \;=\; (a \wedge \overline{b \cdot \overline{c}}) \vdash (b \cdot d). \tag{7}$$

Various authors have noticed that (H3) implies (H2). In matrix algebra this can be verified as follows:

$$\begin{pmatrix} a & b \\ c & d \end{pmatrix} \cdot \mathbb{I} = \begin{pmatrix} a \cdot \top & a \cdot \top + b \\ c \cdot \top & c \cdot \top + d \end{pmatrix}.$$

The matrix on the right-hand side clearly is (H2). So if A is (H3), i.e., if $A = A \cdot \mathbb{I}$, it is also (H2).

For (H4) we calculate

$$(a \vdash b) \cdot \textit{true} \;=\; \begin{pmatrix} \top & \top \\ \overline{a} & \overline{a} + b \end{pmatrix} \cdot \begin{pmatrix} \top & \top \\ \top & \top \end{pmatrix} \;=\; \begin{pmatrix} \top & \top \\ (\overline{a} + b) \cdot \top & (\overline{a} + b) \cdot \top \end{pmatrix},$$

so that $a \vdash b$ satisfies (H4) iff

$$(\overline{a} + b) \cdot \top = \top.$$

Matrices satisfying (H4) are called *feasible* in [5].

Let ND(S) be the set of all normal designs over S. Collecting the stated algebraic properties, we obtain

Lemma 6.2. *The structure* $(\mathrm{ND}(S), +, \cdot, \overline{ok}, \mathbb{I})$ *is a weak semiring.*

There is no analogous result for the feasible normal designs, since there is not even a neutral element w.r.t. addition. This can be shown as follows. A neutral element $t \vdash a$ would have to be least w.r.t. the natural semiring order, i.e., would need to satisfy, for all s, t,

$$t \vdash a \leq s \vdash b \Leftrightarrow s \leq t \wedge s \wedge a \leq b \,.$$

Setting $s = \top$ we obtain $t = \top$ and the residual requirement that $a \leq b$ for all b. So the only candidate would be $\top \vdash 0 = \overline{ok}$ which, however, is not feasible.

7   The Algebra of Prescriptions

Whereas (feasible) designs reflect the semantic view of total correctness, in [3] Dunne models the view of general correctness as introduced in [11, 12, 13] that also allows miraculous program behaviour. To this end Dunne introduces *prescriptions* of the form

$$P \Vdash Q \quad \Leftrightarrow_{df} \quad (ok \,\wedge\, P \Rightarrow ok') \,\wedge\, (ok' \Rightarrow Q \,\wedge\, ok) \,.$$

By investigating the four possible combinations of the values of ok and ok', or by a calculation analogous to the one for designs in Section 2, one obtains the matrix representation

$$P \Vdash Q \Leftrightarrow \begin{pmatrix} true & false \\ \overline{P} & Q \end{pmatrix} \,.$$

Since the first row of our matrices corresponds to the case $ok = false$, this yields immediately Dunne's healthiness condition (HP): A matrix A represents a prescription iff its first row coincides with that of $\overline{ok'}$.

The generalisation to Boolean semirings reads

$$a \Vdash b =_{df} \begin{pmatrix} \top & 0 \\ \overline{a} & b \end{pmatrix} \,.$$

From this it is immediate that, unlike designs, prescriptions can uniquely be decomposed into their constituents:

$$(a \Vdash b) = (c \Vdash d) \Leftrightarrow a = c \,\wedge\, b = d \,. \tag{8}$$

Moreover, since the natural order on matrices works componentwise,

$$(a \Vdash b) \leq (c \Vdash d) \Leftrightarrow c \leq a \,\wedge\, b \leq d \,. \tag{9}$$

Let us now see how addition and composition of prescriptions work out. First,

$$(a \Vdash b) + (c \Vdash d) = \begin{pmatrix} \top & 0 \\ \overline{a} & b \end{pmatrix} + \begin{pmatrix} \top & 0 \\ \overline{c} & d \end{pmatrix} = \begin{pmatrix} \top & 0 \\ \overline{a \wedge c} & b + d \end{pmatrix} = a \wedge c \Vdash b + d \,.$$

Second, since we assume S to be a full semiring,

$$(a \Vdash b) \cdot (c \Vdash d) = \begin{pmatrix} \top & 0 \\ \overline{a} & b \end{pmatrix} \cdot \begin{pmatrix} \top & 0 \\ \overline{c} & d \end{pmatrix} = \begin{pmatrix} \top \cdot \top + 0 \cdot \overline{c} & \top \cdot 0 + 0 \cdot d \\ \overline{a} \cdot \top + b \cdot \overline{c} & \overline{a} \cdot 0 + b \cdot d \end{pmatrix}$$

$$= \begin{pmatrix} \top & 0 \\ \overline{\overline{a} \cdot \top \wedge \overline{b \cdot \overline{c}}} & b \cdot d \end{pmatrix} = (\overline{\overline{a} \cdot \top \wedge \overline{b \cdot \overline{c}}}) \Vdash (b \cdot d) .$$

Summarised,

$$(a \Vdash b) \cdot (c \Vdash d) = (\overline{\overline{a} \cdot \top \wedge \overline{b \cdot \overline{c}}}) \Vdash (b \cdot d) . \tag{10}$$

So, in particular, the set of prescriptions is closed under choice and composition. The formulas for addition and composition coincide with the ones for designs.

The following prescriptions are of particular importance (see Dunne [3] and Nelson [13]):

$$\text{loop} =_{df} 0 \Vdash 0 = \begin{pmatrix} \top & 0 \\ \top & 0 \end{pmatrix} = \overline{ok'} ,$$

$$\text{fail} =_{df} \top \Vdash 0 = \begin{pmatrix} \top & 0 \\ 0 & 0 \end{pmatrix} = \overline{ok} \wedge \overline{ok'} ,$$

$$\text{chaos} =_{df} 0 \Vdash \top = \begin{pmatrix} \top & 0 \\ \top & \top \end{pmatrix} = ok' \rightarrow ok ,$$

$$\text{havoc} =_{df} \top \Vdash \top = \begin{pmatrix} \top & 0 \\ 0 & \top \end{pmatrix} = ok \leftrightarrow ok' ,$$

$$\text{skip} =_{df} \top \Vdash 1 = \begin{pmatrix} \top & 0 \\ 0 & 1 \end{pmatrix} .$$

Since the composition rule for prescriptions is the same as for designs, it is clear that skip (which corresponds to the design $\mathrm{I\!I}$) is a left identity and fail (which corresponds to the design $\overline{ok}$) is a left annihilator w.r.t. composition. Moreover, fail is an identity w.r.t. addition.

Analogously to the case of designs, the *normal* and *feasible* prescriptions are the ones for which skip is also a right identity and fail is also a right annihilator w.r.t. composition. The componentwise algebraic transcriptions of these notions are the same as for designs.

Let $\mathrm{NP}(S)$ be the set of normal prescriptions over a semiring S. Then we have

Lemma 7.1. *The structure* $(\mathrm{NP}(S), +, \cdot, \text{fail}, \text{skip})$ *is a weak semiring.*

The identity in algebraic structure is used in the companion paper [4] to give a uniform treatment of normal designs $t \vdash a$ and normal prescriptions $t \Vdash a$ as pairs (a, t) consisting of a transition part a and a termination condition part t.

For normal prescriptions we obtain again a simplified composition formula that is isomorphic to (7):

$$(a \Vdash b) \cdot (c \Vdash d) = (a \wedge \overline{b \cdot \overline{c}}) \Vdash (b \cdot d) . \tag{11}$$

Finally, we want to relate designs and prescriptions. Following [3], we define

$$relax(a \Vdash b) =_{df} a \Vdash (\overline{a} + b) = \begin{pmatrix} \top & 0 \\ \overline{a} & \overline{a} + b \end{pmatrix} .$$

Except for the 0 entry this is the representation of a design. We can form a proper design representation by adding one of the matrices

$$\begin{pmatrix} 0 & \top \\ 0 & 0 \end{pmatrix} \; = \; \overline{ok \wedge ok'} \; = \; \overline{\text{chaos}} \qquad \text{or} \qquad \begin{pmatrix} \top & \top \\ 0 & 0 \end{pmatrix} \; = \; \overline{ok} \; .$$

This is summarised in part 1. of the following lemma.

Lemma 7.2. *1.* $a \vdash b \;=\; \text{chaos} \rightarrow relax(a \Vdash b) \;=\; ok \rightarrow relax(a \Vdash b).$
2. $relax(a \Vdash b) \;=\; (a \vdash b) \wedge \text{chaos} \;=\; (a \vdash b) \wedge ok.$

Part 2. follows from part 1. by straightforward Boolean algebra.

8   Conditions, Tests and Iteration

As a preparation for our treatment of predicate transformers in the next section, we now show how to algebraically model *state predicates* that describe sets of states. To keep the framework uniform, state predicates have to be embedded into the general set of predicates or relations. If M is the set of all states then in REL(M) there are three basic methods of representing state predicates, i.e., to characterise subsets $N \subseteq M$, as special predicates or relations:

1. Use predicates that do not depend on the output values of variables, corresponding to *right-universal* relations $N \times M$. In a semiring with $\top$ they are abstractly characterised as *right ideals*, i.e., as elements a with $a \cdot \top = a$.
2. Use predicates that do not depend on the input values of variables, corresponding to *left-universal* relations $M \times N$. In a semiring with $\top$ they are abstractly characterised as *left ideals*, i.e., as elements a with $\top \cdot a = a$.
3. Use sub-predicates of skip corresponding to *partial identity* relations of the form $\{(s,s) : s \in N\}$. In an idempotent semiring they are abstractly characterised as elements a with $a \leq 1$.

Each of these approaches has its advantages and disadvantages. Classical UTP uses variant 1, while variant 3 is used in test and modal semirings. Since we are going to import some results from the third framework, we will show some connections between variants 1 and 3 (we do not need variant 2 in the present paper, but the treatment for it would be symmetrical). We only give a summary of the necessary theory; a more thorough treatment can be found in [4].

1. A *(weak) condition semiring* is a pair $(S, \text{cond}(S))$, where S is a (weak) idempotent semiring with a greatest element $\top$ and $\text{cond}(S) \subseteq S$ is a Boolean subalgebra of the set of right ideals of S with $0, \top \in \text{cond}(S)$ and such that the join operation in $\text{cond}(S)$ coincides with $+$ and for every element $a \in S$ and every condition $t \in \text{cond}(S)$ the meet $t \wedge a$, called the *input restriction of a by t*, exists and satisfies $(t + u) \wedge a = (t \wedge a) + (u \wedge a)$ as well as $t \wedge (a + b) = t \wedge a + t \wedge b$. We have the correspondences *false* $\leftrightarrow 0$ and *true* $\leftrightarrow \top$. The negation of t, i.e., its complement relative to $\top$ in $\text{cond}(S)$, is denoted by $\bar{t}$. An example is again REL(M), with the right-universal relations as conditions.

2. A *(weak) test semiring* [8] is a pair $(S, \mathsf{test}(S))$, where S is a (weak) idempotent semiring and $\mathsf{test}(S) \subseteq [0,1]$ is a Boolean subalgebra of the interval
$[0,1]$ of S such that $0, 1 \in \mathsf{test}(S)$ and join and meet in $\mathsf{test}(S)$ coincide with
$+$ and $\cdot$. The negation of test p, i.e., its complement relative to 1 in $\mathsf{test}(S)$,
is denoted by $\neg p$. We have the correspondences *false* $\leftrightarrow 0$ and *true* $\leftrightarrow 1$. In
a test semiring, for $p \in \mathsf{test}(S)$ and $a \in S$, the products $p \cdot a$ and $a \cdot p$ are
the *input* and *output* restrictions of a to those pre-/post-states that satisfy
p. An important example is REL(M) with the partial identities as tests.

We will use the letters $a, b, c, \ldots$ for semiring elements, $p, q, r, \ldots$ for tests and
$s, t, u, \ldots$ for conditions. It should be noted that 0 and $\top$ are always right (and
left) ideals. For 0 this follows from its left annihilation property, while for $\top$ this
is property (2).

By associativity of $\cdot$ and property (2) one has $(p \cdot \top) \cdot \top = p \cdot (\top \cdot \top) = p \cdot \top$,
i.e., the element $p \cdot \top$ is indeed a right ideal. In fact it is easy to show that the
right ideals in a semiring S with $\top$ are exactly the products $a \cdot \top$ for $a \in S$.

It can be shown [4] that $\mathsf{cond}(S)$ and the set $\mathrm{CS}(S) =_{df} \{t \wedge 1 : t \in \mathsf{cond}(S)\}$
of *condition subidentities* are order-isomorphic. Hence every (weak) condition
semiring S can be made into a test (weak) semiring using $\mathsf{test}(S) =_{df} \mathrm{CS}(S)$.

To prepare an example of the use of tests we add an operator for finite iteration. A *left-inductive Kleene algebra*[7] is a structure $(S, *)$ such that S is an
idempotent semiring and the star operation $* : S \to S$ satisfies, for all $a, b, c \in S$,
the *left unfold* and *left induction* axioms

$$1 + a \cdot a^* \le a^* , \qquad b + a \cdot c \le c \Rightarrow a^* b \le c .$$

By these axioms, $a^* \cdot b$ is the least solution of the fixpoint equation $x = b + a \cdot x$.
In particular, the star operator is isotone w.r.t. the natural semiring order. In [4]
we have shown that the design and prescription semirings can be made into
left-inductive Kleene algebras (and even ω-algebras with infinite iteration a^ω).

Assume now a test semiring S that also is a left-inductive Kleene algebra. For
test p and arbitrary element a one can define the loop "while p do a" in UTP
notation as [8]

$$p * a =_{df} (p \cdot a)^* \cdot \neg p .$$

The general unfold and induction axioms yield the laws

$$\neg p + (p \cdot a)^* \cdot (p * a) \le p * a \quad \text{(uf)} , \qquad \neg p + (p \cdot a) \cdot c \le c \Rightarrow t * a \le c \quad \text{(in)} .$$

With them we show the loop merge law L5 in Section 5.5. of [5]:

$$(p * a) \cdot ((p + q) * a) = ((p + q) * a) .$$

We show this as two inequations. Abbreviate the right hand side by d. For $(\le)$
we have by $\neg p \le 1$, isotony of star and (uf), unfold

$$(p \cdot a)^* \cdot \neg p \cdot d \le (p \cdot a)^* \cdot d \le ((p + q) \cdot a)^* \cdot d \le d .$$

The direction ($\geq$) reduces by (in), Boolean algebra ($p + q = p + \neg p \cdot q$) and distributivity to the three inequations

$$\neg(p+q) \leq (p*a)\cdot d \,, \quad p\cdot a\cdot(p*a)\cdot d \leq (p*a)\cdot d \,, \quad \neg p\cdot q\cdot a\cdot(p*a)\cdot d \leq (p*a)\cdot d \,.$$

The first of these holds by (uf) twice, since by Boolean algebra $\neg(p + q) = \neg p \cdot \neg(p + q)$. The second one follows directly from (uf). For the third one we have by the above inequation ($\leq$) and (uf)

$$\neg p \cdot q \cdot a \cdot (p * a) \cdot d \leq \neg p \cdot q \cdot a \cdot d \leq (p * a) \cdot (p + q) \cdot a \cdot d \leq (p * a) \cdot d \leq d \,,$$

which finishes the proof.

Since we will show below that designs and prescriptions form condition and test semirings, this general result also applies to them, showing the mentioned law L5. Unfortunately, an analogous treatment using conditions instead of tests is a bit more cumbersome.

9 Domain and Predicate Transformers

Next we want to characterise the domain of a semiring element a, i.e., the set of states from which corresponding output states may be reached under a. Again, such sets can be modelled by tests or by conditions.

A simple equational axiomatisation for the case of test semirings has been presented in [2]. We repeat it and give a corresponding axiomatisation for the case of condition semirings in parallel.

The domain operations are

$$\ulcorner\;\; : S \rightarrow \text{test}(S) \qquad \ulcorner\!\ulcorner\;\; : S \rightarrow \text{cond}(S)$$

with the respective axioms

$$
\begin{array}{llll}
a \leq \ulcorner a \cdot a & \text{(td1)} & \qquad a \leq \ulcorner\!\ulcorner a \wedge a & \text{(cd1)} \\
\ulcorner(p \cdot a) \leq p & \text{(td2)} & \qquad \ulcorner\!\ulcorner(t \wedge a) \leq t & \text{(cd2)} \\
\ulcorner(a \cdot \ulcorner b) \leq \ulcorner(a \cdot b) & \text{(td3)} & \qquad \ulcorner\!\ulcorner(a \cdot \ulcorner\!\ulcorner b) \leq \ulcorner\!\ulcorner(a \cdot b) & \text{(cd3)}
\end{array}
$$

According to [2] (td1) $\wedge$ (td2) is equivalent to

$$\ulcorner a \leq p \Leftrightarrow a \leq p \cdot a \,. \tag{12}$$

By analogous reasoning we obtain that (cd1) $\wedge$ (cd2) is equivalent to

$$\ulcorner\!\ulcorner a \leq t \Leftrightarrow a \leq t \wedge a \Leftrightarrow a \leq t \,. \tag{GCc}$$

This property has the form of a Galois connection which corresponds to the one for the case of a test semiring with $\top$ (see e.g. [1] and again [2]):

$$\ulcorner a \leq p \Leftrightarrow a \leq p \cdot \top \,. \tag{GCt}$$

By the Galois connections, the domain operations are unique if they exist.

Moreover, one obtains the following consequences.

Lemma 9.1.

$$
\begin{array}{llll}
1. & \ulcorner a \le 0 \;\Leftrightarrow\; a \le 0, & \urcorner a \le 0 \;\Leftrightarrow\; a \le 0. \\
2. & \ulcorner(a+b) = \ulcorner a + \ulcorner b, & \urcorner(a+b) = \urcorner a + \urcorner b. \\
3. & a \le b \;\Rightarrow\; \ulcorner a \le \ulcorner b, & a \le b \;\Rightarrow\; \urcorner a \le \urcorner b. \\
4. & \ulcorner p = p, & \urcorner t = t. \\
5. & \ulcorner(\ulcorner a) = \ulcorner a, & \urcorner(\urcorner a) = \urcorner a. \\
6. & a = \ulcorner a \cdot a, & a = \urcorner a \wedge a. \\
7. & \ulcorner(p \cdot a) = p \cdot \ulcorner a, & \urcorner(t \wedge a) = t \wedge \urcorner a. \\
8. & \ulcorner(a \cdot b) \le \ulcorner(a \cdot \ulcorner b), & \urcorner(a \cdot b) \le \urcorner(a \cdot \urcorner b). \\
9. & \ulcorner(a \cdot \top) = \ulcorner a, & \urcorner(a \cdot \top) = \urcorner a. \\
10. & \ulcorner(a \cdot b) \le \ulcorner a, & \urcorner(a \cdot b) \le \urcorner a. \\
11. & \ulcorner 1 = 1, & \urcorner 1 = \top.
\end{array}
$$

For the proofs in the condition semiring case see [4].

With the help of domain we now define predicate transformers such as wlp and wp that map sets of states to sets of states, both denoted by state predicates. This will allow a more perspicuous representation of the terms involved in the formulas for composition of designs and prescriptions and later the introduction of wlp and wp in the semirings of designs and prescriptions.

The forward modal operators diamond and box are given by

$$
\begin{array}{ll}
\langle a\rangle p =_{df} \ulcorner(a \cdot p), & \langle\!\langle a\rangle\!\rangle t =_{df} \urcorner(a \cdot t), \\[4pt]
[a]p =_{df} \neg\langle a\rangle\neg p, & [\![a]\!]t =_{df} \langle\!\langle a\rangle\!\rangle \bar{t}.
\end{array}
$$

Thus $\langle a\rangle p/\langle\!\langle a\rangle\!\rangle t$ characterise those states for which *some* a-successor state satisfies p/t, whereas $[a]p/[\![a]\!]t$ characterise those states for which *all* a-successor states satisfy p/t. The box operators are the abstract counterparts of the wlp operator [13].

From these definitions the following properties are straightforward [2, 4].

$$
\begin{array}{ll}
\langle 0\rangle p = 0, & \langle\!\langle 0\rangle\!\rangle t = 0, \\
\langle a\rangle(p+q) = \langle a\rangle p + \langle a\rangle q, & \langle\!\langle a\rangle\!\rangle(t+u) = \langle\!\langle a\rangle\!\rangle t + \langle\!\langle a\rangle\!\rangle u, \\
\langle a+b\rangle p = \langle a\rangle p + \langle b\rangle p, & \langle\!\langle a+b\rangle\!\rangle t = \langle\!\langle a\rangle\!\rangle t + \langle\!\langle b\rangle\!\rangle t, \\
\langle p\cdot a\rangle q = p \cdot \langle a\rangle q, & \langle\!\langle t\wedge a\rangle\!\rangle u = t \wedge \langle\!\langle a\rangle\!\rangle u, \\
\langle 1\rangle p = p, & \langle\!\langle 1\rangle\!\rangle t = t, \\
\langle a\cdot b\rangle p = \langle a\rangle\langle b\rangle p. & \langle\!\langle a\cdot b\rangle\!\rangle t = \langle\!\langle a\rangle\!\rangle\langle\!\langle b\rangle\!\rangle t.
\end{array}
$$

Hence $\langle a\rangle$ and $\langle\!\langle a\rangle\!\rangle$ are isotone. Moreover, both diamonds are isotone in their first arguments. If the underlying semiring is full, we obtain additionally

$$
\langle a\rangle 0 = 0 \qquad\qquad \langle\!\langle a\rangle\!\rangle 0 = 0
$$

The box operators enjoy dual laws which we omit, since we will mainly work with diamonds. Because of the importance of modal operators, we call a (weak) test or condition semiring with domain *modal*.

Now we study the special case of the relation semiring. A (weak) semiring S with $\top$ is *ideal-closed*, briefly *id-closed*, if its set $\mathrm{RI}(S)$ of right ideals is a Boolean algebra. The relation semiring REL(M) is id-closed, whereas the semiring of formal languages over an alphabet, under union and concatenation, is not.

We quote the following result from [4]:

Lemma 9.2. *For an id-closed weak semiring S, the pair $(S, \mathrm{RI}(S))$ can uniquely be made into a weak domain semiring by setting*

$$\ulcorner a \urcorner =_{df} a \cdot \top .$$

Hence over an id-closed semiring

$$\langle\!\langle a \rangle\!\rangle t = a \cdot t , \qquad [\![a]\!]t = \overline{a \cdot \bar{t}} .$$

It should be noted that in [5] the notation a wp t is used for $[\![a]\!]t$, although really it ought to be a wlp t. We will give a proper definition of wp for designs and prescriptions in the next section.

With the above representation of $[\![a]\!]t$ in id-closed weak semirings we see that the subterm $\overline{b \cdot \bar{c}}$ occurring in the formulas (6) and (10) for composition of designs and prescriptions can be folded into $[\![b]\!]c$. In the case of a normal design or description, by (7) and (11) the antecedent of the composition therefore simplifies to $a \wedge [\![b]\!]c$.

10   Predicate Transformers for Matrices

Since we have seen that normal designs and prescriptions form weak semirings, we can try to even make them into weak modal semirings. To this end we first need to find out what the potential conditions or tests are in each case. Since, as stated, the condition and test based approaches are isomorphic, we treat only the condition case in the main text, since it is the one used in UTP, and defer the test case to the Appendix.

First we determine the conditions in the design semiring. The greatest (normal) design and also the greatest matrix overall is *true*. So matrix A is an ideal iff $A \cdot true = A$. Now

$$\begin{pmatrix} a & b \\ c & d \end{pmatrix} \cdot \begin{pmatrix} \top & \top \\ \top & \top \end{pmatrix} = \begin{pmatrix} (a+b) \cdot \top & (a+b) \cdot \top \\ (c+d) \cdot \top & (c+d) \cdot \top \end{pmatrix} = \begin{pmatrix} a & b \\ c & d \end{pmatrix}$$

iff

$$a = (a+b) \cdot \top = b \ \wedge \ c = (c+d) \cdot \top = d .$$

Hence the ideals are exactly the row-constant matrices with ideals of S as entries. Therefore a normal design $t \vdash a$ is an ideal iff $\bar{t} + a = \bar{t}$, i.e., iff $a \leq \bar{t}$. Such a row-constant design $\begin{pmatrix} \top & \top \\ \bar{t} & \bar{t} \end{pmatrix}$ has the relative complement $\begin{pmatrix} \top & \top \\ t & t \end{pmatrix}$ within the set of normal designs. Moreover, such a matrix corresponds also to the simpler design $\bar{t} \vdash 0$. The order on the ideals is characterised by $\bar{s} \vdash 0 \leq \bar{t} \vdash 0 \Leftrightarrow s \leq t$. Therefore we have

Theorem 10.1. *If* $(S, \mathrm{cond}(S))$ *is a weak condition semiring, then*

$$(\mathrm{NP}(S), \{\bar{t} \vdash 0 : t \in \mathrm{cond}(S)\})$$

is weak condition semiring. If $\mathrm{cond}(S) = \mathrm{RI}(S)$ *then it is id-closed.*
If $(S, \mathrm{cond}(S))$ *is a modal semiring then* $\mathrm{NP}(S)$ *is a weak modal semiring with domain operation* $^\ulcorner(t \vdash a) = (t \wedge {}^\ulcorner\!a) \vdash 0$.

Proof. The first claim is immediate from the above remarks. For the second claim, we work out what (GCc) means for normal designs: By (4), shunting, lattice algebra, (GCc), 2. and 4. of Lemma 9.1, and Boolean algebra:

$$
\begin{aligned}
& (t \vdash a) \ \le \ (\bar{s} \vdash 0) \\
\Leftrightarrow\ & \bar{s} \le t \ \wedge \ \bar{s} \wedge a \le 0 \\
\Leftrightarrow\ & \bar{t} \le s \ \wedge \ a \le s \\
\Leftrightarrow\ & \bar{t} + a \le s \\
\Leftrightarrow\ & {}^\ulcorner(\bar{t} + a) \le s \\
\Leftrightarrow\ & \bar{t} + {}^\ulcorner\!a \le s \\
\Leftrightarrow\ & \bar{s} \le t \wedge \overline{{}^\ulcorner\!a} \ .
\end{aligned}
$$

Now we check (cd3). By definition of $^\ulcorner$, (5), (7), definition of $^\ulcorner$, Boolean algebra and distributivity, since $a \cdot {}^\ulcorner\!b \le {}^\ulcorner(a \cdot {}^\ulcorner\!b)$ and hence $\overline{{}^\ulcorner(a \cdot {}^\ulcorner\!b)} \le \overline{(a \cdot {}^\ulcorner\!b)}$, by modality, definition of $^\ulcorner$, and (7):

$$
\begin{aligned}
& {}^\ulcorner((s \vdash a) \cdot {}^\ulcorner(t \vdash b)) \\
=\ & {}^\ulcorner((s \vdash a) \cdot (t \wedge \overline{{}^\ulcorner\!b} \vdash 0)) \\
=\ & {}^\ulcorner((s \vdash a) \cdot (t \wedge \overline{{}^\ulcorner\!b} \vdash {}^\ulcorner\!b)) \\
=\ & {}^\ulcorner(s \wedge a \cdot t \wedge \overline{\overline{{}^\ulcorner\!b}} \vdash a \cdot {}^\ulcorner\!b)) \\
=\ & (s \wedge a \cdot t \wedge \overline{{}^\ulcorner\!b} \wedge {}^\ulcorner(a \cdot {}^\ulcorner\!b)) \vdash 0 \\
=\ & (s \wedge a \cdot \bar{t} \wedge \overline{a \cdot {}^\ulcorner\!b} \wedge {}^\ulcorner(a \cdot {}^\ulcorner\!b)) \vdash 0 \\
=\ & (s \wedge a \cdot \bar{t} \wedge {}^\ulcorner(a \cdot {}^\ulcorner\!b)) \vdash 0 \\
=\ & (s \wedge a \cdot \bar{t} \wedge {}^\ulcorner(a \cdot b)) \vdash 0 \\
=\ & {}^\ulcorner(s \wedge a \cdot \bar{t} \vdash a \cdot b) \\
=\ & {}^\ulcorner((s \vdash a) \cdot (t \vdash b)) \ . \qquad\qquad \Box
\end{aligned}
$$

Let us work out the box operator for the case of a modal underlying S: By the definitions, complement of ideal, (5), (7), definition, since $a \cdot \bar{s} \le {}^\ulcorner(a \cdot \bar{s})$, hence $\overline{{}^\ulcorner(a \cdot \bar{s})} \le \overline{a \cdot \bar{s}}$, definition,

$$
\begin{aligned}
& [\![t \vdash a]\!](\bar{s} \vdash 0) \\
=\ & \overline{{}^\ulcorner((t \vdash a) \cdot \overline{\bar{s} \vdash 0)})} \\
=\ & \overline{{}^\ulcorner((t \vdash a) \cdot (s \vdash 0))} \\
=\ & \overline{{}^\ulcorner((t \vdash a) \cdot (s \vdash \bar{s}))} \\
=\ & \overline{{}^\ulcorner(t \wedge \overline{a \cdot \bar{s}}) \vdash a \cdot \bar{s}}
\end{aligned}
$$

$$
\begin{aligned}
&= \overline{t \wedge \overline{a \cdot \overline{s}} \wedge {}^{\top\!\!\top}(a \cdot \overline{s})} \vdash 0 \\
&= \overline{t \wedge {}^{\top\!\!\top}(a \cdot \overline{s})} \vdash 0 \\
&= \overline{t \wedge [\![a]\!]s} \vdash 0 \ .
\end{aligned}
$$

This corresponds precisely to the definition of the wp operator in [13]. That wp is just the wlp of another semiring seems first to have been noted in [10] for a test-based approach.

For the case of prescriptions things work much in the same way. Again we have $t \Vdash a \leq \mathsf{skip} \Leftrightarrow t = \top \wedge a \leq 1$. The ideals have to satisfy $(t \Vdash a) \cdot \mathsf{chaos} = (t \Vdash a)$, which works out to

$$
a \cdot \top = a \wedge a \leq \overline{t} \ .
$$

Hence we can choose the sets of tests and conditions as in the case of designs and obtain a (non-id-closed) weak modal semiring $\mathrm{NP}(S)$.

11   Matrices of Predicate Transformers

In this section we show that the matrix calculus can be extended to predicate transformers, which will allow a lifting of the results of Sections 5 and 7 to predicate transformer algebras. Doing this, we obtain the simplified composition formulas for normal designs with less complicated calculations, while at the same time removing the need for the underlying semiring to be id-closed.

First we show that the diamond operators over a condition semiring form a condition semiring again.

Lemma 11.1. *Set, for $U \subseteq S$ in a weak modal condition semiring $(S, \mathsf{cond}(S))$,*

$$
\langle\!\langle U \rangle\!\rangle \ =_{df} \ \{\langle\!\langle a \rangle\!\rangle : a \in U\} \ .
$$

1. *The structure $\langle\!\langle S \rangle\!\rangle =_{df} (\langle\!\langle S \rangle\!\rangle, +, \circ, \langle\!\langle 0 \rangle\!\rangle, \langle\!\langle 1 \rangle\!\rangle)$ is a (weak) semiring with greatest element $\langle\!\langle \top \rangle\!\rangle$ under the operations*

$$
\langle\!\langle a \rangle\!\rangle + \langle\!\langle b \rangle\!\rangle =_{df} \langle\!\langle a + b \rangle\!\rangle \ , \qquad \langle\!\langle a \rangle\!\rangle \circ \langle\!\langle b \rangle\!\rangle =_{df} \langle\!\langle a \cdot b \rangle\!\rangle \ .
$$

2. *For $s, t \in \mathsf{cond}(S)$ we have $\langle\!\langle t \wedge u \rangle\!\rangle = \langle\!\langle t \rangle\!\rangle \wedge \langle\!\langle u \rangle\!\rangle$, where the meet of diamonds is defined pointwise.*
3. *For $t \in \mathsf{cond}(S)$ we have $\langle\!\langle \overline{t} \rangle\!\rangle = \overline{\langle\!\langle t \rangle\!\rangle}$.*
4. *$\{\langle\!\langle a \rangle\!\rangle : a \in \mathrm{RI}(S)\} \subseteq \mathrm{RI}(\langle\!\langle S \rangle\!\rangle)$.*

Proof.   1. This is immediate from the diamond properties.
2. We calculate, for $u \in \mathsf{cond}(S)$, using Lemma 9.1.7,

$$
\langle\!\langle s \wedge t \rangle\!\rangle u = s \wedge t \wedge \langle\!\langle \top \rangle\!\rangle u = s \wedge \langle\!\langle \top \rangle\!\rangle u \wedge t \wedge \langle\!\langle \top \rangle\!\rangle u = \langle\!\langle s \rangle\!\rangle u \wedge \langle\!\langle t \rangle\!\rangle u \ .
$$

3. First, $\langle\!\langle t \rangle\!\rangle + \langle\!\langle \overline{t} \rangle\!\rangle = \langle\!\langle t + \overline{t} \rangle\!\rangle = \langle\!\langle \top \rangle\!\rangle$. Second, by 2., $\langle\!\langle t \rangle\!\rangle \wedge \langle\!\langle \overline{t} \rangle\!\rangle = \langle\!\langle t \wedge \overline{t} \rangle\!\rangle = \langle\!\langle 0 \rangle\!\rangle$.
   The laws of involution and de Morgan are also easily checked.
4. $a \in \mathrm{RI}(S) \Leftrightarrow a = a \cdot \top \Rightarrow \langle\!\langle a \rangle\!\rangle = \langle\!\langle a \cdot \top \rangle\!\rangle = \langle\!\langle a \rangle\!\rangle \circ \langle\!\langle \top \rangle\!\rangle$.   □

In the remainder we will mostly omit the composition operator $\circ$.

We now define a property that relaxes the one of id-closedness (see Section 9). We call a (weak) modal condition semiring S *Tarskian* if it satisfies

$$\langle\!\langle \top \rangle\!\rangle u = \top \Leftarrow u \in \mathsf{cond}(S)\backslash\{0\} . \qquad\qquad \text{(MTARt)}$$

By Lemma 9.1.9, (MTARt) is equivalent to

$$^\ulcorner(\top \cdot u \cdot \top) = \top \Leftarrow u \in \mathsf{cond}(S)\backslash\{0\} .$$

This is a modal analogue of the Tarski rule $\top \cdot a \cdot \top = \top \Leftarrow a \neq 0$ of the relational calculus, whence our terminology.

Property (MTARt) holds in REL(M), but also in many other semirings that, contrary to REL(M), are not id-closed, e.g. in the semirings of languages of finite and infinite words under concatenation and under fusion product.

We obtain another useful equivalent characterisation:

Lemma 11.2. *S is Tarskian iff $\langle\!\langle t \rangle\!\rangle u = t$ for all $t, u \in \mathsf{cond}(S)$ with $u \neq 0$.*

Proof. ($\Rightarrow$) $\langle\!\langle t \rangle\!\rangle u = t \wedge \langle\!\langle \top \rangle\!\rangle u = t \wedge \top = t$.
($\Leftarrow$) Set $t = \top$. □

Lemma 11.3. *Assume a Tarskian modal condition semiring $(S, \mathsf{cond}(S))$.*

1. *For all $a \in S$ we have $\langle\!\langle a \rangle\!\rangle\langle\!\langle \top \rangle\!\rangle = \langle\!\langle ^\ulcorner a \rangle\!\rangle$.*
2. *$\mathrm{RI}(\langle\!\langle S \rangle\!\rangle) = \{\langle\!\langle t \rangle\!\rangle : t \in \mathsf{cond}(S)\}$.*
3. *$(\langle\!\langle S \rangle\!\rangle, \mathrm{RI}(\langle\!\langle S \rangle\!\rangle))$ is an id-closed and Tarskian modal condition semiring with $^\ulcorner\langle\!\langle a \rangle\!\rangle = \langle\!\langle ^\ulcorner a \rangle\!\rangle$.*

Proof. 1. Since we assume a semiring and not just a weak semiring,

$$\langle\!\langle a \rangle\!\rangle\langle\!\langle \top \rangle\!\rangle 0 = \langle\!\langle a \rangle\!\rangle 0 = 0 = \langle\!\langle ^\ulcorner a \rangle\!\rangle 0 .$$

For $u \neq 0$ we calculate, using Lemma 11.2,

$$\langle\!\langle a \rangle\!\rangle\langle\!\langle \top \rangle\!\rangle u = \langle\!\langle a \rangle\!\rangle\top = {}^\ulcorner a = \langle\!\langle ^\ulcorner a \rangle\!\rangle u .$$

2. By 1. we have $\langle\!\langle a \rangle\!\rangle \in \mathrm{RI}(\langle\!\langle S \rangle\!\rangle) \Leftrightarrow \langle\!\langle a \rangle\!\rangle = \langle\!\langle a \rangle\!\rangle\langle\!\langle \top \rangle\!\rangle \Leftrightarrow \langle\!\langle a \rangle\!\rangle = \langle\!\langle ^\ulcorner a \rangle\!\rangle$.
3. Immediate from 2.,1. and Lemma 9.2. □

Given these results we can now use

$$\begin{pmatrix} \langle\!\langle \top \rangle\!\rangle & \langle\!\langle \top \rangle\!\rangle \\ \langle\!\langle \bar{t} \rangle\!\rangle & \langle\!\langle \bar{t} + a \rangle\!\rangle \end{pmatrix} \quad \text{and} \quad \begin{pmatrix} \langle\!\langle \top \rangle\!\rangle & \langle\!\langle 0 \rangle\!\rangle \\ \langle\!\langle \bar{t} \rangle\!\rangle & \langle\!\langle a \rangle\!\rangle \end{pmatrix}$$

as predicate transformer representations of normal design $t \vdash a$ and prescription $t \Vdash a$, resp., over a Tarskian modal semiring. For the lower left corner element of both $(t \vdash a) \cdot (u \vdash b)$ and $(t \Vdash a) \cdot (u \Vdash b)$ we obtain

$$\langle\!\langle \bar{t} \rangle\!\rangle\langle\!\langle \top \rangle\!\rangle + \langle\!\langle a \rangle\!\rangle\langle\!\langle \bar{u} \rangle\!\rangle = \langle\!\langle \bar{t} \rangle\!\rangle + \langle\!\langle a \rangle\!\rangle\langle\!\langle \bar{u} \rangle\!\rangle = \overline{\langle\!\langle t \rangle\!\rangle \wedge [\![\langle\!\langle a \rangle\!\rangle]\!]\langle\!\langle u \rangle\!\rangle} ,$$

so that things work now smoothly even for non-id-closed underlying semiring S.

12   Conclusion and Outlook

The matrix calculus has proved to be a convenient vehicle for reasoning about general UTP predicates as well as designs and prescriptions. Their modal semi-ring structure allows re-use of the large existing body of results about Kleene/ω algebra with tests and modal Kleene/ω algebra. Recently it has also been shown [6] that designs and prescriptions form a demonic refinement algebra in the sense of von Wright [14], so that that framework can be re-used, too.

It remains to be seen whether a similar approach can be followed when further observation variables are added.

Acknowledgements. I am grateful to Walter Guttmann, Peter Höfner, Kim Solin and the anonymous referees for helpful discussions and remarks.

References

1. Aarts, C. J.: Galois connections presented calculationally. MSc thesis. Dept. of Math. and Comput. Sci., Eindhoven Univ. of Techn. (1992)
2. Desharnais, J., Möller, B., Struth, G.: Kleene algebra with domain. ACM Trans. on Comput. Logic (to appear)
3. Dunne, S.: Recasting Hoare and He's unifying theory of programs in the context of general correctness. In Butterfield, A., Strong, G., Pahl, C., eds.: Proc. of 5th Irish Wksh. on Formal Methods. Electron. Wkshs. in Comput. Sci. British Comput. Soc. (2001)
4. Guttmann, W., Möller, B.: Modal design algebra. Techn. report 2005-15. Inst. für Informatik, Univ. Augsburg (2005) // Revised version in Dunne, S., Stoddart, B., eds.: Proc. of 1st Int. Symp. on Unifying Theories of Programming, UTP 2006. Vol. 4010 of Lect. Notes in Comput. Sci. Springer-Verlag (2006) 236–256
5. Hoare, C. A. R., He, J.: Unifying theories of programming. Prentice Hall (1998)
6. Höfner, P., Möller, B., Solin, K.: Omega algebra, demonic refinement algebra and commands. Techn. Report 2006-11. Inst. für Informatik, Univ. Augsburg (2006)
7. Kozen, D.: A completeness theorem for Kleene algebras and the algebra of regular events. Inform. and Comput. 110(2) (1994) 366–390
8. Kozen, D.: Kleene algebra with tests. ACM Trans. on Program. Lang. and Syst. 19(3) (1997) 427–443
9. Möller, B., Struth, G.: Algebras of modal operators and partial correctness. Theor. Comput. Sci. 351(2) (2006) 221–239
10. Möller, B., Struth, G.: wp is wlp. In MacCaull, W., Winter, M., Düntsch, I., eds.: Selected Revised Papers from 8th Int. Conf. on Relational Methods in Comput. Sci., RelMiCS 2005, 3rd Int. Wksh. on Appl. of Kleene Algebra, Wksh. of COST Action 274 TARSKI. Vol. 3929 of Lect. Notes in Comput. Sci. Springer-Verlag (2006) 200–211
11. Morgan, C.: Data refinement by miracles. Inform. Process. Lett. 26(5) (1988) 243–246
12. Morris, J. M.: Laws of data refinement. Acta Inform. 26(4) (1989) 287–308
13. Nelson, G.: A generalization of Dijkstra's calculus. ACM Trans. on Program. Lang. and Syst. 11(4) (1989) 517–561
14. von Wright, J.: Towards a refinement algebra. Sci. of Comput. Program. 51(1–2) (2004) 23–45

A   Appendix: Test-Based Predicate Transformers

First we determine the tests in the semiring of designs. The multiplicative identity is $\mathbb{I} = \top \vdash 1$ and by (4) we obtain

$$t \vdash a \leq \mathbb{I} \iff (\top \leq t) \wedge (\top \wedge a \leq 1) .$$

So the subidentities are of the form $\top \vdash p$ with $p \leq 1$. Moreover,

$$(\top \vdash p) + (\top \vdash q) = (\top \vdash p + q)$$

and, by (6),

$$(\top \vdash p) \cdot (\top \vdash q) = (\top \vdash p \cdot q) .$$

Hence, if $p \leq 1$ has the relative complement $q \leq 1$ w.r.t. 1 then $\top \vdash q$ is the complement of $\top \vdash p$ relative to $\mathbb{I}$. This shows

Lemma A.1. *If* $(S, \mathsf{test}(S))$ *is a weak test semiring, then so is*

$$(\mathrm{ND}(S), \{\top \vdash p : p \in \mathsf{test}(S)\}) .$$

We use the characterisation (12) of domain to find out whether we can even make $\mathrm{ND}(S)$ into a weak domain semiring if S is one: By (7) and lattice algebra, (4), shunting, lattice algebra, distributivity and (12), and lattice algebra and additivity of domain:

$$
\begin{aligned}
& t \vdash a \; \leq \; \overline{(\top \vdash p)} \cdot (t \vdash a) \\
\iff & t \vdash a \; \leq \; \overline{p \cdot \overline{t}} \vdash p \cdot a \\
\iff & \overline{p \cdot \overline{t}} \leq t \; \wedge \; \overline{p \cdot \overline{t}} \wedge a \leq p \cdot a \\
\iff & \overline{t} \leq p \cdot \overline{t} \; \wedge \; a \leq p \cdot \overline{t} + p \cdot a \\
\iff & \overline{t} \leq p \cdot \overline{t} \; \wedge \; \overline{t} + a \leq p \cdot \overline{t} + p \cdot a \\
\iff & \ulcorner \overline{t} \leq p \; \wedge \; \ulcorner (\overline{t} + a) \leq p \\
\iff & \ulcorner (\overline{t} + a) \leq p .
\end{aligned}
$$

So setting

$$\ulcorner (t \vdash a) =_{df} \top \vdash \ulcorner (\overline{t} + a)$$

we satisfy (td1) and (td2); a straightforward calculation shows that also (td3) holds. Altogether we have shown

Theorem A.2. *If* $(S, \mathsf{test}(S), \ulcorner \;)$ *is a weak modal semiring, then* $\mathrm{ND}(S)$ *can be made into a weak modal semiring.*

For the case of prescriptions things work much in the same way. Again we have $t \Vdash a \leq \mathsf{skip} \iff t = \top \wedge a \leq 1$. Hence we can choose the set of tests as in the case of designs and obtain a test-based weak modal semiring $\mathrm{NP}(S)$.

Next, as in the case of conditions, we investigate the semiring structure of the test-based diamond operators.

Lemma A.3. *Consider a (weak) modal test semiring $(S, \mathsf{test}(S))$ and set, for $U \subseteq S$,*

$$\langle U \rangle =_{df} \{\langle a \rangle : a \in U\} \ .$$

1. *The structure $\langle S \rangle =_{df} (\langle S \rangle, +, \circ, \langle 0 \rangle, \langle 1 \rangle)$ is a (weak) semiring with greatest element $\langle \top \rangle$ under the operations*

$$\langle a \rangle + \langle b \rangle =_{df} \langle a + b \rangle \ , \qquad \langle a \rangle \circ \langle b \rangle =_{df} \langle a \cdot b \rangle \ .$$

2. *For $p, q \in \mathsf{test}(S)$ we have $\langle p \cdot q \rangle = \langle p \rangle \wedge \langle q \rangle$.*
3. *For $a \in S$ we obtain $\langle a \rangle \leq \langle 1 \rangle \Leftrightarrow \langle a \rangle = \langle \ulcorner a \rangle$.*
4. *For $p \in \mathsf{test}(S)$ one has $\langle \neg p \rangle = \neg \langle p \rangle$.*
5. *$\{\langle a \rangle : a \in \mathrm{RI}(S)\} \subseteq \mathrm{RI}(\langle S \rangle)$.*

Proof. 1. This is shown in [9].
2. We calculate, for $r \in \mathsf{test}(S)$,

$$\langle p \cdot q \rangle r = p \cdot q \cdot r = p \cdot r \cdot q \cdot r = \langle p \rangle r \wedge \langle q \rangle r \ .$$

3. By isotony of the diamond we only need to show ($\Rightarrow$). Consider an arbitrary $p \in \mathsf{test}(S)$.

$$\langle \ulcorner a \rangle p = \ulcorner a \cdot p = p \cdot \ulcorner a = p \cdot \ulcorner (a \cdot p + a \cdot \neg p) = p \cdot \ulcorner (a \cdot p) + p \cdot \ulcorner (a \cdot \neg p)$$
$$= p \cdot \langle a \rangle p + p \cdot \langle a \rangle \neg p = \langle a \rangle p + 0 = \langle a \rangle p \ ,$$

since by assumption $\langle a \rangle p \leq p$ and $\langle a \rangle \neg p \leq \neg p$.
4. First, $\langle p \rangle + \langle \neg p \rangle = \langle p + \neg p \rangle = \langle 1 \rangle$. Second, by 2., $\langle p \rangle \wedge \langle \neg p \rangle = \langle p \cdot \neg p \rangle = \langle 0 \rangle$. The laws of involution and de Morgan are also easily checked.
5. $a \in \mathrm{RI}(S) \Leftrightarrow a = a \cdot \top \Rightarrow \langle a \rangle = \langle a \cdot \top \rangle = \langle a \rangle \circ \langle \top \rangle$. $\square$

In the remainder we will again mostly omit the composition operator. Lemma A.3.3 allows us to define domain on diamonds:

Theorem A.4. *Setting $\ulcorner \langle a \rangle =_{df} \langle \ulcorner a \rangle$ makes $(\langle S \rangle, \langle \mathsf{test}(S) \rangle)$ into a modal test semiring.*

Proof. By the previous lemma $\langle \mathsf{test}(S) \rangle$ is a test algebra. So we only need to check the domain axioms.
(cd1) $\ulcorner \langle a \rangle \circ \langle a \rangle = \langle \ulcorner a \rangle \circ \langle a \rangle = \langle \ulcorner a \cdot a \rangle = \langle a \rangle$.
(cd2) $\ulcorner (\langle p \rangle \circ \langle a \rangle) = \ulcorner \langle p \cdot a \rangle = \langle \ulcorner (p \cdot a) \rangle \leq \langle p \rangle$.
(cd3) $\ulcorner (\langle a \rangle \circ \langle b \rangle) = \ulcorner \langle a \cdot b \rangle = \langle \ulcorner (a \cdot b) \rangle = \langle \ulcorner (a \cdot \ulcorner b) \rangle = \ulcorner (\langle a \rangle \circ \langle \ulcorner b \rangle) = \ulcorner (\langle a \rangle \circ \ulcorner \langle b \rangle)$. $\square$

We conclude by relating the test and condition based approaches. A (weak) modal test semiring S is *Tarskian* if satisfies

$$\langle \top \rangle q = 1 \Leftarrow q \in \mathsf{test}(S) \setminus \{0\} \ , \qquad \text{(MTARc)}$$

or, equivalently,

$$\ulcorner (\top \cdot q \cdot \top) = 1 \Leftarrow q \in \mathsf{test}(S) \setminus \{0\} \ .$$

We define the set of *test ideals* of S as $\mathrm{TI}(S) =_{df} \{p \cdot \top : p \in \mathsf{test}(S)\}$. From [2] we know that $\overline{p \cdot \top} = \neg p \cdot \top$ and $p \cdot \top \leq q \cdot \top \Leftrightarrow p \leq q$. Using test ideals we obtain another characterisation of the Tarskian property:

Lemma A.5. S *is Tarskian iff* $\langle p \cdot \top \rangle q = p$ *for all* $p, q \in \mathsf{test}(S)$ *with* $q \neq 0$.

Proof. ($\Rightarrow$) $\langle p \cdot \top \rangle q = \langle p \rangle \langle \top \rangle q = \langle p \rangle 1 = p$.
($\Leftarrow$) Set $p = 1$. $\qquad\qquad\qquad\qquad\qquad\qquad\qquad\qquad\qquad\qquad\qquad$ $\square$

Lemma A.6. *Assume a Tarskian modal test semiring* $(S, \mathsf{test}(S))$.

1. *For all* $a \in S$ *we have* $\langle a \rangle \langle \top \rangle = \langle \ulcorner a \cdot \top \rangle$.
2. $\mathrm{RI}(\langle S \rangle) = \langle \mathrm{TI}(S) \rangle$.
3. $(\langle S \rangle, \langle \mathrm{TI}(S) \rangle)$ *is an id-closed and Tarskian modal condition semiring with*
   $^{\ulcorner}\langle a \rangle = \langle\!\langle \ulcorner a \rangle\!\rangle$.

Proof. 1. Since we assume a semiring and not just a weak semiring,

$$\langle a \rangle \langle \top \rangle 0 = \langle a \rangle 0 = 0 = \langle \ulcorner a \rangle 0 .$$

For $q \neq 0$ we calculate, using Lemma A.5,

$$\langle a \rangle \langle \top \rangle q = \langle a \rangle 1 = \ulcorner a = \langle \ulcorner a \cdot \top \rangle q .$$

2. By 1., $\langle a \rangle \in \mathrm{RI}(\langle S \rangle) \Leftrightarrow \langle a \rangle = \langle a \rangle \langle \top \rangle \Leftrightarrow \langle a \rangle = \langle \ulcorner a \cdot \top \rangle$.
3. Immediate from 2.,1. and Lemma 9.2. $\qquad\qquad\qquad\qquad\qquad\qquad$ $\square$

Therefore we can, over a Tarskian modal test semiring, represent normal designs and prescriptions also in the forms

$$p \vdash a =_{df} \begin{pmatrix} \langle \top \rangle & \langle \top \rangle \\ \langle \neg p \cdot \top \rangle & \langle \neg p \cdot \top + a \rangle \end{pmatrix} \quad \text{and} \quad p \Vdash a =_{df} \begin{pmatrix} \langle \top \rangle & \langle 0 \rangle \\ \langle \neg p \cdot \top \rangle & \langle a \rangle \end{pmatrix}$$

For the lower left corner element of both $(p \vdash a) \cdot (q \vdash b)$ and $(p \Vdash a) \cdot (q \Vdash b)$ we now obtain, with the test ideal $t =_{df} p \cdot \top$ and arbitrary test ideal u,

$$\langle \bar{t} \rangle + \langle a \rangle \langle \bar{u} \rangle = \neg(\langle t \rangle \wedge [\langle a \rangle] \langle u \rangle) ,$$

and things work again smoothly even for non-id-closed underlying semiring S.

The Shadow Knows: Refinement of Ignorance in Sequential Programs

Carroll Morgan

Dept. of Computer Science and Engineering, University of New South Wales,
Sydney 2052, Australia
carrollm@cse.unsw.edu.au

Abstract. Separating sequential-program state into "visible" and "hidden" parts facilitates reasoning about knowledge, security and privacy: applications include zero-knowledge protocols, and security contexts with hidden "high-security" state and visible "low-security" state. A rigorous definition of how specifications relate to implementations, as part of that reasoning, must ensure that implementations reveal no more than their specifications: they must, in effect, preserve ignorance.

We propose just such a definition –a relation of *ignorance-preserving refinement*– between specifications and implementations of sequential programs. Its purpose is to enable a development-by-refinement methodology for applications like those above.

Since preserving ignorance is an extra obligation, the proposed refinement relation restricts (rather than extends) the usual. We suggest general principles for restriction, and we give specific examples of them.

To argue that we do not restrict too much –for "no refinements allowed at all" is trivially ignorance-preserving– we derive The Dining Cryptographers protocol via a program algebra based on the restricted refinement relation. It is also a motivating case study, as it has never before (we believe) been treated refinement-algebraically.

In passing, we discuss –and solve– the *Refinement Paradox*.

1 Introduction

Refinement as a relation between sequential programs is based traditionally on a state-to-state operational model, with a corresponding logic of Hoare-triples $\{\Phi\}$ S $\{\Psi\}$ [1] or equivalently weakest preconditions $wp.S.\Psi$ [2], and it generates an algebra of (in-)equations between program fragments [3, 4]. A specification S1 is said to be *refined by* an implementation S2, written S1 $\sqsubseteq$ S2, just when S2 preserves all logically-expressible properties of S1.

Ignorance is (for us) what an observer doesn't know about the parts of the program state he can't see. If we partition the state into a "visible" part v and a "hidden" part h, and we consider a known program operating over v, h, then we can ask "from the final value of v, what can the observer deduce about the final value of h?" If the program is $v := 0$, what he knows afterwards about h is just what he knew beforehand; if it is $v := h \bmod 2$, then he has learned h's parity; and if it is $v := h$ then he has learned h's value exactly.

T. Uustalu (Ed.): MPC 2006, LNCS 4014, pp. 359–378, 2006.

Traditional refinement does not preserve ignorance. If we assume v, h both to have type T, then "choose v from T" is refinable into "set v to h" — it is simply a reduction of demonic nondeterminism. But that refinement, which we write $v :\in T \sqsubseteq v := h$, is called the "Refinement Paradox" (Sec. 6) precisely because it does not preserve ignorance: program $v :\in T$ tells us nothing about h, whereas $v := h$ tells us everything [5]. *Thus we cannot use traditional refinement "as is" for ignorance-preservation.* We must alter it.

Our first contribution is to propose the following principles that should apply to a *refinement algebra* altered to respect ignorance-preservation:

Pr1. *All traditional "visible-only" refinements are retained* — It would be impractical to search an entire program for hidden variables in order to validate local *visible-only* reasoning in which the hiddens are not even mentioned.

Pr2. *All traditional "structural" refinements are retained* — Associativity of sequential composition, distribution of code into branches of a conditional *etc.* are refinements (actually equalities) that do not depend on the actual code fragments affected: they are *structurally* valid, acting *en bloc*. It would be impractical to have to check through the fragments' interiors (including *e.g.* procedure calls) to validate such familiar rearrangements.

Pr3. *Some traditional "explicit-hidden" refinements are excluded* — Those that preserve ignorance will be retained; the others (*e.g.* the Paradox) will be excluded. For this principle we need a model and a logic.

Our second, and main contribution (Secs. 3–5) is to extend the model and logic of sequential programming (only slightly) to realise the above principles: existing visible-only and structural refinements will all remain sound (Pr1,Pr2); and explicit-hidden (putative) refinements can be checked individually (Pr3) for exclusion (*e.g.* Sec. 6) or retention (*e.g.* Sec. 7).

Ignorance-preserving refinement should be of great utility for developing zero-knowledge- or security-sensitive protocols (at least); and our final contribution (Secs. 7,8) is therefore a case study, the Dining Cryptographer's protocol [6], which will bolster our confidence that Pr3 has not excluded too much.

Sections 2 and 9 are informal, discussions of motivations and of comparisons and conclusions respectively.

2   Realising the Refinement-Algebra of Ignorance

2.1   Guiding Intuitions

The great advantage of having our goals expressed as algebraic principles is that we can conduct early (and intellectually inexpensive) *gedanken* experiments that will inform the subsequent construction of our model and logic. For example...

Does program $v := h; v := 0$ *reveal* h? Yes, it does, because –first– sequential composition ";" remains associative (from Pr2); and $v := 0; v :\in T = v :\in T$ (Pr1);

then $v{:}{\in}\, T \sqsubseteq \mathbf{skip}$ (Pr1), with sequential composition retaining $\sqsubseteq$-monotonicity (Pr2); and finally **skip** is still the identity (Pr2). Thus we can reason

$$(v{:}{=}\, h; v{:}{=}\, 0); v{:}{\in}\, T \;\; = \;\; v{:}{=}\, h; v{:}{\in}\, T; \;\; \sqsubseteq \;\; v{:}{=}\, h; \mathbf{skip} \;\; = \;\; v{:}{=}\, h \;;$$

since the implementation (*rhs*) fails to conceal h, so must the specification (*lhs*) have failed also. Hence our model must have "perfect recall" [7], because escape of h into v is not "erased" by the v-overwriting $v{:}{=}\, 0$ — and that is what allows h to be "copied" by the final $v{:}{\in}\, T$, our algebraic means of detecting the leak.

Arguments like the above –as well as advice[1]– suggest the Logic of Knowledge [8] as a suitable basis (App. A). Here we give the intuitions that basis supplies.

The observed program includes a notion of step-by-step atomicity, and the observer knows at any time what atoms have actually been executed, what effect they potentially had, and what the *visible* variables' values were after each one. With "actually" and "potentially" we are making a distinction between *composite* nondeterminism, written *e.g.* $h{:}{=}\, 0 \sqcap h{:}{=}\, 1$ and acting *between* atoms (or larger structures), and *atomic* nondeterminism, written *e.g.* $h{:}{\in}\, \{0,1\}$ and acting *within* an atom:

- in the composite case, afterwards we know which of atoms $h{:}{=}\, 0$ or $h{:}{=}\, 1$ was executed (actually), and thus we know the value of h too; yet
- in the atomic case, afterwards we know only that the (potential) effects were to set h to 0 or to 1, and thus we know at least (but only) that $h{\in}\{0,1\}$.

Thus atomicity makes $h{:}{=}\, 0 \sqcap h{:}{=}\, 1$ and $h{:}{\in}\, \{0,1\}$ different. (Regularity of syntax however allows $v{:}{=}\, 0 \sqcap v{:}{=}\, 1$ and $v{:}{\in}\, \{0,1\}$ as well; but since in that case we can see v anyway, afterwards, there is no difference between those latter two.) Fig. 1 illustrates this viewpoint with some small examples.

2.2 An Appropriate Logic, Informally

Our logical language is first-order predicate formulae Φ, interpreted conventionally over the variables of the program, but augmented with a "knows" modal operator so that $\mathrm{K}\Phi$ holds in this state just when Φ itself holds in *all* (other) states compatible with the visible part of this state, the program text and what we have seen (as above) about the execution path and earlier visible values.

The dual modality "possibly" is written $\mathrm{P}\Phi$ and defined $\neg\mathrm{K}(\neg\Phi)$; and it is the modality we will use mainly, as it expresses ignorance directly. (Because $\mathrm{K}\Phi$ seems more easily grasped initially, we explain both.)

Fig. 2 illustrates the logic with our earlier examples in Fig. 1.

2.3 Refinement, and the Paradox

Traditional refinement $\sqsubseteq$ between programs allows the reduction of demonic nondeterminism, as in $v{:}{\in}\, \{0,1\} \sqsubseteq v{:}{=}\, 0$.[2] It is a partial order over the program

---

[1] Moses, Engelhardt and van der Meyden have long advocated combining refinement with the Logic of Knowledge; they operate mainly in a concurrent setting.

[2] It also allows elimination of divergence, which we do not treat here.

In each case we imagine that we are at the end of the program given, that the initial values were v_0, h_0, and that *we* are the observer (so we write "we know" *etc.*)

	Program	Informal commentary
1.1	both $v{:}\in \{0,1\}$ and $v{:}=0 \sqcap v{:}=1$	We can see the value of v, either 0 or 1. We know h is still h_0, though we cannot see it.
1.2	(one atomic statement) $h{:}\in \{0,1\}$	We know that h is either 0 or 1, but we don't know which; we see that v is v_0.
1.3	(two atomic statements) $h{:}=0 \sqcap h{:}=1$	We know the value of h, because we know which of atomic $h{:}=0$ or $h{:}=1$ was executed.
1.4	$h{:}\in \{0,1\}$; $v{:}=0 \sqcap v{:}=1$	We don't know whether h is 0 or it is 1: even the $\sqcap$-demon cannot see the hidden variable.
1.5	$h{:}\in \{0,1\}$; $v{:}\in \{h, 1-h\}$	Though the choice of v refers to h it reveals no information, since the statement is atomic.
1.6	$h{:}\in \{0,1\}$; $v{:}=h \sqcap v{:}=1-h$	Here h is revealed, because we know which of the two atomic assignments to v was executed.
1.7	$h{:}\in \{0,1,2,3\}$; $v{:}=h$	We see v; we deduce h since we can see $v{:}=h$ in the program text.
1.8	$h{:}\in \{0,1,2,3\}$; $v{:}=h \bmod 2$	We see v; from that either we deduce h is 0 or 2, or that h is 1 or 3.
1.9	$h{:}\in \{0,1,2,3\}$; $v{:}=h \bmod 2$; $v{:}=0$	We see v is 0; but our deductions about h are as for 1.8, because we saw v's earlier value.

In 1.4 the "$\sqcap$-demon" refers anthropomorphically to unpredictable run-time effects as a demon striving to reduce the utility of the program: the worst alternative is taken whenever choice is offered. If for example these are scheduling choices in a concurrent setting, this adversarial scheduler might be said to be "unable to see" certain variables.

We have assumed throughout that v, h are of type $\{0,1\}$ so that, for example, in 1.5 the choice $h{:}\in \{0,1\}$ reveals nothing.

Fig. 1. Examples of ignorance, informally interpreted

lattice [3] and, as such, satisfies $S1 \sqcap S2 \sqsubseteq S1$ in general; and it is induced by the chosen program logic, so that $S1 \sqsubseteq S2$ just when all expressible properties of $S1$ are preserved in $S2$.

Our expressible properties will be traditional Hoare-style triples (equivalently Dijkstra-style weakest preconditions), *but over formulae whose truth is preserved by increase of ignorance*: those in which all modalities K occur negatively, and all modalities P occur positively. We say that such occurrences of modalities are *ignorant*; and a formula is ignorant just when all its modalities are.

Thus we say that $S1 \sqsubseteq S2$ just when for all *ignorant* formulae Φ, Ψ we have

$$\{\Phi\} \; S1 \; \{\psi\} \quad \text{implies} \quad \{\Phi\} \; S2 \; \{\psi\} \,, \tag{1}$$

although this is informal here because we have not yet given our interpretation of programs (Sec. 3), or formulae (Sec. 4) or their connection (Sec. 5).

We saw that The Refinement Paradox [5] is an issue because traditional refinement allows the "secure" $v{:}\in T$ to be refined to the "insecure" $v{:}=h$ as

The initial values are v_0, h_0. "Valid conclusion" means *true in all final states* and "Invalid conclusion" means *false in some final state*.

	Program	Valid conclusion	Invalid conclusion
2.1	both $v{:}\in \{0,1\}$ and $v{:}=0 \sqcap v{:}=1$	$v \in \{0,1\}$	$v = 0$
2.2	$h{:}\in \{0,1\}$	$\mathrm{P}(h{=}0)$	$\mathrm{K}(h{=}0)$
2.3	$h{:}=0 \sqcap h{:}=1$	$h \in \{0,1\}$	$\mathrm{P}(h{=}0)$
2.4	$h{:}\in \{0,1\}$; $v{:}=0 \sqcap v{:}=1$	$\mathrm{P}(v{=}h)$	$\mathrm{K}(v{\neq}h)$
2.5	$h{:}\in \{0,1\}$; $v{:}\in \{h, 1{-}h\}$	$\mathrm{P}(h{=}0)$ In fact Program 2.5 equals Program 2.4.	$\mathrm{P}(v{=}0)$
2.6	$h{:}\in \{0,1\}$; $v{:}=h \sqcap v{:}=1{-}h$	$v \in \{0,1\}$ But Program 2.6 differs from Program 2.5.	$\mathrm{P}(h{=}0)$
2.7	$h{:}\in \{0,1,2,3\}$; $v{:}=h$	$\mathrm{K}(v{=}h)$	$\mathrm{P}(v{\neq}h)$
2.8	$h{:}\in \{0,1,2,3\}$; $v{:}=h \bmod 2$	$v{=}0$ $\Rightarrow \mathrm{P}(h{\in}\{2,4\})$	$\mathrm{P}(h{=}1)$ $\wedge \mathrm{P}(h{=}2)$
2.9	$h{:}\in \{0,1,2,3\}$; $v{:}=h \bmod 2; \; v{:}=0$	$\mathrm{P}(h{\in}\{1,2\})$	$v{=}0$ $\Rightarrow \mathrm{P}(h{\in}\{2,4\})$

The $v{:}=0$ is an unsuccessful "cover up".

· In 2.3 the invalidity is because $\sqcap$ might resolve to the right: then $h{=}0$ is impossible.
· In 2.6 the invalidity is because ${:}\in$ might choose 1 and the subsequent $\sqcap$ choose $v{:}=h$, in which case v would be 1 and $h{=}0$ impossible.
· In 2.8 the validity is weak: we know h cannot be 4; yet still its membership of $\{2,4\}$ is possible. The invalidity is because the assignment $v{:}=h \bmod 2$ leaves us in no doubt about h's parity; we cannot simultaneously consider both 1 and 2 to be possible.
· In 2.9 the invalidity is v might have been 1 earlier.

Fig. 2. Examples of ignorance logic, informally interpreted

an instance of reduction of demonic nondeterminism. But with (1) we have solved that problem: we can show that the property $\{\mathrm{P}(h{=}C)\}\ v{:}\in T\ \{\mathrm{P}(h{=}C)\}$ is valid, but that property $\{\mathrm{P}(h{=}C)\}\ v{:}=h\ \{\mathrm{P}(h{=}C)\}$ is not valid (Sec. 6).

An operational argument for the refinement's failure is given also.

3   *The Shadow Knows*: An Operational Model

We now give our ignorance-sensitive interpretation of sequential programs; in Sec. 4 we interpret modal formulae; and in Sec. 5 we connect the two via "weakest preconditions" [2], an approach equivalent to Hoare-triples.

Assume a state space with two variables v (visible) and h (hidden). To model knowledge (and hence ignorance) explicitly, we add a third variable H –called the *shadow* of h– and the shadow "knows" all values that h has *potentially* at any point. Thus for example $h{:}\in \{0,1\}$ leads us to either of two states, one with $h{=}0$ and the other with $h{=}1$; but in both of them the shadow H is $\{0,1\}$.

The operational model is thus given by converting "ignorance-sensitive" (that is v, h-) programs to "ordinary" (that is v, h, H-) programs via the scheme of Fig. 3.[3] In the ordinary programs, traditional sequential semantics applies.

For an ignorance-sensitive program S we write $[\![S]\!]$ for its conversion into the shadowed form. In this simplified presentation we exclude declarations, supposing only single variables v, h (ranging over a set D), and then H is simply a set of the potential values for h (thus ranging over the powerset $\mathbb{P}.D$).

On the right the traditional semantics applies: in particular, use of $:\in$ indicates an ordinary nondeterministic choice, from the set given, without any "atomic" implications. Variable e is fresh, just used for the exposition.

Identity	$[\![\mathbf{skip}]\!]$	$\widehat{=}$	$\mathbf{skip}$
Assign to visible	$[\![v := E]\!]$	$\widehat{=}$	$e := E;\ H := \{h : H \mid e = E\};\ v := e$
Choose visible	$[\![v :\in E]\!]$	$\widehat{=}$	$e :\in E;\ H := \{h : H \mid e \in E\};\ v := e$
Assign to hidden	$[\![h := E]\!]$	$\widehat{=}$	$h := E;\ H := \{h : H \cdot E\}$
Choose hidden	$[\![h :\in E]\!]$	$\widehat{=}$	$h :\in E;\ H := (\cup h : H \cdot E)$
Demonic choice	$[\![S1 \sqcap S2]\!]$	$\widehat{=}$	$[\![S1]\!] \sqcap [\![S2]\!]$
Composition	$[\![S1; S2]\!]$	$\widehat{=}$	$[\![S1]\!];\ [\![S2]\!]$

Conditional	$[\![\mathbf{if}\ E\ \mathbf{then}\ S1\ \mathbf{else}\ S2\ \mathbf{fi}]\!]$
$\widehat{=}$	$\mathbf{if}\ E\ \mathbf{then}\ H := \{h : H \mid E\};\ [\![S1]\!]\ \mathbf{else}\ H := \{h : H \mid \neg E\};\ [\![S2]\!]\ \mathbf{fi}$

In Fig. 4 we apply the above to give the shadow semantics for our earlier examples.

Fig. 3. Operational semantics

4 Interpretation of the Logic

As we foreshadowed (Sec. 2.2), our logical language is first-order augmented with a modal operator so that $\mathrm{K}\Phi$ is read "know Φ" [8, 3.7.2]. Here we set out its interpretation.

We give the language function- (including constant-) and relation symbols as needed, among which we distinguish the (program-variable) symbols *visibles* in V and *hiddens* in H; as well there are the usual (logical) variables in L over which we allow $\forall, \exists$ quantification. The visibles, hiddens and variables are collectively the *scalars* $\mathrm{X} \widehat{=} \mathrm{V} \cup \mathrm{H} \cup \mathrm{L}$.

A *structure* comprises a non-empty domain D of values, together with functions and relations over it that interpret the function- and relation symbols mentioned above; within the structure we name the partial functions v, h that interpret visibles, hiddens respectively; we write their types $\mathrm{V} \nrightarrow \mathrm{D}$ and $\mathrm{H} \nrightarrow \mathrm{D}$.

A *valuation* is a partial function from scalars to D, thus typed $\mathrm{X} \nrightarrow \mathrm{D}$; one valuation w_1 can override another w so that for scalar X we have $(w \lhd w_1).\mathrm{X}$ is $w_1.\mathrm{X}$ if w_1 is defined at X and is $w.\mathrm{X}$ otherwise. The valuation $\langle \mathrm{x} \mapsto \mathrm{d} \rangle$ is defined only at X, where it takes value d.

---

[3] Our definitions –in particular the introduction of $H-$ are induced by abstraction, from a lower level given in Sec. A.3.

	(v, h)-program S	(v, h, H)-program $[\![S]\!]$
4.1a	$v:\in\{0,1\}$	$e:\in\{0,1\};\ H:=\{h\colon H\mid e{\in}\{0,1\}\};\ v:=e\ ,$
	and the *rhs* simplifies to $v:\in\{0,1\}$	
4.1b	$v:=0\ \sqcap\ v:=1$	$e:=0;\ H:=\{h\colon H\mid e{=}0\};\ v:=e$
		$\sqcap\ e:=1;\ H:=\{h\colon H\mid e{=}1\};\ v:=e$
	simplifies to $v:\in\{0,1\}$	
4.2	$h:\in\{0,1\}$	$h:\in\{0,1\};\ H:=(\cup h\colon H\cdot\{0,1\})$
	simplifies to $h:\in\{0,1\};\ H:=\{0,1\}$	
4.3	$h:=0\ \sqcap\ h:=1$	$h:=0;\ H:=\{h\colon H\cdot 0\}$
		$\sqcap\ h:=1;\ H:=\{h\colon H\cdot 1\}$
	simplifies to $h:\in\{0,1\};H:=\{h\}$	
4.4	$h:\in\{0,1\};$	$h:\in\{0,1\};\ H:=\{0,1\};$
	$v:=0\ \sqcap\ v:=1$	$v:\in\{0,1\}$
	simplifies to $h:\in\{0,1\};\ H:=\{0,1\};\ v:\in\{0,1\}$	
4.5	$h:\in\{0,1\};$	$h:\in\{0,1\};\ H:=\{0,1\};$
	$v:\in\{h,1{-}h\}$	$v:\in\{h,1{-}h\};\ H:=\{h\colon H\mid v{\in}\{h,1{-}h\}\}$
	which is the same as 4.4	
4.6	$h:\in\{0,1\};$	$h:\in\{0,1\};\ H:=\{0,1\};$
	$v:=h\ \sqcap\ v:=1{-}h$	$v,H:=h,\{h\}\ \sqcap\ v,H:=1{-}h,\{h\}$
	simplifies to $h:\in\{0,1\};\ v:\in\{0,1\};\ H:=\{h\}$	
4.7	$h:\in\{0,1,2,3\};$	$h:\in\{0,1,2,3\};\ H:=\{0,1,2,3\};$
	$v:=h$	$v,H:=h,\{h\}$
	simplifies to $h:\in\{0,1,2,3\};\ v:=h;\ H:=\{h\}$	
4.8	$h:\in\{0,1,2,3\};$	$h:\in\{0,1,2,3\};\ H:=\{0,1,2,3\};$
	$v:=h\bmod 2$	$v:=h\bmod 2;\ H:=\{h\colon H\mid v=h\bmod 2\}$
	simplifies to $(H:=\{0,2\}\sqcap H:=\{1,3\});\ h:\in H;\ v:=h\bmod 2$	
4.9	$h:\in\{0,1,2,3\};$	$h:\in\{0,1,2,3\};\ H:=\{0,1,2,3\};$
	$v:=h\bmod 2;$	$v:=h\bmod 2;\ H:=\{h\colon H\mid v=h\bmod 2\};$
	$v:=0$	$v:=0$
	simplifies to $(H:=\{0,2\}\sqcap H:=\{1,3\});\ h:\in H;\ v:=0$	

Fig. 4. Operational-semantics examples

A *state* (v, h, H) comprises a visible- v, hidden- h and *shadow-* part H; the last, in $\mathbb{P}.(H{\twoheadrightarrow}D)$, is a set of valuations over hiddens only. We require that $h \in H$.[4]

We define truth of Φ at (v, h, H) under valuation w by induction, writing $(v, h, H), w \models \Phi$. Let t be the term-valuation built inductively from the valuation $v \triangleleft h \triangleleft w$. Then we have the following [8, pp. 79,81]:

---

[4] Our state corresponds to Fagin's *Kripke structure and state* together [8]; but our use of Kripke structures is extremely limited (App. A). Not only do we make the Common-Domain Assumption, but we do not allow the structure to vary between worlds except for the interpretation h of hiddens.

To allow for declarations of additional variables, we must make H a set of valuations rather than (as in Sec. 3) simply a set of values. We hope it is clear how the simpler view is a special case of this section's more formal presentation.

- $(v, h, H), w \models R.T_1. \cdots .T_k$ for relation symbol R and terms $T_1 \cdots T_k$ iff the tuple $(t.T_1, \cdots, t.T_k)$ is an element of the interpretation of R.
- $(v, h, H), w \models T_1 = T_2$ iff $t.T_1 = t.T_2$.
- $(v, h, H), w \models \neg \Phi$ iff $(v, h, H), w \not\models \Phi$.
- $(v, h, H), w \models \Phi_1 \wedge \Phi_2$ iff $(v, h, H), w \models \Phi_1$ and $(v, h, H), w \models \Phi_2$.
- $(v, h, H), w \models (\forall L \cdot \Phi)$ iff $(v, h, H), w \triangleleft \langle L \mapsto d \rangle \models \Phi$ for all d in D.
- $(v, h, H), w \models K\Phi$ iff $(v, h_1, H), w \models \Phi$ for all h_1 in H.

We write just $(v, h, H) \models \Phi$ when w is empty, and $\models \Phi$ when $(v, h, H) \models \Phi$ for all v, h, H with $h \in H$, and we take advantage of the usual "syntactic sugar" for other operators (including P as $\neg K \neg$). Thus for example we have $\models \Phi \Rightarrow P\Phi$.

5   Weakest-Precondition Modal Semantics

For practicality, we introduce a weakest-precondition semantics to support direct reasoning at the v, h-level of syntax, *i.e.* without translation to v, h, H-programs. It corresponds to the operational semantics of Fig. 3, given the interpretation in Sec. 4 of the modal formulae.

The predicate-transformer semantics is given in two layers, in Fig. 5 and Fig. 6, because the modal- and classical aspects seem to separate naturally.

Substitute $[e \backslash E]$ Replaces e by E, with alpha-conversion as necessary if distributing through $\forall, \exists$.

Distribution through P however is affected by that modality's implicitly quantifying over hidden variables: if e is a hidden variable, then $[e \backslash E]P\Phi$ is just $P\Phi$; and if E contains hidden variables, the substitution does not distribute into $P\Phi$ at all (which therefore requires simplification by other means).

Shrink shadow $[\Downarrow E]$ Distributes through all classical operators, with renaming; has no effect on classical atomic formulae.

We have $[\Downarrow E]P\Phi \mathrel{\widehat=} P(E \wedge \Phi)$; hidden variables in E are *not* renamed.

Set hidden $[h \leftarrow E]$ Distributes through all operators, including P, with renaming as necessary for $\forall, \exists$ (not P). Replaces h by E.

Set shadow $[h \Leftarrow E]$ Distributes through all classical operators, with renaming; has no effect on classical atomic formulae.

For modal formulae we have $[h \Leftarrow E]P\Phi \mathrel{\widehat=} P(\exists h : E \cdot \Phi)$; note that h's in E (if any) are not captured by the $(\exists h \cdots)$.

Fig. 5. Technical predicate transformers

Visible and hidden variables have separate declarations VIS v and HID h respectively. Declarations within a local scope do not affect visibility: a global hidden variable cannot be seen by the observer; a local visible variable can.

Occurrences of v, h in the rules may be vectors of visible- or vectors of hidden variables, in which case substitutions such as $[h \backslash h']$ apply throughout the vector. We assume *wlog* that modalities are not nested, since we can remove nestings via $\models P\Psi \equiv (\exists c \cdot [h \backslash c]\Psi \wedge P(h=c))$.

Identity	$wp.\textbf{skip}.\Psi$	$\hat{=}$	Ψ
Assign to visible	$wp.(v{:=}E).\Psi$	$\hat{=}$	$[e\backslash E]\,[\Downarrow e{=}E]\,[v\backslash e]\,\Psi$
Choose visible	$wp.(v{:}{\in}E).\Psi$	$\hat{=}$	$(\forall e{:}E \cdot [\Downarrow e{\in}E]\,[v\backslash e]\,\Psi)$
Assign to hidden	$wp.(h{:=}E).\Psi$	$\hat{=}$	$[h{\leftarrow}E]\,\Psi$
Choose hidden	$wp.(h{:}{\in}E).\Psi$	$\hat{=}$	$(\forall e{:}E \cdot [h\backslash e]\,[h{\Leftarrow}E]\,\Psi)$

Demonic choice	$wp.(S1 \sqcap S2).\Psi$	$\hat{=}$	$wp.S1.\Psi \;\wedge\; wp.S2.\Psi$
Composition	$wp.(S1; S2).\Psi$	$\hat{=}$	$wp.S1.(wp.S2.\Psi)$
Conditional	$wp.(\textbf{if } E \textbf{ then } S1 \textbf{ else } S2 \textbf{ fi}).\Psi$		

$$\hat{=} \quad E \Rightarrow [\Downarrow E]\,wp.S1.\Psi \;\wedge\; \neg E \Rightarrow [\Downarrow \neg E]\,wp.S2.\Psi$$

Declare visible	$wp.(\textsc{vis } v).\Psi$	$\hat{=}$	$(\forall e \cdot [v\backslash e]\,\Psi)$	⎫	Note that both these
Declare hidden	$wp.(\textsc{hid } h).\Psi$	$\hat{=}$	$(\forall e \cdot [h{\leftarrow}e]\,\Psi)$	⎭	substitutions propagate within modalities in Ψ.

Logical variable e is fresh.

The *assign to visible* rule has two components conceptually. The first is of course an assignment of E to v, although this is split into two sections $[e\backslash E]\cdots[v\backslash e]$ so that v's initial- and final values are distinguished in between, necessary should v occur in E. The second is the "collapse" of ignorance caused by E's value being revealed: this is inserted as a conjunct, by $[\Downarrow e = E]$, into the body of P-modalities.

Fig. 6. Weakest-precondition modal semantics

The congruence of the transformer- and operational semantics is justified by the following observation:

> If we translate the v, h program fragments into v, h, H fragments via the operational semantics (Fig. 3), and translate correspondingly the modal formulae into ordinary first-order formulae, in both cases we have introduced the shadow H explicitly: in effect our language and logic are both regarded as syntactic sugar for a more basic form. For example (recall Example 2.8),
>
> $$v{:=}h\,\textsf{mod}\,2 \quad \text{becomes} \quad v{:=}h\,\textsf{mod}\,2; \;\; H{:=}\{h{:}H \mid v = h\,\textsf{mod}\,2\}$$
> and $\quad v{=}0 \Rightarrow \textsf{P}(h{\in}\{2,4\}) \quad \text{becomes} \quad v{=}0 \Rightarrow (\exists h{:}H \mid h{\in}\{2,4\}).$
>
> Then the normal wp-semantics [2] is used over the explicit v, h, H program fragments, and the resulting preconditions are translated back from the pure first-order $(\exists h{:}H \cdots)$-form into the modal P-form.

The wp-logic of Figs. 5,6 has the following significant features, which bear directly on the principles we set out in Sec. 1:

1. All visible-only program refinements (hence equalities) are preserved (Pr1).
2. All refinements relying only on Demonic choice, Composition, Identity ("structural") are preserved (Pr2).
3. The transformers defined in Fig. 6 distribute conjunction, as standard transformers do [2]. Thus complicated postconditions can be treated piecewise.
4. Non-modal postconditions can be treated using traditional semantics [1, 2], even if the program contains hidden variables.

5. Because of (3,4) the use of the modal semantics can be restricted to only the modal conjuncts of a postcondition.

Crucially, from (4) we see that we have not *added* refinements. The practical value of (5) is illustrated by the Dining Cryptographers specification (Fig. 10).

6   Avoiding the Refinement Paradox

In this section we see an example of excluding a refinement (Pr3). Fig. 7 uses *wp*-logic to support our claim, in Sec. 2.3 earlier, concerning avoiding the Refinement Paradox on Hoare-triple grounds: if $\not\models wp.S1.\Psi \Rightarrow wp.S2.\Psi$, then $\{wp.S1.\Psi\}$ S1 $\{\Psi\}$ holds (perforce) — but $\{wp.S1.\Psi\}$ S2 $\{\Psi\}$ does not.

$wp.(v{:}{\in}\,T).(\mathrm{P}(h{=}C))$	
$\equiv$	"Choose visible"
$(\forall e{:}T \cdot [\Downarrow e{\in}T]\,[v\backslash e]\,\mathrm{P}(h{=}C))$	
$\equiv$	"v not free"
$(\forall e{:}T \cdot [\Downarrow e{\in}T]\,\mathrm{P}(h{=}C))$	
$\equiv$	"Shrink shadow"
$(\forall e{:}T \cdot \mathrm{P}(e{\in}T \wedge h{=}C)))$	
$\equiv$	"h not free in $e{\in}T$"
$(\forall e{:}T \cdot e{\in}T \wedge \mathrm{P}(h{=}C))$	
$\equiv \mathrm{P}(h{=}C)$.	"e not free in $\mathrm{P}(h{=}C)$"

$wp.(v{:}{=}\,h).(\mathrm{P}(h{=}C))$	
$\equiv$	"Assign to visible"
$[e\backslash h]\,[\Downarrow e{=}h]\,[v\backslash e]\,\mathrm{P}(h{=}C)$	
$\equiv$	"v not free; Shrink shadow"
$[e\backslash h]\,\mathrm{P}(e{=}h \wedge h{=}C)$	
$\equiv [e\backslash h]\,\mathrm{P}(e{=}C \wedge h{=}C)$	"$h{=}C$"
	"h not free in $e{=}C$"
$[e\backslash h]\,(e{=}C \wedge \mathrm{P}(h{=}C))$	
$\equiv h{=}C \wedge \mathrm{P}(h{=}C)$	"e not free"
$\equiv h{=}C$.	"$\models \Phi \Rightarrow \mathrm{P}\Phi$"

We exploit that $\models \mathrm{P}(\Phi \wedge \Psi) \equiv \Phi \wedge \mathrm{P}\Psi$ when Φ contains no hidden variables.

The right-hand side shows that $h{=}C$ is the weakest Φ such that $\{\Phi\}$ $v{:}{=}h$ $\{\mathrm{P}(h{=}C)\}$, yet $(\mathsf{v},\mathsf{h},\mathsf{H}) \models \mathrm{P}(h{=}C) \Rightarrow (h{=}C)$ for all C only when $\mathsf{H} = \{\mathsf{h}\}$. Thus, when the expression T contains no h, the fragment $v{:}{\in}T$ can be replaced by $v{:}{=}h$ only if we know h already.

Fig. 7. Avoiding the Refinement Paradox, seen logically

The corresponding operational view is that we have S1 $\sqsubseteq$ S2 just when for some initial (v_0, h_0, H_0) every possible outcome (v_2, h_2, H_2) of S2 has $v_1{=}v_2 \wedge h_1{=}h_2 \wedge H_1{\subseteq}H_2$ for some outcome (v_1, h_1, H_1) of S1.[5] We illustrate this via Fig. 8, where we have *e.g.* (8.3) $\sqsubseteq$ (8.2), (8.6) $\sqsubseteq$ (8.5) and $((8.7); v{:}{=}0) \sqsubseteq$ (8.9).

Apropos the Paradox we see that $v{:}{\in}T \not\sqsubseteq v{:}{=}h$ because the former's final states are $\{e{:}T \cdot (e, h_0, H_0)\}$ whereas the latter's are just $\{ (h_0, h_0, \{h_0\}) \}$ and, even supposing $h_0{\in}T$, still in general $H_0 \not\subseteq \{h_0\}$.

---

[5] This is the *Smyth* powerdomain-order over an underlying refinement on single triples that allows the H-component *–i.e.* ignorance– to increase [9].

The initial state is $(v_0, h_0, \{h_0\})$.

	Program	Final states in the shadowed model	
8.1	both $v{:}\in \{0,1\}$ and $v:=0 \sqcap v:=1$	$(0, h_0, \{h_0\})$, $(1, h_0, \{h_0\})$	.
8.2	$h{:}\in \{0,1\}$	$(v_0, 0, \{0,1\})$, $(v_0, 1, \{0,1\})$	
8.3	$h:=0 \sqcap h:=1$	$(v_0, 0, \{0\})$, $(v_0, 1, \{1\})$	
8.4	$h{:}\in \{0,1\};$ $v:=0 \sqcap v:=1$	$(0, 0, \{0,1\})$, $(0, 1, \{0,1\})$, $(1, 0, \{0,1\})$, $(1, 1, \{0,1\})$	
8.5	$h{:}\in \{0,1\};$ $v{:}\in \{h, 1-h\}$	$(0, 0, \{0,1\})$, $(1, 0, \{0,1\})$, $(0, 1, \{0,1\})$, $(1, 1, \{0,1\})$	Thus this and 8.4 are equal.
8.6	$h{:}\in \{0,1\};$ $v:=h \sqcap v:=1-h$	$(0, 0, \{0\})$, $(1, 0, \{0\})$, $(0, 1, \{1\})$, $(1, 1, \{1\})$	But this one differs.
8.7	$h{:}\in \{0,1,2,3\};$ $v:=h$	$(0, 0, \{0\})$, $(1, 1, \{1\})$, $(2, 2, \{2\})$, $(3, 3, \{3\})$	
8.8	$h{:}\in \{0,1,2,3\};$ $v:= h \bmod 2$	$(0, 0, \{0,2\})$, $(1, 1, \{1,3\})$, $(0, 2, \{0,2\})$, $(1, 3, \{1,3\})$	
8.9	$h{:}\in \{0,1,2,3\};$ $v:= h \bmod 2;$ $v:=0$	$(0, 0, \{0,2\})$, $(0, 1, \{1,3\})$, $(0, 2, \{0,2\})$, $(0, 3, \{1,3\})$	The final $v{:}{=}0$ does not affect H.

In (8.9) partial information about h remains, represented by two possibilities for H of $\{0,2\}$ and $\{1,3\}$, even though $v{=}0$ in all outcomes.

Fig. 8. Examples (Figs. 1,2) revisited: a relational interpretation

7   The Encryption Lemma

In this section we see an example of retaining a refinement (Pr3); and we prepare for our treatment of the *DC* (Dining Cryptographers') protocol.

When a hidden secret is encrypted with a hidden key and published as a visible message, the intention is that observers ignorant of the key cannot use the message to deduce the secret, even if they know the encryption method. A special case of this occurs in the *DC* protocol, where a secret is encrypted (via exclusive-or) with a key (a hidden Boolean) and becomes a message (is published).

We examine this simple situation in the ignorance logic; the resulting formalisation will provide one of the key steps in the *DC* derivation of Sec. 8.

Lemma 1. Let $s{:}\,S$ be a secret, $k{:}\,K$ a key, and $\oslash$ an encryption method so that $s \oslash k$ is the encryption of s. In a context HID s we have the refinement

$$\mathbf{skip} \quad \sqsubseteq \quad [\![\ \text{VIS } m; \text{HID } k \cdot \quad k{:}\in K; m:= s \oslash k\ ]\!] \ ,$$

which expresses that publishing the encryption as a message m reveals nothing about the secret s, provided the *Key-Complete Condition* (3) of Fig. 9 (*KCC*) is satisfied and the key k is not revealed.[6]

---

[6] The Key-Complete Condition is very strong, requiring as many potential keys as messages; yet it applies to the *DC* protocol, where both are just one bit.

Proof. The calculation is given in Fig. 9. Informally we note that the *KCC* tells us that for every message $s \oslash k$ revealed in m, every guess s' of s we make is supported by some key $k':K$ that could have produced the same m.   □

---

postcondition $s=B \;\wedge\; \mathrm{P}(s=C)$

through $wp.(m:= s \oslash k)$ gives   "Assign visible"
    $[e\backslash s \oslash k]\;[\Downarrow e = s \oslash k]\;[m\backslash e]\;(s=B \;\wedge\; \mathrm{P}(s=C))$
$\equiv$ $s=B \;\wedge\; [e\backslash s \oslash k]\,\mathrm{P}(e = s \oslash k \;\wedge\; s=C)$ "m not free; Shrink shadow"
$\equiv$ $s=B \;\wedge\; [e\backslash s \oslash k]\,\mathrm{P}(e = C \oslash k \;\wedge\; s=C)$ "$s=C$"

through $wp.(k:\in K)$ gives   "Choose hidden"
    $(\forall e: K \cdot [k\backslash e]\;[k\!\Leftarrow\!K]\;(s=B \;\wedge\; [e\backslash s \oslash k]\,\mathrm{P}(e = C \oslash k \;\wedge\; s=C)))$
$\equiv$ $s=B \;\wedge\; (\forall e: K \cdot [k\!\Leftarrow\!K]\;[k\backslash e]\;[e\backslash s \oslash k]\,\mathrm{P}(e = C \oslash k \;\wedge\; s=C))$ "distribute"
$\equiv$ $s=B \;\wedge\; (\forall e: K \cdot [k\!\Leftarrow\!K]\;[e\backslash s \oslash e]\,\mathrm{P}(e = C \oslash k \;\wedge\; s=C))$ "combine subs."
$\equiv$ $s=B \;\wedge\; (\forall e: K \cdot [e\backslash s \oslash e]\;[k\!\Leftarrow\!K]\,\mathrm{P}(e = C \oslash k \;\wedge\; s=C))$ "subs. disjoint"
$\equiv$ $s=B \;\wedge\; (\forall e: K \cdot [e\backslash s \oslash e]\,\mathrm{P}(\exists k': K \cdot e = C \oslash k' \;\wedge\; s=C))$ "Set shadow"
$\equiv$ $s=B \;\wedge\; (\forall e: K \cdot [e\backslash s \oslash e]\,(\exists k': K \cdot e = C \oslash k') \;\wedge\; \mathrm{P}(s=C))$ "distribute"
$\equiv$ $s=B \;\wedge\; \mathrm{P}(s=C) \;\wedge\; (\forall e: K \cdot (\exists k': K \cdot s \oslash e = C \oslash k'))$ "distribute, sub."

We use a subsidiary lemma (App. B) that **skip** $\sqsubseteq$ S if for all A, B, C we have

$$\{v=A \wedge h=B \wedge \mathrm{P}(h=C)\}\quad \mathrm{S}\quad \{v=A \wedge h=B \wedge \mathrm{P}(h=C)\} \, , \tag{2}$$

where v, h are the (vectors of) all variables in context.
In Lem. 1 the context is HID s (and no v), giving the initial calculation boxed above. Because neither m nor k is free in its final line, concluding the calculation by applying the remaining commands VIS m, HID k has no effect. Finally, assuming the precondition, $\forall$-quantifying over B, C, s in their type S, then renaming e, C to k, s', leaves only

$$KCC - \qquad (\forall s, s': S; k: K \cdot (\exists k': K \cdot s \oslash k = s' \oslash k')) \, , \tag{3}$$

which we call the *Key-Complete Condition* for encryption $\oslash$ with key-set K.

Fig. 9. Deriving the Key-Complete Condition for the Encryption Lemma (Sec. 7)

8   Deriving the Dining Cryptographers' Protocol

The Dining Cryptographers Protocol (*DC*) is an example of ignorance preservation [6]. In the original formulation, three cryptographers have finished their meal, and ask the waiter for the bill: he says it has already been paid; they know that the payer is either one of them or is the *NSA*. They devise a protocol to decide which — without however revealing the payer in the former case.

Each two cryptographers flip a Boolean coin, hidden from the third cryptographer; and each publishes (says aloud) the exclusive-or $\oplus$ of the two coins he sees and a Boolean indicating whether he paid. The exclusive-or of the three announcements, each known to all observers, is true iff some cryptographer paid; but it reveals nothing about which one did.

We model this with global Boolean variables p (some cryptographer paid) and p_i (Cryptographer i paid): a typical specification would include $p = p_0 \oplus p_1 \oplus p_2$ as a *post*-condition. If we take the waiter as observer, then from his point of view the postcondition should also include $p \Rightarrow \langle\!\langle p_0\colon \mathbb{B}\rangle\!\rangle \wedge \langle\!\langle p_1\colon \mathbb{B}\rangle\!\rangle \wedge \langle\!\langle p_2\colon \mathbb{B}\rangle\!\rangle$, where in general for hidden (vector) h we introduce this abbreviation:

- *Complete ignorance* $\langle\!\langle h\colon E \mid \varPhi\rangle\!\rangle \; \widehat{=} \; (\forall e\colon E \cdot [h\backslash e]\varPhi \Rightarrow P(h{=}e))^7$

(with omitted $\varPhi$ defaulting to TRUE). It expresses ignorance of h's value beyond its membership in $\{h\colon E \mid \varPhi\}$; thus in this case, even if p holds, still the waiter is to know nothing about whether p_0, p_1 or p_2 hold individually.

As a specification *pre*-condition we would find $\langle\!\langle p_0, p_1, p_2\colon \mathbb{B} \mid \sum_i p_i \leq 1\rangle\!\rangle$ requiring (with an abuse of notation) that the waiter consider any combination possible provided at most one p_i holds. Putting pre- and post- together, the suitability of a specification S could be expressed

$$\{\langle\!\langle p_0, p_1, p_2\colon \mathbb{B} \mid \sum_i p_i \leq 1\rangle\!\rangle\} \;\; \text{S} \;\; \{p = p_0 \oplus p_1 \oplus p_2 \wedge p \Rightarrow \begin{pmatrix} \langle\!\langle p_0\colon \mathbb{B}\rangle\!\rangle \\ \wedge\, \langle\!\langle p_1\colon \mathbb{B}\rangle\!\rangle \\ \wedge\, \langle\!\langle p_2\colon \mathbb{B}\rangle\!\rangle \end{pmatrix}\}, \quad (4)$$

and Fig. 10 shows it indeed is satisfied when S is the assignment $p{:=}\,p_0 \oplus p_1 \oplus p_2$. (Compare Halpern and O'Neill's specification [10]: ours is less expressive because we deal with only one agent at a time.)

---

postcondition $p \Rightarrow \langle\!\langle p_1\colon \mathbb{B}\rangle\!\rangle$

through $wp.(p{:=}\,p_0 \oplus p_1 \oplus p_2)$ gives   "Assign visible"
$\quad [e\backslash p_0 \oplus p_1 \oplus p_2] \, [\Downarrow e = p_0 \oplus p_1 \oplus p_2] \, [p\backslash e] \, (p \Rightarrow \langle\!\langle p_1\colon \mathbb{B}\rangle\!\rangle)$

$\equiv \quad [e\backslash p_0 \oplus p_1 \oplus p_2] \, [\Downarrow e = p_0 \oplus p_1 \oplus p_2] \, (e \Rightarrow \langle\!\langle p_1\colon \mathbb{B}\rangle\!\rangle)$ "substitute"

$\equiv \quad [e\backslash p_0 \oplus p_1 \oplus p_2] \, [\Downarrow e = p_0 \oplus p_1 \oplus p_2] \, (e \Rightarrow (\forall b\colon \mathbb{B} \cdot P(p_1{=}b)))$ "expand $\langle\!\langle \cdot \rangle\!\rangle$"

$\equiv \quad [e\backslash p_0 \oplus p_1 \oplus p_2] \, (e \Rightarrow (\forall b\colon \mathbb{B} \cdot P(e = p_0 \oplus p_1 \oplus p_2 \wedge p_1{=}b)))$ "Shrink shadow"

$\equiv \quad [e\backslash p_0 \oplus p_1 \oplus p_2] \, (e \Rightarrow (\forall b\colon \mathbb{B} \cdot P((p_0 \oplus p_1 \oplus p_2) \wedge p_1{=}b)))$ "e in antecedent"

$\Leftarrow \quad P((p_0{=}p_2) \wedge p_1) \wedge P((p_0 \oplus p_2) \wedge \neg p_1)$ "drop antecedent; expand $\forall$"

$\Leftarrow \quad P(\neg p_0 \wedge \neg p_2 \wedge p_1) \wedge P(\neg p_0 \wedge p_2 \wedge \neg p_1)$ "P is $\Rightarrow$-monotonic"

$\Leftarrow \quad (\forall e_0, e_1, e_2\colon \mathbb{B} \cdot \sum_i e_i \leq 1 \Rightarrow P(p_0, p_1, p_2{=}e_0, e_1, e_2))$ "instantiate $\forall$ twice"

$\equiv \quad \langle\!\langle p_0, p_1, p_2\colon \mathbb{B} \mid \sum_i p_i \leq 1\rangle\!\rangle$.   "contract $\langle\!\langle \cdot \rangle\!\rangle$"

Because wp is conjunctive (Sec. 5 point 3.) we can deal with postcondition conjuncts separately; the standard part follows from ordinary wp (Sec. 5 point 4.); and by symmetry we can concentrate *wlog* on the p_1 case for the remainder.

Fig. 10. Adequacy of the cryptographers' specification (Sec. 8)

Rather than prove (4) for an implementation directly –which could be complex– we can *use program algebra to manipulate a specification for which (4) has already been established.* An implementation reached via ignorance-preserving refinement steps requires no further proof of ignorance-preservation [11].

---

7 Naturally we have *e.g.* $\models \langle\!\langle h\colon E\rangle\!\rangle \Rightarrow P(h{\in}E)$, but in fact the latter is strictly weaker: for example, program $h{:}{\in}\{0, 1\}$ establishes $P(h{\in}\{1, 2\})$ but not $\langle\!\langle h\colon\{1, 2\}\rangle\!\rangle$.

A derivation of the DC protocol, from the specification "validated" in Fig. 10, is given in Fig. 11. To illustrate the possibility of different viewpoints, we observe as Cryptographer 0 –rather than as the waiter– which makes p_0 visible rather than hidden and thus alters our global context to VIS p, p_0; HID p_1, p_2: we can see the final result, and we can "see" whether *we* paid; but we cannot see directly whether Cryptographers 1 or 2 paid.

9   Contributions, Comparisons and Conclusions

Consider this putative refinement in which the variables range over arbitrary integers which, "Boolean-wise" however, are each set initially in $\{0, 1\}$:

$$p := p_0 \oplus p_1 \oplus p_2 \qquad \sqsubseteq^? \qquad \qquad (5)$$

If $c_2, p_1, c_0 = 1, 1, 0$, then visible s_1 will be 2 and hidden $p_1 = 1$ is revealed. *It shouldn't be.*

$$\begin{aligned}
&[\![\text{ VIS } s_0, s_1, s_2, c_1, c_2 \colon \{0, 1\}; \\
&\quad \text{HID } c_0 \colon \{0, 1\} \cdot \\
&\quad s_0 := c_1 + p_0 - c_2; \\
&\quad s_1 := c_2 + p_1 - c_0; \\
&\quad s_2 := c_0 + p_2 - c_1; \\
&\quad p := (s_0 + s_1 + s_2) \bmod 2 \quad]\!] \; .
\end{aligned}$$

The coins c_i cancel just as in Fig. 11, but this time additively. Although Refinement (5) is valid traditionally, the boxed text shows that it does not satisfy *ignorance-preserving* refinement, as we have defined it, in any context where p_1 was declared to be hidden — and so its traditional proof must use some rule excluded by Pr3. Thus, in a sense,

Our contribution has been to <u>disallow</u> this refinement, and others like it.[8]

More generally our contribution is to have altered the rules for refinement of sequential programs, just enough, so that ignorance of hidden variables is preserved. We can still derive correct protocols (Fig. 11), but can no longer mistakenly propose incorrect ones (5).

Compared to the work of Halpern and O'Neill, who apply the Logic of Knowledge to secrecy [7] and anonymity [10], ours is a very restricted special case: we allow just one agent; our (v, h, H) model allows only h to vary in the Kripke model [8]; and our programs are not concurrent. They treat DC, as do Engelhardt, Moses & van der Meyden [12], and van der Meyden & Su [13].

What we add back –having specialised away so much– is reasoning in the *wp*-based assertional/sequential style, thus exploiting the specialisation to preserve traditional reasoning patterns where they can apply.

Comparison with security comes from regarding hidden variables as "high-security" and visible variables as "low-security", and concentrating on program semantics rather than *e.g.* extra syntactic annotations: thus we take the *extensional* view [14] of *non-interference* [15] where security properties are deduced directly from the semantics of a program [16, III-A]. Recent examples of this include elegant work by Leino *et al.* [17] and Sabelfeld *et al.* [18].

---

[8] One role of Formal Methods is to *prevent* people from writing incorrect programs.

The global context VIS p, p_0; HID p_1, p_2 expresses Cryptographer 0's viewpoint; we number the coins so that c_i is opposite p_i, and thus c_0 is the only coin he can't see.

$$p := p_0 \oplus p_1 \oplus p_2 \cdot$$

$=$ **skip**;   "**skip** is identity"
$$p := p_0 \oplus p_1 \oplus p_2$$

$\sqsubseteq$ "Encryption Lemma"
$[\![$ **vis** s_1, c_2; **hid** c_0 ·
$c_0 :\in \mathbb{B}$;
$s_1 := c_2 \oplus p_1 \oplus c_0]\!]$;
$$p := p_0 \oplus p_1 \oplus p_2$$

$=$ "move into block; typed declaration"
$[\![$ VIS s_1, c_2; HID $c_0 : \mathbb{B}$ ·
$s_1 := c_2 \oplus p_1 \oplus c_0$
$\boldsymbol{p := p_0 \oplus p_1 \oplus p_2}]\!]$

$=$ "new inner block equals **skip**"
$[\![$ VIS s_1, c_2; HID $c_0 : \mathbb{B}$ ·
$s_1 := c_2 \oplus p_1 \oplus c_0$
$p := p_0 \oplus p_1 \oplus p_2$
$[\![$ **vis** s_0, s_2, c_1 ·
$s_0 := c_1 \oplus p_0 \oplus c_2$;
$s_2 := p \oplus s_0 \oplus s_1]\!]$ $]\!]$

$=$ "reorder"
$[\![$ VIS s_0, s_1, s_2, c_1, c_2; HID $c_0 : \mathbb{B}$ ·
$s_0 := c_1 \oplus p_0 \oplus c_2$;
$s_1 := c_2 \oplus p_1 \oplus c_0$
$p := p_0 \oplus p_1 \oplus p_2$
$s_2 := p \oplus s_0 \oplus s_1]\!]$

$=$ "Boolean algebra"
$[\![$ VIS s_0, s_1, s_2, c_1, c_2; HID $c_0 : \mathbb{B}$ ·
$s_0 := c_1 \oplus p_0 \oplus c_2$;
$s_1 := c_2 \oplus p_1 \oplus c_0$
$p := p_0 \oplus p_1 \oplus p_2$
$s_2 := c_0 \oplus p_2 \oplus c_1]\!]$

$=$ "reorder"
$[\![$ VIS s_0, s_1, s_2, c_1, c_2; HID $c_0 : \mathbb{B}$ ·
$s_0 := c_1 \oplus p_0 \oplus c_2$;
$s_1 := c_2 \oplus p_1 \oplus c_0$
$s_2 := c_0 \oplus p_2 \oplus c_1$
$p := p_0 \oplus p_1 \oplus p_2]\!]$

The derivation begins at upper-left with the specification, ending with the implementing protocol at right. **Bold text** highlights changes.

The "typed declaration" HID $c_0 : \mathbb{B}$ · abbreviates HID c_0 · $c_0 :\in \mathbb{B}$.

$=$ "Boolean algebra"
$[\![$ VIS s_0, s_1, s_2, c_1, c_2; HID $c_0 : \mathbb{B}$ ·
$s_0 := c_1 \oplus p_0 \oplus c_2$;
$s_1 := c_2 \oplus p_1 \oplus c_0$
$s_2 := c_0 \oplus p_2 \oplus c_1$
$\boldsymbol{p := s_0 \oplus s_1 \oplus s_2}]\!]$.

Local variables c_i (coins) and s_i (Cryptographer i *said*) for $i : 0, 1, 2$ are introduced during the derivation, which depends principally on Key-Completeness and the Boolean algebra of $\oplus$.

In our use of Lem. 1 (Encryption) the message (m) is s_1, the secret (s) is p_1, the encryption $(\oslash)$ is $\cdot (\oplus c_2 \oplus) \cdot$ —which satisfies the Key-Complete Condition (3) for both values of the visible c_2— and the key (k) is c_0.

Other refinements, such as moving statements into blocks where there is no capture, and swapping of statements that do not share variables, are examples of Pr1 and Pr2.

Fig. 11. Deriving the Dining Cryptographers' Protocol

Again we have specialised severely — we do not consider lattices, nor loops (and thus possible divergence), nor concurrency, nor probability. However our "agenda" of Refinement, the Logic of Knowledge, and Program Algebra, has induced four interesting differences from the usual approaches to security:

1. *We do not prove "absolute" security of a program.* Rather we show that it is no less secure than another; this is induced by our refinement agenda. After all, the *DC specification* is not secure in the first place: it reveals whether the cryptographers (collectively) paid or not. To attempt to prove the *DC implementation* (absolutely) secure is therefore pointless.

   However, if we did wish to establish absolute security we would simply prove refinement of an absolutely secure specification (*e.g.* **skip**, or $v{:}\in T$).

2. *We concentrate on* final- *rather than initial hidden values.* This is induced by the Kripke structure of the Logic of Knowledge approach (App. A), which models what other states are possible "now" (rather than "then").

   The usual approach relates instead to hidden *initial* values, so that $h{:=}0$ would be secure and $v{:=}h; h{:}\in T$ insecure; for us just the opposite holds. Nevertheless, we could achieve the same effect by operating on a local hidden copy, thrown away at the end of the block. Thus $[\![$ HID $h'{:}\{h\} \cdot h'{:=}0]\!]$ is secure (for both interpretations), and $[\![$ HID $h'{:}\{h\} \cdot v{:=}h'; h'{:}\in T]\!]$ is insecure.

   A direct comparison with *non-interference* considers the relational semantics R of a program, operating over $v, h{:}T$; the refinement $v{:}\in T \sqsubseteq v{:}\in R.v.h$ then expresses absolute security for the *rhs* with respect to h's initial value. Operational reasoning (App. C) then shows that

$$\textit{Absolute security} — \qquad (\forall v, h, h'{:}T \cdot R.v.h = R.v.h')$$

   is necessary and sufficient, which is non-interference for R exactly [17, 18].

3. *We insist on perfect recall.* This is induced by our algebraic principles (recall the *gedanken* experiment of Sec. 2), and thus we consider $v{:=}h$ to have revealed h's value at that point, no matter what follows.[9] The usual semantic approach allows instead a subsequent $v{:=}0$ to "erase" the information leak.

   Perfect recall is also a side-effect of (thread) concurrency [7],[16, IV-B], but has different causes. We are concerned with ignorance-preservation during program *development*; the concurrency-induces-perfect-recall problem occurs during program *execution*.

   The "label creep" [16, II-E] caused by perfect recall, where the build-up of un-erasable leaks makes the program eventually useless, is mitigated because our knowledge of the *current* hidden values can decrease (via *e.g.* $h{:}\in T$), even though knowledge of *initial*- (or even previous) values cannot.

4. *We do not require "low-view determinism"* [16, IV-B]. This is induced by our explicit policy of retaining abstraction, and of determining exactly when we can "refine it away" and when we cannot. The approach of Roscoe and others instead requires low-level behaviour to be deterministic [19].

---

[9] A similar experiment shows the principles also imply that we can see the program counter.

We conclude that *ignorance refinement* is able to handle examples of simple design, at least — even though their significance may be far from simple. Because *wp*-logic for ignorance retains most structural features of traditional *wp*, we expect that loops and their invariants, divergence, and concurrency via *e.g. action systems* [20] could be feasible extensions.

Adding probability via modal "expectation transformers" [21] is a longer-term goal, but will require a satisfactory treatment of conditional probabilities (the probabilistic version of *Shrink shadow*) in that context.

Acknowledgements. Thanks to Yoram Moses and Kai Engelhardt for the problem, the right approach and the historical background, and to Annabelle McIver, Jeff Sanders, Mike Spivey, Susan Stepney and members of IFIP WG2.1 for suggestions. (Lambert Meertens proposed numbering the cryptographers' coins symmetrically.)

The reviewers were very helpful also.

Michael Clarkson and Chenyi Zhang supplied useful references.

References

1. Hoare, C.: An axiomatic basis for computer programming. Commun. of ACM **12**(10) (1969) 576–80, 583
2. Dijkstra, E.: A Discipline of Programming. Prentice Hall (1976)
3. Back, R.J., von Wright, J.: Refinement Calculus: A Systematic Introduction. Springer-Verlag (1998)
4. Morgan, C.: Programming from Specifications. second edn. Prentice Hall (1994) `http://web.comlab.ox.ac.uk/oucl/publications/books/PfS/`
5. Jacob, J.: Security specifications. In Proc. of 1988 IEEE Symp. on Security and Privacy, S&P '88. IEEE Comput. Soc. Press (1988) 14–23
6. Chaum, D.: The Dining Cryptographers problem: Unconditional sender and recipient untraceability. J. of Cryptol. **1**(1) (1988) 65–75
7. Halpern, J., O'Neill, K.: Secrecy in multiagent systems. In Proc. of 15th IEEE Computer Security Foundations Wksh., CSFW 2002. IEEE Comput. Soc. Press (2002) 32–46
8. Fagin, R., Halpern, J., Moses, Y., Vardi, M.: Reasoning about Knowledge. MIT Press (1995)
9. Smyth, M.: Power domains. J. of Comput. and Syst. Sci. **16** (1978) 23–36
10. Halpern, J., O'Neill, K.: Anonymity and information hiding in multiagent systems. In Proc. of 16th IEEE Computer Security Foundations Wksh., CSFW 2003. IEEE Comput. Soc. Press (2003) 75–88
11. Mantel, H.: Preserving information flow properties under refinement. In Proc. of 2001 IEEE Symp. Security and Privacy, S&P 2001. IEEE Comput. Soc. Press (2001) 78–91
12. Engelhardt, K., Moses, Y., van der Meyden, R.: Unpublished report (2005)
13. van der Meyden, R., Su, K.: Symbolic model checking the knowledge of the Dining Cryptographers. In Proc. of 17th IEEE Computer Security Foundations Wksh., CSFW 2004. IEEE Comput. Soc. Press (2004) 280–291
14. Cohen, E.: Information transmission in sequential programs. ACM SIGOPS Operatings Syst. Review **11**(5) (1977) 133–9

15. Goguen, J., Meseguer, J.: Unwinding and inference control. In Proc. of 1984 IEEE Symp. on Security and Privacy, S&P '84. IEEE Comput. Soc. Press (1984) 75–86

16. Sabelfeld, A., Myers, A.: Language-based information-flow security. IEEE J. of Selected Areas of Commun. **21**(1) (2003)

17. Leino, K., Joshi, R.: A semantic approach to secure information flow. Sci. of Comput. Program. **37**(1–3) (2000) 113–138

18. Sabelfeld, A., Sands, D.: A PER model of secure information flow. Higher-Order and Symb. Comput. **14**(1) (2001) 59–91

19. Roscoe, A.W., Woodcock, J., Wulf, L.: Non-interference through determinism. J. of Comput. Security **4**(1) (1996) 27–54

20. Back, R.J., Kurki-Suonio, R.: Decentralisation of process nets with centralised control. In Proc. of 2nd ACM SIGACT-SIGOPS Symp. on Principles of Distributed Computing, PODC '83. ACM Press (1983) 131–142

21. McIver, A., Morgan, C.: Abstraction, Refinement and Proof for Probabilistic Systems. Technical Monographs in Computer Science. Springer-Verlag (2005)

22. Hintikka, J.: Knowledge and Belief: an Introduction to the Logic of the Two Notions. Cornell University Press (1962) // Available in a new edition, Hendricks and Symonds, Kings College Publ. (2005)

23. Halpern, J.Y., Moses, Y.: Knowledge and common knowledge in a distributed environment. J. of ACM **37**(3) (1990) 549–587

A   The Logic of Knowledge

A.1   Introduction, and Inspiration

The seminal work on formal logic for knowledge is Hintikka's [22], who used Kripke's possible-worlds semantics for the model: he revived the discussion on a subject which had been a topic of interest for philosophers for millennia. It was first related to multi-agent computing by Halpern and Moses [23], and much work by many other researchers followed. Fagin *et al.* summarise the field in their definitive introduction [8].

Engelhardt, Moses, and van der Meyden have earlier treated the *DC* via a refinement-calculus of knowledge and ignorance [12], and their work (and advice from them) is the direct inspiration for what is here. It supports our presentation in the following way.

The standard model for knowledge-based reasoning is based on possible "runs" of a system and participating agents' ignorance of how the runs have interleaved: although each agent knows the (totality of) the possible runs, a sort of "static" knowledge, he does not have direct "dynamic" knowledge of which run has been taken on any particular occasion. Thus he knows a fact in a given global state (of an actual run) iff that fact holds in all possible global states (allowed by other runs) that have the same local state as his.

We severely specialise this view in three ways. The first is that we consider only sequential programs, with explicit demonic choice. As usual, such choice can represent both *abstraction*, that is freedom of an implementor to choose among alternatives (possible refinements), and *ignorance*, that is not knowing which environmental factors might influence run-time decisions.

Secondly, we consider only one agent: informally, we think of this as an observer of the system, whose local state is our system's visible part and who is is trying to learn about (what is for him) the non-local, hidden part.

Finally, we emphasise ignorance rather than (its dual) knowledge, and *loss of ignorance* is sufficient to exclude an otherwise acceptable refinement.

A.2   The Model as a Kripke Structure

We are given a sequential program text, including a notion of atomicity: unless stated otherwise, each *syntactically* atomic element of the program changes the program counter when it is executed. Demonic choice is either a (non-atomic) choice between two program fragments, thus S1 ⊓ S2, or an (atomic) selection of a variable's new value from some set, thus $x :\in X$. For simplicity we suppose we have just two (untyped) variables, the visible v and the hidden h.

The global state of the system comprises both v, h variables' current and all previous values, sequences $\overline{v}, \overline{h}$, together with a history-sequence $\overline{p}$ of the program counter; the observer can see $\overline{v}, \overline{p}$ but not $\overline{h}$. For example, after S1; (S2 ⊓ S3); S4 he can use $\overline{p}$ to "remember" which of S2 or S3 was executed earlier.

The possible runs of a system S are all sequences of global states that could be produced by the successive execution of atomic steps from some initial v_0, h_0, including all outcomes resulting from demonic choice (both ⊓ and :∈).

If the current state is $(\overline{v}, \overline{h}, \overline{p})$, then the set of *possible* states associated with it is the set of triples $(\overline{v}, \overline{h}_1, \overline{p})$ that S can produce from v_0, h_0. We write $(\overline{v}, \overline{h}, \overline{p}) \sim (\overline{v}, \overline{h}_1, \overline{p})$ for this (equivalence) relation, which depends on S, v_0, h_0.

Thus from $\overline{p}$ the observer knows the execution trace; from $\overline{v}$ he knows the successive v values; but of hiddens he knows only h_0 directly. Fig. 1 illustrated this viewpoint with its small examples.

A.3   The Connection with the Shadowed Operational Model

The correspondence between the Kripke model of Sec. A.2 and the shadow model of Sec. 3 is via the abstraction

$$\mathsf{v} = \mathsf{last}.\overline{v} \ \wedge \ \mathsf{h} = \mathsf{last}.\overline{h} \ \wedge \ \mathsf{H} = \{\overline{h}' \mid (\overline{v}, \overline{h}', \overline{p}) \sim (\overline{v}, \overline{h}, \overline{p}) \cdot \mathsf{last}.\overline{h}'\} \ , ^{10}$$

and it determines the operational semantics we gave in Fig. 3.

The abstraction works because programs cannot refer to the full run-sequences directly; what they *can* refer to –the current values of v, h– is just what is captured in the abstraction. The shadow H is used by the modal-logic semantics: it determines the *accessibility* relation with respect to which modalities are interpreted.[11]

---

[10] Read the last as "vary $\overline{h}'$ such that $(\overline{v}, \overline{h}', \overline{p}) \sim (\overline{v}, \overline{h}, \overline{p})$ and take $\mathsf{last}.\overline{h}'$".

[11] In fact the H-component makes h redundant –*i.e.* we can make do with just (v, H)– but this extra "compression" would complicate the presentation subsequently. The redundancy is captured by the healthiness condition

$$wp.S.(\mathsf{K}\varPsi) \quad = \quad \mathsf{K}(wp.S.\varPsi) \ .$$

B   Subsidiary Lemma for Skip (Fig. 9)

Sufficient conditions for **skip** $\sqsubseteq$ S can be obtained operationally. Recall that (operational) refinement includes increase of H, thus being an option available to any refinement of **skip** (which nevertheless must still leave v and h unchanged). Hence the refinement fails only if $[\![S]\!]$ can take some initial v, h, H to some final v', h', H', that is (writing $[\![S]\!]$ as a relation)

$$(v, h, H) \quad [\![S]\!] \quad (v', h', H') , \tag{6}$$

and then we find either v$\neq$v' or h$\neq$h' or H$\not\sqsubseteq$H'. The first two possibilities are excluded directly by the A and B terms in the postcondition of Fig. 9's (2). For the third, we merely pick some C with $C\in$H but $C\not\in$H'; then the initial state satisfies $v=A \wedge h=B \wedge P(h=C)$ for appropriate A, B but the final state does not. Thus the condition (2) excludes this case also.

C   Comparison with Non-interference (Sec. 9)

Consider a program with relational semantics R operating over $v, h: T$, and assume we have $v:\in T \sqsubseteq v:\in R.v.h$. Fig. 3 shows that from initial v, h, H the possible outcomes on the left are t, h, H for all $t: T$, and that on the right they are t', h, $\{h : \mathsf{H} \mid t'\in R.v.h\}$ for all $t': R.v.h$. For refinement from that initial state we must therefore have $t'\in R.v.h \Rightarrow t'\in T$, which is just type-correctness; but also

$$t' \in R.v.h \quad \Rightarrow \quad \mathsf{H} \subseteq \{h : \mathsf{H} \mid t'\in R.v.h\} \tag{7}$$

must hold, both conditions coming from the operational definition of refinement (for which we recall Footnote 5 in Sec. 6). Since (7) constrains all initial states v, h, H, and all t', we close it universally over those variables to give a formula which via predicate calculus and elementary set-theory reduces to the non-interference condition $(\forall v, h, h': T \cdot R.v.h = R.v.h')$ as usually given for demonic programs [17, 18].

Swapping Arguments and Results
of Recursive Functions

Akimasa Morihata[1], Kazuhiko Kakehi[2], Zhenjiang Hu[1], and Masato Takeichi[1]

[1] Graduate School of Information Science and Technology, University of Tokyo
[2] Division of University Corporate Relations, University of Tokyo
7-3-1 Hongo, Bunkyo-ku, 113-8656 Tokyo, Japan
{morihata, kaz}@ipl.t.u-tokyo.ac.jp, {hu, takeichi}@mist.i.u-tokyo.ac.jp

Abstract. Many useful calculation rules, such as fusion and tupling, rely on well-structured functions, especially in terms of inputs and outputs. For instance, fusion requires that well-produced outputs should be connected to well-consumed inputs, so that unnecessary intermediate data structures can be eliminated. These calculation rules generally fail to work unless functions are well-structured. In this paper, we propose a new calculation rule called *IO swapping*. IO swapping exchanges call-time computations (occurring in the arguments) and return-time computations (occurring in the results) of a function, while guaranteeing that the original and resulting function compute the same value. IO swapping enables us to rearrange inputs and outputs so that the existing calculation rules can be applied. We present new systematic derivations of efficient programs for detecting palindromes, and a method of higher-order removal that can be applied to defunctionalize function arguments, as two concrete applications.

1 Introduction

Calculational programming [1] is a methodology for constructing programs, where we first write down a program that may be terribly inefficient but certainly correct, then we improve its efficiency by applying calculation rules, such as fusion [2, 3] and tupling [4, 5, 6, 7]. As an example, consider the problem of checking whether a list is a palindrome or not. A straightforward solution pld0 is given as follows.

```
pld0 x = eqlist(x,reverse x)

eqlist([],[]) = True
eqlist(a:x,b:y) = a==b && eqlist(x,y)

reverse x = rev x []
  where rev [] h = h
        rev (a:x) h = rev x (a:h)
```

The function **reverse** reverses the order of a list, and the function **eqlist** checks whether two lists of the same length are equal. This program is accurate but

T. Uustalu (Ed.): MPC 2006, LNCS 4014, pp. 379–396, 2006.

inefficient on account of multiple traversals over the input list x; both `eqlist` and `reverse` iterate their computation over x. Tupling enables us to eliminate such multiple traversals [4, 5, 6, 7]. For example, Bird [4] derived

```
pldBird x = let (r1,r2) = aux x r2 [] in r1
   where aux [] [] h = (True, h)
         aux (a:x) (b:y) h = let (r1,r2) = aux x y (a:h)
                             in (a==b && r1, r2)
```

Alternatively, Pettorossi and Proietti [6] derived

```
pldPettorossi x = let (r1,r2) = aux x [] in r1 r2
   where aux [] h = (\y->y==[], h)
         aux (a:x) h = let (r1,r2) = aux x (a:h)
                       in (\(b:y)->a==b && r1 y, r2)
```

Both involve a single traversal of x, and tupling plays an important role.

As can be seen in this palindrome detecting problem, calculation rules are useful for developing various kinds of programs if functions are well-structured. For instance, tupling calculation eliminates multiple traversals if two functions have the same structure for the recursion; in facts we succeeded in eliminating multiple traversals in the palindrome detecting problem, because `reverse` and `eqlist` certainly have the same recursion structure. However, These calculation rules generally fail to work unless functions are well-structured.

Let us turn to another improvement to solutions for the palindrome detecting problem. The previous two solutions, namely `pldBird` and `pldPettorossi`, construct intermediate lists in the accumulative arguments (denoted by h). The intermediate lists originate from the function `reverse`, and they are another source of inefficiency. In other words, the intermediate list produced by `reverse` is consumed by `eqlist` as follows.

```
pld1 = eqlist · (id △ reverse)
```

A question that naturally arises is: "Can we derive an efficient palindrome detecting program without an intermediate list?". One obvious idea is to fuse `eqlist` with (id △ reverse), however, applying the fusion rule is not easy, because there are unsuitable connections between `eqlist` and (id △ reverse). Fusion requires that well-produced outputs should be connected to well-consumed inputs so that the intermediate data structure can be eliminated. However, `eqlist` consumes two lists simultaneously while (id △ reverse) produces two lists differently: id produces a list in its *results* while `reverse` produces a list in its accumulative *arguments*.

In this paper, we introduce a novel program transformation called *IO swapping*. IO swapping exchanges call-time computations (occurring in the arguments) and return-time computations (occurring in the results) of a function, while guaranteeing that the original and resulting function compute the same value. IO swapping enables us to rearrange inputs and outputs so that existing calculation rules can be applied. For example, we can derive the following program, `rev_n`, from `reverse` defined above using IO swapping.

```
rev_n x = let ([],r) = rev' x in r
    where rev' [] = (x,[])
          rev' (_:y) = let (a:z,r) = rev' y
                       in (z,a:r)
```

In contrast to `reverse`, function `rev_n` constructs the reversed list at return-time. The production structure of `rev_n` is now the same as `id`, and fusion with `eqlist` successfully derives the program

```
pld1 x = snd (aux x)
    where aux [] = (x, True)
          aux (b:y) = let (a:z,r') = aux y in (z,a==b&&r')
```

This function `pld1` is slightly more efficient than `pldBird` and `pldPettorossi`. Although all three functions `pld1`, `pldBird` and `pldPettorossi` require two traversals, the derived function `pld1` does not require an intermediate list.

The remainder of this paper is organized as follows. We introduce IO swapping in Section 3. We then give two concrete applications of IO swapping in the two sections that follow. The first, in Section 4, is new systematic derivations of efficient programs for detecting palindromes. The second, in Section 5, is a derivation of the transformation of higher-order removal that can be applied to defunctionalize function arguments. Finally, we discuss related work in Section 6 and conclude the paper in Section 7.

2 Preliminaries

2.1 Notations

Throughout the paper, we have mostly used the notation in functional programming language Haskell [8]. Some syntactic notations we have used in this paper are as follows. The backslash \ is used instead of λ for λ-abstraction, and the identity function is written as (\x -> x). The symbol · denotes function composition, i.e., (f·g) x = f(g x). The underscore _ stands for the "don't care" value. We have used the special symbols × and △ to express tupled functions for notational convenience: (f × g) (x,y) = (f x, g y) and (f △ g) x = (f x, g x). Many basic Haskell functions have been used in this paper; their informal definitions are given in Fig. 1. We have assumed that evaluation is based on *lazy evaluation*, data structures are finite, and all patterns are irrefutable except for those of recursion parameters.

2.2 Fusion and Tupling

Functional programming languages provide a compositional way of programming; larger programs are developed through the composition of smaller and simpler functions. Fusion and tupling play an important role in improving the efficiency of compositional programs. Fusion combines the composition of two functions into one and eliminates the intermediate data structure between them.

```
id x = x
fst (a,_) = a
snd (_,b) = b
take m [x₀,x₁,...,xₘ,...,xₙ] = [x₀,x₁,...,xₘ₋₁]
drop m [x₀,x₁,...,xₘ,...,xₙ] = [xₘ,xₘ₊₁,...,xₙ]
length [x₀,x₁,...,xₙ] = n+1
reverse [x₀,x₁,...,xₙ] = [xₙ,xₙ₋₁,...,x₀]
foldr f e [x₀,x₁,...,xₙ] = f x₀ (f x₁ (··· (f xₙ e)···))
foldl f e [x₀,x₁,...,xₙ] = f (···(f (f e x₀) x₁)···) xₙ
div n m = ⌊n/m⌋
```

Fig. 1. Informal definitions of basic functions

Tupling eliminates multiple traversals of the same data if two functions share the same recursion scheme. We will later make use of the following fusion rule [2] and tupling rule [7].

Theorem 1 (Fold Promotion).

```
f · foldr (⊕) e = foldr (⊗) e'
```

provided that $\otimes$ and e' are such that $f (a \oplus y) = a \otimes (f\ y)$ and $f\ e = e'$ hold for any a and y. □

Theorem 2 (Simple Tupling).

```
(f1 △ f2) = foldr (\a (r1,r2)->(k1 a r1, k2 a r2)) (z1,z2)
```

where f1 = foldr k1 z1 and f2 = foldr k2 z2. □

Both Theorems 1 and 2 can be generalized to be polytypic [3, 9, 7].

3   IO Swapping

3.1   IO Swapping for foldl

IO swapping is the new transformation that is used to change the view of recursive functions through the swapping of input (arguments) and output (results). The following theorem shows the IO swapping rule for a typical function, foldl. Before going into the general framework, let us illustrate the basic idea behind IO swapping using this theorem.

Theorem 3 (IO Swapping for foldl). The functions foldl and foldl_n defined below are equivalent.

```
foldl f e [] = e
foldl f e (a:x) = foldl f (f e a) x

foldl_n f e x = let ([],r) = foldl' x in r
  where
    {- foldl' y = (drop (length y) x, foldl f e (take (length y) x)) -}
    foldl' [] = (x,e)
    foldl' (_:y) = let (a:z,r) = foldl' y
                   in (z,f r a)
```

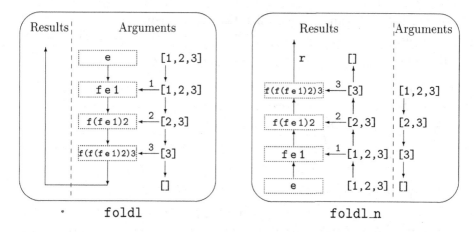

Fig. 2. Models of the computation processes of `foldl` and `foldl_n`

Proof. This is the direct consequence of Theorem 4, which we are going to introduce in Section 3.2. Applying Theorem 4 to `foldl` and removing unnecessary variables yields `foldl_n`.   □

Notice how the result is computed using function parameter `f` of `foldl` and `foldl_n`. While `f` is applied to the accumulation parameter in function `foldl`, it does the computation of the result in `foldl'`. This is because IO swapping is a rule to swap the call-time computation (occurring in the arguments) and the return-time computation (occurring in the results) of the original function.

Fig. 2 illustrates the recursion stacks with the value flows for `foldl` and `foldl_n` (`foldl'`). If we ignore the argument of `foldl'`, we can easily see that `foldl` and `foldl_n` compute exactly the same value, except that the computation is done at different times, call time or return time; moreover, inverting the figure for `foldl` makes it look almost the same figure as that for `foldl_n`. IO swapping swaps call-time and return-time computation without changing the whole process of computation by 'turning the recursion stack upside down', because call-time and return-time computation correspond to top-to-bottom and bottom-to-top computation in the figure, respectively.

Note also that to do swapping we need to estimate the recursion depth from which we should start the computation, because `foldl'` should finish its whole computation exactly at the top of the recursion. We can use the input list to estimate the recursion depth and indeed `foldl'` does this, because there is no difference in the recursion depth between `foldl'` and `foldl`.

3.2   IO Swapping for List Catamorphisms

The idea behind Theorem 3 can be generalized so that it can be applied to higher-order list catamorphisms [3], known to be a generalized form of `foldr` and `foldl`. The following theorem describes the IO swapping rule for higher-order list catamorphisms with circularity [4].

Theorem 4 (IO Swapping for List Catamorphisms). For any suitably-typed g0, g1, g2, and g3, the following two functions, f1 and f2, are equivalent.

```
{- g0::r->h, g1::h->r, g2::a->r->h->h, g3::a->r->h->r -}

f1 :: [a] -> r
f1 x = let r = f1' x (g0 r) in r
  where {- f1' :: [a] -> h -> r -}
        f1' [] h = g1 h
        f1' (a:z) h = let r = f1' z (g2 a r h)
                      in  g3 a r h

f2 :: [a] -> r
f2 x = let ([],h,r') = f2' x (g1 h) in r'
  where {- f2' :: [a] -> r -> ([a],h,r) -}
        f2' [] r = (x, g0 r, r)
        f2' (_:y) r = let (a:z,h,r') = f2' y (g3 a r h)
                      in (z, g2 a r h, r')
```

Proof Sketch

Here we will provide a proof sketch. The full proof can be found in [10].

To prove Theorem 4, we need to assume that all computations terminate with a unique solution. We call the outside (top) of the recursion of the auxiliary function (f1' or f2') the 0-th recursive call and the first call of the auxiliary functions the 1-st recursive call.

Now we can inductively prove that, for all k such that $0 \leq k \leq n$, the first argument, the second argument, and the return value of the k-th recursive call of f1' will be the first element of the return value, the second element of the return value, and the second argument of the $(n-k)$-th recursive call of f2', respectively, without any conflict between recursions. Consequently the values of f1 and f1' determine one solution for f2 and f2', and, from the assumption, it is the only solution for f2 and f2'. Then the result for the whole computation of f1 is the same as the second argument of f2' at the bottom of the recursion. The second argument of f2' at the bottom of the recursion is propagated to the top of the recursion without any updating and eventually becomes the result for the whole recursion of f2. Therefore the results for f1 and f2 are the same.   □

As the same as Theorem 3, Theorem 4 swaps the call-time computation and the return-time computation of the auxiliary function. In the definition for f1, g3 does the return-time computation, but in the definition for f2 it does the call-time computation. In contrast, g2 manages the call-time computation in the function f1, but under f2 it does the return-time computation. The auxiliary function of f2, namely f2', only uses its first argument for estimating the recursion depth, then does the same computation of f1' in the IO-swapped manner. It finally returns the result for whole computation from the bottom of the recursion by the third element of the result of f2'. Fig. 3 outlines the computation process for f1 and f2. We can easily see that inverting the figure

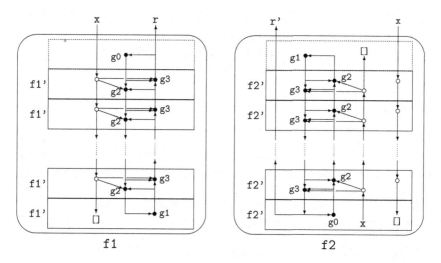

Fig. 3. Models of the computation processes of `f1` and `f2` in Theorem 4

to compute `f1` yields almost the same figure as `f2`, which reflects the fact that swapping the input and output of `f1` yields `f2`. We can generalize Theorem 4 further, so that it can deal with almost every linear recursive function [10].

Note that we have assumed that data structures are finite. We succeed in estimating the recursion depth because of the finiteness of the input list. In other words, `f2` never returns if the input list is infinite, because estimating the recursion depth needs an infinite recursion. Also note that this does not matter for Theorem 3, because `foldl` never returns anyway for an infinite input.

Higher-order list catamorphisms are known as `foldr` functions with higher-order results, and functions `f1` and `f2` are certainly instances of `foldr` with higher-order results as follows.

```
f1 x = let r = foldr k1 g1 x (g0 r) in r
  where  k1 a p = \h -> let r = p (g2 a r h) in g3 a r h
f2 x = let ([],h,r') = foldr k2 z2 x (g1 h) in r'
  where z2 = \r -> (x, g0 r, r)
        k2 _ p = \r -> let (a:z,h,r') = p (g3 a r h)
                       in (z, g2 a r h, r')
```

So Theorem 4 indicates that applying IO swapping to higher-order list catamorphisms results in higher-order list catamorphisms with a projection function. Moreover, applying IO swapping twice produces the original function after constant propagation is removed. It is well known that catamorphisms are suitable for manipulation, and many transformation rules for them have been developed [3, 1, 7]. Theorem 4 therefore allows us to combine IO swapping with other program manipulation techniques.

The list reversing functions provide an example. From Theorem 4, the following function, `reverse2`, is equivalent to `reverse` defined in Section 1.

```
reverse2 x = let ([],h,r') = rev2 x h in r'
  where rev2 [] r = (x, [], r)
        rev2 (_:y) r = let (a:z,h,r') = rev2' y r
                       in (z, a:h, r')
```

Function `reverse2` produces a resulting list in the result of `rev2`, in contrast to `reverse`, which produces a resulting list in the accumulative argument of its auxiliary function `rev`.

It is worth noting that variable `h` at the top of the recursion of `reverse2` describes a circularity [4], i.e., computational dependency from a result to an argument. This circularity is the IO-swapped appearance of computational dependency from an argument to a result; the auxiliary function of `reverse`, namely `rev`, passes its accumulative argument to its result at the bottom of the recursion, and this corresponds to the circularity that passes a result to an argument at the top of the recursion. In general, IO swapping introduces circularities whenever the original function uses its arguments to compute its results. In other words, `f1`, `f1'`, `f2`, and `f2'` are defined using circularities to capture accumulations. In the case of `foldl`, we do not need circularities as can be seen in Theorem 3, because the dependency from arguments to results is unnecessary in `foldl`. In fact, we can remove the circularity in `reverse2` by removing the second argument and the third element of the result of `rev2`, because they just propagate constants. Removing the circularity results in the function `rev_n` that we discussed in the introduction.

4   Detecting Palindromes

To find out how useful IO swapping is in program development, let us demonstrate the derivation of two efficient palindrome detecting programs that have no intermediate lists. The role of IO swapping is to rearrange the structure of functions in order to enable convenient manipulation. We will first derive a simple palindrome detecting program, `pld1`, to show how IO swapping works, and after that we will derive a more involved but efficient one, `pld2`, that only recurses through half the length of the input list.

4.1   Detecting Palindromes Without Intermediate Data

Let us start from the following specification for a palindrome detecting function.

```
pld1 = eqlist · (id △ reverse)
```

The definition for `pld1` has an intermediate list produced by (`id △ reverse`), but Theorem 1 is not sufficient to eliminate it. As explained in the introduction, the production/consumption structure of the intermediate list does not form a suitable connection for the fusion. More concretely, `eqlist` consumes two lists simultaneously while (`id △ reverse`) produces two lists differently: `id` produces a list in its *results* while `reverse` produces a list in its accumulative *arguments*. Let us show how IO swapping can solve this problem.

First of all, we apply IO swapping to `reverse`. Function `reverse` is an instance of `foldl` as follows:

```
reverse x = foldl (\r a->a:r) [] x
```

Theorem 3 yields the following program.

```
rev_n x = let ([],r) = rev' x in r
    where rev' [] = (x,[])
          rev' (_:y) = let (a:z,r') = rev' y
                       in (z,a:r')
```

Note how `rev_n` produces the resulting list at return-time, in the same manner as `id`. Successful fusion of `eqlist` with (`id △ rev_n`) is consequently expected because of suitable connection of the production/consumption structure; (`id △ rev_n`) produces its resulting lists simultaneously, and `eqlist` consumes its input lists simultaneously. Let us confirm it through the following calculation.

We write `id` and `rev_n` in terms of `foldr` as follows, because the `foldr` form is appropriate for the later calculation.

```
id x = foldr (:) [] x
rev_n x = snd (foldr (\_ (a:z,r)->(z,a:r)) (x,[]) x)
```

Tupling (Theorem 2) of `id` and `rev_n` yields the following program.

```
(id △ rev_n) x = snd (foldr (\b (a:z,(r1,r2))->(z,(b:r1,a:r2)))
                            (x,([],[])) x)
```

We now calculate an efficient palindrome detecting function as follows.

```
pld1 x
  = eqlist ((id △ rev_n) x)
  = {- foldr form of (id △ rev_n) -}
    eqlist (snd (foldr (\b (a:z,(r1,r2))->(z,(b:r1,a:r2)))
                      (x,([],[])) x))
  = {- Swapping snd with eqlist -}
    snd ((id×eqlist)(foldr (\b (a:z,(r1,r2))->(z,(b:r1,a:r2)))
                          (x,([],[])) x))
  = {- Fusion (Theorem 1):                                        -}
    {- (id×eqlist)(x,([],[])) = (x,True)                          -}
    {- (id×eqlist)((\b (a:z,(r1,r2))->(z,(b:r1,a:r2))) b r)       -}
    {-    = (z,b==a && eqlist (r1,r2))                            -}
    {-    = (\b (a:z,r')->(z,b==a&&r')) b ((id×eqlist) r)         -}
    snd (foldr (\b (a:z,r')->(z,b==a&&r'))(x,True) x)
```

The resulting function is the one following after `foldr` is unfolded.

```
pld1 x = snd (aux x)
  where aux [] = (x,True)
        aux (b:y) = let (a:z,r') = aux y in (z,a==b&&r')
```

This function, pld1, has no intermediate list. IO swapping creates matching connections between the production/consumption structures, and enables successful fusion.

4.2   Detecting Palindromes Without Intermediate Data and Using Half the Recursion Depth

To check whether a list is a palindrome or not, we do not need to traverse the whole list; half of it is sufficient. This insight yields a more efficient specification as follows.

```
pld2 = eqlist · (takehalf △ revdrophf)
  where takehalf x = take (div (length x) 2) x
        revdrophf x = reverse (drophalf x)
        drophalf x = drop (div (length x) 2) x
```

For simplicity, we have assumed that the length of the input list is even.

First, let us derive efficient definitions for takehalf and drophalf using fusion. We omit the details.

```
takehalf x =  foldr' (\_ r (b:y)->b:r y) (\_->[]) x x
drophalf x =  foldr' (\_ r (_:y)->r y) id x x
```

Function foldr' is defined below, having the similar fusion and tupling rules to foldr [3, 9, 7].

```
foldr' f e [] = e
foldr' f e (a:b:x) = f (a,b) (foldr' f e x)
```

Note that takehalf produces its resulting list in its return-time computation. This indicates that the combination of takehalf and reverse is not suitable to be fused with eqlist. Here, IO swapping has an effect. We adopted the IO-swapped variant rev_n instead of reverse, because its production scheme is the same as that for takehalf.

```
pld2 = eqlist · (takehalf △ revdrophf2)
  where revdrophf2 x = rev_n (drophalf x)
```

We will next calculate an efficient definition for revdrophf2. Here tupling is appropriate, because drophalf does not produce a new list and fusion is not suitable in such a situation. Note that rev_n and drophalf have the same recursion scheme; rev_n and drophalf have the same recursion depth, and rev_n does not use its recursion parameter except for estimating the depth of the recursion. Tupling now yields the following program.

```
revdrophf2 x
  = let ([],r1,dphf)
          = foldr' (\_ r (_:y)->let (a:z,r1,r2) = r y
                                in (z,a:r1,r2))
                   (\y->(dphf,[],y)) x x
    in r1
```

This definition has an uncomfortable dependency denoted by the variable dphf; dphf is computed by the recursion of foldr' and is used at the bottom of the recursion. We can eliminate this uncomfortable dependency because the third element of the result (denoted by r2) remains unchanged throughout the recursion. We can thus obtain the following program.

```
revdrophf2 x
  = let ([],r1) = foldr' (\_ r (_:y)->let (a:z,r1) = r y
                                      in (z,a:r1))
                         (\y->(y,[])) x x
    in r1
```

Finally, we fuse eqlist with (takehalf △ revdrophf2). It is almost the same as that discussed in the previous section. Note that takehalf and revdrophf2 have the same recursion scheme and the same production scheme, and tupling takehalf with revdrophalf2 and fusing it with eqlist is not difficult. We omit the details.

Tupling yields the following definition for (takehalf △ revdrophf2).

```
(takehalf △ revdrophf2)
  =  {- Tupling (Theorem 2) -}
     let ([],r) = foldr' (\_ r (b:y)->let (a:z,(r2,r1)) = r y
                                      in (z,(b:r2,a:r1)))
                         (\y->(y,([],[]))) x x in r
```

Fusion gives the following definition for pld2.

```
pld2 x
  = eqlist ((takehalf △ revdrophf) x)
  = let ([],r) = foldr' (\_ r (b:y)->let (a:z,(r2,r1)) = r y
                                     in (z,(b:r2,a:r1)))
                        (\y->(y,([],[]))) x  x
    in eqlist r

  =  {- Fusion (Theorem 1) -}
     let ([],r) = foldr' (\_ r (b:y)->let (a:z,r') = r y
                                      in (z,b==a&&r'))
                         (\y->(y,True)) x  x
     in r
```

The resulting function is as follows, after foldr' is unfolded.

```
pld2 x = let ([],r) = aux x x in r
   where aux [] y = (y,True)
         aux (_:_:x) (b:y) = let (a:z,r') = aux x y
                             in (z, b==a&&r')
```

This program has no intermediate list and its recursion depth is half the length of the input list.

5 Reinforce the Power of Transformations by IO Swapping

In Section 4, we presented an application of IO swapping as a program transformation. This section demonstrates an application of IO swapping as a *metatransformation*; IO swapping can take a program transformation and return one that is an IO-swapped transformation of the old one. We will present a derivation of a higher-order removal transformation that can be applied to defunctionalize function arguments.

5.1 IO Swapping as a Metatransformation

Consider the higher-order removal problem [11]. It is well known that η-expansion effectively defunctionalizes higher-order results. For example, think about the following function, sumTC, whose auxiliary function sum' returns a function value.

```
sumTC x = let r = sum' x in r 0
  where sum' [] = id
        sum' (a:x) = (sum' x) · (a+)
```

η-expansion yields the usual first-order definition for sumTC as follows.

```
sumTC x = sum' x 0
  where sum' [] h = h
        sum' (a:x) h = sum' x (a+h)
```

Despite such effective defunctionalization of higher-order *results*, η-expansion cannot remove higher-order accumulative *arguments*. That is, it cannot work for the following sumCPS function, whose auxiliary function constructs a higher-order accumulative argument.

```
sumCPS x = sum' x id
  where sum' [] k = k 0
        sum' (a:x) k = sum' x (\v->k(a+v))
```

We have to find another rule to remove higher-order accumulations. It is inefficient to start from scratch. In Section 5.2, we will derive a new method from η-expansion with IO swapping. Here, let us explain the general idea.

The problem is the mismatch between the purpose and the rule; we want to manipulate *arguments*, but η-expansion only defunctionalizes *results*. IO swapping enables us to rearrange the arguments and results to suit manipulation, as seen in Section 4. Applying IO swapping to sumCPS above yields the following function.

```
sumCPS' x = let ([], k) = sum_n' x in k 0
  where sum_n' [] = (x, id)
        sum_n' (_:y) = let (a:z,k) = sum_n' y
                       in  (z,\v->k(a+v))
```

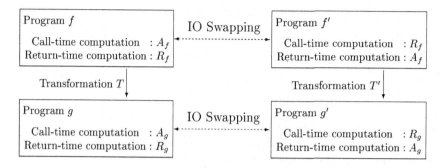

Fig. 4. Framework provided by IO swapping

The auxiliary function sum_n' of sumCPS' constructs a higher-order *result*, and seems suitable for the application of η-expansion. The metatransformation use of IO swapping is derived by generalizing this process, and the idea is summarized in Fig. 4. Assume that there are programs f, g and a program transformation T such that $T[\![f]\!] = g$. IO swapping gives functions equivalent to f and g, namely f' and g'. We can now define a program transformation T' by the relation between f' and g', and T' works as an IO-swapped transformation of T. Note that T' is specified by the sequence of program transformations, that is, applying IO swapping after applying T, after applying IO swapping. Consequently, IO swapping provides the relationship between the manipulation of arguments and that of results for recursive functions.

5.2 Higher-Order Removal for Accumulative Arguments

Let us turn to removing the higher-order accumulation of sumCPS in the previous subsection using IO swapping and η-expansion. First, we apply IO swapping to sumCPS. Because sumCPS is an instance of foldl,

```
sumCPS x = foldl (\k a v->k(a+v)) id x 0
```

we use Theorem 3 and obtain the following program.

```
sumCPS' x = let ([], k) = sum_n' x in k 0
  where sum_n' [] = (x, id)
        sum_n' (_:y) = let (a:z,k) = sum_n' y
                       in (z,\v->k(a+v))
```

In sumCPS', higher-order values only appear in the results, and applying η-expansion is sufficient for higher-order removal. Recall that η-expansion is the rule to pass an extra argument to the higher-order result. We define a function sum_n'' that passes an extra argument to the second element of the result of sum_n' as follows.

```
sum_n'' y v = let (x',k) = sum_n' y in (x',k v)
```

Replacing sum_n' in the definition of sumCPS' with sum_n'' yields the following program.

```
sumCPS' x = let ([], k) = sum_n'' x 0 in k
   where sum_n'' [] v = (x, v)
         sum_n'' (_:y) v = let (a:z,k) = sum_n'' y (a+v)
                           in  (z,k)
```

Higher-order removal is achieved.

We may go further. Since the effect of IO swapping is no longer needed, we eliminate it. Applying Theorem 4 backwards yields the following program.

```
sumCPS x = sum'' x
   where sum'' [] = 0
         sum'' (a:x') = let v = sum'' x'
                        in a+v
```

This is the usual definition of the function summing up all elements of a list. Our strategy, namely applying IO swapping after η-expansion after IO swapping, works successfully.

Let us summarize the transformation above as a formal rule. The point of derivation of an IO-swapped transformation is the step where we apply the original transformation (in this case η-expansion) to the result of IO swapping. Recall that the result for Theorem 4 is the following function.

```
f2 x = let ([],h,r') = f2' x (g1 h) in r'
   where f2' [] r = (x, g0 r, r)
         f2' (_:y) r = let (a:z,h,r') = f2' y (g3 a r h)
                       in (z, g2 a r h, r')
```

If we can define the rule for η-expansion for this function, we can then obtain a higher-order removal rule for accumulative arguments. Although it is not so obvious, we can achieve this by clarifying the intersection for the range of IO swapping and the domain of η-expansion. We then obtain the following lemma.

Lemma 1. For suitably typed functions g0, g1, g2, g3, and g4, the following two functions, f2a and f2b, are equivalent.

```
{- g0::r->v->h, g1::h->r, g2::a->r->v->h->h -}
{- g3::a->r->r, g4::a->r->v->v              -}

f2a :: [a] -> v -> r
f2a x v0 = let ([],h,r') = fa' x (g1 (h v0)) in r'
   where {- fa' :: [a] -> r -> ([a], v->h, r) -}
      fa' [] r = (x, \v->g0 r v, r)
      fa' (_:y) r = let (a:z,h,r') = fa' y (g3 a r)
                    in (z, \v->g2 a r v (h (g4 a r v)), r')

f2a :: [a] -> v -> r
```

```
f2b x v0 = let ([],h,r') = fb' x (g1 h) v0 in r'
  where  {- fb' :: [a] -> r -> v -> ([a], h, r) -}
    fb' [] r v = (x, g0 r v, r)
    fb' (_:y) r v = let (a:z,h,r') = fb' y (g3 a r) (g4 a r v)
                    in (z, g2 a r v h, r')
```

Proof. This is proved by η-expansion, similar to the case of sumCPS' above. Starting from f2a, we define fb' as follows.

```
fb' y r v = let (z,h,r') = fa' y r in (z,h v,r')
```

Then we replace fa' with fb'. We then obtain f2b.   □

We are ready to derive the higher-order removal rule for function arguments. Applying IO swapping to both f2a and f2b, we obtain the following theorem.

Theorem 5 (Higher-order Removal for Function Arguments). For suitably typed functions g0, g1, g2, g3, and g4, the following two functions, f1a and f1b, are equivalent.

```
{- g0::r->v->h, g1::h->r, g2::a->r->v->h->h -}
{- g3::a->r->r, g4::a->r->v->v            -}

f1a :: [a] -> v -> r
f1a x v0 = let r = fa x (\v->g0 r v) in r
  where  {- fa :: [a] -> (v->h) -> r -}
    fa [] h = g1 (h v0)
    fa (a:z) h = let r = fa z (\v->g2 a r v (h (g4 a r v)))
                 in g3 a r

f1b :: [a] -> v -> r
f1b x v0 = let (r,v) = fb x (g0  v) in r
  where    {- fb :: [a] -> h -> (r,v) -}
    fb [] h = (g1 h, v0)
    fb (a:z) h = let (r,v) = fb z (g2 a r v h)
                 in (g3 a r, g4 a r v)
```

Proof. From Lemma 1, currying the arguments of fb' to create a triple, and applying IO swapping backwards to both f2a and f2b, we obtain f1a and f1b respectively.   □

We can use our strategy for other program transformations such as fusion, as discussed in [10].

6   Related Work

We demonstrated the derivation of two palindrome detecting functions, pld1 and pld2, in Section 4. These palindrome detecting functions were given by Danvy and Goldberg [12] as an application of the *There And Back Again* (TABA) pattern. What we demonstrated in Section 4 is, therefore, a derivation of TABA programs based on IO swapping. IO swapping derives TABA programs, on the one hand, because IO swapping turns an iteration over arguments into an iteration over results [13, 14]. IO swapping, on the other hand, is itself an application of TABA pattern; the TABA pattern is necessary for expressing the IO swapping rule. It is worth mentioning that another method based on *defunctionalization* [15] was proposed [16] to derive TABA programs. Although this defunctionalization-based method certainly derives pld1, it is not obvious whether it can cope with pld2.

While it is well known in the functional community that it is difficult to manipulate accumulative programs, we demonstrated in Section 5 a derivation of a manipulation method that could deal with accumulative programs. We found that a combination of the derived method (Theorem 5) and η-expansion works in a similar fashion to the higher-order removal method proposed by Nishimura [17] on the basis of a composition method [18] of attribute grammars [19]. Attribute grammars give a good abstraction of accumulative programs, and many attribute-grammar-based program transformation methods for accumulative functions have been proposed [20, 21, 22, 23]. The reason attribute grammars make manipulations of accumulative functions easy is the symmetric treatments over arguments and results, and this is also what IO swapping aims at.

IO swapping is related to circular programs [4]. There have not been many studies on the application and transformation of circular programs in functional area, since circularities are not intuitive and disturb program manipulation. IO swapping offers the view that circularities, i.e., computational dependencies from results to arguments, are IO-swapped variants of accumulations, which expresses computational dependencies from arguments to results.

IO swapping is related to logic programming or relation-based programs to some extent. From the viewpoint of logic programming, what IO swapping does is to change the order in which a proof tree is constructed. If the original program constructs the proof tree from its root to its leaves, the IO swapped program constructs it from its leaves to its root, but the resulting tree is the same.

Although IO swapping seems related to the inversion of evaluation order [24], our work bears little relationship to it. IO swapping does not change the order of evaluations, but changes the dependency of computation: IO-swapped functions usually compute arguments after results, while ordinary functions compute results after arguments.

7   Conclusion

In this paper, we introduced a novel program transformation, namely IO swapping. IO swapping enables us to rearrange arguments and results to be suitable for manipulation. We demonstrated its effectiveness through two examples, the derivations of efficient palindrome detecting functions, and a higher-order removal transformation to defunctionalize function arguments.

We are currently attempting to extend IO swapping so that it can deal with non-linear recursions. Although many calculational rules have been extended to non-linear recursions using a framework of *constructive algorithmics* [3], we have not yet succeeded in describing the IO swapping rule in terms of constructive algorithmics.

We also consider that IO swapping is related to the synthesis of data structures. IO swapping for list catamorphisms produces a new function, scanning a list from tail to head. In general, IO swapping produces a new function that scans a queue-fashion data structure from an ordinary list-iterating function. It is much more difficult to manipulate queues than lists in a purely functional setting. We hope that IO swapping will enable data structures to be synthesised, e.g., the synthesis of list-like data structure such as queues, doubly linked lists, and circular lists.

Acknowledgements. We are very grateful to Olivier Danvy for introducing us to the TABA work and explaining its relation to defunctionalization and CPS transformation, and to Shin-Cheng Mu and Keisuke Nakano for their inspiring discussions. We are also very grateful to Jeremy Gibbons for editing this paper and giving helpful advice.

References

1. Bird, R., de Moor, O.: Algebra of Programming. Prentice Hall Int. Series in Computer Science. Prentice Hall (1996)
2. Bird, R.: Algebraic identities for program calculation. Computer J. **32**(2) (1989) 122–126
3. Meijer, E., Fokkinga, M., Paterson, R.: Functional programming with bananas, lenses, envelopes and barbed wire. In Hughes, J., ed.: Proc. of 5th ACM Conf. on Functional Programming Languages and Computer Architecture, FPCA '91. Vol. 523 of Lect. Notes in Comput. Sci. Springer-Verlag (1991) 124–144
4. Bird, R.: Using circular programs to eliminate multiple traversals of data. Acta Inform. **21** (1984) 239–250
5. Chin, W.N.: Towards an automated tupling strategy. In Proc. of 1993 ACM SIG-PLAN Symp. on Partial Evaluation and Semantics-Based Program Manipulation, PEPM '93. ACM Press (1993) 119–132
6. Pettorossi, A., Proietti, M.: Rules and strategies for transforming functional and logic programs. ACM Comput. Surveys **28**(2) (1996) 360–414
7. Hu, Z., Iwasaki, H., Takeichi, M., Takano, A.: Tupling calculation eliminates multiple data traversals. In Proc. of 2nd ACM SIGPLAN Int. Conf. on Functional Programming, ICFP '97. ACM Press (1997) 164–175
8. Bird, R.: Introduction to Functional Programming using Haskell. Prentice Hall Int. Series in Computer Science. Prentice Hall (1998)
9. Hu, Z., Iwasaki, H., Takeichi, M.: Deriving structural hylomorphisms from recursive definitions. In Proc. of 1st ACM SIGPLAN Int. Conf. on Functional Programming, ICFP '96. ACM Press (1996) 73–82
10. Morihata, A.: Relationship between arguments and results of recursive functions. Master's thesis. University of Tokyo (2006)

11. Chin, W.N.: Fully lazy higher-order removal. In Proc. of 1992 ACM SIG-PLAN Wksh. on Partial Evaluation and Semantics-Based Program Manipulation, PEPM '92. TR YALEU/DCS/RR-909. Yale University (1992) 38–47

12. Danvy, O., Goldberg, M.: There and back again. In: Proc. of 7th ACM SIGPLAN Int. Conf. on Functional Programming, ICFP'02. ACM Press (2002) 230–234

13. Morihata, A., Kakehi, K., Hu, Z., Takeichi, M.: IO swapping leads you there and back again. In Rutherford, M.J., ed.: Proc. of 7th GPCE Young Researchers Wksh., GPCE-YRW '05. Inst. of Cybernetics, Tallinn (2005) 7–13 Extended abstract of [14].

14. Morihata, A., Kakehi, K., Hu, Z., Takeichi, M.: Reversing iterations: IO swapping leads you there and back again. Techn. Report METR 2005-11, Dept. of Mathematical Informatics, University of Tokyo. (2005)

15. Reynolds, J.C.: Definitional interpreters for higher-order programming languages. Higher-Order and Symb. Comput. **11**(4) (1998) 363–397 // Reprinted from Proc. of 25th ACM Nat. Conf. (1972), with a foreword.

16. Danvy, O., Goldberg, M.: There and back again. Fund. Inform. **66**(4) (2005) 397–413

17. Nishimura, S.: Fusion with stacks and accumulating parameters. In Proc. of 2004 ACM SIGPLAN Wksh. on Partial Evaluation and Semantics-Based Program Manipulation, PEPM '04. ACM Press (2004) 101–112

18. Ganzinger, H., Giegerich, R.: Attribute coupled grammars. In Proc. of 1984 SIG-PLAN Symp. on Compiler Construction. ACM Press (1984) 157–170

19. Knuth, D.E.: Semantics of context-free languages. Math. Syst. Theory **2**(2) (1968) 127–145

20. Kühnemann, A.: Benefits of tree transducers for optimizing functional programs. In Arvind, V., Ramanujam, R., eds.: Proc. of 18th Conf. on Foundations of Software Technology & Theoretical Computer Science, FSTTCS'98. Vol. 1530 of Lect. Notes in Comput. SCi. Springer-Verlag (1998) 146–157

21. Kühnemann, A.: Comparison of deforestation techniques for functional programs and for tree transducers. In Middeldorp, A., Sato, T., eds.: Proc. of 4th Fuji Int. Symp. on Functional and Logic Programming, FLOPS '99. Vol. 1722 of Lect. Notes in Comput. Sci. Springer-Verlag (1999) 114–130

22. Correnson, L., Duris, E., Parigot, D., Roussel, G.: Declarative program transformation: A deforestation case-study. In Nadathur, G., ed.: Proc. of 1st Int. Conf. on Principles and Practice of Declarative Programming, PPDP '99. Vol. 1702 of Lect. Notes in Comput. Sci. Springer-Verlag (1999) 360–377

23. Voigtländer, J.: Using circular programs to deforest in accumulating parameters. Higher-Order and Symb. Comput. **17**(1–2) (2004) 129–163

24. Boiten, E.A.: Improving recursive functions by inverting the order of evaluation. Sci. of Comput. Programming **18**(2) (1992) 139–179

Refinement Algebra with Operators for Enabledness and Termination

Kim Solin* and Joakim von Wright

Turku Centre for Computer Science
Lemminkäinengatan 14 A, FIN-20520 Åbo, Finland
kim.solin@utu.fi, jockum.wright@abo.fi

Abstract. Refinement algebras are abstract algebras for reasoning about programs in a total-correctness framework. We extend a reduct of von Wright's demonic refinement algebra with two operators for modelling enabledness and termination of programs. We show how the operators can be used for expressing relations between programs and apply the algebra to reasoning about action systems.

1 Introduction

Refinement algebras are abstract algebras for reasoning about program refinement [1, 19, 5]. The motivating models are different classes of predicate transformers over a fixed state space, but these should not be seen as exclusive. Applications include reasoning about distributed systems, data refinement, program inversion, and compiler design [21, 22, 23].

In this paper we introduce a reduct of von Wright's demonic refinement algebra [22]. It differs from previous abstract-algebraic approaches to total-correctness reasoning [22, 23, 8, 9] in that it has only one iteration operator: strong iteration. In a program intuition, strong iteration of a statement *either* terminates *or* goes on infinitely. Along the lines of von Wright in [22, 23], we extend the algebra with guards and assertions. Guards should be thought of as programs that check if some predicate holds, skip if that is the case, and otherwise bring about a miracle. Assertions are similar, but instead of performing a miracle when the predicate does not hold, they abort. That is to say, an assertion that is executed in a state where the predicate does not hold establishes no postcondition. In Floyd's terminology, our guards are called assumptions [12].

As the main contribution of this paper, we extend the refinement algebra with two new operators. The first one maps elements in the carrier set to the subset of guards. The intuition is that the operator applied to a program returns a guard that skips in those states in which the program is enabled. This operator is axiomatised in the same way as the domain operator in [10]. The second operator maps a program to an assertion that characterises the set of states in which termination is guaranteed. Different relations between programs, such as

---

* Currently visiting Institut für Informatik, Universität Augsburg.

T. Uustalu (Ed.): MPC 2006, LNCS 4014, pp. 397–415, 2006.

exclusion and a program inversion condition, can be expressed using the new operators. Moreover, with the aid of the enabledness operator, we encode action systems [2, 3, 4] into the refinement algebra and use it for proving refinement relations between them.

Conjunctive predicate transformers over a fixed state space serve as a motivating model for the axiomatisation.

Five papers stand out in the lineage of this paper. Kozen's axiomatisation of Kleene algebra and his introduction of tests into the algebra has been a very significant inspiration for us [15, 16]. The first abstract algebra that was genuinely an algebra for total-correctness was von Wright's demonic refinement algebra [22], which rests upon previous work on algebraic program reasoning by Back and von Wright [6]. Desharnais, Möller and Struth extended Kleene algebra with a domain operator [10] and successfully applied it to reasoning about different structures, such as greedy algorithms [18]. In a slightly different guise, the domain operator appears again in the present paper.

The paper is organised as follows. We begin by presenting a refinement algebra and extend it with guards and assertions. Then we introduce the new operators, investigate their basic algebraic properties and apply them. We end with some concluding remarks and an outlook on future work. Appendix A provides a predicate-transformer model for the algebra.

The purpose of this paper is to introduce the enabledness and the termination operators, settle their basic properties and lay a first ground for more elaborate investigation and application.

Our intended readers are those interested in abstract algebraic reasoning in computer science and those familiar with the research on program refinement. Persons working with action systems might also find the paper worth reading.

2   Refinement Algebra

By a *demonic refinement algebra* (DRA) we shall understand a structure over the signature

$$(\sqcap, ; ,^{\omega}, \top, 1)$$

that satisfies the identities (; is left implicit)

$$x \sqcap (y \sqcap z) = (x \sqcap y) \sqcap z \tag{1}$$
$$x \sqcap y = y \sqcap x \tag{2}$$
$$x \sqcap \top = x \tag{3}$$
$$x \sqcap x = x \tag{4}$$
$$x(yz) = (xy)z \tag{5}$$
$$1x = x \tag{6}$$
$$x1 = x \tag{7}$$
$$\top x = \top \tag{8}$$

$$x(y \sqcap z) = xy \sqcap xz \tag{9}$$

$$(x \sqcap y)z = xz \sqcap yz \tag{10}$$

$$x^{\omega} = xx^{\omega} \sqcap 1 \tag{11}$$

and the equational implication

$$xz \sqcap y \sqcap z = xz \sqcap y \;\Rightarrow\; x^{\omega}y \sqcap z = x^{\omega}y.$$

When $\sqsubseteq$ is defined as

$$x \sqsubseteq y \Leftrightarrow x \sqcap y = x \tag{12}$$

the equational implication can be written as

$$xz \sqcap y \sqsubseteq z \;\Rightarrow\; x^{\omega}y \sqsubseteq z \tag{13}$$

and (3) as $x \sqsubseteq \top$. Note that $\sqsubseteq$ is a partial order with $\top$ as its top element.

The axiomatisation is similar to Kozen's Kleene algebra [15]. The difference is that there is no right annihilation axiom, so $x\top = \top$ does not hold in general, and that * is replaced by $^{\omega}$. The operator $^{\omega}$ is different from the iteration operator in Cohen's ω-algebra [8, 9]. Cohen's infinite iteration operator should be interpreted as an infinite repetition of a program statement, whereas our $^{\omega}$ should be seen as a repetition of a program statement that *either* terminates *or* goes on infinitely. In [14] it is shown that under certain conditions imposed on the omega algebra, Cohen's infinite iteration operator is equal to $(\lambda x \bullet x^{\omega}\top)$. The star operator of Kleene algebra cannot be defined in terms of the other operators of a DRA.

The reason for not having a right annihilation axiom is that we want to reason about non-termination, we want a total-correctness framework. Right annihilation would prevent that (this is elaborated further below, and a semantical clarification is given in Appendix A). In ω-algebra right annihilation holds, which renders it an algebra for partial correctness. The intention to reason about total correctness also motivates the restriction of the signature to one iteration operator. The demonic refinement algebra by von Wright in [22, 23] has two related iteration operators, one equal to our $^{\omega}$ and the other equal to * in Kleene algebra. The intuition for a^* is a terminating repetition of a program statement a (assuming that a is terminating). Since total correctness is what we are actually interested in and the strong iteration operator captures an iteration that will either terminate or go on infinitely we can here exclude * to get a more comprehensible framework.

The elements of the carrier set can be seen as program statements. The operator ; is sequential composition and $\sqcap$ is demonic choice. Executing $x \sqcap y$ performs a choice between x and y over which we have no influence. The iteration a^{ω} is, as mentioned earlier, thought of as a terminating *or* infinitely repeating execution of a program statement a. The order $\sqsubseteq$ is refinement; $x \sqsubseteq y$ means that y establishes anything that x does and possibly more. Finally, $\top$ is interpreted as magic, a non-implementable program statement that establishes *any* postcondition, and 1 is skip. A semantical justification for this intuition is given in terms of predicate transformers in Appendix A.

We define a syntactic constant $\perp$ with the intuition that it stands for an always nonterminating program, an abort statement [22]:

$$\perp = 1^\omega.$$

It is easily seen that $\perp$ is a bottom element

$$\perp \sqsubseteq x \qquad\qquad (14)$$

and that it is a left annihilator

$$\perp x = \perp. \qquad\qquad (15)$$

The axiomatic reason for excluding $x\top = \top$ is now apparent: if $x\top = \top$ would hold, we would have

$$\perp = \perp\top = \top$$

and, then, since $\perp$ is a bottom element we would only have a one-point model.

Many properties of the Kleene-algebra $*$ have analogies for $^\omega$. For example, leapfrog and decomposition,

$$x(yx)^\omega = (xy)^\omega x \qquad\qquad (16)$$

$$(x \sqcap y)^\omega = x^\omega (yx^\omega)^\omega \qquad\qquad (17)$$

and outer inheritance of commutativity

$$yx \sqsubseteq xz \Rightarrow y^\omega x \sqsubseteq xz^\omega \qquad\qquad (18)$$

hold. However, there are differences such as the fact that inner inheritance of commutativity

$$xz \sqsubseteq yx \Rightarrow xz^\omega \sqsubseteq y^\omega x \qquad\qquad (19)$$

does *not* hold in general (take $y = 1$) [22].

3   Guards and Assertions

An element g of the carrier set that has a complement $\bar{g}$ satisfying

$$g\bar{g} = \top \qquad \text{and} \qquad g \sqcap \bar{g} = 1 \qquad\qquad (20)$$

is called a *guard*. It is easily established that the guards form a Boolean algebra over $(\sqcap, ;, {}^-, 1, \top)$, where $\sqcap$ is meet, $;$ is join, $^-$ is complement, 1 is the bottom element, and $\top$ is the top element. Every guard is defined to have a corresponding *assertion*

$$g^\circ = \bar{g}\perp \sqcap 1 \qquad\qquad (21)$$

Thus $^\circ$ is a mapping from guards to a subset of the carrier set, the set of assertions.

Intuitively, guards are statements that check if a predicate holds and, if so, skip, otherwise do magic. Assertions are similar, but abort if the predicate does not hold. The assertions have the properties

$$(g_1 g_2)^\circ = g_1^\circ g_2^\circ = g_1^\circ \sqcap g_2^\circ, \quad g^\circ \bar{g}^\circ = \bot = \bar{g}^\circ g^\circ, \quad \text{and} \quad g^\circ g^\circ = g^\circ \quad (22)$$

These are easily verified; similarly we have

$$g^\circ \sqsubseteq 1 \sqsubseteq g \qquad (23)$$

for any assertion and any guard [22].

The assertions could have been defined implicitly by means of Galois connexions: one part of a Galois connexion is *uniquely* defined by the other and the Galois connexions

$$g^\circ x \sqsubseteq y \;\Leftrightarrow\; x \sqsubseteq gy \quad \text{and} \quad xg \sqsubseteq y \;\Leftrightarrow\; x \sqsubseteq yg^\circ \qquad (24)$$

are satisfied by $g^\circ = \bar{g}\bot \sqcap 1$ [22].

The following propositions summarise some important properties of guards and assertions. First we repeat a proposition reported in [22].

Proposition 1. *Let x be an element in the carrier set of a* DRA *and let g_1 and g_2 be any guards in the same set. Then*

$$\top \sqsubseteq g_1 x \bar{g}_2 \Rightarrow g_1 x g_2 \sqsubseteq g_1 x \quad \text{and} \quad g_1 x g_2 \sqsubseteq g_1 x \Leftrightarrow x g_2 \sqsubseteq g_1 x \qquad (25)$$

hold.

The following two propositions, like the one above, will be useful for the applications in Section 5.

Proposition 2. *Let x be an element in the carrier set of a* DRA *and let g be any guard in the same set. Then*

$$\top \sqsubseteq \bar{g}x \Leftrightarrow gx \sqsubseteq x \qquad (26)$$
$$\bar{g}^\circ x \sqsubseteq \bot \Leftrightarrow x \sqsubseteq g^\circ x \qquad (27)$$

hold.

Proof. Firstly,

$$gx \sqsubseteq x$$
$$\Rightarrow \{\text{isotony}\}$$
$$\bar{g}gx \sqsubseteq \bar{g}x$$
$$\Leftrightarrow \{(20)\}$$
$$\top x \sqsubseteq \bar{g}x$$
$$\Leftrightarrow \{(8)\}$$
$$\top \sqsubseteq \bar{g}x$$

and secondly

$$\top \sqsubseteq \bar{g}x$$
$$\Rightarrow \{\text{isotony}\}$$
$$\top \sqcap gx \sqsubseteq \bar{g}x \sqcap gx$$
$$\Leftrightarrow \{(2, 3, 10)\}$$
$$gx \sqsubseteq (\bar{g} \sqcap g)x$$
$$\Leftrightarrow \{(20)\}$$
$$gx \sqsubseteq 1x$$
$$\Leftrightarrow \{(6)\}$$
$$gx \sqsubseteq x$$

This establishes (26). Then, for one direction of (27) calculate

$$x \sqsubseteq g^\circ x$$
$$\Rightarrow \{\text{isotony}\}$$
$$\bar{g}^\circ x \sqsubseteq \bar{g}^\circ g^\circ x$$
$$\Leftrightarrow \{(22)\}$$
$$\bar{g}^\circ x \sqsubseteq \bot x$$
$$\Leftrightarrow \{(15)\}$$
$$\bar{g}^\circ x \sqsubseteq \bot$$

For the other direction, first note that the left hand side is equivalent to

$$g\bot \sqcap x \sqsubseteq \bot$$

by (21), (10), and (15). Now assume that this holds. Then

$$x$$
$$\sqsubseteq \{(23)\}$$
$$\bar{g}x$$
$$= \{(3)\}$$
$$(\top \sqcap \bar{g})x$$
$$= \{(8)\}$$
$$(\top \bot \sqcap \bar{g})x$$
$$= \{(20)\}$$
$$(\bar{g}g\bot \sqcap \bar{g})x$$
$$= \{(9)\}$$
$$\bar{g}(g\bot \sqcap 1)x$$
$$= \{(10)\}$$
$$\bar{g}(g\bot x \sqcap x)$$
$$= \{(15)\}$$
$$\bar{g}(g\bot \sqcap x)$$
$$\sqsubseteq \{\text{assumption and isotony}\}$$
$$\bar{g}\bot$$

This proves the claim, since $x \sqsubseteq \bar{g}\bot \Leftrightarrow x \sqsubseteq \bar{g}\bot \sqcap x \Leftrightarrow x \sqsubseteq g^\circ x$.   □

Proposition 3. *Let x be an element in the carrier set of a DRA and let g_1 and g_2 be any guards in the same set. Then*

$$g_2 x g_1 \sqsubseteq x g_1 \Leftrightarrow g_2 x \sqsubseteq x g_1 \tag{28}$$

$$x g_1^\circ \sqsubseteq g_2^\circ x g_1^\circ \Leftrightarrow x g_1^\circ \sqsubseteq g_2^\circ x \tag{29}$$

hold.

Proof. Assume $g_2 x g_1 \sqsubseteq x g_1$. Since $1 \sqsubseteq g$ for any guard g, this implies that

$$x g_1 = g_2 x g_1$$

Then

$$g_2 x \sqsubseteq g_2 x g_1 = x g_1$$

Conversely, assume that $g_2 x \sqsubseteq x g_1$. Then

$$g_2 x g_1 \sqsubseteq x g_1 g_1 = x g_1$$

The case for assertions is proved in a similar fashion.   □

4   Enabledness and Termination

In this section we introduce two new operators, the enabledness operator and the termination operator, and investigate their basic properties.

4.1   Enabledness

Let ϵ be a unary operator on a DRA which maps an element of the carrier set to a guard and satisfies the following axioms

$$\epsilon x x = x \tag{30}$$

$$g \sqsubseteq \epsilon(g x) \tag{31}$$

$$\epsilon(x y) = \epsilon(x \epsilon y) \tag{32}$$

We intend ϵ to bind stronger than the other operators, so for example $\epsilon x x$ is $(\epsilon x) x$. The intuition behind ϵ is that it maps any program to a guard that skips in those states in which the program is enabled, that is, in those states from which the program will not terminate miraculously. Axiom (30), for example, says that a program x equals a program that first checks if x is enabled and then executes x.

The enabledness operator, ϵ, is axiomatised as the domain operator of Kleene algebra with domain (KAD) [10]. This means that many properties proved for the domain operator will also hold for ϵ in our algebra, but not necessarily all due to the lack of right annihilation. In [17] Möller shows what can be recovered of KAD when the right annihilation axiom and right distributivity, (9), are dropped, but right isotony of ; is retained. However, the strong iteration operator is different from the iteration operator of KAD and we retain right distributivity, so our framework is not fully symmetric with Möller's.

As shown in [17], the first two axioms of ϵ can be replaced by the equivalence

$$gx \sqsubseteq x \Leftrightarrow g \sqsubseteq \epsilon x \tag{33}$$

and, moreover, the properties

$$\epsilon(x \sqcap y) = \epsilon x \sqcap \epsilon y \tag{34}$$

$$x \sqsubseteq y \Rightarrow \epsilon x \sqsubseteq \epsilon y \tag{35}$$

hold. These are proved by reusing and slightly modifying proofs from [10].

4.2   Termination

Let τ be a unary operator on a DRA which maps an element in the carrier set to an assertion, and satisfies the following axioms

$$x = \tau x x \tag{36}$$

$$\tau(g^\circ x) \sqsubseteq g^\circ \tag{37}$$

$$\tau(x \tau y) = \tau(xy) \tag{38}$$

$$\tau(x \sqcap y) = \tau x \sqcap \tau y \tag{39}$$

By convention, τ has the same precedence as ϵ. As far as we can see, it does not seem possible to derive the fourth axiom from the other three, yet we have no proof of its independence.

The operator τ applied to a program denotes those states from which the program is guaranteed to terminate, that is, states from which it will not abort. Axiom (37) says that a program that checks if the program $g^\circ x$ will terminate is refined by the assertion g°. This holds since the program $g^\circ x$'s termination is determined by the assertion.

Similarly to the enabledness operator, it can be shown that the first two τ-axioms have a characterisation as an equivalence and that τ is isotone.

Proposition 4. *Let x and y be any elements in the carrier set of a DRA and let g be any guard in the same set. Then*

$$x \sqsubseteq g^\circ x \Leftrightarrow \tau x \sqsubseteq g^\circ \tag{40}$$

is equivalent to the axioms (36–37). Moreover, τ is isotone, i.e.,

$$x \sqsubseteq y \Rightarrow \tau x \sqsubseteq \tau y \tag{41}$$

holds.

4.3   Some Basic Properties

In this section we investigate some of the basic properties of ϵ, τ and $^\omega$. The investigation reveals that some propositions that can be shown in KAD regarding the domain operator (δ) and the Kleene star (*), for example the induction rule [10], do not necessarily hold for ϵ and $^\omega$ in a DRA. It also reveals that ϵ and τ are not fully "symmetric".

The following two propositions show that the two operators have some symmetry with respect to the constants.

Proposition 5. *Let* 1, $\top$ *and* $\bot$ *be the constants in a* DRA. *Then*

$$\epsilon g = g \tag{42}$$
$$\tau g^\circ = g^\circ \tag{43}$$
$$\epsilon 1 = 1 \tag{44}$$
$$\tau 1 = 1 \tag{45}$$
$$\epsilon \top = \top \tag{46}$$
$$\tau \bot = \bot \tag{47}$$
$$\epsilon \bot = 1 \tag{48}$$
$$\tau \top = 1 \tag{49}$$

hold.

Proof. The first two statements, (42-43), follow from (7) and (23), and axioms (30–31) and (36–37), respectively. Parts (44-47) are direct consequences of the first two. The seventh part, (48), is proved by (23) and

$$\epsilon \bot$$
$$\sqsubseteq \{(14, 35)\}$$
$$\epsilon 1$$
$$= \{(44)\}$$
$$1$$

The last part, (49), is proved similarly to the seventh.   □

Proposition 6. *Let* x *and* y *be any elements in a* DRA. *Then*

$$\epsilon(\tau x) = 1 = \tau(\epsilon x) \tag{50}$$
$$\epsilon(x \tau y) = \epsilon x \tag{51}$$
$$\tau(x \epsilon y) = \tau x \tag{52}$$

hold.

Proof. For the first part, note that $1 \sqsubseteq \epsilon(\tau x)$ follows from (23), whereas

$$\epsilon(\tau x) \sqsubseteq \epsilon 1 = 1$$

follows from (23) and (44). In turn, $\tau(\epsilon x) \sqsubseteq 1$ follows from (23), whereas

$$1 = \tau 1 1 = \tau 1 \sqsubseteq \tau(\epsilon x)$$

follows from the axioms of τ and (23). The second part follows from

$$\epsilon(x\tau y)$$
$$= \{(32)\}$$
$$\epsilon(x\epsilon(\tau y))$$
$$= \{(50)\}$$
$$\cdot \ \epsilon(x1)$$
$$= \{(7)\}$$
$$\epsilon x$$

The third part is shown similarly as the second.   □

We also have asymmetries, as the following shows.

Proposition 7. *Let x be an element in a* DRA. *Then*

$$(\epsilon x)^\omega \sqsubseteq 1 \tag{53}$$
$$\epsilon(x^\omega) = 1 \tag{54}$$
$$(\tau x)^\omega = \bot \tag{55}$$
$$\tau(x^\omega) \sqsubseteq 1 \tag{56}$$

hold.

Proof. The first part follows from (11). The second part holds since $\epsilon(x^\omega) \sqsubseteq \epsilon 1 = 1$ by (11) and (30), and the converse follows from (23). For the third part, first note that one way follows from $\bot$ being a bottom element. The other direction follows from (23) by $(\tau x)^\omega \sqsubseteq 1^\omega = \bot$. The last part follows from (23). To see that the converse does not hold, take $x = 1$.   □

Similarly to KAD we have unfolding rules.

Proposition 8. *Let x and y be elements in a* DRA. *Then*

$$\epsilon(x^\omega y) = \epsilon(x\epsilon(x^\omega y)) \sqcap \epsilon y \tag{57}$$
$$\tau(x^\omega y) = \tau(x\tau(x^\omega y)) \sqcap \tau y \tag{58}$$

hold.

Proof. The calculation

$$\epsilon(x^\omega y)$$
$$= \{(11)\}$$
$$\epsilon((xx^\omega \sqcap 1)y)$$
$$= \{(10)\}$$
$$\epsilon(xx^\omega y \sqcap y)$$
$$= \{(34)\}$$
$$\epsilon(xx^\omega y) \sqcap \epsilon y$$
$$= \{(32)\}$$
$$\epsilon(x\epsilon(x^\omega y)) \sqcap \epsilon y$$

establishes the first part. The second part is proved in a similar fashion.   □

We do not, however, have an induction rule analogous to the one of KAD.

Proposition 9. *Let x be any element and g be any guard in a* DRA. *Then the implication*

$$g \sqsubseteq \epsilon(xg) \Rightarrow g \sqsubseteq \epsilon(x^\omega g)$$

does not *hold in general. That is, there is an instantiation of x and g, such that*

$$g \sqsubseteq \epsilon(xg)$$

holds, but

$$g \sqsubseteq \epsilon(x^\omega g)$$

does not.

Proof. Take $x = 1$. Then the antecedent becomes $g \sqsubseteq \epsilon g = g$, which clearly holds for any g. The consequent becomes $g \sqsubseteq \epsilon(1^\omega g) = \epsilon(\bot g) = \epsilon\bot = 1$, which clearly does not hold for all g.   □

The reason that this does not hold stems from the fact that we cannot prove (19), that is,

$$xz \sqsubseteq yx \Rightarrow xz^\omega \sqsubseteq y^\omega x$$

in a DRA. This is easily seen when trying to prove the rule along the lines of [10]:

$$g \sqsubseteq \epsilon(xg)$$
$$\Leftrightarrow \{(33)\}$$
$$gxg = xg$$
$$\Leftrightarrow \{(28)\}$$
$$gx \sqsubseteq xg$$
$$\not\Rightarrow \{(19)\}$$
$$gx^\omega \sqsubseteq x^\omega g$$
$$\Leftrightarrow \{(28)\}$$
$$gx^\omega g = x^\omega g$$
$$\Leftrightarrow \{(33)\}$$
$$g \sqsubseteq \epsilon(x^\omega g)$$

But as can be seen from the above (by reading backwards), we do nevertheless have the following result.

Proposition 10. *Let x be any element and g be any guard in a* DRA. *Then*

$$gx^\omega \sqsubseteq x^\omega g \Leftrightarrow g \sqsubseteq \epsilon(x^\omega g) \tag{59}$$

holds.   □

On the other hand, we have an induction rule for τ, which aga in reveals some asymmetry between ϵ and τ.

Proposition 11. *Let x be any element and g be any guard in a* DRA. *Then*

$$\tau(xg^\circ) \sqsubseteq g^\circ \Rightarrow \tau(x^\omega g^\circ) \sqsubseteq g^\circ \tag{60}$$

holds.

Proof. The derivation

$$\tau(xg^\circ) \sqsubseteq g^\circ$$
$$\Leftrightarrow \{(40)\}$$
$$xg^\circ \sqsubseteq g^\circ xg^\circ$$
$$\Leftrightarrow \{(29)\}$$
$$xg^\circ \sqsubseteq g^\circ x$$
$$\Rightarrow \{(18)\}$$
$$x^\omega g^\circ \sqsubseteq g^\circ x^\omega$$
$$\Leftrightarrow \{(29, 40)\}$$
$$\tau(x^\omega g^\circ) \sqsubseteq g^\circ$$

proves the claim. □

5   The Algebra in Action

We show how different relations between programs can be expressed employing the algebra. We also demonstrate the algebra's applicability by using it for proving two properties of action systems.

5.1   Expressing Relations Between Programs

The enabledness and termination operators can be used to express properties between programs; we list here some examples. First note that $\overline{\epsilon x}$ is a guard that skips in those states where x is *disabled*.

Excludes, enables, disables. A program x *excludes* a program y if whenever x is enabled y is not. This can be formalised by saying that x is equal to first executing a guard that checks that y is disabled and then executing x, algebraically: $x = \overline{\epsilon y}x$. A program x *enables* y if y is enabled after having executed x, algebraically: $x = x\epsilon y$. Similarly as above x *disables* y if $x = x\overline{\epsilon y}$.

Using the algebra, we can prove that exclusion is commutative, i.e. x excludes y if and only if y excludes x:

$$x = \overline{\epsilon y}x$$
$$\Leftrightarrow \{(33)\}$$
$$\overline{\epsilon y} \sqsubseteq \epsilon x$$
$$\Leftrightarrow \{\text{guards form a Boolean algebra}\}$$
$$\overline{\epsilon x} \sqsubseteq \epsilon y$$
$$\Leftrightarrow \{(33)\}$$
$$y = \overline{\epsilon x}y$$

We can also express that termination of x requires termination or enabledness of y, $x = \tau yx$ and $x = \epsilon yx$, respectively.

Program inversion. A program x' inverts a program x when execution of the sequence xx' under the same precondition results in the final state being the same as the initial state [13, 7].

If we assume that the precondition is included as part of the program to be inverted, that is

$$x = g^\circ y$$

for some program y and some assertion g° that specifies the precondition, then this means that

$$\tau x = \tau(g^\circ y) \sqsubseteq g^\circ.$$

Program inversion can then be defined as

$$x' \text{ inverts } x \Leftrightarrow \tau x \sqsubseteq xx'.$$

Intuitively, this says that the assertion that skips in those states from which x terminates and aborts in all other states, can be replaced by the program xx': if x terminates and x' inverts x then xx' skips, otherwise xx' aborts.

5.2   Action Systems

Action systems comprise a formalism for reasoning about parallel programs [2, 3, 4]. An *action system*

$$\text{do } x_0 [\!] \ldots [\!] x_n \text{ od}$$

is an iteration of a demonic choice $x_0 \sqcap \cdots \sqcap x_n$ between a fixed number of *actions*, $x_0, \ldots, x_n$, that terminates when none of the actions are any longer enabled. In the refinement algebra, an action system takes the form

$$(x_0 \sqcap \cdots \sqcap x_n)^\omega \overline{\epsilon(x_0)} \ldots \overline{\epsilon(x_n)}.$$

The actions are thus iterated, expressed with the strong iteration operator, until none of them are any longer enabled, expressed with the enabledness operator.
We begin by showing that action systems have a leapfrog property:

$$x; \text{do } y; x \text{ od} \sqsubseteq \text{do } x; y \text{ od}; x$$

We will prove this property in the algebra and at the same time expose a methodology for performing derivations. Action-system leapfrog takes the form

$$x(yx)^\omega \overline{\epsilon(yx)} \sqsubseteq (xy)^\omega \overline{\epsilon(xy)}x \tag{61}$$

in the algebra. We can now embark on proving (61) collecting assumptions, which are then, in turn, proved:

$$
\begin{aligned}
&x(yx)^\omega \overline{\epsilon(yx)} \\
={}& \{(16)\} \\
&(xy)^\omega x \overline{\epsilon(yx)} \\
\sqsubseteq{}& \{\textbf{assume: } x\overline{\epsilon(yx)} \sqsubseteq \overline{\epsilon(xy)}x\} \\
&(xy)^\omega \overline{\epsilon(xy)}x
\end{aligned}
$$

The assumption collected in the second step is shown to hold by the following derivation.

$$\overline{x\epsilon(yx)} \sqsubseteq \overline{\epsilon(xy)x}$$
$\Leftarrow \{(25)\}$
$$\top \sqsubseteq \overline{\epsilon(xy)x\epsilon(yx)}$$
$\Leftrightarrow \{(26)\}$
$$\epsilon(xy)x\epsilon(yx) \sqsubseteq x\epsilon(yx)$$
$\Leftrightarrow \{(33)\}$
$$\epsilon(xy) \sqsubseteq \epsilon(x\epsilon(yx))$$
$\Leftrightarrow \{(32)\}$
$$\epsilon(xy) \sqsubseteq \epsilon(xyx)$$
$\Leftrightarrow \{(32)\}$
$$\epsilon(xy) \sqsubseteq \epsilon(xy\epsilon x)$$
$\Leftarrow \{(23) \text{ and isotony}\}$
True

The same result has been shown in the predicate transformer model [6], but our proof is much cleaner and simpler.

An action system can be decomposed

$$\mathbf{do}\, x \parallel y \,\mathbf{od} = \mathbf{do}\, y \,\mathbf{od};\ \mathbf{do}\, x;\ \mathbf{do}\, y \,\mathbf{od}\,\mathbf{od}$$

provided that x excludes y. In the refinement algebra, action-system decomposition can be encoded as

$$(x \sqcap y)^{\omega}\overline{\epsilon x}\ \overline{\epsilon y} = y^{\omega}\overline{\epsilon y}(xy^{\omega}\overline{\epsilon y})^{\omega}\overline{\epsilon(xy^{\omega}\overline{\epsilon y})} \tag{62}$$

and the assumption as $x = \overline{\epsilon y}x$. This result was also proved already in [6], but again the reasoning in the abstract algebra presented here is more slick and lean. We calculate

$$(x \sqcap y)^{\omega}\overline{\epsilon x}\ \overline{\epsilon y}$$
$= \{(17)\}$
$$y^{\omega}(xy^{\omega})^{\omega}\overline{\epsilon x}\ \overline{\epsilon y}$$
$= \{\text{assumption}\}$
$$y^{\omega}(\overline{\epsilon y}xy^{\omega})^{\omega}\overline{\epsilon x}\ \overline{\epsilon y}$$
$= \{\text{guards form a Boolean algebra}\}$
$$y^{\omega}(\overline{\epsilon y}xy^{\omega})^{\omega}\overline{\epsilon y}\ \overline{\epsilon x}$$
$= \{(16)\}$
$$y^{\omega}\overline{\epsilon y}(xy^{\omega}\overline{\epsilon y})^{\omega}\ \overline{\epsilon x}$$
$= \{\textbf{assume: } \epsilon x = \epsilon(xy^{\omega}\overline{\epsilon y})\}$
$$y^{\omega}\overline{\epsilon y}(xy^{\omega}\overline{\epsilon y})^{\omega}\ \overline{\epsilon(xy^{\omega}\overline{\epsilon y})}$$

One direction ($\sqsubseteq$) of the assumption follows from the fact that

$$\epsilon x = \epsilon(x1) \sqsubseteq \epsilon(x\epsilon y) = \epsilon(xy)$$

for any x and y. The other direction seems, however, harder. One way to prove it would be to show that

$$\epsilon y\bot = y\bot \tag{63}$$

holds. Then the other direction would follow from

$$\epsilon(xy^\omega \overline{\epsilon y}) \sqsubseteq \epsilon x$$
$$\Leftrightarrow \{(7)\}$$
$$\epsilon(xy^\omega \overline{\epsilon y}1) \sqsubseteq \epsilon(x1)$$
$$\Leftrightarrow \{(48)\}$$
$$\epsilon(xy^\omega \overline{\epsilon y}\epsilon\bot) \sqsubseteq \epsilon(x\epsilon\bot)$$
$$\Leftrightarrow \{(32)\}$$
$$\epsilon(xy^\omega \overline{\epsilon y}\bot) \sqsubseteq \epsilon(x\bot)$$
$$\Leftarrow \{(35) \text{ and isotony of } ;\}$$
$$y^\omega \overline{\epsilon y}\bot \sqsubseteq \bot$$
$$\Leftarrow \{(13)\}$$
$$y\bot \sqcap \overline{\epsilon y}\bot \sqsubseteq \bot$$
$$\Leftrightarrow \{\text{provided (63) holds}\}$$
$$\epsilon y\bot \sqcap \overline{\epsilon y}\bot \sqsubseteq \bot$$
$$\Leftrightarrow \{(10)\}$$
$$(\epsilon y \sqcap \overline{\epsilon y})\bot \sqsubseteq \bot$$
$$\Leftrightarrow \{\text{guard property}\}$$
$$1\bot \sqsubseteq \bot$$
$$\Leftrightarrow \{(5,3)\}$$
true

Equation (63) holds in the predicate-transformer model (see Appendix A) so at least in this model it is a valid equation. Nevertheless, it does not seem to follow from the axioms, which indicates that it might have to be taken as an additional axiom for the enabledness operator. Since we have not been able to prove it, but have no proof of its independence either, we leave its status as an open question.

6   Concluding Remarks

We have introduced a demonic refinement algebra restricted to strong iteration and extended it with the enabledness operator and the termination operator. We have shown that the new operators can be used for expressing relations between programs and applied them to reasoning about action systems.

The reduced refinement algebra and its extension deserve further investigation. Since total correctness is what we are interested in, the restriction of the signature to merely the strong iteration operator is motivated. However, some propositions concerning $^\omega$ that were proved in [22] rely on the Kleene-star operator in their proofs. To what extent these types of propositions can be proved in the reduced algebra should be investigated. More generally, the completeness of the axiomatisation with respect to the predicate transformer model and decidability results would be important to settle. Case studies where the new operators are applied to larger problems would also be interesting.

Acknowledgements. Thanks are due to Orieta Celiku, Peter Höfner, Bernhard Möller and Viorel Preoteasa for elucidating discussions and careful scrutiny. The authors are also grateful to several anonymous referees for helpful comments.

References

1. Back, R.-J.: Correctness Preserving Program Refinements: Proof Theory and Applications. Vol. 131 of Mathematical Centre Tracts. Mathematical Centre, Amsterdam (1980)
2. Back, R.-J., Kurki-Suonio, R.: Decentralisation of process nets with centralised control. In Proc. of 2nd Ann. ACM SIGACT-SIGOPS Symp. on Principles of Distributed Computing, PODC '83. ACM Press (1983) 131–142
3. Back, R.-J.: Refining atomicity in parallel algorithms. In Odijk, E., Rem, M., Syre, J.-C., eds.: Proc. of Conf. on Parallel Architectures and Languages Europe, PARLE '89, Vol. 2. Vol. 366 of Lect. Notes in Comput. Sci. Springer-Verlag (1989) 199–216
4. Back, R.-J., Sere, K.: Stepwise refinement of action systems. Structured Programming **12**(1) (1991) 17–30
5. Back, R.-J., von Wright, J.: Refinement Calculus: A Systematic Introduction. Springer-Verlag (1998)
6. Back, R.-J., von Wright, J.: Reasoning algebraically about loops. Acta Inform. **36**(4) (1999) 295–334
7. Chen, W., Udding, J. T.: Program inversion: more than fun! Sci. of Comput. Program. **15**(1) (1990) 1–13
8. Cohen, E.: Hypotheses in Kleene algebra. Unpublished manuscript. Telcordia (1994)
9. Cohen, E.: Separation and reduction. In Backhouse, R. C., Oliveira, J. N., eds.: Proc. of 5th Int. Conf. on Mathematics of Program Construction, MPC 2000. Vol. 1837 of Lect. Notes in Comput. Sci. Springer-Verlag (2000) 45–59
10. J. Desharnais, B. Möller, G. Struth: Kleene Algebra with Domain. ACM Trans. Computational Logic (to appear 2006). Preliminary version: Universität Augsburg, Institut für Informatik, Report No. 2003-07, June 2003
11. Dijkstra, E. W.: A Discipline of Programming. Prentice Hall (1976)
12. Floyd, R. W.: Assigning meanings to programs. In Schwartz, J. T., ed.: Mathematical Aspects of Computer Science. Vol. XIX of Proc. of Symp. on Applied Math. Amer. Math. Soc. (1967) 19–32
13. Gries, D.: The Science of Programming. Springer-Verlag (1981)
14. Höfner, P., Möller, B., Solin, K.: Omega algebra, demonic refinement algebra and commands. Technical Report 2006-11. Inst. für Informatik, Universität Augsburg (2006)
15. Kozen, D.: A completeness theorem for Kleene algebras and the algebra of regular events. Inform. and Comput. **110**(2) (1994) 366–390
16. Kozen, D.: Kleene algebra with tests. ACM Trans. on Program. Lang. and Syst. **19**(3) (1997) 427–443
17. Möller, B.: Lazy Kleene algebra. In Kozen, D., Shanklands, C., eds..: Proc. of 7th Int. Conf. on Mathematics of Program Construction, MPC 2004. Vol. 3125 of Lect. Notes in Comput. Sci. Springer-Verlag (2004) 252–273
18. Möller, B., Struth, G.: Greedy-like algorithms in Kleene algebra. In Berghammer, R., Möller, B., Struth, G., eds.: Revised Selected Papers from 7th Int. Seminar on Relational Methods in Comput. Sci./2nd Int. Wksh. on Appl. of Kleene Algebra, RelMiCS 2003. Vol. 3051 of Lect. Notes in Comput. Sci. Springer-Verlag (2004) 202–215
19. Morgan, C. C.: Programming from Specifications. 2nd edn. Prentice-Hall (1994)
20. Nelson, G.: A generalization of Dijkstra's calculus. ACM Trans. on Program. Lang. and Syst. **11**(4) (1989) 517–561
21. Sampaio, A. C. A.: An Algebraic Approach To Compiler Design. World Scientific (1997)

22. von Wright, J.: From Kleene algebra to refinement algebra. In Boiten, E. A., Möller, B., eds.: Proc. of 6th Int. Conf. on Mathematics of Program Construction, MPC 2002. Vol. 2386 of Lect. Notes in Comput. Sci. Springer-Verlag (2002) 233–262
23. von Wright, J.: Towards a refinement algebra. Sci. of Comput. Program. **51**(1–2) (2004) 23–45

A   Predicate Transformers as a Model

We give a predicate transformer model for the demonic refinement algebra, and look at how the guards and assertions and the enabledness and termination operators are interpreted as predicate transformers.

A.1   Predicate Transformers and Correctness Reasoning

A predicate transformer [11] is a function $S : \wp(\Sigma) \to \wp(\Sigma)$, where Σ is any set. Let $p, q \in \wp(\Sigma)$. If a predicate transformer S satisfies

$$p \subseteq q \Rightarrow S.p \subseteq S.q$$

it is *isotone* (or *monotone*) and if it for a nonempty I satisfies

$$S.(\bigcap_{i \in I} q_i) = \bigcap_{i \in I} S.q_i$$

it is *conjunctive*; it is *universally conjunctive* if S is conjunctive and $S.\Sigma = \Sigma$. Conjunctivity implies isotony.

Programs can be modelled by predicate transformers according to a weakest precondition semantics [11]: $S.q$ denotes those sets of states from which the execution of S is bound to terminate in q. Universally conjunctive predicate transformers cannot properly model non-termination. Too see this, suppose that S is an always non-terminating program, that is,

$$(\forall q \in \wp(\Sigma) \bullet S.q = \emptyset). \tag{64}$$

Now, if S is universally conjunctive, then $S.\Sigma = \Sigma$ so clearly (64) does not hold.

There are three distinguished predicate transformers

$$\mathsf{abort} = (\lambda q \bullet \emptyset)$$
$$\mathsf{magic} = (\lambda q \bullet \Sigma)$$
$$\mathsf{skip} = (\lambda q \bullet q)$$

and a predicate transformer S_1 *is refined by* S_2, written $S_1 \sqsubseteq S_2$, if

$$(\forall q \in \wp(\Sigma) \bullet S_1.q \subseteq S_2.q).$$

This paper deals with three operations on predicate transformers [5, 19] defined by

$$(S; T).q = S.T.q \tag{65}$$
$$(S \sqcap T).q = S.q \cap T.q \tag{66}$$
$$S^{\omega} = \mu.(\lambda X \bullet S; X \sqcap \mathsf{skip}) \tag{67}$$

where μ denotes the least fixpoint with respect to $\sqsubseteq$.

Let Ctran_Σ be the set of conjunctive predicate transformers over a set Σ. Then it is quite easily verified that $(\mathsf{Ctran}_\Sigma, \sqcap, ; , {}^\omega, \mathsf{magic}, \mathsf{skip})$ is a DRA. It is also clear that abort models $\bot$, since it can be shown that $\mathsf{skip}^\omega = \mathsf{abort}$ [5].

We can now give a semantical justification for not having a right annihilation axiom, $x\top = \top$. If we would have right annihilation, then for any predicate transformer S and any $q \in \wp(\Sigma)$

$$S.\Sigma = S.(\mathsf{magic}.q) = \mathsf{magic}.q = \Sigma,$$

so our predicate-transformer model would be universally conjunctive. As noted above, universally conjunctive predicate transformers cannot model non-termination, that is, they do not facilitate our goal: total-correctness reasoning.

A.2   Guards and Assertions

Consider the function $[\cdot] : \wp(\Sigma) \to (\wp(\Sigma) \to \wp(\Sigma))$ such that when $p, q \in \wp(\Sigma)$

$$[p].q = \neg p \cup q$$

where $\neg$ is set complement. These predicate transformers are called *guards*. There is also a dual, an *assertion* and it is defined by

$$\{p\}.q = p \cap q.$$

Complement $\overline{}$ is defined on guards and assertions by $\overline{[p]} = [\neg p]$ and $\overline{\{p\}} = \{\neg p\}$. It follows directly from the definitions that the complement of any guard is also a guard and, moreover, that the guards are closed under the operators $\sqcap, \sqcup$, and ; defined in Section 2.2. If $[p]$ is any guard, it holds that

$$[p].(q_1 \cap q_2) = \neg p \cup (q_1 \cap q_2) = (\neg p \cup q_1) \cap (\neg p \cup q_2) = [p].q_1 \cap [p].q_2$$

for any $q_1, q_2 \in \wp(\Sigma)$. It is also easily established that $(\mathsf{Grd}_\Sigma, \sqcap, ; , \overline{}, \mathsf{skip}, \mathsf{magic})$ is a Boolean algebra, where $\sqcap$ is meet, ; is join, and $\overline{}$ is complement. For example, if $g \in \mathsf{Grd}_\Sigma$, then $g \sqcap \bar{g} = \mathsf{skip}$ as the following shows: Let $[p]$ be any guard and $q \in \wp(\Sigma)$. Then

$$([p] \sqcap \overline{[p]}).q = ([p] \sqcap [\neg p]).q = (\neg p \cup q) \cap (\neg(\neg p) \cup q) = q = \mathsf{skip}.q.$$

The rest of the axioms for Boolean algebra are verified similarly. This means that guards in the predicate-transformer sense constitute a model for the guards in the abstract-algebraic sense. A similar argument shows that assertions in the predicate-transformer sense are a model for assertions in the abstract-algebraic sense.

A.3   Enabledness and Termination

In [5] the *miracle guard* is defined by

$$\neg \left(\bigcap_{q \in \wp(\Sigma)} S.q \right)$$

and the *abortion guard* by

$$\bigcup_{q\in\wp(\Sigma)} S.q.$$

Intuitively, the miracle guard is a predicate that holds in a state $\sigma \in \Sigma$ when the program S is guaranteed to not perform a miracle, that is S does not establish every postcondition starting in σ. The abortion guard holds in a state $\sigma \in \Sigma$ if the program S will always terminate starting in σ, it will establish some postcondition when starting in σ. When S is conjunctive (and thus isotone) the least $S.q$ is $S.\emptyset$ and the greatest $S.\Sigma$, so the miracle guard can be written $\neg(S.\emptyset)$ and the abortion guard $S.\Sigma$; this is the way that Nelson defines *grd* and *hlt*, respectively, in [20].

We want the miracle guard and the termination guard to model the enabledness operator and the termination operator, respectively. To do this, we lift them to the predicate-transformer level and, if x is interpreted as the predicate transformer S, set ϵx to be $[\neg S.\emptyset]$ and τx to be $\{S.\Sigma\}$. It can easily be established that this interpretation is sound for the axioms of ϵ, (30–32) and of τ, (36–39). For example, the axioms (30) and (37) are verified by

$$[\neg S.\emptyset]; S \sqsubseteq S$$
$$\Leftrightarrow \{\text{definitions}\}$$
$$(\forall q \in \wp(\Sigma) \bullet [\neg S.\emptyset].(S.q) \subseteq S.q)$$
$$\Leftrightarrow \{\text{definitions}\}$$
$$(\forall q \in \wp(\Sigma) \bullet S.\emptyset \cup S.q \subseteq S.q)$$
$$\Leftrightarrow \{\text{isotony of } S\}$$
$$(\forall q \in \wp(\Sigma) \bullet \text{True})$$
$$\Leftrightarrow \{\text{logic}\}$$
$$\text{True}$$

and

$$(\forall p \in \wp(\Sigma) \bullet \{(\{p\}; S).\Sigma\} \sqsubseteq \{p\})$$
$$\Leftrightarrow \{\text{definitions}\}$$
$$(\forall p, q \in \wp(\Sigma) \bullet \{\{p\}.(S.\Sigma)\}.q \subseteq \{p\}.q)$$
$$\Leftrightarrow \{\text{definitions}\}$$
$$(\forall p, q \in \wp(\Sigma) \bullet p \cap S.\Sigma \cap q \subseteq p \cap q)$$
$$\Leftrightarrow \{\text{set theory}\}$$
$$(\forall p, q \in \wp(\Sigma) \bullet \text{True})$$
$$\Leftrightarrow \{\text{logic}\}$$
$$\text{True}$$

respectively. The validity of the other axioms can be verified similarly. The calculation

$$[\neg S.\emptyset]; \text{abort}.q = S.\emptyset \cup \emptyset = S.\emptyset = S; \text{abort}.q$$

where $q \in \wp(\Sigma)$, settles that equation (63) holds in this model.

Constructing Rewrite-Based Decision Procedures for Embeddings and Termination

Georg Struth

Department of Computer Science, University of Sheffield,
Regent Court, 211 Portobello Street, Sheffield S1 4DP, UK
g.struth@dcs.shef.ac.uk

Abstract. We prove tractability of ground relational Knuth-Bendix completion procedures. We apply this result to formally develop three dynamic rule-based declarative and tractable decision procedures for termination analysis: for detection of simple and homeomorphic embeddings of ground terms and for termination of ground term rewrite systems. Our algorithms are of general interest for the automated analysis of dynamic reachability, termination and ordering constraints. Our approach is particularly suited for declarative rule-based programming environments.

1 Introduction

Reachability and termination analysis are fundamental for understanding systems and structures based on relations. Applications arise, for instance, in model checking, program correctness, constraint satisfaction problems, word and reachability problems in (ordered) algebras and process algebras. In automated deduction and term rewriting, for instance, the following constraint satisfaction problem is interesting: Is there an instantiation of variables satisfying a set of inequality constraints for some lexicographic or recursive path ordering? For all these purposes it is desirable to integrate specific decision procedures into theorem provers and program analysis tools.

In a companion paper [1], we have proposed a cooperating Knuth-Bendix completion procedure for non-symmetric transitive relations (such as quasiorderings) and equivalences. We have also applied this procedure for formally constructing dynamic graph algorithms for cycle detection and strongly connecting components.

In the present paper, we construct decision procedures related to reachability and termination that are particularly suitable for rule-based declarative programming environments and constraint solving languages. Again, the development uses relational Knuth-Bendix completion [2, 1] as a uniform meta-procedure that supports the integration of declarative and procedural knowledge. For particular algorithms, we augment this procedure with focused rules derived from mathematical specifications. This has several benefits. First, the decision procedures are highly non-deterministic. They can easily be refined to efficient algorithms via execution strategies. Second, correctness proofs and complexity analysis are simple and modular relative to the meta-procedure. Third, most

T. Uustalu (Ed.): MPC 2006, LNCS 4014, pp. 416–432, 2006.

data-structures and implementation details can be hidden in the meta-procedure. Fourth, our algorithms are intrinsically dynamic. Knuth-Bendix completion provides an abstract declarative data structure that maintains reachability information about some set of ground rewrite rules in terms of a graph (cf. [1]). Updates, that is insertion and deletion of inequalities, can be performed locally without any need of recompiling the whole set. Dynamic algorithms are considered as difficult; they are very rare outside the imperative programming paradigm.

Our contributions. First, we show tractability of termination of a ground relational Knuth-Bendix completion procedure from [3, 2] (Theorem 3). This immediately implies tractability of the reachability problem for (possibly non-terminating) ground term rewrite systems [4] and of the uniform word problem for term algebras [5] (Corollary 1). In contrast to the equational case [6], this result is not straightforward; we show non-termination of two naive procedures (Theorem 1, Proposition 1). A side effect of this analysis is a relational completion algorithm with implicit memoisation. Here, because of our applications, we consider only Knuth-Bendix completion for quasiorderings. But it is easy to adapt it to completion for non-symmetric transitive relations and the cooperating procedure for relations and equivalences from [1].

Second, we use this tractability result for formally constructing two novel dynamic rule-based tractable algorithms for detecting embeddings and homeomorphic embeddings induced by ground term rewrite systems from mathematical specifications (Theorem 4, Theorem 5). The main idea is to reduce these problems to cycle detection, which can be handled within the same framework by the completion-based algorithms developed in [1]. Applications of the algorithms are discussed in Section 8.

Third, the tractability result also yields a completion-based reconstruction of a previous tractable decision procedure for termination of ground term rewrite systems (Theorem 7).

Related work. The use of *equational* completion for developing decision procedures has been advocated already by Nelson [7]; its relevance to declarative (congruence closure) algorithms has first been demonstrated by Kapur [8]. Relational completion as a general purpose procedure for reachability analysis in term algebras has been proposed in [3]. In [3, 9] the procedure is used for constructing solutions to word and reachability problems in lattice theory. There, ordered resolution has been proposed as a meta-procedure for constructing focused calculi and completion-based decision procedures. In [1] the approach of the present paper has been first introduced for constructing dynamic cycle detection and strongly connected component algorithms. The development method from [3] differs is several aspects from the present one. There, an irredundant irreducible basis of a given theory specification is constructed. Then inference rules and information about decidability are derived using the interaction of the basis with arbitrary non-theory clauses. This approach, however, does not yield enough information for the decision problems we consider here. We do not ask whether some set of (negated) ground equations is satisfiable modulo some equational theory, but whether the transitive relation or quasiordering presented by some set of ground inequalities has a certain inductively defined property. We therefore do not perform a basis construction, but extend completion with specific rules instead. Our third result provides a completion-based, hence more uniform, alternative to Plaisted's polynomial enumeration procedure for sub-term relations [4] (his Theorem 8). This procedure is the key to tractability of termination of ground term rewrite systems. See Section 7 for further discussion.

2   Preliminaries

This paper focuses on ground rewriting and completion, that is, no variables occur in terms and substitution is meaningless. While the definitions of this section can easily be extended to the non-ground case, the restriction is crucial for the further development of the paper.

Let T_Σ be a set of ground terms with signature Σ. Σ_n denotes the set of n-ary function symbols in Σ. Elements of Σ_0 are constants. Let C be a denumerably infinite set of constants disjoint from Σ. We write $T_\Sigma(C)$ instead of $T_{\Sigma \cup C}$. As usual, terms are identified with Σ-labelled trees with nodes or *positions* in the monoid $\mathbb{N}^*$ and $t|_p$ denotes the subterm of s at position p. We also write $s[t]_p$ if $t = s|_p$. Moreover, $\phi[s/t]$ denotes that all occurrences of ground term s in expression ϕ are replaced by ground term t. For a constant $c \in \Sigma \cup C$, an n-ary function $f \in \Sigma$ and terms $t_1, \ldots, t_n \in T_\Sigma$ we recursively define the *height* $h : T_\Sigma \to \mathbb{N}$ of a term as

$$h(c) = 1, \qquad h(f(t_1, \ldots, t_n)) = 1 + \max\{h(t_1), \ldots, h(t_n)\}.$$

We define the *size* $|.| : T_\Sigma \to \mathbb{N}$ of a ground term as

$$|c| = 1, \qquad |f(t_1, \ldots, t_n)| = 1 + \sum_{i=1}^{n} |t_i|.$$

Let $\to$ be a binary relation on a set A. We write $\leftarrow$ for its converse, $\to^+$ for its transitive closure and $\to^*$ for its reflexive transitive closure. Juxtaposition of relations denotes the relational product. $\to$ is a *quasiordering* if $\to = \to^*$.

Let $\to$ be a binary relation on a ground term algebra A with associated set of ground terms T_Σ. The operation f^A denoted by the n-ary operation symbol f is *isotone* (in each argument), if it satisfies the formula

$$s_1 \to t_1, \ldots, s_n \to t_n \implies f(s_1, \ldots, s_n) \to f(t_1, \ldots, t_n),$$

for all $s_1, \ldots, s_n, t_1, \ldots, t_n \in T_\Sigma$. The relation $\to$ is *compatible* if $s \to t$ implies $r[s]_p \to r[t]_p$ for all $r, s, t \in T_\Sigma$. A ground *rewrite rule* is a pair of ground terms. The ground *rewrite relation* $\to_R$ induced by a set R of ground rewrite rules is the smallest compatible relation containing R. We often write $\to_R$ both for the set of rewrite rules and the associated rewrite relation.

We also consider reduction orderings $\prec$ on ground terms, that is, Noetherian compatible quasiorderings. In addition, we always assume that $\prec$ is assumed to be linear and to contain contain the proper subterm relation.

3   Relational Rewriting and Completion

We presuppose the basic concepts and notation of equational and relational rewriting and completion [10, 11, 3, 2, 1] and briefly recall only the most important notions and ideas. We also restrict our attention to quasiorderings. The adaptation to transitive relations is straightforward.

A (relational) *ground term rewrite system for quasiorderings* (GTRS) is a triple $(R, S, \prec)$ of finite sets R and S of rewrite rules and a reduction ordering $\prec$, also called *syntactic ordering*, such that $l \succ r$ for all $l \to_R r$ and $l \prec r$ for all $l \to_S r$. $I = R \cup S$ induces the quasiordering $\to_I^*$. In relational rewriting, therefore, a set I of inequalities is oriented with respect to a syntactic ordering $\prec$. This yields two disjoint sets R and S of rewrite rules. In contrast, a set of equations is oriented in equational rewriting. This yields one single set of rewrite rules.

Assume that $\to_R \cup \leftarrow_S$ is Noetherian and that for every two-step rewrite sequence of the form $\to_S \to_R$ (a *peak*) there exists a rewrite sequence in $\to_R^* \to_S^*$ (a *valley*) between the same terms. Then reachability in $\to_I^*$ can be decided by searching for a common vertex in the $\to_R$ dag from the initial term and the $\leftarrow_S$ dag from the final term of a query inequality. Since only finitely many rewrite rules apply to each term, the dags are finitely branching. A *critical pair* is a pair of terms connected by a peak that possibly cannot be replaced by a valley.

As usual, a Knuth-Bendix completion procedure (KB-procedure) transforms an initial set of expressions in $\to_I$ into a GTRS that supports this decision procedure. It orients inequalities in I with respect to the syntactic ordering $\prec$, computes critical pairs and simplifies expressions. We call the final GTRS a *normal system*. By definition, in a normal system, all critical peaks can be joined by a rewrite proof, $\to_R$ and $\leftarrow_S$ are Noetherian and no rule from $\to_R$ or $\to_S$ can be deleted.

A KB-procedure implements a state transition system together with a syntactic reduction ordering $\prec$ on terms, on oriented and non-oriented inequalities and on sequences of inequalities and rewrite steps. States are tuples of sets of inequalities or rewrite rules. The transition relation is specified by transition rules of two kinds. First, deductive inference rules add consequences to a state corresponding to critical pair computations. Second, simplification rules combine deduction steps with deletions implementing an (approximate) notion of redundancy: An (oriented) inequality is *redundant*, if it can be replaced by a sequence of smaller steps (oriented or unoriented) with respect to $\prec$.

For a quasiordering presented by a set I_0 of ground inequalities, states of the KB-procedure are of the form $q = (I, R, S)$, where I is a set of ground inequalities and R and S are sets of (decreasing and increasing) rewrite rules. In the initial state q_0, R_0 and S_0 are empty and I_0—the *initial specification*—is irreflexive. The set of transition rules between such states is denoted by C. A *run* of the procedure is a (finite or infinite) sequence $q_0, q_1, q_2, \ldots$ of states such that q_0 is an initial state and between all consecutive states there is a transition that applies some rule in C. A run *fails*, if I is non-empty in the limit. It *succeeds*, if it does not fail and the limit sets R_∞ and S_∞ yield a normal system. A run is *fair*, if every enabled transition is eventually executed. C is *correct*, if every fair run that does not fail succeeds and $\to^*_{R_\infty \cup S_\infty} = \to^*_{I_0}$. The rules of C are defined as follows (c.f. [2]).

$$\frac{(I, R, S)}{(I \cup \{s \to_I t\}, R, S)},$$ (DEDUCE)

if (s, t) is a critical pair. This rule can also be represented as a pair of inference rules.

$$\frac{l_2 \to_S r_2 \quad l_1[r_2]_p \to_R r_1}{l_1[l_2]_p \to_I r_1}, \qquad \frac{l_2 \to_S r_2[l_1]_p \quad l_1 \to_R r_1}{l_2 \to_I r_2[r_1]_p}.$$

$$\frac{(I \cup \{s \to_I t\}, R, S)}{(I, R \cup \{s \to_R t\}, S)}, \qquad \frac{(I \cup \{t \to_I s\}, R, S)}{(I, R, S \cup \{t \to_S s\})}, \qquad \text{(ORIENT)}$$

if $s \succ t$.

$$\frac{(I \cup \{s \to_I t\}, R, S)}{(I, R, S)},$$ (SIMPLIFY)

if $s \to_I t$ is redundant. Analogous rules simplify expressions in $\to_R$ and $\to_S$.

$$\frac{(I \cup \{s \to_I s\}, R, S)}{(I, R, S)},$$ (DELETE)

Simplification rules and in particular DELETE should be applied eagerly.

Theorem 1 ([2]). C *is sound and correct, but need not terminate.*

Proof. Soundness of the procedure means essentially that the relational theory is preserved by the rules of C. The notion of correctness has been defined above.

We only show non-termination. See [3, 2] for a proof of soundness and correctness. Let $b \succ f \succ a$ be a precedence for constants a, b and function f of arity one that is extended to a reduction ordering containing the subterm ordering. The relations $f(b) \to_I b$ and $f(a) \to_I b$ are oriented as $f(b) \to_R b$ and $f(a) \to_S b$. Now inequalities $f^n(a) \to_S b$ can be computed by DEDUCE and ORIENT for arbitrary n. All rules remain irredundant during the entire process, thus can never be simplified.   □

4   Transforming the Initial Specification

We now define a two-step transformation $\tau_{12} = \tau_2 \circ \tau_1$, $\tau_{12} : Q \to Q'$ on states of C that allows us to enforce termination of C. Q is defined with respect to the signature Σ, and Q' with respect to a new signature Σ' defined below.

The first transformation $\tau_1 : T_\Sigma \to T_{\Sigma'}$ maps every $f \in \Sigma$ to a constant $f \in \Sigma'_0$. Σ' contains one single additional binary function symbol @. Terms are transformed as follows.

$$\tau_1(a) = a,$$
$$\tau_1(f(t_1, \ldots, t_n)) = @(f, @(\tau_1(t_1) \ldots @(\tau_1(t_{n-1}), \tau_1(t_n)) \ldots)),$$

for every constant $a \in \Sigma$, function $f \in \Sigma$ of arity n and terms $t_1, \ldots, t_n \in T_\Sigma$. We often write $fc_1 \ldots c_n$ instead of $@(f, @(c_1 \ldots @(c_{n-1}, c_n) \ldots))$. τ_1 is similar to currying in functional languages. τ_1 is extended homomorphically to pairs of terms, states and sets of states. Its main role is to preserve the initial signature.

Example 1. Using τ_1, the term $f(g(a, b), c, d)$ is transformed to the term

$$@(f, @(@(g, @(a, b)), @(c, d))).$$

The second transformation τ_2 flattens expressions by renaming each subterm s of a term t by a fresh constant c_s and by adding a new pair of definitional rewrite rules $s \to_R c_s$ and $c_s \to_S s$ to the initial specification. This renaming will be performed in a purely declarative way by extending states of the Knuth-Bendix completion procedure C to tuples (K, I, R, S), where K is a set of constants and by adding the rule

$$\frac{(K, I[f(\bar{c})], R, S)}{(K \cup \{c_0\}, I[f(\bar{c})/c_0], R \cup \{f(\bar{c}) \to_R c_0\}, S \cup \{c_0 \to_S f(\bar{c})\})} \quad \text{(RENAME)}$$

to C. Here, $\bar{c} = c_1, \ldots, c_n$ is a sequence of constants from K and $c_0 \notin \Sigma \cup K$. RENAME forces subterm-renaming in a bottom up way. Note that in presence of new names, the ordering $\prec$ looses its importance. It could even be constructed on the fly during completion.

Example 2. By τ_2, the inequality $f(g(a)) \le b$ is transformed to $f(c) \le b$ and $c = g(a)$, where c is a fresh constant. $c = g(a)$ is then implicitly split into $c \le g(a)$ and $c \ge g(a)$ and then oriented with respect to $\prec$ as $c \to_S g(a)$ and $g(a) \to_R c$. Terms of greater height are renamed from the leaves to the root.

Proposition 1. C *extended by* RENAME *is sound and correct, but need not terminate.*

Proof. Adding RENAME to C leads to a definitional extension of the theory. Soundness is based on the fact that

$$\phi(s) \Leftrightarrow \forall x.(x = s \Rightarrow \phi(x)) \Leftrightarrow \exists x.x = s \wedge \phi(x)$$

holds in first-order logic. Correctness goes along the lines of the proof of Theorem 1. For non-termination, we adapt the counterexample from the proof of Theorem 1. Consider the rewrite rules $f(b) \to_I b$ and $f(a) \to_I b$ and assume names $c_0, c_1, \cdots \in C$ such that $c_i \succ c_j$ for all $i < j$ and $c_i \prec f$ for all $c_i \in C$ and $f \in \Sigma$. Iterating this, RENAME yields $a \to_R c_0$, $b \to_R c_1$, $f(a) \to_R c_2$, $f(b) \to_R c_3$ and corresponding S-rules in which the arrows are flipped. RENAME, ORIENT and DEDUCE then yield for all $i \ge 0$ the rules $f(c_{2i}) \to_R c_{2i+2}$, $f(c_{2i+1}) \to_R c_{2i+3}$, the corresponding (converse) S-rules, the rules $c_{2i+2} \to_S c_{2i}$, $c_{2i+3} \to_S c_{2i+1}$ and in the respective next step by DEDUCE $f(c_{2i+2}) \to_R c_{2i+2}$, $f(c_{2i+3}) \to_R c_{2i+3}$. This leads to non-termination. $\square$

After application of τ_2 (and orientation), the specification consists of two types of rewrite rules. First, *P-rules* (or *presentation rules*) are of the form

$$f(c_1, \ldots, c_n) \to_{I \cup R} c_0, \qquad c_0 \to_{I \cup S} f(c_1, \ldots, c_n), \qquad c_1 \to_{I \cup R \cup S} c_2$$

for constants $c_1, \ldots, c_n \in C$ and function f of arity n that represent the initial inequalities. Second, *D-rules* (or *definitional rules*) are of the form

$$f(c_1, \ldots, c_n) \to_R c_0, \qquad c_0 \to_S f(c_1, \ldots, c_n),$$

for an n-ary function $f \in \Sigma$ and constants $c_0, \ldots, c_n \in C$ that represent the subterm structure. P- and D-rules are not necessarily disjoint. We also classify these rules in a different way. We call *F-rule* a P- or D-rule involving a function symbol and *C-rule* a P-rule involving only constant symbols. τ_2 is also extended homomorphically to pairs of terms, states and sets of states.

We also extend $|.|$ homomorphically from terms to pairs of terms and states, setting $|(s, t)| = |s| + |t|$ and $|(I, R, S)| = \sum_{(s,t) \in I \cup R \cup S} |(s, t)|$.

The following proposition states that both transformations are conservative.

Proposition 2. *Let Γ be a set of T_Σ-inequalities and let Q denote the quasiordering axioms (reflexivity and transitivity) for the relation $\leq$ together with isotonicity of all functions in Σ. Then for all $s, t \in T_\Sigma$,*

$$\Gamma \cup Q \models s \leq t \Leftrightarrow \tau_1(\Gamma \cup Q) \models \tau_1(s \leq t)$$
$$\Leftrightarrow \tau_2(\Gamma \cup Q) \models \tau_2(s \leq t)$$
$$\Leftrightarrow \tau_{12}(\Gamma \cup Q) \models \tau_{12}(s \leq t).$$

Proof. For the first equivalence, we first consider a proof in T_Σ and reason by induction on the size of proofs.

(i) If $s \leq t \in \Gamma$, then $\tau_1(s) \leq \tau_1(t) \in \tau_1(\Gamma)$.

(ii) If the last step in the proof has been reflexivity, then $s = t$ and therefore $\tau_1(s) = \tau_1(t)$.

(iii) If the last step in the proof has been transitivity, then there exists a T_Σ-term r and proofs of $s \leq r$ and $r \leq t$. The induction hypothesis yields proofs of $\tau_1(s) \leq \tau_1(r)$ and $\tau_1(r) \leq \tau_1(t)$. Then $\tau_1(s) \leq \tau_1(t)$ follows immediately from transitivity.

(iv) If the last step in the proof has been isotonicity, then let $s = f(s_1, \ldots, s_n)$ and $t = f(t_1, \ldots, t_n)$ and the induction hypothesis yields proofs of $s_1 \leq t_1$ to $s_n \leq t_n$ together with proofs of $\tau_1(s_1) \leq \tau_1(t_1)$ to $\tau_1(s_n) \leq \tau_1(t_n)$. Isotonicity of @ then yields in n steps the proofs

$$s_{n-1}s_n \leq t_{n-1}t_n,$$
$$s_{n-2}s_{n-1}s_n \leq t_{n-2}t_{n-1}t_n$$
$$\ldots\ldots$$
$$fs_1 \ldots s_n \leq ft_1 \ldots t_n.$$

The last line is $\tau_1(s) \leq \tau_1(t)$. The converse direction of the first equivalence is similar.

The second equivalence follows from soundness and correctness of C extended by RENAME (Proposition 1).

The third equivalence is immediate from the first and the second one.   □

Moreover, it is easy to see that the transformations τ_1 and τ_2, and therefore also τ_{12}, increase the size of a state q by order $O(|q|)$. We may also assume that they have polynomial running time. Finally, we henceforth assume that all terms are built from one binary non-constant function symbol @, which has maximal weight in the precedence on the signature, and that they are flat, that is, have height at most 2.

5   Termination Analysis

With the two-step transformation τ_{12} and a precedence $\prec$ that gives @ greater weight than all constants, the termination analysis of C is rather simple.

Theorem 2. *Let $q = \tau_{12}(q')$ for some state q' of* C. *Then* C *terminates on q after $O(|q|)$ steps.*

Proof. By assumption, all pairs in q that can contribute to a DEDUCE-step are F- or C-rules of depth at most 2 and size at most 4 of the form

$$c_1 c_2 \to_R c_3, \qquad\qquad c_1 \to_S c_2 c_3, \qquad\qquad (F)$$
$$c_1 \to_R c_2, \qquad\qquad c_1 \to_S c_2, \qquad\qquad (C)$$

where c_1, c_2 and c_3 are constants in C. If k is the number of constants in q, then q contains at most $2k^2(k-1)$ F-rules and $k(k-1)$ C-rules, since both kinds of rules must contain at least two different constants. This and the sizes of F- and C-rules imply that $|q| \leq 8k^3 - 6k^2 - 2k$. Let n be the number of (P- and D-)rules in q. We analyse the possible DEDUCE-steps.

– F/F-overlaps. Consider the DEDUCE-step

$$\frac{c_1 \to_S c_2 c_3 \qquad c_2 c_3 \to_R c_4}{c_1 \to_I c_4}.$$

The conclusion is a C-rule. This is the only way two F-rules can overlap.
– F/C-overlaps. Consider the DEDUCE-steps

$$\frac{c_1 \to_S c_2 \qquad c_2 c_3 \to_R c_4}{c_1 c_3 \to_I c_4}, \qquad\qquad \frac{c_1 \to_S c_2 c_3 \qquad c_3 \to_R c_4}{c_1 \to_I c_2 c_4}.$$

The conclusions are F-rules. There are two similar cases, where the C-rule matches with c_3 in the left-hand and with c_2 in the right-hand F rule.
– C/C-overlaps. Consider the DEDUCE-step

$$\frac{c_1 \to_S c_2 \qquad c_2 \to_R c_3}{c_1 \to_I c_3}.$$

The conclusion is a C-rule. This is the only way two C-rules can overlap.

The DEDUCE-steps produce only F- and C-rules; no new constants from C are introduced. So their number is bounded by the total number of rules in Q as $2k^3 - k^2 - k - n$. At most k rules can be deleted; at most $2k^3 - k^2 - k - n$ rules can be oriented or simplified. Thus the overall number of steps in C is $O(k^3)$, which by our above estimation for $|q|$ is equal to $O(|q|)$. □

A subtlety is that no new constants are introduced during the completion process. If one would continue renaming during the completion procedures and introduce a new constant for every new term that is generated by a DEDUCE step (as in the proof of Proposition 1), then the procedure need not terminate.

Theorem 3. C *terminates in polynomial time.*

Proof. Let q_0 be the initial specification with $R_0 = S_0 = \emptyset$. According to the results of Section 4, the transformation $\tau_{12} : q_0 \mapsto q$ takes polynomial running time and increases the size of q_0 by a linear factor. According to Theorem 2, C takes polynomially many steps in the size of q, hence also in the size of q_0.

We may assume that each DEDUCE, ORIENT and DELETE step may be executed in constant (or at least polynomial) time. See [8] for a discussion of a related procedure. It remains to consider the cost of SIMPLIFY.

Unlike the equational KB-procedures, the SIMPLIFY-steps of C are search-based. We represent q as a directed graph with vertices consisting of constants or pairs of constants from C. There is an edge between vertices for every rule $l \rightarrow_{I \cup R \cup S} r$ in q. If q is built from k constants, then there may be at most $k + k^2$ vertices. According to the proof of Theorem 2, there are at most $k(k-1)$ edges corresponding to C-rules and $2k^2(k-1)$ edges corresponding to F-rules. We can then check for simplification by depth-first or breadth-first search along these edges. This is linear in the number of vertices plus the number of edges. Thus every SIMPLIFY-step takes polynomial time and the whole procedure therefore has running time polynomial in the size of the initial specification. □

Correctness of C does not depend on performing SIMPLIFY-steps. Thus the running time can be considerably improved by using no or an approximate implementation of SIMPLIFY. The proof of Theorem 3 has the following consequences.

Corollary 1.

(i) *The running time of the decision procedure of ground relational rewriting (c.f. Section 3) is polynomial in the size of the normal GTRS.*

(ii) *([4]) Reachability in GTRSs is tractable.*

(iii) *([5]) The uniform word problem for term algebras is tractable.*

For Corollary 1(ii), note that this result applies in particular to non-terminating rewrite systems. For Corollary 1(iii), note that every word problem can be rephrased as a reachability problem.

Example 3. Consider again the GTRS from the proof of Theorem 1. We use the notation introduced in Section 4. The transformation τ_{12} yields the rewrite rules $fb \rightarrow_R b$ and $fa \rightarrow_R b$. There are no critical pairs.

6   Detecting Embeddings

We now apply C as a meta-procedure to the development of two rule-based declarative and (incrementally) dynamic algorithms for detecting simple and homeomorphic embeddings in a state transition or constraint system represented by a set of ground inequalities. The inference rules are highly non-deterministic and therefore characterise classes of algorithms rather than particular instances. Concrete algorithms can be obtained by refinement, imposing execution strategies. The correctness proofs of algorithms are simple and concise. They are relative to total correctness of C.

We first define a simple *embedding relation* $\trianglelefteq$ by $t \trianglelefteq f(\dots, t, \dots)$ for all $t \in T_\Sigma$. We say that a term s is *embedded* into a term t if $s \trianglelefteq^* t$. Let $q = (I, R, S)$ be a state. A $\rightarrow_{I \cup R \cup S}$-sequence $s = t_0, t_1, \dots$ *contains an embedding*, if $t_i \trianglelefteq^* t_j$ holds for some t_i, t_j in s and $i \leq j$.

We first present two simple technical lemmata.

Lemma 1. $s \trianglelefteq^* t$ *iff* $t = t[s]_p$ *for some position* p.

The proof is obvious.

Lemma 2. s *is a subterm of* t *iff* $\tau_1(s)$ *is a subterm of* $\tau_1(t)$.

Proof. We ignore positions of terms in the proof to simplify notation.

(i) $t = t[s]$ implies $\tau_1(t) = \tau_1[\tau_1(s)]$ by induction on the size of t. If $t \in \Sigma_0$, then the result follows trivially from the definition of τ_1. If $t = f(t_1, \dots, t_n)$, then either $s = t$ or $t_i = t_i[s]$ for some $1 \leq i \leq n$. The first case is trivial. In the second case, the induction hypothesis yields $\tau_1(t_i) = \tau_1(t_i)[\tau_1(s)]$. Then $i - 1$ applications of @ yield $\tau_1(t) = \tau_1(t)[\tau_1(s)]$, according to the definition of τ_1.

(ii) $\tau_1(t) = \tau_1(t)[\tau_1(s)]$ implies $t = t[s]$ by induction on the size of terms. The base case is similar to (i). Let $\tau_1(t) = f\tau_1(t_1)\dots\tau_1(t_n)$. Then either $s = t$ (which is trivial) or $\tau_1(t_i) = \tau_1(t_i)[\tau_1(s)]$ for some $1 \leq i \leq n$. Then the induction hypothesis yields $t_i = t_i[s]$. This implies $t = t[s]$ by definition of τ_1. □

We assume that all rules are labelled with P, D or both, depending on whether they are P- or D-rules.

Lemma 3. *Let* $q = (I, R, S)$ *be a state. The following statements are equivalent.*

(i) $s \rightarrow^*_{I \cup R \cup S} t$ *is an embedding.*
(ii) $\tau_1(s) \rightarrow^*_{I' \cup R' \cup S'} \tau_1(t)$ *is an embedding, where* $(I', R', S') = \tau_1(q)$.
(iii) $\tau_{12}(s) \rightarrow^*_{I'' \cup R'' \cup S''} \tau_{12}(t)$ *holds in the state* $\tau_{12}(q) = (I'', R'', S'')$, *where* $\tau_{12}(s)$ *names a subterm of* $\tau_1(t)$ *and all rules in the sequence are P-rules.*

Proof. ((i) equivalent to (ii)). First note that $s \rightarrow^*_{I \cup R \cup S} t$ iff $\tau_1(s) \rightarrow^*_{I' \cup R' \cup S'} \tau_1(t)$ by Proposition 2. Moreover, $s \trianglelefteq^* t$ iff s is a subterm of t by Lemma 1, iff $\tau_1(s)$ is a subterm of $\tau_1(t)$ by Lemma 2, iff $\tau_1(t) = \tau_1(t)[\tau_1(s)]$ again by Lemma 1.

((ii) equivalent to (iii)). $\tau_1(s) \rightarrow^*_{I' \cup R' \cup S'} \tau_1(t)$ iff $\tau_{12}(s) \rightarrow_{I'' \cup R'' \cup S''} \tau_{12}(t)$ by Proposition 2, obviously by a sequence of P-rules. Now let $\tau_1(s) \trianglelefteq^* \tau_1(t)$. By Lemma 1, this is equivalent to the fact that $\tau_1(s)$ is a subterm of $\tau_1(t)$. By definition of τ_2, equivalently, $\tau_{12}(s)$ names a subterm of $\tau_1(t)$. □

Lemma 3 is the basis for detecting embeddings.

Theorem 4. *Let $q_0 = (I_0, R_0, S_0)$ be an initial specification and $q = \tau_{12}(q_0) = (I, R, S)$. Let C_e be C together with the rule*

$$\frac{(I, R \cup \{c_1 c_2 \rightarrow_R^D c_3\}, S)}{(I \cup \{c_3 \rightarrow_I^P c_1, c_3 \rightarrow_I^P c_2\}, R \cup \{c_1 c_2 \rightarrow_R^D c_3\}, S)}. \qquad \text{(BACK)}$$

(i) *An I_0-sequence in q_0 contains an embedding iff a fair run of C_e constructs a cycle of P-rules from q.*
(ii) *C_e detects all embeddings in q_0 in polynomial time.*

Proof. (ad i) By Lemma 3, q_0 contains an embedding iff q contains a rewrite sequence of P-rules that connects the name c_s of the initial term s with the (name c_t of the) final term t of the embedding. By Lemma 1, s must be a subterm of t. By Lemma 2 and Lemma 3, subterms and embeddings are preserved by τ_1. Thus for each name of a term in q_0, BACK-steps eventually produce a rewrite sequence to the names of all its subterms. This yields a cycle iff there is an embedding.

(ad ii) By Theorem 3, C terminates in polynomial time. The number of rules generated by BACK is $O(|q|)$ and therefore $O(|q_0|)$ by properties of the transformation τ_{12}; the closure under BACK can also be done in polynomial time. Cycle detection can also be done in polynomial time with C and therefore C_e. This has been shown for graph structures in [1]. The basic idea, which applies also here, is that by the ordering constraints, every cycle must contain at least an R- and an S-step, hence a critical peak. Each cycle with k-edges can therefore eventually be collapsed into a cycle with two edges, which is simple to detect (in polynomial time). Therefore detection of embeddings has polynomial running time in the size of q_0. □

The intuition behind the algorithm is rather simple. If a rewrite sequence contains an embedding, then, on the one hand, there is a sequence of P-rewriting steps from the embedded term to the embedding term. On the other hand, there is a sequence of D-rewriting steps from the embedding term to the embedded term along the D-rules that form the edges of the tree corresponding to the embedding term. This obviously yields a cycle.

The cycle detection algorithm can be refined to the running time of depth-first search using a strategy and an on-the-fly construction of the precedence. See [1] for details.

We now consider a more complex kind of embedding. A binary relation $\trianglelefteq$ on T_Σ is a (ground) *homeomorphic embedding*, if the following holds (cf. [12]). For all $s = f(s_1, \ldots, s_m)$ and $t = g(t_1, \ldots, t_n)$ in T_Σ, $s \trianglelefteq t$ iff either

(h1) $f \preceq g$ and $s_i \trianglelefteq t_{j_i}$ for all $i = 1, \ldots, m$ and some $j_1, \ldots, j_m$ with $1 \leq j_1 < j_2 < \cdots < j_m \leq n$, or
(h2) $s \trianglelefteq t_i$ for some $i = 1, \ldots, n$, or
(h3) $s \preceq t$ if $s, t \in \Sigma_0$.

Intuitively, an unlabelled tree s can be homeomorphically embedded in an unlabelled tree t, if the root of s can be mapped to some node i of t and all other nodes of s are injectively mapped to successors of i such that s can be rebuilt in the subtree of t by considering paths of t as edges of s. For labelled trees, this is generalised with respect to $\preceq$ on the signature.

The following lemma says that τ_1 preserves homeomorphic embeddings.

Lemma 4. *Let $q = (I, R, S)$ be a state. Then $s \to_{I \cup R \cup S} t$ is a homeomorphic embedding iff $\tau_1(s) \to_{I' \cup R' \cup S'} \tau_1(t)$ is a homeomorphic embedding, where $(I', R', S') = \tau_1(q)$.*

Proof. $s \to_{I \cup R \cup S} t$ iff $\tau_1(s) \to_{I' \cup R' \cup S'} \tau_1(t)$ follows from Proposition 2.

(i) Let $s \trianglelefteq t$. We argue by induction on the size of terms and assume that the precedence $\prec$ of Σ is inherited by Σ'. If $t \in \Sigma_0$, then $s \preceq t$ and therefore also $\tau_1(s) \preceq \tau_1(q)$ by (h3), since $\tau_1(s), \tau_1(q) \in \Sigma'_0$ by definition of τ_1.

Now let $s = f(s_1, \ldots s_m)$ and $t = g(t_1, \ldots, t_n)$.

(Case h1). Let $f \preceq g$ and $s_i \trianglelefteq t_{j_i}$ for all $1 \leq i \leq m$ and some $j_1, \ldots, j_m$ such that $1 \leq j_1 < j_2 < \cdots < j_m \leq n$. Then by definition of τ_1, $\tau_1(f), \tau_1(g) \in \Sigma'_0$ and $\tau_1(f) \preceq \tau_1(g)$, therefore also $\tau_1(f) \trianglelefteq \tau_1(g)$. Moreover the induction hypothesis yields $\tau_1(s_i) \trianglelefteq \tau_1(t_{j_i})$. Applying (h1) m times and (h2) $n - m$ times yields $f\tau(s_1) \ldots \tau(s_m) \trianglelefteq g\tau_1(t_1) \ldots \tau_1(t_n)$, hence $\tau_1(s) \trianglelefteq \tau_1(t)$. Here, (h2) is used to fill in those $\tau_1(t_j)$ that are not related by $\trianglelefteq$ to a $\tau_1(s_i)$.

(Case h2). Let $s \trianglelefteq t_i$ for some $1 \leq i \leq n$. Then the induction hypothesis yields $\tau_1(s) \trianglelefteq \tau_1(t_i)$. Then n applications of (h2) yield $\tau_1(s) \trianglelefteq g\tau_1(t_1) \ldots \tau_1(t_n)$, hence $\tau_1(s) \trianglelefteq \tau_1(t)$.

(ii) Let $\tau_1(s) \trianglelefteq \tau_1(t)$. We argue again by induction on the size of terms. The cases are similar to those in (i), only the packing and unpacking of terms is done in the opposite direction. $\qquad\square$

Lemma 5. *Let $q = (I, R, S)$ be a state. Then $s \to_{I \cup R \cup S} t$ is a homeomorphic embedding iff*

(i) $\tau_{12}(s) \to_{I'' \cup R'' \cup S''} \tau_{12}(t)$ holds in the state $\tau_{12}(q) = (I'', R'', S'')$ and
(ii) $\tau_{12}(s) \trianglelefteq \tau_{12}(t)$ follows from the embedding axioms

$$c_1 \trianglelefteq c'_1, c_2 \trianglelefteq c'_2, c_1 c_2 \to^D_R c_3, c'_1 c'_2 \to_R c'_3 \Rightarrow c_3 \trianglelefteq c'_3, \tag{h1'}$$

$$c \trianglelefteq c'_1, c'_1 c'_2 \to^D_R c'_3 \Rightarrow c \trianglelefteq c'_3, \tag{h2'}$$

$$c \trianglelefteq c'_2, c'_1 c'_2 \to^D_R c'_3 \Rightarrow c \trianglelefteq c'_3, \tag{h2'}$$

$$c \preceq c' \Rightarrow c \trianglelefteq c', \qquad \text{if } c, c' \in \Sigma_0. \tag{h3'}$$

All elements of Σ preserve their names and the precedence on Σ is inherited.

Proof. $s \to_{I \cup R \cup S} t$ iff $\tau_{12}(s) \to_{I'' \cup R'' \cup S''} \tau_{12}(t)$ holds by Proposition 2. Homeomorphic embeddings are preserved under τ_1 by Lemma 4. The remainder follows from the correctness of the encoding of (h1), (h2) and (h3), which is straightforward. In particular, the $\to_R$-rules in the definition trigger the choice of subterms according to (h1), (h2) and (h3). $\qquad\square$

Lemma 5 is the basis for detecting homeomorphic embeddings.

Theorem 5. *Let* $q_0 = (I_0, R_0, S_0)$ *be an initial specification and* $q = \tau_{12}(q_0) = (I, R, S)$. *Let* C_h *be* C *together with the rules*[1]

$$\frac{c_1 \to_I^h c_1' \quad c_2 \to_I^h c_2' \quad c_1 c_2 \to_R^D c_3 \quad c_1' c_2' \to_R^D c_3'}{c_3 \to_I^h c_3'} \tag{H1}$$

$$\frac{c_1' \to_I^h c \quad c_1' c_2' \to_R^D c_3'}{c_3' \to_I^h c} \qquad \frac{c_2' \to_I^h c \quad c_1' c_2' \to_R^D c_3'}{c_3' \to_I^h c} \tag{H2}$$

$$\frac{c \preceq c'}{c' \to_I^h c} \qquad \text{if } c, c' \in \Sigma_0. \tag{H3}$$

All h-rules are considered also as P-rules. (H1), (H2) and (H3) are eagerly applied[2].

(i) An I_0-sequence in q_0 contains an embedding, iff a fair run of C_h constructs a cycle of P-rules from q that contains precisely one h-rule.

(ii) C_h detects all homeomorphic embeddings in q_0 in polynomial time.

Proof. (ad i) By Lemma 5, q_0 contains a homeomorphic embedding, iff q contains a rewrite sequence of P-rules that connects the name c_s of the initial term s with the (name c_t of the) final term t of the embedding. The rules (H1), (H2) and (H3) are constructed such that all homeomorphic embeddings are enumerated according to the rules (h1'), (h2') and (h3') in Lemma 5. The two rule sets are identical (which establishes correctness of (H1), (H2) and (H3)), only the arrows $\to_I^h$ are inverted with respect to $\preceq$. Therefore, a cycle containing precisely one h-rule is eventually constructed by C_h iff there is an embedding.

(ad ii) By Theorem 3, C terminates in polynomial time. The rules (H1), (H2) and (H3) do not introduce any new constants. (H3) introduces at most $|\Sigma_0|^2$ edges, that is C-rules. Also (H1) and (H2) introduce only C-rules. Their number is bounded by $k(k-1)$, where k is the number of constants in C that occur in q and therefore in $O(|q_0|)$. The closure under these rules can be done in polynomial time. The remainder of the proof is analogous to that of Theorem 4. In addition one must use an execution strategy for C_h that ensures that only one h-rule is used for every cycle detection. □

The concept of homeomorphic embedding may be difficult to grasp at first sight. The fact that our detection algorithm is nevertheless simple and has been constructed from the mathematical specification in a few short formal steps indicates the power of our approach. The (H2)-rules of C_h are essentially the BACK-rule of C_e read backwards. Generally, C_e uses a top-down approach to cycle construction, whereas C_h takes a bottom-up approach. We have chosen the bottom-up approach, since it is then easier to model axiom (h1'), but in principle also a top-down approach should be possible. There should also be much space for refining

---

[1] They are written as inference rules because of their length.

[2] Alternatively, and more non-deterministically, similar rules for R and S should be used.

the algorithms, using different execution strategies on the deduction and simplification rules of C_e and C_h. The algorithms can also easily be combined with other rule-based extensions of C and integrated into the combined KB-procedure for equalities and inequalities in [1].

Our algorithms for embeddings and homeomorphic embeddings are inherently dynamic. When a new rule $s \rightarrow_I t$ is inserted into a state q, it must first be transformed by τ_{12}. The transformation with τ_1 is completely local. The transformation τ_2 is non-local. Names of subterms that appear in q might be relevant to s and t, but conversely, the addition has no impact on q. Insertion of new rules is therefore also local. The abstract declarative data structure represented by the completion algorithm need not be recompiled when the rule is inserted. Only the new critical pairs that arise between the new rule and the precompiled rules must be computed. Deletion of a rule is more complex. It requires tracking and revision of critical pair computations of presentational rules, but fortunately no revision of definitional rules. In particular, rules stemming from critical pair computations with the deleted rule must be deleted, unless they can be produced by other rules. This procedure is again local.

Example 4. Consider the one step rewrite sequence $s \rightarrow_I t$ for terms $s = \neg(\neg 0 \vee 1)$ and $t = \neg(\neg(\neg 1 \wedge (1 \vee (\neg 0 \vee 1))))$, where $\Sigma = \{0, 1, \vee, \wedge, \neg\}$ is the signature of the two-element Boolean algebra. Assume a precedence $\prec$ for which all elements of Σ are incomparable (for homeomorphic embeddings, $\prec$ needs only be a quasiordering). It is easy to check with (h1), (h2) and (h3) that $s \trianglelefteq t$ (cf. [12]). Let $\Sigma' = \{0, 1, \vee, \wedge, \neg, @\}$ be a new signature for which $\neg$, $\vee$ and $\wedge$ are constants. We obtain

$$\tau_1(s) = @(\neg, @(\vee, @(@(\neg, 0), 1))) = (\neg(\vee(\neg 0)1)),$$
$$\tau_1(t) = @(\neg, @(\neg, @(\wedge, @(@(\neg, 1), @(\vee, @(1, @(\vee, @(@(\neg, 0), 1))))))))$$
$$= (\neg(\neg(\wedge(\neg 1)(\vee 1(\vee(\neg 0)1))))).$$

τ_2 yields the following rewrite rules.

$$1c_2 \rightarrow_R^D c_4, \quad (5)$$
$$\vee c_4 \rightarrow_R^D c_5, \quad (6)$$
$$\neg 0 \rightarrow_R^D c_0, \quad (1)$$
$$\neg 1 \rightarrow_R^D c_6, \quad (7)$$
$$c_0 1 \rightarrow_R^D c_1, \quad (2)$$
$$c_6 c_5 \rightarrow_R^D c_7, \quad (8)$$
$$c_3 \rightarrow_I^P c_{10}. \quad (12)$$
$$\vee c_1 \rightarrow_R^D c_2, \quad (3)$$
$$\wedge c_7 \rightarrow_R^D c_8, \quad (9)$$
$$\neg c_2 \rightarrow_R^D c_3, \quad (4)$$
$$\neg c_8 \rightarrow_R^D c_9, \quad (10)$$
$$\neg c_9 \rightarrow_R^D c_{10}, \quad (11)$$

We then obtain

$$\frac{c_2 \preceq c_2}{c_2 \rightarrow_I^h c_2} \qquad \{\text{by (H3)}\}, \tag{13}$$

$$\frac{c_2 \rightarrow_I^h c_2 \quad 1c_2 \rightarrow_R^D c_4}{c_4 \rightarrow_I^h c_2} \qquad \{\text{by (H2), (13), (5)}\}, \tag{14}$$

$$\frac{c_4 \rightarrow_I^h c_2 \quad \vee c_4 \rightarrow_R^D c_5}{c_5 \rightarrow_I^h c_2} \qquad \{\text{by (H2), (14), (6)}\}, \tag{15}$$

$$\frac{c_5 \rightarrow_I^h c_2 \quad c_6 c_5 \rightarrow_R^D c_7}{c_7 \rightarrow_I^h c_2} \qquad \{\text{by (H2), (15), (8)}\}, \tag{16}$$

$$\frac{c_7 \rightarrow_I^h c_2 \quad \wedge c_7 \rightarrow_R^D c_8}{c_8 \rightarrow_I^h c_2} \qquad \{\text{by (H2), (16), (9)}\}, \tag{17}$$

$$\frac{\neg \preceq \neg}{\neg \rightarrow_I^h \neg} \qquad \{\text{by (H2)}\}, \tag{18}$$

$$\frac{c_8 \rightarrow_I^h c_2 \quad \neg \rightarrow_I^h \neg \quad \neg c_8 \rightarrow_R^D c_9 \quad \neg c_2 \rightarrow_R^D c_3}{c_9 \rightarrow_I^h c_3} \qquad \{\text{by (H1), (17), (18)}\}, \tag{19}$$

$$\frac{c_9 \rightarrow_I^h c_3 \quad \neg c_9 \rightarrow_R^D c_{10}}{c_{10} \rightarrow_I^h c_3} \qquad \{\text{by (H2), (19), (11)}\}. \tag{20}$$

We have thus obtained the 2-cycle $c_3 \rightarrow_I c_{10} \rightarrow_I^h c_3$ from (12) and the conclusion of (20), which can easily be detected.

7   Termination of Ground Term Rewrite Systems

Tractability of termination for GTRSs has already been shown in [4]. The method is based mainly on two facts.

Theorem 6 ([4]). *Let R be a GTRS. The set of all $r \rightarrow_R^* s$, where r is a subterm of a right-hand side and s is a subterm of a left-hand side of a rule in R, can be computed in polynomial time.*

Proof. We give an alternative to the proof in [4] that is based on KB-completion. By Theorem 3, R can be completed in polynomial time. By Proposition 2, τ_{12} preserves reachability. So reachability between polynomially many pairs of subterms (in the size of the input GTRS) must be tested. This can be done with the decision procedure of relational rewriting in polynomial time by Corollary 1. Consequently, the whole procedure has polynomial running time.   □

The second fact expresses that every non-terminating GTRS contains a rewrite sequence of a particular shape: a so-called *constricting* sequence.

Theorem 7 ([4]). *A GTRS R is non-terminating iff there is a sequence $\alpha = r_1 \ldots r_k$ of left-hand sides of rules in R such that* *(i)* $r_1 = r_k$,

(ii) for all pairs (r_i, r_{i+1}) in α there is a rule $r_i \to s$ in R, r_{i+1} is the left-hand side of a rule in R and $s|_p \to_R^* r_{i+1}$ for some position p.

Moreover, the existence of such a sequence can be decided in polynomial time.

Proof. For the polynomial time part, we use KB-completion and Theorem 6 to generate all pairs that satisfy condition (ii) in polynomial time. We then run a cycle detection algorithm to satisfy condition (i). This can also be based on relational completion, as shown in [1]. □

8   Conclusion and Further Work

We have shown that ground KB-completion for quasiorderings terminates in polynomial time, using a two-step transformation on the initial specification. This result immediately transfers to completion for non-symmetric transitive relations from [3] and to various extensions, including combined ground KB-completion for relations and equivalences (cf. [3, 1]). A main application of reachability analysis based on KB-completion is the proof support for algebraic calculi for programs and processes and for ordered algebras in general. The question how far our results can be generalised to these richer structures is very interesting. Related results for certain lattices are contained in [9].

We have also developed two novel rule-based, declarative and dynamic algorithms to detect embeddings and homeomorphic embeddings in ground rewrite sequences, using KB-completion as a meta-procedure. We envision applications in termination analysis of term rewrite systems and programs, in constraint satisfaction problems for lexicographic or recursive path orderings (cf. [4]), in the context of automated deduction, in constraint-based analysis, partial evaluation and program transformation. In the context of termination analysis, the presence of embeddings is a necessary, but not sufficient condition for non-termination [13], whereas the absence of homeomorphic embeddings is a necessary, but not sufficient condition for termination [13]. For the analysis of ordering constraints in automated deduction, the fact that our algorithms are incrementally dynamic is of particular interest. The present algorithms are only decision procedures for the ground case. In general, it is undecidable, whether a term rewrite system contains a homeomorphic embedding [14], but extensions of the algorithms can be used as semi-decision procedures. Homeomorphic embeddings also arise in the field of partial deduction with logic programs and termination analysis of logic programs [15, 16]. In the field of (online) partial evaluation and program transformation or optimisation, the technique of supercompilation (cf. [17]) is based on dynamic detection of homeomorphic embeddings. It seems promising to reconstruct supercompilation in the Knuth-Bendix completion framework.

References

1. Struth, G.: Knuth-Bendix completion as a data structure. In MacCaull, W., Düntsch, I., Winter, M., eds.: Selected Revised Ppaers from 8th Int. Conf. on Relational Methods in Computer Science, RelMiCS 2005, 3rd Int. Wksh. on Applications of Kleene Algebra, Wksh. of COST Action 274 TARSKI. Vol. 3929 of Lect. Notes in Comput. Sci. Springer-Verlag (2006)
2. Struth, G.: Knuth-Bendix completion for non-symmetric transitive relations. In van den Brand, M., Verma, R., eds.: Proc. of 2nd Int. Wksh. on Rule-Based Programming, RULE 2001. Vol. 59 of Electron. Notes in Theor. Comput. Sci. Elsevier (2001)
3. Struth, G.: Canonical Transformations in Algebra, Universal Algebra and Logic. PhD thesis. Inst. für Informatik, Univ. des Saarlandes (1998)
4. Plaisted, D.A.: Polynomial termination and constraint satisfaction tests. In Kirchner, C., ed.: Proc. of 5th Int. Conf. on Rewriting Techniques and Applications, RTA '93. Volume 690 of Lect. Notes in Comput. Sci. Springer-Verlag (1993) 405–420
5. Kozen, D.: Complexity of finitely presented algebras. Techn. Report TR-76-294, Dept. of Computer Science, Cornell Univ. (1979)
6. Snyder, W.: Efficient ground completion: an $O(n \ log \ n)$ algorithm for generating reduced sets of ground rewrite rules equivalent to a set of ground equations E. In Kirchner, C., ed.: Proc. of 3rd Int. Conf. on Rewriting Techniques and Applications, RTA '89. Vol. 355 of Lect. Notes in Comput. Sci. Springer-Verlag (1989) 419–433
7. Nelson, G.: Techniques for program verification. Techn. Report CSL-81-10, Xerox Palo Alto Research Center (1981)
8. Kapur, D.: Shostak's congruence closure as completion. In Comon, H., ed.: Proc. of 8th Int. Conf. on Rewriting Techniques and Applications, RTA '97. Vol. 1232 of Lect. Notes in Comput. Sci. Springer-Verlag (1997) 23–37
9. Struth, G.: An algebra of resolution. In Bachmair, L., ed.: Proc. of 11th Int. Conf. on Rewriting Techniques and Applications, RTA 2000. Vol. 1833 of Lect. Notes in Comput. Sci. Springer-Verlag (2000) 214–228
10. Baader, F., Nipkow, T.: Term Rewriting and All That. Cambridge University Press (1998)
11. Levy, J., Agustí, J.: Bi-rewrite systems. J. of Symb. Comput. **22** (1996) 279–314
12. Wechler, W.: Universal Algebra for Computer Scientists. Springer-Verlag (1992)
13. Dershowitz, N.: Termination of rewriting. J. of Symb. Comput. **3** (1987) 69–116
14. Plaisted, D. A.: The undecidability of self-embedding for term rewriting systems. Inform. Proc. Lett. **20** (1985) 61–64
15. Bol, R.: Loop checking in partial deduction. J. of Logic Programming **16** (1993) 25–46
16. Leuschel, M.: On the power of homeomorphic embedding for online termination. In Levi, G., ed.: Proc. of 5th Int. Static Analysis Symposium, SAS '98. Vol. 1503 of Lect. Notes in Comput. Sci. Springer-Verlag (1998) 230–245
17. Glück, R., Sørensen, M.H.: A roadmap to metacomputation by supercompilation. In Danvy, O., Glück, R., Thiemann, P., eds.: Selected Papers from Int. Seminar on Partial Evaluation. Vol. 1110 of Lect. Notes in Comput. Sci., Springer-Verlag (1996) 137–160

Quantum Predicative Programming

Anya Tafliovich and Eric C.R. Hehner

Dept. of Computer Science, University of Toronto,
Toronto, ON M5S 3G4, Canada
anya@cs.toronto.edu, hehner@cs.toronto.edu

Abstract. The subject of this work is quantum predicative programming — the development of programs intended for execution on a quantum computer. We look at programming in the context of formal methods of program development, or programming methodology. Our work is based on probabilistic predicative programming, a recent generalisation of the well-established predicative programming. It supports the style of program development in which each programming step is proven correct as it is made. We inherit the advantages of the theory, such as its generality, simple treatment of recursive programs, time and space complexity, and communication. Our theory of quantum programming provides tools to write both classical and quantum specifications, develop quantum programs that implement these specifications, and reason about their comparative time and space complexity all in the same framework.

1 Introduction

Modern physics is dominated by concepts of quantum mechanics. Today, over seventy years after its recognition by the scientific community, quantum mechanics provides the most accurate known description of nature's behaviour. Surprisingly, the idea of using the quantum mechanical nature of the world to perform computational tasks is very new, less than thirty years old. Quantum computation and quantum information is the study of information processing and communication accomplished with quantum mechanical systems. In recent years the field has grown immensely. Scientists from various fields of computer science have discovered that thinking physically about computation yields new and exciting results in computation and communication. There has been extensive research in the areas of quantum algorithms, quantum communication and information, quantum cryptography, quantum error-correction, adiabatic computation, measurement-based quantum computation, theoretical quantum optics, and the very new quantum game theory. Experimental quantum information and communication has also been a fruitful field. Experimental quantum optics, ion traps, solid state implementations and nuclear magnetic resonance all add to the experimental successes of quantum computation.

The subject of this work is quantum programming — the developing programs intended for execution on a quantum computer. We assume a model of a quantum

T. Uustalu (Ed.): MPC 2006, LNCS 4014, pp. 433–454, 2006.

computer proposed by Knill [1]: a classical computer with access to a quantum device that is capable of storing quantum bits (called *qubits*), performing certain operations and measurements on these qubits, and reporting the results of the measurements.

We look at programming in the context of formal methods of program development, or programming methodology. This is the field of computer science concerned with applications of mathematics and logic to software engineering tasks. In particular, the formal methods provide tools to formally express software specifications, prove correctness of implementations, and reason about various properties of specifications (e.g. implementability) and implementations (e.g. time and space complexity). Today formal methods are successfully employed in all stages of software development, such as requirements elicitation and analysis, software design, and software implementation.

In this work the theory of quantum programming is based on probabilistic predicative programming, a recent generalisation of the well-established predicative programming [2, 3], which we deem to be the simplest and the most elegant programming theory known today. It supports the style of program development in which each programming step is proven correct as it is made. We inherit the advantages of the theory, such as its generality, simple treatment of recursive programs, and time and space complexity. Our theory of quantum programming provides tools to write both classical and quantum specifications, develop quantum programs that implement these specifications, and reason about their comparative time and space complexity all in the same framework.

The rest of this work is organised as follows. Section 2.1 is the introduction to quantum computation. It assumes that the reader has some basic knowledge of linear algebra and no knowledge of quantum computing. Section 2.2 contains the introduction to probabilistic predicative programming. The reader is assumed to have some background in logic, but no background in programming theory is necessary. The contribution of this work is section 3 which defines the quantum system, introduces programming with the quantum system, and several well-known problems, their classical and quantum solutions, and their formal comparative time complexity analyses. Section 4 states conclusions and outlines directions for future research.

1.1   Related Work

Traditionally, quantum computation is presented in terms of quantum circuits. Recently, there has been an attempt to depart from this convention for the same reason that classical computation is generally not presented in terms of classical circuits. As we develop more complex quantum algorithms, we will need ways to express higher-level concepts with control structures in a readable fashion.

In 2000 Ömer [4] introduced the first quantum programming language QCL. Following his work, Bettelli *et. al.* [5] developed a quantum programming language with syntax based on C++. These two works did not involve any verification techniques.

Sanders and Zuliani in [6] introduced a quantum language qGCL, which is an extension of pGCL [7], which in turn generalises Dijkstra's guarded-command language to include probabilism. Zuliani later extends this attempt at formal program development and verification in [8], which discusses treatment of non-determinism in quantum programs, and in [9], where the attempt is made to build on Aharonov's work [10] to reason about mixed states computations. Zuliani also provides tools to approach the task of compiling quantum programs in [11]. A very similar approach was used in [12] to formally prove the bound on the running time of Grover's algorithm, previously established in [13].

A large amount of work in the area was performed in the past two years. In [14], [15], and [16] process algebraic approaches were explored. Tools developed in the field of category theory were successfully employed by [17], [18], [19], [20], [21], and others to reason about quantum computation. In [22] and [23] a functional language with semantics in a form of a term rewrite system is introduced and a notion of linearity and how it pertains to quantum systems are examined. A functional language QML with design guided by its categorical semantics is defined in [24]. Following on this work, [25] provides a sound and complete equational theory for QML. Weakest preconditions appropriate for quantum computation are introduced in [26]. This work is interesting, in part, because it diverts from the standard approach of reducing a quantum computation to a probabilistic one. It also provides semantics for the language of [21]. Other interesting work by the same authors includes reasoning about knowledge in quantum systems ([27]) and developing a formal model for distributed measurement-based quantum computation ([28]). A similar work is introduced in [29], where a language CQP for modelling communication in quantum systems is defined. The latter approaches have an advantage over process algebraic approaches mentioned earlier in that they explicitly allow a quantum state to be transmitted between processes. Building on the work of [30], [31] defines a higher order quantum programming language based on a linear typed lambda calculus, which is similar to the work of [32].

1.2   Our Contribution

Our approach to quantum programming amenable to formal analysis is very different from almost all of those described above. Work of [6], [8], [9] is the only one which is similar to our work. The contribution of this paper is twofold. Firstly, by building our theory on that in [3], we inherit the advantages it offers. The definitions of specification and program are simpler: a specification is a boolean (or probabilistic) expression and a program is a specification. The treatment of recursion is simple: there is no need for additional semantics of loops. The treatment of termination simply follows from the introduction of a time variable; if the final value of the time variable is ∞, then the program is a non-terminating one. Correctness and time and space complexity are proved in the same fashion; moreover, after proving them separately, we naturally obtain the conjunction. Secondly, the way Probabilistic Predicative Programming is extended to Quantum Predicative Programming is simple and intuitive. The use of Dirac-like notation makes it easy to write down specifications and develop algorithms. The treatment of computation with mixed states does not require any additional mechanisms. Quantum Predicative Programming fully preserves Predicative Programming's treatment of parallel programs and communication, which provides for a natural extension to reason about quantum communication protocols, such as BB84 ([33]), distributed quantum algorithms, such as distributed Shor's algorithm ([34]), as well as their time, space, and entanglement complexity.

2   Preliminaries

2.1   Quantum Computation

In this section we introduce the basic concepts of quantum mechanics, as they pertain to the quantum systems that we will consider for quantum computation. The discussion of the underlying physical processes, spin-$\frac{1}{2}$-particles, etc. is not our interest. We are concerned with the model for quantum computation only. A reader not familiar with quantum computing can consult [35] for a comprehensive introduction to the field.

The *Dirac notation*, invented by Paul Dirac, is often used in quantum mechanics. In this notation a vector v (a column vector by convention) is written inside a *ket*: $|v\rangle$. The dual vector of $|v\rangle$ is $\langle v|$, written inside a *bra*. The inner products are *bra-kets* $\langle v|w\rangle$. For n-dimensional vectors $|u\rangle$ and $|v\rangle$ and m-dimensional vector $|w\rangle$, the value of the inner product $\langle u|v\rangle$ is a scalar and the outer product operator $|v\rangle\langle w|$ corresponds to an m by n matrix. The Dirac notation clearly distinguishes vectors from operators and scalars, and makes it possible to write operators directly as combinations of bras and kets.

In quantum mechanics, the vector spaces of interest are the Hilbert spaces of dimension 2^n for some $n \in \mathbb{N}$. A convenient orthonormal basis is what is called a *computational basis*, in which we label 2^n basis vectors using binary strings of length n as follows: if s is an n-bit string which corresponds to the number x_s, then $|s\rangle$ is a 2^n-bit (column) vector with 1 in position x_s and 0 everywhere else. The tensor product $|i\rangle \otimes |j\rangle$ can be written simply as $|ij\rangle$. An arbitrary vector in a Hilbert space can be written as a weighted sum of the computational basis vectors.

Postulate 1 (state space). Associated to any isolated physical system is a Hilbert space, known as the *state space* of the system. The system is completely described by its *state vector*, which is a unit vector in the system's state space.

Postulate 2 (evolution). The evolution of a closed quantum system is described by a *unitary transformation*.

Postulate 3 (measurement). Quantum measurements are described by a collection $\{M_m\}$ of *measurement operators*, which act on the state space of the system being measured. The index m refers to the possible measurement outcomes. If the state of the system immediately prior to the measurement is described by a vector $|\psi\rangle$, then the probability of obtaining result m is $\langle\psi|M_m^\dagger M_m|\psi\rangle$, in which case the state of the system immediately after the measurement is described by the vector $\dfrac{M_m|\psi\rangle}{\sqrt{\langle\psi|M_m^\dagger M_m|\psi\rangle}}$. The measurement operators satisfy the *completeness equation* $\sum m \cdot M_m^\dagger M_m = I$.

An important special class of measurements is *projective measurements*, which are equivalent to general measurements provided that we also have the ability to perform unitary transformations.

A projective measurement is described by an *observable* M, which is a Hermitian operator on the state space of the system being measured. This observable has a spectral decomposition $M = \sum m \cdot \lambda_m \times P_m$, where P_m is the projector onto the eigenspace of M with eigenvalue λ_m, which corresponds to the outcome of the measurement. The probability of measuring m is $\langle\psi|P_m|\psi\rangle$, in which case immediately after the measurement the system is found in the state $\dfrac{P_m|\psi\rangle}{\sqrt{\langle\psi|P_m|\psi\rangle}}$.

Given an orthonormal basis $|v_m\rangle$, $0 \le m < 2^n$, measurement with respect to this basis is the corresponding projective measurement given by the observable $M = \sum m \cdot \lambda_m \times P_m$, where the projectors are $P_m = |v_m\rangle\langle v_m|$.

Measurement with respect to the computational basis is the simplest and the most commonly used class of measurements. In terms of the basis $|m\rangle$, $0 \le m < 2^n$, the projectors are $P_m = |m\rangle\langle m|$ and $\langle\psi|P_m|\psi\rangle = |\psi_m|^2$. The state of the system immediately after measuring m is $|m\rangle$.

For example, measuring a single qubit in the state $\alpha \times |0\rangle + \beta \times |1\rangle$ results in the outcome 0 with probability $|\alpha|^2$ and outcome 1 with probability $|\beta|^2$. The state of the system immediately after the measurement is $|0\rangle$ or $|1\rangle$, respectively.

Suppose the result of the measurement is ignored and we continue the computation. In this case the system is said to be in a *mixed state*. A mixed state is not the actual physical state of the system. Rather it describes our knowledge of the state the system is in. In the above example, the mixed state is expressed by the equation $|\psi\rangle = |\alpha|^2 \times \{|0\rangle\} + |\beta|^2 \times \{|1\rangle\}$. The equation is meant to say that $|\psi\rangle$ is $|0\rangle$ with probability $|\alpha|^2$ and it is $|1\rangle$ with probability $|\beta|^2$. An application of operation U to the mixed state results in another mixed state, $U(|\alpha|^2 \times \{|0\rangle\} + |\beta|^2 \times \{|1\rangle\}) = |\alpha|^2 \times \{U|0\rangle\} + |\beta|^2 \times \{U|1\rangle\}$.

Postulate 4 (composite systems). The state space of a composite physical system is the tensor product of the state spaces of the component systems. If we have systems numbered 0 up to and excluding n, and each system i, $0 \le i < n$, is prepared in the state $|\psi_i\rangle$, then the joint state of the composite system is $|\psi_0\rangle \otimes |\psi_1\rangle \otimes \ldots \otimes |\psi_{n-1}\rangle$.

While we can always describe a composite system given descriptions of the component systems, the reverse is not true. Indeed, given a state vector that describes a composite system, it may not be possible to factor it to obtain the state vectors of the component systems. A well-known example is the state $|\psi\rangle = |00\rangle/\sqrt{2} + |11\rangle/\sqrt{2}$. Such a state is called an *entangled* state.

2.2   Probabilistic Predicative Programming

This section introduces the programming theory of our choice, on which our work on quantum programming is based — probabilistic predicative programming. We briefly introduce parts of the theory necessary for understanding section 3 of this work. For a course in predicative programming the reader is referred to [2]. An introduction to probabilistic predicative programming can be found in [3].

Predicative programming. In predicative programing a specification is a boolean expression. The variables in a specification represent the quantities of interest, such as prestate (inputs), poststate (outputs), and computation time and space. We use primed variables to describe outputs and unprimed variables to describe inputs. For example, specification $x' = x + 1$ in one integer variable x states that the final value of x is its initial value plus 1. A computation *satisfies* a specification if, given a prestate, it produces a poststate, such that the pair makes the specification true. A specification is *implementable* if for each input state there is at least one output state that satisfies the specification.

We use standard logical notation for writing specifications: $\land$ (conjunction), $\lor$ (disjunction), $\Rightarrow$ (logical implication), $=$ (equality, boolean equivalence), $\neq$ (non-equality, non-equivalence), and **if then else**. The larger operators $==$ and $\Longrightarrow$ are the same as $=$ and $\Rightarrow$, but with lower precedence. We use standard mathematical notation, such as $+ - * / mod$. We use lowercase letters for variables of interest and uppercase letters for specifications.

In addition to the above, we use the following notations: σ (prestate), σ' (poststate), ok ($\sigma' = \sigma$), and $x := e$ ($x' = e \land y' = y \land \ldots$). The notation ok specifies that the values of all variables are unchanged. In the assignment $x := e$, x is a state variable (unprimed) and e is an expression (in unprimed variables) in the domain of x.

If R and S are specifications in variables $x, y, \ldots$, then R'' is obtained from R by substituting all occurrences of primed variables $x', y', \ldots$ with double-primed variables $x'', y'', \ldots$, and S'' is obtained from S by substituting all occurrences of unprimed variables $x, y, \ldots$ with double-primed variables $x'', y'', \ldots$, then the *sequential composition* of R and S is defined by

$$R; S == \exists x'', y'', \ldots \cdot R'' \land S''$$

Various laws can be proven about sequential composition. One of the most important ones is the substitution law, which states that for any expression e of the prestate, state variable x, and specification P,

$$x := e; P == \text{(for } x \text{ substitute } e \text{ in } P)$$

Specification S *is refined by* specification P if and only if S is satisfied whenever P is satisfied:

$$\forall \sigma, \sigma' \cdot S \Leftarrow P$$

Specifications S and P are equal if and only if they are satisfied simultaneously:

$$\forall \sigma, \sigma' \cdot S = P$$

Given a specification, we are allowed to implement an equivalent specification or a stronger one.

Informally, a *bunch* is a collection of objects. It is different from a set, which is a collection of objects in a package. Bunches are simpler than sets; they don't have a nesting structure. See [3] for an introduction to bunch theory. A bunch of one element is the element itself. We use upper-case to denote arbitrary bunches and lower-case to denote elements (an element is the same as a bunch of one element). A, B denotes the union of bunches A and B. $A : B$ denotes bunch inclusion — bunch A is included in bunch B. We use notation $x, ..y$ to mean from (including) x to (excluding) y.

If x is a fresh (previously unused) name, D is a bunch, and b is an arbitrary expression, then $\lambda x : D \cdot b$ is a *function* of a variable (parameter) x with domain D and body b. If f is a function, then Δf denotes the domain of f. If $x : \Delta f$, then fx (f applied to x) is the corresponding element in the range. A function of n variables is a function of 1 variable, whose body is a function of $n - 1$ variables, for $n > 0$. A predicate is function whose body is a boolean expression. A relation is a function whose body is a predicate. A higher-order function is a function whose parameter is a function.

A *quantifier* is a unary prefix operator that applies to functions. If p is a predicate, then $\forall p$ is the boolean result, obtained by first applying p to all the elements in its domain and then taking the conjunction of those results. Taking the disjunction of the results produces $\exists p$. Similarly, if f is a numeric function, then $\sum f$ is the numeric result, obtained by first applying f to all the elements in its domain and then taking the sum of those results.

For example, applying the quantifier $\sum$ to the function $\lambda i : 0, ..2^n \cdot |\psi i|^2$, for some function ψ, yields: $\sum \lambda i : 0, ..2^n \cdot |\psi i|^2$, which for the sake of tradition we abbreviate to $\sum i : 0, ..2^n \cdot |\psi i|^2$. In addition, we allow a few other simplifications. For example, we can omit the domain of a variable if it is clear from the context. We can also group variables from several quantifications. For example, the sum $\sum i : 0, ..2^n \cdot \sum j : 0, ..2^n \cdot 2^{-m-n}$ can be abbreviated to $\sum i, j : 0, ..2^n \cdot 2^{-m-n}$.

A *program* is an implemented specification. For simplicity we only take the following to be implemented: ok, assignment, **if then else**, sequential composition, booleans, numbers, bunches, and functions.

Given a specification S, we proceed as follows. If S is a program, there is no work to be done. If it is not, we build a program P, such that P refines S, i.e. $S \Leftarrow P$. The refinement can proceed in steps: $S \Leftarrow ... \Leftarrow R \Leftarrow Q \Leftarrow P$.

One of the best features of Hehner's theory is its simple treatment of recursion. In $S \Leftarrow P$ it is possible for S to appear in P. No additional rules are required to prove the refinement. For example, it is trivial to prove that

$$x \geq 0 \Rightarrow x' = 0 \Longleftarrow \textbf{if } x = 0 \textbf{ then } ok \textbf{ else } (x := x - 1; x \geq 0 \Rightarrow x' = 0)$$

The specification says that if the initial value of x is non-negative, its final value must be 0. The solution is: if the value of x is zero, do nothing, otherwise decrement x and repeat.

How long does the computation take? To account for time we add a time variable t. We use t to denote the time at which the computation starts, and t'

to denote the time at which the computation ends. In case of non-termination, $t' = \infty$. This is the only characteristic by which we distinguish terminating programs from non-terminating ones. See [36] for a discussion on treatment of termination. We choose to use a *recursive time* measure, in which we charge 1 time unit for each time P is called. We replace each call to P to include the time increment as follows:

$$P \Longleftarrow \text{if } x = 0 \text{ then } ok \text{ else } (x := x - 1; t := t + 1; P)$$

It is easy to see that t is incremented the same number of times that x is decremented, i.e. $t' = t + x$, if $x \geq 0$, and $t' = \infty$, otherwise. Just as above, we can prove:

$$x \geq 0 \wedge t' = t + x \vee x < 0 \wedge t' = \infty$$
$$\Longleftarrow \text{if } x = 0 \text{ then } ok$$
$$\text{else } (x := x - 1; \ t := t + 1; \ x \geq 0 \wedge t' = t + x \vee x < 0 \wedge t' = \infty)$$

Probabilistic predicative programming. Probabilistic predicative programming was introduced in [2] and was further developed in [3]. It is a generalisation of predicative programming that allows reasoning about probability distributions of values of variables of interest. Although in this work we apply this reasoning to boolean and integer variables only, the theory does not change if we want to work with real numbers: we replace summations with integrals.

A *probability* is a real number between 0 and 1, inclusive. A *distribution* is an expression whose value is a probability and whose sum over all values of variables is 1. For example, if n is a positive natural variable, then 2^{-n} is a distribution, since for any n, 2^{-n} is a probability, and $\sum n \cdot 2^{-n} = 1$. In two positive natural variables m and n, 2^{-n-m} is also a distribution. If a distribution of several variables can be written as a product of distributions of the individual variables, then the variables are *independent*. For example, m and n in the previous example are independent. Given a distribution of several variables, we can sum out some of the variables to obtain a distribution of the rest of the variables. In our example, $\sum n \cdot 2^{-n-m} = 2^{-m}$, which is a distribution of m.

To generalise boolean specifications to probabilistic specifications, we use 1 and 0 for boolean *true* and *false*, respectively.[1] If S is an implementable deterministic specification and p is a distribution of the initial state $x, y, ...$, then the distribution of the final state is

$$\sum x, y, ... \cdot S \times p$$

For example, if the initial joint distribution of integers x and y is

$$(x = 0) \times (y = 1)/3 + (x = 1) \times (y = 0) \times 2/3$$

---

[1] Readers familiar with $\top$ and $\bot$ notation can notice that we take the liberty to equate $\top = 1$ and $\bot = 0$.

then after executing the program $x := x + 1$, the distribution is

$$\sum x, y \cdot (x' = x + 1) \times (y' = y) \times$$
$$((x = 0) \times (y = 1)/3 + (x = 1) \times (y = 0) \times 2/3)$$
$$= (x' = 1) \times (y' = 1)/3 + (x' = 2) \times (y' = 0) \times 2/3$$

If R and S are specifications in variables $x, y, \dots$, R'' is obtained from R by substituting all occurrences of primed variables $x', y', \dots$ with double-primed variables $x'', y'', \dots$, and S'' is obtained from S by substituting all occurrences of unprimed variables $x, y, \dots$ with double-primed variables $x'', y'', \dots$, then the *sequential composition* of R and S is defined by

$$R; S = \sum x'', y'', \dots \cdot R'' \times S''$$

If p is a probability and R and S are distributions, then

if p **then** R **else** $S = p \times R + (1 - p) \times S$

Various laws can be proven about sequential composition. One of the most important ones, the substitution law, introduced earlier, applies to probabilistic specifications as well.

To implement a probabilistic specification we use a random (or pseudo-random) number generator. For a positive natural variable n, we say that *rand* n produces a random natural number uniformly distributed in $0, ..n$. To reason about the values supplied by the random number generator consistently, we replace every occurrence of *rand* n with a fresh variable r whose value has probability $(r : 0, ..n)/n$. If *rand* occurs in a context such as $r = rand\ n$, we replace the equation by $(r : 0, ..n)/n$. If *rand* occurs in the context of a loop, we parametrise the introduced variables by the execution time.

Recall the earlier example. Let us change the program slightly by introducing probabilism:

$$P \Longleftarrow \textbf{if } x = 0 \textbf{ then } ok \textbf{ else } (x := x - rand\ 2; t := t + 1; P)$$

In the new program at each iteration x is either decremented by 1 or it is unchanged, with equal probability. Our intuition tells us that the revised program should still work, except it should take longer. Let us prove it. We replace *rand* with $r : time \rightarrow (0, 1)$ with rt having probability $1/2$. We choose the domain *time* according to the task at hand: reals, integers, naturals, etc. Ignoring time we can prove:

$$x \geq 0 \Rightarrow x' = 0$$
$$\Longleftarrow \textbf{if } x = 0 \textbf{ then } ok \textbf{ else } (x := x - rand\ 2; x \geq 0 \Rightarrow x' = 0)$$

As for the execution time, we can prove that it takes at least x time units to complete:

$$t' \geq t + x$$
$$\Longleftarrow \textbf{if } x = 0 \textbf{ then } ok \textbf{ else } (x := x - rand\ 2; t := t + 1; t' \geq t + x)$$

How long should we expect to wait for the execution to complete? In other words, what is the distribution of t'? Consider the following distribution of the final states:

$$(0 = x' = x = t' - t) + (0 = x' < x \leq t' - t) \times \binom{t' - t - 1}{x - 1} \times \frac{1}{2^{t'-t}},$$

$$\text{where} \quad \binom{n}{m} = \frac{n!}{m! \times (n - m)!}$$

We can prove that:

$$\sum rt \cdot \frac{1}{2} \times \Bigg(\text{ if } x = 0 \text{ then } ok$$

$$\textbf{else} \left(x := x - rt; \ t := t + 1; \right.$$

$$(0 = x' = x = t' - t) +$$

$$\left. (0 = x' < x \leq t' - t) \times \binom{t' - t - 1}{x - 1} \times \frac{1}{2^{t'-t}} \right) \Bigg)$$

$$= (0 = x' = x = t' = t) \ + (0 = x' < x \leq t' - t) \times \binom{t' - t - 1}{x - 1} \times \frac{1}{2^{t'-t}}$$

Now, since for positive x, t' is distributed according to the negative binomial distribution with parameters x and $\frac{1}{2}$, its mean value is

$$\sum t' \cdot (t' - t) \times \Bigg((0 = x = t' - t) + (0 < x \leq t' - t) \times \binom{t' - t - 1}{x - 1} \times \frac{1}{2^{t'-t}} \Bigg)$$

$$= 2 \times x + t$$

Therefore, we should expect to wait $2 \times x$ time units for the computation to complete. Notice that the theory tells us more than the expected time; it tells us the distribution of times.

3   Quantum Predicative Programming

This section is the contribution of the paper. Here we define the quantum system, introduce programming with the quantum system and several well-known problems, their classical and quantum solutions, and their formal comparative time complexity analyses. The proofs of refinements are omitted for the sake of brevity. The reader is referred to [37] for detailed proofs of some of the algorithms.

3.1   The Quantum System

Let $\mathbb{C}$ be the set of all complex numbers with the absolute value operator $|\cdot|$ and the complex conjugate operator $*$. Then a state of an n-qubit system is a function $\psi : 0, ..2^n \to \mathbb{C}$, such that $\sum x : 0, ..2^n \cdot |\psi x|^2 = 1$.

If ψ and ϕ are two states of an n-qubit system, then their *inner product*, denoted by $\langle\psi|\phi\rangle$, is defined by[2]:

$$\langle\psi|\phi\rangle = \sum x : 0, ..2^n \cdot (\psi x)^* \times (\phi x)$$

A *basis* of an n-qubit system is a collection of 2^n quantum states $b_{0,..2^n}$, such that $\forall i, j : 0, ..2^n \cdot \langle b_i|b_j\rangle = (i = j)$.

We adopt the following Dirac-like notation for the computational basis: if x is from the domain $0, ..2^n$, then $\mathbf{x}$ denotes the corresponding n-bit binary encoding of x and $|\mathbf{x}\rangle : 0, ..2^n \to \mathbb{C}$ is the following quantum state:

$$|\mathbf{x}\rangle = \lambda i : 0, ..2^n \cdot (i = x)$$

If ψ is a state of an m-qubit system and ϕ is a state of an n-qubit system, then $\psi \otimes \phi$, the tensor product of ψ and ϕ, is the following state of a composite $m + n$-qubit system:

$$\psi \otimes \phi = \lambda i : 0, ..2^{m+n} \cdot \psi(i \ div \ 2^n) \times \phi(i \ mod \ 2^n)$$

We write $^{\otimes n}$ to mean *tensored with itself n times*.

An operation defined on an n-qubit quantum system is a higher-order function, whose domain and range are maps from $0, ..2^n$ to the complex numbers. An *identity* operation on a state of an n-qubit system is defined by

$$I^n = \lambda\psi : 0, ..2^n \to \mathbb{C} \cdot \psi$$

For a linear operation A, the *adjoint* of A, written $A^\dagger$, is the (unique) operation, such that for any two states ψ and ϕ, $\langle\psi|A\phi\rangle = \langle A^\dagger\psi|\phi\rangle$.

The *unitary transformations* that describe the evolution of an n-qubit quantum system are operations U defined on the system, such that $U^\dagger U = I^n$.

In this setting, the *tensor product* of operators is defined in the usual way. If ψ is a state of an m-qubit system, ϕ is a state of an n-qubit system, and U and V are operations defined on m and n-qubit systems, respectively, then the tensor product of U and V is defined on an $m + n$ qubit system by $(U \otimes V)(\psi \otimes \phi) = (U\psi) \otimes (V\phi)$.

Just as with tensor products of states, we write $U^{\otimes n}$ to mean *operation U tensored with itself n times*.

Suppose we have a system of n qubits in state ψ and we measure it. Suppose also that we have a variable r from the domain $0, ..2^n$, which we use to record the result of the measurement, and variables $x, y, \ldots$, which are not affected by the measurement. Then the measurement corresponds to a probabilistic specification that gives the probability distribution of ψ' and r' (these depend on ψ and on the type of measurement) and states that the variables $x, y, \ldots$ are unchanged.

For a general quantum measurement described by a collection $M = M_{0,..2^n}$ of measurement operators, which satisfy the completeness equation, the specification is **measure**$_M \psi r$, where

---

[2] We should point out that this kind of function operations is referred to as *lifting*.

$$\textbf{measure}_M \, \psi \, r \ = \ \langle \psi | M_{r'}^{\dagger} M_{r'} \psi \rangle \times \left(\psi' = \frac{M_{r'} \psi}{\sqrt{\langle \psi | M_{r'}^{\dagger} M_{r'} \psi \rangle}} \right) \times (\sigma' = \sigma)$$

where $\sigma' = \sigma$ is an abbreviation of $(x' = x) \times (y' = y) \times \dots$ and means "all other variables are unchanged".

To obtain the distribution of, say, r' we sum out the rest of the variables as follows:

$$\sum \psi', x', y', \dots \cdot \langle \psi | M_{r'}^{\dagger} M_{r'} \psi \rangle \times \left(\psi' = \frac{M_{r'} \psi}{\sqrt{\langle \psi | M_{r'}^{\dagger} M_{r'} \psi \rangle}} \right) \times (\sigma' = \sigma)$$

$$= \langle \psi | M_{r'}^{\dagger} M_{r'} \psi \rangle$$

For projective measurements defined by an observable $O = \sum m \cdot \lambda_m \times P_m$, where P_m is the projector on the eigenspace of O with eigenvalue λ_m:

$$\textbf{measure}_O \, \psi \, r \ = \ \langle \psi | P_{r'} \psi \rangle \times \left(\psi' = \frac{P_r' \psi}{\sqrt{\langle \psi | P_r' \psi \rangle}} \right) \times (\sigma' = \sigma)$$

Given an arbitrary orthonormal basis $B = b_{0,\dots 2^n}$, measurement of ψ in basis B is:

$$\textbf{measure}_B \, \psi \, r \ = \ |\langle b_{r'} | \psi \rangle|^2 \times (\psi' = b_{r'}) \times (\sigma' = \sigma)$$

Finally, the simplest and the most commonly used measurement in the computational basis is:

$$\textbf{measure} \, \psi \, r \ = \ |\psi r'|^2 \times (\psi' = |\textbf{r'}\rangle) \times (\sigma' = \sigma)$$

In this case the distribution of r' is $|\psi r'|^2$ and the distribution of the quantum state is:

$$\sum r' \cdot |\psi r'|^2 \times (\psi' = |\textbf{r'}\rangle)$$

which is precisely the mixed quantum state that results from the measurement.

In order to develop quantum programs we need to add to our list of implemented things from section 2.2. We add variables of type quantum state as above and we allow the following three kinds of operations on these variables. If ψ is a state of an n-qubit quantum system, r is a natural variable, and M is a collection of measurement operators that satisfy the completeness equation, then:

1. $\psi := |0\rangle^{\otimes n}$ is a program
2. $\psi := U\psi$, where U is a unitary transformation on an n-qubit system, is a program
3. $\textbf{measure}_M \, \psi \, r$ is a program

The special cases of measurements, described in section 2.1, are therefore also allowed: for an observable O, **measure**$_O$ $q\,r$ is a program; for an orthonormal basis B, **measure**$_B$ $q\,r$ is a program; finally, **measure** $q\,r$ is a program.

The *Hadamard* transform, widely used in quantum algorithms, is defined on a 1-qubit system and in our setting is a higher-order function from $0,1 \to \mathbb{C}$ to $0,1 \to \mathbb{C}$:

$$H = \lambda \psi : 0,1 \to \mathbb{C} \cdot i : 0,1 \cdot (\psi 0 + (-1)^i \times \psi 1)/\sqrt{2}$$

The operation $H^{\otimes n}$ on an n-qubit system applies H to every qubit of the system. Its action on a zero state of an n-qubit system is:

$$H^{\otimes n}|0\rangle^{\otimes n} = \sum x : 0,..2^n \cdot |\mathbf{x}\rangle/\sqrt{2^n}$$

On a general state $|\mathbf{x}\rangle$, the action of $H^{\otimes n}$ is:

$$H^{\otimes n}|\mathbf{x}\rangle = \sum y : 0,..2^n \cdot (-1)^{\mathbf{x}\cdot\mathbf{y}} \times |\mathbf{y}\rangle/\sqrt{2^n}$$

where $\mathbf{x} \cdot \mathbf{y}$ is the inner product of $\mathbf{x}$ and $\mathbf{y}$ modulo 2.

Another important definition is that of the quantum analog of a classical oracle f:

$$U_f = \lambda \psi : 0,1 \to \mathbb{C} \cdot x : 0,1 \cdot (-1)^{fx} \times \psi x$$

3.2   Deutsch Algorithm

In this section we look at one of the most famous quantum algorithms, Deutsch's algorithm [38]. The task is: given an oracle function $f : 0,1 \to 0,1$, compute $f0 \oplus f1$. For now, we ignore the restriction on the number of queries to the oracle. With natural x, the specification is:

$$x' = f0 \oplus f1$$

A simple classical solution is $x := f(0) \oplus f(1)$.

Let us develop a quantum solution. With a state ψ of a 1-qubit system:

$$
\begin{aligned}
&x' = f0 \oplus f1 && \text{arithmetic}\\
&= |\,(((-1)^{f0}/2 + (-1)^{f1}/2) \times |0\rangle + \\
&\quad\ ((-1)^{f0}/2 - (-1)^{f1}/2) \times |1\rangle)\,x'|^2 && \text{measure}\\
&= \textbf{measure}\ (((-1)^{f0}/2 + (-1)^{f1}/2) \times |0\rangle + \\
&\qquad\qquad\ ((-1)^{f0}/2 - (-1)^{f1}/2) \times |1\rangle)\ x && \text{arithmetic}\\
&= \textbf{measure}\ ((-1)^{f0}/2 \times (|0\rangle + |1\rangle) + \\
&\qquad\qquad\ (-1)^{f1}/2 \times (|0\rangle - |1\rangle))\ x && \text{Hadamard}\\
&= \textbf{measure}\ ((-1)^{f0}/\sqrt{2} \times (H|0\rangle) + (-1)^{f1}/\sqrt{2} \times (H|1\rangle))\ x && \text{linearity}
\end{aligned}
$$

$$\begin{aligned}
&= \textbf{measure } H((-1)^{f0}/\sqrt{2} \times |0\rangle + (-1)^{f1}/\sqrt{2} \times |1\rangle) \, x && \text{Oracle}\\
&= \textbf{measure } H(U_f|0\rangle/\sqrt{2} + U_f|1\rangle/\sqrt{2}) \, x && \text{linearity}\\
&= \textbf{measure } H(U_f(|0\rangle/\sqrt{2} + |1\rangle/\sqrt{2})) \, x && \text{Hadamard}\\
&= \textbf{measure } H(U_f(H|0\rangle)) \, x && \text{substitutions}\\
&= \psi := |0\rangle;\ \psi := H\psi;\ \psi := U_f\psi;\ \psi := H\psi;\ \textbf{measure } \psi \, x
\end{aligned}$$

So far we have two solutions — a simple classical one and a complicated quantum one. Let us add the restriction on the number of allowed calls to the oracle. We add a time variable t and decide to charge 1 unit of time for a call to the oracle, leaving all other operations free. The new specification is:

$$x' = f0 \oplus f1 \wedge t' = t + 1$$

The above quantum solution still works:

$$\begin{aligned}
& x' = f0 \oplus f1 \wedge t' = t + 1\\
&= \psi := |0\rangle;\ \psi := H\psi;\ t := t + 1;\ \psi := U_f\psi;\ \psi := H\psi;\ \textbf{measure } \psi \, x
\end{aligned}$$

The new specification with the above way of charging time is clearly unimplementable classically. The corresponding strongest classically implementable specification is:

$$x' = f0 \oplus f1 \wedge t' \leq t + 2$$

3.3   Deutsch-Jozsa Algorithm

Deutsch-Jozsa's problem ([39]), an extension of Deutsch's Problem, is an example of the broad class of quantum algorithms that are based on the quantum Fourier transform ([40]). The task is: given a function $f : 0, ..2^n \rightarrow 0, 1$, such that f is either constant or balanced, determine which case it is. Without any restrictions on the number of calls to f, we can write the specification (let us call it S) as follows:

$$(f \text{ is constant} \vee f \text{ is balanced}) \implies b' = f \text{ is constant}$$

where b is a boolean variable and the informally stated properties of f are defined formally as follows:

$$\begin{aligned}
f \text{ is constant} &= \forall i : 0, ..2^n \cdot fi = f0\\
f \text{ is balanced} &= \left| \sum i : 0, ..2^n \cdot (-1)^{fi} \right| = 0
\end{aligned}$$

It is easy to show that

$$\begin{aligned}
&(f \text{ is constant} \vee f \text{ is balanced})\\
&\implies (f \text{ is constant} = \forall (i : 0, ..2^{n-1} + 1) \cdot fi = f0)
\end{aligned}$$

That is, more than half of the values need to be equal to $f0$.

In our setting, we need to implement the specification R defined as follows:

$$b' == \forall i : (0, ..2^{n-1} + 1) \cdot fi = f0$$

The quantum solution is a direct generalisation of Deutsch's algorithm. The idea is to create a suitable superposition for state ψ, so that a measurement of ψ produces 0 if and only if f is constant, so that:

$$S \Longleftarrow Q; \; b := (r = 0) \qquad , \text{ where}$$
$$Q == f \text{ is constant} \vee f \text{ is balanced} \Rightarrow f \text{ is constant} = (r' = 0)$$

To implement Q we notice that:

$$f \text{ is constant} == \left(\left| \sum x \cdot (-1)^{fx} / 2^n \right| = 1 \right)$$
$$f \text{ is balanced} == \left(\left| \sum x \cdot (-1)^{fx} / 2^n \right| = 0 \right)$$

We can show that if f is constant $\vee$ f is balanced, variables $x, y,$ and z are from the domain $0, ..2^n$, and $\mathbf{x} \cdot \mathbf{z}$ is the dot product of $\mathbf{x}$ and $\mathbf{z}$, then:

$$f \text{ is constant} = (r' = 0)$$
$$\Longleftarrow \left| \left(\sum z, x \cdot (-1)^{\mathbf{x} \cdot \mathbf{z} + fx} / 2^n \times |\mathbf{z}\rangle \right) r' \right|^2$$
$$= \mathbf{measure} \left(\sum x \cdot (-1)^{fx} / \sqrt{2^n} \times \left(\sum z \cdot (-1)^{\mathbf{x} \cdot \mathbf{z}} / \sqrt{2^n} \times |\mathbf{z}\rangle \right) \right) r$$
$$= \mathbf{measure} \left(H^{\otimes n} (U_f (H^{\otimes n} |0\rangle^{\otimes n})) \right) r$$
$$= \psi := |0\rangle^{\otimes n}; \; \psi := H^{\otimes n} \psi; \; \psi := U_f \psi; \; \psi := H^{\otimes n} \psi; \; \mathbf{measure} \; \psi r$$

The complete solution is:

$$\psi := |0\rangle^{\otimes n}; \; \psi := H^{\otimes n} \psi; \; \psi := U_f \psi; \; \psi := H^{\otimes n} \psi; \; \mathbf{measure} \; \psi r; \; b := (r' = 0)$$

Let us add to the specification a restriction on the number of calls to the oracle by introducing a time variable. Suppose the new specification is:

$$(f \text{ is constant} \vee f \text{ is balanced} \Longrightarrow b' = f \text{ is constant}) \wedge (t' = t + 1)$$

where we charge 1 unit of time for each call to the oracle and all other operations are free. Clearly, the above quantum solution works.

Classically the specification is unimplementable. The strongest classically implementable specification is

$$(f \text{ is constant} \vee f \text{ is balanced} \Longrightarrow b' = f \text{ is constant}) \wedge (t' \le t + 2^{n-1} + 1)$$

3.4   Grover's Search

Grover's quantum search algorithm ([41], [42]) is well-known for the quadratic speed-up it offers in the solutions of NP-complete problems. The algorithm is optimal up to a multiplicative constant ([13]). The task is: given a function $f : 0, ..2^n \to 0, 1$, find $x : 0, ..2^n$, such that $f x = 1$. For simplicity we assume that there is only a single solution, which we denote x_1, i.e. $f x_1 = 1$ and $f x = 0$ for all $x \neq x_1$. The proofs are not very different for a general case of more than one solutions.

As before, we use a general quantum oracle, defined by

$$U_f |\mathbf{x}\rangle = (-1)^{fx} \times |\mathbf{x}\rangle$$

In addition, we define the *inversion about mean* operator as follows:

$$M : (0, ..N \to \mathbb{C}) \to (0, ..N \to \mathbb{C})$$

$$M\psi = \lambda x : 0, ..N \cdot 2 \times \left(\sum i : 0, ..N \cdot \psi i / N \right) - \psi x$$

where $N = 2^n$.

Grover's algorithm initialises the quantum system to an equally weighted superposition of all basis states $|\mathbf{x}\rangle$, $x : 0, ..N$. It then repeatedly applies U_f followed by M to the system. Finally, the state is measured. The probability of error is determined by the number of iterations performed by the algorithm.

The algorithm is easily understood with the help of a geometric analysis of the operators. Let α be the sum over all x, which are not solutions, and let β be the solution:

$$\alpha = \frac{1}{\sqrt{N-1}} \times \sum x \neq x_1 \cdot |\mathbf{x}\rangle$$

$$\beta = |\mathbf{x}_1\rangle$$

Then the oracle U_f performs a *reflection* about the vector α in the plane defined by α and β. In other words, $U_f(a \times \alpha + b \times \beta) = a \times \alpha - b \times \beta$. Similarly, the inversion about mean operator is a reflection about the vector ψ in the plane defined by α and β. Therefore, the result of U_f followed by M is a *rotation* in this plane. We define θ to be the rotation angle:

$$\theta = 2 \times \arcsin \sqrt{1/N}$$

Since each rotation leaves us in the plane defined by α and β, then the state of the system after i rotations by θ radians is:

$$\psi_i = \cos((2 \times i + 1) \times \theta/2) \times \alpha + \sin((2 \times i + 1) \times \theta/2) \times \beta$$

Suppose we charge one unit of time for each call to the oracle and all other operations are free. The specification of the problem is then:

$$S = \left(\sin \left((2 \times (t' - t) + 1) \times \arcsin \sqrt{1/N} \right) \right)^2 \times (r' = x_1) +$$
$$\left(1 - \left(\sin \left((2 \times (t' - t) + 1) \times \arcsin \sqrt{1/N} \right) \right)^2 \right) \times (r' \neq x_1)/(N - 1)$$

where r is the result variable from the domain $0,..N$. The specification says that we want the solution $\left(\sin((2 \times (t' - t) + 1) \times \arcsin \sqrt{1/N})\right)^2$ of the time, where $t' - t$ is the number of times we use the oracle.

As before, we want to specify the quantum state that, when measured, gives the desired distribution. With a quantum state variable $\psi : 0,..N \to \mathbb{C}$, we can show

$$S \Longleftarrow \psi' = \sin((2 \times (t' - t) + 1) \times \theta/2) \times \beta +$$
$$\cos((2 \times (t' - t) + 1) \times \theta/2) \times \alpha;$$

measure $\psi\ r$

Let P be the description of the quantum state immediately before the measurement.

$$P \Longleftarrow \psi' = \psi_{t'-t}$$

Since $\psi_{t'-t}$ is the state obtained by $t' - t$ rotations by θ radians, we define the specification R to describe the rotation. With a natural k that represents the number of iterations performed:

$$R \Longleftarrow \psi = \psi_i \Rightarrow \psi' = \psi_k \wedge t' = t + k - i$$

Adding initialisation, we prove:

$$P \Longleftarrow i := 0;\ \psi := \psi_0;\ R$$

Our task has been simplified. We now need to implement $\psi := \psi_0$ and R and we are done. Implementing the assignment is trivial:

$$\psi := |0\rangle^{\otimes n};\ \psi := H^{\otimes n}\psi$$

Having understood the geometry of Grover's algorithm, implementing R is easy. After adding the time increment before the call to the oracle, we can show:

$$R \Longleftarrow \text{if } i = k \text{ then } ok \text{ else } (i := i + 1;\ t := t+1;\ \psi := U_f\psi;\ \psi := M\psi;\ R)$$

Note that specification R is recursive. The ease with which recursion is treated in Predicative Programming allows us to easily translate our geometric understanding of the problem into an implementable specification.

The complete quantum solution is

$$S \Longleftarrow \left(\sin\left((2 \times (t' - t) + 1) \times \arcsin \sqrt{1/N}\right)\right)^2 \times (r' = x_1) +$$
$$\left(1 - \left(\sin\left((2 \times (t' - t) + 1) \times \arcsin \sqrt{1/N}\right)\right)^2\right) \times$$
$$(r' \neq x_1)/(N - 1)$$
$$= P;\ \textbf{measure } \psi\ r$$

$$P \Longleftarrow i := 0;\ \psi := |0\rangle^{\otimes n};\ \psi := H^{\otimes n}\psi;\ R$$
$$R \Longleftarrow \textbf{if } i = k \textbf{ then } ok$$
$$\textbf{else } (i := i+1;\ t := t+1;\ \psi := U_f\psi;\ \psi := M\psi;\ R)$$

Specification S carries a lot of useful information. For example, it tells us that the probability of finding a solution after k iterations is

$$\left(\sin((2 \times k + 1) \times \arcsin\sqrt{1/N})\right)^2$$

Or we might ask how many iterations should be performed to minimise the probability of an error. Examining first and second derivatives, we find that the above probability is minimised when $t' - t = (\pi \times i)/(4 \times \arcsin\sqrt{1/N}) - 1/2$ for integer i. Of course, the number of iterations performed must be a natural number. It is interesting to note that the probability of error is periodic in the number of iterations, but since we don't gain anything by performing extra iterations, we pick $i = 1$. Finally, assuming $1 \ll N = 2^n$, we obtain an elegant approximation to the optimal number of iterations: $\lceil \pi \times \sqrt{2^n}/4 \rceil$, with the probability of error approximately $1/2^n$.

3.5 Computing with Mixed States

As we have discussed in section 2.1, the state of a quantum system after a measurement is traditionally described as a *mixed state*. An equation $\psi = \{|0\rangle\}/2 + \{|1\rangle\}/2$ should be understood as follows: the state ψ is $|0\rangle$ with probability $1/2$ and it is $|1\rangle$ with probability $1/2$. In contrast to a pure state, a mixed state does not describe a physical state of the system. Rather, it describes our knowledge of what state the system is in.

In our framework, there is no need for an additional mechanism to compute with mixed states. Indeed, a mixed state is not a system state, but a distribution over system states, and all our programming notions apply to distributions. The above mixed state is the following distribution over a quantum state ψ of a single-qubit system: $(\psi = |0\rangle)/2 + (\psi = |1\rangle)/2$. This expression tells us, for each possible value in the domain of ψ, the probability of ψ having that value. For example, ψ is the state $|0\rangle$ with probability $(|0\rangle = |0\rangle)/2 + (|0\rangle = |1\rangle)/2$, which is $1/2$; it is $|1\rangle$ with probability $(|1\rangle = |0\rangle)/2 + (|1\rangle = |1\rangle)/2$, which is also $1/2$; for any scalars α and β, not equal to 0 or 1, ψ is equal to $\alpha \times |0\rangle + \beta \times |1\rangle$ with probability $(\alpha \times |0\rangle + \beta \times |1\rangle = |0\rangle)/2 + (\alpha \times |0\rangle + \beta \times |1\rangle = |1\rangle)/2$, which is 0. One way to obtain this distribution is to measure an equally weighted superposition of $|0\rangle$ and $|1\rangle$:

$$\psi' = |0\rangle/\sqrt{2} + |1\rangle/\sqrt{2};\ \textbf{measure } \psi\, r \qquad\qquad \text{measure}$$
$$= \psi' = |0\rangle/\sqrt{2} + |1\rangle/\sqrt{2};\ |\psi r'|^2 \times (\psi' = |\mathbf{r'}\rangle) \qquad \text{sequential composition}$$
$$= \sum r'', \psi'' \cdot (\psi'' = |0\rangle/\sqrt{2} + |1\rangle/\sqrt{2}) \times |\psi''r'|^2 \times (\psi' = |\mathbf{r'}\rangle)$$
$$= |(|0\rangle/\sqrt{2} + |1\rangle/\sqrt{2}) r'|^2 \times (\psi' = |\mathbf{r'}\rangle)$$
$$= (\psi' = |\mathbf{r'}\rangle)/2$$

Distribution of the quantum state is then:

$$\sum r' \cdot (\psi' = |\mathbf{r'}\rangle)/2 \;=\; (\psi' = |0\rangle)/2 + (\psi' = |1\rangle)/2$$

as desired.

Similarly, there is no need to extend the application of unitary operators. Consider the following toy program:

$$\psi := |0\rangle; \; \psi := H\psi; \; \textbf{measure } \psi\, r; \; \textbf{if } r = 0 \textbf{ then } \psi := H\psi \textbf{ else } ok$$

In the second application of Hadamard the quantum state is mixed, but this is not evident from the syntax of the program. It is only in the analysis of the final quantum state that the notion of a mixed state is meaningful. The operator is applied to a (pure) system state, though we are unsure what that state is.

$$\psi := |0\rangle; \; \psi := H\psi; \; \textbf{measure } \psi\, r;$$

$$\qquad \textbf{if } r = 0 \textbf{ then } \psi := H\psi \textbf{ else } ok \qquad\qquad\qquad \text{as before}$$

$$= (\psi' = |\mathbf{r'}\rangle)/2;$$

$$\qquad \textbf{if } r = 0 \textbf{ then } \psi := H\psi \textbf{ else } ok \qquad\qquad \text{sequential composition}$$

$$= \sum r'', \psi'' \cdot (\psi'' = |\mathbf{r''}\rangle)/2 \times$$
$$\qquad\qquad ((r'' = 0) \times (\psi' = H\psi'') \times (r' = r'') +$$
$$\qquad\qquad (r'' = 1) \times (\psi' = \psi'') \times (r' = r'')) \qquad \text{one point law}$$

$$= ((\psi' = H|0\rangle) \times (r' = 0) + (\psi' = |1\rangle) \times (r' = 1))/2$$

$$= (\psi' = |0\rangle/\sqrt{2} + |1\rangle/\sqrt{2}) \times (r' = 0)/2 +$$
$$\quad (\psi' = |1\rangle) \times (r' = 1)/2$$

The distribution of the quantum state after the computation is:

$$\sum r' \cdot (\psi' = |0\rangle/\sqrt{2} + |1\rangle/\sqrt{2}) \times (r' = 0)/2 + (\psi' = |1\rangle) \times (r' = 1)/2$$
$$= (\psi' = |0\rangle/\sqrt{2} + |1\rangle/\sqrt{2})/2 + (\psi' = |1\rangle)/2$$

A lot of properties of measurements and mixed states can be proven from the definitions of measurement and sequential composition. For example, the fact that a measurement in the computational basis, performed immediately following a measurement in the same basis, does not change the state of the system and yields the same result as the first measurement with probability 1, is proven as follows:

$$\textbf{measure } \psi\, r; \; \textbf{measure } \psi\, r \qquad\qquad\qquad\qquad \text{measure}$$

$$= |\psi\, r'|^2 \times (\psi' = |\mathbf{r'}\rangle); \; |\psi\, r'|^2 \times (\psi' = |\mathbf{r'}\rangle) \qquad \text{sequential composition}$$

$$= \sum \psi'', r'' \cdot |\psi\, r''|^2 \times (\psi'' = |\mathbf{r''}\rangle) \times |\psi''\, r'|^2 \times (\psi' = |\mathbf{r'}\rangle) \quad \text{one point law}$$

$$= |\psi\, r'|^2 \times (\psi' = |\mathbf{r'}\rangle) \qquad\qquad\qquad\qquad\qquad \text{measure}$$

$$= \textbf{measure } \psi\, r$$

In case of a general quantum measurement, the proof is similar, but a little more computationally involved.

4   Conclusion and Future Work

We have presented a new approach to developing, analysing, and proving correctness of quantum programs. Since we adopt Hehner's theory as the basis for our work, we inherit its advantageous features, such as simplicity, generality, and elegance. Our work extends probabilistic predicative programming in the same fashion that quantum computation extends probabilistic computation. We have provided tools to write quantum as well as classical specifications, develop quantum and classical solutions for them, and analyse various properties of quantum specifications and quantum programs, such as implementability, time and space complexity, and probabilistic error analysis uniformly, all in the same framework.

Current research and research in the immediate future involve reasoning about distributed quantum computation. Current work involves expressing quantum teleportation, dense coding, and various games involving entanglement, in a way that makes complexity analysis of these quantum algorithms simple and natural. These issues will be described in a forthcoming paper. We can easily express teleportation as refinement of a specification $\phi' = \psi$, for distinct qubits ϕ and ψ, in a well-known fashion. However, we are more interested in the possibilities of simple proofs and analysis of programs involving communication, both via quantum channels and exhibiting the LOCC (local operations, classical communication) paradigm. Future work involves formalising quantum cryptographic protocols, such as BB84 [33], in our framework and providing formal analysis of these protocols. This will naturally lead to formal analysis of distributed quantum algorithms (e.g. distributed Shor's algorithm of [34]).

References

1. Knill, E.: Conventions for quantum pseudocode. Techn. Report LAUR-96-2724. Los Alamos National Laboratory (1996)
2. Hehner, E.: A Practical Theory of Programming. Springer-Verlag (1993) New edition available free at http://www.cs.utoronto.ca/~hehner/aPToP/.
3. Hehner, E.: Probabilistic predicative programming. In Kozen, D., Shankland, C., eds.: Proc. of 7th Int. Conf. on Mathematics of Program Construction. Vol. 3125 of Lect. Notes in Comput. Sci. Springer-Verlag (2004) 169–185
4. Ömer, B.: Quantum programming in QCL. Master's thesis. TU Vienna (2000)
5. Bettelli, S., Calarco, T., Serafini, L.: Toward an architecture for quantum programming. European Physical J. D **25**(2) (2003) 181–200
6. Sanders, J.W., Zuliani, P.: Quantum programming. In Backhouse, R.C., Oliveira, J.N., eds.: Proc. of 5th Int. Conf. on Mathematics of Program Construction. Vol. 1837 of Lect. Notes in Comput. Sci. Springer-Verlag (2000) 80–99
7. Morgan, C., McIver, A.: pQCL: formal reasoning for random algorithms. South African Computer J. **22** (1999) 14–27
8. Zuliani, P.: Non-deterministic quantum programming. In: QPL 2004. (2004) 179–195
9. Zuliani, P.: Quantum programming with mixed states. In: QPL 2005. (2005)
10. Aharonov, D., Kitaev, A., Nisan, N.: Quantum circuits with mixed states. In Proc. of 30th Ann. ACM Symp. on Theory of Computing, STOC 98. ACM Press (1998) 20 – 30

11. Zuliani, P.: Compiling quantum programs. Acta Inform. **41**(7-8) (2005) 435–474
12. Butler, M.J., Hartel, P.H.: Reasoning about grover's quantum search algorithm using probabilistic wp. ACM Trans. on Program. Lang. and Syst. **21**(3) (1999) 417–429
13. Boyer, M., Brassard, G., Høyer, P., Tapp, A.: Tight bounds on quantum searching. In: Fortschritte der Physik. (1998) 493–506
14. Adao, P., Mateus, P.: A process algebra for reasoning about quantum security. In QPL 2005. (2005)
15. Lalire, M., Jorrand, P.: A process algebraic approach to concurrent and distributed quantum computation: operational semantics. In QPL 2004. (2004) 109–126
16. Jorrand, P., Lalire, M.: Toward a quantum process algebra. In Proc. of 1st ACM Conf. on Computing Frontiers. ACM Press (2004) 111–119
17. Abramsky, S.: High-level methods for quantum computation and information. In Proc. of 19th Ann. IEEE Symp. on Logic in Computer Science, LICS 2004. IEEE Comput. Soc. Press (2004) 410–414
18. Abramsky, S., Coecke, B.: A categorical semantics of quantum protocols. In Proc. of 19th Ann. IEEE Symp. on Logic in Computer Science, LICS 2004. IEEE Comput. Soc. Press (2004) 415–425
19. Abramsky, S., Duncan, R.: A categorical quantum logic. In QPL 2004. (2004) 3–20
20. Coecke, B.: The logic of entanglement. quant-ph/0402014 (2004)
21. Selinger, P.: Towards a quantum programming language. Math. Struct. in Comput. Sci. **14**(4) (2004) 527–586
22. Arrighi, P., Dowek, G.: Operational semantics for formal tensorial calculus. In QPL 2004. (2004) 21–38
23. Arrighi, P., Dowek, G.: Linear-algebraic lambda-calculus. In QPL 2005. (2005)
24. Altenkirch, T., Grattage, J.: A functional quantum programming language. In Proc. of 20th Ann. IEEE Symp. on Logic in Computer Science, LICS '05. IEEE Comput. Soc. Press (2005) 249–258
25. Altenkirch, T., Grattage, J., Vizzotto, J.K., Sabry, A.: An algebra of pure quantum programming. In QPL 2005. (2005)
26. D'Hondt, E., Panangaden, P.: Quantum weakest precondition. In QPL 2004. (2004) 75–90
27. D'Hondt, E., Panangaden, P.: Reasoning about quantum knowledge. quant-ph/0507176 (2005)
28. Danos, V., D'Hondt, E., Kashefi, E., Panangaden, P.: Distributed measurement-based quantum computation. In QPL 2005. (2005)
29. Gay, S.J., Nagarajan, R.: Communicating quantum processes. In Proc. of 32nd ACM SIGACT-SIGPLAN Symp. on Principles of Programming Languages, POPL 2005. ACM Press (2005) 145–157
30. Selinger, P.: Towards a semantics for higher-order quantum computation. In QPL 2004. (2004)
31. Valiron, B.: Quantum typing. In QPL 2004. (2004) 163–178
32. van Tonder, A.: A lambda calculus for quantum computation. SIAM J. of Computing **33**(5) (2004) 1109–1135
33. Bennet, C.H., Brassard, G.: Quantum cryptography: Public key distribution and coin tossing. In Proc. of 1984 IEEE Int. Conf. on Computers, Systems and Signal Processing. IEEE (1984) 175–179
34. Yimsiriwattana, A., Jr, S.J.L.: Distributed quantum computing: A distributed Shor algorithm. `quant-ph/0403146` (2004)
35. Nielsen, M.A., Chuang, I.L.: Quantum Computation and Quantum Information. Cambridge University Press (2000)

36. Hehner, E.: Retrospective and prospective for unifying theories of programming. In Proc. of 1st Int. Symp. on Unifying Theories of Programming, UTP 2006, Lect. Notes in Comput. Sci. Springer-Verlag (to appear)
37. Tafliovich, A.: Quantum programming. Master's thesis, University of Toronto (2004)
38. Deutsch, D.: Quantum theory, the Church-Turing principle and the universal quantum computer. Proc. of Royal Society of London A **400** (1985) 97–117
39. Deutsch, D., Jozsa, R.: Rapid solution of problems by quantum computation. Proc. of Royal Society of London A **439** (1992) 553–558
40. Jozsa, R.: Quantum algorithms and the Fourier transform. Proc. of Royal Society of London A **454** (1998) 323–337
41. Grover, L.K.: A fast quantum mechanical algorithm for database search. In Proc. of 28th Ann. ACM Symp. on Theory of Computing, STOC '96. ACM Press (1996) 212–219
42. Ambainis, A.: Quantum search algorithms. SIGACT News **35**(2) (2004) 22–35

Author Index

Lecture Notes in Computer Science

For information about Vols. 1–3960

please contact your bookseller or Springer

Vol. 4005: G. Lugosi, H.U. Simon (Eds.), Learning Theory. XI, 656 pages. 2006. (Sublibrary LNAI).

Vol. 4004: S. Vaudenay (Ed.), Advances in Cryptology - EUROCRYPT 2006. XIV, 613 pages. 2006.

Vol. 4003: Y. Koucheryavy, J. Harju, V.B. Iversen (Eds.), Next Generation Teletraffic and Wired/Wireless Advanced Networking. XVI, 582 pages. 2006.

Vol. 4001: E. Dubois, K. Pohl (Eds.), Advanced Information Systems Engineering. XVI, 560 pages. 2006.

Vol. 3999: C. Kop, G. Fliedl, H.C. Mayr, E. Métais (Eds.), Natural Language Processing and Information Systems. XIII, 227 pages. 2006.

Vol. 3998: T. Calamoneri, I. Finocchi, G.F. Italiano (Eds.), Algorithms and Complexity. XII, 394 pages. 2006.

Vol. 3997: W. Grieskamp, C. Weise (Eds.), Formal Approaches to Software Testing. XII, 219 pages. 2006.

Vol. 3996: A. Keller, J.-P. Martin-Flatin (Eds.), Self-Managed Networks, Systems, and Services. X, 185 pages. 2006.

Vol. 3995: G. Müller (Ed.), Emerging Trends in Information and Communication Security. XX, 524 pages. 2006.

Vol. 3994: V.N. Alexandrov, G.D. van Albada, P.M.A. Sloot, J. Dongarra (Eds.), Computational Science – ICCS 2006, Part IV. XXXV, 1096 pages. 2006.

Vol. 3993: V.N. Alexandrov, G.D. van Albada, P.M.A. Sloot, J. Dongarra (Eds.), Computational Science – ICCS 2006, Part III. XXXVI, 1136 pages. 2006.

Vol. 3992: V.N. Alexandrov, G.D. van Albada, P.M.A. Sloot, J. Dongarra (Eds.), Computational Science – ICCS 2006, Part II. XXXV, 1122 pages. 2006.

Vol. 3991: V.N. Alexandrov, G.D. van Albada, P.M.A. Sloot, J. Dongarra (Eds.), Computational Science – ICCS 2006, Part I. LXXXI, 1096 pages. 2006.

Vol. 3990: J. C. Beck, B.M. Smith (Eds.), Integration of AI and OR Techniques in Constraint Programming for Combinatorial Optimization Problems. X, 301 pages. 2006.

Vol. 3989: J. Zhou, M. Yung, F. Bao, Applied Cryptography and Network Security. XIV, 488 pages. 2006.

Vol. 3987: M. Hazas, J. Krumm, T. Strang (Eds.), Location- and Context-Awareness. X, 289 pages. 2006.

Vol. 3986: K. Stølen, W.H. Winsborough, F. Martinelli, F. Massacci (Eds.), Trust Management. XIV, 474 pages. 2006.

Vol. 3984: M. Gavrilova, O. Gervasi, V. Kumar, C.J. K. Tan, D. Taniar, A. Laganà, Y. Mun, H. Choo (Eds.), Computational Science and Its Applications - ICCSA 2006, Part V. XXV, 1045 pages. 2006.

Vol. 3983: M. Gavrilova, O. Gervasi, V. Kumar, C.J. K. Tan, D. Taniar, A. Laganà, Y. Mun, H. Choo (Eds.), Computational Science and Its Applications - ICCSA 2006, Part IV. XXVI, 1191 pages. 2006.

Vol. 3982: M. Gavrilova, O. Gervasi, V. Kumar, C.J. K. Tan, D. Taniar, A. Laganà, Y. Mun, H. Choo (Eds.), Computational Science and Its Applications - ICCSA 2006, Part III. XXV, 1243 pages. 2006.

Vol. 3981: M. Gavrilova, O. Gervasi, V. Kumar, C.J. K. Tan, D. Taniar, A. Laganà, Y. Mun, H. Choo (Eds.), Computational Science and Its Applications - ICCSA 2006, Part II. XXVI, 1255 pages. 2006.

Vol. 3980: M. Gavrilova, O. Gervasi, V. Kumar, C.J. K. Tan, D. Taniar, A. Laganà, Y. Mun, H. Choo (Eds.), Computational Science and Its Applications - ICCSA 2006, Part I. LXXV, 1199 pages. 2006.

Vol. 3979: T.S. Huang, N. Sebe, M.S. Lew, V. Pavlović, M. Kölsch, A. Galata, B. Kisačanin (Eds.), Computer Vision in Human-Computer Interaction. XII, 121 pages. 2006.

Vol. 3978: B. Hnich, M. Carlsson, F. Fages, F. Rossi (Eds.), Recent Advances in Constraints. VIII, 179 pages. 2006. (Sublibrary LNAI).

Vol. 3977: N. Fuhr, M. Lalmas, S. Malik, G. Kazai (Eds.), Advances in XML Information Retrieval and Evaluation. XII, 556 pages. 2006.

Vol. 3976: F. Boavida, T. Plagemann, B. Stiller, C. Westphal, E. Monteiro (Eds.), Networking 2006. Networking Technologies, Services, and Protocols; Performance of Computer and Communication Networks; Mobile and Wireless Communications Systems. XXVI, 1276 pages. 2006.

Vol. 3975: S. Mehrotra, D.D. Zeng, H. Chen, B. Thuraisingham, F.-Y. Wang (Eds.), Intelligence and Security Informatics. XXII, 772 pages. 2006.

Vol. 3973: J. Wang, Z. Yi, J.M. Zurada, B.-L. Lu, H. Yin (Eds.), Advances in Neural Networks - ISNN 2006, Part III. XXIX, 1402 pages. 2006.

Vol. 3972: J. Wang, Z. Yi, J.M. Zurada, B.-L. Lu, H. Yin (Eds.), Advances in Neural Networks - ISNN 2006, Part II. XXVII, 1444 pages. 2006.

Vol. 3971: J. Wang, Z. Yi, J.M. Zurada, B.-L. Lu, H. Yin (Eds.), Advances in Neural Networks - ISNN 2006, Part I. LXVII, 1442 pages. 2006.

Vol. 3970: T. Braun, G. Carle, S. Fahmy, Y. Koucheryavy (Eds.), Wired/Wireless Internet Communications. XIV, 350 pages. 2006.

Vol. 3969: Ø. Ytrehus (Ed.), Coding and Cryptography. XI, 443 pages. 2006.

Vol. 3968: K.P. Fishkin, B. Schiele, P. Nixon, A. Quigley (Eds.), Pervasive Computing. XV, 402 pages. 2006.

Vol. 3967: D. Grigoriev, J. Harrison, E.A. Hirsch (Eds.), Computer Science – Theory and Applications. XVI, 684 pages. 2006.

Vol. 3966: Q. Wang, D. Pfahl, D.M. Raffo, P. Wernick (Eds.), Software Process Change. XIV, 356 pages. 2006.

Vol. 3965: M. Bernardo, A. Cimatti (Eds.), Formal Methods for Hardware Verification. VII, 243 pages. 2006.

Vol. 3964: M. Ü. Uyar, A.Y. Duale, M.A. Fecko (Eds.), Testing of Communicating Systems. XI, 373 pages. 2006.

Vol. 3963: O. Dikenelli, M.-P. Gleizes, A. Ricci (Eds.), Engineering Societies in the Agents World VI. XII, 303 pages. 2006. (Sublibrary LNAI).

Vol. 3962: W. IJsselsteijn, Y. de Kort, C. Midden, B. Eggen, E. van den Hoven (Eds.), Persuasive Technology. XII, 216 pages. 2006.